SO-ASG-543

FLORIDA STATE
UNIVERSITY LIBRARIES

JAN 0 9 2002

TALLAHASSEE, FLORIDA

SOMETHING ABOUT THE AUTHOR®

Something about
the Author *was named*
an "Outstanding
Reference Source,"
the highest honor given
by the American
Library Association
Reference and Adult
Services Division.

ISSN 0276-816X

SOMETHING ABOUT THE AUTHOR®

**Facts and Pictures about Authors
and Illustrators of Books for Young People**

volume 126

GALE GROUP

THOMSON LEARNING

Detroit • New York • San Diego • San Francisco
Boston • New Haven, Conn. • Waterville, Maine
London • Munich

NSL
REF
PN
451
.56
v.126

STAFF

Scot Peacock, *Managing Editor, Literature Product*
Mark W. Scott, *Publisher, Literature Product*

Frank Castronova, Lisa Kumar, *Senior Editors;* Katy Balcer, Sara Constantakis, Kristen A. Dorsch, Marie Lazzari, Thomas McMahon, *Editors;* Alana Joli Foster, Arlene M. Johnson, Jennifer Kilian, Michelle Poole, Anita Sundaresan, Thomas Wiloch, *Associate Editors;* Karen Abbott, Madeline Harris, Maikue Vang, Denay L. Wilding, *Assistant Editors;* Anna Marie Dahn, Judith L. Pyko, *Administrative Support;* Joshua Kondek, Mary Ruby, *Technical Training Specialists*

Dwayne Hayes, Joyce Nakamura, *Managing Editors*
Susan M. Trosky, *Literature Content Coordinator*

Victoria B. Cariappa, *Research Manager;* Tracie A. Richardson, *Project Coordinator;* Barbara McNeil, Gary J. Oudersluys, Cheryl L. Warnock, *Research Specialists;* Tamara C. Nott, *Research Associates;* Nicodemus Ford, *Research Assistant;* Michelle Campbell, *Administrative Assistant*

Maria L. Franklin, *Permissions Manager;* Kim Davis, *Permissions Associate*

Mary Beth Trimper, *Manager, Composition and Prepress;* Dorothy Maki, *Manufacturing Manager;* Stacy Melson, *Buyer*

Barbara J. Yarrow, *Manager, Imaging and Multimedia Content;* Randy Bassett, *Imaging Supervisor;* Robert Duncan, Dan Newell, *Imaging Specialists;* Pamela A. Reed, *Imaging Coordinator;* Dean Dauphinais, *Senior Editor;* Robyn V. Young, *Project Manager;* Kelly A. Quin, *Editor*

While every effort has been made to ensure the reliability of the information presented in this publication, Gale Research does not guarantee the accuracy of the data contained herein. Gale accepts no payment for listing; and inclusion of any organization, agency, institution, publication, service, or individual does not imply endorsement of the editors or publisher. Errors brought to the attention of the publisher and verified to the satisfaction of the publisher will be corrected in future editions.

This publication is a creative work fully protected by all applicable copyright laws, as well as by misappropriation, trade secret, unfair competition, and other applicable laws. The authors and editors of this work have added value to the underlying factual material herein through one or more of the following: unique and original selection, coordination, expression, arrangement, and classification of the information.

All rights to this publication will be vigorously defended.

Copyright © 2002
Gale Group, Inc.
27500 Drake Rd.
Farmington Hills, MI 48331-3535

Gale Group and Design is a trademark used herein under license.
All rights reserved including the right of reproduction in whole or in part in any form.

Library of Congress Catalog Card Number 72-27107

ISBN 0-7876-4714-4
ISSN 0276-816X

Printed in the United States of America

10 9 8 7 6 5 4 3 2 1

Contents

Authors in Forthcoming Volumes

Below are some of the authors and illustrators that will be featured in upcoming volumes of *SATA*. These include new entries on the swiftly rising stars of the field, as well as completely revised and updated entries (indicated with *) on some of the most notable and best-loved creators of books for children.

Meg Cabot: Cabot is a popular writer who has quickly earned a reputation for capturing the essence of the way adolescents think and talk. Cabot is best known as the author of the 2000 novel *The Princess Diaries*, a story about a fourteen-year-old New Yorker whose ordinary troubles are magnified the day her father returns to reveal that he is a prince of a small European country.

R. Gregory Christie: Christie is an artist whose intensely colored paintings filled with elongated figures have graced the pages of several award-winning children's books. *The Palm of My Heart: Poetry by African American Children* was named a Coretta Scott King honor book in 1997, as was *Only Passing Through: The Story of Sojourner Truth* in 2001.

Christine Davenier: Davenier is a French writer and illustrator whose pen and-ink and watercolor draw-ings are considered charming and humorous. Her self-illustrated works include *León et Albertine* (pub-lished in the United States as *Leon and Albertine*). Davenier has brought her breezy, expressive style to others' stories, including Paul B. Janeczko's collection *Very Best (Almost) Friends: Poems of Friendship*.

*Dougal Dixon: Scottish-born author Dixon blends a passionate interest in geology and zoology in his award-winning books about prehistoric life forms as well as speculative life forms of the future. *Dougal Dixon's Amazing Dinosaurs,* published in numerous editions for all levels of readers, has attracted young and old to the topic.

Don Gillmor: Canadian writer Gillmor has penned a number of award-winning books for children that have been praised for their originality and whimsy. Titles like *When Vegetables Go Bad!* and *Yuck, a Love Story* reflect Gillmor's unique approach to writing for children. Two of his works, *The Fabulous Song* and *The Christmas Orange,* have been shortlisted for the Governor General's Award.

Janet Hickman: Hickman, a lecturer at Ohio State University, has written a number of novels for middle-grade readers that focus on American history. The stresses that occur during wartime are the subject of several of Hickman's works, among them *The Stones* and *Zoar Blue*. In her 1998 work *Susannah,* Hickman follows the title character, a fourteen-year-old girl living in a Shaker community in the early 1800s.

*Else Holmelund Minarik: Danish-born author Minarik has written many acclaimed books for children, but she is probably best known for her beloved "Little Bear" series, which began with *Little Bear,* pub-lished in 1957. Minarik's work has been augmented with illustrations by some of the most noted artists working in children's books in the twentieth century, among them Maurice Sendak, James Stevenson, and Garth Williams.

*Meredith Ann Pierce: Pierce's novels, which include the trilogies "Darkangel" and "Firebringer," are highlighted by their imaginative plots and settings, poetic language, and determined, independent charac-ters. Her most noted work, the "Darkangel" fantasy trilogy, relates a young girl's struggle to free herself, her friends, and her world from an evil witch. Pierce released a self-contained fantasy novel, *Treasure at the Heart of Tanglewood,* in 2001.

*Martin Waddell: A citizen of Belfast, Northern Ireland, Waddell writes children's mysteries, picture books, slapstick comedies, football stories, and ghost stories under his own name. He has also written emotionally charged young adult titles under the pseudonym Catherine Sefton, and has penned books for adults, as well. In 2001, Waddell published three children's books: *Webster J. Duck, Tom Rabbit,* and *A Kitten Called Moonlight*.

*Nancy Willard: Willard is the award-winning, versatile author of over sixty volumes of children's fic-tion and poetry, as well as novels, poetry, short stories, and literary criticism for adults. She was the first recipient of a Newbery Medal for a volume of poetry, for *A Visit to William Blake's Inn: Poems for Innocent and Experienced Travelers.* Willard's collection for children, *The Moon and Riddles Diner and the Sunnyside Café,* was published in 2001.

Introduction

Something about the Author (*SATA*) is an ongoing reference series that examines the lives and works of authors and illustrators of books for children. *SATA* includes not only well-known writers and artists but also less prominent individuals whose works are just coming to be recognized. This series is often the only readily available information source on emerging authors and illustrators. You'll find *SATA* informative and entertaining, whether you are a student, a librarian, an English teacher, a parent, or simply an adult who enjoys children's literature.

What's Inside SATA

SATA provides detailed information about authors and illustrators who span the full time range of children's literature, from early figures like John Newbery and L. Frank Baum to contemporary figures like Judy Blume and Richard Peck. Authors in the series represent primarily English-speaking countries, particularly the United States, Canada, and the United Kingdom. Also included, however, are authors from around the world whose works are available in English translation. The writings represented in *SATA* include those created intentionally for children and young adults as well as those written for a general audience and known to interest younger readers. These writings cover the entire spectrum of children's literature, including picture books, humor, folk and fairy tales, animal stories, mystery and adventure, science fiction and fantasy, historical fiction, poetry and nonsense verse, drama, biography, and nonfiction.

Obituaries are also included in *SATA* and are intended not only as death notices but also as concise overviews of people's lives and work. Additionally, each edition features newly revised and updated entries for a selection of *SATA* listees who remain of interest to today's readers and who have been active enough to require extensive revisions of their earlier biographies.

New Autobiography Feature

Beginning with Volume 103, *SATA* features two or more specially commissioned autobiographical essays in each volume. These unique essays, averaging about ten thousand words in length and illustrated with an abundance of personal photos, present an entertaining and informative first-person perspective on the lives and careers of prominent authors and illustrators profiled in *SATA*.

Two Convenient Indexes

In response to suggestions from librarians, *SATA* indexes no longer appear in every volume but are included in alternate (odd-numbered) volumes of the series, beginning with Volume 57.

SATA continues to include two indexes that cumulate with each alternate volume: the Illustrations Index, arranged by the name of the illustrator, gives the number of the volume and page where the illustrator's work appears in the current volume as well as all preceding volumes in the series; the Author Index gives the number of the volume in which a person's biographical sketch, autobiographical essay, or obituary appears in the current volume as well as all preceding volumes in the series.

These indexes also include references to authors and illustrators who appear in Gale's *Yesterday's Authors of Books for Children, Children's Literature Review,* and *Something about the Author Autobiography Series.*

Easy-to-Use Entry Format

Whether you're already familiar with the *SATA* series or just getting acquainted, you will want to be aware of the kind of information that an entry provides. In every *SATA* entry the editors attempt to give as complete a picture of the person's life and work as possible. A typical entry in *SATA* includes the following clearly labeled information sections:

- *PERSONAL:* date and place of birth and death, parents' names and occupations, name of spouse, date of marriage, names of children, educational institutions attended, degrees received, religious and political affiliations, hobbies and other interests.

- *ADDRESSES:* complete home, office, electronic mail, and agent addresses, whenever available.

- *CAREER:* name of employer, position, and dates for each career post; art exhibitions; military service; memberships and offices held in professional and civic organizations.

- *AWARDS, HONORS:* literary and professional awards received.

- *WRITINGS:* title-by-title chronological bibliography of books written and/or illustrated, listed by genre when known; lists of other notable publications, such as plays, screenplays, and periodical contributions.

- *ADAPTATIONS:* a list of films, television programs, plays, CD-ROMs, recordings, and other media presentations that have been adapted from the author's work.

- *WORK IN PROGRESS:* description of projects in progress.

- *SIDELIGHTS:* a biographical portrait of the author or illustrator's development, either directly from the biographee—and often written specifically for the *SATA* entry—or gathered from diaries, letters, interviews, or other published sources.

- *BIOGRAPHICAL AND CRITICAL SOURCES:* cites sources quoted in "Sidelights" along with references for further reading.

- *EXTENSIVE ILLUSTRATIONS:* photographs, movie stills, book illustrations, and other interesting visual materials supplement the text.

How a SATA Entry Is Compiled

A *SATA* entry progresses through a series of steps. If the biographee is living, the *SATA* editors try to secure information directly from him or her through a questionnaire. From the information that the biographee supplies, the editors prepare an entry, filling in any essential missing details with research and/or telephone interviews. If possible, the author or illustrator is sent a copy of the entry to check for accuracy and completeness.

If the biographee is deceased or cannot be reached by questionnaire, the *SATA* editors examine a wide variety of published sources to gather information for an entry. Biographical and bibliographic sources are consulted, as are book reviews, feature articles, published interviews, and material sometimes obtained from the biographee's family, publishers, agent, or other associates.

Entries that have not been verified by the biographees or their representatives are marked with an asterisk (*).

Contact the Editor

We encourage our readers to examine the entire *SATA* series. Please write and tell us if we can make *SATA* even more helpful to you. Give your comments and suggestions to the editor:

BY MAIL: Editor, *Something about the Author,* The Gale Group, 27500 Drake Rd., Farmington Hills, MI 48331-3535.

BY TELEPHONE: (800) 877-GALE

BY FAX: (248) 699-8054

Something about the Author Product Advisory Board

The editors of *Something about the Author* are dedicated to maintaining a high standard of excellence by publishing comprehensive, accurate, and highly readable entries on a wide array of writers for children and young adults. In addition to the quality of the content, the editors take pride in the graphic design of the series, which is intended to be orderly yet inviting, allowing readers to utilize the pages of *SATA* easily and with efficiency. Despite the longevity of the *SATA* print series, and the success of its format, we are mindful that the vitality of a literary reference product is dependent on its ability to serve its users over time. As literature, and attitudes about literature, constantly evolve, so do the reference needs of students, teachers, scholars, journalists, researchers, and book club members. To be certain that we continue to keep pace with the expectations of our customers, the editors of *SATA* listen carefully to their comments regarding the value, utility, and quality of the series. Librarians, who have firsthand knowledge of the needs of library users, are a valuable resource for us. The *Something about the Author* Product Advisory Board, made up of school, public, and academic librarians, is a forum to promote focused feedback about *SATA* on a regular basis. The five-member advisory board includes the following individuals, whom the editors wish to thank for sharing their expertise:

- **Eva M. Davis,** Teen Services Librarian, Plymouth District Library, Plymouth, Michigan

- **Joan B. Eisenberg,** Lower School Librarian, Milton Academy, Milton, Massachusetts

- **Francisca Goldsmith,** Teen Services Librarian, Berkeley Public Library, Berkeley, California

- **Monica F. Irlbacher,** Young Adult Librarian, Middletown Thrall Library, Middletown, New York

- **Caryn Sipos,** Librarian--Young Adult Services, King County Library System, Washington

Acknowledgments

Grateful acknowledgment is made to the following publishers, authors, and artists whose works appear in this volume.

ACKERMAN, KAREN. Gammell, Stephen, illustrator. From a cover of *Song and Dance Man,* by Karen Ackerman. Dragonfly Books, 1988. Illustrations copyright © 1988 by Stephen Gammell. Reproduced by permission of Alfred A. Knopf, Inc./ Stock, Catherine, illustrator. From a cover of *By the Dawn's Early Light,* by Karen Ackerman. Aladdin Paperbacks, an imprint of Simon & Schuster, 1994. Illustrations copyright © 1994 by Catherine Stock. Reproduced by permission./ Moser, Barry, illustrator. From a jacket of *Bingleman's Midway,* by Karen Ackerman. Caroline House, 1995. Illustrations copyright © 1995 by Barry Moser. Reproduced by permission.

ADLER, C(AROLE) S(CHWERDTFEGER). de Groat, Diane, illustrator. From a jacket of *Daddy's Climbing Tree,* by C. S. Adler. Clarion Books, a Houghton Mifflin Company imprint, 1993. Reproduced by permission./ Clapp, John, illustrator. From a cover of *Youn Hee & Me,* by C. S. Adler. Harcourt Brace & Company, 1995. Jacket illustration copyright © 1995 by John Clapp. Reproduced by permission of Harcourt, Inc./ Adler, C. S. From a cover of *The Magic of the Glits,* by C. S. Adler. iUniverse.com, Inc., 2000. All rights reserved. Copyright © 1979, 2000 by C. S. Adler. Reproduced by permission./ Adler, C. S., photograph by Arnold R. Adler. Reproduced by permission of C. S. Adler.

ARONSON, MARC. Aronson, Marc, photograph. From a jacket of his *Sir Walter Ralegh and the Quest for El Dorado.* Clarion Books, a Houghton Mifflin Company imprint, 2000. Reproduced by permission of Marc Aronson.

BAGGETTE, SUSAN K. Moriarty, William J., photographer. From a cover of *Jonathan & Papa,* by Susan K. Baggette. The Brookfield Reader, 1999. Copyright © 1999 Susan K. Baggette. Reproduced by permission.

BARASCH, LYNNE. Barasch, Lynne, illustrator. From a jacket of her *Old Friends.* Frances Foster Books, 1998. Copyright © 1998 by Lynne Barasch. Reproduced by permission./ Barasch, Lynne, photograph. Reproduced by permission.

BARR, NEVADA. From a cover of *Ill Wind,* by Nevada Barr. Avon Books, 1996. Reproduced by permission of HarperCollins Publishers. In the UK by permission of Penguin Putnam Inc./ From a cover of *Endangered Species.* Avon Books, 1998. Reproduced by permission of HarperCollins Publishers. In the UK by permission of Penguin Putnam Inc./ Barr, Nevada, photograph by Judy Lawne. Reproduced by permission of Nevada Barr.

BARRON, T(HOMAS) A(RCHIBALD). Sweet, Darrell K., illustrator. From a cover of *The Ancient One,* by T. A. Barron. Tom Doherty Associates, LLC, 1992. Reproduced by permission of St. Martin's Press, Inc./ Sweet, Darrell K., illustrator. From a cover of *The Merlin Effect,* by T. A. Barron. Tor Books, 1996. Illustration copyright © 1995 by Anthony Bacon Venti. Reproduced by permission./ A cover of *The Fires of Merlin,* by T. A. Barron. Philomel Books, 1998. Reproduced by permission of Philomel Books, a division of Penguin Putnam Inc./ A cover of *The Seven Songs of* Merlin, by T. A. Barron. Philomel Books, 1997. Reproduced by permission of Philomel Books, a division of Penguin Putnam Inc./ Barron, T. A., photograph by Currie C. Barron. Reproduced by permission of T. A. Barron.

BARTON, BYRON. Barton, Byron, illustrator. From a cover of his *Where's Al?,* Clarion Books, 1972. Copyright © 1972 by Byron Barton. Reproduced by permission./ Barton, Byron, illustrator. From an illustration in his *Buzz Buzz Buzz.* Aladdin Paperbacks, 1995. Copyright © 1973 by Byron Barton. Reproduced by permission.

BELL, KRISTA (ANNE BLAKENEY). Bell, Krista, photograph. Reproduced by permission.

BING, CHRISTOPHER (H). Bing, Christopher, illustrator. From an illustration in *Casey at the Bat: A Ballad of the Republic Sung in the Year 1888,* by Ernest Lawrence Thayer. Handprint Books, 2000. Illustrations © 2000 by Christopher Bing. Reproduced by permission.

BLACKALL, BERNIE. Cross, Malcolm, photographer. From a cover of *Softball,* by Bernie Blackall. Heinemann Interactive Library, 1998. © 1998 Reed Educational & Professional Publishing. Reproduced by permission.

BOND, FELICIA. Bond, Felicia. From an illustration in *If You Give a Mouse a Cookie,* by Laura Joffe Numeroff. HarperCollins, 1985. Illustration copyright © 1985 by Felicia Bond. Reproduced by permission of HarperCollins Publishers, Inc.

CHOI, SOOK NYUL. Opening author portrait taken by Lovella Beres. Closing author portrait taken by Christine Reynolds at Boston College. All other photographs reproduced by permission of the author.

CLARK, MARGARET (D). Clark, Margaret, photograph. Reproduced by permission.

COLLIER, BRYAN. Collier, Bryan, photograph. From a jacket of *Freedom River,* by Doreen Rappaport. Reproduced by permission of Bryan Collier./ Collier, Bryan, illustrator. From an illustration in *Freedom River,* by Doreen Rappaport. Jump at the Sun, Hyperion Books for Children, 2000. Illustrations copyright © 2000 by Bryan Collier. Reproduced by permission.

COLLINS, PAUL. Rogers, Gregory, cover illustration from *The Dog King,* by Paul Collins. Reproduced by permission./ Collins, Paul, photograph. Reproduced by permission.

DESAI, ANITA. Desai, Anita, photograph. © Jerry Bauer. Reproduced bypermission.

DRAWSON, BLAIR. Drawson, Blair, illustrator. From an illustration in *Arachne Speaks,* by Kate Hovey. Margaret K. McElderry Books, 2000. Illustrations copyright © 2000 by Blair Drawson. Reproduced by permission.

DUNNE, KATHLEEN. Dunne, Kathleen, standing in her studio, photograph. © Vorpal Gallery, 1998. Reproduced by permission.

FANELLI, SARA. Fanelli, Sara, illustrator. From a cover of her *Dear Diary.* Candlewick, 2000. Copyright © 2000 by Sara Fanelli. All rights reserved. Reproduced by permission.

FLEMING, DENISE. Fleming, Denise, illustrator. From an illustration in her *In the Tall, Tall Grass.* Henry Holt and Company, LLC, 1991. Copyright © 1991 by Denise Fleming. All rights reserved. Reproduced by permission./ Fleming, Denise, illustrator. From an illustration in her *Where Once There Was a Wood.* Henry Holt and Company, LLC, 1996. Copyright © 1996 by Denise Fleming. All rights reserved. Reproduced by permission./ Fleming, Denise, illustrator. From an illustration in her *The Everything Book.* Henry Holt and Company, LLC, 2000. Copyright © 2000 by Denise Fleming. All rights reserved. Reproduced by permission.

GAY, MARIE-LOUISE. Gay, Marie-Louise, illustrator. From *Lizzy's Lion,* by Dennis Lee. Stoddart, 1984. Illustrations copyright © 1984 Marie-Louise Gay. Reproduced by permission./ Illustration from *Rainy Day Magic,* by Marie-Louise Gay. Stoddart Publishing Co., Limited, 1987. Copyright © 1987 Marie-Louise Gay. All rights reserved. Reproduced by permission of Marie-Louise Gay./ Gay, Marie-Louise, illustrator. From an illustration in *When Vegetables Go Bad!,* by Don Gillmor. Firefly Books, 1998. Copyright © 1994 illustrations by Marie-Louise Gay. Reproduced by permission./ Gay, Marie-Louise, illustrator. From anillustration in her *Stella: Star of the Sea.* Groundwood Books, 2001. Copyright © 1999 by Marie-Louise Gay. All rights reserved. Reproduced by permission./ Gay, Marie-Louise, photograph. Reproduced by permission.

GIBBS, ADREA. Cover illustration from her *Let's Put on a Show!: A Beginner's Theatre Handbook for Young Actors.* Meriwether Publishing Ltd., 1999. © Copyright MCMXCIX Meriwether Publishing Ltd. Reproduced by permission.

GROSSMAN, BILL. Hawkes, Kevin, illustrator. From a cover of *My Little Sister Ate One Hare,* by Bill Grossman. Dragonfly Books, 1996. Illustrations copyright © 1996 by Kevin Hawkes. Reproduced by permission.

HARPER, BETTY. Harper, Betty, illustrator. From an illustration in *Enid and the Dangerous Discovery* ("Our Neighborhood" series), by Cynthia G. Williams. Broadman & Holman Publishers, 1999. Illustration © 1999 Betty Harper. Reproduced by permission./ Harper, Betty, photograph. From a jacket of *Enid and the Dangerous Discovery* ("Our Neighborhood" series), by Cynthia G. Williams. Reproduced by permission of Betty Harper.

HEHENBERGER, SHELLY. Hehenberger, Shelly, illustrator. From an illustration in *Isn't My Name Magical?: Sister and Brother Poems,* by James Berry. Simon & Schuster Books for Young Readers, 1999. Illustrations copyright © 1999 by Shelly Hehenberger. Reproduced by permission

HILL, KIRKPATRICK. Knorr, Peter, illustrator. From a cover of *Toughboy and Sister,* by Kirkpatrick Hill. Aladdin Paperbacks, 2000. Cover illustration copyright © 2000 by Peter Knorr. Reproduced by permission./ Knorr, Peter, illustrator. From a jacket of *The Year of Miss Agnes,* by Kirkpatrick Hill. Margaret K. McElderry Books, 2000. Jacket illustration copyright © by Peter Knorr. Reproduced by permission.

HOL, COBY. Hol, Coby, illustrator. From an illustration in her *Lisa and the Snowman.* North-South Books, Inc., 1989. Copyright © 1989 by Nord-Sud Verlag, AG, Gossau Zurich, Switzerland. Reproduced by permission./ Hol, Coby, photograph. Reproduced by permission.

HOWE, NORMA. Dynamic Duo Studio, illustrator. From a cover of her *The Adventures of Blue Avenger: A Novel.* Henry Holt and Company, Inc., 1999. Reproduced by permission of Henry Holt and Company, LLC./ Frendak, Rodney, illustrator. From a cover of *Blue Avenger Cracks the Code,* by Norma Howe. Henry Holt and Company, LLC, 2000. Jacket illustration copyright © 2000 by Rodney Frendak/Rocket Studios. Reproduced by permission.

KALLEN, STUART A(RNOLD). Cover photograph by Bettmann from *The Nazis Seize Power, 1933-1941* ("The Holocaust" series), by Stuart A. Kallen. Abdo & Daughters, 1994. Copyright © 1994 by Abdo Consulting Group, Inc., Pentagon Tower, P.O. Box 36036, Minneapolis, Minnesota 55435 USA. Reproduced by permission./ Peter Arnold, Inc., photographer. From a cover of *Manx Cats,* by Stuart A. Kallen. Abdo & Daughters, 1996. Copyright © 1996 by Abdo Consulting Group, Inc., Pentagon Tower, P.O. Box 36036, Minneapolis, Minnesota 55435. Reproduced by permission./ Cover illustration from *Life on the American Frontier* ("The Way People Live" series), by Stuart A. Kallen. Lucent Books, 1999. Copyright 1999 by Lucent Books, Inc., P.O. Box 289011, San Diego, California 92198-9011. Reproduced by permission.

KANER, ETTA. Cupples, Pat, illustrator. From a cover of *Bridges,* by Etta Kaner. Kids Can Press, 1994. Illustrations copyright © 1994 by Pat Cupples. Reproduced by permission./ Stephens, Pam, illustrator. From a cover of *Animal Defenses: How Animals Protect Themselves,* by Etta Kaner. Kids Can Press, 1999. Illustrations copyright © 1999 by Pat Stephens. Reproduced by permission./ Kaner, Etta, 1996, photograph. Reproduced by permission.

KIMBALL, VIOLET T(EW). Kimball, Violet T., photograph. Reproduced by permission.

KLASS, SHEILA SOLOMON. Opening author portrait taken by Morton Klass. All other photographs reproduced by permission of the author.

KOLÍBALOVÁ, MARKÉTA. Prachatická, Markéta (pseudonym for Markéta Kolíbalová), illustrator. From a cover of *Sheep Don't Go to School,* edited by Andrew Fusek Peters. Bloodaxe Books Ltd., 1999. Drawings © Markéta Prachatická 1999. Reproduced by permission.

KONIGSBURG, E(LAINE) L(OBL). Konigsburg, E. L., illustrator. From an illustration in her *From the Mixed-up Files of Mrs. Basil E. Frankweiler*. Atheneum, 1967. Copyright © 1967 by E. L. Konigsburg. All rights reserved. Reproduced with permission of Atheneum Publishers, a division of Simon & Schuster, Inc./ da Vinci, Leonardo, illustrator. From a cover of *The Second Mrs. Giaconda,* by E. L. Konigsburg. Aladdin Paperbacks, 1998. Copyright © 1975 by E. L. Konigsburg. Reproduced by permission of Aladdin Paperbacks, an imprint of Simon & Schuster Macmillan./ Konigsburg, E. L., illustrator. From a cover of her *Father's Arcane Daughter.* Aladdin Paperbacks, 1999. Copyright © 1976 by E. L. Konigsburg. Reproduced by permission of Aladdin Paperbacks, an imprint of Simon & Schuster Macmillan./ Konigsburg, E. L., illustrator. From a cover of her *Silent to the Bone.* Atheneum Books for Young Readers, 2000. Copyright © 2000 by E. L. Konigsburg. Reproduced by permission of Atheneum Books for Young Readers, an imprint of Simon & Schuster Macmillan./ Konigsburg, E. L., photograph. Reproduced by permission.

KURTZ, KATHERINE (IRENE). Call, Greg, illustrator. From a cover of *The Temple and the Stone,* by Katherine Kurtz and Deborah Turner Harris. Warner Books, Inc., 1999. Copyright © 1998 by Katherine Kurtz and Deborah Turner Harris. Reproduced by permission./ Kurtz, Katherine, photograph by Beth Gwinn.Reproduced by permission of Katherine Kurtz.

LACE, WILLIAM W. Lace, William W., photograph. Reproduced by permission of the Bagwell Studio, Weatherford, Texas.

LAMSTEIN, SARAH MARWIL. Cote, Nancy, illustrator. From a jacket of *I Like Your Buttons!,* by Sarah Marwil Lamstein. Albert Whitman & Company, 1999. Illustrations copyright © 1999 by Nancy Cote. Reproduced by permission./ Lamstein, Sarah Marwil, photograph. Reproduced by permission.

LAROCHE, GILES. Laroche, Giles, illustrator. From an illustration in *The Color Box,* by Dayle Ann Dodds. Little, Brown and Company, 1992. Illustrations copyright © 1992 by Giles Laroche. Reproduced by permission.

LAWSON, JULIE. Mombourquette, Paul, illustrator. From a jacket of *Emma and the Silk Train,* by Julie Lawson. Kids Can Press Ltd., 1998. Illustrations copyright © 1997 by Paul Mombourquette. Reproduced by permission./ Campbell, Ken, illustrator. From a cover of *The Ghost of Avalanche Mountain,* by Julie Lawson. Stoddart Kids, 2000. Reproduced by permission./ Lawson, Julie, photograph. From a jacket of her *Blown Away.* Reproduced by permission.

MARRIN, ALBERT. From a jacket of *Virginia's General: Robert E. Lee and the Civil War.* Atheneum, 1994. Copyright © 1994 by Albert Marrin. All rights reserved. Reproduced by permission of Art Resource, New York./ Brady, Matthew, photographer. From a cover of *Unconditional Surrender: U.S. Grant and the Civil War,* by Albert Marrin. Atheneum Books for Young Readers, 1994. Copyright © by National Portrait Gallery/Art Resource, New York. Reproduced by permission./ Marrin, Albert, photograph. Reproduced by permission.

MARTIN, ANN M. Colin, Paul, illustrator. From a jacket of *P. S. Longer Letter Later,* by Paula Danziger and Ann M. Martin. Scholastic Press, 1998. Jacketillustration copyright © 1998 by Paul Colin. Reprinted by permission of Scholastic Inc./ Selznick, Brian, illustrator. From a jacket of *The Doll People,* by Ann M. Martin and Laura Godwin. Hyperion

Books, 2000. Illustrations copyright © by Brian Selznick. Reproduced by permission./ Tauss, Marc, photographer. From a jacket of *Snail Mail No More,* by Paula Danziger and Ann M. Martin. Scholastic Press, 2000. Copyright © 2000 by Paula Danziger Copyright © 2000 by Ann M. Martin. Reproduced by permission.

MARTIN, MARVIN. Martin, Marvin, photograph. Reproduced by permission.

MCCOURT, MALACHY. McCourt, Malachy, photograph by Michael O'Neill. From a cover of his *A Monk Swimming: A Memoir.* Hyperion, 1998. Copyright © 1998 by Malachy McCourt. Reproduced by permission./ McCourt, Malachy, 1998, photograph. AP/Wide World Photos. Reproduced by permission.

CKILLIP, PATRICIA A(NNE). Griesbach/Martucci, illustrator. From a cover of *The Forgotten Beasts of Eld,* by Patricia A. McKillip. Magic Carpet Books/Harcourt, Inc., 1996. Copyright © 1974 by Patricia A. McKillip. Reproduced by permission./ McKillip, Patricia A., photograph by David Lunde. Reproduced by permission of Patricia A. McKillip.

MODARRESSI, MITRA. Modarressi, Mitra, illustrator. From a cover of *Knead It, Punch It, Bake It!: The Ultimate Breadmaking Book for Parents and Kids,* by Judith and Evan Jones. Houghton Mifflin Company, 1998. Illustrations copyright © 1998 by Mitra Modarressi. Reproduced by permission.

MORI, KYOKO. All photographs reproduced by permission of the author.

MURPHY, SHIRLEY ROUSSEAU. Murphy, Shirley Rousseau, photograph by Patrick Murphy. Reproduced by permission of Shirley Rousseau Murphy.

REIDER, KATJA. von Roehl, Angela, illustrator. From a cover of *Snail Started It!,* by Katja Reider. North-South Books, 1997. Copyright © 1997 by Nord-Sud Verlag AG, Gossau Zurich, Switzerland. Reproduced by permission./ Reider, Katja, photograph. Reproduced by permission.

RUELLE, KAREN GRAY. Ruelle, Karen Gray, illustrator. From a jacket of her *The Monster in Harry's Backyard.* Holiday House, 1999. Text and illustrations copyright © 1999 by Karen Gray Ruelle. Reproduced by permission./ Ruelle, Karen Gray, illustrator. From a cover of her *The Thanksgiving Beast Feast.* Holiday House Books, 1999. Copyright © 1999 by Karen Gray Ruelle. All rights reserved. Reproduced by permission./ Ruelle, Karen Gray, photograph by Lee Ruelle. Reproduced by permission of Karen Gray Ruelle.

SCHMID, ELEONORE. Schmid, Eleonore, illustrator. From a cover of her *The Living Earth.* North-South Books, 1994. Copyright © by Nord-Sud Verlag AG, Gossau Zurich, Switzerland. Reproduced by permission./ Schmid, Eleonore, illustrator. From an illustration in her *Hare's Christmas Gift.* North-South Books, 2000. Copyright © 2000 by Nord-Sud Verlag AG, Gossau Zurich, Switzerland. Reproduced by permission.

SIMONT, MARC. Simont, Marc, illustrator. From an illustration in *Many Moons,* by James Thurber. Harcourt Brace & Company, 1990. Artwork copyright © 1990 by Marc Simont. Reproduced by permission./ Simont, Marc, illustrator. From an illustration in *Nate the Great Saves the King of Sweden,* by Marjorie Weinman Sharmat. Bantam Doubleday Dell Books for Young Readers, 1999. Illustrations copyright © 1997 by Marc Simont. Reproduced by permission.

SMALL, DAVID. Small, David, illustrator. From an illustration in *The Gardener,* by Sarah Stewart. Sunburst/Farrar Straus Giroux, 2000. Illustrations copyright © 1997 by David Small. Reproduced by permission./ Small, David, illustrator. From an illustration in *So You Want to Be President?,* by Judith St. George. Philomel Books, 2000. Illustrations copyright © 2000 by David Small. Reproduced by permission./ Small, David, photograph by Doug Hren. Reproduced by permission of David Small.

SOMMER, CARL. James, Kennon, illustrator. From a cover of *Light Your Candle,* by Carl Sommer. Advance Publishing, Inc., 2000. Copyright © 2000 by Advance Publishing, Inc. Reproduced by permission./ Sommer, Carl, photograph. Reproduced by permission.

SOREL, EDWARD. Sorel, Edward, illustrator. From an illustration in *The Saturday Kid,* by Edward Sorel in collaboration with Cheryl Carlesimo. Margaret K. McElderry Books, 2000. Illustrations copyright © 2000 by Edward Sorel. Reproduced by permission./ Sorel, Edward, photograph. Reproduced by permission.

STILLE, DARLENE R(UTH). Cover photographs by Archive Photos from *Extraordinary Women of Medicine,* by Darlene R. Stille. Children's Press, 1997. © 1997 Children's Press ®, a Division of Grolier Publishing Co. Reproduced by permission./ Stille, Darlene R., photograph. Reproduced by permission.

SURFACE, MARY HALL. Surface, Mary Hall, photograph by Kevin Reese. Reproduced by permission of Mary Surface Hall.

THALER, SHMUEL. Thaler, Shmuel, photographer. From an illustration in *Pumpkin Circle: The Story of a Garden,* by George Levenson. Tricycle Press, 1999. Text copyright © 1999 by George Levenson. Photograph © 1999 by Shmuel Thaler. Reproduced by permission.

VIOLA, HERMAN J(OSEPH). Shaw, Charles, illustrator. From a cover in *Sitting Bull* ("Native American Stories" series), by Herman J. Viola. Raintree Steck-Vaughn, 1992. Copyright © 1990 Pinnacle Press, Inc. doing business as RiviloBooks. Reproduced by permission.

WALTERS, CELESTE. Walters, Celeste, photograph. Reproduced by permission.

WATKINS, DAWN L. Watkins, Dawn L., photograph. Reproduced by permission.

WHITE, NANCY. White, Nancy, photograph. Reproduced by permission.

WINTER, JANET. Winter, Janet, photograph by Robert A. Winter. Reproduced by permission of Janet Winter.

WOJCIECHOWSKI, SUSAN. Lynch, P. J., illustrator. From a jacket of *The Christmas Miracle of Jonathan Toomey,* by Susan Wojciechowski. Candlewick Press, 1995. Illustrations copyright © 1995 by P. J. Lynch. All rights reserved. Reproduced by permission./ Natti, Susanna, illustrator. From a jacket of *Beany and the Dreaded Wedding,* by Susan Wojciechowski. Candlewick Press, 2000. Illustrations copyright © 2000 by Susanna Natti. All rights reserved. Reproduced by permission.

YOUNG, DAN. Young, Dan, photographer. From a cover of *Big Brother Dustin,* by Alden R. Carter. Albert Whitman & Company, 1997. Photographs copyright © 1997 by Dan Young. Reproduced by permission.

SOMETHING ABOUT THE AUTHOR

ACKERMAN, Karen 1951-

Personal

Born 1951, in Cincinnati, OH; married.

Addresses

Home—Cincinnati, OH. *Office*—c/o Author Mail, St. Paul Books and Media, Boston, MA. *E-mail*—KAbooks@webtv.net.

Career

Poet, playwright, and author of children's books.

Awards, Honors

Parents' Choice Award, 1986, for *Flannery Row;* Society of Midland Authors award for Juvenile Fiction, 1989, for *Song and Dance Man.*

Writings

FOR CHILDREN

Flannery Row, illustrated by Karen Ann Weinhaus, Atlantic Monthly (Boston, MA), 1986.
Song and Dance Man, illustrated by Stephen Gammell, Knopf (New York, NY), 1989.
Araminta's Paint Box, illustrated by Betsy Lewin, Atheneum (New York, NY), 1990.

The Banshee, illustrated by David Ray, Philomel (New York, NY), 1990.
Just Like Max, illustrated by George Schmidt, Knopf (New York, NY), 1990.
Moveable Mabeline, illustrated by Linda Allen, Philomel (New York, NY), 1990.
The Tin Heart, illustrated by Michael Hays, Atheneum (New York, NY), 1990.
The Leaves in October, Atheneum (New York, NY), 1991.
The Broken Boy, Philomel (New York, NY), 1991.
I Know a Place, illustrated by Deborah Kogan Ray, Houghton (Boston, MA), 1992.
This Old House, illustrated by Sylvie Wickstrom, Atheneum (New York, NY), 1992.
When Mama Retires, illustrated by Alexa Grace, Knopf (New York, NY), 1992.
Walking with Clara Belle, illustrated by Debbie Mason, St. Paul Books (Boston, MA), 1993.
The Night Crossing, illustrated by Elizabeth Sayles, Knopf (New York, NY), 1994.
By the Dawn's Early Light, illustrated by Catherine Stock, Atheneum (New York, NY), 1994.
Bingleman's Midway, illustrated by Barry Moser, Boyds Mills Press (Honesdale, NJ), 1995.
The Sleeping Porch, illustrated by Liz Sayles, Morrow (New York, NY), 1995.
In the Park with Dad: A Story for Kids Whose Parents Don't Live Together, illustrated by Linda Crockett-Blassingame, St. Paul Books (Boston, MA), 1996.

Author's works have been translated into Spanish.

Complete with bowler hat and gold-tipped cane, Grandpa performs a vaudeville routine for his grandchildren in Karen Ackerman's award winner. (Cover illustration by Stephen Gammell.)

OTHER

(Collector) Emily Dickinson, *A Brighter Garden: Poetry,* illustrated by Tasha Tudor, Philomel (New York, NY), 1990.

Adaptations

The Song and Dance Man was narrated by Danny Gerard and recorded on audiocassette by American School Publishers, 1991.

Work in Progress

Bean's Big Day; Letters from the Nowhere Room.

Sidelights

Karen Ackerman opens a window into the American past through her picture books for young readers. *Flannery Row* hearkens back to the early nineteenth century as it introduces readers to a whaling ship captain and his large family, while *Araminta's Paint Box* takes readers west on a covered wagon. In *Just Like Max,* Ackerman depicts what it was like growing up in the city during the early twentieth century. Each of her books centers on house and home, even on less traditional homes, where Mom works the night shift, or where family members struggle with adversity in its many forms. Ackerman's books have benefitted from

the work of many talented illustrators, among them Stephen Gammell who earned a Caldecott Award for his illustrations for Ackerman's 1988 picture book, *Song and Dance Man.*

In Ackerman's award-winning *Flannery Row,* published in 1986, Commander Ahab Flannery is preparing to take leave of his twenty-six children and set sail for another whaling voyage off the coast of New England. With twenty-six children to keep track of, the captain and his wife have started each child's name with a different letter of the alphabet. Now that it's time for goodbyes, the only way he can be sure of seeing each one is to have them line up in alpha order, a process Ackerman recounts in a bouncy, rhythmic text that *New York Times Book Review* contributor Michael Patrick Hearn dubbed "a charming memory game." In her *School Library Journal* review, Virginia Opocensky praised the ABC book as "a charmer" due to its upbeat humor and the use of "old-fashioned names" like Blanche, Caleb, Upton, Xavier, Yancy, and Zack.

In the tradition of Rachel Field's classic *Hitty, Araminta's Paint Box* recounts the history of Americans moving West as Ackerman follows the path of a lost paintbox. In 1847 Araminta Darling is a passenger in the covered wagon carrying her family from Boston to California. During a stop in northern Pennsylvania, her father buys her a boxed set of paints for the trip, but when the wagon breaks a wheel and tips over, the paintbox becomes lost. A Mennonite family finds the box while following the same trail shortly afterward; the box continues on its trip, transported via coach, river boat, and mule, before ending up in the possession of a gold prospector who, miraculously, returns it to Araminta's doorstep. Calling *Araminta's Paint Box* a "sweet, lively book" in her *New York Times Book Review* appraisal, Jennifer Allen added that "It's a pleasure to find a frontier book specially appealing to ... early-grade children, readers or not." Allen's praise was echoed by Denise Wilms in her *Booklist* review, who dubbed the work "a satisfying tale that also shows what mid-nineteenth-century westward travel was like."

The shift from generation to generation figures strongly in many of Ackerman's picture books, such as *Moveable Madeline,* wherein young Mimi and Isobel long for a beautiful porcelain doll with moveable arms and legs and eyes that open and close. Sitting in the window of a local toy store in the late nineteenth century, Moveable Mabeline is something new, and when the doll suddenly vanishes from the shop window, the two girls excitedly hope that she might find her way to their home. But she never does, and it is only decades later that Mimi and Isobel, now elderly women, discover the doll waiting for them in an antique shop and buy it as a gift for a young relative. Noting Ackerman's ability to make her story "poignant, but not saccharine," *Horn Book* contributor Mary M. Burns added that *Moveable Madeline* "touches the heart without seeming manipulative." Young readers "will recognize the longing and disappointment the girls feel," added *Booklist* reviewer Stephanie Zvirin, noting that "the artwork and text convey [both] with ... dignity and understanding."

Also focusing on generations is *Just Like Max.* In this story, Aaron's Great-Uncle Max works as a tailor on the fourth floor of a brownstone. Aaron is fascinated by Max's job making patterns, cutting fabric, and creating beautiful clothing for his fashionable clients. When Max suffers a stroke, Aaron attempts to take over the tailor shop, although his skills are not totally up to the task. It is not until forty years pass that readers meet up again with Aaron, working as hard as Max once had, and the subject of fascination to his own nephews who climb the four stories to watch him at work as a writer. A *Kirkus Reviews* critic called *Just Like Max* a "touching, well-shaped intergenerational story," while in *Booklist* Leone McDermott praised Ackerman's text as "simple, precise, and affecting in its understated nostalgia and devotion." *Just Like Max* was also compared by several reviewers to Ackerman's 1989 book *Song and Dance Man,* in which a beloved grandfather recounts his early years as a vaudevillian. "Grandparents are a bridge to the past," noted Eda LeShan in her *New York Times Book Review* article on *Song and Dance Man.* "This engaging and ebullient storybook puts grandparents in the spotlight—where most of [them] want to be."

While nostalgic about the past, Ackerman also recognizes that many in her young readership have a different concept of family: some families have only mom or dad

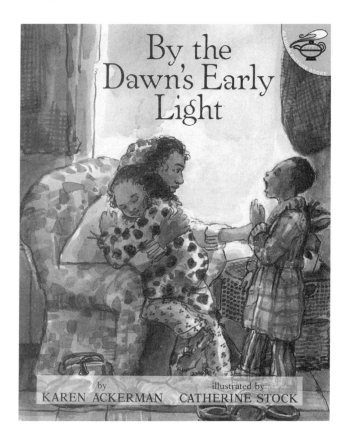

Rachel and her little brother spend early mornings with their mother when she comes home from her nighttime factory job. (Cover illustration by Catherine Stock.)

at the helm, while others must deal with poverty or other difficulties. In *By the Dawn's Early Light,* she focuses on an African-American family where Grandma takes charge every night after Mom leaves for her factory job on the graveyard shift. While Nana and Josh do not like being different from their friends, whose two-parent families are together in the evening, they make the best of things in a book that *School Library Journal* contributor Claudia Cooper called "a reassuring affirmation of intergenerational love, regardless of circumstances." Mothers at work outside the home are not a new phenomenon, as Ackerman makes clear in her 1992 book *When Mama Retires.* Set during World War II, the story finds three boys "motherless" as well as "fatherless" after Dad goes off to war and Mom gets a job as a riveter at a nearby factory, making airplanes for the war effort. Ackerman's book "offers children an opportunity to engage family members in discussion about their memories of life at home during a momentous period in our history," according to *Horn Book* contributor Hanna B. Zeiger. Commenting on the technological differences children will be sure to pick up from Alexa Grace's stylized illustrations, Lee Bock added in *School Library Journal* that *When Mama Retires* reflects the fact that "Styles have changed, but the substance of family remains constant."

Ackerman's 1991 book *The Leaves in October* touches upon another family disruption: poverty. Nine-year-old Livvy and her little brother, suddenly find themselves homeless after their father loses his job at the factory. Now in a city-run homeless shelter, Livvy tries to earn money making tissue-paper flowers, and hopes that by autumn the family will find their own apartment. Other problems arise after her dad finds a new job: it requires him to be on the road most of the time, and the children's mother has long since abandoned the family, leaving the children to fend for themselves. "Livvy will capture hearts with her sensitivity, tenacity, and courage," noted *School Library Journal* contributor Gerry Larson, praising the book for its depiction of homelessness as an emotionally difficult time for all family members. *The Broken Boy,* a longer, novel-length work for young readers, focuses on another family torn by tragic circumstances. Ackerman's 1991 book deals with old age and senility, disability, mental illness, and death through the narration of Solly Freedom, a teen with a mentally-retarded younger brother and a disjointed family life. A *Kirkus Reviews* critic found "the dialogue ... witty and offbeat, the situation engrossing, the characters perceptively drawn, and the outcome moving and credible."

Biographical and Critical Sources

PERIODICALS

Belles Lettres, summer, 1994, Bettina Berch, review of *By the Dawn's Early Light,* p. 44.

Booklist, February 1, 1990, Denise Wilms, review of *Araminta's Paint Box,* p. 1081; November 1, 1990, Stephanie Zvirin, review of *Moveable Mabeline,* pp. 524-525; December 1, 1990, Leone McDermott,

Ackerman drew upon her childhood memories for her story of a carnival's powerful spell on a young boy. (Cover illustration by Barry Moser.)

review of *Just Like Max,* p. 748; December 15, 1990, Leone McDermott, review of *The Tin Heart,* p. 850; February 1, 1991, Hazel Rochman, review of *The Leaves in October,* p. 1127; July, 1991, Hazel Rochman, review of *The Broken Boy,* p. 2045; January 15, 1992, Carolyn Phelan, review of *When Mama Retires,* p. 946; April 1, 1992, Kay Weisman, review of *I Know a Place,* p. 1455; October 15, 1992, Ilene Cooper, review of *This Old House,* p. 436.

Children's Book Review Service, November, 1990, Lee Beasley, review of *The Tin Heart,* p. 30; February, 1991, review of *Moveable Mabeline,* p. 73; April, 1992, Lee Beasley, review of *I Know a Place,* p. 97.

Horn Book, November, 1990, Mary M. Burns, review of *Moveable Mabeline,* pp. 737-738; March, 1992, Hanna B. Zeiger, review of *When Mama Retires,* p. 189.

Kirkus Reviews, January 1, 1990, review of *Araminta's Paint Box,* p. 43; August 15, 1990, review of *Just Like Max,* p. 1165; May 1, 1991, review of *The Broken Boy,* p. 601; February 1, 1992, review of *I Know a Place,* p. 179; April 1, 1994, review of *The Night Crossing,* p. 477; May 1, 1994, review of *By the Dawn's Early Light,* p. 625; October 15, 1995, review of *Bingleman's Midway,* p. 1486.

New York Times Book Review, July 13, 1986, Michael Patrick Hearn, review of *Flannery Row,* p. 22; February 12, 1989, Eda LeShan, review of *Song and Dance Man,* p. 25; September 16, 1990, Jennifer Allen, review of *Araminta's Paint Box,* p. 14; November 11, 1990, Betsy Wade, review of *Just Like Max,* p. 57.

Publishers Weekly, May 30, 1986, Diane Roback, review of *Flannery Row,* p. 62; October 23, 1995, review of *Bingleman's Midway,* p. 69

School Library Journal, May, 1986, Virginia Opocensky, review of *Flannery Row,* p. 67; November, 1990, Marcia Hupp, review of *Just Like Max,* p. 74; March, 1991, Gerry Larson, review of *The Leaves in October,* p. 192; June, 1991, Carol A. Edwards, review of *The Broken Boy,* p. 122; April, 1992, Lee Bock, review of

When Mama Retires, p. 86; August, 1992, Lucy Young Clem, review of *I Know a Place,* p. 132; March, 1993, J. J. Votapka, review of *This Old House,* p. 170; June, 1994, Claudia Cooper, review of *By the Dawn's Early Light,* p. 94; May, 1995, Jane Marino, review of *The Sleeping Porch,* p. 81.

Washington Post Book World, August 10, 1986, Arthur Yorinks, review of *Flannery Row,* p. 8; May 13, 1990, Selma G. Lanes, review of *Araminta's Paint Box,* p. 22.*

*   *   *

ADLER, C(arol) S(chwerdtfeger) 1932-

Personal

Born February 23, 1932, in Long Island, NY; daughter of Oscar Edward (a car mechanic and chief petty officer in the Naval Reserve) and Clarice (an office manager; maiden name, Landsberg) Schwerdtfeger; married Arnold R. Adler (an engineer), June, 1952; children: Steven and Clifford (twins), Kenneth. *Education:* Hunter College (now Hunter College of the City University of New York), B.A. (cum laude), 1953; Russell Sage College, M.A., 1967.

Addresses

Home—7041 North Cathedral Rock Pl., Tucson, AZ 85718 (winter); Box 11, Wellfleet, MA 02667 (summer).

Career

Worthington Corp., Harrison, NJ, advertising assistant, 1952-54; Niskayuna Middle Schools, Niskayuna, NY, English teacher, 1968-77; writer, 1977—. Volunteer worker in child abuse and protection program at local children's shelter, and as tutor of foster children. *Member:* Society of Children's Book Writers and Illustrators, Author's Guild, Author's League of America, Phi Beta Kappa.

Awards, Honors

Golden Kite Award for Fiction, Society of Children's Book Writers and Illustrators, Children's Choice award, International Reading Association and the Children's Book Council, and Child Study Association of America's Children's Books of the Year selection, all 1979, and William Allen White Children's Book Award, 1982, all for *The Magic of the Glits;* Children's Choice Book, International Reading Association, 1981, for *In Our House Scott Is My Brother;* Best Young Adult Books of the Year selection, American Library Association, 1983, for *The Shell Lady's Daughter;* Child Study Children's Book Award, Child Study Center's Book Committee at Bank Street College of Education (NY), 1985, for *With Westie and the Tin Man.*

Writings

The Magic of the Glits, illustrated by Ati Forberg, Macmillan (New York, NY), 1979.
The Silver Coach, Coward (New York, NY), 1979.
In Our House Scott Is My Brother, Macmillan (New York, NY), 1980.
Shelter on Blue Barns Road, Macmillan (New York, NY), 1981.
The Cat That Was Left Behind, Clarion (New York, NY), 1981.
Down by the River, Coward (New York, NY), 1981.
Footsteps on the Stairs, Delacorte (New York, NY), 1982.
Some Other Summer (sequel to *The Magic of the Glits),* Macmillan (New York, NY), 1982.
The Evidence That Wasn't There, Clarion (New York, NY), 1982.
The Once in a While Hero, Coward (New York, NY), 1982.
Binding Ties, Delacorte (New York, NY), 1983.
Get Lost, Little Brother, Clarion (New York, NY), 1983.
Roadside Valentine, Macmillan (New York, NY), 1983.
The Shell Lady's Daughter, Coward (New York, NY), 1983.
Fly Free, Coward (New York, NY), 1984.
Good-bye, Pink Pig, Putnam (New York, NY), 1985.
Shadows on Little Reef Bay, Clarion (New York, NY), 1985.
With Westie and the Tin Man, Macmillan (New York, NY), 1985.
Split Sisters, illustrated by Mike Wimmer, Macmillan (New York, NY), 1986.
Kiss the Clown, Clarion (New York, NY), 1986.
If You Need Me, Macmillan (New York, NY), 1987.
Carly's Buck, Clarion (New York, NY), 1987.
Eddie's Blue-winged Dragon, Putnam (New York, NY), 1988.
Always and Forever Friends, Clarion (New York, NY), 1988.
One Sister Too Many (sequel to *Split Sisters),* Macmillan (New York, NY), 1989.
The Lump in the Middle, Clarion (New York, NY), 1989.
Ghost Brother, Clarion (New York, NY), 1990.
Help, Pink Pig! (sequel to *Good-bye, Pink Pig),* Putnam (New York, NY), 1990.
A Tribe for Lexi, Macmillan (New York, NY), 1991.
Mismatched Summer, Putnam (New York, NY), 1991.
Tuna Fish Thanksgiving, Clarion (New York, NY), 1992.
Daddy's Climbing Tree, Clarion (New York, NY), 1993.
Willie, the Frog Prince, Clarion (New York, NY), 1994.
That Horse Whiskey!, Clarion (New York, NY), 1994.
Youn Hee and Me, Harcourt (New York, NY), 1995.
Courtyard Cat, Clarion (New York, NY), 1995.
What's to Be Scared of, Suki?, Clarion (New York, NY), 1996.
More than a Horse, Clarion (New York, NY), 1997.
Her Blue Straw Hat, Harcourt (New York, NY), 1997.
Not Just a Summer Crush, Clarion (New York, NY), 1998.
Winning, Clarion (New York, NY), 1999.
One Unhappy Horse, Clarion (New York, NY), 2001.
The No Place Cat, Clarion (New York, NY), 2002.

Contributor of articles and stories to periodicals, including *American Girl, Co-Ed,* and *Ingenue.* Adler's books

C. S. Adler

have been published in Japan, Germany, England, Denmark, Sweden, France, and Austria.

Adaptations

Get Lost, Little Brother was adapted for audio cassette, Talking Books, 1983.

Sidelights

C. S. Adler may have gotten a late start in publishing books for young readers—she was in her late forties when *The Magic of the Glits,* her first novel, was released—but she has more than made up for lost time with some forty books to her credit. Adler writes for middle graders and young adults, penning books about magic, family relations, and emotional problems. Praised for her characters, both male and female, who demonstrate humor as well as pathos, and for the upbeat tone of her writing, Adler tries to draw a realistic picture of the world in her books. A teacher turned writer, she brings to her books the real-life concerns of her intended readers, running a gamut of topics from dyslexia and skate boarding to latchkey kids and horseback riding.

Adler's award-winning books include *The Magic of the Glits, In Our House Scott Is My Brother, The Shell Lady's Daughter,* and *With Westie and the Tin Man.* The immediacy of her writing is in part due to the fact that she draws heavily upon her personal experience when shaping plot and characters. "Looking back," Adler once wrote, "it almost seems as if everything bad and good in my life served to mold me into the writer I became."

Born in 1932 in Rockaway Beach, Long Island, Adler was brought up in the Bronx, Brooklyn, and Manhattan. "We moved every couple of years because I had a restless father who was never happy with his boss," Adler once noted. Her father was a car mechanic and a chief petty officer in the Naval Reserve and her mother a bookkeeper and office manager. Much of Adler's early care fell to her maternal grandmother, "a soft, clinging woman" according to Adler, who had lost her own husband when she was still young and who doted on her young granddaughter, overprotecting Adler in the process. Suffering from asthma and a heart murmur, Adler was not allowed to take part in many youthful games, and early on found comfort in reading and roaming about the city. An only child, she was shy with her peers, and her supposed physical limitations only served to set her further apart. "I wasn't allowed to participate in gym class," Adler once recalled, adding the observation that "Being a nonparticipant in sports stamps a school child as a misfit." Nonetheless, she usually managed to find at least one other outsider to befriend wherever she lived, and her aunt, "the bright and lively baby of the family" although twenty years Adler's senior, served as a surrogate older sister to Adler.

Adler was in fact raised in a household of women, for her father left their home when she was twelve to marry another woman. A "cold and distant man," he was never very close to his daughter. Still, there were memories of spending happy hours with him in a rowboat on Long Island Sound, or of going to with him to his parents' farm in the Adirondacks to pick blackberries. Some of her love of nature was inherited from her father as well, and when he left, a part of Adler's life left with him. "Certainly many of the broken families in my books are comprehensible to me because of my own background," the writer once noted.

With the departure of her father, Adler and her extended family moved to Manhattan, where her mother was soon busier than ever, single-handedly supporting the family. Throughout all her childhood ups and downs, Adler found one constant: books. "The minute I learned to read, I lived my life in books," Adler once commented. "There I could happily escape being me.... I became daring and beautiful and lovable—all the things I knew I wasn't in real life." Never a re-reader of books, Adler always pushed on for new reading experiences, devouring Louisa May Alcott, *Doctor Dolittle, The Secret Garden,* and *Hans Brinker; or, The Silver Skates* among others. "I spent my most philosophical moments on rooftops communing with what I called 'god' via sunsets and clouds and stars. I was a pantheist early on." She also began writing early on, "publishing" her stories between cardboard covers held together by rubber bands.

Tall and gawky as a preteen, Adler came into her own as a teenager. Appearing older than her years, she attended college dances while still a student at Hunter High School. It was at one such dance that she met her future husband, a World War II veteran studying mechanical engineering. She was sixteen, he was twenty-two; it was only several months later that he found out her true age. "It was after I met [Arnold] and we began to 'go steady' that I started to be happy, consistently happy," Adler once commented. The couple soon determined to marry, but only after Adler completed college, which she did in three years. "Despite my rush to be done with higher education," she recalled, "I found some of my English major courses stimulating, and I was fascinated by anthropology." Graduating cum laude, Adler was soon married and settled into a more or less typical role as a young wife of the 1950s. "The ignoble truth was that getting married and having babies were the major goals in my life in my late teens."

Life in the suburbs was not all diapers and birthday parties, however, for Adler continued writing—at night, while the children were napping, and at any other odd

An Authors Guild Backinprint.com Edition

"Adler infuses her first book with sympathy and sharp insights and she writes with professionalism."

—*Publishers Weekly*

The Magic of the Glits

C.S. ADLER

Twelve-year-old Jeremy invents the magical Glits, who make wishes come true, to help Lynnette overcome the death of her mother.

moment she could. She had twin boys and then a third boy in quick succession, but still managed to turn out several adult novels and a quantity of short stories—all unpublished—before her children reached school age. "One of my virtues as a writer is persistence," Adler once noted. She collected drawers full of rejection slips, but kept on writing, always dreaming of the day when she would be invited to an editor's office and told that her book was going to be published. Her husband's work also took the family from New Jersey to Cincinnati, Ohio, and back to New York state. All the while, Adler wrote and kept up contact with other writers through writing and reading groups.

Eventually Adler's persistence paid off. A short story she had written with a protagonist very much like her as a teenager was bought by *American Girl* magazine. Adler, then thirty-two, was momentarily elated, but ultimately did not feel she had reached her goal of "real" publication. Her short story was published and forgotten almost immediately. The same fate befell the sixteen more short stories she would sell over the next years. While her goal remained before her, these early stories taught her a primary writer's lesson: write about what you know about. Meantime, she returned to college to get a master's degree in elementary education, and spent much of the next ten years teaching in the Niskayuna schools in suburban Schenectady, New York. Never a great disciplinarian, Adler did know how to inspire her sixth and eighth graders to write, and almost decided to give up the notion of becoming a writer.

A summer vacation on Cape Cod helped to refuel Adler's childhood dream of becoming a "real" writer. Sitting on the dunes while her husband fished the breakers, she began a story about fairies that might live in the wave tops, a story she told from the point of view of a boy she had once taught in an English class. She wrote fifty pages, and then put the work away at the start of another school year. Although she didn't realize it at the time, that year would prove to be Adler's last as a teacher. Taking a course in children's literature in the evening, she dusted off her summertime story, turned it into a novel, and sent it off to Macmillan. When she got the telltale manuscript package back, she at first thought it was another rejection. In this case, however, it was a request for revisions—her novel had found a home. That June she quit teaching and began living the life of a full-time writer.

The Magic of the Glits is told from the point of view of twelve-year-old Jeremy, whose summer on Cape Cod is apparently ruined by the twin disasters of a broken leg and having to look after seven-year-old Lynette, whose mother has died. Reluctantly, Jeremy begins to feel responsible for Lynette, and invents the Glits, magical beings, and she responds to him with both trust and love. A contributor to *Publishers Weekly* noted that Adler "infuses her first book with sympathy and sharp insights, [writing] with the professionalism achieved as a published author of short stories." *Horn Book* critic Virginia Haviland called Adler's debut a "perceptive story," and both readers and award committees agreed; *The Magic*

Caitlin wants her adopted Korean brother's newfound sister to become part of the family. (Cover illustration by John Clapp.)

of the Glits won the Golden Kite Award from the Society of Children's Book Writers and Illustrators, an auspicious beginning. Adler continued the adventures of her two young protagonists in the sequel *Some Other Summer,* in which Lynette's affection for Jeremy grows into a definite crush that their age difference ultimately thwarts.

Several of Adler's books contain elements of magic, though Adler herself has claimed not to be interested in magic herself. In her second book, *The Silver Coach,* the miniature coach of the title enables those who know how to use it to live out daydreams. Again, the theme of the book is larger than that of magic; in this case the breakup of a marriage is viewed from the vantage point of a twelve-year-old girl and her sister. "The important quality of the book is the depth of understanding of family relationships and its ability to reproduce them faithfully in lively style," commented a reviewer for

Junior Bookshelf, who concluded, "This is an author worth watching."

Adler's third title, *In Our House Scott Is My Brother,* is another award winner, the story of a blended family and the adjustments that are ultimately required in order for such an arrangement to have a chance to work. The book focuses on the relationship between new half-siblings Jodi and Scott. According to a reviewer for *Bulletin of the Center for Children's Books,* the "writing style is fluid and the characterization has depth, but the outstanding facet of the book is [the] protective love" the children have for their parents. Mary M. Burns described the work in *Horn Book* as a "poignant first-person narrative with a credible heroine." Other Adler titles dealing with the fallout from broken families include *Tuna Fish Thanksgiving* and the novel duo *Split Sisters* and *One Sister Too Many.*

The loneliness Adler recalled from her own childhood came into play in the writing of her novels *Good-bye, Pink Pig, A Tribe for Lexi,* and *The Cat That Was Left Behind.* In the last novel, thirteen-year-old Chad is a foster child with few illusions left about adults. A new family seems nice at first, but Chad waits for the other shoe to drop, and meanwhile finds solace in a stray cat he takes in. He dreams that some day he will be reunited with his mother, but when a letter from her advises him otherwise, he is forced to face reality. His foster family wants to adopt him, but Chad must deal with his past before he is able and willing to accept new emotional bonds. A reviewer in *Bulletin of the Center for Children's Books* called *The Cat That Was Left Behind* "smoothly written" and "perceptive." As in *The Silver Coach,* in *Good-bye, Pink Pig* a figurine brings magical daydreams, this time to lonely, ten-year-old Amanda, who ultimately finds a friend in her grandmother. Eleanor K. MacDonald observed in *School Library Journal* that Adler's "sensitive story should appeal to children who have suffered from the 'lonelies'." Amanda and her pink pig are also featured in the sequel *Help, Pink Pig!*

Adler has also turned her hand to young adult fiction with *Down by the River, Roadside Valentine, The Shell Lady's Daughter, Binding Ties, Kiss the Clown,* and *If You Need Me.* Teen love figures largely in these books, but as Hildegarde Gray noted in a *Best Sellers* review of *Down by the River,* Adler has presented a "love story in which the man and woman learn to need and like each other long, long before the meeting of the bodies in delicate, heart-felt, better than heat-felt, physical love." An American Library Association Best Book for Young Adults title, *The Shell Lady's Daughter* is another thoughtful story from Adler, this time dealing with a nervous breakdown and a daughter's attempts to help her mother. *Booklist* contributor Ilene Cooper noted "the fluidity of the writing" which made the book one "in which readers will find themselves caught up." Cooper concluded that the "talented Adler continues to hone her craft." In another YA title, *Kiss the Clown,* an unusual combination of dyslexia and Guatemala forms the backdrop for a triangular love story, while in *If You Need Me,* school activities, responsibilities to friends, and divorce concerns and blended families each take center stage.

In 1986 and again in 1988, Adler suffered personal losses that deeply affected her writing. Her mother died in 1986, and one of her twin sons was killed in a car accident two years later. She once recalled an incident shortly before these deaths, when she was doing a school presentation. One young member of the audience asked if Adler had written any books about people in one's family dying. "'No,' I told him, 'I've been lucky. Old as I am, I haven't lost anyone close to me.' I didn't feel confident writing about death with no experience of it. Well, now I'm confident." Both *Ghost Brother* and *Daddy's Climbing Tree* were inspired by those deaths, the former a tribute to her son.

In addition to mining her own life for ideas, Adler gets inspiration for her fiction from reading the newspaper, even from fans. *The Lump in the Middle,* a story about a middle child, was the result of a personal request by Adler's tennis partner; *A Tribe for Lexi* was the result of an overheard dinner conversation about a girl who built

Eleven-year-old Jessica cannot accept her father's death in a car accident and looks for him at his house with the climbing tree in Adler's story. (Cover illustration by Diane de Groat.)

a raft and set off to look for Indians along a Catskills river. Something of a workaholic as far as her books are concerned, she writes everywhere—at her desk, at the kitchen table, while waiting for a plane, or driving in the car with her husband. During the winter in her home in Tucson, Arizona, she writes six hours a day, usually from noon to six. In the summer Adler retreats to her house on Cape Cod, gets up early and writes five pages, and then has the rest of the day for household concerns and guests. She publishes at least one title per year, providing her fans with a continuing supply of stories told from both male and female points of view: novels of suspense such as *The Evidence That Wasn't There, Footsteps on the Stairs,* and *Shadows on Little Reef Bay;* novels about friendship in *Always and Forever Friends* and *Willie, the Frog Prince;* about school traumas in *The Once in a While Hero;* and about horses in *That Horse Whiskey!* and *One Unhappy Horse.*

Foremost, though, Alder's books are all about family. Her 1995 novel *Youn Hee and Me* enlarges on her characteristic theme of family when eleven-year-old Caitlin insists that her adopted Korean brother's real sister in Korea also become part of the family, with unexpected results. Deborah Stevenson, reviewing the title in *Bulletin of the Center for Children's Books,* summed up much of Adler's other work as well, noting that she "has a flair for ... vivid and slightly unusual family stories." Family communication plays a pivotal role in 1998's *Not Just a Summer Crush,* in which twelve-year-old Hana struggles with her parents' and siblings' reactions to her crush on her sixth grade teacher. Although she and Mr. Crane become good friends during the summer break, their relationship remains steadfastly platonic. When Hana develops romantic feelings for her teacher, her parents grow suspicious of Mr. Crane's intentions, and Hana must force them to realize that the romance is strictly one-sided. *Horn Book* contributor Jennifer M. Brabander found that "Adler's bittersweet narrative shrewdly captures the wretchedness of feeling completely misunderstood and being neither a child nor an adult."

Her flair for portraying real young people in situations that illustrate the support and resilience of many different types of families has made Adler a popular writer. As she once admitted, "In a sense I'm still teaching. Since I am an optimist, I think things work out well for *most* people. Children tend to despair because they have no idea that tomorrow could bring a sunny day. I can remind them of that.... I hope that my books will make kids more positive about life as well as more sympathetic to others. I also hope that I can entertain them. I'd like them to feel good about themselves when they finish one of my books."

Biographical and Critical Sources

BOOKS

Contemporary Literary Criticism, Volume 35, Gale (Detroit, MI), 1985.

Something about the Author Autobiography Series, Volume 15, Gale (Detroit, MI), 1994.

PERIODICALS

Best Sellers, January, 1982, Hildegarde Gray, review of *Down by the River,* p. 400.
Book Report, September-October, 1997, Sharon Johnson Oothoudt, review of *More than a Horse,* p. 30.
Booklist, June 1, 1983, Ilene Cooper, review of *The Shell Lady's Daughter,* p. 1270; May 15, 1991, p. 1797; April 15, 1994, p. 1533; November 1, 1994, pp. 490-491; April 15, 1995, p. 1497; August, 1995, pp. 1945-1946; November 1, 1996, Susan Dove Lempke, review of *What's to Be Scared of, Suki?,* p. 497; March 15, 1997, Chris Sherman, review of *More than a Horse,* p. 1241; September 1, 1997, Lauren Peterson, review of *Her Blue Straw Hat,* p. 121; November 15, 1998, Shelle Rosenfeld, review of *Not Just a Summer Crush,* p. 586.
Bulletin of the Center for Children's Books, March, 1980, review of *In Our House Scott Is My Brother,* p. 125; December, 1981, review of *The Cat That Was Left Behind,* p. 61; May, 1990, p. 207; April, 1992, p. 197; July, 1993, p. 340; December, 1994, p. 118; March, 1995, Deborah Stevenson, review of *Youn Hee and Me,* p. 226; September, 1995, p. 4; September, 1997, p. 5; October, 1998, p. 51.
Horn Book, April, 1979, Virginia Haviland, review of *The Magic of the Glits,* p. 187; June, 1980, Mary M. Burns, review of *In Our House Scott Is My Brother,* p. 293; July, 1993, pp. 455-456; November, 1998, Jennifer M. Brabander, review of *Not Just a Summer Crush,* p. 724.
Junior Bookshelf, August, 1981, review of *The Silver Coach,* p. 154.
Kirkus Reviews, April 15, 1993, p. 523.
Publishers Weekly, February 5, 1979, review of *The Magic of the Glits,* p. 95; June 23, 1997, review of *Her Blue Straw Hat,* p. 92.
School Library Journal, December, 1985, Eleanor K. MacDonald, review of *Good-bye, Pink Pig,* pp. 84-85; June, 1994, p. 124; November, 1994, p. 102; May, 1995, p. 104; October, 1996, Susan W. Hunter, review of *What's to Be Scared of, Suki?,* p. 120; April, 1997, review of *More than a Horse,* p. 134; September, 1997, p. 210; November 1, 1998, Francisca Goldsmith, review of *Not Just a Summer Crush,* p. 116; September, 1999, Connie Tyrrell Burns, review of *Winning,* p. 218; April, 2001, Carol Schene, review of *One Unhappy Horse,* p. 138.

—Sketch by J. Sydney Jones

*   *   *

ALBERTSON, Susan
See WOJCIECHOWSKI, Susan

ARONSON, Marc

Personal

Married Marina Budhos (an author); children: one son. *Education:* Earned a Ph.D. in American history.

Addresses

Home—New York, NY. *Office*—c/o Author Mail, Carus Publishing, 315 5th St., Peru, IL 61354.

Career

Harper & Row, New York, NY, and later, Henry Holt Books for Young Readers, New York, NY, editor of books for children and young adults, became senior editor; Carus Publishing, Chicago, IL, editorial director and vice president of nonfiction development, 2000—; *zooba.com*, managing editor; writer. Instructor in publishing courses at New York University, Simmons College, and the Radcliffe Publishing program.

Awards, Honors

Publishers Weekly Best Book of the Year and *New York Times* Notable Book citations, both 1998, both for *Art Attack: A Short Cultural History of the Avant-Garde;* *Boston Globe-Horn Book* Award for nonfiction, 2000, Blue Ribbon Award from *Bulletin of the Center for Children's Books,* 2000, and Robert F. Sibert Award for "most distinguished informational book for children," American Library Association, 2001 (first year awarded), all for *Sir Walter Ralegh and the Quest for El Dorado.*

Marc Aronson

Writings

YOUNG ADULT NONFICTION

(With Thomas Leonard and Cynthia Crippen) *Day by Day: The Seventies,* two volumes, Facts on File (New York, NY), 1988.
(With Ellen Meltzer) *Day by Day: The Eighties,* two volumes, Facts on File (New York, NY), 1995.
Art Attack: A Short Cultural History of the Avant-Garde, Clarion Books (New York, NY), 1998.
Exploding the Myths: The Truth about Teens and Reading, Scarecrow Press (Lanham, MD), 2000.
Sir Walter Ralegh and the Quest for El Dorado, Clarion Books (New York, NY), 2000.

Contributor to *The Holocaust in Literature for Youth,* edited by Edward T. Sullivan, Scarecrow Press (Lanham, MD), 1999.

Sidelights

Marc Aronson writes nonfiction titles for young adults that have been praised for their engrossing prose style and unique approach to source materials. For example, in *Art Attack: A Short Cultural History of the Avant-Garde,* Aronson explains that throughout history avant-garde artists have challenged the world with their personal visions, and that young artists, even adolescents, have often taken the greatest risks to bring their art to the public. "What an exciting invitation to a brisk but rigorous survey that connects Marcel Duchamp, the Russian avant-garde and Mondrian to Charles Ives and the Sex Pistols!," observed a reviewer in the *New York Times Book Review.* Indeed, it is through such cross-cultural and cross-generic connections that *Art Attack* manages to offer fresh insights into the history of twentieth-century art despite its brevity, according to reviewers. Throughout the volume, art movements and the work of individual artists are explored in conjunction with the evolution of twentieth-century music. "In fact, what is unique and appealing in Aronson's cultural history is his placing of experimental and popular music within the art world," remarked Shirley Wilton in *School Library Journal.* Thus, Aronson juxtaposes the artwork of the Dadaists and rap music, Jean-Michel Basquiat's expressive scribbles and the jazz innovations of Philip Glass. The result is "an exceptional resource," Wilton concluded.

Aronson turned to the more distant past in *Sir Walter Ralegh and the Quest for El Dorado,* a work for which he was named the first winner of the Robert F. Sibert Award for the "most distinguished informational book for children" published in 2000. Ralegh (as the man himself rendered his name) was both an exceptional figure, in his talents, ambition, and willingness to take large risks, and representative of his times, in that his talents, ambition, and willingness to take risks were all pointed towards exploring and conquering the New World. Ralegh's intelligence and drive took him from rural obscurity to courtier in Queen Elizabeth's court to fame and fortune through his journeys to North and South America. The resulting story of his life is an exciting tale. "Aronson not only details Ralegh's career as soldier, sailor, explorer, writer, and schemer but consistently discusses causes, effects, and the broader significance of events large and small," commented a reviewer for *Kirkus Reviews.* Aronson's skills as a writer of histories for young people were extolled by reviewers. Ilene Cooper, writing in *Booklist,* noted that at just over 200 pages, there is not space enough to discuss every topic presented by the multifaceted life of Sir Walter Ralegh, but added that "the book is beautifully researched, and it is written with wit and passion." A reviewer for the *Los Angeles Times* praised Aronson's portrait of Ralegh as "both provocative and tantalizing, revealing his subject as a person of canny wit and magnetism with all-to-human shortcomings." In conclusion, Cooper dubbed *Sir Walter Ralegh and the Quest for El Dorado* "sweeping, multilayered nonfiction."

Aronson's experience as a publisher, editor, and critic comes to the fore in *Exploding the Myths: The Truth about Teens and Reading,* a collection of his speeches and articles that touches on the development of young adult literature as well as its major controversies. In a review for *Booklist,* Hazel Rochman found the author's style "clear, chatty, and tough" while pointing out that Aronson "shows that teenagers today are often more open to challenge and diversity in narrative and format than their adult guardians are." *School Library Journal* contributor Vicki Reutter called *Exploding the Myths* a "thought-provoking collection [that] should be not missed."

Biographical and Critical Sources

PERIODICALS

Booklist, July, 1998, Stephanie Zvirin, review of *Art Attack: A Short Cultural History of the Avant-Garde;* August, 2000, Ilene Cooper, review of *Sir Walter Ralegh and the Quest for El Dorado,* p. 2130; March 15, 2001, Hazel Rochman, review of *Exploding the Myths: The Truth about Teenagers and Reading,* p. 1406.

Horn Book, September-October, 2000, Peter D. Seiruta, review of *Sir Walter Ralegh and the Quest for El Dorado,* p. 593.

Kirkus Reviews, May 15, 2000, review of *Sir Walter Ralegh and the Quest for El Dorado,* p. 710.

Los Angeles Times, October 22, 2000, review of *Sir Walter Ralegh and the Quest for El Dorado,* p. 6.

New York Times Book Review, February 14, 1999, review of *Art Attack,* p. 26.

School Library Journal, June, 1995, Linda Diane Townsend, review of *Day by Day: The Eighties,* pp. 144-145; July, 1998, Shirley Wilton, review of *Art Attack,* p. 102; December, 2000, review of *Sir Walter Ralegh and the Quest for El Dorado,* p. 52; May, 2001, Vicki Reutter, review of *Exploding the Myths,* p. 179.*

B

BAGGETTE, Susan K. 1942-

Personal

Born November 27, 1942, in Berwyn, IL; daughter of Frank J. (an engineer) and Marcella Ann (a teacher; maiden name, Lapitz) Kessel; married Richard B. Freeman (marriage ended); married Harold D. Baggette (a program manager), August 30, 1991; children: (first marriage) Jason, Sean Pietri, Timothy, Melodie V. Whitbey. *Education:* Attended Northwestern University, 1960-63; California State University—Long Beach, B.A., 1965. *Religion:* United Methodist. *Hobbies and other interests:* Gardening, reading, activities with grandchildren.

Addresses

Home and office—137 Peyton Rd., Sterling, VA 20165. *E-mail*—info@brookfieldreader.com.

Career

National Wildlife Federation, Vienna, VA, renewal manager, 1984-89; American Society for Psychoprophy-laxis in Obstetrics/Lamaze, Arlington, VA, associate director of membership, 1989; League of Women Voters, Washington, DC, director of membership, 1989-90; SWL, Inc., Vienna, director of marketing, 1990-96; Brookfield Reader, Inc., Sterling, VA, publisher, 1996—. Loudoun County Chamber of Commerce, member. *Member:* Publishers Marketing Association, American Library Association, American Booksellers Association, SPAN.

Awards, Honors

Named entrepreneur of the year, Loudoun County Chamber of Commerce, 1998; named small press publisher of the year, Quality Books, 1999.

Jonathan gets a ride in Grandpa's wheelchair when he spends a day with the author and her husband in one of the board books in Susan K. Baggette's "Jonathan Adventures" series. (Cover photo by William J. Moriarty.)

Writings

"JONATHAN ADVENTURES" SERIES

Jonathan Goes to the Library, Brookfield Reader (Sterling, VA), 1998.
Jonathan Goes to the Doctor, Brookfield Reader (Sterling, VA), 1998.
Jonathan Goes to the Grocery Store, Brookfield Reader (Sterling, VA), 1998.
Jonathan Goes to the Airport, Brookfield Reader (Sterling, VA), 1998.

Jonathan Goes to the Post Office, Brookfield Reader
   (Sterling, VA), 1998.
Jonathan Goes to the Fire Station, Brookfield Reader
   (Sterling, VA), 1998.
Jonathan and Papa, Brookfield Reader (Sterling, VA),
   1999.

OTHER

The Night the Moon Slept, Brookfield Reader (Sterling,
   VA), 2000.

Work in Progress

Victory or Death, completion expected in 2002; research
on the Civil War, the Revolutionary War, and immigra-
tion to the United States.

Sidelights

Susan K. Baggette told *SATA:* "Children frequently ask
me: 'How can I become a writer?' Just write, I advise.
Keep writing. Make it a regular part of your day, like
brushing your teeth. Start a journal and reveal everything. I wrote my first book when I was eight. It was a
book of poetry, and I wanted it bound like a real book.
So I got out some yellow cotton and stitched the cover
and sewed in the pages on my mother's sewing
machine—my first effort at Smyth sewn. No one ever
told me to do these things. I just loved to read and write,
and I grew up with people who loved to read, visit
museums, listen to good music, and explore.

"It occurred to me that a hole existed in books for young
children. Dr. Benjamin Spock, in his last interview with
Parenting magazine, talked about how important it was
for young children to understand their connections to
friends, family, and their communities. This is the hole I
wanted to fill, and that's why I started the Brookfield
Reader. 'The Jonathan Adventures,' a series of board
books for toddlers and preschoolers, is all about a
youngster's connections to his family, friends, and
community. 'Big people' in the series gently demonstrate their real-life responsibilities, and Jonathan understands.

"*Jonathan and Papa* will always be special to me. Papa
happens to be my husband, who has progressive
supranuclear palsy. Jonathan, our grandson, comes to
visit. Despite Papa's physical and mental challenges, he
and Jonathan have more fun than a barrel of monkeys:
exercising side by side wearing their walkie talkies,
racing to the playground on their respective wheels,
reading a story together (and when Papa's eyes get tired,
Jonathan tells him about the pictures). *Jonathan and
Papa* is all about simple pleasures and the incredible
bond between grandparents and grandchildren.

"I have always admired courage under fire. *The Night
the Moon Slept* demonstrates that quality. Here's a
mischievous little cloud who just can't 'do right,' but
when he really makes a big mistake, he is sorry and
admits it. And, he's forgiven. Furthermore, his father,

King Cumulus, gives him a cool new responsibility that
makes Nimbus feel good about himself.

"At the Brookfield Reader, we look for manuscripts that
are meaningful, that convey a message to children and
are fun to read. At the Brookfield Reader, the good guys
always win.

"I have a lot of people to thank for getting me this far.
My parents and brothers gave me a perfectly perfect
childhood to build upon; my children, Jay, Pietri, Tim,
and Melodie, were constant sources of creative inspiration; the bright, patient, kind people at R. R. Donnelley
and Sons always keep me on track; and Tomie dePaola
is my forever hero. His children's entertainments, *The
Clown of God, Nana Upstairs and Nana Downstairs,*
and *Watch Out for the Chicken Feet in Your Soup,* are
the best of the best of children's literature. I read them
often for inspiration.

"If one child somewhere, after she's read one of my
books, discovers she loves to read more than anything
else in the whole world, I will have been successful."

Biographical and Critical Sources

PERIODICALS

Book Reader, May, 2000.

*   *   *

BALLARD, Robin 1965-

Personal

Born on May 21, 1965, in Los Angeles, CA; married
Martin Rohner (an economist), October 21, 1994;
children: Jasper, Sebastian. *Education:* Cooper Union
School of Art, B.F.A.

Career

Author and illustrator of children's books and designer,
1990—.

Writings

FOR CHILDREN; SELF-ILLUSTRATED

Cat and Alex and the Magic Flying Carpet, HarperCollins
   (New York, NY), 1991.
Granny and Me, Greenwillow Books (New York, NY),
   1992.
My Father Is Far Away, Greenwillow Books (New York,
   NY), 1992.
Gracie, Greenwillow Books (New York, NY), 1993.
Good-bye House, Greenwillow Books (New York, NY),
   1995.
Carnival, Greenwillow Books (New York, NY), 1995.
When I Am a Sister, Greenwillow Books (New York, NY),
   1998.
When We Get Home, Greenwillow Books (New York, NY),
   1999.

Tonight and Tomorrow, Greenwillow Books (New York, NY), 2000.

My Day, Your Day, Greenwillow Books (New York, NY), 2001.

I Used to Be the Baby, Greenwillow Books (New York, NY), 2002.

FOR CHILDREN; ILLUSTRATOR

Liz Rosenberg, *The Scrap Doll,* HarperCollins (New York, NY), 1991.

Fran Manushkin, *The Best Toy of All,* Dutton (New York, NY), 1992.

Boots, Scholastic (New York, NY), 1994.

Sidelights

Robin Ballard noted on her Web site that she has always known that she wanted to be an artist. Although Ballard began her training as an artist with the intention of becoming a graphic designer, a year spent in Berlin, Germany, where she found herself in a program for children's book illustration, changed the direction she would take as an artist. Her first book was *Cat and Alex and the Magic Flying Carpet,* a tale in which Alex and his best friend, Cat, take a trip to the moon on a flying carpet. Reviewing this work in the *School Library Journal,* Virginia Opocensky remarked on the "stylized, muted, watercolors" Ballard used in the artwork.

Ballard noted on her Web site that her books reflect themes that are an integral part of her own life, both as a child and an adult. *Granny and Me* recounts the activities Annie and her grandmother do together, including such simple tasks as reading books and baking cookies. The relationship between the two is easygoing and loving, noted Nancy Seiner in *School Library Journal,* and serves as a reminder about loving relationships. In *Booklist* Ilene Cooper also praised Ballard's depiction of the relationship between grandmother and granddaughter, characterizing the work as a "nice look at an intergenerational relationship" that also provides a simple introductory lesson in family history. In *My Father Is Far Away* a little girl muses about her father's activities during his travels, making comparisons with the things she does herself during the day. *School Library Journal* reviewer Judy Constantinides lauded Ballard for a "quiet, contemplative book for children who miss an absent parent."

Ballard continues to focus on issues relevant to children with *Gracie,* a book that deals with divorce and its affect on a child's life. Although the work is meant to reassure children whose parents are going through a divorce, Ilene Cooper, writing in *Booklist,* appreciated Ballard's acknowledgment of Gracie's anxiety over the separation. And although the artwork, according to Cooper, is "deceptively simple, [the book] is full of emotion." In *Good-bye House,* Ballard deals with another important childhood event: moving from one house to another. As her parents pack the truck, a little girl moves from one room to the other in the house they are leaving behind. Each space she wanders through brings back fond memories as she reluctantly prepares to leave, yet the

book ends on a positive note as the family arrives at the new house and the little girl immediately makes a friend, declaring "I think I will like it here." A reviewer for *Publishers Weekly* was particularly appreciative of Ballard's artwork in this book, praising her for "so accurately chronic[ling] one of childhood's important transitions."

Ballard returns to the issues surrounding families and change in a young child's life with *When I Am a Sister,* a book that explores Kate's anxiety as she spends the summer with her father and pregnant stepmother. Each page is devoted to a question by Kate, followed by a reassuring and realistic answer from her father. *Booklist* critic Carolyn Phelan called the book "thoughtfully designed," with each page presenting an artistically rendered contrast between Kate's fears, which are represented by small, gray illustrations, and her father's reassuring answers, which are rendered in large, water-color illustrations.

A bedtime routine is the subject of *When We Get Home.* During a journey in her mother's car, a young girl anticipates her bedtime routine. Once again, Ballard uses her artwork to contrast the two situations. On one page she traces the car's progression towards home, while the opposite page depicts the activities that will lead up to the little girl's bedtime. A similarly reassuring work for young children is Ballard's *Tonight and Tomorrow,* where a young boy talks about the things in his room as he prepares to go to bed. Reviewing this book for *Booklist,* Todd Morning said that Ballard "manages to capture the comfort children feel" when they are surrounded by familiar and comfortable things.

Focusing again on daily routines, *My Day, Your Day* shows children the jobs adults do while youngsters spend the day in child care. For each event in day care, presented on one side of a page, Ballard illustrates what happens in the workplace through a picture on the opposite page. For instance, as children play with blocks, Ballard details the workings of a construction site, and as children sit around a circular table for snack time, the author/illustrator shows a woman leading a business meeting with all the participants seated around a conference table. According to a *Publishers Weekly* reviewer, "Ballard ... effectively and inventively draws parallels between the routines of parent and child in this upbeat picture book." "Done in pen and ink and watercolors," *School Library Journal* reviewer Joy Fleishhacker remarked that "the cartoon artwork is colorful and pleasing."

Biographical and Critical Sources

PERIODICALS

Booklist, April 15, 1992, Ilene Cooper, review of *Granny and Me,* pp. 1534-1535; September, 15, 1992, Hazel Rochman, review of *My Father Is Far Away,* p. 153; February 15, 1993, Ilene Cooper, review of *Gracie,* pp. 1065-1066; March 15, 1994, Mary Harris Veeder, review of *Good-bye House,* p. 1369; February 15, 1995, Ilene Cooper, review of *Carnival,* p. 1088;

March 1, 1998, Carolyn Phelan, review of *When I Am a Sister,* p. 1139; April 1, 1999, Stephanie Zvirin, review of *When We Get Home,* p. 1419; April 15, 2000, Todd Morning, review of *Tonight and Tomorrow,* p. 1550; January 1, 2001, Hazel Rochman, review of *My Day, Your Day,* p. 966.

Bulletin of the Center for Children's Books, May, 2000, Janice M. Del Negro, review of *Tonight and Tomorrow,* pp. 305-306.

Horn Book Guide, fall, 1992, Suzanne Wolfe, review of *Granny and Me,* p. 222; fall, 1995, Carolyn Shute, review of *Carnival,* p. 257; fall, 1998, Suzy Schmidt, review of *When I Am a Sister,* p. 268; fall, 1999, Patricia Riley, review of *When We Get Home,* p. 228.

Kirkus Reviews, April 1, 2000, review of *Tonight and Tomorrow,* p. 470.

Publishers Weekly, February 28, 1994, review of *Good-bye House,* p. 86; January 15, 2001, review of *My Day, Your Day,* p. 75.

School Library Journal, June, 1991, Virginia Opocensky, review of *Cat and Alex and the Magic Flying Carpet,* p. 72; September, 1992, Judy Constantinides, review of *My Father Is Far Away,* pp. 196, 198; October, 1992, Nancy Seiner, review of *Granny and Me,* pp. 78, 80; January, 1994, Lori A. Janick, review of *Gracie,* p. 82; June, 1994, Anna Biagioni Hart, review of *Good-bye House,* p. 96; June, 1995, Karen James, review of *Carnival,* p. 76; June, 1999, Martha Topol, review of *When We Get Home,* p. 85; June, 2001, Joy Fleishhacker, review of *My Day, Your Day,* p. 100.

ON-LINE

Robin Ballard Web site, http://www.pair.com/rballard/ (May 6, 2001).*

*   *   *

BARASCH, Lynne 1939-

Personal

Born March 23, 1939, in New York, NY; daughter of Robert Julius and Elaine (Haas) Marx; married Kenneth Robert Barasch (an ophthalmologist), June 20, 1958; children: Wendy, Jill (deceased), Nina (deceased), Cassie, Dinah. *Education:* Attended Rhode Island School of Design, 1957-58; Parsons School of Design, B.A., 1976. *Politics:* Democrat. *Religion:* Jewish. *Hobbies and other interests:* Theater, ballet, art.

Addresses

Home and office—455 East 57th St., New York, NY 10022.

Career

Children's author and illustrator. *Member:* Authors Guild.

Awards, Honors

Notable Children's Book selection, Smithsonian Institute, 2000, Notable Children's Book selection, American Library Association, 2001, Pick of the Lists, American Booksellers Association, Best Children's Books of the Year selection, Bank Street College, and Oppenheimer Gold Award, all for *Radio Rescue.*

Writings

SELF-ILLUSTRATED PICTURE BOOKS

Rodney's Inside Story, Orchard Books (New York, NY), 1992.

A Winter Walk, Ticknor & Fields (New York, NY), 1993.

Old Friends, Farrar, Straus, and Giroux (New York, NY), 1998.

Radio Rescue, Frances Foster Books (New York, NY), 2000.

The Reluctant Flower Girl, HarperCollins (New York, NY), 2001.

Sidelights

Lynne Barasch once told *SATA* that she found "picture books ... a very gratifying means of expression." Although Barasch had been drawing and painting all her life, it was not until her daughter Cassie was ten years old that she began writing and illustrating in earnest. One of her first books was *A Winter's Walk,* a quiet tale

Lynne Barasch

Lonely after the loss of her best friend, Henrietta makes friends with a little dog who seems to know her. (Cover illustration by Barasch.)

of a day in winter when Sophie and her mother go for a walk. Describing the outdoors in simple text, Barasch accompanied the story with watercolor illustrations, eliciting praise from a *Kirkus Reviews* contributor for putting together a "quiet book with special appeal for the observant child."

In another book, *Old Friends,* Barasch explores the unusual topic, for picture books, of reincarnation. Henrietta is an older woman who has outlived her acquaintances, and very much misses her childhood friend, Anna. One day, she meets a little dog who seems to communicate with her, reminding her of Anna. Henrietta realizes a connection with the dog and they remain friends until she dies. Reviewing this work for the *School Library Journal,* Jody McCoy lauded Barasch's "soft focus" illustrations and "thoughtful text."

In 2001, Barasch wrote and illustrated *The Reluctant Flower Girl,* a book about young April and the wedding

of her older sister, Annabel. Fearing she is losing her best friend, April attempts to thwart the upcoming nuptials, telling her sister's fiancé that Annabel both snores and wets the bed. However, discovering that her brother-in-law has a fine sense of humor and play, April realizes that she is not losing a sister, but instead gaining a brother. Writing in *Publishers Weekly,* a critic remarked that "Barasch gets to the heart of a girl's jumble of feelings regarding her sister's wedding with both humor and honesty." "In simple, perfectly paced text and appealing pen-and-watercolor drawings," found *Booklist* reviewer Gillian Engberg, the author/illustrator "nicely captures a young girl's sense of loss, leavening it with plenty of humor and lighthearted detail."

Biographical and Critical Sources

PERIODICALS

Booklist, May 1, 2001, Gillian Engberg, review of *The Reluctant Flower Girl,* p. 1688.

Children's Book Review Service, November, 1993, review of *A Winter's Walk,* p. 25.

Five Owls, February, 1995, review of *A Winter's Walk,* p. 55.

Kirkus Reviews, July 15, 1993, review of *A Winter's Walk,* p. 930; January 15, 1998, review of *Old Friends,* p. 109.

Publishers Weekly, April 30, 2001, review of *The Reluctant Flower Girl,* p. 76.

School Library Journal, September, 1993, Starr LaTronica, review of *A Winter's Walk,* p. 204; April, 1998, Jody McCoy, review of *Old Friends,* p. 91.*

*   *   *

BARR, Nevada 1952-

Personal

Born March 1, 1952, in Yerington, NV; daughter of a pilot and a pilot, mechanic, and carpenter; divorced. *Education:* California Polytechnical University, B.A.; University of California—Irvine, M.F.A.

Addresses

Home—Clinton, MS. *Office*—c/o Putnam Publishing Group, 375 Hudson St., New York, NY 10014.

Career

Novelist and park ranger. Classic Stage Company, New York, NY, performer in shows Off-Broadway; performed in television commercials and corporate and industrial films, Minneapolis, MN; United States National Park Service, law enforcement ranger in National Parks, including Guadalupe Mountains, TX, Isle Royale, MI, Mesa Verde, CO, Natchez Trace Parkway, MS, and Horsefly Fire Camp, ID, 1989—.

Awards, Honors

Anthony Award for Best First Novel and Agatha Award for Best First Novel, both 1994, both for *Track of the Cat;* Prix du Roman (French national crime fiction award), 1995, for *Firestorm.*

Writings

"ANNA PIGEON" MYSTERIES

Track of the Cat, Putnam (New York, NY), 1993.
A Superior Death, Putnam (New York, NY), 1994.
Ill Wind, Putnam (New York, NY), 1995.
Firestorm, Putnam (New York, NY), 1996.
Endangered Species, Putnam (New York, NY), 1997.
Blind Descent, Putnam (New York, NY), 1998.
Liberty Falling, Putnam (New York, NY), 1999.
Deep South, Putnam (New York, NY), 2000.
Blood Lure, Putnam (New York, NY), 2001.
Hunting Season, Putnam (New York, NY), 2002.

OTHER

Bittersweet (novel), St. Martin's (New York, NY), 1984.

(Contributor, with others) *Naked Came the Phoenix: A Serial Novel,* St. Martin's Minotaur (New York, NY), 2001.

Several of Barr's short stories have appeared in the *Mary Higgins Clark Mystery Magazine.*

Sidelights

Popular novelist Nevada Barr is best known for her mystery series starring amateur detective and National Park Service ranger Anna Pigeon. Born in Nevada in 1952, Barr was named for a character in one of her father's favorite books. The daughter of two pilots, she grew up in the small California town of Susanville and later went on to college at California Polytechnical in San Luis Obispo, California, and then to the University of California—Irvine where she earned her M.F.A. in acting. After graduation, Barr pursued an acting career, moving to New York for five years and then to Minneapolis. For eighteen years Barr worked in acting: on stage, in commercials, in industrial training films, and in voice-overs for radio. During these same years, Barr became interested in the environmental movement, married a man who worked for the National Park Service, and worked summers in the National Parks in Michigan, Texas, New Mexico, and Mississippi. In 1978 she began to write, and her career as a published author was inaugurated in 1984 with an historical novel set in the American West.

Bittersweet, Barr's second book but first published work, tells the story of a schoolteacher, Imogene Grelznik, who, when falsely accused of having a love affair with a female pupil, leaves her native Philadelphia for a smaller Pennsylvania town where she really does have a love affair with a female pupil: a sixteen-year-old abused wife named Sarah. Imogene and Sarah flee to Nevada, become innkeepers, and maintain their independence in the face of a rough, male-dominated world that does not understand them. The plot—an unusual premise for western fiction, according to commentators—attracted critical notice, as did the quality of Barr's craftsmanship. Sister Avila, writing for *Library Journal,* called *Bittersweet* "a first novel of power and vitality that will grip the reader." A *Booklist* reviewer stated, "Despite the novel's flaws ... Barr succeeds in conveying the meaning of these brave and desperate lives."

Though Barr followed *Bittersweet* with three other books, they remained unpublished. Meanwhile, she had taken a job with the National Park Service, working as a law enforcement ranger in such locations as Guadalupe Mountains National Park in west Texas, Mesa Verde National Park in Colorado, and Natchez Trace Parkway in Mississippi. This professional experience was to prove fruitful for Barr's writing career, for it became the basis for her popular mystery series featuring park ranger and amateur sleuth, Anna Pigeon. As she told *Booklist* interviewer John Rowen, "In 1991 ... I started writing with a character like me in a murder mystery." The result was a mystery series acclaimed for its

Nevada Barr

originality and vivid descriptions of its spectacular natural settings.

In *Track of the Cat,* the first book in the series, Anna Pigeon is working in Mesa Verde National Park when the body of a dead ranger is found, apparently killed by a mountain lion. Anna does not believe the obvious explanation, however, and investigates the lives and circumstances of everyone around her. At times, she is helped by her sister Molly, a New York City psychiatrist whose telephone conversations with Anna become an enjoyable staple of the series. *Track of the Cat* earned considerable praise as well as both the Anthony and Agatha awards for best first novel—much to Barr's amusement, she told Rowen, since the book was really her fifth novel. Reviewer Paul Skenazy, writing in the *Washington Post Book World,* raised the issue of uneven writing and "overripe" prose in the first third of the book, but called the novel "a wonderful and absorbing tale." Barr, he wrote, "knows her countryside and writes about it with a naturalist's eye.... She also does a fine job putting us inside a woman who looks at the world as a woman," with the result, he claimed, that the novel's "inner geography" matched its landscapes. Charles Champlin, of the *Los Angeles Times Book Review,* regretted that Anna's physical isolation forced her to use her horse excessively as a Dr. Watson-type sounding-board, but that was a minor quibble; Champlin hailed

Track of the Cat as "an eventful, characterful story with a slam-bang denouement, all set in a wilderness environment Barr knows, loves and describes with poetic passion." A scholarly review in *Women's Review of Books* more than a year after the novel's publication treated Barr's work as inspiringly "ecofeminist." The critic, Mimi Wesson, praised Barr for allowing her protagonist a realistic ambivalence on social and human issues: "Some of the most rewarding parts of the narrative depict Anna's struggles to understand and satisfy her own needs for human connection," she declared.

The next seven Anna Pigeon mysteries attracted consistent critical praise. The follow-up to *Track of the Cat, A Superior Death,* found Anna in Isle Royale National Park in the middle of Lake Superior, halfway between the Upper Peninsula of Michigan and Canada. The location provided the author with a chance to give her heroine a fear of the immeasurable, as well as the spunk to conquer that trepidation. An assorted group of possible suspects, including park employees and tourists, can be found in the otherwise thinly populated area; this time the trigger for the mystery plot is the discovery of an experienced diver's dead body on a sunken wreck shortly after his wedding. Skenazy, again reviewing Barr for the *Washington Post Book World,* called *A Superior Death* "a wonderfully satisfying read." He particularly noted Barr's "tangled, rich descriptive language" which, to him, had "an engrossing pull." Marilyn Stasio, the *New York Times Book Review* crime expert, also singled out the descriptions for praise: "Ms. Barr's sternly beautiful style is best displayed in natural settings—like her eerie underwater landscapes of sunken ships and floating corpses—where human life makes itself scarce." Chicago *Tribune Books* critic Dick Adler was another critic who enjoyed *A Superior Death* and found Barr best at nature portraits. Envisioning happily the further expansion of the Anna Pigeon series, he wrote, "Think of all the national parks Barr has left in which to turn Anna loose."

The third Anna novel, 1995's *Ill Wind,* returns to an old stomping ground, Mesa Verde National Park. This time a disliked park ranger's body is found at a "pathologically neat" murder scene. Surrounding this mystery are questions about the fate of the Anasazi Indians and about local construction practices. Anna assists FBI agent Frederick Stanton in solving the crime, and their interactions provide a developing focus for human relationships in the book. This Literary Guild and Mystery Guild selection won good reviews; a critic for *Publishers Weekly* commended the "common sense and appreciation for nature that makes Anna Pigeon such good company." Stasio, writing in the *New York Times Book Review,* applauded the intelligence with which Barr answered the questions the novel posed and added, "Her stirring style is best illustrated by vibrant descriptions of the order and disorder in the natural world. In vivid images of life ... and death ... she shows us the very face of nature." Chicago *Tribune Books* critic Gary Dretzka used *Ill Wind* as an opportunity to say of the Anna Pigeon books in general, "This is a rich new series, enlivened by unusual settings and a three-dimensional protagonist."

The 1996 entry in the series, *Firestorm,* brought a change of setting and the challenge of a different kind of mystery. The place is a forest on fire in northern California, and the subplot is of the locked room mystery style which, according to Maureen Corrigan in *Washington Post Book World,* Barr "ingeniously resurrects." While helping fight the fire, Anna and eight others in her squad, one of whom is injured, are trapped in a canyon as the fire advances upon them. For survival, they take shelter inside the individual, fireproof tents they carry for just such occurrences. The fire passes through, burning the entire landscape around them; and when (twelve minutes later) the firefighters emerge from their foil cocoons they are unharmed—except for one of them, who is found dead, with a knife in his back. The question of who could have committed murder during the twelve minutes of the firestorm, and why, is the locked-room puzzle. "*Firestorm* is a brilliantly executed mystery," applauded Corrigan, who went on to favorably compare the forest fire descriptions with Dorothy Sayers' descriptions of flood in *The Nine Tailors,* a mystery classic. Some of the fire scenes even "approach the reverent terror of Norman Maclean's posthumous 1992 masterpiece, *Young Men and Fire,*" Corrigan declared. *Tribune Books* contributor Adler went a step further, calling the fire scenes "the best I've read anywhere." He called the novel "good, dirty, escapist fun of the first rank." Dick Lochte of the *Los Angeles Times Book Review* told readers that *Firestorm* describes natural disaster "with such authenticity and in such chilling detail that you can smell the smoke and taste the ashes." Lochte continued, "Barr is a splendid storyteller, but it's her knowledge of the territory that ignites this fast-paced and suspenseful whodunit." *New York Times Book Review* critic Stasio put a slightly different spin on her equally high praise, saying, "The striking visceral quality . . . is all the more remarkable because she writes with such a cool, steady hand about the violence of nature and the cruelty of man."

As she continued the series, Barr placed her protagonist in increasingly diverse park settings. *Endangered Species* placed Anna on temporary assignment at Georgia's Cumberland Island National Seashore, where she investigates the deaths of a pilot and a district ranger in a plane crash. *Blind Descent* found Anna back in the West, at Carlsbad Caverns National Park in Colorado, where she is challenged by claustrophobia when she is asked to help rescue a woman injured while exploring a cave. And in *Liberty Falling,* Anna goes to New York City to visit her critically ill sister. Gateways Park, which includes Liberty and Ellis Islands, becomes the backdrop for several fatal falls that Anna eventually traces to nefarious doings.

In *Deep South,* Anna takes a post at Natchez Trace Parkway in Mississippi, where she discovers an undercurrent of violence and tragic history beneath the deaths of two white girls. A reviewer for *Booklist* found that the novel "offers the same strengths as its predecessors:

vivid prose, a surprising plot, and a cast of sympathetic, well-rounded characters," and that Barr "effectively captures the beauty and menace of nature below the Mason Dixon Line and provides thoughtful insights into teens, race, and the Civil War." A reviewer for *Publishers Weekly* offered similar praise, commending the book as "another suspenseful and highly atmospheric mystery, illuminated even in this new setting by [Barr's] trademark lyricism in writing about the natural world."

In *Blood Lure,* the ninth Anna Pigeon mystery, Anna has to deal with the nastier side of nature. After accepting a training assignment at Watertown-Glacier International Peace Park on the border of Montana and Canada, Anna has to come to terms with a vicious bear attack. But though the victim might have been killed by a bear, the victim's face was removed by a knife—the perverse act of a disturbed human. "Overall, *Blood Lure* is an engrossing story made better by the vivid descriptions of nature through obviously appreciative eyes," wrote Linda Brinson in the *Winston-Salem Journal. Milwaukee*

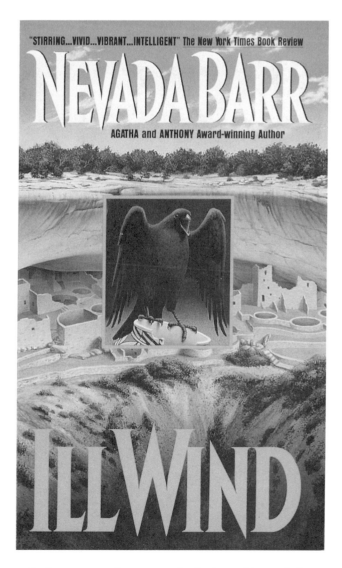

Park ranger and amateur sleuth Anna Pigeon helps solve a mystery involving the fate of the Anasazi Indians in Barr's third mystery in the "Anna Pigeon" series.

Journal Sentinel reviewer Dorman T. Shindler praised Anna's inner struggle, saying that Barr's "biggest triumph is in detailing Pigeon's 'falling out' with nature, and her inner journey back to trust." But a *Booklist* reviewer criticized *Blood Lure* as weaker than the previous novels in the series: "Barr takes too long to set up the action ... and, most surprising of all, the landscape is not as vividly described as usual." *People Weekly* reviewer Jean Reynolds was enthusiastic about the scenery, however, writing, "Readers can take pleasure in Barr's descriptions of the natural setting. ... Her fans can only be grateful that there are still plenty of national parks left for Anna Pigeon to visit."

In the course of her "Anna Pigeon" series, Barr told Rowen, she has done considerable physical research. "Often, I've worked at the parks in my books, and those parks struck me as marvelous," she said. "To me, it's so important to be where you're writing about. In the 'Anna Pigeon' series, the parks where she works become major characters." Anna's character, too, is central. "Anna started out like me, but she has evolved into herself," Barr explained. "Anna's grown older and relies less on physical ability. She has grown more tolerant of others over the years. But she has also become more of a loner, more vulnerable."

Biographical and Critical Sources

PERIODICALS

Booklist, July, 1984, p. 1520; February 14, 1997, p. 1006; December 15, 1998, p. 728; April 15, 1999, p. 1462; April 15, 1999, John Rowen, "The *Booklist* Interview: Nevada Barr," p. 1542; January 1, 2000, John Rowen, review of *Deep South,* p. 882; December 15, 2000, p. 289; March 1, 2001, p. 1295.

Library Journal, September 1, 1984, p. 1684; February 1, 1997, p. 111; March 15, 1998, p. 91; March 15, 1999, p. 108; January, 2000, p. 167; February 15, 2000, p. 214; June 14, 2001, p. 121.

Los Angeles Times Book Review, May 23, 1993, p. 8; April 28, 1996, p. 11.

Milwaukee Journal Sentinel, February 4, 2001, Dorman T. Shindler, "Nature's Beauty, Danger Enfold Mystery," p. 6.

New York Times Book Review, April 18, 1993, p. 24; April 17, 1994, p. 19; April 2, 1995, p. 25; March 24, 1996, Marilyn Stasio, review of *Firestorm,* p. 24; April 3, 1997, p. 24; April 5, 1998, p. 32; April 4, 1999, p. 20; March 19, 2000, Marilyn Stasio, review of *Deep South;* February 4, 2001, Marilyn Stasio, review of *Blood Lure.*

People Weekly, February 5, 2001, Jean Reynolds, review of *Blood Lure,* p. 39.

Publishers Weekly, January 30, 1995, p. 87; January 6, 1997, p. 244; February 2, 1998, p. 245; January 24, 2000, review of *Deep South,* p. 294; January 15, 2001, review of *Blood Lure,* p. 56.

Tribune Books (Chicago, IL), March 6, 1994, p. 6; April 2, 1995, p. 7; March 3, 1996, p. 6.

Washington Post Book World, July 18, 1993, p. 6; March 20, 1994, p. 6; July 2, 1995, p. 12; April 21, 1996, p. 6.

Winston-Salem Journal, January 28, 2001, Linda Brinson, "Descriptions of Nature Make Tale All the Better in Latest Barr Mystery," p. A18.

Women's Review of Books, January, 1995, review of *Track of the Cat,* p. 22.

ON-LINE

National Parks Conservation Association, http://www.npca.org/ (September 20, 1995).

Nevada Barr, http://www.members.tripod.com/ (July 28, 2001).

Nevada Barr Web site, http://www.nevadabarr.com/ (July 28, 2001).

Outside Magazine, http://www.outside.starwave.com/ (April, 1996).

Putnam Berkley Group, http://univstudios.com/putnam/ (October 21, 1997).

Putnam Berkley Online, http://www.mca.com/putnam/ (October 21, 1997).

In this work, Anna is on temporary assignment at Georgia's Cumberland Island National Seashore to investigate the death of a pilot and district ranger.

University of Mississippi, http://www.olemiss.edu/ (November 24, 1997).*

*   *   *

BARRON, T(homas) A(rchibald) 1952-
(Tom Barron)

Personal

Born March 26, 1952, in Boston, MA; son of Archibald (a hotel operator) and Gloria (a geologist and museum founder) Barron; married Currie Cabot; children: three boys and two girls, "all named after mountains." *Education:* Princeton University, B.A., 1974; attended Oxford University on a Rhodes scholarship, graduated, 1978; Harvard University, M.B.A. and J.D., both 1982. *Hobbies and other interests:* Reading, traveling, hiking, cross-country skiing, "playing any sports that my kids like to play."

Addresses

Home and office—545 Pearl St., Boulder, CO 80302.

Career

Author and environmentalist. Businessman, c. 1979-89, positions included president, venture capital firm, New York, NY; general partner, Sierra Ventures; chairman, Swiss Army Knives Corporation. Full-time writer, 1989—. Founder, Environmental Studies Program at Princeton University and Gloria Barron Prize for Young Heroes; former Princeton University trustee and trustee of the Nature Conservancy of Colorado. Has led workshops in environmental preservation and restoration; speaker at conferences on literature, education, and the environment as well as at schools and libraries. *Member:* Nature Conservancy, Wilderness Society (member of board).

Awards, Honors

Best Books of the Year, *Parents Magazine* and *Voice of Youth Advocates,* 1992, Best Books for the Teen Age, New York Public Library, 1993, and Young Adult Choice List, International Reading Association, 1994, all for *The Ancient One;* Colorado Book Award, 1995, Texas Lone Star Book Award, 1997, Utah Book Award, Children's Literature Association of Utah, 1998, and Best of the Texas Lone Star Reading Lists, 2000, all for *The Merlin Effect;* Robert Marshall Award, the Wilderness Society, for environmental work, 1997; "Not Just for Children Anymore" Award, Children's Book Council, 1997, Oppenheim Portfolio Gold Award, 2000, both for *The Lost Years of Merlin;* "Not Just for Children Anymore" Award, 1998, for *The Seven Songs of Merlin;* Best Books of the Year, *Voice of Youth Advocates,* Best Fantasy Books List, *Booklist,* both 1999, both for *The Fires of Merlin;* Booksense Bestseller List, 2000, and Nautilus Award for outstanding contribution to literature, 2001, for *The Wings of Merlin;* Colorado Book Award nominee, 2000, for both *The Mirror of Merlin*

and *The Fires of Merlin,* and 2001, for *Where Is Grandpa?*

Writings

To Walk in Wilderness: A Rocky Mountain Journal (adult nonfiction), photographs by John Fielder, Westcliffe Publishers (Englewood, CO), 1993.

(With Enos Mills and John Fiedler) *Rocky Mountain National Park: A 100 Year Perspective* (adult nonfiction) photographs by Enos Mills and John Fielder, Westcliffe Publishers (Englewood, CO), 1995.

Where Is Grandpa? (picture book), illustrated by Chris K. Soenpiet, Philomel (New York, NY), 2000.

Tree Girl (middle-grade fiction), Philomel (New York, NY), 2001.

"HEROIC KATE" SERIES (ALSO KNOWN AS "THE KATE ADVENTURES")

Heartlight, Philomel Books (New York, NY), 1990.

The Ancient One, Philomel Books (New York, NY), 1992.

The Merlin Effect, Philomel Books (New York, NY), 1994.

"THE LOST YEARS OF MERLIN" SERIES

The Lost Years of Merlin (also see below), Philomel Books (New York, NY), 1996.

The Seven Songs of Merlin (also see below), Philomel Books (New York, NY), 1997.

The Fires of Merlin (also see below), Philomel Books (New York, NY), 1998.

The Mirror of Merlin, Philomel Books (New York, NY), 1999.

The Wings of Merlin, Philomel Books (New York, NY), 2000.

A T. A. Barron Collection (omnibus; includes *The Lost Years of Merlin, The Seven Songs of Merlin,* and *The Fires of Merlin*), Philomel Books (New York, NY), 2001.

OTHER

Contributor to periodicals, including *Book Links, New York Times, Parents Magazine, School Library Journal,* and *Voice of Youth Advocates.* Some work appears under the name Tom Barron. Barron's books have been translated into several languages, including German and Spanish.

Adaptations

The Lost Years of Merlin was released on audio cassette by Listening Library, 2001.

Work in Progress

A Throne in the Clouds, a historical picture book about a Colorado girl who became the youngest person ever to climb Long's Peak, expected 2004; *The Hero's Trek,* essays about "the meaning of heroism and the ways young people can make a positive difference to the world," expected 2002, for Philomel; another nature book for adults; a book of essays for adults.

T. A. Barron

Sidelights

A popular, prolific American author of fiction for children and young adults and nature books for adults, T. A. Barron is regarded as both a master storyteller and a gifted nature writer. As a novelist, he is often compared favorably to such writers as J. R. R. Tolkien, T. H. White, Lloyd Alexander, and, especially, Madeleine L'Engle. Barron is perhaps best known as the author of two series of coming-of-age tales set in imaginary worlds: the "Heroic Kate" trilogy, which is also called "The Kate Adventures," and "The Lost Years of Merlin" five-book epic. The "Kate" series, which is comprised of *Heartlight, The Ancient One,* and *The Merlin Effect,* blends such elements as science fiction, history, mythology, metaphysics, and ecology in contemporary adventures that feature Kate Prancer Gordon, a courageous, resourceful teenager. The "Merlin" series, which includes *The Lost Years of Merlin, The Seven Songs of Merlin, The Fires of Merlin, The Mirror of Merlin,* and *The Wings of Merlin,* focuses on the teenage years of the legendary magician, a period that is not represented in traditional Arthurian literature. Barron describes Merlin's search for identity and spiritual balance as well as his adventures with both human characters—such as Ector, the boy who is to become King Arthur—and supernatural characters, such as spirits, ogres, dwarves, and shape-shifters. Barron has also received praise for *Where Is Grandpa?,* an autobiographical picture book that describes how the young narrator is helped to adjust to the death of his beloved grandfather by the image of heaven that his father presents. In addition, the author has been lauded for the prose and poetry that he contributed to two nature books for adults, *To Walk in*

Wilderness: A Rocky Mountain Journal, and *Rocky Mountain National Park: A 100 Year Perspective.*

Thematically, Barron is noted for addressing issues that relate directly to both his young audience and to the universal human condition. He explores such themes as the connections among people, cultures, and other forms of life; the ultimate meaning of existence; the power of love; the power of every individual to make a difference with their lives; death as part of a grand design; the bond between generations; the need to preserve the environment; the spiritual value of wilderness; and the light and darkness within ourselves. In the "Kate" and "Merlin" series, Barron takes his protagonists on both literal and figurative journeys. The young heroes face enormous—and often dangerous—obstacles, situations that require Kate and Merlin to make difficult, sometimes life-threatening, decisions that lead them to a greater sense of self-confidence and maturity as well as to a deeper sense of how they can contribute to the world. As a writer, Barron characteristically favors a clear, lyrical prose style. He is commended for his use of descriptive language; for his creation of exciting plots, which often include twists at the end; and for his inclusion of strong female and sensitive male characters. Although some observers have criticized Barron for overwriting, most critics applaud him as a talented writer whose well crafted blend of adventure, fantasy, and spirituality has led to the creation of insightful, moving books.

Writing on the Web site for the National Resources Defense Council (NRDC), Barron stated, "My childhood was spent in two places: a New England town full of apple orchards, Native American lore, and Shaker craftspeople, and a ranch in Colorado where I learned to yip and yap like a coyote and hoot like a great horned owl." Barron credits his parents and several of his teachers with fostering his innate love and nature and interest in traditional cultures. His father was owner and operator of one of the oldest hotels in Colorado, the historic Alamo Hotel in Colorado Springs. Barron has recalled that his first memory is being carried on his father's shoulders to an old chestnut tree near his home. In an article for *Book Links,* the author wrote, "I remember him lifting me up to peer into a dark hole in the trunk. To my surprise, a family of baby raccoons, their eyes as bright as lanterns, peered back at me. Whenever I think of that man, I think of all the places that he shared. And the memories, like the eyes of those raccoons, are lantern-bright. Small wonder that, for me, place is far more than landscape." Barron concluded that the diversity of the imaginary worlds in his fiction is a result of "my own grounding in the natural world. And a good deal of that grounding I owe to my father, a man who knew how to hear the many voices of a stream." Barron was later to use his father, and his passing, as the basis for *Where Is Grandpa?* After the youngest of Barron's six brothers and sisters started school, his mother Gloria went back to college to study geology. Later, she founded the Touch Museum, a hands-on nature museum for children, at the Colorado School for the Deaf and Blind. "By word and example," Barron wrote in a media piece entitled "Colorado's Heroic

Kids," his mother "instilled in each of her seven children the idea that one individual can make a lasting difference in the lives of others." In 2001, Barron established the Gloria Barron Young Heroes Prize, an award that celebrates Colorado young people who make a major contribution to that state or to the world.

"As a kid growing up in Colorado," Barron wrote in "Colorado's Heroic Kids," I learned early on the power of heroes—through books. The more I read about heroes such as Abe Lincoln, Winston Churchill, Martin Luther King, and Mahatma Gandhi, the more I felt that I, too, could do great things to help the world." In an article in *Voice of Youth Advocates,* Barron stated, "My own background as a writer is rooted in nature, having grown up reading Henry David Thoreau, Rachel Carson, and John Muir long before I ever dipped into Madeleine L'Engle, Lloyd Alexander, Ursula Le Guin, E. B. White, or J. R. R. Tolkien." Barron has noted that, as a boy, he also enjoyed reading world mythology, sports stories, and biographies—but no fantasy. Barron's earliest writings were nature journals; at the age of nine, he wrote "Autobiography of a Big Tree," the story of the old chestnut tree in which the family of raccoons had lived that his father had shown him. In an *Booklist* interview with Sally Estes, Barron said, "As a kid, I often dreamed up stories and poems—especially about nature." When his family moved to a ranch, Barron continued writing outside under the ponderosa pine trees. In middle school, he wrote, illustrated, and published his own humor magazine, *The Idiot's Odyssey.*

Barron also enjoyed outdoor pursuits, especially hiking and camping. He joined the Boy Scouts of America, worked summers as a counselor at a local scout camp, and became an Eagle Scout. After winning a national speech competition sponsored by the Scouts, he was sent to Washington, D.C., to meet the President. After graduating from high school, Barron attended Princeton University, where he continued to write. "Then," he wrote on his Web site, "I encountered Tolkien, and a new world opened before my eyes." Barron founded two literary publications at Princeton. As a senior, he won the Pyne Prize, the university's highest honor for an undergraduate; the prize honors outstanding service to Princeton by one of its students. After winning a Rhodes scholarship, Barron set off for Oxford University in England.

Barron told the NDRC, "As a youth, my education was mostly through exploring the outdoors, and through travels abroad on a Rhodes, though I did very much enjoy my undergrad years at Princeton." At Oxford, Barron studied, but took time out to write stories and poems while sitting under an English oak that he dubbed "Merlin's Tree." He took a year off from school to travel, exploring the British Isles (especially Scotland); going to Russia and Uzbekistan; trekking in Alaska above the Arctic Circle; living in Africa, India, and Nepal; and helping build a thatched-roof home in a remote Japanese village, among other adventures. After returning to Oxford, he wrote his first novel, and

collected dozens of rejection letters for it. Barron then came back to the United States and enrolled in law school at Harvard University, hoping to become an environmental lawyer. He changed his mind, got his MBA, and went to New York City to work as a venture capitalist, acquiring and building small and medium-size businesses for his firm.

While working in New York, Barron married Currie Cabot, a woman whom he had met while cross-country skiing in the Catskill Mountains; the couple now have five children, three boys and two girls. Throughout his various careers, Barron continued to write, even stopping to jot a few lines while running the Boston Marathon. He gave a manuscript of his first novel for young people, *Heartlight,* to Madeleine L'Engle, an author who had influenced him and to whom he is often compared. L'Engle saw promise in the manuscript and passed it on to her agent. After this, Barron's wife Currie suggested that the fledgling author quit his day job. In 1989, Barron resigned from his firm and moved his family to a Colorado ranch so that he could become a full-time writer. *Heartlight* was published the following year.

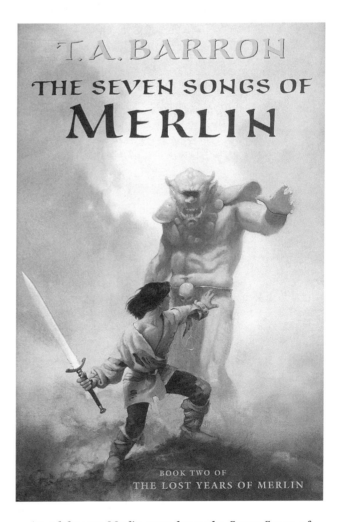

An adolescent Merlin must learn the Seven Songs of Wisdom in order to obtain an elixir to save his ill mother.

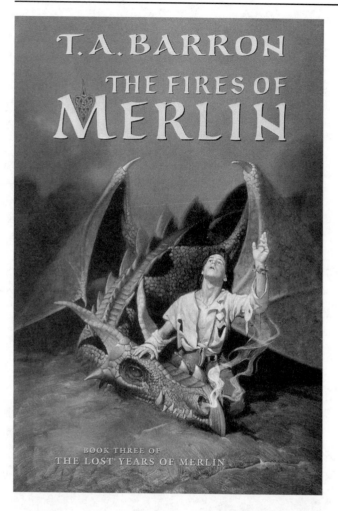

Merlin continues to develop as a wizard and young man on his quest to rid Fincayra of a dragon.

In *Heartlight*, thirteen-year-old Kate and her beloved grandfather, a renowned astrophysicist who has done research on the nature of light and its relationship to the human soul, travel to a distant galaxy by liberating their souls (or "heartlights") to find out why the Earth's sun is losing power. They discover that the star Trethonial, which should have become a black hole, has begun to drain the energy from other suns in order to live forever. Kate and her grandfather battle a demonic force that is seeking eternal life. The Darkness, a dark cloud, fights with the Pattern, the force that keeps the universe in balance, before order is restored at last.

In *The Ancient One*, Kate and her great-aunt Melanie work to save a forest of redwood trees from being cut down; the forest is located near the logging town of Blade, Oregon, on Native American holy ground. After Kate is transported five hundred years into the past, she encounters the Halamis, a tribe of Native Americans who are facing a volcanic eruption that will wipe them out. The eruption is being caused by Gashra, an evil being that wants to rule the world. Kate enlists the help of the Ancient One, the oldest living tree in the forest, to save the Halamis and the redwood forest and return to her own time. Kate must risk her life to restore this

balance; in addition, she must learn to become a tree. She succeeds, sending Gashra back into the earth. Tragically, Kate returns to the present just in time to see a logger felling the Ancient One right before a protective injunction is put into place.

In the final book of the series, *The Merlin Effect*, Kate accompanies her father, a leading Arthurian scholar, to the coast of Baja, California. Here, he hopes to discover one of Merlin's lost treasures, a drinking horn that has powers of immortality, on a sunken Spanish galleon. After Kate saves a whale that gets tangled in the expedition's equipment, she is sucked into a whirlpool that takes her to the ocean's floor. She and her companions engage in a battle with the enchantress Nimue and her army of sea demons, who want to use the horn for their own evil purposes. In order to save herself, her father, his friends, and the Horn of Merlin, Kate must find a way to regain her free will; finally, she encounters Merlin, rescues the horn, and returns it to its rightful place.

Noted for its perceptive exploration of complex ideas, difficult choices, and adult/child relationships, the "Heroic Kate" series interweaves mythological imagery, metaphysical philosophy, scientific theories, and environmental issues with the exciting adventures—and personal growth—of its heroine. Generally, reviewers have lauded the series. A critic in *Publishers Weekly* wrote that *Heartlight* "shines as a bold, original effort worthy of repeat readings."

After finishing *The Merlin Effect*, Barron was intrigued greatly by what he discovered in researching the character of Merlin. He was also surprised by what he did not find in Celtic literature: information on the wizard's youth. Barron decided to write "The Lost Years of Merlin" to cover this missing period of Merlin's life. Though the series was originally scheduled to be a trilogy, Barron concluded that, in just three volumes, the young Merlin could not believably grow from the nameless boy who washes ashore in the first pages to the legendary wizard and sage of Camelot he is destined to become. So Barron decided to add two more books to the series. In his five-book epic, Barron profiles Merlin before he realizes his calling as a wizard, taking him through time and space in a series of adventures that prepare him for his role as the greatest mage of all time. Merlin learns about love, grief, humility, rebirth, transformation, nature, compassion, and the ability to see with his heart while battling his own insecurity, vulnerability, and hubris as well as the powers of darkness. Merlin is aided on his quests by humans, animals, and supernatural creatures, several of whom must risk danger or sacrifice themselves in order to save him. Finally, Merlin discovers his own inner gifts, his own magic, and is ready to become the legendary mentor to King Arthur.

In the first volume of the series, *The Lost Years of Merlin*, twelve-year-old Emrys is washed up on a Welsh beach with a woman who claims to be his mother. The boy has lost all of his memories, including knowing his real name; his mother, Branwen, refuses to tell him about his past. Emrys discovers that he has developing magical powers. Emrys defends his mother, who is about to be burned at the stake by a vicious mob, through telekinesis—but his action also burns the leader of the mob, the town bully Dinatius. When Merlin leaps into the fire to save the boy, Emrys loses his own eyesight. Recovering from his burns in an abbey, Emrys vows never to use his powers in anger, and after developing second sight to replace his lost eyesight, sets off on a journey to find out who he really is. Emrys lands on Fincayra, an enchanted island between Heaven and the Otherworld that connects them both. He goes on a dangerous quest to save Fincayra from a blight that was caused by a pact between its king, Stangmar, and the evil Rhita Gawr, the power-mad warlord of the spirit world whose glance means certain death. At the end of the novel, Emrys learns that Stangmar is really his father; that Elen, the woman who helped him, is truly his mother; and that he is really Merlin. In *The Seven Songs of Merlin,* the thirteen-year-old has been appointed to heal the barren lands of Fincayra. However, he uses his powers irresponsibly to bring his mother to the island. She is stricken with a death shadow—a poison meant for her son—by Rhita Gawr. In order to save his mother's life, Merlin must find and master the legendary riddle called the Seven Songs of Wisdom; in addition, he must go to the Otherworld and get a magic potion that will act as an antidote to the death shadow. Merlin encounters giants and monsters and kills the ogre that took the life of his grandfather Tuatha, a great but arrogant wizard. Merlin also finds the magical sword Excalibur that one day will belong to King Arthur. Most precious of all, he finds his lost sister, Rhia, who saves his life. Finally, Merlin completes his tasks and rescues his mother. Through his experiences, Merlin learns about responsibility, intuition, and the worth of all living things.

In *The Fires of Merlin,* fourteen-year-old Merlin has earned his wizard's staff and is learning the ways of a wizard. However, his powers are still new. The last dragon emperor, Valdearg, who is also called Wings of Fire, was put to sleep by Merlin's grandfather, the wizard Tuatha. When the eggs containing the dragon's last offspring are destroyed, he wakes up, and is led to believe that Merlin is the culprit. The evil Rhita Gawr has made a deal with dwarf queen Urnalda to steal Merlin's magical powers in return for a promise of safety for the dwarves. Before he can confront the dragon, Merlin must face a series of dangers and fight the raging fires within himself. He reaches deep inside to find the source of his magic, his compassion, and his readiness to sacrifice himself for the common good. It is his practical knowledge of herbs and his act of saving Valdearg's last surviving hatchling that allow Merlin to succeed in his quest. In 2001, an omnibus volume containing the first three volumes of "The Lost Years of Merlin" was published as *A T. A. Barron Collection.*

The fourth volume of the series, *The Mirror of Merlin,* finds fifteen-year-old Merlin deep in the Haunted Marshes of Fincarya, where he is searching for his stolen sword. The theft of his sword is a trap set by the

sorceress Nimue, who wants to destroy Merlin. She infects the teen with a deadly, incurable condition. Merlin meets Ector, a boy who feels that his master can cure young Merlin's illness. Merlin goes through the Mists of Time into the future. Through a magical mirror, he meets his much older self, trapped in the Crystal Cave by Nimue. Before he can return to his own time, Merlin must confront his deepest fears; however, he also learns about the choices open to him. He sees the Round Table and forecasts a society based on justice. At the end of his adventure, Merlin is cured of his condition and gains a greater sense of both his identity and his powers.

In the final volume of the series, *The Wings of Merlin,* Rhita Gawr and his henchmen are preparing to invade Fincayra. Within a two-week time frame, Merlin must get all of the Fincaryan creatures and races to put aside their mistrust of each other and band together to battle the evil forces. A masked warrior, a man with swords for

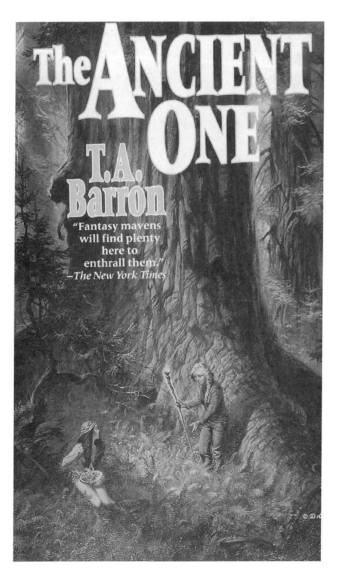

Working to save a stand of redwood trees, Kate Gordon is thrown back five hundred years to struggle with an evil volcanic creature. (Cover illustration by Darrell K. Sweet.)

Barron blends Arthurian legend and oceanography as Kate is drawn by the power of a magical drinking horn into an undersea battle with ancient forces. (Cover illustration by Anthony Bacon Venti.)

arms who calls himself Slayer, attacks orphaned children in an attempt to lure Merlin into a duel with him. Merlin's father, Stangmar, escapes from his imprisonment, and saves Merlin and Elen from Slayer before sustaining fatal injuries. As he dies, Stangmar is forgiven by Elen, although Merlin cannot bring himself to forgive his father for all his misdeeds. In their quest for safety, Merlin, Elen, and a large group of children go to the Forgotten Island, a place considered haunted by Fincayrans; Slayer, who follows them there, reveals himself to be Dinatius, Merlin's boyhood nemesis. After he lost his arms in the fire that blinded Merlin, Dinatius was given steel, swordlike arms by Rhita Gawr, who also gave him the power to use Merlin's own magic against him. Merlin eventually defeats Slayer and decides to spare his life, an act of mercy that brings about the rejoining of the Forgotten Island with Fincayra. Merlin and his friends succeed in uniting the Fincayrans, who win the terrible battle with Rhita Gawr

and work together in its aftermath. Then, a cosmic shift occurs: Fincayra and the Otherworld transform into one world, while the Forgotten Island becomes Avalon. Merlin learns his true name—Olo Eopia, which means man of many worlds and many times—and is at last able to whisper words of forgiveness to his dead father, Stangmar. Finally, Merlin makes his hardest decision yet: to leave his beloved Fincayra for the earthly island of Britannia, where he will become mentor to King Arthur as well as the celebrated wizard of story and song.

The "Merlin" books are praised for fitting well into the Arthurian literary canon while providing young readers with a unique, imaginative, and relevant depiction of the legendary character. Barron blends Celtic folklore, Christian and Druid spirituality, psychological realism, drama, and humor, among other elements, as he describes Merlin's journey of self-discovery. In the *NAPRA Review,* Antoinette Botsford wrote, "Through the adventures of young Merlin and his fellow travelers, Barron—more than any other on my sagging shelf of Merlin books—helps readers of all ages confront ... vital topics with renewed vigor and deepened insight.... I believe his work inspires us to hang onto our dreams— no matter what." Writing about the series in *Newspapers in Education,* Laura Farrell stated, "Much like his best-selling character, Merlin, renowned children's author T. A. Barron has a marvelous talent. While young Merlin has the gift of magic, T. A. Barron has an extraordinary way with words that can be described as no less than magical." Sara Pearce of the *Cincinnati Enquirer* urged, "I know this is asking a lot, but I want you to set aside Harry Potter and pick up Merlin." In an interview with Ken Trainer in the *Chicago Parent,* Barron said that Merlin is "a boy who has enormous struggles to learn the basic lessons of wisdom, truth, humility, power, and love. Merlin's journey is a metaphor for the hero that's in every one of us." Writing on his Web site, Barron concluded that Merlin's story "is, in truth, a metaphor— for the idea that all of us, no matter how weak or confused, have a magical person down inside, just waiting to be discovered."

With *Where Is Grandpa?,* Barron took his writing in a new direction. In this work, which was inspired by the death of his own father, he created a picture book for young children that uses the concept of nature to explain the cycle of life. Barron and illustrator Chris K. Soenpiet depict a young boy, sitting with his family on the day that his grandfather has passed away. Each member of his family shares a memory of Grandpa, but the boy stays silent. Finally, he asks where his grandfather is. The narrator's father answers that Grandpa is in heaven, which is, among other things, any place where people who have loved each other have some shared time together. Grandpa has been present in many places, such as at the tree house, at the waterfall, and at the door, ready to carve Halloween pumpkins. The boy decides that, for Grandpa, heaven is perhaps not so far away. He realizes that his grandfather can be with him in all of the places that they shared, and he begins to feel that it might be okay to go back to those special spots.

Reviewer considered *Where Is Grandpa?* a sincere and effective homage to a deceased parent. A critic in *Kirkus Reviews* stated that Barron "makes a heartfelt tribute." Writing in *School Library Journal,* Virginia Golodetz called *Where Is Grandpa?* "[a] helpful introduction to death and the grieving process," while a critic in *Publishers Weekly* dubbed it a "useful springboard for dialogue between bereaved adults and children."

Barron told Antoinette Botsford of *NAPRA Review* that he hoped that his tales "will give people a sense of their own wondrous gifts." Barron told Kylene Beers of *Emergency Librarian* that he writes for "children of all ages," and that he hopes that his books will "speak truthfully to human experience ... [and] bring to life some of our most basic yearnings and hopes and fears." On his Web site, Barron talked about why he often writes quest novels about imaginary places rather than realistic or historical fiction: "I write books I would like to read. That means each story must have a character, a relationship, a place, a dilemma, and an idea that I care about. A lot. I like a story where an individual must deal with personal issues as well as overarching issues. The mythic quest—call it fantasy if you prefer—allows me to incorporate all of these qualities. " He continued, "In addition, the mythic quest gives me a great opportunity to wrestle with some of life's biggest questions in the context of a good old-fashioned page-turner." In their *Booklist* interview, Barron told Sally Estes that, since he became a full-time writer, "I haven't had a moment of regret. I feel very, very lucky to get to follow my deepest passion in life."

Biographical and Critical Sources

PERIODICALS

Booklist, April 15, 2001, Sally Estes, "The *Booklist* Interview: T. A. Barron," p. 1560.
Chicago Parent, March, 1999, Ken Trainer, "Teaching the Difference between Celebrities and Heroes."
Cincinnati Enquirer, October 29, 1999, Sara Pearce, "Youngsters Can Find Magic in 'Merlin.'"
Denver Post, October 28, 1998, Claire Martin, "Colorado Author Is Living His Dream."
Emergency Librarian, Vol. 24, no. 4, 1997, Kylene Beers, "Where Fantasy Flies: An Interview with T. A. Barron," pp. 61-63.
Kirkus Reviews, December 1, 1999, review of *Where Is Grandpa?,* p. 1880.
NAPRA Review, April, 1997, Antoinette Botsford, "Merlin in Our Midst."
Parents Magazine, November, 1998, T. A. Barron, "Merlin's Message."
Publishers Weekly, June 29, 1990, review of *Heartlight,* p. 102; January 11, 2000, review of *Where Is Grandpa?,* p. 103.
School Library Journal, February, 2000, Virginia Golodetz, review of *Where Is Grandpa?,* p. 91.
Voice of Youth Advocates, April, 1999, T. A. Barron, "Vision, Voice and the Power of Creation: A Young Adult Author Speaks Out."

ON-LINE

Book Links, http://www.tabarron.com/ (July 24, 2001), T. A. Barron, "A Place for Love: The Story Behind 'Where Is Grandpa?'."
Children's Book Page, http://www.bookpage.com/ (July 24, 2001), "Meet the Kids' Author: T. A. Barron."
NAPRA—ALA, http://www.napra.com/ (July 21, 2001), Antoinette Botsford, "To Think as a Tree, to Act as a Man."
Natural Resources Defense Council, http://www.ndrc.org/ (July 24, 2001), "Profile—T. A. Barron."
Newspapers in Education, http://www.activedayton.com/ (July 24, 2001), Laura Farrell, "Students Give Feedback on T. A. Barron *Interview.*"
The Worlds of T. A. Barron (T. A. Barron's official Web site), http://www.tabarron.com/ (July 24, 2001).
Young Heroes Prize, http://www.youngheroesprize.org/ (July 24, 2001), T. A. Barron, "Colorado's Heroic Kids" (op-ed piece for media).*

—Sketch by Gerard J. Senick

*   *   *

BARRON, Tom
See BARRON, T(homas) A(rchibald)

*   *   *

BARTON, Byron 1930-

Personal

Born Byron Vartanian, September 8, 1930, in Pawtucket, RI; son of Toros and Elizabeth (Krekorian) Vartanian; changed surname in 1953; married Harriett Wyatt, December, 1967 (divorced, April, 1973). *Education:* Attended Los Angeles City College, CA, 1948-50, and Chouinard Art Institute, 1953-56.

Addresses

Home—2 Washington Square Village, New York, NY 10012.

Career

Freelance writer, illustrator, and designer. Studio 7 Los Angeles, Los Angeles, CA, illustrator, 1956-57; Equitable Life Assurance Co., New York, NY, designer, 1957-60; Columbia Broadcasting System, Inc., New York, NY, designer, 1960-66. *Military service:* U.S. Army, 1950-52.

Awards, Honors

Spring Book Festival Middle Honor, *New York Herald Tribune,* 1969, for *A Girl Called Al; New York Times* Choice of Best Illustrated Children's Books of the Year, 1972, for *Where's Al?,* and 1988, for *I Want to Be an Astronaut;* Children's Book Showcase Title, Children's Book Council, 1972, for *The Paper Airplane Book,* and

1973, for *Where's Al?*; *Airport* was selected a *New York Times* Notable Book, 1982; Please Touch Award, Please Touch Museum for Children, 1990, for *Dinosaurs, Dinosaurs*.

Writings

FOR CHILDREN; SELF-ILLUSTRATED

Elephant, Seabury Press (New York, NY), 1971.

Where's Al?, Seabury Press (New York, NY), 1972.

Applebet Story, Viking (New York, NY), 1973.

Buzz Buzz Buzz, Puffin (New York, NY), 1973.

Harry Is a Scaredy-Cat, Macmillan (New York, NY), 1974.

Jack and Fred, Macmillan (New York, NY), 1974.

Hester, Greenwillow (New York, NY), 1975.

Wheels, Crowell (New York, NY), 1979.

Building a House, Greenwillow (New York, NY), 1981, published as *Building a House: Big Book* and *Building a House: Small Book*, Hampton-Brown, 1992.

Airport, Crowell (New York, NY), 1982.

Airplanes, Crowell (New York, NY), 1986.

Boats, Crowell (New York, NY), 1986, published as *Boats Board Book*, HarperCollins (New York, NY), 1996.

Trains, Crowell (New York, NY), 1986, published as *Trains Board Book*, HarperCollins (New York, NY), 1996.

Trucks, Crowell (New York, NY), 1986, published as *Trucks Board Book*, HarperCollins (New York, NY), 1996.

Machines at Work, Crowell (New York, NY), 1987, published as *Machines at Work Board Book*, Harper-Collins (New York, NY), 1997.

I Want to Be an Astronaut, Crowell (New York, NY), 1988, published as *I Want to Be an Astronaut Board Book*, HarperCollins, 1997.

Dinosaurs, Dinosaurs, Crowell (New York, NY), 1989, published as *Dinosaurs, Dinosaurs Board Book*, Har-perCollins (New York, NY), 1994.

Bones, Bones, Dinosaur Bones, Crowell (New York, NY), 1990.

(Reteller) *The Three Bears*, HarperCollins (New York, NY), 1991, published as *Three Bears Big Book*, HarperCollins (New York, NY), 1994.

(Reteller) *The Little Red Hen*, HarperCollins (New York, NY), 1993, published as *Little Red Hen Big Book*, HarperCollins (New York, NY), 1994.

Planes, HarperCollins (New York, NY), 1994, published as *Planes Board Book*, HarperCollins, 1998.

The Wee Little Woman, HarperCollins (New York, NY), 1995.

Big Machines, HarperCollins (New York, NY), 1995.

Dinosaurs, HarperCollins (New York, NY), 1995.

Tools, HarperCollins (New York, NY), 1995.

Zoo Animals, HarperCollins (New York, NY), 1995.

Trucks and Trains, HarperCollins (New York, NY), 2000.

My Car, Greenwillow (New York, NY), 2001.

ILLUSTRATOR

Constance C. Greene, *A Girl Called Al*, Viking (New York, NY), 1969.

Alan Venable, *The Checker Players*, Lippincott (Philadel-phia, PA), 1973.

Seymour Simon, *The Paper Airplane Book*, Viking (New York, NY), 1973.

Franklyn Branley, *How Little and How Much: A Book about Scales*, Crowell (New York, NY), 1976.

Robert Froman, *Angles Are Easy as Pie*, HarperCollins (New York, NY), 1976.

Paula D. Schwartz, *You Can Cook*, Macmillan (New York, NY), 1976.

Rosamond Dauer, *Bullfrog Builds a House*, Greenwillow (New York, NY), 1977.

David A. Adler, *Roman Numerals*, Crowell (New York, NY), 1977.

Jack Prelutsky, *Snopp on the Sidewalk, and Other Poems*, Greenwillow (New York, NY), 1977.

Russell Hoban, *Arthur's New Power*, HarperCollins (New York, NY), 1978.

Jan Wahl, *Drakestail*, Greenwillow (New York, NY), 1978.

Melvin and Gilda Berger, *The New Food Book*, HarperCol-lins (New York, NY), 1978.

Marjorie Weinman Sharmat, *Gila Monsters Meet You at the Airport*, Simon & Schuster (New York, NY), 1980.

Mirra Ginsburg, *Good Morning, Chick*, Greenwillow (New York, NY), 1980.

Rosamond Dauer, *Bullfrog Gertrude Camp*, HarperCollins (New York, NY), 1980.

Robert Kalan, *Jump, Frog, Jump!*, Greenwillow (New York, NY), 1981.

David A. Adler, *My Dog and the Key Mystery*, F. Watts (New York, NY), 1982.

Charlotte Pomerantz, *Where's the Bear?*, Greenwillow (New York, NY), 1984.

Diane Siebert, *Truck Song*, Crowell (New York, NY), 1984.

Constance C. Greene, *Al's Blind Date*, Puffin (New York, NY), 1991.

Constance C. Greene, *Ask Anybody*, Puffin (New York, NY), 1991.

Charlotte Pomerantz, *The Tamarindo Puppy*, Greenwillow (New York, NY), 1993.

Sarah Weeks, *Little Factory*, HarperCollins/Laura Geringer (New York, NY), 1998.

Sidelights

Through the use of simple text and bright, bold illustrations with thick black outlines, children's author and illustrator Byron Barton makes such activities as building a house, going on a space mission, and reassembling dinosaur bones accessible to young read-ers. With just a few rhythmic words running along the bottom of his illustrations, Barton tells his stories with pictures that give readers all the necessary details about his subject. Barton is "a master of simplicity," declared a reviewer in *Publishers Weekly*, while in *Children's Books and Their Creators* an essayist noted that his books "embody an understanding of the drama inherent in information, and he makes nonfiction subjects avail-able and attractive to the youngest reader." Cathryn A. Camper, writing in *Five Owls*, praised Barton's colorful, well-defined drawings which make "his books fun even for children too young to read." Among Barton's many books are such titles as *Harry Is a Scaredy-Cat*, *I Want to Be an Astronaut,* and *The Wee Little Women;* many of his preschool texts have been issued as board books.

Born in Pawtucket, Rhode Island, Barton's home was often his playground because of his father's job—he sold coal and wood during the winter and ice during the summer. "To a small boy, our home with its woodpiles, barns, and attics, made an ideal playground," Barton once told *SATA.* However, all this would be left behind the year Barton entered the fourth grade, when the family of seven moved to Los Angeles, California. It was in this new state that Barton's interest in drawing and art began, mostly because of the different teaching methods used in his new school. "In class, when subjects I had already learned came up, I was allowed to go to the back of the room to play with paints," Barton explained. "I remember making large paintings of Indians in their canoes, alongside their tepees, and hunting animals. My pictures were hanging all over the back walls of the class and cloakroom. I became known as 'the artist.'"

Barton's early art interest was developed during formal art training at Los Angeles City College and Chouinard Art Institute. Having received a scholarship to Chouinard, Barton was forced to leave when he was drafted into the U.S. Army and sent to Korea; it was only after his discharge that he was able to complete his art training. A move to New York City brought Barton jobs as an illustrator for an advertising agency and as an animated film designer for CBS-TV. These experiences led to assignments illustrating other author's works and eventually the writing and illustrating of his own children's books. Barton's first illustration assignment was for *A Girl Called Al,* which was published in 1969 and which went on to win a *New York Herald Tribune*'s Spring Book Festival award. The book's author, Constance C. Greene, was pleased with Barton's efforts, and the two would collaborate on several more books, including *Al's Blind Date* and *Ask Anybody,* both published in 1991. Other authors benefitting from Barton's stylized renderings include Jack Prelutsky, Russell Hoban, Marjorie Weinman Sharmat, and Charlotte Pomerantz. Reviewing his illustrations for Sarah Weeks' 1998 *Little Factory, School Library Journal* contributor Marian Drabkin called Barton's work "attractive and childlike," adding that "Barton's multiethnic, stylized figures ... [are] presented in flat, bright primary colors against contrasting backgrounds."

Published in 1971, Barton's first self-authored children's book contains no text. In *Elephant* Barton illustrates a young girl's journey through fantasy and reality by showing young readers all the different shapes and sizes in which elephants may appear. A reviewer for *Publishers Weekly* asserted that no words are necessary to convey Barton's theme because the "bold, cheerful drawings ... send the imagination soaring." This first picture book has since been joined by numerous others, each with Barton's trademark illustration style and simple text.

A very timid young boy is the focus of *Harry Is a Scaredy-Cat,* published in 1974. Afraid of everything,

Byron Barton's illustrations reveal the events that take place during a young boy's search for his lost puppy in the big city. (Cover illustration by Barton.)

from other children to animals to cars, Harry is forced to face his fears during a trip to the circus with his father. Terrified of everything around him, Harry finds himself entangled in a bunch of balloons, lifted high into the air, and then dropped. Despite the hair-raising adventure, he discovers that the circus is not as scary as he thought. A critic writing in *Publishers Weekly* praised Barton's "dazzling, non-stop-action text," while *Horn Book* reviewer Ethel L. Heins compared Barton's illustrations to a "firmly drawn, concise, and spirited" comic strip, although with much brighter colors.

Action plays a large role in most of Barton's stories, especially those that teach children about a certain activity, such as the construction of a house. His 1981 book *Building a House* starts with a plot of land being surveyed, moves on to laying the foundation, describes the electrical wiring and plumbing process, shows the walls being painted, and concludes with a family moving into the finished product. "In *Building a House* I wanted to show, with simple words and pictures, the different workers coming one after the other to do their part: digging the hole, making the floor, putting up the walls, putting in the plumbing," explained Barton in *Junior Literary Guild.* "Then, when all the work is done, the family comes to live inside the house."

As with *Building a House,* other books by Barton have a technological focus, and explain the way the world works. Within a simple storyline, such books as *Trucks, Wheels, Planes,* and *Airport* feature illustrations that allow young people to learn about basic machines which shape their lives. With *Airport,* Barton reveals to his young audience the activities in an airport that surround the preparations for a flight before it takes off. Mary M. Burns showered praise on Barton in her *Horn Book* review for capturing all the "excitement and bustle of a major airport" while keeping the flow of events in a clear, well-focused order. A contributor to *Publishers Weekly* pointed out that the picture book is filled with

Barton's hallmark "flashy primary colors and inspired characterizations" and dubbed *Airport* "a wonder."

Airplanes are described again as part of Barton's series focusing on different forms of transportation. *Trucks, Boats, Airplanes,* and *Trains* feature illustrations of different vehicles that fall into these categories, as well as some of the activities surrounding them, such as a boat docking and a train stopping to pick up passengers. Linda Wicher, writing in *School Library Journal,* related that all the books in the series feature "brightly colored illustrations" which present many "accurate details that preschoolers find so fascinating." A critic in *Publishers Weekly* applauded Barton's understandable concepts and illustrations, noting that "a little says a great deal here."

The details of a trip to outer space are the focus of Barton's *I Want to Be an Astronaut.* A crew of six children who want to be astronauts now, as opposed to waiting until they grow up, make up the crew of the space shuttle. Along with enjoying the new sensations of weightlessness and ready-to-eat space food, the young crew also fixes a satellite and builds a space factory before journeying back to earth. In *I Want to Be an Astronaut,* "Barton has provided an especially evocative early career book," according to Zena Sutherland in *Bulletin of the Center for Children's Books. Horn Book*

contributor Nancy Vasilakis praised Barton's illustrations, stating that "astronauts, spaceships, and the earth itself unite in dramatic visual harmonies." Writing in the *New York Times Book Review,* Roger Sutton described the author/illustrator's vision of space as "downright giddy," going on to conclude: "*I Want to Be an Astronaut* has a sense of adventure that enlarges its context beyond space to the realm of imaginative journey."

A far different profession is explored in *Bones, Bones, Dinosaur Bones.* Six young paleontologists methodically dig up dinosaur bones, carefully package their findings, and then travel with them to the natural history museum. The process of cleaning each bone and then assembling them into a recognizable dinosaur skeleton is detailed at the museum. And once the project is complete, the young workers leave in search of more bones, starting the cycle over again. *Horn Book* contributor Ellen Fader applauded Barton's "accuracy, simplicity, appropriateness, appeal for intended audience, and timeliness" in describing paleontological work. In *Five Owls,* Camper called *Bones, Bones, Dinosaur Bones* "a gentle rainbow procession of discovery, mixing a little magic into this search for bones."

Disaster follows after the bee stings the bull in Buzz Buzz Buzz, *written and illustrated by Barton.*

In a departure from his fact-based stories, Barton describes a day in the life of a tiny woman in *The Wee Little Woman.* The wee little woman starts her day by milking her wee little cow, placing the milk on her wee little table. Things go awry, though, when her wee little cat drinks the milk and runs away for a wee little time after being scolded. By the time the cat returns home, all is forgiven and a new bowl of milk is waiting for the petite feline. "This reassuring story is told in simple words with lots of repetition," observed Leone McDermott in *Booklist.* And Marcia Hupp, writing in *School Library Journal,* noticed that the illustrations in *The Wee Little Woman* "have a satisfying heft well suited to this most satisfying little tale."

In 2001, Barton produced a new title on transportation, *My Car.* Again geared to the younger set, *My Car* shows how Sam takes care of his bright red vehicle. Readers learn not only how cars operate, but also receive lessons on road safety from Sam as well as a twist at the end of the picture book. Writing in *Booklist,* Carolyn Phelan found that "for young children intrigued by cars, this book is simply wonderful." A *Publishers Weekly* reviewer observed that Barton's "minimalist text has a plainspoken eloquence and subtle rhythm that will survive countless readings," while *School Library Journal* contributor Roxanne Burg remarked favorably upon Barton's blending of words and illustrations, writing "the illustrations are simple and stylized, but perfectly suited to the text."

Biographical and Critical Sources

BOOKS

Silvey, Anita, editor, *Children's Books and Their Creators,* Houghton (Boston, MA), 1995.

PERIODICALS

Booklist, July, 1995, Leone McDermott, review of *The Wee Little Woman,* p. 1882.

Bulletin of the Center for Children's Books, October, 1975, p. 21; September, 1979, p. 2; May, 1982, p. 162; October, 1988, Zena Sutherland, review of *I Want to Be an Astronaut,* p. 26; September, 1989, p. 3; January, 1992, p. 117; July, 2001, Carolyn Phelan, review of *My Car,* p. 2008.

Five Owls, November-December, 1990, Cathryn A. Camper, review of *Bones, Bones, Dinosaur Bones,* p. 28.

Horn Book, June, 1974, Ethel L. Heins, review of *Harry Is a Scaredy-Cat,* p. 271; June, 1979, pp. 290-291; August, 1981, p. 412; Mary M. Burns, review of *Airport,* April, 1982, pp. 152-153; January-February, 1988, pp. 49-50; July-August, 1988, Nancy Vasilakis, review of *I Want to Be an Astronaut,* p. 476; May-June, 1989; November-December, 1990, Ellen Fader, review of *Bones, Bones, Dinosaur Bones,* pp. 724-725.

Junior Literary Guild, March, 1981.

Kirkus Reviews, July 15, 1973, p. 750; March 1, 1982, p. 269; June 15, 1986, p. 935; June 15, 1988, p. 896; July 15, 1991, p. 937.

New York Times Book Review, May 5, 1974, p. 46; October 26, 1975, p. 17; April 29, 1979, p. 45; November 13, 1988, Roger Sutton, "Don't Worry, Be Giddy," p. 46.

Publishers Weekly, October 4, 1971, Review of *Elephant,* p. 60; September 18, 1972, p. 73; February 25, 1974, review of *Harry Is a Scaredy-Cat,* p. 114; January 29, 1982, review of *Airport,* p. 67; May 30, 1986, review of *Trucks, Boats, Airplanes,* and *Trains,* p. 61; August 10, 1990, p. 443; November 1, 1991, p. 79; May 3, 1993, pp. 304-305; May 8, 1995, p. 294; July 2, 2001, review of *My Car,* p. 74.

School Library Journal, April, 1979, p. 39; April, 1981, p. 108; September, 1986, Linda Wicher, review of *Airplanes, Boats, Trains,* and *Trucks,* p. 116; May, 1988, p. 76; July, 1993, p. 80; August, 1995, Marcia Hupp, review of *The Wee Little Woman,* p. 114; January, 1999, Marian Drabkin, review of *Little Factory,* p. 106; August, 2001, Roxanne Burg, review of *My Car,* p. 142.*

*   *   *

BELL, Janet
See CLYMER, Eleanor

*   *   *

BELL, Krista (Anne Blakeney) 1950-

Personal

Born January 27, 1950, in Sydney, Australia; daughter of John Spencer (an engineer) and Lurline Joyce (Rawlinson) Blakeney; married Douglas Bell (a transport planner), July 16, 1983; children: Ben, Damien, Henry. *Education:* Attended St. Vincent's College (Potts Point, Sydney, Australia), Catholic Ladies College (Melbourne, Victoria, Australia), and Monash University (Melbourne, Victoria, Australia). *Hobbies and other interests:* Watercolor painting, recycled book and clothing shops, animals and birds, "growing things."

Addresses

Home—12 Valley View Road, Glen Iris, Victoria, Australia 3146. *E-mail*—kristabell@bigpond.com.au.

Career

Australian Broadcasting Commission (ABC) Radio, book reviewer, 1984-96; freelance book reviewer for newspapers and literary magazines, 1985-2000; full-time writer 2000—. Writer, producer, and presenter of *The Children's Hour,* on Radio for the Print Handicapped, Melbourne, Australia, 1990-95; presents workshops and talks at libraries and schools; coordinator of the Virtuoso Literary Weekends, 1997-99. *Member:* Children's Book Council, The Dromkeen Society, Actor's Equity, Australian Society of Authors.

Awards, Honors

Jezza was shortlisted for the 1992 Young Australians Best Book Awards (YABBA); *Where Do You Get Your Ideas?* was shortlisted for the Australia Publishers

Education Excellence Awards, and was a Children's Book Council Notable Book, both 1997.

Writings

Jezza, illustrated by Kym Lardner, Macmillan, 1991.
Where Do You Get Your Ideas?: Interviews with Australian Authors of Children's Books, Reed Library, Cardigan Street (Port Melbourne, Victoria, Australia), 1996.
Pidge, illustrated by Ann James, Allen & Unwin, 1997.
That's Our Henry, Era, 1997.
Read My Mind! (young adult novel), Lothian Books, 2000.
Get a Life! (young adult novel), Lothian Books, 2001.
The Kindest Family (picture book), Nelson, 2001.
Rory's Big Chance (picture book), Nelson, 2001.

"TOP SHOTS" SERIES

The Slammers, illustrated by Kevin Burgemeestre, Allen & Unwin, 1995.
Star Rookie, illustrated by Kevin Burgemeestre, Allen & Unwin, 1995.
Camp Phantom, illustrated by Kevin Burgemeestre, Allen & Unwin, 1996.
Nothing But Net, illustrated by Kevin Burgemeestre, Allen & Unwin, 1996.

OTHER

Contributor of story "Off to Duncan's Paddock" to *Saddle Up Again—More Australian Horse Stories,* compiled by Mary Small, Blue Gum Press, 1995; contributor of story "Double or Nothing" to *Thrillogy: Cliff Hangers,* Longman, 2001; book reviews published in *Classroom Magazine, The Author, Magpies, Literature Base, Australian Book Review, Herald Sun* (Melbourne, Australia), *Pets and Vets Australia,* and *Writing Australia.*

Work in Progress

Getting It Right ..., a young teen novel, due in 2002, from Lothian Books.

Sidelights

Krista Bell told *SATA:* "I was a bookseller, and then a publicist before reviewing books on radio for about fifteen years, as well as being a critic for literary magazines and newspapers. When I finally started to write fiction for children, I was terrified that no one would take my writing seriously—but luckily they did.

"Since 2000 I've been writing fiction full time, and it's been like 'coming home.' My one career regret is that I didn't become an author before I was forty—so many books to write, and so little time! If I had attended Bennington College, Vermont, in 1970, as I originally intended, while my parents were living in New York, perhaps my career would have taken off far earlier. But I returned to Australia instead!

"My advice to would-be writers is to do it *now*—there's no 'right time to write,' just as there's no 'right way to

Krista Bell

write.' Write now, do it your way and find your own unique voice.

"When I give writing workshops, I tell children that I write not fiction, but 'fibtion.' To create my stories, I take my own experiences and stories that I've been told, or overheard, and then I use a portion of truth, mixed with a large dollop of imaginative fibs. That's fibtion!"

Bell has written picture books, chapter books, and young adult novels. Her "Top Shots" series plays off the growing popularity of basketball among young Australians. In this series of four novels, Bell centers on a team of youngsters called the Slammers. The series' first novel, *The Slammers,* introduces the members of the team who go from fans of the sport to players in the course of the novel, with the help of a former professional basketball player. "When the Slammers finally face their opponents, the tension builds sharply, players have to leave the court, and the chance of victory seems certain to slip from their fingers," remarked Russ Merrin in *Magpies.* In *Top Shots,* the second novel in the series, the team must raise money for new uniforms and shoes but the injury of their best player puts their ability to win against the Mighty Mixtures in doubt. "It is action and fun all the way," Merrin stated. These novels were recommended for their accessibility to young readers. Further, the use of basketball as the sport at the center of the plot will give the books a built-in audience, Merrin noted. "Krista Bell's story-telling captures the modern idiom well, and cleverly manages to describe tips, hints, strategies and rules of the game," Merrin concluded.

Bell drew upon her years with the radio show *The Children's Hour* for the text of her book, *Where Do You Get Your Ideas?: Interviews with Australian Authors of Children's Books.* Here, thirty-one of the children's book authors and illustrators she interviewed for the program are showcased with brief biographical information and a selection of between three and five questions and answers from the original interviews. Each subject gets a two-page spread with a photograph and an illustration or two from their books. The subject matter dealt with is almost entirely devoted to the writing of picture books, noted Joan Zahnleiter in *Magpies,* though the topic is not discussed in a manner that the picture-book audience would find accessible. Zahnleiter concluded that though it was difficult to pinpoint the intended audience for *Where Do You Get Your Ideas?,* "Teachers and teacher-librarians would find it useful for extension work."

Biographical and Critical Sources

PERIODICALS

Magpies, September, 1995, Russ Merrin, review of *The Slammers* and *Star Rookie,* p. 24; September, 1996, Joan Zahnleiter, review of *Where Do You Get Your Ideas?: Interviews with Australian Authors of Children's Books,* p. 43; November, 2000, Debbie Mulligan, review of *Read My Mind,* p. 37.

Reading Time, Volume 44, number 4, 2000, review of *Read My Mind,* p. 24.

ON-LINE

Krista Bell Web site, http://www.uses.bigpond.com/Kristabell/ (September 22, 2001).

*   *   *

BIALA
See BRUSTLEIN, Janice Tworkov

*   *   *

BING, Christopher (H.)

Personal

Married, wife's name, Wendy; children: three. *Education:* Attended Rhode Island School of Design.

Addresses

Home—Lexington, MA. *Office*—c/o Author Mail, Handprint Books, 413 Sixth Ave., Brooklyn, NY 11215.

Career

Editorial illustrator for the *New York Times, Washington Post, Christian Science Monitor,* Japan Airlines, and *Wall Street Journal,* among others. Children's book illustrator.

Awards, Honors

Blue Ribbon Book citation, *Bulletin of the Center for Children's Books,* 2000, and Caldecott Honor Book and Notable Children's Book selection, American Library Association, both 2001, all for *Casey at the Bat: A Ballad of the Republic Sung in the Year 1888.*

Illustrator

Ernest L. Thayer, *Casey at the Bat: A Ballad of the Republic Sung in the Year 1888,* Handprint Books (Brooklyn, NY), 2000.
Henry Wadsworth Longfellow *The Midnight Ride of Paul Revere,* Handprint Press (Brooklyn, NY), 2001.

Also illustrator of cover art for the following titles: *The Orphan's Tent* and *Chill Series,* both by Tom De Haven, Atheneum (New York, NY), 1996; *The Angry Angel* by Chelsea Quinn Yarbro, Morrow/Avon (New York, NY), 1998; *Sisters of the Night* by Chelsea Quinn Yarbro, Morrow/Avon (New York, NY), 1999.

Work in Progress

Illustrations for *Little Black Sambo* by Helen Bannerman, for Handprint Press, expected 2002.

Sidelights

Christopher Bing is a professional illustrator, contributing editorial and political cartoons to such nationally prominent periodicals as the *New York Times* and the *Washington Post.* "I draw for a living, and I love it," he told *Publishers Weekly*'s Heather Frederick Vogel. But when the constraints of newspaper illustrating began to wear on him, the idea of producing a new, historically piquant, version of Ernest L. Thayer's classic nineteenth-century baseball poem, "Casey at the Bat," rejuvenated him as an artist. In *Casey at the Bat: A Ballad of the Republic Sung in the Year 1888,* Bing uses a pen-and-ink on scratchboard technique he learned from children's illustrator Chris Van Allsburg at the Rhode Island School of Design, to create the look of a century-old scrapbook. The pages of this "scrapbook" are filled with weathered newsprint upon which are printed lines of the poem and nineteenth-century style illustrations. Each page of newsprint is also surrounded by baseball memorabilia of the era such as game tickets and baseball cards, as well as advertisements, editorials, and other clippings on topics suggested by the text of the poem. The result is "a stunning example of contemporary bookmaking," according to Bill Ott writing in *Booklist.*

Christopher Bing "copiously and faithfully" illustrated Ernest L. Thayer's classic poem with period artifacts, ads, tickets, and other memorabilia. (*From* Casey at the Bat: A Ballad of the Republic Sung in the Year 1888.)

"When people pick up one of my books," Bing told Vogel, "I want them to become absorbed into the work and feel like they are experiencing the time and the period of the event that they're looking at or reading about." In pursuit of this ideal, Bing mixed images of actual and fabricated items to round out the poem in his book, including baseball cards, ads, Thayer's obituary, and stereopticon illustrations from newspapers of the era. "The yellowed, crumbling pages of this manufactured artifact look authentic, and notes contained within the book attest to the care with which artist, designer, and publisher took in their re-creation," remarked a contributor to the *Horn Book*. The poem itself recounts the crushing defeat of the fictional baseball team of the Mudville Nine, and their arrogant star player, Casey, who strikes out in the bottom of the ninth inning. The nineteenth-century poem, when read in conjunction with Bing's surrounding ephemera, gives a fascinating glimpse of the game and of the country at the time, according to critics. Though some feared that text and artistry alike would be above the heads of younger baseball fans, others envisioned parents and children poring over the book together, taking in all the details. A contributor to *Publishers Weekly* concluded: "Though Casey and the Mudville nine strike out in the end, this exceptionally clever picture book is definitely a winner."

Biographical and Critical Sources

PERIODICALS

Booklist, February 15, 2001, Bill Ott, review of *Casey at the Bat,* p. 1136.
Horn Book, March, 2001, review of *Casey at the Bat,* p. 222.
Publishers Weekly, November, 2000, review of *Ernest L. Thayer's Casey at the Bat,* p. 89; December 18, 2000, Heather Frederick Vogel, "Christopher Bing," p. 27.
School Library Journal, January, 2001, Wendy Lukehart, review of *Ernest L. Thayer's Casey at the Bat,* p. 124.

*   *   *

BLACKALL, Bernie 1956-

Personal

Born April 6, 1956, in Murchison, Victoria, Australia; son of William and Catherine Blackall; married Kim Elizabeth (a banker), August 13, 1983; children: Andrew, Maddie, Emily. *Education:* Earned a B.A. in physical education and outdoor education. *Hobbies and other interests:* Swimming, surfing, cycling, running.

Addresses

Home—9 Villeroy St., Hampton, 3188 Victoria, Australia.

Career

Ministry of Education, Victoria, Australia, department head, 1979-89; Xavier College, Australia, department head, 1990-97; Camp Endeavour, Australia, founding director, 1998—. Certified navy diver, 1975-85.

Writings

Australian Physical Education, Book 1, Macmillan Australia (South Melbourne, Australia), 1986.

Australian Physical Education, Book 2, Macmillan Australia (South Melbourne, Australia), 1987.

(With Damien Davis) *Outdoor Education,* Macmillan Australia (South Melbourne, Australia), 1988.

Australian Rules Football, Macmillan Australia (South Melbourne, Australia), 1989.

Netball, Macmillan Australia (South Melbourne, Australia), 1989.

Cricket, Macmillan Australia (South Melbourne, Australia), 1989.

Tennis, Macmillan Australia (South Melbourne, Australia), 1989, Heinemann Library (Des Plains, IL), 1999.

Softball, Macmillan Australia (South Melbourne, Australia), 1989, Heinemann Library (Des Plains, IL), 1998.

Baseball, Macmillan Australia (South Melbourne, Australia), 1990, Heinemann Library (Des Plains, IL), 1998.

Volleyball, Macmillan Australia (South Melbourne, Australia), 1990, Heinemann Library (Des Plains, IL), 1998.

Athletics, Macmillan Australia (South Melbourne, Australia), 1990.

Rugby, Macmillan Australia (South Melbourne, Australia), 1990.

Basketball, Macmillan Australia (South Melbourne, Australia), 1990, Heinemann Library (Des Plains, IL), 1999.

Table Tennis, Heinemann Library (Port Melbourne, Australia), 1991.

Golf, illustrated by Vasja Koman, photographs by Malcolm Cross, Heinemann Library (Port Melbourne, Australia), 1997, Heinemann Library (Des Plains, IL), 1998.

Gymnastics, Heinemann Library (Port Melbourne, Australia, and Des Plains, IL), 1998.

Martial Arts, illustrated by Vasja Koman, Heinemann Library (Port Melbourne, Australia, and Des Plains, IL), 1998.

Soccer, Heinemann Library (Port Melbourne, Australia), 1998, Heinemann Library (Des Plains, IL), 1999.

Swimming, Heinemann Library (Port Melbourne, Australia), 1998, Heinemann Library (Des Plains, IL), 1999.

Hockey, Heinemann Library (Port Melbourne, Australia), 1999.

Badminton, Heinemann Library (Port Melbourne, Australia), 1999.

Rugby League, Heinemann Library (Port Melbourne, Australia), 1999.

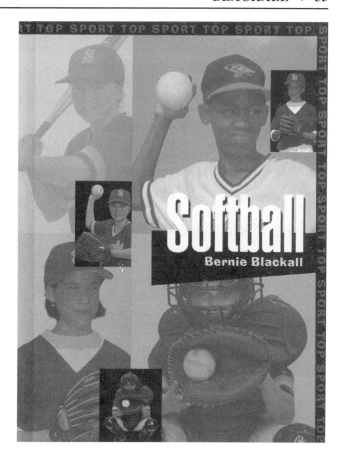

Bernie Blackall teaches the reader everything needed to start playing softball. *(Cover photos by Malcolm Cross.)*

Track and Field, Heinemann Library (Port Melbourne, Australia, and Des Plains, IL), 1999.

(With Neil Champion) *Rock Climbing,* Heinemann Library, 1999.

(With Kirk Bizley) *In-Line Skating,* Heinemann Library, 1999.

(With Andy Fraser) *Snowboarding,* Heinemann Library, 2000.

Sidelights

When sports and recreation enthusiast and educator Bernie Blackall is not running Camp Endeavour, a children's holiday adventure program in Australia that he founded in the 1990s, he enjoys participating in sports himself. As a natural extension of these activities, he has written more than two dozen books about sports and outdoor activities. In his books about popular sports, Blackall offers readers picture-book length titles that include full-color and black-and-white photographs, and diagrams that show warm-up positions, skills, and diagrams of playing fields. Each title in this series presents rudimentary information on a sport, such as basic rules and skills. These books have been adapted for sale in Australia, the United Kingdom, and the United States, each with a brief history of the sport and highlights of the careers of sports stars from the country where the book is to be marketed. About the volumes *Tennis* and *Soccer,* Blair Christolon wrote in a *School*

Library Journal review that they would make "adequate additions for libraries needing more on these subjects."

Biographical and Critical Sources

PERIODICALS

Horn Book Guide, fall, 1999, Susan Halperin, review of *Gymnastics, Martial Arts,* and *Volleyball,* p. 363.

School Library Journal, December, 1999, Blair Christolon, review of *Soccer* and *Tennis,* p. 146.*

*   *   *

BOND, Felicia 1954-

Personal

Born July 18, 1954, in Yokohama, Japan; daughter of Oliver James (a retired civil engineer) and Mary Elizabeth (a high school English teacher; maiden name, Stengel) Bond. *Education:* University of Texas—Austin, B.F.A., 1976.

Addresses

Home—Austin, TX. *Office*—c/o Author Mail, Harper-Collins Publishers, 10 East 53rd St., New York, NY 10022.

Career

Illustrator and educator. Spring Branch Science Center, Houston, TX, botanical illustrator, 1971-78; puppeteer in Austin, TX, wrote and adapted text, designed and made puppets, and performed, 1979-80; Reader's Digest Books, New York, NY, designer's assistant, 1980-81; Margaret K. McElderry Books, New York, NY, art director, 1981-83; freelance designer and illustrator, 1983—. Substitute grade school art teacher and instructor in painting for adults in continuing education program, Houston, TX, 1980.

Awards, Honors

Child Study Association of America Children's Book of the Year designations, 1985, for *Poinsettia and Her Family* and *If You Give a Mouse a Cookie;* Book of the Year Award, American Booksellers Association, 1999, for *If You Give a Pig a Pancake.*

Writings

SELF-ILLUSTRATED

Poinsettia and Her Family, Crowell (New York, NY), 1981.

Mary Betty Lizzie McNutt's Birthday, Crowell (New York, NY), 1983.

Four Valentines in a Rainstorm, Crowell (New York, NY), 1983.

The Halloween Performance, Crowell (New York, NY), 1983, published as *The Halloween Play,* HarperCollins (New York, NY), 1999.

Christmas in the Chicken Coop, Crowell (New York, NY), 1983.

Poinsettia and the Firefighters, Crowell (New York, NY), 1984.

Wake up, Vladimir, Crowell (New York, NY), 1987.

The Chick's Christmas, HarperCollins (New York, NY), 1988.

Make Your Own Valentines!, HarperCollins (New York, NY), 1994.

Tumble Bumble, Front Street (Arden, NC), 1996.

The Day It Rained Hearts, HarperCollins (New York, NY), 2001.

ILLUSTRATOR

Roma Gans, *When Birds Change Their Feathers,* Crowell (New York, NY), 1980.

Franklyn M. Branley, *The Sky Is Full of Stars,* Crowell (New York, NY), 1981.

Joseph Slate, *How Little Porcupine Played Christmas,* Crowell (New York, NY), 1982, reprinted, HarperCollins (New York, NY), 2001.

Carol Kendall, *The Firelings,* Atheneum (New York, NY), 1982.

Maria Polushkin, *Mama's Secret,* Four Winds Press (New York, NY), 1984.

Laura Joffe Numeroff, *If You Give a Mouse a Cookie,* Harper (New York, NY), 1985.

Stephen P. Kramer, *Getting Oxygen: What Do You Do if You're Cell Twenty-two?,* Crowell (New York, NY), 1986.

Stephen P. Kramer, *How to Think like a Scientist: Answering Questions by the Scientific Method,* Crowell (New York, NY), 1987.

Linda Beech, *Everyone Write,* Sniffen Court, 1988.

Margaret Wise Brown, *Big Red Barn,* Harper (New York, NY), 1989, published as *Big Red Barn Big Book,* HarperCollins (New York, NY), 1991.

Jeff Sheppard, *The Right Number of Elephants,* Harper (New York, NY), 1990, published as *The Right Number of Elephants Big Book,* HarperCollins (New York, NY), 1993.

Laura Joffe Numeroff, *If You Give a Moose a Muffin,* HarperCollins (New York, NY), 1991.

Candice Ransom, *The Big Green Pocketbook,* HarperCollins (New York, NY), 1993.

Nola Buck, *Christmas in the Manger,* HarperCollins (New York, NY), 1994.

Laura Joffe Numeroff, *Mouse Cookies: Ten Easy-to-Make Cookie Recipes with a Story in Pictures,* HarperCollins (New York, NY), 1995.

Laura Joffe Numeroff, *If You Give a Pig a Pancake,* HarperCollins (New York, NY), 1998.

Laura Joffe Numeroff, *The Best Mouse Cookie,* HarperCollins (New York, NY), 1999.

Laura Joffe Numeroff, *If You Take a Mouse to School,* HarperCollins (New York, NY), 2000.

Laura Joffe Numeroff, *If You Take a Mouse to the Movies,* HarperCollins (New York, NY), 2000.

Contributor of illustrations to periodicals, including *Cricket* and *Family Circle.* Illustrator of *Moose Sticker Book.* Works illustrated by Bond have appeared in

Spanish, German, French, Danish, Japanese, and Afrikaans.

Adaptations

Works adapted as filmstrip-audiocassette packages include *Four Valentines in a Rainstorm, The Halloween Performance, Mary Betty Lizzie McNutt's Birthday,* and *Christmas in the Chicken Coop,* all Listening Library, all 1984. *Poinsettia and Her Family* was presented on *Reading Rainbow,* PBS-TV, 1984. *If You Give a Mouse a Cookie* was recorded on audiocassette, HarperCollins, 1992; a stuffed toy mouse based on Bond's illustration was included in the boxed set. *Poinsettia and the Firefighters* and *If You Give a Mouse a Cookie* were recorded on audiocassette, Random House, 1986; *If You Take a Mouse to the Movies* was recorded on audiocassette, HarperCollins, 2001.

Work in Progress

If You Give a Bear a Brownie, If You Give a Cat a Cupcake, If You Give a Pig a Pumpkin, Pig Pancakes, and *Pig Stroller Songs,* all to be published by Harper-Collins (New York, NY).

Sidelights

In a career spanning several decades, illustrator Felicia Bond is most known for her popular illustrations for Laura Joffe Numeroff's *If You Give a Mouse a Cookie,* first published in 1995. In addition to that book, as well as the many books the pair have since collaborated on—all of which involve tempting animals with a variety of tasty treats—Bond has also illustrated the works of authors such as Margaret Wise Brown, Candice Ransom, and Stephen P. Kramer. Bond has also taken on the role of author/illustrator for such titles as *Poinsettia and Her Family, Tumble Bumble,* and *Christmas in the Chicken Coop,* all of which feature her humorous anthropomorphized animal characters.

Born in 1954 and raised in a family of seven children, Bond grew up in Bronxville, New York. Bond wanted to be an artist from an early age, once recalling the very moment to *SATA:* "I was standing in the doorway of my bedroom in the late afternoon. The room was dark, except for a brilliant but soft beam of sunlight filtering through the window. At the base of the window was a red leather window seat, and it glowed a rich, dark color. I was moved somehow, and decided I had to capture that feeling of poignancy and time passing. Art seemed to me to be the best way to do this. My feelings about light and what it represents have not changed to this day."

By the time she was six years old, Bond had received enough encouragement from her parents to be creative that in school she quickly gained a reputation as an artistic talent. Her teacher's request that she draw the class mural boosted her own sense of skill. That year, too, she gained an "awareness that artists have an opportunity to be different." As Bond realized, "They don't always have to do the same old boring things that

Felicia Bond illustrated the popular **If You Give a Mouse a Cookie,** *written by Laura Joffe Numeroff.*

other people do. I found [art] was a way to stand out and (at that age) to get attention. As I grew older, I developed an intellectual appreciation for art, but it is primarily the early impressions that motivate and inspire me."

Bond's favorite artist as a child was Charles Schulz. "His work was precise, alive, and very specific in its movements and expressions of the characters' bodies and faces," she later explained. "I devoured all his books from first grade on, as did all of my six brothers and sisters. In sixth grade I 'wrote' a class play adapted from a selection of Schulz's cartoons."

Bond moved with her family to Houston, Texas, when she was thirteen, and continued her interest in drawing. Attending the University of Texas after high school graduation, she majored in painting, and graduated with a B.F.A. in 1976. A brief move to Edmonton, Alberta, Canada, followed, during which time she became interested in book illustration. Inspired by the classic fairy tale illustrations of Edmund Dulac, Kay Neilson, and Arthur Rackham, the twenty-two-year-old Bond decided to create enough illustrations to fill a portfolio. After a move back to New York City, she supported herself by working various jobs. On the strength of her completed portfolio came her first assignment, working for publisher T. Y. Crowell. While illustrating *When Birds Change Their Feathers,* a "Let's Read and Find Out" science book authored by Roma Gans, she "pieced together enough other work to stay in New York," Bond recalled.

Bond remained in New York City for ten years and built a successful career as a children's book illustrator. "I did my first couple of books slowly," she explained to *SATA,* "and I started writing.... I found it more interesting to invent stories of my own, although they were more vignettes than well-crafted stories. I did not, however, think of myself as a writer. But my editor encouraged me, and in 1980 I wrote *Poinsettia and Her Family.* I couldn't believe how hard it was to see the book through to completion. My entire life came to a halt as I executed it. Nor could I believe how good I felt when it was finished. When it did reasonably well, I had more confidence from my publisher and in myself. I really was hooked—there was no turning back."

As an artist, Bond has won praise from critics for what *School Library Journal* reviewer Denise Anton Wright termed a "puckish sense of humor"; Wright went on to note that the effectiveness of Jeff Sheppard's *The Right Number of Elephants* "rests solely on Bond's well-executed watercolor, ink, and colored-pencil illustrations." Her work for Stephen P. Kramer's *How to Think like a Scientist: Answering Questions by the Scientific Method* is also surprisingly light-hearted, according to *New York Times Book Review* critic Katherine Bouton. "Bond's illustrations are charming and sometimes down-right funny," Bouton noted, "and give the anecdotes a wry dimension that the text ... can't achieve on its own." The new illustrations Bond created for Margaret Wise Brown's 1956 picture book *Big Red Barn* were praised by Eldon Younce in *School Library Journal* as "stylized," and with "a strong sense of detail and reality," while her "perky watercolor-and-line drawings, packed with delicious details, enhance" author Candice Ransom's *The Big Green Pocketbook,* in the opinion of *Booklist* contributor Deborah Abbott.

When Bond talks to young people about her career as an author/illustrator, she explains that many of her books are based on small things that caught her interest, or things she cared about. "Some of my ideas spring forth full-grown, others sometimes gestate for years," she explained to *SATA.* "I write down things in my sketchbook which now has more words in it than drawings. I try to stay 'free-form' about my ideas so they don't become stiff or mechanical. The process is a personal one and not the same for any two people. It is open and flexible but by no means casual." While Bond has found her job as an author/illustrator "sometimes

frustrating" due to both the isolation it requires and the fact that it is sometimes not viewed as a serious career, she views it as rewarding overall. "When I look at my past books, I remember a strong sense of freedom mixed with the hard work, and when I look ahead to future books, I feel happy."

Biographical and Critical Sources

PERIODICALS

Booklist, July, 1993, Deborah Abbott, review of *The Big Green Pocketbook,* pp. 1976-1977.

New York Times Book Review, May 17, 1987, Katherine Bouton, "Calling a Guppy a Guppy," p. 34.

School Library Journal, May, 1987, Margaret L. Chatham, review of *How to Think like a Scientist,* p. 101; June, 1989, Eldon Younce, review of *Big Red Barn,* p. 84; November, 1990, Denise Anton Wright, review of *The Right Number of Elephants,* p. 98; July, 1993, Lisa Dennis, review of *The Big Green Pocketbook,* p. 69; November, 1995, Carolyn Jenks, review of *Mouse Cookies,* p. 92.*

*   *   *

BRUSTLEIN, Janice Tworkov 1903-2000
(Biala, Janice)

OBITUARY NOTICE—See index for *SATA* sketch: Born October 18, 1903, in Biala, Russia; died September 24, 2000, in Paris, France. Artist and author. Brustlein painted vibrant scenes of city, seaside, and countryside under the name Biala and wrote a number of children's books under the name Janice. Her first published work, *It's Spring! It's Spring!* appeared in 1956, and *Lonely Little Lady and Her Garden* followed in 1958. Her later works include *Minette, Angelique, Little Bear's New Year's Party* and *Mrs. Button's Wonderful Watchdogs.* As Biala, she exhibited her paintings consistently in both Paris and New York. Her first American exhibit came in 1937 at the George Passedoit Gallery, and her last, at the Kouros Gallery, took place in 1999. Biala's artwork stands in the permanent collections of such museums as the Museum Lausanne in Switzerland.

OBITUARIES AND OTHER SOURCES:

PERIODICALS

Independent (London, England), November 30, 2000, p. 6.

New York Times, October 12, 2000, p. A25.

C

Sook Nyul Choi

1937-

The first time I dreamed of leaving Korea for America was when I was in high school and read Henry Wadsworth Longfellow's poem "I Shot an Arrow." I wondered what it would be like to travel to the country where he had lived and where he had gained his inspiration. The more I studied American literature, the more I daydreamed about traveling across the Pacific to America. And yet, it was never something that I talked about with my friends and family. The Korean War had ended recently, and everyone was so busy just trying to survive and rebuild their lives, there was really no time or place for talking about such daydreams with anyone. Besides, my family had very clear plans for me: after finishing high school, I would attend Ewha Women's University in Seoul, and then I would enter the convent—just as my older sister had done before me. Seventeen years older than I, she was already a Reverend Mother and supervised the Convent's hospital, orphanage, school, and nursing home. Once I finished my schooling, I would join her and help her in this good work.

Ever since I was little, my sister had been telling me what a glorious life it was to be a part of the religious order. My sister was beautiful and very charming. She told me many exciting Bible stories of famous women saints and heroines like Joan of Arc, who changed the world by dedicating their lives to God. Moreover, throughout the terrible period of the Japanese Occupation and World War II, our Catholic faith had been a great source of hope and strength for us. During secret visits with my sister and the other nuns, they always exuded such peace and discipline as they adhered to their devout schedule of praying, meditation, and Bible reading. After World War II ended and after we escaped from North Korea to the South, we were finally able to practice our religion freely. It was wonderful to visit my sister in the convent and hear her speak about the path I would take to make my life a worthy one before God and my family. I admired my sister and

wanted to do all I could to have a worthy and important life like hers.

Nevertheless, the dream of going to America always stayed with me. One day, during my senior year in high school, I decided that I would at least try to take the test necessary to earn a visa to the United States. At that time, the Korean Government administered a very rigorous test and only a handful of the highest scorers were able to get visas to leave the country. Many of my older brothers' friends, who had already graduated from college and taken the test multiple times, had not yet succeeded.

When I told my family that I wanted to try to take the test, they were gently amused. First of all, I did not yet have the college-level coursework in science, economics, and history that was required to even be allowed to take the test. And secondly, and more importantly, I was a girl. The Korean government would rather give the chance to go abroad to a man. Finally, even if I were able to take the test, no one imagined that I would succeed where my brothers' friends had failed. However, they figured that it wouldn't hurt for me to study hard to try—and they were thoroughly confident I would eventually decide to just stay in Seoul and enter the convent.

After graduating high school, I started at Ewha University as an English major, but I also took a full course load at night school to meet the requirements for the government's test. After a year and a half of attending classes day and night, I would have all the requisite credits and could sign up for the test.

I also needed to get a letter of acceptance from an American university before I could take the test. I approached Bishop Ro of the Myungdong Cathedral and asked for his help in obtaining a scholarship. He referred me to the American nuns at the Convent of the Sacred Heart. I went and introduced myself to the Reverend Mother, Mother McCarthy, and offered to teach her nuns

Korean in exchange for her help in applying for a scholarship. She was gracious, but I saw her amused smile. She said she was, in fact, thinking of hiring a language teacher for her nuns, but she was thinking of a more mature woman, perhaps a Korean nun. At that point I mentioned that I was a poet and that several of my poems had been published in the Seoul newspaper's section for young adults. She smiled, looked at me for a while, and then gave me the job of teaching her nuns on weekends. Because the convent was so far from my house, the nuns invited me to stay at the convent on weekends. Sister Reilly, one of the nuns I met there, helped me fill out all the necessary paperwork to apply to Manhattanville, an all-women's college run by the sisters of the Sacred Heart in Purchase, New York. After several months, I received a letter of acceptance from Manhattanville to start in the fall. Still, without passing the government exam that would permit me to leave the country, it was just a nice pipe dream.

One weekend, my entire family came by to meet the Sacred Heart nuns. My mother brought a big bundle of her beautiful chrysanthemums, and my father and brothers presented a huge cake to the nuns. My third brother teased me that I was already a nun, a little weekend nun. My parents smiled when the nuns told them how wonderful it was to have me there with them. They felt even more sure that I would be entering the convent soon myself.

The day of the big test finally arrived and I went to the huge building packed with hundreds of stern-faced men filling row after row of desks. They all looked at me as if I were an errand girl who had stumbled into the wrong room. One of the proctors told me to leave and get out of the way, but I told him I had registered for the test and was not leaving. He towered over me and brusquely asked for my name. When I told it to him, he found it on the list and looked puzzled. He then rudely pointed me toward an empty desk in the back corner of the room. I looked around and realized that I was the only girl in that entire room. But once the test began, I forgot all about that as I answered one question after another about science, economics, Korean history and literature, world history, European and American culture, music, and art. The test took all day.

Two weeks later, I anxiously stood in front of the huge bulletin board among throngs of men talking and smoking nervously. I had to push my way to the front so I could see the list. To my great surprise, I saw my name posted among the short list of people who had passed.

For the first time, I realized that my daydream of going to America was actually coming true. Although I had dreamed about it for so long, I never really expected that I would be leaving home so soon. Suddenly, I wasn't sure whether if I had done the right thing. Perhaps, I had not thought through my life plan carefully. Now, it was too late to go back and rethink things. I was too far down the road now and had no choice but to move forward. I had blindly followed my heart. I worried about myself for being so impulsive. I always depended on my feelings too much. I knew my family valued rational thinking before making big decisions, but I kept making big decisions impulsively. I walked around town for a long time. When I went home late that night, I simply told everyone that I had passed the test and would be getting ready to leave the country soon.

They were all stunned and looked at each other in silence. My third brother cleared his throat and asked me if

Sook Nyul Choi

I had been mistaken. Perhaps I had seen on the list a man's name similar to my own. It was true that my name sounds rather masculine. Most of my female friends had names like Plum Blossom, Humble Obedience, Thousand Patience, Good Follower, or Inner Peace. But my father had chosen for my name the Chinese characters meaning Clear and Passion. Words like that were normally given to boys. I realized then that perhaps that was why the proctor at the test site had looked so puzzled when I told him my name. Perhaps I only got permission to take the test because they had thought from my name that I was a boy!

The next day, my brother went to double-check the list. He came home and announced, that I had indeed passed. I would become the first one in my family to travel across the Pacific Ocean to receive a college education.

Suddenly, there was not enough time to prepare for the September departure. It was hard to see my mother's pale face as she rushed around to get my things ready for me. She hugged me and told me how proud everyone was of me, but she could not hide her worry and sadness over my impending departure to a faraway and unknown land.

I went to see my sister to let her know that I would depart as soon as my visa arrived. She was full of excitement and said it would be wonderful for me to have an American education. We would be able to do more of God's work with my broad knowledge of the western world. She began giving me a list of all the things I should do while at Manhattanville. First, I needed to study and learn all I could about American culture. Of course, I should write her every day so that we could grow together in our new discoveries. Second, I must go to graduate school and earn a doctorate. Third, I must never forget even for a minute that I am from Korea and that I am representing my country. I must be always cheerful and keep myself and my room immaculate at all times.

As I was leaving, she mentioned again that while I was in America, I should write her every day to keep her informed of all my feelings and activities so that we would know each other's thoughts and grow together and be ready to work together without wasting time catching up after our years of separation. There would be only physical separation, not spiritual separation, she said. I nodded my head as I intently listened to her as I had always done. I promised myself that I would work hard and do all that she asked of me and make her proud of me.

My mother hurriedly began to make me a Korean outfit for each season so that I would have them to show to my college friends. She carefully pressed and folded my best outfits and embroidered many handkerchiefs and towels so that I would have something to give as gifts to the nuns and to people I might visit. Even with all these special preparations, however, I only had two tiny suitcases of possessions to take with me as I embarked on my new life. My mother also gathered up all the money she could. She emptied all of her savings and her emergency money. She put a single $100 bill into my shoe for safekeeping. Into my purse, she placed one $10 bill, one $5 bill, one $1 bill, one quarter, one dime, one nickel and one penny.

The day I left Seoul was a warm September day in 1958. All my family, relatives, and friends came out to say goodbye and asked me to write them and let them know what it was like to live in America. I promised them all that I would, and we said our teary goodbyes. The images of my mother's pale face and forced smile, the solemn faces of my four brothers, and my father's tall figure standing stoically behind my mother, all were etched deeply into my heart.

I looked up at the sky and I saw the image of my sister praying for me in her chapel and reiterating all she had said to me. She was counting the days until my return so that we could start our ambitious task of furthering God's great work. I felt nervous, but honored and privileged to have a sister who cared for me so much. I told myself that I must be successful and make her proud of me and sank down in my seat for the long flight to America. It was my first airplane trip and my first trip outside my homeland.

When I arrived at Kennedy Airport (then called Idlewild Airport), I looked around for the group of Manhattanville seniors who were to be waiting to greet me and take me to school. I had imagined the smiling seniors, all with beautiful blonde hair, waving eagerly to me as I deplaned. But, though I waited and waited, there was no one there to meet me. My spirits sinking, I finally found someone to help me call the college. The operator who

Sook, pretending she isn't tired as she is caught by her mother studying till 3 a.m. for the government exams, in Seoul, 1956

Author's family on the lawn in front of one of the palaces in Seoul: (from left) second brother Tom, third brother Callistus, mother, younger brother Francis, author, oldest brother Augustus, and his son, Matthew at the end, 1958

answered told me to hurry up and get myself to school. All the other new students had already arrived and the orientation was almost over. It was my first telephone conversation in English and I had a hard time writing the directions down fast enough. I just hoped that I hadn't missed any important part of the directions. Gripping the scrap of paper I had written on, I ventured out, hoping I wouldn't end up in the wrong place.

I took a bus to Grand Central Station, then found the train to White Plains, New York, and then finally took a taxi to the college campus. By the time I got in the cab, all I had left was the $100 bill in my shoe. I carefully unfolded it and handed it to the cab driver. I asked him to include whatever the right tip should be for himself, and to give me the change. I was not used to American money and the tipping system, and I felt it was best to ask the driver in order to avoid the mistake of tipping too little. The kind driver smiled and gave me the change.

As I got out of the cab clutching my change and my two small suitcases, a tall nun dashed down and said, "Oh, my stars, you are here already. We thought you were coming tomorrow! How did you get here all by yourself?" It was my freshmen class warden, Mother Hargrove. I was glad she recognized me from the pictures I had been asked to send her. She asked whether I had had enough money, and I told her I had given the cab driver my $100 bill. She grabbed the change to count it and breathed a sigh of relief. "Thank goodness, he was an honest man."

I put the money securely in my side pocket. I knew that I could expect no more money from home, and that this money would have to last until I could figure out how to earn book money and pocket money. It had only been five years since the Korean War ended, and things were hard for everyone at home. My family had already spent lots of money to send me to America. I knew my mother borrowed from everyone she knew and had not told anything to my father and brothers. She did not want to make them feel inadequate. The college provided me tuition and room and board in return for maintaining good grades, performing thirty-five hours of scholarship work each week, and participating in a "cultural exchange" program to educate people about Korea. The rest was my responsibility.

As I had arrived late and missed freshmen orientation completely, the first week of college was hectic. I scrambled around to find the right classrooms and to get to know my classmates. Doing thirty-five hours of scholarship work in the dining hall was difficult as it took much needed time away from reading the weekly assignments. There were twenty-five freshmen scholarship students who served dinner and cleaned up after the students had left. As we rushed around to clean up the dining hall, we spoke and got to know each other. Among the scholarship students there was a special bond. We did not have the luxury of going out for dinner and to the movies in town. But, we were all so excited to be at such a wonderful school, and were determined to make it all work.

I quickly came to realize the great responsibility of being the only Korean student at the school. My classmates were curious and interested in learning more about my native country and me. My desire to be anonymous and hide in the library studying could not be fulfilled. The nuns often asked me to get dressed in my flowing Korean silk outfit to greet college guests. The nuns said, "Your national costume is so beautiful and graceful, we just love to see you walking about our beautiful campus in that." I smiled and did as they asked and answered all the questions I was asked about my country and its customs. But my Korean outfit was so cumbersome and uncomfortable for me as a college freshman who needed to dash about to get her work done. It robbed me of my time to study and work, and I began to feel worried and torn. I wanted to do all that was asked of me by the nuns and my new friends at school, but I did not want my family to receive a poor report card at the end of the year.

In the hallways of the dorms, there hung several posters of Korean orphans, sitting amidst the debris from the bombings, begging for rice with their thin arms outstretched with a rice bowl. Below these posters were big jars with a note asking everyone who passed to donate their spare change. Even though I was across the ocean, I could not avoid being reminded of the plight of my homeland. Next to the sad posters of the Korean War orphans, there were beautiful posters of cherry blossoms and the peaceful temples of Japan. It pained me to see that most of my college friends knew Korea only as an impoverished war-torn land devoid of beauty, culture, and history. People I

"My last visit to my older sister, the nun Sister Caritas, with my mother, before I left for America," Our Lady of Perpetual Help, Seoul, 1958

met on campus did not know how beautiful and wonderful Korean people were, nor how exquisite the little country was and how greatly it had suffered over the years at the hands of the bigger nations around it.

Often, the Maryknoll missionary nuns came to Manhattanville and paged me, asking me to teach them some Korean, as they would soon be heading off to Korea to help the war orphans. I was touched and grateful for their concern for my country, but at the same time I was frustrated and scared about failing my courses. Feeling that it was my responsibility to accommodate them, I dutifully helped out for an hour or two, but at night tears came to my eyes because I did not have enough time to study.

Due to this lack of time, I could not keep the promise I made to write my sister and family every day. My sister began to send me letters worrying that I may have lost sight of my goal and may have been swept away by life in a rich country. Because I knew my mother would worry about me, I never mentioned my lack of sleep, my scholarship work, my lack of pocket money, and my continual struggle with the English language. Since I had so little time to write, and didn't want my mother to worry, I just sent weekly postcards home. I simply said that I was happy and that all was well.

In trying to keep up with all my obligations and my studying, I did not sleep more than five hours a night at most. The college dorm rule was to be in bed at ten. A lights-out bell rang at 9:50 p.m. and at 10:00, the class wardens patrolled the hallways to make sure all lights were out and all girls were securely tucked in bed. The nuns wanted to make sure we got to bed early so we could be up early for morning mass. Their girls should be healthy, spiritually strong, and morally sound.

But I went to bed each night fully dressed with my book bag all packed and hidden under the covers. After my roommate began to snore softly and the nuns and senior hall proctors were all gone, I tip toed out into the dark and silent hall with my book bag, pillow, and blanket. I went to the bathroom, which was the only place where lights were kept on all night long. Between two long lines of shower stalls, there were two bathtubs. I laid out my blanket and pillow in one of the tubs and studied with the shower curtain drawn tightly. I read and wrote papers until two or three in the morning and then tiptoed back to my room and quietly slipped into my bed and collapsed. When my roommate's alarm went off at six o'clock, I jumped out of bed and said a cheery good morning and got ready for 6:30 mass. During mass, I often dozed and closed my eyes and hoped none of the nuns would see me yawn.

For several months, I avoided being caught. But one rainy night, I fell asleep in the tub and woke up at four with a sharp pain in my stomach. I bundled my things together and headed toward my room, but I fainted in the hallway. When I woke up, I was in the infirmary with Mother Hargrove, my class warden, and Mother Cavanaugh, the vice president, staring down at me with great concern. I cried feeling helpless and weak, realizing that my secret nighttime studying was over. I did not know how I could manage to do all the scholarship work and still study enough to earn decent grades and make my family proud of me. Also, I was ashamed to have woken up the nuns and to have worried them.

The nuns did not scold me, but firmly told me that I must get enough sleep and not break the "lights out" rule. While I was recovering at the college infirmary for a week, many of my classmates came to visit me. It was then that I realized how many good friends I had already made, even though my English was so halting and my time to spend with them was so limited.

During my sophomore year, I had more time to concentrate on my studies as I had done most of my scholarship work during the summer. I had a chance to get to know more of my classmates and began to accept invitations to spend weekends with them at their homes. By junior year, my English had gotten much better, and I began to study French and Art. I was pleased with my choices of majoring in History and minoring in French and Art. I began to write longer letters home every other week. Sometimes, when writing to my family, I wished that they understood English because, often in describing my new experiences, it seemed that only an English expression could explain them in just the right way.

My senior year seemed to fly by. Between my courses, my scholarship work, and my growing number of friends, I was as happy and busy as I had ever been. The one nagging disappointment, however, was that I was not going to be able to go straight to graduate school, as I had planned. Although it was not much money to most people, the application fees for graduate school—combined with the money needed to travel to schools to interview for scholarships—was more than I could afford. Even though I had started working as a teacher's aide at a nearby high

At a park after Sunday High Mass near Myungdong Cathedral before leaving Seoul, 1958

school to earn extra money, I was not able to save the money I needed to apply to graduate school. I resigned myself to the fact that I would have to spend a year or two working to save enough money to go to graduate school.

Nevertheless, graduation was a joyous occasion. My friends and teachers were all so proud of me and were so effusive in praising me when they introduced me to other students' parents. After my Korean upbringing in which I was always expected to achieve and was never praised for merely meeting those expectations, this generous praise was wonderful and surprising to me. I felt embarrassed that I was getting praised for merely getting through college, even when I had not gotten all A's as I always had in Korea. Graduation day flew by in a blur of celebration. At the end of the day, my roommate and I sat in our room and chatted about our life ahead. I told her that I had been offered a full-time teaching job in New York City, which I was very excited about, since I had just loved my work as a teacher's aide. Still, I was worried about not fulfilling my sister's plan for me to go to graduate school right away. My roommate, normally a sunny and sweet girl, suddenly exploded with exasperation. "Live your own life. It is your life, not your sister's. For goodness sakes, don't bother re-reading her long lecturing letters again, and don't worry about what she thinks and says. You are here now, not there. Who knows what the future has in store for us? You loved teaching and maybe this will lead to just the right thing for you." I didn't know what to say. I had never had someone shout at me, and I had never had anyone tell me to make myself happy. Without a word, I hugged her and squeezed her tightly.

Living on my own in New York City and teaching school did indeed bring many changes. I loved meeting the children and marveled at how outspoken, independent, and curious they were to learn and try new things. I loved the American style of encouraging children, praising them, and helping them strike out on their own. Their enthusiasm to learn awakened a deep and lasting love in me for teaching. Now, when I go to schools to lecture and read my books to students, it is always like a wonderful return to my earliest days of teaching.

B ut the biggest, most unexpected development in my life was meeting Mark. Much like myself, he was the first in his family to have left Korea and ventured across the Pacific to go to college. He was in business school when we met, and I found myself suddenly, surprisingly, deeply in love. I had never been in love before and, when he asked me to marry him, I decided to follow my heart. I knew that falling in love and getting married was not part of the plan, but I heard myself say yes to his proposal.

I knew my family would be surprised, but I convinced myself that they just wanted me to be happy and that, as soon as I explained how in love I was and how wonderful Mark was, they would give their blessing. I could not imagine anyone being unhappy with Mark and with the happiness I had found with him. With confidence and excitement, I wrote to my mother, and enclosed several pictures of us taken together during the engagement party that Mark's friends and mine threw in New York.

My sister wrote me back telling me it was a terrible mistake to throw my life away for a mere man and waste

Speaking to alumnae at Manhattanville College, New York, in 1962

my life doing his chores for him. I was made for something better than washing a man's socks and cooking for him, she said. My brothers wrote saying I must cancel the wedding until they could come to see me and talk to me in person.

Stunned by their response, I went to Manhattanville to visit my favorite nuns. Surely they would understand me and rejoice with me and give me their blessings. They would see how happy and thrilled I was about the new life ahead of me. I showed them my engagement ring and spoke of my marriage to Mark. The nuns looked at my beautiful diamond ring and told me it could be a fake and that Mark could be a gambler or drunkard for all I knew. They asked me what I knew about his family and how long

I had known him. I knew nothing much about his family history other than the little he had told me. All I knew was that we were in love and that I wanted to be with him. The nuns told me to give the ring back and think about my family and my future. They all said it was a hasty and ridiculous decision that was surely brought on by the pressures of living alone in New York City away from the sheltered environment in which I had felt so secure for four years.

After listening to all my favorite nuns, I got scared and decided to listen to these wonderful people who loved me. I called Mark and said I needed to give his ring back as I had made a rash decision. Mark was quiet on the phone for a

Welcoming Crown Princess Michiko of Japan at Manhattanville College in the fall of 1960

long while. He sighed and asked me calmly, "Please, make an appointment for me with the nuns. I will come tomorrow and meet with all the nuns who want to talk to me. Let them see me and talk to me and then they can judge for themselves whether if I am right for you or not. Please tell them I will come early in the morning and stay as long as necessary."

Mark's family was Buddhist. He had never been inside a Catholic church and had never seen a nun. But Mark arrived early in the morning, dressed in his best, light-gray, pinstriped suit, and sat in the parlor as one nun after another came through to interview him. First he spoke with Mother O'Byrne, the college president, for an hour; then Mother Cavanagh, the vice president; Mother Hargrove, my freshmen warden; then three other wardens who had watched over me. I paced nervously in the foyer and watched Mark sitting in the convent parlor talking to all the nuns. My heart broke as I saw him grilled by nun after nun till late afternoon. At the end of the day, the nuns gathered together, sat me down, and told me they unanimously

found him to be truly wonderful and handsome. They gave their blessing to go ahead with our wedding plans. Mark then joined us, and we all relaxed and talked some more.

It was then Mark quietly told us that he had already taken three Catechism lessons from Monsignor Campbell at Corpus Christi Church near his apartment in New York City. He planned to be confirmed by the same Monsignor and to make his first confession before he got married. Mark then gave the nuns Msgr. Campbell's address and phone number in case they wanted to contact him. When the nuns did call, the Monsignor confirmed that he found Mark to be a rare young man; much to our surprise, he told the nuns he was planning on performing the marriage ceremony.

After that day, we set the wedding date for November and I sent the invitation to my family. I got another telegram telling me to stop all plans until my brothers could come to speak with me. But Mark and I went ahead with our plans, and were married before they had a chance to get their visas to come.

I felt sad to be married without their blessings and presence, but I was one of the first to be married in my class and almost all of my classmates came to my wedding. The nuns could not come, but they invited us to the college and gave us a reception in the same beautiful parlor where they had grilled Mark all day with zillions of questions.

Since my sister and brothers were disappointed with me and did not write to congratulate me, I kept my silence. But my mother wrote me every week, repeatedly giving her blessings as if to make up for the other blessings that did not come my way. Each time I read her sweet and calm letters, I felt deep pain and sadness for disappointing her and the rest of the family.

I planned on bringing my mother to New York to live with us once we got settled more comfortably. But soon after we married, my mother died. The last memory I have of my mother is of her standing at Seoul Kimpo Airport waving her white handkerchief to me. My family, wanting to spare me the shock and sorrow, did not tell me the news until the funeral was over. They relied on Father Lee, my favorite priest, to come and break the news to me in person. On his way to Rome for a meeting, he made a special stop in New York to tell me of the death of my mother.

It was sad for me to be so far away from home and from the rest of my family. My sister and brothers and I started writing each other more, and I helped arrange to have two of my brothers and their wives come to the U.S. Other family members began to travel to New York and even my sister came several times on her way to Rome for her meetings. It was good to be able to see family once again.

Life in New York was very busy. Mark and I were raising our two daughters, and I continued to teach all the while. When our daughters were born, my husband and I decided to become American citizens and joined our children in their new nationality. Mark and I did not want to live as perpetual visitors. Once we were citizens, we no longer felt like rootless foreigners struggling to belong. Our small family worked hard and our days were busy trying to make a life for ourselves in our new country.

When I was teaching, my students often asked me to tell them about life in Korea. When we studied World War II, I often wished there were a book I could recommend about life in Korea during that period, but I could find none. The textbooks we used barely mentioned anything about what was happening in Asia during that period. The students kept asking me about my life growing up in Korea during that time. Those memories seemed so distant, and I did not wish to journey back to that difficult

Choi and her husband-to-be Mark as they celebrated their engagement in New York City in 1962

era. It would be too painful to delve into my memories of the grim days in northern Korea under the brutal Japanese occupation and the subsequent Soviet occupation, and finally, my perilous crossings of the 38th Parallel to freedom in South Korea.

When I told my students that we had many more chapters to cover before school ended and that we needed to move on to the next subject, they asked me to write a book about my life. I smiled and said that maybe someday I would. But the thought of writing a book about those dark days of Korean history made me wince. That part of my life was long gone and buried deep in my heart. The best way for me to live was to live in the present, and focus on teaching and on raising my family. My life was full, and I was happy as a wife, mother, and teacher in New York City.

Suddenly, one cold February day in 1980, I was in class teaching, when the principal suddenly came in and whispered in my ear. Mark had collapsed and had been taken by ambulance to the hospital.

Two days later, Mark left this world. To this day, I still cannot find the appropriate words to express my shock and grief at such a profound loss.

Suddenly, I had become the head of our little family, and all responsibilities rested on my shoulders. My small teacher's salary was not enough to support us all. Yet, I had no business expertise and was not equipped to take over the company, which Mark had worked so hard to build.

The day after the funeral, I went to my school to thank all my students for their support. I asked for a leave of absence and the nuns and the priests at school told me to take all the time I needed.

I went to Mark's office and stood in front of the door and stared at his name engraved on the big, brown wooden door. I had not been to his office very often, nor did he discuss his business with me when he came home. He was always so interested in hearing about my teaching and about our children's activities that we rarely spoke about his work.

After a long pause, I pushed the door open, expecting to face a cold, lifeless office. I was afraid of my reaction to not seeing Mark sitting there smiling and welcoming me as he had the last time I had stopped by. But the office felt surprisingly warm and inviting. The sun splashed across Mark's big brown leather chair, and on his big wooden desk, the letters, phone messages, and files were all out as if Mark had just dashed out for a minute for a cup of coffee.

Although I knew nothing of his import and export business, I impetuously decided then and there to run his business. I promised myself that I would learn the business quickly and would make a go of it, no matter what it took. I simply could not close the office and see all his hard work be reduced to nothing.

The next day, I called my school and told the principal that I was going to try to run the business using sheer determination, hard work, and blind faith. I learned the business and ran the company for five years at the Empire State Building.

I t was while I was running the business that I began to write *Year of Impossible Goodbyes,* my first book. Long days at the office left me exhausted, yet I kept typing out

the story until the wee hours of the morning. Suddenly, I had a deep desire to write the book. Perhaps, it was out of fear that I, too, might die suddenly like Mark. I suddenly worried that if I didn't write this, nothing would ever be written telling of the experiences that my family and many others like us lived through. Because I had been a teacher, I realized how important and powerful it would be to have a book that accurately portrayed life in Korea in the 1940s.

In Korean culture, it is taboo to speak of past sufferings. One should move on and concentrate on bettering the present and building a new life. The generations that truly suffered were too tired and simply wanted to forget and to move on. The younger generation did not know much, as their elders did not want to talk of the past. Had I stayed in Korea all these years, I, too, would have thought it inappropriate to speak of our sad history. But, after living in the U.S. and teaching for so many years, my ideas had changed. I knew it was important for students to learn about what happened in the 1940s in Korea. The school history books did not cover this, and I felt that if I didn't write, perhaps no one would.

It was painful to journey back to my childhood days. I understood why my parents and older siblings chose never to speak of those horrible times. I, too, had never before spoken of those times. It took several years to write *Year of Impossible Goodbyes,* and the original version was over

Choi at a friend's wedding in Cambridge, Massachusetts, in the mid-1990s

600 pages. It was only after much difficult editing that I cut it down to 170 pages.

In 1991, *Year of Impossible Goodbyes* was finally published. I felt relieved and happy to hold the first copy of the book in my hands. It had been a long journey. I told myself that I had done my job and could move on and perhaps write a happy, even funny book the next time. No more looking back, I said to myself.

But within a few months after the publication of my first book, letters, phone calls, and faxes streamed in, asking me what happened to Sookan, the young protagonist of the book. And, to my great surprise, I began to receive many invitations to speak at schools, libraries, and literary institutions all across the U.S. Each time I spoke to a group, the audience asked me about what became of Sookan. My many readers inspired me and gave me renewed courage to write the sequel. Thus, *Echoes of the White Giraffe* was born.

The second book speaks of how young Sookan and her family lived through the turbulent years of the Korean War. This book was also warmly received, and, once again, many schools and literary institutions invited me to speak. Again, my readers urged me to write yet another sequel describing Sookan's life in America. *Gathering of Pearls*, the third book, speaks of how Sookan makes the transition to American college life. The book speaks of the cultural differences between East and West, and how one person deals with bridging these differences, and beginning a new life in a new country. I drew great strength from my readers, my students, librarians, and teachers. Their interest and encouragement provided me great support and inspiration over the years.

Many grammar, middle and high schools as well as universities include these novels as part of their curriculum, and I travel a great deal to speak with different groups. I was frequently asked by readers to write picture books for little children so that young children might learn about Korean culture. Since I had taught kindergarten and elementary school for many years, I was delighted to draw on my experiences with young children, and wrote three picture books. *Halmoni and the Picnic* deals with Yunmi, a third grader whose Halmoni (meaning grandmother in Korean) came from Korea. Her classmates invited Yunmi's grandmother to a class picnic. Although Yunmi loves her grandmother, she is afraid that her classmates might make fun of her grandmother for being so different. Yunmi especially worries that her grandmother's strange food might embarrass her and her grandmother. But her classmates and her grandmother surprise Yunmi and all goes well at the picnic.

When I taught third and fourth grades in New York City, I often took my class for field trips: trips to Theodore Roosevelt's birth place, Abigail Adam Smith's House, and numerous educational sights and museums. I also took them often to Central Park. Each time we ventured out, I asked my students to ask their grandparents to join us as class chaperones. The grandparents were wonderful chaperones and they often brought special food for the children to eat. It was heartwarming to see the proud and loving grandparents. The children as well loved sharing their school life with their grandparents. So, my first picture book was drawn from my fond memories of grandparents who came, enjoyed, and helped us with our class trips.

Choi giving a reading at Boston College, Boston, Massachusetts, 1993

The second picture book, *Yunmi and Halmoni's Trip*, is about Yunmi's going to visit Korea with her grandmother. Yunmi, who was born and raised in America, learns of her grandmother's culture and experiences life in Korea through her young cousins, whom she finally has a chance to meet.

The third picture book, *The Best Older Sister*, deals with the feelings a young girl experiences when a younger brother is born. In each picture book I wrote, I wanted to talk about feelings common to us all against the backdrop of a different culture. In this way, I thought children could explore their own feelings while also learning about cultures different from their own.

As I look back on my life, I can't help but feel a deep gratitude for the ultimate joy life brings. It was grace I prayed for and received that enabled me to endure dark times, survive them, and ultimately rejoice in the many blessings I have been granted.

As I travel to many schools and literary institutions to speak, I meet many wonderful readers and I hope to meet many more. It pleases me to know that my books are read in many foreign countries as well. Some of my books have been translated into French, Korean, Japanese, Italian, and Spanish. I have received many letters from readers all over the U.S., Canada, South America, and Europe, and from as far away as Singapore and Thailand.

I hope that my books continue to teach readers about the unique history and culture of Korea. I am constantly touched by the way readers have taken Sookan and the other characters in my books into their hearts. I am forever grateful to my readers and hope they continue to enjoy and learn from their reading adventures.

Writings

NOVELS FOR YOUNG ADULTS

Year of Impossible Goodbyes, Houghton Mifflin (Boston, MA), 1991.

Echoes of the White Giraffe, Houghton Mifflin (Boston, MA), 1993.
Gathering of Pearls, Houghton Mifflin (Boston, MA), 1994.

PICTURE BOOKS

Halmoni and the Picnic, illustrated by Karen Milone-Dugan, Houghton Mifflin (Boston, MA), 1993.
The Best Older Sister, illustrated by Cornelius Van Wright and Ying-Hwa Hu, Delacorte (New York, NY), 1997.
Yunmi and Halmoni's Trip, illustrated by Karen Milone-Dugan, Houghton Mifflin (Boston, MA), 1997.

CLARK, Margaret (D.) 1943-
(Lee Striker)

Personal

Born in 1943; married John Clark (divorced); children: Stuart, Fiona. *Education:* Toorak Teacher's College, B.Ed. (with honors), 1985; Deakin University, M.A. (education), 1990, Ph.D. (children's literature), c. 2001. *Hobbies and other interests:* Gardening, reading, walking on the beach, researching.

Addresses

Office—P.O. Box 454, Geelong, Victoria 3220, Australia. *E-mail*—margaretclark43@hotmail.com.

Career

Educator and author. Geelong schools, Victoria, Australia, classroom teacher, 1962-72, preschool teacher, 1972-82; Deakin University, Victoria, Australia, lecturer in education, 1982-85; Victoria Health Department, Alcohol and Drug Centre, Victoria, Australia, education officer and counselor, 1985-95; freelance author, 1995—. Margaret Clark (Pugwall) Pty. Ltd., director. *Member:* Australian Society of Authors, Fellowship of Australian Writers, Australian Council of Education, Deakin University Alumni.

Awards, Honors

White Raven award, *Wally the Whiz Kid;* numerous award short-lists.

Writings

FOR JUNIOR READERS

Tina Tuff, Omnibus, 1991.
Plastic City, Random House, 1992.
Ghost on Toast, Random House, 1994.
Calvin the Clutterbuster, Omnibus, 1994.
Tina Tuff in Trouble, Omnibus, 1995.
Meatball's Good Dog Day, Random House, 1997.
(With Paul Collins) *Shivers I* (includes *Brain Drain*), Angus & Robertson (Pymble, New South Wales, Australia), 1997.
Hot Stuff, illustrated by Tom Jellett, Omnibus, 1998.
A Wee Walk, 2001.

Also author of *The Biggest Boast,* Random House; *Ripper and Fang,* Omnibus; *Mystery of the Talking Tail* ("Supa Doopa" series), Addison Wesley Longman; and *Lucky Last Luke* ("Supa Doopa" series), Addison Wesley Longman.

FOR YOUNG ADULTS

Pugwall, Penguin, 1987.
Pugwall's Summer, Penguin, 1989.
The Big Chocolate Bar, Random House, 1991.
Hold My Hand—or Else, Random House, 1993.
Fat Chance ("Lisa Trelaw" series), Random House, 1993.
Living with Leanne, Random House, 1994.
Hot or What ("Lisa Trelaw" series), Random House, 1995.
Back on Track: Diary of a Street Kid, Random House, 1995.
Pulling the Moves, Random House, 1996.
Care Factor Zero, Random House, 1997, Morrow (New York, NY), 2000.
Web Watchers, Random House, 1997.
On Ya, Sonya, Addision Wesley Longman, 1997.
Annie with Attitude, Addison Wesley Longman, 1998.
No Fat Chicks, Random House, 1998.

Margaret Clark

Cool Chrissie, illustrated by Bettina Gutheridge, Red Fox (Milsons Point, New South Wales, Australia), 1998.
No Standing Zone, Random House, 1999.
Kiss and Make Up ("Lisa Trelaw" series), Random House, 1999.
Secret Girls' Stuff, Random House, 1999.
Coolini Beach: The Search, Random House, 1999.
Coolini Beach: Cool Bananas, Random House, 2000.
More Secret Girls' Stuff, Random House, 2001.
Rave On, Random House, 2001.
Hooking Up ("Lisa Trelaw" series), Random House, 2001.
(With Dr. Claire Fox) *What to Do When Life Sucks*, 2001.

Also author of *Bad Girl*, Random House; *Famous for Five Minutes*, Random House; *Love on the Net*, Penguin.

HORROR NOVELS; "HAIR RAISERS" SERIES; AS LEE STRIKER

Revenge of the Vampire Librarian, Red Fox (Milson's Point, New South Wales), 1995.
Body Parts, Random House, 1996.
Murder on the Ghoul Bus, Random House, 1997.
Curse of the Mummy, Random House, 1997.

Also author of *The House of the Living Dead*, Random House; *Evil at Camp Starr*, Random House; *Dead Kids Tell No Tales*, Random House; *Humans for Breakfast*, Random House; *Bat Attack*, Random House; *Teacher Torture*, Random House; *Bite Your Head Off*, Random House; and (with Claire Carmichael and Christine Harris) *Deadly Friends* (contains "Out of Control"), Random House.

"MANGO STREET" SERIES

Weird Warren, illustrated by Bettina Guthridge, Penguin, 1993.
Butterfingers, illustrated by Bettina Guthridge, Penguin, 1994.
Britt the Boss, Penguin, 1995.
Wally the Whiz Kid, Penguin, 1995.
Millie the Moaner, Penguin, 1997.
Bold as Brass, Penguin, 1997.
Mango Street Mania!, Penguin, 2001.

Also author of *Copy Cat*, Penguin, and *Wacky Mac*, Penguin.

"AUSSIE ANGELS" SERIES

Okay Koala, Hodder, 1999.
Whale of a Time, Hodder, 1999.
Seal with a Kiss, Hodder, 1999.
Hello Possum, Hodder, 1999.
Wannabe Wallaby, Hodder, 2000.
Cocky Too, Hodder, 2000.
Sheila the Heeler, Hodder, 2000.
A Horse of Course, Hodder, 2000.
Operation Wombat, Hodder, 2000.
Dollar for a Dolphin, Hodder, 2000.
Dog on the Job, Hodder, 2001.
Mouse Pad, Hodder, 2001.
Camel Breath, Hodder, 2001.
Duck for Luck, Hodder, 2001.

"CHICKABEES" SERIES

Hot and Spicy, Penguin, 1998.
Stars, Penguin, 1998.
Sugar Sugar, Penguin, 1999.
Brush with Fame, Penguin, 1999.
Far from Phoneys, Penguin, 1999.
Bewitched, Penguin, 1999.

"EGG" SERIES; PICTURE BOOKS

Egg's Cup, illustrated by Bettina Guthridge, Hodder, 2000.
Egg's Cosy Day, illustrated by Bettina Guthridge, Hodder, 2000.
Egg's Shell, illustrated by Bettina Guthridge, Hodder, 2000.
Egg's Box, illustrated by Bettina Guthridge, Hodder, 2000.
Egg's Tent, illustrated by Bettina Guthridge, Hodder, 2001.
Egg Goes Fishing, illustrated by Bettina Guthridge, Hodder, 2001.

"ASSORTED SHORTS" SERIES

Footy Shorts, Penguin, 2000.
Board Shorts, Penguin, 2000.
Boxer Shorts, Penguin, 2000.
Dirty Shorts, Penguin, 2000.
Holey Shorts, Penguin, 2000.
Stinky Shorts, Penguin, 2001.
Cool Shorts (contains *Footy Shorts, Board Shorts, Boxer Shorts, Dirty Shorts, Holey Shorts,* and *Stinky Shorts*), Penguin, 2001.

"AUSSIE BITES" SERIES

Snap!, Penguin, 1997.
Crackle!, Penguin, 1999.

Pop!, Penguin, 1999.
Great Aussie Bites (includes *Snap!, Crackle!,* and *Pop!*),
    Penguin, 2000.
S.N.A.G., illustrated by Terry Denton, Penguin, 2001.
Silent Knight, Penguin, 2001.

Adaptations

Pugwall was adapted as a television series.

Work in Progress

Working on the novel *Nightworks* for Random House.

Sidelights

With over ninety books to her credit during her first
dozen years as a children's author, prolific writer
Margaret Clark stands among the top-selling women
authors in her native Australia. Clark first made a splash
with her debut novel *Pugwall,* which was adapted as a
popular Australian television series. Her books, which
range in audience from picture books to young adult
novels, include *Weird Warren, Hold My Hand—or
Else!,* and *Rave On.* Series for young readers include her
"Aussie Angels" novels, featuring a pair of animal-
loving kids whose adventures on an Australian nature
preserve provide Clark with the opportunity with sharing
a wealth of facts about that fascinating continent.

Born in Geelong, Victoria, Australia, in 1943, Clark first
trained as a teacher. After lecturing at Deakin University
between 1982 and 1985, she left academia to work as a
consultant and counselor for an alcohol and drug
rehabilitation center in Geelong. Her experiences there
would provide the raw material for several works of
young adult fiction, among them *Back on Track: Diary
of a Street Kid* and *Care Factor Zero,* a controversial
novel that was published in the United States in 2000. In
Back on Track, fifteen-year-old Simone leaves home
with her boyfriend, and finds out that life on the streets
is not as romantic or glamorous as she thought. Noting
that the book "reads like a catalogue of the awful, and no
doubt authentic," *Magpies* contributor Jo Goodman
praised Clark for writing a novel that "pulls no punches,
neither trivialising nor romanticising" the predicaments
of her teen protagonist. Another fifteen year old is
featured in *Care Factor Zero,* as foster child Larceny
Leyton suspects she is in over her head after a visit to
her "fence" results in murder. Although *Bulletin of the
Center for Children's Books* contributor Deborah Stevenson maintained that Clark's "portrayal of Larceny is
oddly romanticized," a reviewer for *Publishers Weekly*
praised the "intriguing characters" introduced in the
novel.

Other books for older teen readers include *No Standing
Zone,* a 1999 novel that finds Link and his sister caught
off guard after they discover that their father has a whole
other family living in New Zealand. When Dad decides
to desert his Australian family for good, Link's mother
is forced to sell the upscale family home and relocate to
a less affluent neighborhood; ultimately both kids find

themselves out of private schools and in public schools,
where they are forced to deal with their tough, streetwise
classmates.

Involved with personal issues, such as body image, are
Clark's "Lisa Trelaw" novels, which focus on a super
model wannabe. 1994's *Fat Chance* finds Lisa obsessing
about her figure as she begins to plan a future in
modeling. *Hot or What* finds Lisa achieving her dream
as a top teen model, and then questioning whether the
model's lifestyle is really what she wanted after all. In
Kiss and Make Up, Lisa is stuck at home helping her
mother in volunteer efforts, while her boyfriend, Mike,
seems more interested in surfing that in spending time
with her. "As well as undermining the mindset which
places ... concerns [about weight and dating] above all
others, Clark challenges the media hype and peer group
pressure which make nonconformity so difficult," commented *Magpies* contributor Cathryn Crowe in a review
of *Fat Chance. Hold My Hand—or Else!* introduces Sam
Studley, a young man smitten with the charms of
Belinda, and yet not quite up to the task of maintaining a
serious romance. While Belinda tries to force the issue,
she eventually realizes that she is more mature, and
settles for Sam as a good friend and a surfing mentor, in
a conclusion that *Magpies* contributor Virginia Lowe
dubbed "satisfying." In *Living with Leanne,* Sam must
contend with older sister Leanne and her efforts to
subvert her mother's authority, first by ignoring her
curfew, and then by running away and tracking down the
father she hopes will allow her a more active social life.
Praising the novel's humor, *Magpies* critic Scott Johnston added that "Clark's sure comic touch is bound to
further enhance her reputation [as] ... a fun read as well
as discussing a serious issue." Sam and Leanne return in
Pulling the Moves, as the pair become involved in such
activities as reckless driving, sexual experimentation,
and drug use.

In addition to longer fiction for middle-school and high-
school readers, Clark has penned her "Eggs" series for
the story-hour set, while her beginning readers books
include *The Biggest Boast, Meatball's Good Dog Day,*
and the "Mango Street," "Aussie Angels," and "Chicka-
bee" series. Her "Assorted Shorts" novels are geared
toward boys, their upbeat humor designed to attract even
the most reluctant reader. Among Clark's most popular
books for middle-grade readers are the horror novels she
pens under the pseudonym Lee Striker. Among these
"Hair Raisers" are *Revenge of the Vampire Librarian,
Evil at Camp Star,* and *Bite Your Head Off,* their titles
hinting at the humor behind the frightening goings-on.

In between her heavy writing schedule, Clark finds time
to travel from her home in Geelong, Victoria, to speak
with school students and at writers' conferences. Her
Secret Girls' Stuff, published in 1999, contains letters
and e-mails from fans of her diverse fiction. Intersperse-
ing these with her own diary entries and comments on
the life of a writer, Clark also touches on a number of
teen issues. The book "comes across as a sympathetic
ear prepared to take teenage concerns seriously and offer
choices and options for the reader to consider," noted

Lynne Babbage in her positive *Magpies* review. A sequel, *More Secret Girls' Stuff,* was released in 2001, as was a follow-up cowritten with Dr. Claire Fox, *What to Do When Life Sucks.*

Biographical and Critical Sources

PERIODICALS

Bulletin of the Center for Children's Books, April, 2000, Deborah Stevenson, review of *Care Factor Zero,* p. 274.

Magpies, September, 1993, Virginia Lowe, review of *Hold My Hand—or Else!,* p. 32; July, 1994, Cathryn Crowe, review of *Fat Chance,* p. 31; November, 1994, Scott Johnston, review of *Living with Leanne,* p. 31; March, 1995, Nola Allen, review of *Ghost on Toast,* p. 24; July, 1995, Terri Cornish, review of *Hot or What,* p. 28; September, 1995, Jo Goodman, review of *Back on Track,* p. 34; September, 1996, John Murray, review of *Pulling the Moves,* pp. 36-37; March, 1998, Fran Knight, review of *On Ya, Sonya,* p. 36; May, 1998, Cynthia Anthony, review of *Hot Stuff,* p. 29; May, 1999, Helen Purdie, reviews of *Hot and Spicy, Stars, Sugar Sugar, Brush with Fame, Far from Phonies,* and *Bewitched,* p. 21; September, 1999, Jo Goodman, review of *No Standing Zone,* pp. 36-37, Cecile Grumelart, review of *Kiss and Make Up,* p. 37, Fran Knight, reviews of *Okay Koala, Whale of a Time, Seal with a Kiss,* and *Hello, Possum,* pp. 33-34; November, 1999, Lynne Babbage, review of *Secret Girls' Stuff,* pp. 41-42; March, 2000, Sally Harding, review of *The Search,* p. 37.

Publishers Weekly, March 6, 2000, review of *Care Factor Zero,* p. 111.

School Librarian, May, 1995, Jocelyn Hanson, reviews of *Weird Warren* and *Butter Fingers,* p. 62.

ON-LINE

Margaret Clark Web site, http://www.margaretclark.com (July 7, 2001).

*   *   *

CLYMER, Eleanor 1906-2001
(Janet Bell, Elizabeth Kinsey)

OBITUARY NOTICE—See index for *SATA* sketch: Born January 7, 1906, in New York, NY; died March 31, 2001, in Haverford, PA. Author. Eleanor Clymer was the prolific author of over fifty books for children who created stories with threads of the fabric from her own familial experiences. A mother who valued nature-based, realistic, emotionally moving literature for children, she set out to write such works of fiction as *My Brother Stevie,* which earned her the Woodward School Zyra Lourie book award in 1968, and *The Spider, the Cave, and the Pottery Bowl,* which won her the Juvenile Literature Award from the Border Regional Library Association in Texas. Clymer's *Get-Away Car,* a story based on a Clymer family vehicle owned during the 1930s, won the 1978 Sequoyah Book Award of the Oklahoma Library Association.

OBITUARIES AND OTHER SOURCES:

BOOKS

St. James Guide to Children's Writers, 5th Edition, St. James Press (Detroit, MI), 1999.

PERIODICALS

Los Angeles Times, April 3, 2001, p. B6.
New York Times, April 1, 2001, p. A21.
Washington Post, April 2, 2001, p. B7.

*   *   *

COLLIER, Bryan

Personal

Male. *Education:* Pratt Institute, B.F.A. (with honors), 1989.

Addresses

Home—Harlem, NY. *Office*—c/o Author Mail, Henry Holt Inc., 115 West 18th St., New York, NY 10011.

Career

Illustrator and author of children's books. Harlem Horizon Art Studio, Harlem Hospital Center, New York, NY, assistant director, 1989—; Unity Through Murals, Harlem Hospital Center, New York, NY, art director,

Bryan Collier

1991—; Simone Nissan Films, Inc., art director, 1994—. *Exhibitions:* Collier's work has been displayed at Apercu Gallery, Brooklyn, NY, 1989; Pratt Institute, Brooklyn, NY, 1989; Art Institute and Gallery, Salsbury, MD, 1989; Manhattan Community College, New York, NY, 1990, University of Maryland Eastern Shore, Princess Ann, MD, 1990; Gallery Sixty Nine, Bronx, NY, 1991; Tar Studio, New York, NY, 1992; Arsenal Gallery, New York, NY, 1992; Afriworks, New York, NY, 1993; Emmanuel Baptist Church, Brooklyn, NY, 1993, 1996, and 1997; Zoom Gallery, 1995, Essence Music Festival, New Orleans, LA, 1996; Gallerie 500, Washington, DC, 1996; LiaZan Gallery, New York, NY, 1996; Lewis Gallery, Brooklyn, NY, 1996; City College, New York, NY, 1997; Grace Baptist Church, Mt. Vernon, NY, 1997; Exhibition 1A, New York, NY, 1998.

Awards, Honors

First place in Congressional Competition, U.S. Congress, 1985; first place winner in Wicomico Art Council Show (Maryland), 1987; Brio Award, Bronx Council of the Arts, 1994 and 1995; National Black Arts Festival Poster selection, National Black Arts Festival of Atlanta, Georgia, 1994; Coretta Scott King Award for Illustration, American Library Association (ALA), and Ezra Jack Keats New Illustrator Award, New York Public Library and Ezra Jack Keats Foundation, both 2001, both for *Uptown;* Coretta Scott King Honor for Illustration, ALA, 2001, for *Freedom River.*

Writings

SELF-ILLUSTRATED

Uptown, Henry Holt (New York, NY), 2000.
To All My Sisters, Henry Holt (New York, NY), 2001.

ILLUSTRATOR

Hope Lynne Price, *These Hands,* Hyperion (New York, NY), 1999.
Doreen Rappaport, *Freedom River,* Jump at the Sun (New York, NY), 2000.
Doreen Rappaport, *Martin's Big Words,* Jump at the Sun (New York, NY), 2001.

Collier's murals were featured in the 1992 movie *Above the Rim* and in a 1992 episode of *Sesame Street.*

Sidelights

Bryan Collier is an artist who works in paint-and-photo collages. His illustrations for Hope Lynne Price's picture book, *These Hands,* effectively portray the happiness and confidence of the African-American girl at the center of the story, according to Alicia Eames in *School Library Journal.* Price's short, rhyming text celebrates the many things that this girl can do, including playing, drawing, helping, and praying at the end of the day. Throughout, her "confidence and joy are captured by Collier's deeply hued, evocative collages," Eames stated.

Freedom River, *the true story of John Parker's courage and faith in leading slaves to freedom along the Underground Railroad, features Collier's collage-with-watercolor illustrations. (Written by Doreen Rappaport.)*

In *Uptown,* Collier provided his own text along with the illustrations in celebration of Harlem, the traditionally African-American enclave in New York City where he lives and works. A tour of the area as seen through the eyes of a young boy, *Uptown* provides readers with a glimpse of some typical activities, such as shopping on 125th Street, eating chicken and waffles, listening to jazz, and playing basketball, as well as some special sights, such as the Apollo Theater, the brownstones (which Collier depicts using photos of chocolate bars for the bricks), and viewing James Van Der Zee photographs. *Booklist* contributor Gillian Engberg praised the "gorgeous, textured collages" Collier created for the story. *Uptown* garnered the prestigious Coretta Scott King Award and the first Ezra Jack Keats New Illustrator Award, both in 2001.

Biographical and Critical Sources

PERIODICALS

Black Issues Book Review, November, 2000, Khafre K. Abif and Kelly Ellis, review of *Uptown,* p. 82.
Booklist, June 1, 2000, Gillian Engberg, review of *Uptown,* p. 1906.
Publishers Weekly, June 19, 2000, review of *Uptown,* p. 78.
School Library Journal, December, 1999, Alicia Eames, review of *These Hands,* p. 111; July, 2000, Alicia Eames, review of *Uptown,* p. 70; October, 2000, Cynde Marcengill, review of *Freedom River,* p. 152; May, 2001, interview with Bryan Collier, p. 21.

ON-LINE

Bryan Collier Web site, http://www.bryancollier.com/ (September 19, 2001).
School Library Journal Online News, http://www.slj.com/ (September 19, 2001), interview with Bryan Collier.*

COLLINS, Paul 1954-
(Marilyn Fate; Roger Wilcox, a joint pseudonym)

Personal

Born May 21, 1954, in England; immigrated to New Zealand, then to Australia; son of Ernest William and Jean Collins. *Hobbies and other interests:* Gym, kickboxing, tennis.

Addresses

Home—P.O. Box 1339, Collingwood, Victoria 3066, Australia. *Agent*—Cherry Weiner Literary Agency, 28 Kipling Way, Manalapan, NJ 07726. *E-mail*—cherry8486@aol.com.

Career

Author and editor. Founder of *Void* (a magazine, and later publishing imprint), 1975-81; cofounder of Cory & Collins (a publishing company), 1980-85.

Awards, Honors

William Atheling Award, and Aurealis Convenor's Award shortlist, both for *The MUP Encyclopaedia of Australian Science Fiction & Fantasy;* Notable Book,

Paul Collins

Children's Book Council, and Clayton's Award shortlist, both 2000, both for *The Dog King;* cowinner of Aurealis Convenor's Award, 2001, for the series "Spinouts Bronze"; recipient of numerous Ditmars (Australian Science Fiction Achievement Awards) nominations and shortlists.

Writings

FOR CHILDREN

The Wizard's Torment, HarperCollins (Pymble, Australia), 1995.

The Hyper Kid, Addison Wesley Longman Australia (Melbourne, Australia), 1997.

The Shadow Factory, Macmillan Education Australia (South Yarra, Australia), 1998.

(Editor) *Fantastic Worlds,* HarperCollins (Pymble, Australia), 1998.

Double Trouble, Addison Wesley Longman Australia (Melbourne, Australia), 1999.

Out of This World, illustrated by Steven Woolman, Koala Books (Mascot, Australia), 1999.

The Dog King, Lothian, 1999.

Cyberboy, Longman (Melbourne, Australia), 2000.

Nasty Bump ("Just Kids" series), Pearson Educational (South Melbourne, Australia), 2000.

Little Mark ("Just Kids" series), illustrated by Gaston Vanzet, Pearson Educational (South Melbourne, Australia), 2000.

Movie World, Pearson Educational (South Melbourne, Australia), 2001.

The Ultimate Skates, Pearson Educational (South Melbourne, Australia), 2001.

The Great Ferret Race, Lothian Books (South Melbourne, Australia), 2001.

Adventures of the Dragon Family, Barrie Publishing (Kew, Australia), 2001.

How I Saved the Earth, Barrie Publishing (Kew, Australia), 2001.

Also author of (with Meredith Costain) *Old Bones, Spaced Out!, Rude Cars, Replicas,* (with Howard Goldsmith) *The Tooth Fairy Mystery, The Gold Diggers, 2 Real 2000,* (with Sean McMullen) *Moko's Earrings,* and *Pitstop.* Author of e-book *Street Kid. The Wizard's Torment* is also available as an e-book from New Concepts Publishing.

"SUPA DOOPERS" SERIES

Tricking, illustrated by Kevin Burgemeestre, Longman (Melbourne, Australia), 1998, published as *Tricksters,* Sundance (Littleton, MA), 1999.

Castle Rock, illustrated by Kevin Burgemeestre, Longman (Melbourne, Australia), 1999.

Flying High, illustrated by Gus Gordon, Longman (Melbourne, Australia), 1999.

"SUPA DAZZLERS" SERIES

The Knockout, illustrated by Peter Foster, Longman (Melbourne, Australia), 1999.

The Great Escape, illustrated by Peter Foster, Longman (Melbourne, Australia), 1999.

The Final Countdown, illustrated by Peter Foster, Longman (Melbourne, Australia), 1999.

EDITOR WITH MEREDITH COSTAIN; "SPINOUTS" SHORT STORY SERIES

Dragon Tales, Longman (Melbourne, Australia), 1999.
Heroic Feats, Longman (Melbourne, Australia), 1999.
Techno Terror, Longman (Melbourne, Australia), 1999.
Alien Invasions, Longman (Melbourne, Australia), 1999.
It Came from the Lab, Longman (Melbourne, Australia), 1999.
Time Zones, Longman (Melbourne, Australia), 1999.
Last Gasps, Longman (Melbourne, Australia), 1999.
Freaks of Nature, Longman (Melbourne, Australia), 1999.
Tales from Beyond, Longman (Melbourne, Australia), 1999.
Ghosts and Ghoulies, Longman (Melbourne, Australia), 1999.
Spooky Tales, Longman (Melbourne, Australia), 1999.
Tales from the Deep, Longman (Melbourne, Australia), 1999.
Altered States, Longman (Melbourne, Australia), 1999.
Lost in Space, Longman (Melbourne, Australia), 1999.

EDITOR WITH MEREDITH COSTAIN; "SPINOUTS BRONZE" SHORT STORY SERIES

Other Times, Pearson Educational (South Melbourne, Australia), 2000.
Alien Encounters, Pearson Educational (South Melbourne, Australia), 2000.
Winners Are Grinners, Pearson Educational (South Melbourne, Australia), 2000.
On the Edge, Pearson Educational (South Melbourne, Australia), 2000.
Creepy Crawlies, Pearson Educational (South Melbourne, Australia), 2000.
Distant Shores, Pearson Educational (South Melbourne, Australia), 2000.
Eerie Tales, Pearson Educational (South Melbourne, Australia), 2000.
School Daze, Pearson Educational (South Melbourne, Australia), 2000.
Noises in the Dark, Pearson Educational (South Melbourne, Australia), 2000.
Beyond the Grave, Pearson Educational (South Melbourne, Australia), 2000.
Warps and Wormholes, Pearson Educational (South Melbourne, Australia), 2000.
The Bold and the Brave, Pearson Educational (South Melbourne, Australia), 2000.
Spacebound, Pearson Educational (South Melbourne, Australia), 2000.
Into the Future, Pearson Educational (South Melbourne, Australia), 2000.
Space Mates, Pearson Educational (South Melbourne, Australia), 2000.

EDITOR WITH MEREDITH COSTAIN; "THRILLOGY" SHORT STORY SERIES

Cliffhangers, Longman (Melbourne, Australia), 2001.
Ribticklers, Longman (Melbourne, Australia), 2001.
Playing to Win, Longman (Melbourne, Australia), 2001.
Beast Feast, Longman (Melbourne, Australia), 2001.

Spider Mania, Longman (Melbourne, Australia), 2001.
Wild Things, Longman (Melbourne, Australia), 2001.
Double Agents, Longman (Melbourne, Australia), 2001.
Whodunit, Longman (Melbourne, Australia), 2001.
On the Case, Longman (Melbourne, Australia), 2001.
Do or Dare, Longman (Melbourne, Australia), 2001.
Treasure Seekers, Longman (Melbourne, Australia), 2001.
Seafarers, Longman (Melbourne, Australia), 2001.
Thrills and Spills, Longman (Melbourne, Australia), 2001.
Crimestoppers, Longman (Melbourne, Australia), 2001.
Riding High, Longman (Melbourne, Australia), 2001.

"MARTIAL ARTS" SERIES

Judo, Chelsea House (Philadelphia, PA), 2002.
Karate, Chelsea House (Philadelphia, PA), 2002.
Kung Fu, Chelsea House (Philadelphia, PA), 2002.
Taekwondo, Chelsea House (Philadelphia, PA), 2002.
Kendo, Chelsea House (Philadelphia, PA), 2002.
Ninjutsu, Chelsea House (Philadelphia, PA), 2002.
Muay Thai, Chelsea House (Philadelphia, PA), 2002.
Samurai, Chelsea House (Philadelphia, PA), 2002.

WITH MEREDITH COSTAIN; "MACMILLAN COUNTRIES" SERIES (AUSTRALIA); "COUNTRIES OF THE WORLD" SERIES (UNITED STATES)

Welcome to Brazil, Macmillan Library (South Yarra, Australia), 2000, Chelsea House (Philadelphia, PA), 2001.
Welcome to China, Macmillan Library (South Yarra, Australia), 2000, Chelsea House (Philadelphia, PA), 2001.
Welcome to France, Macmillan Library (South Yarra, Australia), 2000, Chelsea House (Philadelphia, PA), 2001.
Welcome to Greece, Macmillan Library (South Yarra, Australia), 2000, Chelsea House (Philadelphia, PA), 2001.
Welcome to Indonesia, Macmillan Library (South Yarra, Australia), 2000, Chelsea House (Philadelphia, PA), 2001.
Welcome to Italy, Macmillan Library (South Yarra, Australia), 2000, Chelsea House (Philadelphia, PA), 2001.
Welcome to Japan, Macmillan Library (South Yarra, Australia), 2000, Chelsea House (Philadelphia, PA), 2001.
Welcome to Russia, Macmillan Library (South Yarra, Australia), 2000, Chelsea House (Philadelphia, PA), 2001.
Welcome to South Africa, Macmillan Library (South Yarra, Australia), 2000, Chelsea House (Philadelphia, PA), 2001.
Welcome to the United Kingdom, Macmillan Library (South Yarra, Australia), 2000, Chelsea House (Philadelphia, PA), 2001.
Welcome to the United States of America, Macmillan Library (South Yarra, Australia), 2000, Chelsea House (Philadelphia, PA), 2001.
Welcome to Germany, Macmillan Library (South Yarra, Australia), 2000, Chelsea House (Philadelphia, PA), 2002.
Welcome to India, Macmillan Library (South Yarra, Australia), 2001, Chelsea House (Philadelphia, PA), 2001.

Wishing for a dog of his own, Keiren comes to love the dog stories told by a drifter, stories written long ago by author Henry Lawson. (Cover illustration by Gregory Rogers.)

Welcome to Canada, Macmillan Library (South Yarra, Australia), 2001, Chelsea House (Philadelphia, PA), 2001.
Welcome to Mexico, Macmillan Library (South Yarra, Australia), 2001, Chelsea House (Philadelphia, PA), 2001.
Welcome to Spain, Macmillan Library (South Yarra, Australia), 2001, Chelsea House (Philadelphia, PA), 2001.
Welcome to Egypt, Macmillan Library (South Yarra, Australia), 2001, Chelsea House (Philadelphia, PA), 2001.

FOR ADULTS; EDITOR

Void: Science Fiction and Fantasy, Void (Fortitude Valley, Australia), 1977.
Envisaged Worlds: From the Editor of Void, Australia's First Original Science Fiction Anthology, Void (St. Kilda, Australia), 1978.
(With Ron Graham) *Ron Graham Presents Other Worlds,* Void (St. Kilda, Australia), 1978.
Alien Worlds, Void (St. Kilda, Australia), 1979.

Distant Worlds, Cory and Collins (St. Kilda, Australia), 1981.
Metaworlds: Best Australian Science Fiction, Penguin (New York, NY), 1994.
Strange Fruit: Tales of the Unexpected, Penguin (Ringwood, Australia), 1995.
(Editor) *Tales from the Wasteland: Stories from the 13th Floor,* Hodder Headline (Rydalmere, Australia), 2000.

FOR ADULTS

Hot Lead—Cold Sweat, Void (St. Kilda, Australia), 1975.
The Government in Exile and Other Stories, Sumeria Press (Melbourne, Australia), 1994.
Selling Your Fiction & Poetry Made Easy, TPT Technical Publications of TAFE (Perth, Australia), 1996.
The MUP Encyclopaedia of Australian Science Fiction & Fantasy, Melbourne University Press (Carlton South, Australia), 1998.
Cyberskin, Hybrid Publishers (Melbourne, Australia), 2000.
Stalking Midnight, Cosmos Books (New Jersey), 2001.

Cyberskin is also available as an e-book from clocktowerfiction.com; *Stalking Midnight* is also available as an e-book from www.wildsidepress.com.

OTHER

(With Meredith Costain) *Spinouts Teacher's Book,* Longman (Melbourne, Australia), 1999.
(With Meredith Costain) *Spinouts Bronze Teacher's Idea Book,* Longman (Melbourne, Australia), 2000.
(With Meredith Costain) *Thrillogy Teacher's Ideas Book,* Longman (Melbourne, Australia), 2001.

Also editor of *The Second Void Science Fiction and Fantasy* and *Void Science Fiction and Fantasy, the Fourth Dimension,* both published by Void; *SF aus Australien,* Goldmann Verlag (Germany); *Frontier Worlds; Dream Weavers;* and the "Shivers" series. Author of over 140 short stories published in anthologies, including *Gothic Ghosts, Urban Fantasies, Alien Shores,* and *Dreaming Down-Under,* and magazines throughout the world, including *Weirdbook, Eidolon, Aurealis, PC User, Orbit, Challenge, Pursuit,* and *Cicada.* Collins's work has appeared in Germany. Author of several e-books, including *Dead Easy Money,* published by dnovel.com, and *The Wizard's Torment, Wizard Trouble,* and *The Earthborn,* all published by New Concepts Publishing. Some of Collins's work appears under the names Marilyn Fate and Roger Wilcox, the latter a joint pseudonym with Sean McMullen.

Work in Progress

Dragonlinks, for Penguin; *The Earthborn,* for Tor; "Book People: Meet Australia's Favourite Children's Author's and Illustrators" series, for Macmillan.

Sidelights

Science fiction writer and editor Paul Collins told *SATA* that he began his writing career "when I was seventeen because I wanted to be *someone,* perhaps leave my mark upon the world. I wasn't anything special at sports, and knew that racing cars and motorbikes would probably get me killed. A typewriter saved the day."

Born in England and raised in New Zealand, Collins decided to make his mark in Australia at age eighteen. A few years after his arrival, his first published book, a Western called *Hot Lead—Cold Sweat,* appeared, followed by his own venture into magazine publishing, the science fiction and fantasy periodical *Void.* In 1978, Collins ended the run of *Void* magazine, turning the company into a publisher of science fiction books. In the 1980s, after closing Void Publishing, Collins opened another publishing company with Rowena Cory, called Cory & Collins. The company provided an outlet for several Australian science fiction authors, including Wynne Whiteford, Jack Wodhams, A. Bertram Chandler, Russell Blackford, and David Lake. However, Collins eventually closed Cory & Collins in 1985 to concentrate on his own works for children and adults.

Discussing his working habits, Collins told *SATA,* "It's always a slow start. Get up about nine, make coffee, have breakfast, read the major newspaper, collect the mail from my post office box. About eleven I collect e-mails and respond to them—about lunchtime and it's time to eat. If I'm working on a book, I try to start by about one in the afternoon, and sometimes go through until dinner, then even until late at night, depending on how the writing is going. I work seven days a week if the work is there."

When asked about the inspiration for his 1999 award-winning book *The Dog King,* Collins replied, "Basically Australia's national newspapers were bewailing the fact that kids don't read this country's classics. I realised that Henry Lawson had written several stories featuring dogs—perhaps his best-known short fiction was called 'The Loaded Dog.' So I worked a plot around the fact that Henry Lawson comes back from the dead and tells his stories to kids who really, really want a dog. You don't find out for sure that the ghost was actually Henry Lawson. I figured that this was a good way to get kids reading the classics again—naturally I had to modernize the stories a little."

Reviewers responded favorably to Collin's efforts starring a young boy named Keiren who wishes for a dog of his own. Teased and bullied at school, Keiren strikes up a friendship with Jack Ellis, a drifter staying at his mother's boarding house. Still mourning the loss of his father, the young boy comes to love the stories that Jack tells about all kinds of dog, tales that the reader, but not Keiren, realizes came from the pen of Henry Lawson years ago. Eventually Keiren does find a canine friend and Jack moves on to another town. With his new companion, the young boy enters his school's annual dog show with a newfound confidence and hope for the future. Reviewing *The Dog King* in *Magpies,* Russ Merrin described the book as "a warm, moving tale of the acceptance of change and loss—and the importance of family and friends." "Collins draws his characters

with a deft pen," wrote a *Reading Time* critic, who went on to call *The Dog King* "a good read for younger readers."

Collins is perhaps as equally well known for the anthologies of science fiction he edits for both children and adults. Among his collections for young adult readers are *Strange Fruit,* a book of horror stories, *Dream Weavers,* a grouping of heroic fantasy tales, and *Fantastic Worlds,* a gathering of science fiction and fantasy writings. Reviewing *Fantastic Worlds* in *Magpies,* critic Michael Gregg remarked that "the consistency of the writing makes it useful and entertaining for those who have already had a first taste of the genre." Collins has also edited several series of books with Meredith Costain. Ranging from short story collections to nonfiction works on world countries, some of the series have been published in both Australia and the United States. One prolific collection of science fiction stories, the "Spinouts Bronze" series, received the Aurealis Convenor's Award in 2001.

Adding to his work in the field of science fiction, Collins edited *The MUP Encyclopaedia of Australian Science Fiction & Fantasy* in 1998, a reference book covering the works of Australian authors. Including both writers for children and adults, *The MUP Encyclopaedia of Australian Science Fiction & Fantasy* focuses on work in the genre produced after 1950 and includes biographies on well-known authors. Claiming that "the coverage is extensive, the research exhaustive, and the thematic essays are fascinating," *Magpies* reviewer Helen Purdie described the book as "a very handy tool for readers and book buyers." Though noticing a few errors, *Locus* contributor Jonathan Strahan felt the work contained "an impressive and significant amount of useful information on Australian science fiction and fantasy, and the editors deserve applause for their achievement."

Asked about what he hopes to achieve through the books he writes, Collins told *SATA* that, "I'd like to think that my work encourages kids to read. I try to make them action-based, more plot driven than character driven." Of influences on his work, the author said "Meredith Costain has influenced the way I write. She's always made herself available to read my material and offer suggestions. I think any aspiring writer, and even established writers, need a sort of mentor to guide them sometimes. I read heaps of different authors and don't have a particular favorite."

His advice to aspiring writers? "Get a mentor!," Collins explained to *SATA.* "You'd be surprised how some established authors can be flattered to be asked. It only takes a letter in care of the publisher."

Biographical and Critical Sources

BOOKS

The Encyclopedia of Science Fiction, edited by John Clute and Peter Nicholls, St. Martin's Press (New York, NY), 1993.

PERIODICALS

Australian SF News, May, 1999, Sue Bursztynski, review of *The Dog King,* p. 9.

Locus, April, 1999, Jonathan Strahan, review of *The MUP Encyclopaedia of Australian Science Fiction & Fantasy,* p. 31.

Magpies, May, 1998, Michael Gregg, review of *Fantastic Worlds,* p. 37; September, 1998, Helen Purdie, "Of Professional Interest," p. 20; November, 1999, Russ Merrin, review of *The Dog King,* p. 33.

Meanjin, April, 1995, Kerry Greenwood, "Peel Me a Grape," pp. 672-676.

Reading Time, Vol. 43, no. 4, review of *The Dog King,* p. 32.

ON-LINE

Paul Collins Web site, http://www.plasticine.com/pcollins (July 27, 2001).

D

DAWSON, Imogen (Zoë) 1948-

Personal

Born April 18, 1948, in England; children: two sons. *Education:* University of Sussex, B.A. *Hobbies and other interests:* Travel, reading and historical research, taking photographs, cooking and eating a wide variety of food, running.

Addresses

Office—c/o Zoë Books Ltd., 15 Worth Ln., Winchester, Hampshire SO23 7AB, England.

Career

Author and publisher of children's information books; founder of Zoë Books Ltd., 1990—.

Writings

Food and Feasts in the Middle Ages ("Food and Feasts" series), New Discovery Books (Parsippany, NJ), 1994.
Food and Feasts in Ancient Greece ("Food and Feasts" series), New Discovery Books (Parsippany, NJ), 1995.
Food and Feasts with the Aztecs ("Food and Feasts" series), New Discovery Books (Parsippany, NJ), 1995.
Clothes and Crafts in Aztec Times ("Clothes and Crafts in History" series), Dillon Press (Parsippany, NJ), 1997.
Middle Ages ("Clothes and Crafts" series), Zoë Books, 1997, published in the United States as *Clothes and Crafts in the Middle Ages* ("Clothes and Crafts in History" series), Dillon Press (Parsippany, NJ), 1997.

Sidelights

Imogen Dawson's "Food and Feasts" books describe the way food is used in various cultures, as well as the differences within those cultures. For example, in *Food and Feasts in the Middle Ages* she describes the differences in the food consumed by farmers and city dwellers in medieval Europe. Dawson not only provides information on how crops and animals were raised and how food was prepared and served, but she also details the kinds of foods reserved for special occasions in rural and urban areas. With the help of photographs of artifacts and works of art, recipes, maps, and nursery rhymes, the author fills in details about the culture and history that produced the food and its surrounding rituals. Deborah Stevenson wrote in *Bulletin of the Center for Children's Books* that the "Food and Feasts" series offers "an appealing social history with a tasty theme."

Dawson has also contributed several books to a series on "Clothes and Crafts." One of those titles, *Middle Ages* (published in the United States as *Clothes and Crafts in the Middle Ages*) emphasizes the materials that were available in medieval times and how people transformed these few materials into items of necessity or beauty. In her review of *Middle Ages* for *School Librarian,* Liz Baynton-Clarke noted that the "range of information given is comprehensive and attractively presented."

Biographical and Critical Sources

PERIODICALS

Booklist, June 1, 1996, Denia Hester, review of *Food and Feasts in Ancient Greece,* p. 1706; January 1, 2001, Carolyn Phelan, review of *Clothes and Crafts in the Middle Ages,* p. 944.
Bulletin of the Center for Children's Books, October, 1994, Deborah Stevenson, review of *Food and Feasts in the Middle Ages,* p. 41.
Horn Book Guide, spring, 1995, p. 157.
New Advocate, winter, 1995, M. Jean Greenlaw, review of *Food and Feasts in the Middle Ages,* p. 53.
School Librarian, spring, 1998, Liz Baynton-Clarke, review of *Middle Ages,* pp. 38, 40.
School Library Journal, December, 1994, Joyce Adams Burner, review of *Food and Feasts in the Middle Ages,* p. 120; September, 1995, Joyce Adams Burner, review of *Food and Feasts in Ancient Greece,* p. 206.*

DESAI, Anita 1937-

Personal

Born June 24, 1937, in Mussoorie, India; daughter of D. N. (an engineer) and Toni (Nimé) Mazumbar; married Ashvin Desai (an executive), December 13, 1958; came to United States, 1987; children: Rahul, Tani, Arjun, Kiran. *Education:* Delhi University, B.A. (with honors), 1957.

Addresses

Home—Cambridge, MA. *Office*—c/o c/o The Program in Writing and Humanistic Studies, Massachusetts Institute of Technology, Cambridge, MA 02139. *Agent*—c/o Deborah Rogers Ltd., 20 Powis Mews, London W11 1JN, England.

Career

Writer. Smith College, Northampton, MA, Elizabeth Drew Professor, 1987-88; Mount Holyoke College, South Hadley, MA, Purington Professor of English, 1988-93; Massachusetts Institute of Technology, Cambridge, MA, professor of writing, 1993—. *Member:* Royal Society of Literature (fellow), American Academy of Arts and Letters (honorary fellow).

Awards, Honors

Winifred Holtby Prize, Royal Society of Literature, 1978, for *Fire on the Mountain;* Sahitya Academy award, 1979; shortlisted for the Booker Prize, 1980, for *Clear Light of Day; Guardian* Prize for Children's Fiction, 1983, for *The Village by the Sea;* shortlisted for the Booker Prize, 1984, for *In Custody;* Girton College, University of Cambridge, Helen Cam Visiting Fellow, 1986-87, honorary fellow, 1988; Clare Hall, University of Cambridge, Ashby Fellow, 1989, honorary fellow, 1991; *Hadassah* Prize, *Hadassah* (magazine), 1989, for *Baumgartner's Bombay;* Padma Sri, 1990; Literary Lion Award, New York Public Library, 1993; Neil Gunn Fellowship, Scottish Arts Council, 1994; shortlisted for the Booker Prize, 1999, for *Feasting, Fasting;* Moravia Award, Rome, 1999.

Writings

NOVELS; FOR CHILDREN

The Peacock Garden, India Book House (Bombay, India), 1974.
Cat on a Houseboat, Orient Longmans (Bombay, India), 1976.
The Village by the Sea: An Indian Family Story, Heinemann (London, England), 1982.

NOVELS; FOR ADULTS

Cry, the Peacock, P. Owen (London, England), 1963.
Voices in the City, P. Owen (London, England), 1965.
Bye-Bye, Blackbird, Hind Pocket Books (New Delhi, India), 1968, InterCulture (Thompson, CT) 1971.

Where Shall We Go This Summer?, Vikas Publishing House (New Delhi, India), 1975.
Fire on the Mountain, Harper (New York, NY), 1977.
Clear Light of Day, Harper (New York, NY), 1980.
In Custody, Heinemann (London, England), 1984, Harper (New York, NY), 1985.
Baumgartner's Bombay, Knopf (New York, NY), 1989.
Journey to Ithaca, Knopf (New York, NY), 1995.
Fasting, Feasting, Chatto & Windus (London, England), 1999, Houghton Mifflin (Boston, MA), 2000.

OTHER

Games at Twilight and Other Stories (short stories) Heinemann (London, England), 1978, Harper (New York, NY), 1980.
(Author of introduction) Lady Mary Wortley Montagu, *Turkish Embassy Letters,* edited by Malcolm Jack, University of Georgia Press (Athens, GA), 1993.
Diamond Dust: Stories, Houghton Mifflin (Boston, MA), 2000.

Contributor of short stories to periodicals, including *Thought, Envoy, Writers Workshop, Quest, Indian Literature, Illustrated Weekly of India, Fesmina,* and *Harper's Bazaar.*

Adaptations

The Village by the Sea was adapted for film in 1992, and *In Custody* was adapted for film in 1993.

Sidelights

Anita Desai focuses her novels upon the personal struggles of her East Indian characters to cope with the problems of contemporary life. In this way, she manages to portray the cultural and social changes that her native country has undergone since the departure of the British. One of Desai's major themes is the relationships between family members, and especially the emotional tribulations of women whose independence is suppressed by Indian society. Her first novel, *Cry, the Peacock,* concerns a woman who finds it impossible to assert her individuality; the theme of the despairing woman is also explored in Desai's *Where Shall We Go This Summer?* Other novels explore life in urban India (*Voices in the City*), the clash between eastern and western cultures (*Bye-Bye, Blackbird*), and the differences between the generations (*Fire on the Mountain*). Desai has been shortlisted for Britain's prestigious Booker Prize three times: in 1980, for *Clear Light of Day;* in 1984, for *In Custody;* and in 1999, for *Fasting, Feasting.*

Desai is also "acquiring an increasingly strong international reputation as a children's writer," according to a contributor for *St. James Guide to Children's Writers.* This reputation is due largely to two books, *The Peacock Garden* and *The Village by the Sea: An Indian Family Story.* Unlike her adult literature, in which all societal and traditional constructs are called into question, Desai's work for younger readers posits the family as "a safe harbor on the sea of change—and that of all social entities, the family is most effective in nurturing individuals through tragedy and crisis in facilitating growth and reformation," as the critic for *St. James Guide to Children's Writers* pointed out. Her first children's novel, *The Peacock Garden,* is told from the perspective of a young Muslim girl whose family manages to escape race riots and find safety thanks to an old Hindu man. Taking refuge in the enclosed garden of a mosque, the family face adversity and tragedy, and finally prepare themselves to face the outside world once again. In *The Village by the Sea,* adapted for a film in 1992, two young children are forced to accept adult responsibilities at an early age. With the mother of the family hospitalized and the irresponsible father off drinking, the twelve-year-old son leaves for Bombay to earn money for the family, leaving his thirteen-year-old sister to rebuild the family structure. The writer for *St. James Children's Writers* felt that, while *The Village by the Sea* was "less structured" and "less focused in characterization or theme" than *The Peacock Garden,* it was nevertheless "a richer and more engaging novel despite its flaws" and "provides an engaging and enlightening view of life earlier in this century." The same critic concluded, "Sensitive students will be rewarded for the time they spend with Desai: they will come away from her novels knowing they have been taught."

In her adult novels, Desai continues with some of the themes explored in her children's novels, and expands these to look at a range of subjects and topics. Exile—physical as well as psychological—is also a prominent theme. In *Baumgartner's Bombay,* Desai (who is half-Indian and half-German) details the life of Hugo Baumgartner, a German Jew who flees Nazi Germany for India, where he "gradually drifts down through Indian society to settle, like sediment, somewhere near the bottom," wrote Rosemary Dinnage in the *New York Review of Books.* She added: "Baumgartner is a more thoroughly displaced person than Anglicized Indians, and more solitary, for Desai's Indian characters are still tied to family and community, however irksomely. She has drawn on her dual nationality to write on a subject new, I think, to English fiction—the experience of Jewish refugees in India." Pearl K. Bell made a similar statement. "Baumgartner is the loneliest, saddest, most severely dislocated of Desai's fictional creatures," she noted in the *New Republic.* "But [he] is also a representative man, the German Jew to whom things happen, powerless to resist the evil wind that swept him like a vagrant weed from Berlin to India." Jean Sudrann of the *Yale Review* praised Desai's narrative skill "in making us feel the cumulative force of Hugo's alienation."

The author's descriptive powers are acclaimed by several critics. In the *New Leader,* Betty Falkenberg called *Baumgartner's Bombay* "a mathematical problem set and solved in exquisite prose." Bell observed that "there is a Dickensian rush and tumble to her portrayals of the bazaars, the crowded streets, the packed houses of an Indian metropolis." In general, Desai's "novels are quite short, but they convey a sharply detailed sense of

Anita Desai

the tangled complexities of Indian society, and an intimate view of the tug and pull of Indian family life."

While noting Desai's mixed German-Indian ancestry, *Spectator* contributor Caroline Moore nonetheless commended the author for the authentic Indian flavor of her works. "Westerners visiting India find themselves reeling under the outsider's sense of 'culture shock,' which is compounded more of shock than culture," the critic wrote. "To Anita Desai, of course, the culture is second nature. Yet that intimacy never becomes mere familiarity: her achievement is to keep the shock of genuine freshness, the eyes of the perpetual outsider." This particular engagement with India is evident in many of Desai's novels, as A. G. Mojtabai noted in the *New York Times Book Review.* "Anita Desai is a writer of Bengali-German descent, who stands in a complicated but advantageous relation to India," said the reviewer. "Insiders rarely notice this much; outsiders cannot have this ease of reference." Mojtabai found that Desai is able to delineate characters, settings, and feelings intricately, yet economically, without extraneous detail or excessively populated scenes: "This author has no need of crowds. Properly observed, a roomful of people is crowd enough, and in the right hands—as Anita Desai so amply illustrates—*world* enough."

The complexities of outsiders facing Indian culture form the basis of Desai's 1995 novel, *Journey to Ithaca.* The story revolves around a hippie-era European couple who travel to India for quite different reasons—the husband to find enlightenment, the wife to enjoy a foreign experience. As the husband, Matteo, becomes involved with a spiritual guru known as the Mother, his wife, Sophie, goes on a quest of her own—to find the guru's roots in an effort either to debunk or to understand her. Calling the work "a kind of love triangle set against the madness of extreme spiritual searching," *New York Times* reviewer Richard Bernstein added of *Journey to Ithaca:* "Ms. Desai writes with intelligence and power. She has a remarkable eye for substance, the things that give life its texture. Nothing escapes her power of observation, not the thickness of the drapes that blot out the light in a bourgeois Parisian home, or the enamel bowl in the office of an Indian doctor." Moore, in the *Spectator,* though commenting that the main characters are drawn rather sketchily, commended the book as "superbly powerful ... emotionally and intellectually haunting, teasing and tugging our minds even through its imperfections."

Desai's *Fasting, Feasting,* her third novel to be shortlisted for the Booker Prize, "tells the apparently spare story of one Indian family and the varying fates of its two daughters and single son; it is only on the novel's final, quiet page that Desai's intricate structure becomes clear and the complexity of her emotional insight makes itself felt," explained Sylvia Brownrigg in *Salon.com.* Uma, the oldest daughter, is charged with the care of her demanding parents. Uma's sister Aruna is unhappily married, but has escaped the responsibilities that hinder her older sister. Arun, the brother, is the focus of the second half of the novel. He is smothered by his parents' expectations of his life, and he eventually finds his way to Boston where he attends school, staying with an American family, named the Pattons, during a break between semesters. "Arriving in the United States, Arun had exulted in his newfound anonymity: 'no past, no family ... no country.' But he has not escaped family after all, just stumbled into a plastic representation of it," commented J. M. Coetzee in the *New York Review of Books.* The Pattons, with their excesses, counter the Indian household. "Arun himself, as he picks his way through a minefield of puzzling American customs, becomes a more sympathetic character, and his final act in the novel suggests both how far he has come and how much he has lost," explained a critic for *Publishers Weekly.*

Critics were nearly universally positive in their assessment of the novel. "*Fasting, Feasting* is a novel not of plot but of comparison," wrote Brownrigg. "In beautifully detailed prose Desai draws the foods and textures of an Indian small town and of an American suburb. In both, she suggests, family life is a complex mixture of generosity and meanness, license and restriction." Donna Seaman commented in *Booklist:* "Desai has been compared to Jane Austen, and, indeed, she is a deceptively gracious storyteller, writing like an embroiderer concealing a sword as she creates family microcosms that embody all the delusions and cruelties of society-at-large." Though Coetzee faulted Desai's America as feeling "as if it comes out of books," he lauded her

writing, particularly her portraits of India. "Desai's strength as a writer has always been her eye for detail and her ear for the exact word ... her gift for telling metaphor, and above all her feel for sun and sky, heat and dust, for the elemental reality of central India."

In addition to her novels, Desai has also written two volumes of short stories: *Games at Twilight and Other Stories* and *Diamond Dust: Stories.* While the former volume, published in 1978, contains stories mainly set in Desai's native India, *Diamond Dust,* published in 2000, has a more international flavor. Three of its nine stories deal with life in the United States, where Desai has lived since 1987. "The best story in the collection," wrote Shyamala A. Narayan in a *World Literature Today* review of *Diamond Dust,* "'Winterscape,' deals with the relationship between a young American girl and her Indian mothers-in-law." *Library Journal*'s Faye A. Chadwell, reviewing *Diamond Dust,* noted, "Desai here demonstrates whey she has been chosen as a Booker Prize finalist not once but three times." Chadwell concluded, "Desai's exquisite descriptions of settings, her perceptive insights into human nature, and her bountiful humor make this book a valuable addition to a multitude of library collections."

Desai is frequently praised by critics for her ability to capture the local color of her country and the ways in which Eastern and Western cultures have blended together there, and for developing this skill further with each successive novel. A large part of this skill is due to her use of imagery, one of the most important devices in Desai's novels. Because of this emphasis on imagery, Desai is referred to by such reviewers as *World Literature Today* contributor Madhusudan Prasad as an "imagist-novelist.... [Her use of imagery is] a remarkable quality of her craft that she has carefully maintained in all her later fiction" since *Cry, the Peacock.* Employing this imagery to suggest rather than overtly explain her themes, Desai's stories sometimes appear deceptively simple; but, as Anthony Thwaite pointed out in the *New Republic,* "she is such a consummate artist that she [is able to suggest], beyond the confines of the plot and the machinations of her characters, the immensities that lie beyond them—the immensities of India." In the *Observer,* Salman Rushdie described Desai's books as being "illuminated by the author's perceptiveness, delicacy of language and sharp wit."

Biographical and Critical Sources

BOOKS

Afzal-Khan, Fawzia, *Cultural Imperialism and the Indo-English Novel: Genre and Ideology in R. K. Narayan, Anita Desai, Kamala Markandaya, and Salman Rushdie,* Pennsylvania State University Press (University Park, PA), 1993.

Bellioppa, Meena, *The Fiction of Anita Desai,* Writers Workshop, 1971.

Choudhury, Bidulata, *Women and Society in the Novels of Anita Desai,* Creative Books (New Delhi, India), 1995.

Contemporary Literary Criticism, Gale (Detroit, MI), Volume 19, 1981, Volume 37, 1986.

Contemporary Novelists, 6th edition, St. James Press (Detroit, MI), 1996.

Feminist Writers, St. James Press, (Detroit, MI), 1996.

Khanna, Shashi, *Human Relationships in Anita Desai's Novels,* Sarup and Sons (New Delhi, India), 1995.

Parker, Michael, and Roger Starkey, editors, *Postcolonial Literature: Achebe, Ngugi, Desai, Walcott,* St. Martin's (New York, NY), 1995.

Pathania, Usha, *Human Bonds and Bondages: The Fiction of Anita Desai and Kamala Markandaya,* Kanishka Publishers (New Delhi, India), 1992.

St. James Guide to Children's Writers, 5th edition, St. James Press (Detroit, MI), 1999.

Sharma, Kajali, *Symbolism in Anita Desai's Novels,* Abhinav Publications (New Delhi, India), 1991.

Singh, Sunaina, *The Novels of Margaret Atwood and Anita Desai: A Comparative Study in Feminist Perspectives,* Creative Books (New Delhi, India), 1994.

Sivanna, Indira, *Anita Desai as an Artist: A Study in Image and Symbol,* Creative Books (New Delhi, India), 1994.

Solanki, Mrinalini, *Anita Desai's Fiction: Patterns of Survival Strategies,* Kanishka Publishers (New Delhi, India), 1992.

PERIODICALS

Belles Lettres, summer, 1989, p. 4.

Booklist, December 15, 1999, Donna Seaman, review of *Fasting, Feasting,* p. 739.

Boston Globe, August 15, 1995, p. 26.

Chicago Tribune, September 1, 1985.

Globe and Mail (Toronto, Canada), August 20, 1988.

Kirkus Reviews, June 15, 1995, p. 799.

Library Journal, February 1, 2000, Dianna Moeller, review of *Fasting, Feasting,* p. 115; June 1, 2000, Faye A. Chadwell, review of *Diamond Dust,* p. 206.

Los Angeles Times, July 31, 1980.

Los Angeles Times Book Review, March 3, 1985; April 9, 1989.

New Leader, May 1, 1989, Betty Falkenberg, review of *Baumgartner's Bombay.*

New Republic, March 18, 1985; April 3, 1989, Pearl K. Bell, review of *Baumgartner's Bombay;* April 6, 1992, p. 36; August 15, 1994, p. 43.

New York Review of Books, June 1, 1989, Rosemary Dinnage, review of *Baumgartner's Bombay;* December 6, 1990, p. 53; January 16, 1992, p. 42; March 3, 1994, p. 41; May 23, 1996, p. 6; May 25, 2000, J. M. Coetzee, review of *Fasting, Feasting,* pp. 33-35.

New York Times, November 24, 1980; February 22, 1985; March 14, 1989; August 30, 1995, Richard Bernstein, review of *Journey to Ithaca,* p. B2.

New York Times Book Review, November 20, 1977; June 22, 1980; November 23, 1980; March 3, 1985, p. 7; April 9, 1989, p. 3; January 27, 1991, p. 23; September 17, 1995, p. 12.

Observer (London, England), October 7, 1984, p. 22.

Publishers Weekly, December 6, 1999, review of *Fasting, Feasting,* p. 55.

Spectator, June 3, 1995, Caroline Moore, review of *Journey to Ithaca,* pp. 41-42.

Time, July 1, 1985; August 21, 1995, p. 67.

Times (London, England), September 4, 1980.

Times Higher Education Supplement, April 7, 1995, pp. 16-17.

Times Literary Supplement, September 5, 1980; September 7, 1984; October 19, 1984; July 15-21, 1988, p. 787; June 2, 1995, Gabriele Annan, review of *Journey to Ithaca,* p. 501.

Tribune Books (Chicago, IL), August 23, 1981; March 5, 1989.

Wall Street Journal, August 24, 1995, Brooke Allen, review of *Journey to Ithaca,* p. A14.

Washington Post Book World, January 11, 1981, p. 3; October 7, 1984; March 31, 1985; February 26, 1989.

World Literature Today, summer, 1984, pp. 363-369; winter, 1997, p. 221; winter, 2001, Shyamala A. Narayan, review of *Diamond Dust,* p. 104.

Yale Review, spring, 1990, Jean Sudrann, review of *Baumgartner's Bombay,* p. 414.

ON-LINE

Salon.com, http://www.salon.com/ (February 17, 2001), Sylvia Brownrigg, review of *Fasting, Feasting.*

*   *   *

DRAWSON, Blair 1943-

Personal

Born October 16, 1943, in Winnipeg, Manitoba, Canada; son of Richard Robert and Florence Carter Drawson; married Noel Saville (divorced, 1973); married Bibi Caspari (a mime and dancer), October 19, 1974; children: two. *Education:* Attended Ontario College of Art, 1963-66. *Politics:* "Anti-political." *Religion:* "Religious, but no church affiliation."

Addresses

Home and office—69 Westmoreland Ave., Toronto, Ontario M5H 2Z8, Canada. *Agent*—John Locke, 15 East 76th St., New York, NY 10021.

Career

Illustrator in Toronto, Ontario, Canada, 1966-70, 1975—, in St. Helena, CA, 1970-73, and in Norwalk, CT, 1974-75. *Exhibitions:* Drawson's work has been exhibited at Vintage 1864, Yountville, CA, 1972, and in England, France, Italy, and Japan.

Awards, Honors

Gold Medal, Society of Illustrators, 1988, 1989; Governor General's Literary Award nomination, Canada Council for the Arts, 1997, for *Flying Dimitri.*

Writings

SELF-ILLUSTRATED

The Bug and Her Friends, Harcourt, 1976.

I Like Hats!, Gage (Agincourt, Ontario, Canada), 1977.

Do Something Special on Your Birthday, Gage (Agincourt, Ontario, Canada), 1977.

Blair Drawson's stunning artwork illustrates the poetic retelling of a teenage Arachne's fateful weaving contest with the goddess Athena. (From Arachne Speaks, *written by Kate Hovey.)*

Flying Dimitri, Groundwood Books, 1978, Orchard Books (New York, NY), 1997.

Arthur, Their Very Own Child, Gage (Agincourt, Ontario, Canada), 1979.

Mary Margaret's Tree, Groundwood Books, 1980, Orchard Books (New York, NY), 1996.

The Special Birthday Book, Annick Press (Toronto, Ontario, Canada), 1982.

ILLUSTRATOR

Barbara Brenner, *Mystery of the Plumed Serpent,* Houghton (Boston, MA), 1972.

Eleanor Kay, *Read about the School Nurse,* F. Watts (New York, NY), 1972.

Addie, *The Silly Book of Animals,* Golden Press (New York, NY), 1973.

Jerry Lane, *In the Zoo,* Ginn (Lexington, MA), 1974.

Patty Wolcott, *I'm Going to New York to Visit the Queen,* Addison-Wesley (Reading, MA), 1974, Lippincott (New York, NY), 1985.

Patty Wolcott, *Pickle, Pickle, Pickle Juice,* Addison-Wesley (Reading, MA), 1975, Random House (New York, NY), 1991.

Kate Hovey, *Arachne Speaks,* M. K. McElderry Books (New York, NY), 2000.

Illustrations have appeared in various magazines throughout the United States and Canada, including *Esquire, Time, Saturday Night, Rolling Stone,* and the *New York Times Magazine.*

Sidelights

Blair Drawson once told *SATA:* "It seems that the work of the artist is to provide a gentle reminder of what we may have lost in 'growing up.' When we were children, the world looked, felt, smelled, and tasted in ways which are more or less only faintly recalled in adult life. The impressions we received then—terrifying as they were at times—were fueled and made exquisite by our great innocent sense of possibility. This was the possibility of find things and finding things out."

These characteristics, especially the nearly surreal perception of the world, a world in which the child's imagination is unbounded, are ably displayed in Drawson's self-illustrated picture books. For example, a reviewer for *Publishers Weekly* described Drawson's book, *Mary Margaret's Tree,* in the following way: "This unpredictable fantasy of a girl's adventures in a tree is illustrated in a style that suggests Grandma Moses on hallucinogens."

Drawson's story centers on Mary Margaret, who tires as she plants a tree and, looking up, finds herself shrinking even as the tree itself grows to great heights. Mary Margaret climbs up into the tree to observe life there among the green leaves, birds, and insects, and eventually winters over in a cave with a crowd of wild animals that includes a bear and a tiger. In the spring, she herself grows roots and becomes a tree, until the sound of her mother's call to dinner wakes her, and she is back at the base of the newly-planted tree. *Booklist* reviewer Michael Cart called this "an affectionate celebration of both the natural world and a little girl's imagination." And a reviewer for *Kirkus Reviews* dubbed *Mary Margaret's Tree* "both engaging and imaginative."

Drawson recounted the inspiration for the story of *Flying Dimitri* to *SATA:* "Until I was about nine, I thought myself to be the only person in the world named Blair. It seemed to me that there was perhaps a magical property to my name. On several occasions a curious thing happened to demonstrate this. While washing my face or brushing my teeth at the bathroom sink, I would find myself staring at my reflection in the mirror. I would then begin to whisper, over and over, the incantation, 'Blair, Blair, your name is *Blair.*' This released a mechanism whereby I would seem to float up in the air, and sort of hover there in the vicinity of the light fixture. From there I could look down at the back of my head and see my own face gazing at its image in the glass. It was altogether an awesome sensation, and one which I came to write about in a book titled *Flying Dimitri.*"

In *Flying Dimitri,* a boy gives his father a tie for his birthday, and then an image of himself flies out of his head and out the window while he brushes his teeth. The boy plays with whales and rescues a queen on Mars whom he thinks might be his mother before returning home to be tucked into bed by his father, now wearing the birthday tie. Reviews were mixed in their response to the unusual plot of *Flying Dimitri.* A reviewer for *Publishers Weekly* called Drawson's art "stylized, protean illustrations [that] flirt with the surreal," but complained that "the overall mood ... and lonely characters ... may leave children feeling frightened." For *Booklist* contributor Julie Corsaro, however, "the striking pictures and simple, well-crafted text perfectly evoke the logic of a dream." Corsaro contended that Drawson's fantasy is both personal and universal, and thus is capable of a potentially "powerful" reading to those willing to surrender to its fancy.

Drawson has also provided the illustrations for others' stories, including Kate Hovey's adaptation of the Greek myth of Arachne. Here, in a mixed rhyme and free verse text, is the story of Arachne, who outrages Athena, the goddess of weaving, with her pride in her own achievements and is ultimately punished by being turned into a spider. Drawson's strongly colored illustrations garnered critical notice from a *Publishers Weekly* reviewer who stated: "Drawson's art ... reconciles Hovey's contemporary interpretation of a classical subject with a visual approach that quotes classical motifs but uses stylish perspectives and emphasizes—if not exaggerates—the figures' emotions." Writing in *School Library Journal,* critic Nancy Call felt that the "brilliant illustrations, strong in golds and blues, perfectly embody Arachne's anger and Athena's wrath."

Biographical and Critical Sources

PERIODICALS

Booklist, October 1, 1996, Michael Cart, review of *Mary Margaret's Tree,* p. 358; December 15, 1997, Julie Corsaro, review of *Flying Dimitri,* p. 702.

Canadian Children's Literature, no. 26, 1982, Joan McGrath, review of *The Special Birthday Book,* pp. 93-94.

Horn Book, January, 2001, Anita L. Burkam, review of *Arachne Speaks,* p. 100.

Kirkus Reviews, July 1, 1996, review of *Mary Margaret's Tree,* p. 966.

Publishers Weekly, July 8, 1996, review of *Mary Margaret's Tree,* p. 83; October 13, 1997, review of *Flying Dimitri,* p. 73; December 18, 2000, review of *Arachne Speaks,* p. 78.

School Library Journal, October, 1996, Susan M. Moore, review of *Mary Margaret's Tree,* p. 91; April, 1998, John Peter, review of *Flying Dimitri,* p. 98; March, 2001, Nancy Call, review of *Arachne Speaks,* p. 268.*

*   *   *

DUNNE, Kathleen 1933-

Personal

Born March 5, 1933, in Bryn Mawr, PA; daughter of Thomas (a policeman) and Marion (a homemaker; maiden name, Reep) Dunne; children: Kerry Hardin, Chris McCarthy. *Education:* Attended Philadelphia Museum School of Art.

Addresses

Home—3191 Deronda Dr., Los Angeles, CA 90068. *Agent*—Vorpal San Francisco, 393 Grove St., San Francisco, CA 94102.

Career

Freelance illustrator, 1974—. Painter, with work exhibited in San Francisco, CA, and New York, NY. Worked as art director for the advertising firm of Ogilby & Mather. Church of Religious Science, licensed practitioner.

Illustrator

(With Terry Anderson) Angela Abraham and Ken Abraham, *The Hosanna Bible,* Word Publishing (Dallas, TX), 1993, published as *Jesus Loves Me Bible,* Tommy Nelson (Nashville, TN), 1999.

Luella Connelly, *Let's Measure It,* Creative Teaching Press (Huntington Beach, CA), 1995.

Rozanne Lanczak Williams, *There's a Monster in the Tree,* Creative Teaching Press (Huntington Beach, CA), 1995.

Rozanne Lanczak Williams, *Mr. Noisy,* Creative Teaching Press (Huntington Beach, CA), 1995.

Rozanne Lanczak Williams, *Where Do Monsters Live?,* Creative Teaching Press (Huntington Beach, CA), 1995.

(With Terry Anderson) Angela Abraham and Ken Abraham, *Praise and Worship: A Devotional for Little Ones,* Word Publishing, 1996, published as *Jesus Loves Me Devotional,* Tommy Nelson, 1999.

Rozanne Lanczak Williams, *Five Little Monsters,* Creative Teaching Press (Huntington Beach, CA), 1996.

Rozanne Lanczak Williams, *Mr. Noisy's Book of Patterns,* Creative Teaching Press (Huntington Beach, CA), 1996.

Kathleen Dunne

Rozanne Lanczak Williams, *Ten Monsters in Bed,* Creative Teaching Press (Huntington Beach, CA), 1996.

Fun and Fantasy Resource Guide, edited by Joanne Corker, Creative Teaching Press (Huntington Beach, CA), 1996.

Science Resource Guide, edited by Rozanne Lanczak Williams, Creative Teaching Press (Huntington Beach, CA), 1996.

Math Resource Guide, edited by Rozanne Lanczak Williams, Creative Teaching Press (Huntington Beach, CA), 1996.

Rozanne Lanczak Williams, *Mr. Noisy's Helpers,* Creative Teaching Press (Huntington Beach, CA), 1996.

Joel Kupperstein, *Safety Counts!,* Creative Teaching Press (Huntington Beach, CA), 1996.

Rozanne Lanczak Williams, *Five Little Monsters Went to School,* Creative Teaching Press (Huntington Beach, CA), 1997.

Luella Connelly, *Mr. Noisy Builds a House,* Creative Teaching Press (Huntington Beach, CA), 1997.

Rozanne Lanczak Williams, *Mr. Noisy's Helpers,* Creative Teaching Press (Huntington Beach, CA), 1997.

Will Barber, *Monster's Tea Party,* Creative Teaching Press (Huntington Beach, CA), 1997.

Joel Kupperstein, *Mr. Noisy Paints His House,* Creative Teaching Press (Huntington Beach, CA), 1997.

Social Studies Resource Guide, edited by Joel Kupperstein, Creative Teaching Press (Huntington Beach, CA), 1998.

Sandi Hill, *Playground Problem Solvers,* Creative Teaching Press (Huntington Beach, CA), 1998.

Marcia S. Gresko, *Monster Stew,* Creative Teaching Press (Huntington Beach, CA), 1998.

Margaret Allen, *Mr. Noisy at the Dude Ranch,* Creative Teaching Press (Huntington Beach, CA), 1999.

Instant Math Centers: Hands-On Independent Math Activities (two-book collection), edited by Ruth B. Simon, Creative Teaching Press (Huntington Beach, CA), 2001.

Illustrator of other books for Creative Teaching Press and for other publishers.

Work in Progress

Painting.

Sidelights

Kathleen Dunne told *SATA:* "I have always been an artist. Even as a young girl I made my own paper dolls and drew and painted all the time. I was fortunate to have a very good art teacher in high school who encouraged me to take art classes on weekends and helped me put a portfolio together for entrance into one of the finest art schools on the East Coast. It was an enormous leap of faith that I took about ten years ago into the world of painting, and I have not regretted it one bit. I built a studio onto my house in the Hollywood Hills and now spend every day in it, working on canvases as large as eight feet. My subjects are inspired from trips I take to Italy, France, England, and the most recent—Greece. It's a nice life."

Biographical and Critical Sources

ON-LINE

Kathleen Dunne Web site, http://www.kathleendunne.com/ (April 13, 2001).

F

FANELLI, Sara 1969-

Personal

Born July 20, 1969, in Florence, Italy; daughter of Giovanni (a university professor) and Rosalia (an art historian; maiden name, Bonito) Fanelli. *Education:* City and Guilds of London Art School, Foundation Course Diploma, 1989; attended Florence Academy of Fine Arts, 1989-90; Camberwell College of Arts, B.A. (honors), 1993; Royal College of Art, M.A., 1995.

Addresses

Home—Piazza Duomo 7, Florence, Italy 50122; Flat 11, Howitt Close, Howitt Road, London NW3 4LX, England. *Agent*—Riley Illustration, 155 West 15th Street, New York, NY 10011; Heart Agency, Top Floor, 100 DeBeauvior Rd., London N1 4EN, England.

Career

Artist, illustrator, and designer. *Exhibitions:* Macmillan Prize show, Royal College of Art, London, England, 1991, 1992, 1993; Maastricht 4th Biennial of European Academies of Visual Arts, Maastricht, Germany, 1993; Camberwell College of Arts Degree Show, London, 1993; Folio Society Award, Royal College of Art, London, 1994; "Still There Will Be Stories," Royal College of Art, London, 1994; "Hidden Treasures," Djanogly Art Gallery, Nottingham, England, 1995; National Library Illustration Award exhibition, Victoria and Albert Museum, London, 1995, 1997, 1998; "L'Art a la Page," Paris, France, 1996; "Post Impressions: An Exhibition of the Royal Mail Millennium Collection," British Library, London, 1999; "Peter Blake: About Collage," Tate Gallery, Liverpool, England, 2000. *Member:* AIG.

Awards, Honors

Macmillan Prize, 1992, for *Button;* Folio Society Award, 1994; shortlisted for the Mother Goose Award, 1995; Parallel Prize, Royal College of Art, 1995; National Art Library Illustration first prize, Victoria and Albert Museum, 1995; National Art Library Illustration commendation, Victoria and Albert Museum, 1997, 1998, and 2000; Kall-Kwik Award, Images 24, Association of Illustrators (London, England), 1999; Kate Greenaway Medal nomination, British Library Association, 2000; Kall-Kwik Award, Images 25, Association of Illustrators (London, England), 2000; special prize for winning awards in four different years, National Art Library Illustration Competition, Victoria and Albert Museum, 2000.

Writings

SELF-ILLUSTRATED PICTURE BOOKS

Button, ABC (London, England), 1993, Little, Brown (Boston, MA), 1994.
My Map Book, ABC (London, England), 1994, HarperCollins (New York, NY), 1995.
Pinocchio ("Picture Box" series), ABC (London, England), 1995, HarperCollins (New York, NY), 1996.
Cinderella ("Picture Box" series), ABC (London, England), 1995, HarperCollins (New York, NY), 1996.
Wolf!, Heinemann (London, England), Dial (New York, NY), 1997.
The Doggy Book, Running Press (Philadelphia, PA), 1998, published as *A Dog's Life,* Heinemann (London, England), 1998.
It's Dreamtime, Heinemann (London, England), 1999.
Dear Diary, Candlewick Press (Cambridge, MA), 2000.
The New Faber Book of Children's Verse, Faber and Faber (London, England), 2001.

ILLUSTRATOR

G. Barker, *Dibby Dubby Dhu,* Faber and Faber (London, England), 1997.
The Folio Book of Short Novels, Folio Society (London, England), 1998.

Also provided a stamp design for the Royal Mail Millennium Collection. Creator of theater posters and leaflets for Edinburgh Festival, Royal Exchange Theatre,

Lyric Theatre, and Fernando Kinas. Illustrator of book jackets for publishers, including Penguin, Orion, Bloomsbury, Random House, Pan Macmillan, and Faber and Faber. Illustrations have appeared in magazines in the United States and England, including *New Yorker, Time, New Scientist, Times Educational Supplement, Readers Digest, Radio Times, Daily Telegraph,* and *Independent on Sunday.*

Fanelli's work has been translated into other languages, including French, Dutch, Japanese, German, and Portugese.

Sidelights

Sara Fanelli is an award-winning artist whose illustrations combine collage and sketches in crayon to create effects critics find striking and humorous. Although the stories of her picture books have sometimes been considered less compelling than her spectacular illustrations, many critics have also noted that Fanelli's whimsy extends beyond her illustrations to the presentation of her story and its unusual plot elements.

Lucy, Spider, Knife and Fork, Ladybug, Firefly, Chair, and Bubu the dog record the events of the same day in their diaries. (Cover illustration by Fanelli.)

In *Button,* Fanelli's first picture book, an adventurous button pops off his owner's jacket to go in search of new experiences. First he becomes a toy for a little girl, then a wheel for a farmer's wagon. A hungry wolf uses the former button as a plate, and then one of the three little pigs turns him into a weather vane for his house. Finally, the button is blown off the roof and onto the back of a homeless snail, and together the two travel the world until the day the button's owner finds them and reclaims his long lost companion. The illustrations are brightly colored collages including bits of newsprint upon which the characters are scribbled in crayon. The text crawls along the borders of the page, circling the pictures in what critics found an apt echoing of the circular story.

The critical response to *Button* was largely favorable, though some reviewers felt that the unusual story lacked the imaginative flair of Fanelli's illustrations. "Fanelli's abundant visual energy drives this offbeat story," wrote a reviewer in *Publishers Weekly,* who felt that the book's playful design and illustrations were intended to "shift ... the emphasis away from the meager plot." Similarly, *New York Times Book Review* critic Paul O. Zelinsky observed that while Fanelli's illustrations are executed "with verve and a fine sense of humor," some of the visual details of *Button* "make no sense except design sense." Some suggested that *Button* would find its best audience among art-oriented children's book lovers and older art students. "It is an unusual but curiously engaging story," according to *School Library Journal* contributor Kathy Piehl.

Fanelli once told *SATA:* "I have always been encouraged to look at art and to draw by my parents. My family and the environment where I grew up in Florence are the prime source of my education in the art field. I have been studying in London ... and I find this city very exciting. I think illustration is a most interesting field which keeps expanding its limits. I appreciate the freedom and self-expression which illustration allows nowadays (although these remain by the nature of illustration closely related to some narrative idea).

"I enjoy surreal and ironic situations, finding excitement and the fantastic aspect in everyday life. I believe it is very important to show children different ways to look at the world, so that they may find their own personal view to help them in life. My favorite contemporary children's books are mostly American."

Fanelli followed up *Button* with another visually exciting picture book, *My Map Book.* Here, in characteristic mixed-media collages with drawings, the author/illustrator presents a series of maps that locate her protagonist not only in her neighborhood, but within her family, along with "detail" maps including one of her heart, another of her stomach, and so forth. "The energetic art is childlike in design and rendering, with no text except the labels found on each map," remarked Lolly Robinson in *Horn Book.* Reviewers noted that the artist thoughtfully left spaces for her readers to map out some element in their own life. *My Map Book* stands apart from some of Fanelli's other picture books, which reviewers occasionally hinted were intended for the adults who love children's books rather than for children themselves. However, a reviewer in *Publishers Weekly* reflected: "Fields of rich color and easygoing disregard of perspective make the work seem approachable and sophisticated at the same time."

The story of Fanelli's next book, *Wolf!*, is simple but satisfying, according to reviewers, and the pages are brimming with her stunning collages and unusual text presentation. A wolf's decision to visit a nearby city is mostly disastrous as he frightens everyone he meets. But when he flees for his life, he meets a sympathetic female wolf and manages to convince the city dwellers that their fears are groundless, and they all enjoy a picnic together. *Booklist* reviewer Michael Cart allowed that Fanelli's story is "episodic," but added "Fanelli's art is absolutely arresting, the naive style outrageously inventive and quirky." Like other reviewers, a critic in *Publishers Weekly* observed that "Wolf's triumph may seem simplistic to adults," but concluded nonetheless that "Fanelli's eclectic and artful illustrations will win over many readers of all ages."

The Doggy Book, like *My Map Book* before it, does not pretend to have a narrative, but is rather theme-oriented. Here, Fanelli's distinctive collages present various aspects of dogs, including tails and ears, as well as flights of fancy in which, for example, a St. Bernard rescue dog is shown with a ring of miniature dogs flying around its head in the shape of a halo. The book itself becomes a dog, when ears, legs, and tail are unfolded, and there is a dog bone bookmark thrown in for good measure. Although this effort seemed intended for adults rather than children, according to some reviewers, others were delighted by Fanelli's latest visual extravaganza. "For readers who love dogs, their accessories, and the most whimsical of artwork, this book is made in doggy heaven," concluded a reviewer in *Publishers Weekly*.

Fanelli attempts another unusual approach to storytelling in *Dear Diary,* which purports to be a page from the diary of young Lucy, as well as pages from the diaries of Chair, Spider, Firefly, Knife and Fork, the family dog, and Ladybug for the same day. Thus, Lucy tells the story of walking Bubu the dog to the park and then attending a dinner party; in the pages that follow, the reader finds the same story told from these other perspectives, each with accompanying doodles and handwriting to match each character. A reviewer for *Publishers Weekly* found Fanelli's book populated by "an enchanting community of committed diarists," and suggested: "This volume is sure to inspire both secret and self-proclaimed diarists."

Biographical and Critical Sources

PERIODICALS

Booklist, May 15, 1997, Michael Cart, review of *Wolf!,* p. 1578.
Books for Keeps, May, 1998, John Lawrence, review of *Button* and *Wolf!,* p. 4; March, 1999, George Hunt, review of *A Dog's Life,* p. 20.

Horn Book, January-February, 1996, Lolly Robinson, review of *My Map Book,* p. 63.
Kirkus Reviews, May 1, 1997, review of *Wolf!,* p. 719.
New York Times Book Review, May 21, 1995, Paul O. Zelinsky, "More Fun Than a Zipper," p. 29; February 25, 1996, Martha Davis Beck, review of *My Map Book,* p. 25.
Publishers Weekly, March 20, 1995, review of *Button,* p. 60; August 14, 1995, review of *My Map Book,* p. 84; April 7, 1997, review of *Wolf!,* p. 90; November 2, 1998, review of *The Doggy Book,* p. 80; April 3, 2000, review of *Dear Diary,* p. 81.
School Library Journal, April, 1995, Kathy Piehl, review of *Button,* p. 101; February, 1996, Lucinda Snyder Whitehurst, review of *My Map Book,* p. 84; July, 1997, Marcia Hupp, review of *Wolf!,* p. 67; May, 2000, Jackie Hechtkopf, review of *Dear Diary,* p. 140.

*   *   *

FATE, Marilyn
See COLLINS, Paul

*   *   *

FLEMING, Denise 1950-

Personal

Born January 31, 1950, in Toledo, OH; daughter of Frank (a realtor) and Inez (a homemaker; maiden name, Campbell) Fleming; married David Powers (a designer), October 9, 1971; children: Indigo (daughter). *Education:* Graduated from Kendall College of Art and Design, 1970. *Hobbies and other interests:* Gardening, natural habitats.

Addresses

Home—Toledo, OH. *Office*—c/o Author Mail, Henry Holt Inc., 115 West 18th St., New York, NY 10011.

Career

Children's book author and illustrator.

Awards, Honors

American Library Association notable book, *American Bookseller* Pick of the List, *Booklist* Editor's Choice selection, *School Library Journal* Best Book citation, *Redbook* Children's Picture Book Award, all 1991, *Boston Globe-Horn Book* Award honor book and International Reading Association-Children's Book Council Children's Choices selection, both 1992, all for *In the Tall, Tall Grass;* American Library Association notable book, 1992, for *Lunch; Publishers Weekly* Fifty Best Books of 1992, for *Count!; American Bookseller* Pick of the List, 1993, *Publishers Weekly* Best Books of 1993, *School Library Journal* Best Books of 1993, *Booklist* Notable Books of 1994, Caldecott honor book and American Library Association notable book, all

1994, all for *In the Small, Small Pond; American Bookseller* Pick of the List, 1994, for *Barnyard Banter; Booklist* Notable Books of 1997, for *Where Once There Was a Wood.*

Writings

SELF-ILLUSTRATED

In the Tall, Tall Grass, Holt (New York, NY), 1991.

Count!, Holt (New York, NY), 1992.

Lunch, Holt (New York, NY), 1992.

In the Small, Small Pond, Holt (New York, NY), 1993.

Barnyard Banter, Holt (New York, NY), 1994.

Denise Fleming's Painting with Paper, Holt (New York, NY), 1994.

Where Once There Was a Wood, Holt (New York, NY), 1996.

Time to Sleep, Holt (New York, NY), 1997.

Mama Cat Has Three Kittens, Holt (New York, NY), 1998.

The Everything Book, Holt (New York, NY), 2000.

Pumpkin Eye, Holt (New York, NY), 2001.

Buster, Holt (New York, NY), in press.

ILLUSTRATOR

Edith Adams, *The Charmkins Discover Big World,* Random House (New York, NY), 1983.

The Charmkins Sniffy Adventure, Random House (New York, NY), 1983.

Alice Low, *All through the Town,* Random House (New York, NY), 1984.

It Feels Like Christmas! A Book of Surprises to Touch, See, and Sniff, Random House (New York, NY), 1984.

Peggy Kahn, *The Care Bears Help Santa,* Random House (New York, NY), 1984.

Ernie's Sesame Street Friends, Random House (New York, NY), 1985.

This Little Pig Went to Market, Random House (New York, NY), 1985.

Count in the Dark with Glow Worm, Random House (New York, NY), 1985.

Deborah Shine, *Little Puppy's New Name,* Random House (New York, NY), 1985.

Teddy's Best Toys, Random House (New York, NY), 1985.

The Merry Christmas Book: A First Book of Holiday Stories and Poems, Random House (New York, NY), 1986.

Linda Hayward, *This Is the House,* Random House (New York, NY), 1988.

Linda Hayward, *D Is for Doll,* Random House (New York, NY), 1988.

Linda Hayward, *Tea Party Manners,* Random House (New York, NY), 1988.

Natalie Standiford, *Dollhouse Mouse,* Random House (New York, NY), 1989.

Sidelights

During the 1980s, Denise Fleming achieved some success illustrating children's books by other authors, including drawing licensed characters such as the Care Bears and Charmkins, but, as she told Shannon Maughan in *Publishers Weekly:* "It wasn't really what I ultimately wanted to do." Then she and her sister enrolled in a papermaking class, a subject Fleming found so fascinating she took a further course. It was with the knowledge Fleming gleaned there that she eventually developed her own technique of forcing cotton pulp through hand-cut stencils to make the distinctive art that accompanies her own picture books. Even though the techniques are completely different, Fleming's work is compared to the collage of children's book author and

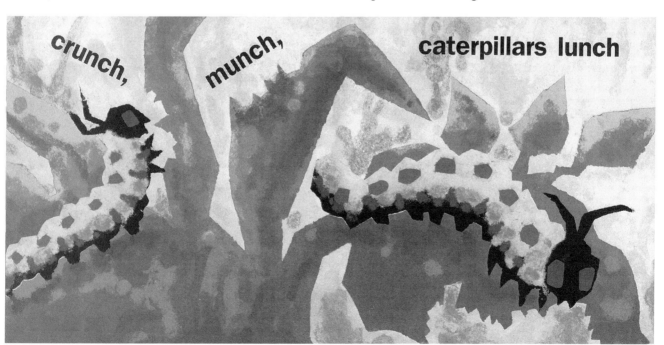

With rhyming text and bold illustrations, Denise Fleming tours the backyard from the point of view of a caterpillar in her **In the Tall, Tall Grass.**

illustrator Eric Carle, and critics often single out the stunningly vibrant colors in her creations.

Fleming's first solo effort, *In the Tall, Tall Grass,* follows a caterpillar through a backyard jungle from afternoon until evening. The author's "bold, bright, stylized ... illustrations" offer the caterpillar's point of view on the myriad of other creatures in the yard, from hummingbirds to bees, ants, and snakes, according to Virginia Opocensky in *School Library Journal.* A *Publishers Weekly* reviewer commented: "The ultimate kaleidoscope effect makes this title ideal for sharing with young explorers." The illustrations are accompanied by a simple rhyming text that emphasizes the activity of each creature. Ellen Fader, writing in *Horn Book,* remarked: "This book holds appeal for a wide range of children."

Count!, the author's next work, introduces young audiences to numbers with the help of Fleming's signature pulp paintings. Each spread features animals exhibiting characteristic behavior accompanied by a short, exclamatory phrase that identifies the animal and its behavior. "This introduction to the numbers ... also serves as a lively romp through the wild kingdom," remarked a *Publishers Weekly* contributor. Writing in *School Library Journal,* Liza Bliss dubbed *Count!* "very bright, very hip!" A small paperback edition of the book is included in *Denise Fleming's Painting with Paper,* a kit that contains instructions and equipment for making art with paper pulp and stencils, just like the artist.

Fleming's next book, *Lunch,* employs a format similar to *In the Tall, Tall Grass.* In *Lunch,* a greedy mouse eats his way through a vegetarian feast and consequently teaches young children the names and colors of common foods. *Booklist* contributor Kathryn Broderick commented: "Fleming's vibrant handmade paper paintings ... flaunt big blotches of colors and a funny, piggy mouse." Karen James, writing in *School Library Journal,* called *Lunch* a "well designed, joyous romp." *Horn Book* reviewer Fader concluded: "Delectable fun, and, with the simple yet engaging plot, sure to be requested over and over by the youngest readers."

Many critics compared Fleming's *In the Small, Small Pond* to her earlier *In the Tall, Tall Grass* for its close-to-the-ground view of an enclosed natural system. In this work, the author focuses on a frog and his interaction with other creatures associated with pond life. The rhyming text again emphasizes the activities of the animals depicted, and the illustrations lead the reader through the seasons from spring to winter. Like many other critics, *Booklist* contributor Ilene Cooper emphasized Fleming's compositions in her review, concluding: "The art has both a fluidity of design and a precision of definition that make it a pleasure to view." Judy Constantinides commented in *School Library Journal:* "Another truly stunning picture book from Fleming."

Animal life is again the focus of Fleming's *Barnyard Banter,* in which each barnyard animal makes an appearance and spouts its characteristic noise accompanied by the refrain "Where's goose?" "Lush colors, startled, wide-eyed animals, and bold, black print make each page ... jump with activity," observed a contributor to *Kirkus Reviews.* Reviewing *Time to Sleep* in *School Library Journal,* critic Marcia Hupp called Fleming's story about animals preparing for a long winter hibernation, "a gem of a picture book." As in

a meadow

Fleming discusses how communities and schools can provide homes for wildlife displaced by development in her self-illustrated **Where Once There Was a Wood.**

Fleming wrote and illustrated **The Everything Book,** *which introduces colors, shapes, numbers, nursery rhymes, finger games, and more.*

Barnyard Banter, Fleming's simple story in *Time to Sleep* serves to introduce a wide variety of animals. Here, Bear realizes that it is time to hibernate for the winter and tells Snail, who tells Skunk, who tells Turtle, and so forth until Ladybug wakes up the already slumbering Bear to inform him that it is indeed, time to sleep. The book is "subtly informative and poetic in its simplicity," according to Hupp, who predicted that *Time to Sleep* would make regular appearances at afternoon story-hours in the autumn months.

Mama Cat Has Three Kittens celebrates individuality in the form of one little kitten, Boris, who sleeps while Mama leads Fluffy and Skinny, her other two kittens, through their paces. But when the rest of the family settles down for a nap, Boris leaps into action. A reviewer for *Publishers Weekly* noted that Fleming's love for cats is evident in every spread "as she accurately captures feline behavior and movement." Fleming adds visual interest to her signature poured-fiber art in jewel tones by placing small creatures in unobtrusive places in each illustration. "The repetition of simple phrases and actions is also sure to be a hit with toddlers," this critic continued. "Preschoolers will request repeat readings of this delightful story," Blair Christolon likewise predicted in *School Library Journal.*

Reviewers commended Fleming's seamless blend of artwork and text, of story and message in *Where Once There Was a Wood,* in which the author reminds readers that while a new housing development may mean a new community to humans, it displaces a community of animals and other creatures. Fleming pairs a gently rhyming text with vibrantly colored and richly textured illustrations comparing and contrasting the animal habi-

tat and the human. "An ecology lesson it surely is," remarked a contributor to *Kirkus Reviews,* "but it's also a celebration of the earth and its creatures." Fleming does not abandon her audience to the dilemma she has exposed; the conclusion of *Where Once There Was a Wood* includes simple suggestions that encourage the wildlife in one's own yard, such as planting butterfly or hummingbird gardens. Sarabeth Kalajian called this "A book to be shared and enjoyed by a wide audience," in her review for *School Library Journal.*

For a much younger audience, Fleming has produced *The Everything Book,* a compendium of nursery rhymes, peek-a-boo, the alphabet, games involving counting objects, naming body parts, playing with kitchen utensils, learning the creatures commonly found in one's own backyard, and other useful and amusing pastimes for parents and their very young offspring. "All the first concepts children learn are endearingly presented in Fleming's vibrant, distinctively textured style," recounted Julie Yates Walton in the *New York Times Book Review.* Walton jocularly compared *The Everything Book* to E. D. Hirsch's books purporting to contain all the information one should know by the time he or she has achieved a certain age or grade level, and concluded that "with her warm, intuitively childlike touch, Fleming's book could be properly billed as 'What Every Pre-Kindergartner Wants to Know.'"

Biographical and Critical Sources

PERIODICALS

Booklist, November 1, 1992, Kathryn Broderick, review of *Lunch,* p. 519; September 1, 1993, Ilene Cooper,

review of *In the Small, Small Pond,* p. 67; March 15, 1994, review of *In the Small, Small Pond,* p. 1351; April 1, 1997, review of *Where Once There Was a Wood,* p. 1296.
Horn Book, January-February, 1992, Ellen Fader, review of *In the Tall, Tall Grass,* pp. 56-57; January-February, 1993, Ellen Fader, review of *Lunch,* pp. 74-75.
Kirkus Reviews, March 15, 1994, review of *Barnyard Banter,* p. 395; April 1, 1996, review of *Where Once There Was a Wood,* p. 528.
New York Times Book Review, November 19, 2000, Julie Yates Walton, "Everything You Always Wanted to Know," p. 36.
Publishers Weekly, September 13, 1991, review of *In the Tall, Tall Grass,* p. 78; December 13, 1991, review of *Count!,* p. 55; December 20, 1991, Shannon Maughan, interview with Denise Fleming, p. 24; September 7, 1992, p. 94; July 5, 1993, p. 69; October 10, 1994, review of *Painting with Paper,* p. 71; January 27, 1997, review of *Count!,* p. 108; July, 1998, review of *Mama Cat Has Three Kittens,* p. 217.
School Library Journal, September, 1991, Virginia Opocensky, review of *In the Tall, Tall Grass,* pp. 232-233; March, 1992, Liza Bliss, review of *Count!,* p. 228; December, 1992, Karen James, review of *Lunch,* pp. 81-82; September, 1993, Judy Constantinides, review of *In the Small, Small Pond,* pp. 206-207; June, 1996, Sarabeth Kalajian, review of *Where Once There Was a Wood,* p. 116; November, 1997, Lisa Falk, review of *Time to Sleep,* p. 80; November, 1998, Blair Christolon, review of *Mama Cat Has Three Kittens,* p. 84.
Tribune Books (Chicago, IL), January 13, 1992, p. 6.

*   *   *

FRENETTE, Liza

Personal

Daughter of James and Susanne (Hull) Frenette; children: Jasmine. *Education:* Morrisville College, A.A., 1978; State University of New York—Albany, B.A., 1991, M.A., 1994.

Addresses

Office—c/o Author Mail, North Country Books, Richardson Place, 2 Church St., Burlington, VT 05401.

Career

Press Republican, Plattsburgh, NY, reporter and photographer, 1985-88; *Folio,* Stamford, CT, associate editor, 1988-89; *Voice,* Albany, NY, writer, 1996—. Visiting writer at elementary school and college workshops. Big Brothers and Big Sisters, volunteer big sister. *Member:* Children's Literature Connection.

Awards, Honors

First place award, United Press International, 1985, for news writing; first place award, Associated Press of New York State, 1986, for feature writing, and 1987, for column writing; first place award, *Writer's Voice* national contest, c. 1998, for *Soft Shoulders.*

Writings

Soft Shoulders, illustrated by Jane Gillis, North Country Books (Utica, NY), 1998.
Dangerous Falls Ahead (sequel to *Soft Shoulders*), North Country Books (Utica, NY), 2001.

Work represented in anthologies, including *The Little Magazine,* 1991.

Sidelights

Liza Frenette told *SATA:* "I've always wanted to be a writer. I dare say it's the only thing I've ever been sure of (okay, that and the fact that I love chocolate and swimming). My life has been filled with detours and zigzags. I've always loved books: reading them aloud to my daughter, listening to authors read their work, or just reading myself. I find books for children uplifting; they almost always help me see things a new way, or they refresh me. I love the illustrations, especially since I can't draw myself. I like oral storytelling, too, and always made up stories for my daughter when she was younger. We'd tell the same ones over and over. I read a lot of adult literature as well, mostly fiction, some nonfiction. I like the woods a lot, and water, and city lights, and a good band. I like bookstores that have cafés and stay open late. I like movies, not just for entertainment, but because they can be so creative. They mix art, music, sometimes literature, acting, and cinematography. Plays are creative the same way. They remind us about human nature and zigzags!"

G

GAY, Marie-Louise 1952-

Personal

Born June 17, 1952, in Québec City, Québec, Canada; daughter of Bernard Roland (a sales representative) and Colette Fontaine (a homemaker) Gay; married, c. 1972 (husband died, c. 1975); companion of David Toby Homel (an author and translator); children: (with Homel) Gabriel Reubens, Jacob Paul. *Education:* Attended Institute of Graphic Arts of Montréal, 1970-71; graduated from Montréal Museum of Fine Arts School, 1973; attended Academy of Art College (San Francisco, CA),

Marie-Louise Gay

1977-79. *Religion:* Raised Roman Catholic. *Hobbies and other interests:* Reading, traveling, cycling, cross-country skiing, canoeing, and writing.

Addresses

Home—773 Davaar, Montréal, Québec H2V 3B3, Canada. *Office*—c/o Groundwood Books, 720 Bathurst St., Ste. 500, Toronto, Ontario M5S 2R4, Canada.

Career

Author/illustrator, playwright, graphic artist, cartoonist, animator, sculptor, and set, costume, and clothing designer. Actress on Canadian television and in local theater, c. 1961-62. Editorial illustrator for Canadian and American periodicals, 1972-87; graphic designer for magazines *Perspectives* and *Decormag,* 1974-76; La Courte Echelle (publishing company), Montréal, Québec, art director, 1980; University of Québec—Montréal, lecturer in illustration, 1981—; visiting lecturer in illustration, Ahuntsic College, 1984-85. Host of or speaker at workshops and conferences at schools and libraries, 1981—. Designer of children's clothing, 1985—; set designer of animated film *La Boite,* 1989. *Exhibitions:* Man and His World, Humor Pavillion, Montréal, Canada, 1974; "Books for Children," Montréal Museum of Contemporary Art, and "Sketches of Greece and Italy," San Francisco, CA, 1979; "Animals and Women" solo exhibition, Galerie 858, Montréal, Canada, 1980; "Books for Kids," Communication-Jeunnesse, Montréal, Canada, 1981-86; Toronto Art Directors' Club Show, Toronto, Canada, 1982-83; "Current Wave," Los Angeles, CA, 1985; "Humour," Galerie Articule and Centre culturel NDG, Montréal, Canada, 1984-86; "Once upon a Time," Vancouver Art Gallery, Vancouver, Canada, and throughout Canada, 1988-90; "Quebec Illustration," Montréal, Canada, 1989; "Willy Nilly and Company," solo exhibition, Mable's Fable's, Toronto, Canada, 1990; "Canada at Bologne," Bologne, Italy, Rome, Italy, Milan, Italy, Munich, Germany, Paris, France, and Tokyo, Japan, 1990-91; "Colora il nostra compleanno," Bologna Fiere and UNICEF, Bologna,

Big sister Stella has the answers to Sam's questions about the sea, but will he ever come into the water? *(From* Stella, Star of the Sea, *written and illustrated by Gay.)*

Italy, Tokyo, Japan, Paris, France, and New York, NY, 1991; "La giraffe québécoise," Québec, Canada, 1992-94; "International Year of Family," Ottawa, Canada, 1994; "L'espace théâtral" (costumes and sets), Montréal, Canada, 1994; "L'envers du décor" (exhibition of drawings of puppets, costumes, and sets), Montréal, Canada, 1999; "L'illustration pour enfants," Drummond-ville, Canada, and solo exhibition at Ceperley House Gallery, Burnaby, Canada, both 2000. *Member:* Canadian Children's Book Center, IBBY Canada.

Awards, Honors

Alvine-Belisle Prize (best French-Canadian children's book of the year), 1984, for *La soeur de Robert;* Canada Council Children's Literature Prize (Illustrator), 1984, for the "Drôle d'école" series (French-Canadian prize) and for *Lizzy's Lion* (English-Canadian prize); Amelia Frances Howard-Gibbon Illustrator's Award, Canadian Association of Children's Librarians, 1986, for *Moonbeam on a Cat's Ear;* Governor General's Literary Award (Children's Literature—Illustration), 1987, and Amelia Frances Howard-Gibbon Illustrator's Award, 1988, both for *Rainy Day Magic;* shortlisted, Governor General's Literary Award Children's Literature—Illustration), 1989, for *Angel and the Polar Bear;* White Ravens Selection, International Youth Library, Munich, 1993, for *Mademoiselle Moon;* Ehrenliste zum Oster-reichiscchen Kinder-und Jugenbuchpreis, 1995, for *Fat Charlie's Circus* (German edition); shortlisted, Governor General's Literary Award Children's Literature—Illustration), 1996, for *Berthold et Lucréce;* shortlisted, Governor General's Literary Award Children's Literature—Illustration), Mr. Christie's Book Award, and Honor Title designation, Storytelling World Awards in Atlanta (GA), all 1997, all for *The Fabulous Song;* shortlisted, Governor General's Literary Award Children's Literature—Illustration), and Mr. Christie's Book Award shortlist, both 1998, both for *Rumpelstiltskin;*

second prize, Alcuin Citations, Design Citations for Canadian Publishers, 1999, for *Dreams Are More Real than Bathtubs;* Governor General's Literary Award (Children's Literature—Illustration), 2000, for *Yuck: A Love Story;* shortlisted, Governor General's Literary Award (Children's Literature—Illustration), 2000, for *Sur mon île* (French edition); Ruth Schwartz Children's Book Award, Ontario Arts Council, Mr. Christie's Book Award, Amelia Howard-Gibbon Illustrator's Award nomination, and IBBY Honours List designation, all 2000, all for *Stella, Star of the Sea;* Governor General's Literary Award Children's Literature—Illustration), and Canadian Booksellers Association Illustrator of the Year Award shortlist, both 2000, both for *Yuck: A Love Story;* shortlisted, Ruth Schwartz Award, Mr. Christie's Book Award nomination, Elizabeth Mazrik-Cleaver Award, and Talking Book of the Year Award, all 2001, all for *Stella, Queen of the Snow;* Children's Illustrator of the Year, Canadian Booksellers Association, 2000. In addition, she has received recognition for her work as a freelance illustrator and graphic designer, including the Claude Neon National Billboard Award, 1972; Western Art Directors Club Award, San Francisco, 1978; Society of Illustrators Award, 1979; and Toronto Art Directors Club Award, 1983 and 1985.

Writings

FOR CHILDREN; SELF-ILLUSTRATED PICTURE BOOKS

De zéro à minuit (title means "From Zero to Midnight"), La Courte Echelle (Montréal, Canada), 1981.

La soeur de Robert (title means "Robert's Sister"), La Courte Echelle (Montréal, Canada), 1983.

The Garden (board book), Lorimer (Toronto, Canada), 1985, originally published as *Mon Potager,* Ovale (Québec, Canada), 1985.

Moonbeam on a Cat's Ear, Silver Burdett (Don Mills, Canada, and Morristown, New Jersey), 1986, reissued with new design, Stoddart (Toronto, Canada), 1992, originally published as *Voyage au Clair de Lune,* Heritage (Saint-Lambert, Canada), 1986.

Rainy Day Magic, Stoddart (Don Mills, Canada), 1987, Whitman (Morton Grove, IL), 1989, originally published as *Magie d'un jour de pluie,* Heritage (Saint-Lambert, Canada), 1986.

Angel and the Polar Bear, Stoddart (Don Mills, Canada), 1988, Kane/Miller (Brooklyn, NY), 1997, originally published as *Angèle et l'ours polaire,* Heritage (Saint-Lambert, Canada), 1988.

Fat Charlie's Circus, Stoddart (Don Mills, Canada), 1989, originally published as *Le Cirque de Charlie Chou,* Heritage (Saint-Lambert, Canada), 1989.

Willy Nilly (adapted from the author's puppet play, *Bonne fête Willy;* also see below), Whitman (Morton Grove, IL), 1990.

Mademoiselle Moon, Stoddart (Don Mills, Canada), 1992.

Rabbit Blue, Stoddart (Don Mills, Canada), 1993, originally published as *Lapin bleu,* Heritage (Saint-Lambert, Canada), 1993.

Midnight Mimi, Stoddart (Don Mills, Canada), 1994, originally published as *Mimi-la-Nuit,* Heritage (Saint-Lambert, Canada), 1994.

Qui a peur de Loulou?: théâtre (adapted from the author's puppet play; also see below), Editions VLB (Montréal, Canada), 1994.

(Reteller) *The Three Little Pigs,* Groundwood Books (Toronto, Canada), 1994, Publishers Group West, 1996.

(Reteller) *Rumpelstiltskin,* Groundwood Books (Toronto, Canada), 1997, Publishers Group West, 1997.

Stella, Star of the Sea (also see below), Publishers Group West, 1999, Douglas & McIntyre/Groundwood (Toronto, Canada), 1999.

Princesse Pistache, Dominique at Compagnie (Montréal, Canada), 1999.

Le jardin de Babel: théâtre (adapted from the author's puppet play; also see below), Lanctot (Québec, Canada), 1999.

On My Island (originally published in France as *Sur mon ile*), Douglas & McIntyre/Groundwood (Toronto, Canada), 2000.

Stella, Queen of the Snow (sequel to *Stella, Star of the Sea*), Groundwood Books (Toronto, Canada), 2000.

"DRÔLE D'ÉCOLE" SERIES; BOARD BOOKS FOR PRESCHOOLERS

Rond comme ton visage, Ovale (Québec, Canada), 1984.
Blanc comme neige, Ovale (Québec, Canada), 1984.
Petit et grand, Ovale (Québec, Canada), 1984.
Un léopard dans mon placard, Ovale (Québec, Canada), 1984.

ILLUSTRATOR; FOR CHILDREN

Dennis Lee, *Lizzy's Lion,* Stoddart (Don Mills, Canada), 1984.

Tim Wynne-Jones, *The Last Piece of Sky,* Groundwood Books (Toronto, Canada), 1993.

Don Gillmor, *When Vegetables Go Bad!,* Doubleday Canada (Toronto, Canada), 1993.

Christiane Duchesne, *Berthold & Lucrèce: roman,* Québec-Amerique Jeunesse, 1994.

(Contributor) *Mother Goose: A Canadian Sampler,* Groundwood (Toronto, Canada), 1994.

Don Gillmor, *The Fabulous Song,* Stoddart (Don Mills, Canada), 1996, Kane-Miller (Brooklyn, NY), 1998.

Lois Wyse and Molly Rose Goldman, *How to Take Your Grandmother to the Museum,* Workman (New York, NY), 1998.

Don Gillmor, *The Christmas Orange,* General Distribution Services, 1999.

Susan Musgrave, *Dreams Are More Real than Bathtubs,* Orca Book Publishers (Custer, WA, and Victoria, Canada), 1999.

Don Gillmor, *Yuck: A Love Story,* Stoddart Kids (Don Mills, Canada), 2000.

Marilyn Singer, *Didi & Daddy on the Promenade,* Clarion (New York, NY), 2001.

PICTURE BOOK TRILOGY, WRITTEN BY BERNARD GAUTHIER

Hou Ilva, La Tamanoir (Montréal, Canada), 1976.
Dou Ilvien, La Courte Echelle (Montréal, Canada), 1978.
Hébert Lué, La Courte Echelle (Montréal, Canada), 1980

"SOPHIE/MADDIE" SERIES; PRIMARY GRADE FICTION; WRITTEN BY LOUISE LeBLANC

That's Enough, Maddie, Formac Publishing, 1990, originally published as *Ça suffit, Sophie,* La Courte Echelle (Montréal, Canada), 1990.

Maddie in Goal, Formac Publishing, 1991, originally published as *Sophie lance et compte,* La Courte Echelle (Montréal, Canada), 1991.

Ça va mal pour Sophie, La Courte Echelle (Montréal, Canada), 1992, translated as *Maddie Wants Music,* Formac Publishing, 1993.

Maddie Goes to Paris, Formac Publishing, 1993, originally published as *Sophie part en voyage,* La Courte Echelle (Montréal, Canada), 1993.

Maddie in Danger, Formac Publishing, 1994, originally published as *Sophie est en danger,* La Courte Echelle (Montréal, Canada), 1994.

Maddie in Hospital, Formac Publishing, 1995, originally published as *Sophie fait des folies,* La Courte Echelle (Montréal, Canada), 1995.

Sophie in Trouble, Formac Publishing, 1996, originally published as *Sophie vit un cauchemar,* La Courte Echelle (Montréal, Canada), 1996.

Sophie devient sage ..., La Courte Echelle (Montréal, Canada), 1997.

Sophie vent vivre sa vie, La Courte Echelle (Montréal, Canada), 1999.

Maddie Tries to Be Good, Formac Publishing, 2000.
Maddie Wants New Clothes, Formac Publishing, 2001.
Sophie court apres la fortune, La Courte Echelle (Montréal, Canada), 2001.

"JULIA" SERIES; PRIMARY GRADE FICTION; WRITTEN BY CHRISTIANE DUCHESNE

Julia et le chef des Pois, Boreal (Montréal, Canada), 1999.
Julia et les fantômes, Boreal (Montréal, Canada), 1999.
Julia et le voleur de nuit, Boreal (Montréal, Canada), 2000.

OTHER

(Illustrator) Anne Taylor, *Hands On: A Media Resource Book for Teachers* (nonfiction) National Film Board of Canada (Montréal, Canada), 1977.

(Contributing illustrator) Michel Rivard and others, *La Vache et d'autres animaux* (nonfiction), La Courte Echelle (Montréal, Canada), 1982.

Graphic designer of *Crapauds et autres animaux* by Francine Tougas and others, 1981. Illustrator of *Monsieur Soleil* by Lucie Papineau and *Le Beurre de Doudou* by Sylvie Nicolas, both 1997. Gay wrote and designed three puppet plays, *Bonne fête Willy,* 1989-91; *Qui a peur de Loulou?,* 1993-95; and *Le jardin de Babel,* 1999; all were produced by the Theatre de l'oeil in Québec, Canada and *Bonne fête Willy* was also produced in Europe. Also contributor of illustrations to periodicals, including *Mother Jones, Psychology Today,* and *Saturday Night.* Gay's books have been published in several languages, including Dutch, Danish, Norwegian, Spanish, Swedish, German, Portuguese, Greek, and Korean.

Adaptations

Gay is the subject of the video *Meet the Author/Illustrator: Marie-Louise Gay,* School Services of Canada, 1991.

Sidelights

A Canadian author, illustrator, and reteller, Marie-Louise Gay is considered one of Canada's most prominent contemporary creators of children's literature. She directs her picture books—humorous, action-filled works and more reflective titles—to youngsters ranging from preschool to the early primary grades. She has also provided the art for picture books and stories by such writers as Dennis Lee, Louise LeBlanc, Tim Wynne-Jones, Don Gillmor, Susan Musgrave, and Marilyn Singer. Popular and prolific, Gay is often praised for her originality, imagination, and understanding of children and their world. Characteristically, Gay blends fantasy and reality to describe how her young protagonists launch themselves into amazing adventures that take them to such places as the sky or under the sea before they return home safely. The author is noted for celebrating children's natural joyfulness and love of

Then the robber shooed the lion,
Using every name he knew;
But each time he shooed, the lion
Merely took another chew.

The lion that Lizzy keeps in her room eats a burglar in Dennis Lee's Lizzy's Lion, *illustrated by Gay.*

exuberant, often chaotic, play. However, she also depicts the less sunny parts of the lives of the young, such as embarrassment, terror, loneliness, and the need for emotional support. Through both imaginative play and exploration of the world around them, Gay's characters ultimately confront their fears and experience personal growth. These boys and girls often bring home souvenirs of their journeys, such as a starfish or a slice of moon, which are introduced subtly in Gay's pictures.

As a writer, Gay generally favors simple but lively prose and verse. As an illustrator, she uses mediums such as watercolor, pen and ink, colored pencil, and collage to depict and amplify the adventures of her characters, whom she draws in a cartoon-like style that stresses their large bodies, broad faces, tiny limbs, and spiked hair. Gay often extends her drawings beyond their usual confines to provide viewers with parallel stories, visual details, clues, and witty touches; these asides are often represented by the actions of secondary characters such as cats and mice. She is often lauded for the energy, freshness, and colorful, expressionistic quality of her art as well as for her inventive page designs and distinctive use of perspective. Occasionally, however, Gay has been criticized for creating books without morals, works that give negative ideas to children while showing adults in a less than favorable light; some of her texts are also considered slight, especially in relation to her illustrations. However, many observers revere Gay as a multi-talented artist and writer whose works capture the interest of children with their humor, accessibility, and emotional resonance.

Reviewers have often commented on Gay's contributions to children's literature. Writing in *Canadian Children's Literature,* Joan McGrath called Gay "the mistress of 'what-if'.... Her perfect recall of a child's free-ranging, fresh-eyed delight coupled with the adult artistry to bring joyful fantasy to life on brilliant pages, makes her work a nursery treasure, and an ornament to the growing collection of Canadian picture books." Janet McNaughton stated in *Quill & Quire,* "At her best, Marie-Louise Gay captures the whimsical side of childhood in a way that few author/illustrators can. Her pictures are so full of life and motion that they appear to be on the verge of spilling out of the book. Her most successful texts are sparse poems that understate the action of the illustrations, allowing pre-literate children to fill in the blanks with their own observations. This is the kind of interplay between child and book one always hopes for." A critic writing in the *St. James Guide to Children's Writers* said that Gay is "one of Canada's foremost interpreters of young children's perceptions of important real and imaginary elements of their lives."

Born in Québec City, Québec, Gay is the daughter of Bernard Roland, a sales representative whose jobs took him and his family across Canada, and Colette Fontaine Gay. When she was five, her family moved from the French-speaking province of Québec to Oakville, Ontario, a city that she described in her *Something about the Author Autobiography Series* (*SAAS*) essay as "a totally English environment." The author recalled, "It was

frightening to discover that I couldn't communicate with children my own age. I remember feeling confused and lonely. But total immersion and the intense desire to belong helped me learn English." Shortly after moving to Oakville, Gay taught herself to read—in English. She was sitting with one of H. A. and Margret Rey's "Curious George" books on her lap and spelling out words from it to her mother, when, as Gay wrote, "Those strange lines and squiggles became words and sentences.... All of a sudden, the famous cartoon lightbulb went off over my head. I c-o-u-l-d r-e-a-d! That was the beginning of my addiction to reading. With books, I could find friends wherever we went."

When she was seven, Gay moved with her family to West Vancouver in Canada. The Gays lived halfway up a mountain in an isolated neighborhood. Since her father was often away on business and her mother did not drive, Gay and her younger sister Marie-Claude were, as Marie-Louise wrote in *SAAS,* "prisoners of the mountain. It was a lovely prison, though...." When her father would return from his trips, he would take his daughters to the beach, to the park, and to the public library. Here, Gay recalled, "I would stock up on books for the week (at least six or seven at a time), enough to feed my voracious appetite. I read constantly: at meals, before bed, in the bathroom, in the school bus, and even during classes, hiding a book beneath the textbook being used at the time. It strained my eyes to read secretly while pretending to be attentive to the teacher, but it was worth it." Even today, Gay loves to read. She told Marie Davis in *Canadian Children's Literature,* "I am an avid reader—I need a fix. I have to read all the time. And I have been like that since I was five years old."

While she was living in Vancouver, Gay made her debut as an actress. Her parents were part of a local amateur theater group, and Gay would help them to learn their roles. When the need arose for a young girl to play a small but important role in the play *Speaking of Murder,* Gay auditioned for, and won, the part. "My father," she wrote in *SAAS,* "was the leading man and, fittingly enough, I played the role of his daughter." On opening night, Gay was "discovered" by a television producer who was in the audience. This man invited Gay to audition for a part in a television drama, *Raft in the Middle of Noon.* The drama featured two boys who played games of pirates and castaways on their home-made raft. Gay recalled, "I played the younger sister who would continually intrude upon their game, breaking the magical mood which, of course, they resented. While I enjoyed this new acting experience, I didn't like playing the role of the one who brought them down to earth; I would have preferred playing the role of one of the boys. I would have chosen their flights of fantasy over boring reality. This has become a leitmotif in almost all the books I have written." Gay then began to act in children's television serials, including *Tidewater Tramp* and *Friday Morning Series.* However, as she noted, "after a heady year of stardom, our family moved again, back to Montréal. A promising career bit the dust."

In Montréal, Gay was immersed once again in a French environment. She attended a French private school where, she said, "I was completely miserable because I didn't fit in with the rich students; my school marks roller-coasted all over the place." She continued, "My way of escape during those difficult teenage years, when money was the cause of much friction in our home and when my parents' marriage disintegrated, was reading." She took refuge in science fiction by authors such as C. S. Lewis, Ursula K. Le Guin, and John Wyndham, and in novels by such writers as Colette, Lawrence Durrell, and Gabriel Garcia Marquez. Gay was also fascinated, as she recalled, "by a type of literature which came mainly from France and Belgium: *la bande dessinée,* illustrated albums, astonishing because of their innovative visual impact and highly humorous and intellectual content. I pored over these drawings and realize now that they had an enormous influence on my style of illustration." Gay noted, "I discovered another way to escape my problems: I, who had never displayed a particular talent in art, and who would yawn out of boredom during the stuffy traditional art classes we were given in school, art classes that were designed to immediately stifle any little show of originality.... I began to doodle on any piece of paper I could get my hands on." In school, Gay would cover her notebooks with "all manner of strange cartoon creatures flying in between math equations, weaving in and out of grammar rules, skiing down equilateral triangles, or squashing chemistry problems to death. It was obvious my mind was elsewhere!" Gay's mother, Colette, suggested that her daughter go to art school. Gay remembered, "It was like opening the wardrobe in *The Lion, the Witch, and the Wardrobe* by C. S. Lewis. I stepped into another world. A world that suited me." In an interview with *SATA* the author recalled, "What a revelation for me! I started having fun in school! I quickly realized that this was really what I wanted to do."

From 1970 through 1971, Gay attended the Institute of Graphic Arts of Montréal, where she studied typography, perspective, and art history. "It was such a relief," she wrote in *SAAS,* "to be studying things that interested me, that inspired me, and to discover that I at least had some talent. I was enjoying myself thoroughly but, at the same time, I had the nagging suspicion that I could be doing something more creative, less confining. It was like learning to waltz while you secretly learned to tap dance." Gay then transferred to the Montréal Museum of Fine Arts School, where she discovered what she called "the wonderful and wacky world of animation." She added, "That was more like it!" She drew and painted a variety of what she described as "whimsical and batty characters," using them as the subjects of animated films; she wrote in *SAAS,* "I was having the time of my life." After a year, Gay decided to try selling some of her art to magazines in order to finance her filmmaking and her school tuition. She began shopping around some of her original cartoon strips, having little success until she met with what she called "one prescient art director" at *Perspectives* magazine who sent her home to rework her drawings—several times. Gay noted, "When he finally accepted and purchased three of my cartoon strips, I was

on top of the world! I had learned two very important things: to be very critical about my own work and not to be afraid of throwing a drawing away and redoing it." Gay spent the next several months reworking her portfolio. She then returned to the same magazines and publishing houses that had previously rejected her work. This time, however, Gay started to gain acceptance. She illustrated magazine articles, textbooks, book covers, flyers, posters, billboards, and T-shirts, among other things. As she wrote in *SAAS,* "I was off and running."

When Gay was twenty, she married a man whom she had met in art school who, like herself, was now working as an artist and illustrator. Gay wrote, "For three years, we shared ideas and creative enthusiasms, encouraging each other to explore new techniques and styles. Then he died of cancer. As you can imagine, it was terribly difficult to accept that someone so young could die. I couldn't face it. I ran away. I ran away to a place where I didn't know a soul. I packed up my pencils and brushes, my watercolors and inks and, in 1977, I moved to San Francisco." Gay enrolled at the Academy of Arts College, a school that specialized in illustration. Since she had been working professionally for five years, Gay was allowed to choose the classes that she took. She decided to concentrate on drawing. Writing in *SAAS,* she stated, "I wanted to understand what went on beneath the skin of my whimsical characters, my flying rabbits, my acrobatic mice. How did the characters that I created move? Where should shadows fall? How do snakes and lizards smile?" At the Academy of Arts, Gay took such classes as anatomy, life drawing, portraits, and illustration techniques. She immersed herself in work, trying to forget what she had left behind in Montréal. She battled loneliness and confusion but, as she noted, "time and hard work will heal." Slowly, Gay became inspired by the physical beauty of San Francisco and the uninhibited attitude and unconventional ideas of many of its people. She noted, "The gray, white, and ice-blue tones of the Montréal winters gave way to fuschias and orange, turquoise and lime green." During her three years in San Francisco, Gay worked sporadically as an editorial illustrator, and also illustrated textbooks. She also traveled to France, Greece, and Italy, as well as to the southern United States. One day, after coming back from one of these trips, she realized that it was time to return to what she called "my real home.... I was ready to go back to Montréal."

Back in Montréal, Gay began working part-time as art director and production manager of La Courte Echelle, a company that specialized in publishing books for children. Gay chose the illustrators for book projects, designed the books, and supervised the printing process. She also provided the pictures for a trilogy of French-language children's books by Bernard Gauthier, an author who had seen Gay's work in magazines and asked her if she would be interested in illustrating a book for children. "Believe it or not," she wrote in *SAAS,* "with all the books I had read and enjoyed as a child, it never occurred to me that I could do something like that. I was greatly excited by the prospect."

Victor and Joey fantasize about being in the jungle in Gay's self-illustrated **Rainy Day Magic.**

Although Gay enjoyed working on her illustrations for the trilogy, which introduced the new palette of colors that were inspired by her life in San Francisco, she found Gauthier's texts less than effective. She noted in *SAAS,* "I felt there was something missing, as if the story was meant for adults: clever, witty, urbane, not really addressing the emotional needs of children. It certainly didn't address the emotional needs I had in myself. Enough griping! I had to risk it and try my hand at writing *my* stories, at inventing *my* world." She told Leacy O'Brien in *Canadian Materials,* "I felt it was important to talk to children on a level they can appreciate . . . to take children seriously."

In 1981 Gay wrote and illustrated the first of her books for children, *De zéro à minuit.* The success of this work, a French-language picture book that has yet to be translated into English, led her to create another picture book in French, *La soeur de Robert,* which won the Alvine-Belisle Prize for the best French-Canadian picture book of 1983. The next year, Gay produced the "Drôle d'école" series, a quartet of board books for preschoolers that won the Canada Council Children's Literature Prize in illustration for a French-Canadian title. Gay also provided the illustrations for *Lizzy's Lion,* a picture book in verse by well-known Canadian poet Dennis Lee. This work features a little girl who keeps a lion in her bedroom; because she knows his Secret Lion Name, Lizzy can handle the beast. When a burglar breaks into Lizzy's home, the lion eats him; Lizzy wakes up in time to put his head, toes, and tummy in the garbage. *Lizzy's Lion*—which became one of the most censored books in Canada due to its violence—brought Gay to national attention. Writing in *Books in Canada,* Mary Ainslie Smith called her pictures "great—funny and eccentric," while John Bemrose and others, writing in *Maclean's,* concluded that Gay's "mischievously

exaggerated illustrations prevent sober judgment from spoiling the fun." Her illustrations for *Lizzy's Lion* brought Gay the Canada Council Literature Prize in illustration for an English-language book. Gay won this prize in 1984, the same year that she won for her "Drôle d'école" series. Her joint win of the Canada Council prize made Gay the first author to receive this award in both the French-language and English-language categories. In 1985, Gay produced *Mon Potager,* a board book for preschoolers that was the first of her works to be translated into English. Published in English as *The Garden,* this work introduces young children to the concept of vegetables. From this point onward, most of Gay's books have been published in both English and French.

Moonbeam on a Cat's Ear, is a picture book in verse about how two small children, Rose and Toby Toby, lasso and ride the moon before being driven back inside by a thunderstorm. A reviewer in *Children's Book News* called the work "a lovely book [that] has all the elements of a classic picturebook." Writing in *Books in Canada* about the reissued version of the book, Rhea Tregebov called the interplay of layout, text, and illustrations "not merely coherent, but brilliant"; she added that Gay's text "is marvellous poetry. Gay's use of rhyme and metre is so effective that the words have an inevitable feel to them, a hypnotic effect that only such poets as Dennis Lee and Gay seem able to create." In 1986, *Moonbeam on a Cat's Ear* received the Amelia Frances Howard-Gibbon Illustrator's Award.

Gay's next book, *Rainy Day Magic,* describes how two friends, Victor and Joey, engage in a fantasy that takes them to the jungle and under the sea after they are sent to the basement for being too loud. At the end of the book, the children are called back upstairs for dinner; however,

Joey sports a mauve starfish in her hair from her aquatic adventure. Compared to Maurice Sendak's classic picture book *Where the Wild Things Are, Rainy Day Magic* was praised for its charming story and energetic illustrations, and it received the Governor General's Literary Award for Illustration in 1987 and the Amelia Frances Howard-Gibbon Illustrator's Award in 1988.

Fat Charlie's Circus is one of Gay's most popular books. Fat Charlie is a small boy who wants to be a famous circus performer when he grows up. He practices stunts at home, such as lion-taming with his cat, walking the clothesline for a tightrope, training his goldfish to jump through a hoop, and juggling dinner plates. The results of his practicing often cause Fat Charlie's parents to get upset. In order to show his folks how wonderful he can be, Charlie decides to do a diving act: he intends to jump from the tallest tree in his backyard into a tiny glass of water. Once he is in the tree, Charlie realizes that he is too scared to dive or to come down; he is crestfallen and alone. Then, Charlie's grandmother climbs the tree, intending, she claims, to jump with Charlie. In helping her down, Charlie reaches safety on the ground while retaining his dignity. The book ends with Charlie and his grandmother working as a team, practicing their Bicycle Balancing Act. Writing in *Canadian Children's Literature,* Marie Davis commented, "Gay's narrative clearly moves towards insights about the relationship between imagination and reality and, more importantly, about the child's need for uncritical emotional support. And these insights are embedded in the text; like Charlie's grandmother, they are heartwarming and emerge naturally and quietly." Davis concluded that Fat Charlie's Circus has "an unusual depth—both in the carefully-shaded illustrations and the subtlety of the text." Writing in *Quill & Quire,* Callie Israel predicted that *Fat Charlie's Circus* was "sure to be a story-hour favorite," while Alison Mews, writing in *Canadian Materials,* called it a "wonderful story that begs to be shared with children."

The Three Little Pigs is Gay's first attempt at retelling an already popular story. In her version of the familiar tale in which the porcine characters defeat a predatory wolf, the author incorporates some techniques used in oral storytelling, such as colloquial expressions and asides to the audience. As for her illustration work, according to Joanne Findon in *Quill & Quire,* Gay's watercolors and figure drawings "are filled with colour and energy, spilling out of their borders and across the text pages.... Small details—leaves flying and raindrops blowing out of the illustrations and across the adjacent white spaces—create a satisfying sense of the oneness of words and pictures." Findon concluded by calling *The Three Little Pigs* a "lovely book that breathes life into a well-known tale." Gay's second picturebook retelling, *Rumpelstiltskin,* is often praised for the originality of its presentation. Dave Jenkinson noted in *Canadian Materials,* "Gay's text and illustrations soften the story for the intended audience. For example, the little man is comical, almost jester-like in appearance, and it is only the cobwebs in his hat, plus the creatures trailing behind him, that hint of his true

sinister nature." Writing in *School Library Journal,* Jeanne Clancy Watkins stated, "In this age of the lavishly illustrated fairy tale, Gay gives readers a version of the well-worn Grimm tale that is surprisingly and refreshingly childlike." *Rumpelstiltskin* was shortlisted for the Governor General's Literary Award for illustration in 1997.

Gay's two picture books about young siblings Stella and Sam—*Stella, Star of the Sea* and *Stella, Queen of the Snow*—have brought her special recognition. In the first story, which was inspired by Gay's childhood memories, little Stella and her younger brother, Sam, spend a day at the seashore. Sam is afraid of the water but curious about it. Since Stella had been at the sea once before, she is quick to answer his many questions with replies that blend realism with imagination. Finally, Sam joins his sister in the ocean. Gay uses watercolor and collage for her illustrations, which contain many visual details and, according to a reviewer in *Publishers Weekly,* "suggest an air of holiday abandon." *Canadian Materials* critic Helen Norrie predicted, "Children will identify with the reluctant Sam and enjoy both his questions and Stella's answers." In 2000, *Stella, Star of the Sea* received the Ruth Schwartz Children's Book Award and the Mr. Christie's Book Award.

Stella, Queen of the Snow continues the adventures of Stella and Sam. In this work, Sam sees his first snowstorm. He approaches the white world with caution and asks question after question about it. His big sister, the self-dubbed Queen of the Snow, answers them with a humorous combination of fantasy and fact. The children eat snowflakes, have a snowball fight, and make snow angels, among other activities. At the end of the book, Sam assures Stella that he can hear the snow angels singing. Writing in *School Library Journal,* Grace Oliff called *Stella, Queen of the Snow* "a charming story of successful sibling mentoring, simply but effectively told." Oliff added that Gay's line-and-watercolor illustrations "complement both the humor and the message of the tale."

In the picture book *On My Island,* a young boy and his animal companions—three ants, two cats, a wolf, and a bat—float on the sea on a small island. The boy complains that his life is boring. However, fantastic events take place all around him: a dragon swims past, kites rise to the sky, elephants parachute into the water, and a train circles the island. The irony lies in the fact that the boy and his friends are always looking the other way while these activities are going on. Gay's watercolor and collage art incorporates flower petals, fabrics, and bits of newspaper, while her use of type size—for example, when the narrator shouts over a stiff wind, the text is huge—takes on different configurations. According to *Booklist* contributor Carolyn Phelan, "the short, direct text, the well-composed double-page spreads, and the abundance of action in the illustrations combine to make this satisfying and enjoyable." In *School Library Journal,* Holly Belli noted that while it may be parents who appreciate the irony of the tale, "children will pore over the pictures and imagine islands of their own."

After she began working as a professional author and illustrator, Gay met David Homel, an award-winning American writer and translator. The couple have two sons, Gabriel and Jacob, who have served as the inspiration for several of Gay's works. In 1987 Gay decided to suspend her work as an editorial illustrator for adults in order to concentrate on writing and illustrating books for children. She wrote in *SAAS,* "The more specialized I became, the more I was offered projects addressed to children." Gay illustrated textbooks and posters and designed children's clothing and sets for animated films. In addition, she wrote three puppet plays and designed the puppets, costumes, and sets; these plays were performed by the Theatre de l'oeil, a Québec group that produces plays featuring puppets. Gay is also a regular speaker at schools and in conferences on children's literature. Since 1981 she has also been teaching illustration to students at the university level. As a writer, she is equally comfortable working in English and French. She told *SATA,* "I start writing something, and for some reason it just comes out in French or in English—and that's just the way it stays. I don't illustrate in French or English. I just illustrate, there's no language; that's the beauty of illustration." She continued, "I feel that I'm concentrating on a particular medium because it's for kids. I am geared towards kids in what I want to talk about to them and how to make them laugh, whether in clothing design, in the plays, or in the books. I'm happy about that. I finally got to where I don't have to worry about the rush of the adult world and the quick throwaway feeling you have."

Gay's themes often center on the power that children find in their imagination. She told *SATA,* "I try to tell children that there are other kinds of power [than that held by adults], such as the power of imagination, of learning, and the power of humor, being able to laugh at one's self. You find out as you are growing up that it is not necessary to envy the power that your parents have. That form is actually not the most important one." Regarding her own work, Gay told Marie Davis in *Canadian Children's Literature,* "Something that's exciting and that emotionally touches you: that's what I try to get when I write. . . . I want kids to identify with the kids in the story—even if they don't look like those kids, I want them to identify with the feel, the aura around the kids I draw." Gay wrote in *SAAS,* "When I write and illustrate for children, my primary concern is to tell a good story, a story that will capture their heart and minds. I want to create characters and emotional situations that children will recognize. I want children to identify with the joy, anger, frustration, laughter, fear, loneliness, doubt, and happiness of my characters. I accomplish this in two ways: the first, of course, is the story itself, which in most cases is inspired by an ordinary event, a domestic situation. . . . The other way

Ivy woke up and saw a turnip in the middle of her bedroom. It was almost as big as she was.
"I am a turnip," the turnip cried.
"I taste so good," the turnip lied.

A young girl who refuses to eat her vegetables faces unpleasant consequnces in **When Vegetables Go Bad!** *written by Don Gillmor and illustrated by Gay.*

to ensure emotional identification is through illustration. I want children to identify visually with my characters. That's why I've created a series of rather funny-looking kids ... not particularly pretty kids, but real kids! ... Another important aspect in the visual environment in my stories is the different subplots I introduce in the illustrations." She concluded, "When I hear people (adults, of course) saying that children are more interested in videos, electronic games and so on, and that books will disappear altogether in a few decades, I do not believe it for one minute. What's disappearing is the time to read books, the time to tell stories. Children are naturally curious, open to new ideas, ready to trade reality for fiction. They are still open to other ways of thinking, their prejudices yet to come. If children are exposed to a wide range of books, reading will eventually become an important aspect of their lives. I, for my part, will continue writing for them."

Biographical and Critical Sources

BOOKS

St. James Guide to Children's Writers, fifth edition, St. James Press (Detroit, MI), 1999.
Something about the Author Autobiography Series, Volume 21, Gale (Detroit, MI), 1996.

PERIODICALS

Booklist, March 15, 2001, Carolyn Phelan, review of *On My Island,* p. 1403; April 1, 2001, Shelle Rosenfeld, review of *Didi and Daddy on the Promenade,* p. 1480.
Books in Canada, December, 1984, Mary Ainslie Smith, review of *Lizzy's Lion,* p. 12; summer, 1992, Rhea Tregebov, review of *Moonbeam on a Cat's Ear,* p. 37.
Canadian Children's Literature, no. 54, 1989, Joan McGrath, review of *Moonbeam on a Cat's Ear,* pp. 67-69; no. 59, 1990, Marie Davis, "The Fantastic and the Familiar in 'Fat Charlie's Circus,'" pp. 75-77.
Canadian Materials, March, 1989, Leacy O'Brien, interview with Marie-Louise Gay, pp. 54-55; March, 1990, Alison Mews, review of *Fat Charlie's Circus,* p. 64; November 28, 1997, Dave Jenkinson, review of *Rumpelstiltskin;* November 28, 1999, Helen Norrie, review of *Stella, Star of the Sea.*
Children's Book News (Toronto, Ontario, Canada), June, 1986, review of *Moonbeam on a Cat's Ear,* p. 4.
Maclean's, December 10, 1984, John Bemrose and others, review of *Lizzy's Lion,* pp. 62-63.
Publishers Weekly, July 28, 1997, review of *Rumpelstiltskin,* p. 74; March 29, 1999, review of *Stella, Star of the Sea,* p. 102; November 20, 2000, review of *Yuck: A Love Story,* p. 67; February 12, 2001, review of *Didi and Daddy on the Promenade,* p. 210; March 26, 2001, review of *On My Island,* p. 92.
Quill & Quire, December, 1989, Callie Israel, review of Fat Charlie's Circus, p. 22; Number 60, 1990, interview with Marie Davis, pp. 52-74; December, 1993, Janet McNaughton, review of *Rabbit Blue,* p. 33; October, 1994, Joanne Findon, review of *The Three Little Pigs,* p. 41.
School Library Journal, November, 1997, Jeanne Clancy Watkins, review of *Rumpelstiltskin,* p. 107; October, 2000, Grace Oliff, review of *Stella, Queen of the Snow,* p. 125; July, 2001, Holly Belli, review of *On My Island,* p. 75.

ON-LINE

Canadian Children's Book Centre, http://www3.sympatico.ca/ (June 29, 2001), "Marie-Louise Gay."
Children's Literature by Canadian Authors, http://www.macabees.ab.ca/ (June 29, 2001), Marie-Louise Gay, commentary on *Stella, Star of the Sea.*
Groundwood Books, http://www.groundwoodbooks.com/ (June 29, 2001), "Authors: Marie-Louise Gay."
National Library of Canada, http://www.nlc-bnc.ca/ (June 28, 2001), "Cartoon Art: Marie-Louise Gay."
Online Guide to Writing in Canada, http://track0.com/ (June 28, 2001), "Online Guide to Canadian Authors Marie-Louise Gay."

—*Sketch by Gerard J. Senick*

*   *   *

GIBBS, Adrea 1960-

Personal

Born 1960, in Arcadia, CA. *Education:* La Salle University, M.S. (summa cum laude); Columbus University, Ph.D. (summa cum laude).

Addresses

Home—Simi Valley, CA. *Office*—c/o Author Mail, Meriwether Publishing, 885 Elkton Dr., Colorado Springs, CO 80907. *E-mail*—M2BSY@aol.com.

Career

Pacific International Consulting and Management, Taipei, Taiwan, director of entertainment and recreation, 1995-98; Boys and Girls Club of Hollywood, Hollywood, CA, program director, 1998-99; Oakbridge Athletic Club, Simi Valley, CA, director of children's programming. Director and choreographer for international and national programs; consultant to corporations, including Disneyland, Kidzfit International, and Gymboree, and the cultural ministries of Germany and Czechoslovakia. *Member:* International Association of Amusement Parks and Attractions, American Association of Fitness and Aerobics, IDEA, National Storytelling Network, Society of Children's Book Writers and Illustrators.

Writings

(Self-illustrated) *Let's Put On a Show! A Beginner's Theatre Handbook for Young Actors,* Meriwether Publishing (Colorado Springs, CO), 1999.

Let's Put On A Show!

A beginner's theatre handbook for young actors

ADREA GIBBS

Adrea Gibbs's handbook includes information on scripting, casting, sets, costumes, and makeup.

Work in Progress

"Physically fit" fairy tales; *The Story of Aunt Dia; Kidzfit Letters,* for Kidzfit International; research on women of the Old West.

Sidelights

Adrea Gibbs told *SATA:* "Imagination and creativity are my watch-words, particularly as our day-to-day existence becomes electronically possessed. I am inspired by my own love of reading and writing and my desire to see both youth and adults rediscover their own capacity for flexing their creative muscle."

*   *   *

GREEN, Cliff(ord) 1934-

Personal

Born December 6, 1934, in Melbourne, Victoria, Australia; son of Aubrey George (a draftsman) and Dorothy Jessie (a telegraphist; maiden name, Dowden) Green; married Judith Irene Painter (a secretary and manager), May 16, 1959; children: Amanda Susan Green Bence, Katherine Ann Green Ewart, Fiona Helen, David Michael. *Education:* Received primary teachers' certificate from Toorak Teachers' College.

Addresses

Home and office—23 Webb St., Warrandyte, Victoria 3113, Australia. *Agent*—Rick Raftos Management, P.O. Box 445, Paddington, NSW 2021, Australia.

Career

Apprentice in the printing trade in Melbourne, Victoria, Australia, 1951-56; Education Department of Victoria, head teacher in primary grades, 1960-69; Crawford Productions, Melbourne, Victoria, Australia, staff writer, beginning in 1969; freelance writer. Teacher of screen-writing at Victorian Council of Adult Education, Western Australian Institute of Technology, Australian Film and Television School, and Victorian College of the Arts; dramaturge at Australian National Playwrights' Conference. Founding member of board of directors of Victorian Film Corporation, 1977-84; founding vice president of Melbourne Writers' Theatre, 1983-84; member of convocation of Australian Film, Television and Radio School. *Member:* Australian Writers Guild (vice president, 1975-76; former member of national council), Warrandyte Historical Society (president, 1983-85).

Awards, Honors

Awards from Australian Writers' Guild, 1972, for documentary film *Moving On,* 1973, for quartet *Marion,* 1974, for feature film *Picnic at Hanging Rock,* 1976, for television adaptation *Power without Glory,* 1978, for television play *End of Summer,* 1979, for television adaptation *Lawson's Mates,* 1990, for television play *Boy Soldiers,* and 1992, for television drama *Phoenix;* Penguin Award from Television Society of Australia, 1974, for *Marion,* 1976, for *Power without Glory,* 1978, for *End of Summer,* and 1980, for television play *Burn the Butterflies;* Sammy Award, Variety Club of Australia, 1978, for *End of Summer;* best writer nomination for U.S. Science Fiction Film Awards, 1978, for *Picnic at Hanging Rock;* Liv Ullman Peace Prize, Chicago International Festival of Children's Films, 1990, for *Boy Soldiers;* Richard Lane Award, Australian Writers Guild, 1990, for service and dedication to the Guild; AFI nomination, 1992, for *Phoenix,* and 1995, for *Janus;* Australian Human Rights Award, 1995, for *Janus* episode "Fit to Plead."

Writings

The Incredible Steam-Driven Adventures of Riverboat Bill (for children; also see below), Hodder & Stoughton (London, England), 1975, Walter McVitty Books, 1995.

Break of Day (novel), Hodder & Stoughton (London, England), 1976.

The Sun Is Up (stories), Drummond, 1978.

The Further Adventures of Riverboat Bill (for children), Hodder & Stoughton (London, England), 1981.

The Art of Dale Marsh, privately printed, 1981.

Evergreen: The Story of a Family, privately printed, 1984.

Riverboat Bill Steams Again (for children), Hodder & Stoughton (London, England), 1985.

Boy Soldiers (for children; also see below), McPhee Gribble/Penguin Books, 1990.

STAGE PLAYS

Cop Out! (first produced in Melbourne, Victoria, Australia, at Russell Street Theatre, 1977), Yackandandah Playscripts, 1983.

Four Scripts, Hyland House, 1978.

Plays for Kids, Primary Education Publishing, 1981.

(Contributor) *Senior Drama,* Macmillan (New York, NY), 1985.

SCREENPLAYS

Picnic at Hanging Rock, Picnic Productions, 1975, published as *Picnic at Hanging Rock: A Film,* F. W. Cheshire, 1975.

Break of Day, Clare Beach Films, 1977.

Summerfield, Clare Beach Films, 1977.

(With Ellen Green) *Baby ... Secret of the Last Legend,* Touchstone Films, 1985.

Bless the Child (first draft, with Ellen Green), Paramount Pictures, 2000.

DOCUMENTARY FILMS

Big River, Australian Broadcasting Corp., 1969.

Light the Empty Places, Crawford Productions, 1970.

People on the Edge, Australian Broadcasting Corp., 1971.

The Lost People of Chowilla, Australian Broadcasting Corp., 1972.

(With Anne Brooksbank) *Moving On,* Commonwealth Film Unit, 1972.

One Good Reason, Commonwealth Film Unit, 1973.

TELEVISION SCRIPTS

Christmas at Boggy Creek (for children), Australian Broadcasting Corp., 1963.

The Ballad of Riverboat Bill (for children), Australian Broadcasting Corp., 1965.

The Treasure Hunters (for children), Murray-Golburn Television, 1968.

Marion (quartet; Australian Broadcasting Corp., 1973), Heinemann Educational, 1974.

End of Summer, Australian Broadcasting Corp., 1977.

Lawson's Mates (Australian Broadcasting Corp., 1978-79), Hyland House, 1980.

Burn the Butterflies (Australian Broadcasting Corp., 1979), Currency Press, 1979.

All the Green Year, Australian Broadcasting Corp., 1980.

Lucinda Brayford, Australian Broadcasting Corp., 1980.

I Can Jump Puddles, Australian Broadcasting Corp., 1980-81.

Mud, Bloody Mud, Australian Broadcasting Corp., 1985-86.

(With Mac Gudgeon) *The Petrov Affair* (mini-series), PBL Productions, 1986.

The Steam-Driven Adventures of Riverboat Bill (for children, animated), Phantascope, 1986.

Boy Soldiers (for children; also see writings above) Australian Children's Television Foundation, 1989.

Creator of, and writer for, television series *Mercury,* Australian Broadcasting Corp., 1995-96. Writer for popular television series, including *Homicide,* Crawford Productions, 1969-70; *Matlock Police,* Crawford Productions, 1970-71; *The Spoiler,* Gemini Productions, 1972; *Behind the Legend,* Australian Broadcasting Corp., 1972; *The Rise and Fall of Wellington Boots,* Australian Broadcasting Corp., 1973; *Rush,* Australian Broadcasting Corp., 1974; *Seven Ages of Man,* Australian Broadcasting Corp., 1975; *Power without Glory,* Australian Broadcasting Corp., 1975-76; *Against the Wind,* Pegasus Productions, 1978; *A Country Practice,* JNP Productions, 1984; *Special Squad,* Crawford Productions, 1984; *City West,* SBS/Ferryman Productions, 1984; *The Flying Doctors,* Crawford Productions, 1988, 1990; *Mission: Impossible,* Paramount, 1989; *Skirts,* Simpson Le Mesurier Films, 1990; *Phoenix,* Australian Broadcasting Corp., 1991; *Embassy,* Grundy/Australian Broadcasting Corp.; and *Janus,* Australian Broadcasting Corp., 1994. Writer for television adaptations, including *The Norman Lindsay Festival,* Australian Broadcasting Corp., 1973; *Power without Glory,* Australian Broadcasting Corp., 1975-76; and *I Can Jump Puddles,* Australian Broadcasting Corp., 1980-81.*

*   *   *

GROSSMAN, Bill 1948-

Personal

Born April 21, 1948, in Cleveland, OH; son of George (an engineer and company founder) and Phyllis (a homemaker; maiden name, Schmitt) Grossman; married Donna Anischik, May 29, 1977 (divorced, 1992); children: Joshua, Adam, Sally. *Education:* Renselaer Polytechnic Institute, B.S., 1976, M.B.A., 1977, M.S., 1979; University of Hartford, M.Ed., 1989. *Hobbies and other interests:* Storytelling.

Addresses

Home and office—Windsor, CT. *Agent*—Ginger Knowlton, Curtis Brown, Ltd., 10 Astor Place, New York, NY 10003.

Career

Computer software engineer and systems analyst in Connecticut, 1977-83; insurance actuary in Hartford, CT, 1983-88; Hebrew Academy of Greater Hartford, Bloomfield, CT, teacher, 1989-90; University of Hartford, West Hartford, CT, adjunct professor of mathematics, 1990—; writer. Worked variously as a "fast food griller, grounds crew laborer, art school model, telephone technician, warehouse worker, grave digger, factory laborer, construction worker, coal shoveler, assembly line worker, patent research assistant, moving and storage flunky, entrepreneur, Fuller Brush salesperson, steelworker, ski equipment salesperson, janitor, and

Little sister eats an increasing number of creatures in Bill Grossman's counting book. (Cover illustration by Kevin Hawkes.)

forklift operator," 1968-75. Coach for youth baseball, basketball, and soccer leagues, 1987—. *Military service:* U.S. Marine Corps Reserves, 1969-75. *Member:* Society of Children's Book Writers and Illustrator.

Awards, Honors

Publishers Weekly Editor's Choice Award, 1989, for *Tommy at the Grocery Store; Tommy at the Grocery Store* appeared on the Library of Congress List of Books for Children, 1989; Children's Choice Awards, Children's Book Council and International Reading Association, 1989, for *Donna O'Neeshuck Was Chased By Some Cows,* and 1991, for *The Guy Who Was Five Minutes Late;* Georgia Picture Storybook Award Masterlist nominations, 1989, for *Donna O'Neeshuck Was Chased By Some Cows,* and 1990, for *Tommy at the Grocery Store;* California Young Reader Medal Masterlist nomination, 1991, for *Tommy at the Grocery Store;* Colorado Children's Book Award Masterlist nomination, 1992, for *Tommy at the Grocery Store.*

Writings

Don't Keep Your Head Down, Vantage (New York, NY), 1987.
Donna O'Neeshuck Was Chased By Some Cows, illustrated by Sue Truesdell, Harper (New York, NY), 1988.
Tommy at the Grocery Store, illustrated by Victoria Chess, Harper (New York, NY), 1989.

The Guy Who Was Five Minutes Late, illustrated by Judy Glasser, Harper (New York, NY), 1990.
Cowboy Ed, illustrated by Florence Wint, Harper (New York, NY), 1993.
The Banging Book, illustrated by Robert Zimmerman, HarperCollins (New York, NY), 1995.
My Little Sister Ate One Hare, illustrated by Kevin Hawkes, Crown (New York, NY), 1996.
The Bear Whose Bones Were Jezebel Jones, illustrated by Jonathan Allen, Dial (New York, NY), 1997.
My Little Sister Hugged an Ape, Random House (New York, NY), 1999.
Timothy Tunny Swallowed a Bunny, illustrated by Kevin Hawkes, Laura Geringer Books (New York, NY), 2000.

Also author of *Children's Verses,* Harper (New York, NY); *The Horrible Singing,* Harper (New York, NY); and *What's Wrong with the Way That I Look?,* Harper (New York, NY). Contributor of stories to *Northeast* and *Marlow RFD.*

Sidelights

Bill Grossman is the author of humorous, rhyming picture books. He once told *SATA* that he has been telling stories all his life, learning to do so from his parents, who would make up bedtime stories for him and his siblings. Grossman's interest in rhyme and poetry began in high school, when he often had to memorize lengthy poems on Saturdays as a punishment for his tardiness. He related to *SATA* that, "although those Saturday sessions did not correct my character flaws, they did instill in me a greater appreciation for rhyming verse and showed me enough examples of it to guide me in formulating my own opinions as to how such verse should be written. I am sure that it is no coincidence that the rhyming verse stories I write today are generally similar in structure and length to the poems I had to memorize. . . ."

Although much of Grossman's writing contains rhyming verse, he began his publishing career by issuing several adult short stories in such periodicals as *Northeast.* Soon thereafter, however, Harper & Row (now HarperCollins) accepted his first rhyming picture book, *Donna O'Neeshuck Was Chased by Some Cows,* for publication. Since then, although he has held several jobs, including being a teacher, mathematician, and college professor, Grossman has continued to write rhyming stories, including such titles as *Cowboy Ed, The Guy Who Was Five Minutes Late,* and *Timothy Tunny Swallowed a Bunny.*

In *The Guy Who Was Five Minutes Late,* Grossman tells the story of a baby who was born five minutes late, and grows up being five minutes tardy for everything. That is until he meets Princess Carrie, his true love, whose hand he wins because she also does not like being on time. Mary Harris Veeder, writing in Chicago *Tribune Books,* noted that Grossman is a writer who deserves the moniker " 'rollicking' " for his work, going on to declare that this tale in particular is a "wonderful read-aloud."

Similarly, *Cowboy Ed* tells, in rhyming verse, the tale of Ed, a cowboy who takes a journey into a fantasy frontier, a place where horses ride the cowboys and people "put their underwear on last." A reviewer for *Publishers Weekly* praised both the humorous text and colorful illustrations of this work, calling it a "pithy plug for independent thinking."

Grossman's *The Banging Book* conveys the value of building things versus breaking them in this story about four children who, amidst alliterative rhymes, break apart several toys and then put them back together. A *Kirkus Reviews* contributor noted that while children will enjoy the action of this book, parents reading to them will also relish the tongue-in-cheek aspect of the book's message.

In his next book, *The Bear Whose Bones Were Jezebel Jones,* Grossman tells the tale of a little girl who jumps into a bear's skin while the bear is out snorkeling. Unfortunately, she realizes only after she is in the skin that no one except the bear can unzip her. In *My Little Sister Ate One Hare,* Grossman recounts the epicurean adventures of the narrator's little sister, who eats everything from ants to snakes and bats. As J. Patrick Lewis noted in the *New York Times Book Review,* both the characters in the book as well as its readers will "gawk" at this book in "bug-eyed wonder." Grossman's next book, *Timothy Tunny Swallowed a Bunny,* offers readers a collection of eighteen short verses about characters with funny names who meet equally funny fates. Multiple noses, ballooning waistlines, and flat-tened characters abound in this "promising read-aloud choice" said a reviewer for *Publishers Weekly.* Connie Fletcher noted in *Booklist* that the breakneck rhymes and wordplays in the book "will appeal to young children's love of the outlandish," while *School Library Journal* reviewer Louise L. Sherman predicted that "these ridiculously funny rhymes will tickle funny bones."

Biographical and Critical Sources

PERIODICALS

Booklist, February 15, 2001, Connie Fletcher, review of *Timothy Tunny Swallowed a Bunny,* p. 1140.

Horn Book, March, 2001, review of *Timothy Tunny Swallowed a Bunny,* p. 221.

Kirkus Reviews, May 1, 1995, review of *The Banging Book,* p. 634.

New York Times Book Review, July 4, 1993, review of *Cowboy Ed,* p. 16; March 16, 1997, J. Patrick Lewis, review of *My Little Sister Ate One Hare,* p. 26.

Publishers Weekly, June 7, 1993, review of *Cowboy Ed,* p. 69; May 29, 1995, review of *The Banging Book,* p. 83; July 21, 1997, review of *The Bear Whose Bones Were Jezebel Jones,* p. 201; October 5, 1998, review of *My Little Sister Ate One Hare,* p. 93; December 18, 2000, review of *Timothy Tunny Swallowed a Bunny,* p. 77.

School Library Journal, March, 2001, Louise L. Sherman, review of *Timothy Tunny Swallowed a Bunny,* p. 236.

Tribune Books (Chicago, IL), March 11, 1990, Mary Harris Veeder, review of *The Guy Who Was Five Minutes Late,* p. 6.*

H

HANDLER, Daniel
See SNICKET, Lemony

*   *   *

HANNA, William (Denby) 1910-2001

OBITUARY NOTICE—See index for *SATA* sketch: Born July 14, 1910, in Melrose, NM; died March 22, 2001, in North Hollywood, CA. Animator, director, producer, and author. Hanna was co-animator, co-author, and co-director, with Joseph Barbera, of such cartoon series as *The Flintstones,* a Golden Globe winner, *Tom and Jerry,* which earned seven Academy Awards, and *The Jetsons.* The duo came together first in 1937 while working for MGM studios, where they captured audiences with cartoon-spliced films such as *Anchors Aweigh.* In 1957 they founded Hanna-Barbera Productions, and in the years thereafter created and drew numerous cartoons. In addition to the dozens of cartoons he developed with Barbera, Hanna's other creative work includes serving as producer of *The Flintstones* movie, and as director of such cartoon shorts as *Hard Luck Duck.*

OBITUARIES AND OTHER SOURCES:

BOOKS

Contemporary Theatre, Film and Television, Volume 30, Gale (Detroit, MI), p. 171.

PERIODICALS

Chicago Tribune, March 23, 2001, section 2, p. 10.
Los Angeles Times, March 23, 2001, p. B6.
New York Times, March 23, 2001, p. A16.
Times (London, England), March 24, 2001.
Washington Post, March 23, 2001, p. B7.

HARPER, Betty 1946-

Personal

Born October 4, 1946, in Bartow, FL; daughter of Dorsey E. (in the Air Force) and Mary A. (a homemaker) Hall; children: Brian W., Jr., Esther Kaplan, Bridget, Loretta, James. *Education:* Attended Abilene Christian University and the American Academy in Paris.

Betty Harper

From **Enid and the Dangerous Discovery,** *written by Cynthia Williams and illustrated by Harper.*

Addresses

Home and office—274 Old Shackle Is. Rd., Hendersonville, TN 37075. *E-mail*—betjam911@aol.com.

Career

Artist and illustrator. Formerly employed at J. Robert Gallery, Hendersonville, TN. Has designed numerous album covers for RCA, Jim Reeves Enterprises, Loretta Lynn, and others; provided design and drawings for the Graceland International Tribute Week, 1982-86, and other commissioned paintings and drawings. *Exhibitions:* Harper's work has been exhibited at the American Pop Culture Gallery, Nashville, TN, Local Color Gallery, Nashville, TN, Memphis Music and Heritage Festival, Memphis, TN, Gestine's Gallery, Memphis, TN, Tennessee Artist Gallery, Nashville, TN, and in Tokyo, Japan.

Writings

SELF-ILLUSTRATED

Elvis: Newly Discovered Drawings of Elvis Presley, Bantam Books (New York, NY), 1979.
Suddenly and Gently: Visions of Elvis through the Art of Betty Harper, St. Martin's Press (New York, NY), 1987.

Also author of *Magic of Elvis,* 1985.

ILLUSTRATOR

Cynthia G. Williams, *Enid and the Church Fire,* Doorway (Nashville, TN), 1999.
Cynthia G. Williams, *Enid and the Dangerous Discovery,* Broadman & Holman (Nashville, TN), 1999.
Cynthia G. Williams, *Enid and the Great Idea,* Broadman & Holman (Nashville, TN), 2000.
Cynthia G. Williams, *Enid and the Homecoming,* Broadman & Holman (Nashville, TN), 2000.
Muriel F. Blackwell, *How Do I Become a Christian?,* Broadman & Holman (Nashville, TN), 2000.

Illustrator for James Wright's *Legendary Tales of the Old South,* 2000. Cover art provided for a number of books published by Propwash Publishing, including *Elvis through My Eyes, The Sun Years,* and *The Tupelo Years,* all by Bill E. Burk, and *Soldier Boy Elvis,* by Burk and Ira Jones, and for *Presleyana,* by Jerry Osborne, and *Dispelling the Myths,* by Todd Rheingold.

Sidelights

Betty Harper told *SATA:* "I want my drawings to have so much emotional impact that the subject becomes secondary. Drawing has been my life, my means of expression of all that I think and feel."

Biographical and Critical Sources

ON-LINE

Betty Harper Web site, http://www.bettyharper.com (December 14, 2000).

*   *   *

HEHENBERGER, Shelly 1968-

Personal

Born May 14, 1968, in Ohio; daughter of Jackie Grafton Houg (a medical transcriptionist); married Thomas Hehenberger (a student), October 5, 1990. *Education:* Indiana University, degree in fine arts and graphic design, 1990; University of Cincinnati, M.F.A., 1994. *Religion:* Lutheran.

Addresses

Home—4205 Horry St. #A-7, Columbia, SC 29203. *Agent*—HK Portfolio, 666 Greenwich St. #860, New York, NY 10014. *E-mail*—tshehenberger@hotmail.com.

Career

Freelance illustrator, 1995—. Former art teacher in Cincinnati, OH.

Illustrator

A Surprising Summer, Scholastic (New York, NY), 1997.
The Cowboys of Argentina, Scott Foresman, 1998.
Ellen Levine, *If You Lived with the Iroquois,* Scholastic (New York, NY), 1998.

Shelly Hehenberger's richly colored art illustrates James Berry's Isn't My Name Magical? *in which dreamer Dreena and skateboarder Delroy write poems about themselves, their family, and their friends.*

James Berry, *Isn't My Name Magical?: Sister and Brother Poems,* Simon & Schuster (New York, NY), 1999.

B. J. Reinhard, *Sanji's Seed,* Bethany Backyard (Minneapolis, MN), 2000.

Juwanda G. Ford, *Together for Kwanzaa,* Random House (New York, NY), 2000.

Joyce Milton, *Pocahontas: American Princess,* Grosset & Dunlap (New York, NY), 2000.

Joyce Milton, *Sacajawea,* Putnam (New York, NY), 2001.

Work in Progress

A young adult fiction work titled *The Burning Ground.*

Sidelights

Shelly Hehenberger told *SATA:* "Ever since I was very young, I have always loved making pictures and telling stories. I am particularly interested in themes that are cross cultural, or that teach specific ideas/virtues. I had many picture books as a child and continue collecting to this day. My most successful project has been *Sanji's Seed,* which teaches the value of honesty. In the future, I look forward to writing the books that I illustrate, and/or writing young adult fiction titles. I have been an art teacher, working with all ages, since 1993, and am currently working with ages 4-6 at an early childhood development center."

Hehenberger is an illustrator who works in pastels and colored pencils, lending the stories and poems she portrays a richly colored palette. In James Berry's *Isn't My Name Magical? Sister and Brother Poems,* for example, Hehenberger chose a bright color for the background of each spread, and in the foreground realistically depicted Dreena and Delroy in a busy, ordinary milieu. Brother and sister's different perspectives on family, friends, and favorite activities are highlighted in the poems that each sibling narrates. Hehenberger's illustrations were credited with augmenting the emotional impact of the poems. "Rich hues of magenta, purple, and blue declare the magic of Dreena and Delroy's ordinary world," remarked Susan P. Bloom in *Horn Book. Booklist* reviewer Susan Dove Lempke remarked that "Hehenberger's intensely glowing pastel-and-colored-pencil drawings" will increase the attractiveness of *Isn't My Name Magical* for students, teachers, and parents, while *School Library Journal* contributor Nancy Menaldi-Scanlan concluded: "This will be a good choice for encouraging youngsters to write poetry about the people and activities that form the basis of their own lives."

Hehenberger is also the illustrator for *Together for Kwanzaa,* a story written by Juwanda G. Ford about a girl anxiously awaiting the arrival of her older brother from school, where he is snowed in over the holiday. The story teaches readers about the seven days of

Kwanzaa, the seven candles, and the seven principles associated with them, including Swahili names.

Biographical and Critical Sources

PERIODICALS

Booklist, February 15, 1999, Susan Dove Lempke, review of *Isn't My Name Magical?,* p. 1072.

Horn Book, March, 1999, Susan P. Bloom, review of *Isn't My Name Magical?,* p. 215.

Publishers Weekly, May 3, 1999, "Kindred Poems," p. 78; September 25, 2000, Elizabeth Devereaux, "Kwanzaa Note," p. 67.

School Library Journal, March, 1999, Nancy Menaldi-Scanlan, review of *Isn't My Name Magical?,* p. 190.

ON-LINE

H K Portfolio, http://www.hkportfolio.com/ (September 23, 2001), biography of Shelly Hehenberger.*

*   *   *

HILL, Kirkpatrick 1938-

Personal

Born April 30, 1938; daughter of William Clifton Hill (a mining engineer) and Isabel Stirling Matson (an office worker); divorced; children: Matt, Shannon, Kirk, Crystal, Mike, Sean. *Education:* Attended University of Alaska; Syracuse University, B.S., 1969. *Politics:* "Liberal." *Hobbies and other interests:* Music, art history, cooking, books, animals, film.

Addresses

Home—Box 53, Ruby, AK 99768 (summer); Box 84435, Fairbanks, AK 99708 (winter). *E-mail*—kirkpatrick@mosquitonet.com.

Career

Author and educator. Elementary school teacher in Alaska, 1969-91.

Awards, Honors

Toughboy and Sister was named a Junior Literary Guild Selection, 1990; Blue Ribbon Award, Bulletin of the Center for Children's Books, 1991; Children's Book Award Master List citations in Rhode Island, Alaska, and Kansas, 1993; Berlin Senate Commissioner for Foreigners' Affairs Award, 1997, for *Winter Camp;* Once upon a World Book Award, Simon Wiesenthal Center, Museum of Tolerance, for The Year of Miss Agnes, 2001; Dorothy Canfield Fisher Award finalist, 2002. Has also received nominations for the Young Hoosier Award, William Allen White Children's Book Award, Rebecca Caudill Young Reader's Book Award, Dorothy Canfield Fisher Children's Book Award, Penn, Norma Klein Award, and the Nebraska Golden Sower Award.

Writings

Toughboy and Sister, Margaret K. McElderry (New York, NY), 1990.

Winter Camp, Margaret K. McElderry (New York, NY), 1993.

The Year of Miss Agnes, Margaret K. McElderry (New York, NY), 2000.

Toughboy and Sister and *Winter Camp* have been translated into German, Danish, Italian, and braille.

Sidelights

Kirkpatrick Hill is the author of several short novels that introduce young readers to life in the Alaskan wilderness areas known as the bush. In *Toughboy and Sister, The Winter Camp,* and *The Year of Miss Agnes,* Hill "lets the audience live inside her story, and in fortifying her characters she fortifies readers too," according to Elizabeth Devereaux in the *New York Times Book Review.* The novels are told entirely from their child protagonist's point of view, allowing readers to identify with the fear, grief, and resolve these young people experience

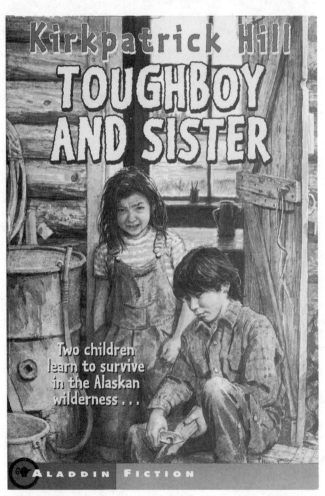

Eleven-year-old Toughboy and his sister are stranded at a fishing cabin on the Yukon River after the death of their drunken father in Kirkpatrick Hill's survival story. (Cover illustration by Peter Knorr.)

while surviving the harsh conditions of Alaska. "If good children's books got the attention they deserve, Kirkpatrick Hill would be a name known to everyone," Devereaux concluded.

Hill was born in 1938, and spent her first years in a mining camp outside Fairbanks, Alaska. "We moved into Fairbanks so I could go to school," she once related to *SATA*. After graduating from high school, she enrolled at the University of Alaska, but left when she got married. With one, then two, then three children at home, Hill found the time to go back to school to complete her studies, and received her bachelor's degree from Syracuse University in 1969. Three more children followed, after Hill began a teaching career that took her back to the Alaskan bush.

"One day, when I'd taken a year off from teaching to be home with my youngest child," Hill remembered, "I decided that it was the right time to write. I was going to write the Great Alaskan Novel. There are Alaskan novels, of course, but most are romantic clichés, full of absurd situations which could never happen in Alaska. Jack London's stories of Alaska and the Yukon Territory are incredibly popular all over the world. But Jack was only here a year. He got some things right, but he got a whole lot wrong. For the next five months I wrote the Great Alaskan Novel. It was pretty terrible."

Hill decided that she needed some practice in writing in different genres, and one summer, when circumstances allowed her the time, she decided to try her hand at writing a children's book. "I wanted to write a truly realistic children's book about real Yukon village kids, something especially for the kids I taught. I wanted it to be absolutely authentic, without any romanticizing about Alaskan life."

She quickly discovered writing for young people to be "engrossing, demanding, and exhilarating. I felt rather foolish for not having tried it to begin with. After all, I had literally spent my entire life with children. First I *was* a child, and then I had six of my own, and then I began teaching, so it was kids, kids, kids, all day long, all my life long. I thought like a kid, had a kid's point of view, remembered what it felt like to be a kid, and found that in a group of people I always gravitated towards the kids. So of course I like writing for kids."

Hill's editor, the author noted, "pointed out things in the book which would be obscure to a non-Alaskan kid, words we use differently, perhaps, or objects they'd never seen, like a fish-wheel or a kicker. But she let me leave in all the Yukon-ese, all the down-river speech patterns. That was very important to me because the speech has to be right if the book's going to be an authentic picture of our life."

With the editor's help, *Toughboy and Sister* was published in 1990. The book tells the story of two Athabascan Indian children, who are forced to survive on their own after their mother dies during childbirth and their father, an alcoholic who cannot get over the loss of

Ten-year-old Frederika describes a year spent under the tutelage of the inspiring Miss Agnes in her 1948 Alaskan village. (Cover illustration by Peter Knorr.)

his wife, meets his death in a boating accident at a fishing camp on the Yukon river. Eleven-year-old John and his sister, nine-year-old Annie Laurie, find themselves left in this remote area and must rely on their wits to survive. Calling *Toughboy and Sister* a "strong, satisfying short novel accessible to very young readers," Betty Levin added in the *New York Times Book Review* that "Hill has achieved a sense of a world that spans two cultures and a feeling for two children whose clear and convincing voices speak to us across the divide."

Hill was pleased that the publisher "didn't shy away from the grim aspects of *Toughboy and Sister*. There are a lot of bad things that happen to the children in this book and they didn't ask me to water it down. Life in Alaskan villages is decidedly rough. We have the highest rate of alcoholism in the United States, the highest accident rate, and the highest infant mortality rate. You probably wouldn't believe some of the things our kids go through on a day-to-day basis. I want to write about those things honestly."

In Hill's second novel, 1994's *Winter Camp,* Toughboy and Sister return. They have found a new home with their neighbor, an elderly Alaskan woman named Natasha, who brings them with her to her winter trapping camp during the month of October. Falls through the ice, attacks by moose, and the endless search for enough firewood to keep the trappers warm punctuate an experience during which Sister learns to abhor the cruelty of animal trapping. Praising the novel, a *Kirkus Reviews* critic noted that Hill's "portrayal of these competent, courageous children battling the intense cold is compelling."

In her third novel, *The Year of Miss Agnes,* Hill introduces readers to ten-year-old Frederika, whose feelings about schoolwork change drastically when a new teacher named Miss Agnes comes to the small, one-room schoolhouse in Frederika's remote Abathascan village. While many teachers have come and gone—some lasting only a few weeks—Miss Agnes is here to stay, and inspires Fred and her friends with her creativity and excitement over learning. Told in what *Horn Book* reviewer Roger Sutton described as Fredrerika's "distinct and definite voice," Hill captivates her readers with "the anecdotes about Miss Agnes's masterful teaching methods," creating a novel Sutton dubbed "always true and involving."

When Hill receives letters from children, they often ask her if the things that happen in her books are true. "Almost all of the events that pop into my head are real and have happened to my family or to someone else I know," Hill explained. "Life in the Alaskan bush is very adventurous, and strange things are always happening. My six kids have enough mishaps between them to keep me writing for years!"

Hill and her youngest daughter spend the summers in their large house near the Yukon village of Ruby. "The house is full of dogs and cats and kids and books and music. In between working on the house, starting the light plant, hauling water, cutting wood, baking bread, and all the innumerable bush chores, I keep trying to find the time to write. In the winter we live in Fairbanks, where all my children work at their various jobs and I maintain what my son calls 'mission control.'

"Having a book published is like dropping a rock in a pond," Hill once told *SATA.* "The ripples—like getting letters from readers—continually surprise me. I can't believe that the ripples have spread so far, and for so long. Maybe I'll be getting letters ten, twenty, thirty years from now. All from the work of a few summer weeks. It's quite amazing. And now *Toughboy and Sister* is ... translated into German, so there will be German kids reading about my Yukon River kids. That's a trans-Atlantic ripple!"

Biographical and Critical Sources

PERIODICALS

Horn Book, November, 2000, Roger Sutton, *The Year of Miss Agnes,* p. 755.
Kirkus Reviews, November 15, 1993, review of *Winter Camp,* p. 1461.
New York Times Book Review, April 14, 1991, Betty Levin, review of *Toughboy and Sister,* p. 19; March 13, 1994, review of *Winter Camp,* p. 20; January 21, 2001, Elizabeth Devereaux, review of *The Year of Miss Agnes,* p. 24.
School Library Journal, December, 2000, review of *The Year of Miss Agnes,* pp. 53-54.

*　　*　　*

HOL, Coby 1943-

Personal

Born October 22, 1943, in Leiden, Netherlands; married Frans W. M. Hol, November 27, 1969; children: Esther, Martijn. *Education:* Received degree from the Royal Academy of Fine Arts (The Hague), 1968; also earned teaching certificates in drawing, handicraft, and textiles from 1970 to 1984. *Religion:* Roman Catholic.

Addresses

Office—Van Vreumingenstraat 3, 2801 AV Gouda, Netherlands.

Career

Teacher of drawing in secondary schools 1975-79, and of handicraft and textiles at a primary school, 1979—; illustrator and author of picture books, 1989—. *Member:* Stichting Schrijvers School and Samenleving.

Coby Hol

Writings

A Visit to the Farm, North-South, 1989, published in the Netherlands as *De Zonnehoeve,* Christofoor (Zeist, Netherlands), 1989.

Lisa and the Snowman, North-South, 1989, published in the Netherlands as *Sanne en de sneeuwpop,* De Vier Windstreken, 1989.

Tippy Bear Goes to a Party, North-South, 1991, published in the Netherlands as *Tippie viert carnaval,* De Vier Windstreken, 1991.

Tippy Bear Hunts for Honey, North-South, 1991, published in the Netherlands as *Tippie zoekt honing,* De Vier Windstreken, 1991.

Tippy Bear and Little Sam, North-South, 1992, published in the Netherlands as *Een neefje voor Tippie,* De Vier Windstreken, 1992.

Tippy Bear's Christmas, North-South, 1992, published in the Netherlands as *Het kerstfeest van Tippie,* De Vier Windstreken, 1992.

Henrietta Saves the Show, North-South, 1992, published in the Netherlands as *Het avontuur van de kleine witte pony,* De Vier Windstreken, 1992.

Niki's Little Donkey, North-South, 1993, published in the Netherlands as *Niki's ezeltje,* De Vier Windstreken, 1993.

Punch and His Friends, Floris Books, 1994, published in the Netherlands as *Jan Klaassen zoekt zijn vriendjes,* Christofoor (Zeist, Netherlands), 1994.

Tom et Puce, Hatier Littérature Générale (Paris, France), 1996.

Petit Nuage, Hatier Littérature Générale (Paris, France), 1996, published in the Netherlands and Belgium as *Wolkje,* De Eenhoorn (Wielsbeke, Belgium), 1999.

La naissance de la lune, Hatier Littérature Générale (Paris, France), 1998, published in the Netherlands and Belgium as *Een licht in de nacht,* De Eenhoorn (Wielsbeke, Belgium), 1998, translated by Sibylle Kazeroid as *The Birth of the Moon,* North-South, 2000.

Le secret de l'étoile; une histoire de Noël, Hatier Littérature Générale (Paris, France), 1999, published in the Netherlands and Belgium as *Een ster met een geheim,* De Eenhoorn (Wielsbeke, Belgium), 1999.

Petit Agneau et l'arc-en-ciel, Hatier Littérature Générale (Paris, France), 2000, published in the Netherlands and Belgium as *Lammetje en de regenboog,* De Eenhoorn (Wielsbeke, Belgium), 2000.

Les petit princes, Hatier Littérature Générale (Paris, France), 2001, published in the Netherlands and Belgium as *Koningskindern,* De Eenhoorn (Wielsbeke, Belgium), 2001.

Hol's works have been translated and published in ten languages, including German, Japanese, and Korean.

Work in Progress

A new picture book, expected to be published in 2002.

Sidelights

A native of the Dutch city of Leiden, Coby Hol writes and illustrates picture books for young readers that have been published throughout Europe and other parts of the world. Most of her works have also been translated into English. An art teacher to young children by profession, Hol creates colorful collages from magazine paper to illustrate charming stories that often feature curious and gentle animals.

Coby told *SATA,* "I started making picture books when my two children were young. We often visited a so-called 'children's farm.' There children in cities in Holland can see, feed, and caress several farm animals. There were also school gardens and an herb garden. It was a little paradise for me and the children. I often made sketches there, and afterwards at home I made collages from torn magazine paper. That was the beginning of my first picture book, *A Visit to the Farm,* published in English in 1989 by North-South, with my own children in the central role."

A Visit to the Farm was the first of her works to appear also in English translation. The story revolves around a little boy and his sister who have been sent to the local farmer to buy eggs, milk, and cheese. First, however, they pay visits to all their favorite animals, including the cow, a goat, and some pigs. Toward the close, the farmer's wife provides them with a filled basket to take home. "Hol convincingly transmits the headiness of a day in the country," noted a *Publishers Weekly* reviewer who also praised Hol's collage illustrations as "truly remarkable."

In another work that appeared in 1989, *Lisa and the Snowman* features a little girl who loses her favorite red hat after a day of winter fun. She and her mother head out in the snow the next day to find it and take it from the head of a snowman, who seems dejected to lose it. Lisa comes back with a bag of hats from home and tries all of them on him, and it is her grandfather's battered fedora that seems to please him finally. "Hol has composed expressive, articulated figures with a three-dimensional effect," observed Virginia Opocensky in a *School Library Journal* review. Hol told *SATA* that "memories from my own youth in the snow, my day-to-day life with my children and winter holidays in Austria are some of the sources" for *Lisa and the Snowman.*

In *Henrietta Saves the Show,* Hol's 1992 torn-paper collage story, the title character is a sweet white pony who works on a farm. When the star horse in a local circus becomes ill, Henrietta is recruited to stand in and thoroughly enjoys her brief foray into show business. Nancy Seiner's *School Library Journal* review called it a "tidy, satisfying story," and found that Hol's collage figures "form pleasing patterns."

Hol has also written and illustrated several works starring little Tippy Bear, a likable animal with whom preschoolers might identify. Her titles include *Tippy Bear Goes to a Party* and *Tippy Bear and Little Sam,* a 1992 work in which Tippy visits his infant cousin and learns about caring for newborns.

When Lisa woke up one Sunday morning, she heard her friends laughing and shouting outside. She jumped up and went to the window.
"Hurray!" she said. "It snowed last night!"
She quickly got dressed. She put on a warm yellow sweater and the red hat that her grandmother had knitted for her.

Lisa's snowman needs just the right hat in Hol's **Lisa and the Snowman,** *illustrated with torn-paper collages on watercolor backdrops.*

In *Niki's Little Donkey,* published in the United States in 1993, a little girl on a Greek island becomes upset when she learns that her parents plan to sell the new little donkey recently born on their property. Niki and her grandmother devise an alternative plan, and instead of whiling away her idle hours at play, Niki helps out at her grandmother's home and even waits tables at the local café owned by her uncle. When market day comes, she surprises her family by buying the little donkey herself with her savings. Ilene Cooper, reviewing the title for *Booklist,* praised Hol's magazine-paper collages as "delightful and an excellent choice to portray" the blue skies and white stone dwellings of this part of the Mediterranean.

The Birth of the Moon imagines a long-ago time when the sky was completely dark at night. Animals could not see, and so a group of them—three ducks, a snake, and a turtle—ask the sun to shed a bit of its light in the evening hours as well. The sun obliges and arranges for a crescent moon to hang overhead, but it is still not enough for them. The animals pester the sun until he makes the moon grow into a full orb—and then the sun becomes angry when the animals do not seem very grateful for his services. In retaliation, he shrinks the moon down again. A compromise is reached that pleases all—and reminds the animals not to take such marvels for granted. "As befits a story about cosmic origins, the world Hol details feels newly minted and poignantly fragile," commented a *Publishers Weekly* reviewer. Carolyn Phelan, writing in *Booklist,* called Hol's collages "quite satisfying in their simplicity, beauty, and narrative clarity."

"*The Birth of the Moon,*" Hol told *SATA,* "is one of my favorites. I discovered the white ducks on the island of Samos in Greece, where we spent our holidays. I made a lot of drawings of them and tried some stories. Later I decided it had to be a story with the white ducks and the moon. During a later stay on the island of Ikaria in Greece, my husband got the idea to tell a story about the birth of the moon and why it waxes and wanes. This book is now published in five languages and will be published in Korea and Brazil also."

Hol told *SATA* about *Punch and His Friends:* "For *Punch and His Friends,* published in English in 1994 by Floris Books, I made drawings in some of the old historical cities of Holland like Leiden, Delft, and Amsterdam. For the past seven years I have lived in one of these old cities, Gouda, where I also had spent my school period. The idea for this picture book started with a miniature toy of Punch. One can move his arms and legs. I have used toys for a story several times.

"In my work as a teacher of handicrafts at a primary school," Hol continued, "it is my most important goal to stimulate the children to be creative themselves. I am very fond of the things they make and the joy that it gives to them. Of course they inspire me a lot, too!

"Important for me when I started to make pictures books were Eric Carle and Leo Leonni. They also use the collage technique, and I like them very much. Max Velthuijs, one of the most prominent illustrator/writers of picture books in Holland and one of my former teachers at the Academy of Fine Arts, advised me in 1987 to show my work to publishers at the International Children's Book Fair in Bologna, Italy. I also like the work of Susanne Rotraut Berner, Wolf Erlbruch, Kveta Pacovska, Lucy Cousins, Anna Höglund, and many more. During my work, I always listen to music.... Every picture book is a new adventure. I hope to make a lot more!"

Biographical and Critical Sources

PERIODICALS

Booklist, June 1, 1993, Ilene Cooper, review of *Niki's Little Donkey,* pp. 1857-1858; June 1, 2000, Carolyn Phelan, review of *The Birth of the Moon,* pp. 1908-1909.

Horn Book, July, 1991, review of *Henrietta Saves the Show,* p. 486.

Publishers Weekly, April 28, 1989, review of *A Visit to the Farm,* p. 78; August 30, 1991, review of *Tippy Bear Goes to a Party,* p. 81; February 28, 2000, review of *The Birth of the Moon,* p. 79.

School Library Journal, November, 1989, Eldon Younce, review of *A Visit to the Farm,* pp. 83-84; December, 1989, Virginia Opocensky, review of *Lisa and the Snowman,* p. 82; January, 1992, Nancy Seiner, review of *Henrietta Saves the Show,* p. 91; June, 1992, Anna Biagioni Hart, review of *Tippy Bear and Little Sam,* p. 95; May, 2000, Susan Knell, review of *The Birth of the Moon,* p. 142.

*   *   *

HOWE, Norma 1930-

Personal

Born February 7, 1930, in San Jose, CA; daughter of Daniel and Josephine (DiVittorio) Nadeau; married Bob Howe (a teacher, education administrator, and author; retired), 1951; six children. *Education:* San Jose State University, B.A. (English), 1959.

Addresses

Home—P.O. Box 980672, West Sacramento, CA, 95798-0672. *Agent*—Russell Galen, Scovil Chichak Galen Literary Agency, New York, NY 10016-8806. *E-mail*—BlueAvengerGuy@aol.com.

Career

Writer. Also worked as a telephone operator, newspaper circulation department clerk, prune picker, and cannery worker.

Awards, Honors

Outstanding Books of the Year list, University of Iowa Books for Young Adults Program, 1985, for *God, the Universe, and Hot Fudge Sundaes;* Recommended Book for Reluctant Readers, American Library Association, 1988, for *In with the Out Crowd;* California Young Reader Medal nomination, 2001-2002, for *The Adventures of Blue Avenger.*

Writings

YOUNG ADULT NOVELS

God, the Universe, and Hot Fudge Sundaes, Houghton (Boston, MA), 1984.

In with the Out Crowd, Houghton (Boston, MA), 1986.

The Game of Life, Crown (New York, NY), 1989.

Shoot for the Moon, Crown (New York, NY), 1992.

The Adventures of Blue Avenger, Holt (New York, NY), 1999.

Blue Avenger Cracks the Code, Holt (New York, NY), 2000.

Adaptations

God, the Universe, and Hot Fudge Sundaes was adapted as an Emmy-award winning segment of *Schoolbreak Special,* Columbia Broadcasting Corp. (CBS), 1986. *The Adventures of Blue Avenger* has been optioned by Nickelodeon for a television pilot.

Work in Progress

A third Blue Avenger novel for Cricket Books, expected 2002.

Sidelights

A reviewer for *Booklist* said it succinctly in a review of Norma Howe's second novel, *In with the Out Crowd:* "Howe tries ... to make readers think for themselves." In six novels for young adults, Howe does exactly that, exploring themes from creationism, peer group pressure,

In Norma Howe's novel, sixteen-year-old David Schumacher changes his name to Blue Avenger after a comic-strip hero he created and sets himself the tasks of abolishing handguns, winning the love of the new girl in school, and discovering the answer to the question of free will.

and sexuality to questions of free will and gun control in her novels, but never forgetting the human touch with humor and memorable characters. "Howe creates rare heroes—exceptional people who happen to be in their teens," explained Janice Green in a *San Francisco Chronicle* review of *The Game of Life*. Blending wry humor with unexpected romance, Howe serves up young adult novels that appeal on several levels. As the author noted on her Web site, "For most of my life I've been interested in two philosophical questions: the conflict between faith and reason, and free will versus determination. I tackled the faith versus reason problem in my first novel . . . but I couldn't figure out how to handle the topic of free will in a young adult novel in a non-boring way. So I wrote about peer pressure (*In with the Out Crowd*), the foolishness of astrology and the randomness of life (*The Game of Life*), and the awakenings of a young girl to the wonders of the world outside of her little sphere of existence (*Shoot for the Moon*). Finally it was time to direct my thoughts to the question of free will." This theme Howe took on in two related titles, *The Adventures of Blue Avenger* and its sequel, *Blue Avenger Cracks the Code*.

Howe was born in San Jose, California. Her father worked nights for the railroad, so the children in the family were admonished to keep quiet around the house, as their father slept during the days. "No shouting, screaming, or door-banging was allowed," she noted on her Web site. Howe's mother was an Italian immigrant from a small Sicilian town who came to the United States as a young child; she only became a U.S. citizen when Howe was in elementary school. Later in her life, Howe's mother wrote poetry and short articles for local newspapers, and even crafted a never-published novel about the fortunes of a young Italian immigrant.

Howe had two brothers, one older and one younger. With the older one she played tennis, and with the younger she was the built-in babysitter. From first grade through college in San Jose, Howe's favorite subject was always English. "I loved writing the required weekly essays and always got excellent grades," she reported on her Web site. In high school she took journalism classes, and worked on the school paper, along with the boy who would eventually become her husband, Bob Howe. In college Howe majored in English, and was introduced to the work of masters such as William Thackery, Thomas Hardy, Mark Twain, John Steinbeck, Sherwood Anderson, James T. Farrell, and John Dos Passos. "I wrote a few short stories in a required creative writing class in college," she recalled, "and the thought crossed my mind that I might want to write more some day." But as she grew up in the 1940s and 1950s, Howe was still imbued with the cultural ethos of the day. Her major dream was to one day become a good wife and mother.

Also during these years, Howe worked at a series of jobs to help pay her way. Even as a child of ten she was working in the fruit orchards that once filled the landscape of San Jose—this was long before the silicon chip had turned the area into the wall-to-wall condominiums and businesses of today's Silicon Valley. Later she also worked in canneries, as a soda jerk at a drug store soda fountain, and as a part-time evening clerk in the circulation department of the *San Jose Evening News,* ready to explain to irate subscribers why their newspaper might not have arrived that afternoon.

During her third year in college, Norma married Bob Howe, whom she had known since seventh grade. After Bob received his teaching credentials, the couple moved to San Bernardino, California, where he began his high school teaching career. They spent several summers in San Jose taking classes at San Jose State University until Howe received her B.A. in English in 1959, while her husband obtained his M.A. degree. After reading an article in a writer's magazine about how to write for confession magazines, Howe tried her hand at it, and sold her first story immediately. These stories were easy and fun to write even while caring for several toddlers, and Howe began to place them fairly regularly in magazines such as True Story and Modern romances at the going rate of three cents per word. Meanwhile, she promised herself that she would work on more serious literature once her children were older and she had more time.

The Howes moved to Sacramento, California, when Bob accepted a position with the California State Department of Education. In 1981 the couple went abroad for the

Blue Avenger solves several lesser evils while trying to discover the true author of Shakespeare's plays. (Cover illustration by Rodney Frendak.)

first time. "We had such a great time roaming around Europe with our backpacks and Eurail Pass, we try to go back whenever we can," Howe noted on her Web site. Italy, ancestral home of her mother, remains a favorite among the countries she visits, and Italian scenes have made their way into three of her books.

Finally, Howe felt she had the time and space to start work on a serious book. She began writing her first novel on the day her youngest son received his driver's license, inspired by the widely publicized "Scopes Two" trial she attended in Sacramento in 1981, at which her husband was called to testify. Once she finished the manuscript, she sent it off with a reader's fee to the Scott Meredith Literary Agency in New York. A young associate there named Russell Galen told her he loved the book, and quickly sold it to Houghton Mifflin. Galen and Howe have worked together ever since.

God, the Universe, and Hot Fudge Sundaes, Howe's debut novel, tells about the hardest week in the life of sixteen-year-old Alfie. Her little sister dies, and she falls in love with the most unlikely of people. Alfie attends a trial between evolutionists and creationists vying over which version of the origin of life should be taught in schools. Alfie thinks that the trial might be a diversion from the tensions she is experiencing at home, with her little sister dying and her parents—a skeptical father and a born-again Christian mother—forever bickering. At the trial she meets Kurt, a spectator who has come to support the evolutionists, and she is strongly attracted to him. Kurt does not simply supply soft words of regret when Alfie's sister finally dies; instead he challenges Alfie's unexamined religious convictions. Caught in this emotional cauldron, Alfie must find her own way between faith and reason.

Readers and critics responded positively to this first effort by Howe. A reviewer for *Booklist* felt that *God, the Universe, and Hot Fudge Sundaes* was a "promising novel sure to have YA appeal, especially to those going through their own religious questioning," while a contributor to *School Library Journal* observed that Howe's book is "a thought-provoking novel that should appeal to YA's." Ann A. Flowers, writing in *Horn Book,* remarked that in spite of the serious themes, "there is much humor in the dialogue and in Alfie's relations with her friends." Flowers concluded that "Alfie herself is a thoughtful, intelligent heroine with a contemporary problem." Similarly, a contributor to *Bulletin of the Center for Children's Books* called *God, the Universe, and Hot Fudge Sundaes* an "impressive first novel that has strong characterization, a smooth writing style, and universal theme." In *Voice of Youth Advocates* a reviewer concluded that the "controversial nature of this book makes it excellent for booktalks and discussions."

With her second novel, *In with the Out Crowd,* Howe tackles the theme of peer pressure and the question of when it is appropriate for teens to begin sexual activity. Once again dealing with a sixteen-year-old protagonist, Howe takes readers into the life of Robin, one-time member of the in crowd at school, the "double-A tens."

Pretty and popular, Robin has always been on the inside, and she also is dating Bill, the cutest guy in her junior class. But when Bill wants to move beyond the kissing stage to making love, Robin refuses. Bill is mad at her for turning him down and her friends start turning on her for refusing to lose her virginity. Suddenly, Robin finds herself locked out of the popular group at school and begins to look at things differently than before. The jokes she used to laugh at no longer seem so funny and the way the "cool" guys and girls act with each other seems painfully juvenile to her. The kids she formerly considered losers begin to appear more interesting to her, especially one boy, thought to be the school nerd, for whom she forms a particular attachment.

Critics again responded warmly to Howe's vision and humor. Carolyn Noah, writing in *School Library Journal,* maintained that Howe "tells a perceptive, entertaining story of a teen who chooses to stand apart from the in crowd and enjoys it." A contributor to *Voice of Youth Advocates* called the novel a "[w]ell written account of a girl refusing to give up her virginity just because 'everybody's doing it.'" Remarking that there are many adolescent novels dealing with such issues of peer pressure, a reviewer for *Bulletin of the Center for Children's Books* wrote that Howe's book "is just better than most of them; more smoothly written, with characters who have depth and who change and grow." And Patricia Holt concluded in the *San Francisco Chronicle* that "running jokes keep us laughing and even a tragic death of long ago combine with Robin's budding romance with the school nerd to teach us all something new about individualism."

With *The Game of Life* Howe lets her humorous imagination take over in a tale of Cairo Hays, a young woman who desperately needs to stop her older sister Heather, an astrology freak, from making the mistake of her life by marrying an abusive jerk who appears to be a professional protestor. But Cairo has not got her mind set on just one such rear-guard action. What about helping out her Aunt Lucille who desperately wants to lose weight? And then there is Rocky Nevin who seems to have a few thoughts of his own about Cairo. Throughout it all, Cairo tries to find meaning for her young life and escape the jaws of simple fate. Rocky seems the perfect soul mate for such an escape, and together they talk about topics from the meaning of life to tennis.

Marilyn S. Burrington, reviewing this third novel in *School Library Journal,* called *The Game of Life* a "sparkling gem replete with nuggets of wit and wisdom," while a reviewer for *Publishers Weekly* described it as a "rich, realistic portrait of a young woman's life." "The best thing in the book is the funny, thought-provoking attack on astrology," wrote a contributor to *Booklist.* Janice Green, writing in the *San Francisco Chronicle,* pointed out Howe's "invisibly smooth" writing, and concluded that *The Game of Life* is "an exceptional novel."

For her fourth novel, *Shoot for the Moon,* Howe travels farther afield than American suburbia. Gina Gari, yo-yo artist supreme, never figured that her talent with the yo-yo would serve for much in the world, but suddenly she wins a ten-day trip to Italy as first prize in a yo-yo contest sponsored by a toy company. When Gina gets to Italy, she experiences much more than a mere change of scene. Life abroad, and a romance with an intense young Dutchman named Stefan, combine to open the eyes of this naïve girl from California to a world beyond comfortable borders. Gina is a "refreshingly different ... YA heroine," in the opinion of a reviewer for *Publishers Weekly.* The same contributor further noted that "splendidly evoked locales, well-drawn characters and a subtle yet moving theme add up to a beguiling book." *Booklist* contributor Chris Sherman praised Howe's "whirlwind pacing and interesting characters," while *School Library Journal* reviewer Connie Tyrrell Burns called *Shoot for the Moon* "[z]any and witty." Burns went on to note that *Shoot for the Moon* is "an appropriate metaphor for a novel about growing up, laced with "poignancy" and "conveying teen humor."

Howe was ready to deal with the issue of free will with her fourth novel, *The Adventures of Blue Avenger.* After many false starts, Howe realized she needed humor in the mix to hold her readers' attention. She gained some inspiration from a friend of one her sons who changed his name to that of a cartoon creation; she also decided to write from an omniscient point of view and make her protagonist male. The result was Blue Avenger, who ponders the heavy questions of life. Does free will exist? Do we really have any choices in life? Sixteen-year-old David Bruce Schumacher has been drawing a super-hero comic book for several years—ever since his father died—when finally he decides to tackle the world's problems himself; to become the hero of his own strip. David, now the Blue Avenger, wears his father's fishing vest as part of his super hero costume; with a towel wrapped around his head like Lawrence of Arabia he is transformed into the hero of his dreams. He saves the school principal from killer bees, then goes on to tackle handgun violence in addition to creating a recipe for dripless lemon meringue pie. Falling in love with a girl named Omaha Nebraska Brown is also all in a day's work for the Blue Avenger.

The Adventures of Blue Avenger drew critical praise from a wide assortment of publications. A contributor to *Publishers Weekly* noted that Howe "interpolates her loopy plot with serious discussions of philosophy ... and finely honed characterizations.... The story's teasingly open ending will inspire delighted conjecture." Michael Cart, reviewing the novel in the *San Francisco Chronicle,* commented particularly on Howe's "light touch" which is "just right for painlessly provoking thought about personal responsibility and love's habit of conspiring with fate to change young lives." Writing in the *Bulletin of the Center for Children's Books,* Elizabeth Bush called the book "at once ingeniously plotted and howlingly funny," while a *Kirkus Reviews* contributor dubbed it "a funny, warmly romantic tale" that has "priceless moments and is the perfect respite from all the

bleak YA fiction out there." Joel Shoemaker joined the chorus of hoorays, in *School Library Journal* describing *The Adventures of Blue Avenger* as "funny, tender, a bit manic, and thoroughly entertaining." "Smart teens will enjoy the freewheeling tone of the book," concluded *Booklist* contributor Susan Dove Lempke.

Howe reprised her popular teen super hero in *Blue Avenger Cracks the Code.* This tale takes our hero to Venice along with twin childhood pals Louie and Drusie, only to follow the trail of a mystery hundreds of years old: the true authorship of the works attributed to Shakespeare. Along the way, Blue also helps to work out a more contemporary mystery. "Blue Avenger ... strikes again in Norma Howe's rollicking sequel," noted Veronica Schwartz in *School Library Journal.* Ruth Cox, writing in *Voice of Youth Advocates,* commended Howe's "quirky sense of humor and unique writing style," while a contributor to *Publishers Weekly* observed that *Blue Avenger Cracks the Code* "is just as eccentric and intellectually engaging" as the first. Reviewing the book for *School Library Journal,* contributor Barbara Jo McKee concluded, "Readers will find romance, mystery, and literary intrigue in this funny book about a boy with many causes." Referring to the book's exploration of the possibility that Edward de Vere, the seventeenth Earl of Oxford, was the real author of Shakespeare's works, a reviewer for *U.S. News & World Report* rated the novel a "top pick," calling it "an absorbing Oxfordian primer." A writer for *Kirkus Reviews* also had kind words for Howe, as well as a look to the future. Commenting on the "quirky cast" which "inspires continued admiration and affection," the reviewer concluded, "stay tuned."

Howe herself is staying tuned, not only to her own muse, but to the voice of contemporary youth. "I enjoy writing for young adults because I can so readily identify with people of that age group," she concluded on her Web site. "Perhaps it's because I am short and have always been what used to be called a tomboy that I have the feelings I have never really grown up. Somehow, I got stuck at about age thirteen. Maybe some day I'll get over that, but I doubt it. In the meantime, I'll see just how long I can get away with wearing my jeans and sweat shirt everywhere I go."

Biographical and Critical Sources

PERIODICALS

Best Sellers, June, 1984.
Booklist, April 15, 1984, review of *God, the Universe, and Hot Fudge Sundaes;* November 1, 1986, review of *In with the Out Crowd;* October 15, 1989, review of *The Game of Life;* February 15, 1992, Chris Sherman, review of *Shoot for the Moon,* p. 1099; March 15, 1999, Susan Dove Lempke, review of *The Adventures of Blue Avenger,* p. 1325; February 1, 2001, review of *Blue Avenger Cracks the Code,* p. 1064.
Book Report, January-February, 1987; September-October, 1992, p. 48.
Bulletin of the Center for Children's Books, July-August, 1984, review of *God, the Universe, and Hot Fudge*

Sundaes; January, 1987, review of *In with the Out Crowd;* March, 1999, Elizabeth Bush, review of *The Adventures of Blue Avenger;* October, 2000, review of *Blue Avenger Cracks the Code.*

Children's Book Review Service, August, 1984.

English Journal, December, 1985, p. 95; December, 1985, p. 55.

Horn Book, June-July, 1984, Ann A. Flowers, review of *God, the Universe, and Hot Fudge Sundaes,* pp. 337-338.

Kirkus Reviews, January 15, 1999, review of *The Adventures of Blue Avenger;* August 15, 2000, review of *Blue Avenger Cracks the Code.*

Publishers Weekly, November 28, 1986, p. 78; March 24, 1989, review of *The Game of Life,* p. 73; January 13, 1992, review of *Shoot for the Moon,* p. 57; March 29, 1999, review of *The Adventures of Blue Avenger,* p. 105; March 15, 2000, p. 1341; August 21, 2000, p. 75; September 11, 2000, review of *Blue Avenger Cracks the Code,* p. 92; November 20, 2000, p. 32.

San Francisco Chronicle, August 5, 1984; November 19, 1986, Patricia Holt, review of *In with the Out Crowd;* September 24, 1989, Janice Green, review of *The Game of Life;* May 30, 1999, Michael Cart, review of *The Adventures of Blue Avenger.*

School Library Journal, August, 1984, review of *God, the Universe, and Hot Fudge Sundaes,* p. 84; January, 1987, Carolyn Noah, review of *In with the Out Crowd,* p. 83; October, 1989, Marilyn S. Burrington, review of *The Game of Life,* pp. 133-34; Connie Tyrrell Burns, review of *Shoot for the Moon,* p. 146; April, 1999, Joel Shoemaker, review of *The Adventures of Blue Avenger,* p. 136; September, 2000, Barbara Jo McKee, review of *Blue Avenger Cracks the Code,* p. 231; March 2001, Veronica Schwartz, review of *Blue Avenger Cracks the Code,* pp. 88, 89.

Teacher Librarian, May, 1999, p. 45.

U.S. News & World Report, September 4, 2000, p. 65.

Voice of Youth Advocates, October, 1984, review of *God, the Universe, and Hot Fudge Sundaes;* December, 1986, review of *In with the Out Crowd;* December, 2000, Ruth Cox, review of *Blue Avenger Cracks the Code,* p. 350.

Wilson Library Bulletin, May, 1990, p. S5.

ON-LINE

Young Adult Novels by Norma Howe, http://www.members.aol.com/normahowe/ (May 10, 2001).

J–K

JANICE
See BRUSTLEIN, Janice Tworkov

* * *

KALLEN, Stuart A(rnold) 1955-

Personal

Born August 24, 1955, in Cleveland, OH; son of Edward Samuel (a salesperson) and Ruth (a secretary) Kallen; married P. Marlene Boekhoff (a writer). *Education:* Attended Ohio University. *Politics:* "Frankly, I'm appalled." *Religion:* Jewish. *Hobbies and other interests:* Playing music, art photography, travel, cooking, reading, humor.

Addresses

Home—3253 Via Arcilla, San Diego, CA 92111.

Career

Freelance writer and musician.

Awards, Honors

Mid-American Publishers Association award, for *Recycle It! Once Is Not Enough.*

Writings

NONFICTION; FOR CHILDREN

Recycle It! Once Is Not Enough ("We Can Save the Earth" series), Abdo & Daughters (Minneapolis, MN), 1990.
Before the Communist Revolution: Russian History through 1919 ("Rise and Fall of the Soviet Union" series), Abdo & Daughters (Minneapolis, MN), 1992.
The Brezhnev Era, 1964-1982 ("Rise and Fall of the Soviet Union" series), Abdo & Daughters (Minneapolis, MN), 1992.

Exploring the Origins of the Universe ("Secrets of Space" series), Twenty-first Century (New York, NY), 1997.
Egypt ("Modern Nations of the World" series), Lucent (San Diego, CA), 1999.
The Rolling Stones ("People in the News" series), Lucent (San Diego, CA), 1999.
Rosie O'Donnell ("People in the News" series), Lucent (San Diego, CA), 1999.
The Salem Witch Trials ("World History" series), Lucent (San Diego, CA), 1999.
(Editor) *The 1950s* ("America's Decades"), Greenhaven Press (San Diego, CA), 2000.
(Editor) *The 1990s* ("America's Decades"), Greenhaven Press (San Diego, CA), 2000.
Witches ("Mystery Library"), Lucent (San Diego, CA), 2000.
(With wife, P. M. Boekhoff) *Leonardo da Vinci* ("Importance Of" series), Lucent (San Diego, CA), 2000.
The War at Home ("American War Library"), Lucent (San Diego, CA), 2000.
The Home Front: Americans Protest the War ("American War Library"), Lucent (San Diego, CA), 2001.
(Editor) *The 1400s* ("Headlines in History" series), Greenhaven Press (San Diego, CA), 2001.
(Editor) *The 1700s* ("Headlines in History" series), Greenhaven Press (San Diego, CA), 2001.
(Editor) *Sixties Counterculture,* Greenhaven Press (San Diego, CA), 2001.
(With P. M. Boekhoff) *Lasers,* Kidhaven Press (San Diego, CA), 2001.
The Mayans ("Lost Civilizations" series), Lucent (San Diego, CA), 2001.
Spiders ("Nature's Predators" series), Kidhaven Press (San Diego, CA), 2001.
Understanding The Catcher in the Rye ("Understanding Great Literature" series), Lucent (San Diego, CA), 2001.
The Gold Rush, Kidhaven Press (San Diego, CA), 2001.
Shintoism ("Religions of the World" series), Lucent (San Diego, CA), 2001.
The Baby Boom ("Turning Points" series), Greenhaven Press (San Diego, CA), 2001.

Stuart A. Kallen's book is written for fourth to sixth graders.

(Editor) *Roaring Twenties,* Greenhaven Press (San Diego, CA), 2002.

Alligators ("Nature's Predators" series), Kidhaven Press (San Diego, CA), 2002.

John Lennon ("Importance Of" series), Lucent (San Diego, CA), 2002.

Dolphins and Porpoises ("Endangered Animals and Habitats" series), Lucent (San Diego, CA), 2002.

(Editor) *The Age of Revolution,* Greenhaven Press (San Diego, CA), 2002.

(With P. M. Boekhoff) *Plains Indian Village* ("Daily Life" series), Kidhaven Press (San Diego, CA), 2002.

(With P. M. Boekhoff) *Dr. Seuss* ("Inventors and Creators" series), Kidhaven Press (San Diego, CA), 2002.

(With P. M. Boekhoff) *Mercury* ("Eyes on the Sky" series), Kidhaven Press (San Diego, CA), 2002.

"HISTORY OF ROCK 'N' ROLL" SERIES

Roots of Rock, two volumes, Abdo & Daughters (Minneapolis, MN), 1989.

Renaissance of Rock: The British Invasion, Abdo & Daughters (Minneapolis, MN), 1989.

Renaissance of Rock: The Sixties—Sounds of America, Abdo & Daughters (Minneapolis, MN), 1989.

The Revolution of Rock: The 1970s, Abdo & Daughters (Minneapolis, MN), 1989.

Rock in Retrospect: The 1980s, Abdo & Daughters (Minneapolis, MN), 1989.

"BUILDING A NATION" SERIES

Newcomers to America, 1400-1650, Abdo & Daughters (Minneapolis, MN), 1990.

Life in the Thirteen Colonies, 1650-1750, Abdo & Daughters (Minneapolis, MN), 1990.

The Road to Freedom, 1750-1783, Abdo & Daughters (Minneapolis, MN), 1990.

A Nation United, 1780-1850, Abdo & Daughters (Minneapolis, MN), 1990.

A Nation Divided, 1850-1900, Abdo & Daughters (Minneapolis, MN), 1990.

A Modern Nation, 1900-1990, Abdo & Daughters (Minneapolis, MN), 1990.

"BLACK HISTORY" SERIES

The Lost Kingdoms of Africa, Abdo & Daughters (Minneapolis, MN), 1990, revised as *Kingdoms of Africa,* Abdo Publishing (Edina, MN), 2001.

Days of Slavery: A History of Black People in America, 1619-1863, Abdo & Daughters (Minneapolis, MN), 1990, revised, Abdo Publishing (Edina, MN), 2001.

The Civil War and Reconstruction: A History of Black People in America, 1830-1880, Abdo & Daughters (Minneapolis, MN), 1990, revised, Abdo Publishing (Edina, MN), 2001.

The Twentieth Century and the Harlem Renaissance, Abdo & Daughters (Minneapolis, MN), 1990, revised as *The Harlem Renaissance,* Abdo Publishing (Edina, MN), 2001.

The Civil Rights Movement: The History of Black People in America, 1930-1980, Abdo & Daughters (Minneapolis, MN), 1990, revised, Abdo Publishing (Edina, MN), 2001.

The Struggle into the 1990s: A History of Black People from 1968 to the Present, Abdo & Daughters (Minneapolis, MN), 1990, revised as *Striving into 2000,* Abdo Publishing (Edina, MN), 2001.

"GHASTLY GHOST STORIES" SERIES

How to Catch a Ghost, Abdo & Daughters (Minneapolis, MN), 1991.

(And illustrator) *Haunted Hangouts of the Undead,* Abdo & Daughters (Minneapolis, MN), 1991.

Phantoms of the Rich and Famous, Abdo & Daughters (Minneapolis, MN), 1991.

Vampires, Werewolves, and Zombies, Abdo & Daughters (Minneapolis, MN), 1991.

Monsters, Dinosaurs, and Beasts, Abdo & Daughters (Minneapolis, MN), 1991.

Ghosts of the Seven Seas, Abdo & Daughters (Minneapolis, MN), 1991.

World of the Bizarre, Abdo & Daughters (Minneapolis, MN), 1991.

Witches, Magic, and Spells, Abdo & Daughters (Minneapolis, MN), 1991.

"WORLD RECORD LIBRARY"

Human Oddities, Abdo & Daughters (Minneapolis, MN), 1991.

Spectacular Sports Records, Abdo & Daughters (Minneapolis, MN), 1991.

Incredible Animals, Abdo & Daughters (Minneapolis, MN), 1991.

Awesome Entertainment Records, Abdo & Daughters (Minneapolis, MN), 1991.

Super Structures, Abdo & Daughters (Minneapolis, MN), 1991.

Amazing Human Feats, Abdo & Daughters (Minneapolis, MN), 1991.

"SECOND REVOLUTION" SERIES

Princes, Peasants, and Revolution, Abdo & Daughters (Minneapolis, MN), 1992.

The Rise of Lenin, Abdo & Daughters (Minneapolis, MN), 1992.

Stalin: Man of Steel, Abdo & Daughters (Minneapolis, MN), 1992.

Khrushchev: The Coldest War, Abdo & Daughters (Minneapolis, MN), 1992.

Brezhnev: Before the Dawn, Abdo & Daughters (Minneapolis, MN), 1992.

Gorbachev-Yeltsin: The Fall of Communism, Abdo & Daughters (Minneapolis, MN), 1992.

"FABULOUS FUN LIBRARY"

Ridiculous Riddles (Giggles, Gags, and Groaners), illustrated by Terry Boles, Abdo & Daughters (Minneapolis, MN), 1992.

Tricky Tricks (Simple Magic Tricks), Abdo & Daughters (Minneapolis, MN), 1992.

Mad Scientist Experiments (Safe, Simple Science Experiments), Abdo & Daughters (Minneapolis, MN), 1992.

Math-a-Magical Fun (Fun with Numbers), Abdo & Daughters (Minneapolis, MN), 1992.

Puzzling Puzzles (Brain Teasers), Abdo & Daughters (Minneapolis, MN), 1992.

Silly Stories (Funny, Short Stories), Abdo & Daughters (Minneapolis, MN), 1992.

Funny Answers to Foolish Questions, Abdo & Daughters (Minneapolis, MN), 1992.

The Giant Joke Book, Abdo & Daughters (Minneapolis, MN), 1992.

"TARGET EARTH" SERIES

If the Clouds Could Talk, Abdo & Daughters (Minneapolis, MN), 1993.

If Trees Could Talk, Abdo & Daughters (Minneapolis, MN), 1993.

If the Sky Could Talk, Abdo & Daughters (Minneapolis, MN), 1993.

If the Waters Could Talk, Abdo & Daughters (Minneapolis, MN), 1993.

If Animals Could Talk, Abdo & Daughters (Minneapolis, MN), 1993.

Eco-Games, Abdo & Daughters (Minneapolis, MN), 1993.

Precious Creatures A-Z, Abdo & Daughters (Minneapolis, MN), 1993.

Eco-Fairs and Carnivals: A Complete Guide to Raising Funds for the Environment, Abdo & Daughters (Minneapolis, MN), 1993.

Earth Keepers, Abdo & Daughters (Minneapolis, MN), 1993.

Eco-Arts and Crafts, Abdo & Daughters (Minneapolis, MN), 1993.

"I HAVE A DREAM" SERIES

Maya Angelou: Woman of Words, Deeds, and Dreams, Abdo & Daughters (Minneapolis, MN), 1993.

Arthur Ashe: Champion of Dreams and Motion, Abdo & Daughters (Minneapolis, MN), 1993.

Martin Luther King Jr.: A Man and His Dream, Abdo & Daughters (Minneapolis, MN), 1993.

Thurgood Marshall: A Dream of Justice for All, Abdo & Daughters (Minneapolis, MN), 1993.

Quincy Jones, Abdo Publishers (Edina, MN), 1996.

"FAMOUS ILLUSTRATED SPEECHES AND DOCUMENTS" SERIES

The Statue of Liberty: "The New Colossus," Abdo & Daughters (Minneapolis, MN), 1994.

The Gettysburg Address, Abdo & Daughters (Minneapolis, MN), 1994.

Pledge of Allegiance, Abdo & Daughters (Minneapolis, MN), 1994.

Star-Spangled Banner, Abdo & Daughters (Minneapolis, MN), 1994.

The Declaration of Independence, illustrated by Michael Birawer, Abdo & Daughters (Minneapolis, MN), 1994.

"IF THE DINOSAURS COULD TALK" SERIES

Brontosaurus, illustrated by Kristen Copham, Abdo & Daughters (Minneapolis, MN), 1994.

Stegosaurus, illustrated by Kristen Copham, Abdo & Daughters (Minneapolis, MN), 1994.

Tyrannosaurus Rex, illustrated by Kristen Copham, Abdo & Daughters (Minneapolis, MN), 1994.

Pterandon, illustrated by Kristen Copham, Abdo & Daughters (Minneapolis, MN), 1994.

Plesiosaurus, illustrated by Kristen Copham, Abdo & Daughters (Minneapolis, MN), 1994.

Kallen tells about the only cat in the world without a tail. *(Cover photo by Peter Arnold.)*

Triceratops, illustrated by Kristen Copham, Abdo & Daughters (Minneapolis, MN), 1994.

"THE HOLOCAUST" SERIES

The History of a Hatred: 70 A.D. to 1932, Abdo & Daughters (Minneapolis, MN), 1994.
The Nazis Seize Power: 1933-1939, Abdo & Daughters (Minneapolis, MN), 1994.
The Holocaust: 1939-1945, Abdo & Daughters (Minneapolis, MN), 1994.
Bearing Witness: Liberation and the Nuremberg Trials, Abdo & Daughters (Minneapolis, MN), 1994.
Holocausts in Other Lands, Abdo & Daughters (Minneapolis, MN), 1994.
The Faces of Resistance, Abdo Publishing (Edina, MN), 1994.

"DOGS" SERIES

German Shepherds, Abdo Publishing (Edina, MN), 1995.
Cocker Spaniels, Abdo Publishing (Edina, MN), 1996.
Dalmatians, Abdo Publishing (Edina, MN), 1996.
Golden Retrievers, Abdo Publishing (Edina, MN), 1996.
Poodles, Abdo Publishing (Edina, MN), 1996.
Labrador Retrievers, Abdo Publishing (Edina, MN), 1996.
Mutts, Abdo Publishing (Edina, MN), 1996.
Yorkshire Terriers, Abdo Publishing (Edina, MN), 1996.
Beagles, Abdo Publishing (Edina, MN), 1998.
Collies, Abdo Publishing (Edina, MN), 1998.
Dachshunds, Abdo Publishing (Edina, MN), 1998.
Old English Sheepdogs, Abdo Publishing (Edina, MN), 1998.

"CATS" SERIES

Abyssinian Cats, Abdo Publishing (Edina, MN), 1995.
Maine Coon Cats, Abdo Publishing (Edina, MN), 1996.
Manx Cats, Abdo Publishing (Edina, MN), 1996.
Persian Cats, Abdo Publishing (Edina, MN), 1996.
Russian Blue Cats, Abdo Publishing (Edina, MN), 1996.
Tabby Cats, Abdo Publishing (Edina, MN), 1996.
Siamese Cats, Abdo Publishing (Edina, MN), 1996.
American Curl Cats, Abdo Publishing (Edina, MN), 1998.
Balinese Cats, Abdo Publishing (Edina, MN), 1998.
Devon Rex Cats, Abdo Publishing (Edina, MN), 1998.
Exotic Shorthair Cats, Abdo Publishing (Edina, MN), 1998.
Oriental Shorthair Cats, Abdo Publishing (Edina, MN), 1998.

"BEARS" SERIES

Black Bears, Abdo Publishing (Edina, MN), 1996.
Alaskan Brown Bears, Abdo Publishing (Edina, MN), 1998.
Giant Pandas, Abdo Publishing (Edina, MN), 1998.
Grizzly Bears, Abdo Publishing (Edina, MN), 1998.
Polar Bears, Abdo Publishing (Edina, MN), 1998.
Sun Bears, Abdo Publishing (Edina, MN), 1998.

"GIANT LEAPS" SERIES

The Apollo Moonwalkers, Abdo Publishing (Edina, MN), 1996.
The Gemini Spacewalker, Abdo Publishing (Edina, MN), 1996.
The Mercury Seven, Abdo Publishing (Edina, MN), 1996.

The Race to Space, Abdo Publishing (Edina, MN), 1996.
Space Shuttles, Abdo Publishing (Edina, MN), 1996.

"FIELD TRIPS" SERIES

The Farm, Abdo Publishing (Edina, MN), 1997.
The Museum, Abdo Publishing (Edina, MN), 1997.
The Fire Station, Abdo Publishing (Edina, MN), 1997.
The Police Station, Abdo Publishing (Edina, MN), 1997.
The Airport, Abdo Publishing (Edina, MN), 1997.
The Zoo, Abdo Publishing (Edina, MN), 1997.

"THE WAY PEOPLE LIVE" SERIES

Life among the Pirates, Lucent (San Diego, CA), 1999.
Life on the American Frontier, Lucent (San Diego, CA), 1999.
Life in the Amazon Rain Forest, Lucent (San Diego, CA), 1999.
Life on the Underground Railroad, Lucent (San Diego, CA), 2000.
Life in America during the 1960s, Lucent (San Diego, CA), 2001.
Life in Tokyo, Lucent (San Diego, CA), 2001.
Life During the American Revolution, Lucent (San Diego, CA), 2002.

"CULTURAL HISTORY OF THE UNITED STATES" SERIES

The 1950s Lucent (San Diego, CA), 1999.
The 1980s, Lucent (San Diego, CA), 1999.
The 1990s, Lucent (San Diego, CA), 1999.

"HISTORY MAKERS" SERIES

Native American Chiefs and Warriors, Lucent (San Diego, CA), 1999.
Great Composers, Lucent (San Diego, CA), 2000.
Great Male Comedians, Lucent (San Diego, CA), 2000.

"INDIGENOUS PEOPLES OF NORTH AMERICA" SERIES

Native Americans of the Northeast, Lucent (San Diego, CA), 2000.
Native Americans of the Great Lakes, Lucent (San Diego, CA), 2000.
Native Americans of the Southwest, Lucent (San Diego, CA), 2000.
The Pawnee, Lucent (San Diego, CA), 2001.

"FOUNDING FATHERS" SERIES

Alexander Hamilton, Abdo Publishing (Edina, MN), 2001.
Benjamin Franklin, Abdo Publishing (Edina, MN), 2001.
George Washington, Abdo Publishing (Edina, MN), 2001.
James Madison, Abdo Publishing (Edina, MN), 2001.
James Monroe, Abdo Publishing (Edina, MN), 2001.
John Adams, Abdo Publishing (Edina, MN), 2001.
John Hancock, Abdo Publishing (Edina, MN), 2001.
John Jay, Abdo Publishing (Edina, MN), 2001.
Thomas Jefferson, Abdo Publishing (Edina, MN), 2001.
John Marshall, Abdo Publishing (Edina, MN), 2001.
John Marshall, Abdo Publishing (Edina, MN), 2001.
Patrick Henry, Abdo Publishing (Edina, MN), 2001.
Samuel Adams, Abdo Publishing (Edina, MN), 2002.

"SEEDS OF A NATION" SERIES; WITH P. M. BOEKHOFF

California, Kidhaven Press (San Diego, CA), 2001.
New York, Kidhaven Press (San Diego, CA), 2001.

Illinois, Kidhaven Press (San Diego, CA), 2001.
Minnesota, Kidhaven Press (San Diego, CA), 2001.
Delaware, Kidhaven Press (San Diego, CA), 2001.
Ohio, Kidhaven Press (San Diego, CA), 2002.
Indiana, Kidhaven Press (San Diego, CA), 2002.

FOR ADULTS

Beer Here: A Traveler's Guide to American Brewpubs and Microbreweries, Citadel Press, 1995.
The Fifty Greatest Beers of the World: An Expert's Ranking of the Very Best, Carol Publishing (Secaucus, NJ), 1997.
The Complete Idiot's Guide to Beer, Alpha (New York, NY), 1997.

OTHER

Also author of numerous articles for magazines.

Sidelights

Prolific children's author Stuart A. Kallen, with dozens of books for young readers to his credit, has allowed his curiosity as a writer to lead him to gather information about a variety of topics, from history to science to fun and games. One case in particular, Kallen's award-winning *Recycle It! Once Is Not Enough,* which identifies ways to reduce waste, piqued his writer's curiosity more than usual; further study led Kallen to write a ten-book series, "Target Earth," which focuses on ecology and the natural world.

In his "The History of Rock 'n' Roll" series, Kallen offers a chronological look at the story of rock music. The sounds of the 1950s are represented in the two-volume *Roots of Rock.* The two volumes of *Renaissance of Rock,* covering the 1960s, are separated into American music and the sounds of the British Invasion. The music of the 1970s is discussed in *Revolution of Rock,* and Kallen closes his series with *Rock in Retrospect: The 1980s,* a look at the nostalgic influences that shaped much of the popular rock and roll of the 1980s.

American history is another subject to which Kallen has devoted dozens of books. His "Building of a Nation" series is a collection of books that covers the American experience from the age of exploration and colonialism through the Revolutionary and Civil War periods to the twentieth century. In *The Salem Witch Trials,* Kallen begins with a discussion of goddess cults before describing how the European tradition of witch-hunting made its way to colonial Massachusetts, his attention to detail prompting *School Library Journal* contributor Laura Glaser to recommend the book as "an excellent resource." Figures such as Thomas Jefferson, George Washington, and John Jay receive attention in Kallen's "Founding Fathers" series. Praising the author for his "highly readable" text, *Booklist* reviewer Ilene Cooper remarked that in the volume *The 1950s,* Kallen "does an excellent job of surveying the decade and placing it in the larger context of American history." The history of African Americans is covered in even greater detail in "Black History and the Civil Rights Movement," a six-volume series. And Kallen's "I Have a Dream" books

Kallen discusses the lives of the trailblazers, fur trappers, mountain men, Native Americans, miners, cowboys, and pioneers of the American frontier.

contain biographies of notable black Americans such as civil rights activist Martin Luther King, Jr., author Maya Angelou, tennis player Arthur Ashe, and Supreme Court Justice Thurgood Marshall.

In books such as *Native Americans of the Northeast* and *Native American Chiefs and Warriors,* Kallen addresses the life of North America's indigenous peoples, illustrating for young readers the daily life, religion, social habits, and warring habits of the tribes that inhabited the American continent prior to the arrival of white Europeans. *Native American Chiefs and Warriors* recounts the biographies of such warriors as Wampanoag chief King Philip, Ottawa chief Pontiac, Apache leader Geronimo, and Sioux leader Crazy Horse, "cover[ing] basic information in an interesting and genuine manner," according to *School Library Journal* contributor Sarah O'Neal. *Booklist* reviewer Susan Dove Lempke also had praise for the volume, citing in particular Kallen's use of primary source materials. Calling Kallen "sympathetic to, yet realistic about, Indian causes," Cris Riedel noted in a *School Library Journal* review of *Native Americans of the Northeast* that "while the ideas presented are occasionally complex, the writing is straightforward." In *Native Americans of the Great Lakes, Booklist* contributor Karen Hutt noted that "detailed descriptions ... illustrate the differences as well as the similarities between the tribes," and recommended Kallen's book for its "wealth of information."

Kallen's curiosity has also led him to examine conflicts on distant shores, as in *The Nazis Seize Power: 1933-39* and *Bearing Witness: Liberation and the Nuremberg Trials,* two of the books in his series describing the torments endured by millions of European Jews and others during the Holocaust of World War II. The volumes in "The Second Revolution" series allow readers to explore the rise and fall of yet another world power, the Communist empire of the former Soviet Union, from its prerevolutionary days as Mother Russia through the Cold War era and *glasnost* to the fall of the Soviet Union and the efforts of small Eastern European nations to create free-market democracies after achieving independence. Focusing on a different kind of violence, Kallen's *Life in the Amazon Rainforest* describes the way of life in this endangered region before discussing the destruction wrought by sixteenth-century European explorers, and modern-day gold miners, rubber tapers, and those whose cut-and-burn policy has provided the region more farmland at a cost to the entire planet.

Subjects of scientific interest also benefit from Kallen's curiosity. In *Exploring the Origins of the Universe,* the author reviews several ancient theories about the creation of the universe before embarking on a discussion that stretches from Pythagoras through the development of the telescope to the theories of Stephen Hawking. His "Giant Leaps" series describes the history of the U.S. space program through such titles as *The Apollo Moonwalkers, The Mercury Seven,* and *The Race to Space.*

In addition to his many volumes of nonfiction, Kallen has written a number of books in a much lighter vein. *Witches, Magic, and Spells, Haunted Hangouts of the Undead,* and *Phantoms of the Rich and Famous* are just a few of the titles in Kallen's "Ghastly Ghost Stories" series. And the books he has compiled for his "The Fabulous Fun Library" series provide young readers with a host of ideas for fun and games that include brain teasers, magic tricks, riddles, jokes, math games, and simple science experiments.

A writer who tries to project his great enthusiasm for learning beyond the pages of his books, Kallen has strong feelings about his readers. "I believe there are only three solutions to the problem facing America today," he told *SATA.* "Education, education, and education. But learning must be exciting and fun. I believe in piquing a reader's curiosity with humor to generate interest in the topic at hand. I was not the greatest student back in the 1960s, but books have been some of my best friends since childhood. I read the 'Lord of the Rings' trilogy in sixth grade, all the while getting low marks in English class. As my list of published works can attest, one is never too old to keep learning and growing. Writing is a gift, but it is also one that needs to be nurtured and fed with an open book and an open mind."

Biographical and Critical Sources

PERIODICALS

Booklist, January 1, 1999, Ilene Cooper, review of *The 1950s,* pp. 866, 868; August, 1999, Ilene Cooper, review of *Rosie O'Donnell,* p. 2054; January 1, 2000, Susan Dove Lempke, review of *Native American Chiefs and Warriors,* and Mary Romano Marks, review of *War at Home,* pp. 890, 896; March 1, 2000, Karen Hutt, review of *Native Americans of the Great Lakes,* p. 1235; June 1, 2000, Roger Leslie, review of *The 1990s,* p. 1876; September 1, 2000, Anne O'Malley, review of *Witches,* p. 73; February 15, 2001, Carolyn Phelan, review of *Sixties Counterculture,* pp. 1124, 1126.

Library Journal, May 1, 1995, review of *Beer Here,* p. 121.

School Library Journal, May, 1993; February, 1995; March, 1995, Cathryn A. Camper, review of *Brontosaurus,* p. 198; April, 1995, Sharon Grover, reviews of *The Nazis Seize Power* and *Holocausts in Other Lands,* p. 143; June, 1997, John Peters, review of *Exploring the Origins of the Universe,* p. 132; March, 1999, Andrew Medlar, review of *Life among the Pirates,* and Cindy Darling Codel, review of *The 1950s,* pp. 222-223; July, 1999, Kathy Piehl, review of *Life in the Amazon Rain Forest,* p. 109; September, 1999, Laura Glaser, review of *The Salem Witch Trials,* p. 236; October, 1999, Steve Matthews, review of *Egypt,* p. 170; January, 2000, Sarah O'Neal, review of *Native American Chiefs and Warriors,* p. 148; May, 2000, Cris Riedel, review of *Native Americans of the Northeast,* and Starr E. Smith, *A Live on the Underground Railroad,* p. 184; September, 2000, Susan Shaver, review of *The 1950s,* Sean George, review of *Native Americans of the Southwest,* and Ann G. Brouse, review of *Witches,* pp. 249-250; April, 2001, Jane Halsall, review of *Sixties Counterculture,* p. 162, Eldon Younce, *The Home Front: Americans Protest the War,* p. 162, and Herman Sutter, review of *Understanding* The Catcher in the Rye, p. 162; May, 2001, Carol Wichman, review of *The Mayans,* p. 166; June, 2001, DeAnn Tabuchi, review of *Life in Tokyo,* p. 174.

*   *   *

KANER, Etta 1947-

Personal

Born October 17, 1947; daughter of Meilech (a furrier) and Sally (a homemaker; maiden name, Rosenfeld) Kaner; married David Nitkin (an ethicist), 1970; children: two daughters. *Education:* University of Toronto, B.A. (honors); University of Wisconsin, M.A. *Hobbies and other interests:* Gardening, reading, dancing.

Addresses

Office—c/o Kids Can Press Ltd., 29 Birch Ave., Toronto, Ontario, Canada M4V 1E2.

Career

Elementary school teacher in Ontario, Canada, 1972—; teacher of gifted children and those with learning disabilities. Presents workshops based on her books to school and library groups.

Awards, Honors

Science in Society Award, 1994, for *Bridges;* Silver Birch awards, shortlist, 1994, for *Bridges,* shortlist, 1995, for *Towers and Tunnels,* regional award winner, 1999, for *Animal Defenses.*

Writings

Balloon Science, illustrated by Louise Phillips, Kids Can Press (Toronto, Canada), Addison-Wesley (Reading, MA), 1989.

I Am Not Jenny, Groundwood Press, 1991.

Sound Science, illustrated by Louise Phillips, Kids Can Press (Toronto, Canada), Addison-Wesley (Reading, MA), 1991.

Bridges, illustrated by Pat Cupples, Kids Can Press (Toronto, Canada), 1994.

Towers and Tunnels, illustrated by Pat Cupples, Kids Can Press (Toronto, Canada), 1995.

Animal Defenses: How Animals Protect Themselves, illustrated by Pat Stephens, Kids Can Press (Toronto, Canada), 1999.

Animals at Work, Kids Can Press (Toronto, Canada), 2001.

Animal Talk: How Animals Communicate, Kids Can Press (Toronto, Canada), 2002.

Contributor of book reviews to *Quill & Quire.*

Work in Progress

Research for *Animal Social Groups* (working title).

Sidelights

Canadian author Etta Kaner is an elementary school teacher with a knack for introducing young people to the role science plays in everyday life. Designed to appeal to young people from ages seven through eleven, Kaner's books, which include *Balloon Science, Animal Defenses: How Animals Protect Themselves,* and *Towers and Tunnels,* feature riddles, hands-on activities, easy-to-do experiments, and interesting facts with which readers can amaze and impress their teachers, parents, and friends. In deciding what to include in her books, Kaner uses what she described to *SATA* as the "wow" test. For example, when writing a book on wildlife, "I choose animals that will cause readers to say 'wow' when they read about them. I also try to write with a sense of humor and a sense of wonder. After all, the world of animals is truly a wonderful place!"

"I guess that I've always enjoyed words in one form or another," Kaner told *SATA,* "whether it was listening to my father tell humorous stories about members of our family or participating in speech contests and plays in

Etta Kaner

school or voraciously reading books from the local library." Among her favorite writers while growing up during the 1950s and early 1960s were C. S. Lewis, E. B. White, Hugh Lofting, and Laura Ingalls Wilder. "I remember feeling terribly disappointed when I found out that I had reached the end of the 'Little House on the Prairie' series," Kaner recalled. "In my mind's eye, I can still see the shelf in the library where that series was kept and myself wishing that the author would write some more books about those characters that I had come to love."

Hearing stories told aloud and reading books by favorite authors was one thing, but writing was something else, according to Kaner. "Although I often got A's on my stories in school, writing them was pure torture. I used to write stories with a lot of descriptive language ... adjectives describing trees, water, mountains, and plants in different seasons. I always felt I had to find the perfect word to describe these various elements of nature and I went through agony trying to think of it. I finally took the advice of my grade-eight teacher and bought a thesaurus." While the writing aide helped, putting stories down on paper remained far from Kaner's favorite pastime.

After high school, Kaner attended the University of Toronto and then moved to the United States briefly to earn a master's degree at the University of Wisconsin. "Once I graduated from university ... my creative energies went into making planters, curtains, and wall hangings out of macrame, acting in community theaters in Toronto, and teaching," the author explained. "Being a teacher is very similar to being a writer. Teachers are generally creative, curious, good problem solvers, and enjoy learning and being with children. I think that's what writers of children's books are too."

It was only after her oldest daughter had started school and Kaner's days at home were more relaxed, with only her four-year-old to care for, that she was inspired to began writing again. "One day, my younger daughter and I were mucking about with balloons," she recalled. "We were painting faces on them and attaching paper springs for arms and legs. I wondered what else could be done with balloons, and since I didn't know much about them, I started to do some research. Part of that research was going to the library and part of it was going on a fascinating but smelly tour of a balloon factory. (The smell came from the ammonia used in the manufacturing process.) I soon realized that I had enough material for a book, and that's how *Balloon Science* was born."

For a year, Kaner developed more than forty experiments using balloons, repeating each one many times to be sure it worked. She also interviewed people, composed the text, and then went back and edited her work. Another year would pass while *Balloon Science* was designed, illustrations were drawn, and it was printed. Finally, in 1989, Kaner became a published author.

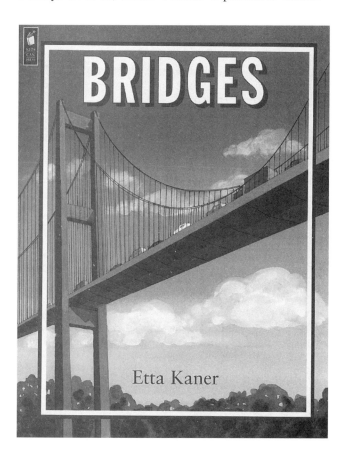

Readers ages eight to twelve can investigate and experiment with the science of building beam, arch, moveable, and suspension bridges. (Cover illustration by Pat Cupples.)

Although Kaner has written some fiction, most of her books since *Balloon Science* have been nonfiction works that explore the world of science. Interviews are her favorite part of the writing process. "Sometimes I get strange but interesting information that I wasn't looking for," Kaner explained. "I once interviewed a train engineer about train whistles for my book *Sound Science.* He told me about the time he worked in northern Ontario. He said that when moose heard a train coming, they would run onto the track because they thought the train whistle was the love call of another moose. To avoid further accidents, train whistles were changed to a higher pitch."

Bridges came about when Kaner grew interested in all the different types of bridges in the world and wondered how different bridge designs came about. Soon her mind was filled with questions. Why do many bridges use arches? What makes a bridge strong enough to support cars, trucks, and people? Why do bridges come in so many different shapes? Answering these questions with the help of experts, and then organizing all she had learned into a book that children could understand took Kaner nearly twelve months. When *Bridges* was published in 1994, it earned its author critical recognition, including the Science in Society Award. Citing the book's "essentially technical but also interesting and easy-to-grasp style" in his review for *Quill & Quire,* Martin Dowding also poked fun at Kaner's inclusion of what he deemed "dreadfully droll jokes, no doubt included to take the sting out of 'too much science,' [but that] add to the fun." Brenda Partridge also had praise for *Bridges* in her *Canadian Materials* review, calling the work "very non-threatening" because its technical subject matter is balanced by colorful illustrations and Kaner's "easy-to-understand language."

Researching *Towers and Tunnels* allowed Kaner to learn more about famous places she knew of but had never before studied, including the Eiffel Tower of Paris, France; Toronto's C.N. Tower; and the Eurotunnel linking Great Britain and France under the English Channel. Each of these engineering feats was accomplished through the work of designers, engineers, workmen, and visionaries. Talking with engineers, Kaner was able to design experiments that allow her readers to better understand the building techniques used and the physical science in play in each construction project. Calling the book "highly informative, readable, and very brightly illustrated," *Quill & Quire* contributor Phyllis Simon praised *Towers and Tunnels* for the depth of its research and its discussion of how a skyscraper is made: from studying the earth on which it is to be built to designing the building to the materials used in its construction.

Being a nonfiction author has provided Kaner with an excellent outlet for her natural curiosity, her desire to "find ... out about things I didn't already know." Researching her 1999 book, *Animal Defenses,* required sifting through dozens of books to learn how different animals—everything from porcupines to dolphins, butterflies to armadillos—defend themselves. "I found it

Kaner describes the unusual methods some animals use to defend themselves. (Cover illustration by Pat Stephens.)

fascinating that animals, unlike people, rarely fight to get out of a tight spot," Kaner explained to *SATA*. "They only fight if all the other ways they've tried to get rid of their enemy have failed." Kaner's book includes a section titled "Strange but True" in which she explains a number of eye-opening defenses animals have developed: "from playing tricks to pretending to be a snake or some other scary creature to using special protective gear. I was especially interested in the way animals form partnerships with other species to help each other out. I could hardly believe that a tiny fish like the Luther's goby could act as a guide to a blind shrimp while the shrimp could warn the goby of danger." Praised by critics for its organization and breadth of coverage, *Animal Defenses* presents information "in a particularly accessible way" according to *Booklist* contributor Carolyn Phelan.

In addition to being a writer and a teacher, Kaner is devoted to her husband and two daughters, and the family's summers used to be spent at a country cottage, swimming, hiking, picking wild blueberries, and enjoying the Canadian wildlife. "I liked to take advantage of these trips to pick my family's brains for riddles for whatever book I happen to be working on," Kaner admitted. "To paraphrase a well-known expression, I find that four heads are better than one. Family trips also give me ideas for new books. I always enjoy meeting

people and learning about new things, since I never know what might turn into a book!"

Biographical and Critical Sources

PERIODICALS

Booklist, April 15, 1999, Carolyn Phelan, review of *Animal Defenses,* p. 1533.

Canadian Materials, March, 1990, Eve Williams, review of *Balloon Science,* p. 70; September, 1994, Brenda Partridge, review of *Bridges,* pp. 136-137.

Hungry Mind Review, summer, 1999, Ralph Blythe, review of *Animal Defenses,* p. 44.

Quill & Quire, May, 1994, Martin Dowding, review of *Bridges,* p. 36; May, 1995, Phyllis Simon, review of *Towers and Tunnels,* p. 50.

School Library Journal, June, 1992, Tina Smith Entwistle, review of *Sound Science,* p. 133; June, 1999, Arwen Marshall, review of *Animal Defenses,* p. 116.

*　　*　　*

KIMBALL, Violet T(ew) 1932-

Personal

Born May 27, 1932, in Sampson County, NC; daughter of Perlie A. (a farmer and justice of the peace) and Daisy (a homemaker; maiden name, McLamb) Tew; married Stanley B. Kimball (a professor of history), June 25, 1953; children: Chase, Hope Kimball Montgomery, Kay, April Kimball Hunt. *Education:* University of Missouri—St. Louis, B.A.; Southern Illinois University—Edwardsville, graduate study.

Awards, Honors

Home and office—15 Crestwood Dr., Glen Carbon, IL 62034. *E-mail*—v.kimball@aol.com.

Career

Substitute teacher at schools in St. Louis County, MO, 1975-85; freelance writer and photographer in Missouri and Illinois, 1982-95. Southern Illinois University, Edwardsville, IL, member of board of directors, Friends of Music; volunteer for local political, civic, and charitable causes; gives readings from her books. *Member:* Oregon/California Trails Association, Mormon Historical Association, John Whitmer Historical Society.

Awards, Honors

Award for best nonfiction article in *North County Writers,* 1982; first-place awards for photography, St. Louis Camera Club, between 1990 and 1995; Spur Award for best western juvenile nonfiction, Western Writers of America, Book of the Year Award in Young Adult Nonfiction, *Foreword* magazine, and Young Adult Nonfiction Award, Independent Book Publishers, all for *Stories of Young Pioneers: In Their Own Words;*

Violet T. Kimball

Writings

(With husband, Stanley B. Kimball) *Mormon Trail, Voyage of Discovery: The Story behind the Scenery,* photographs by Gary Ladd, KC Publications (Las Vegas, NV), 1995.

(And contributor of photographs) *Stories of Young Pioneers: In Their Own Words,* Mountain Press Publishing (Missoula, MT), 2000.

Contributor to magazines and newspapers, including *Children's Friend, Today's Christian Woman, Cobblestone, Quilt World, Ensign, Ford Times,* and *Woman's World. Mormon Trail, Voyage of Discovery* was translated into German.

Work in Progress

Villages on Wheels: A Social History of the Mormon Trek West, with Stanley B. Kimball, publication expected in 2003; *Southern Sisters,* a novel based on the author's family history and accounts by soldiers and civilians in the Civil War in North Carolina; *First Ladies in America: The Noble and the Notorious,* "which is not," Kimball emphasizes, "about the wives of the presidents."

Sidelights

Violet T. Kimball told *SATA:* "I started writing about twenty years ago. I sold articles and features to national publications and local newspapers and magazines. I usually submitted my own photographs, and they were used. I have won a few prizes with photos and articles, and some of my images have won first place in camera club contests. I have also sold some of my images.

"I came to the writing and research arena late in life. I decided to quit standing on the sidelines being a wallflower, listening to my husband, who is the authority on the Mormon Trail, give talks. About fifteen years ago I jumped in. I went with my husband on several student trail/study trips. I used to think history of the West was boring, but that is because I was reading the edited, sanitized version in an easy chair. One needs to get on boots and see where it all happened. I enjoy reading the real thing, not what an editor said someone said. I've discovered it in the wonderful trail diaries and journals and recollections of the young people who marched west from 1843 to 1867.

"I started writing my book on young pioneers about five years ago. I have been doing research and traveling along the trail for twenty years, however. As I read their stories, it dawned on me that the adults on the trail seldom mentioned their children and the contributions they made. I began to be awed by the children's stories. They amazed me with their diligence, cheerfulness, and dependability. They seemed to say, 'tell *our* story.' I have tried to do that.

"Parents and young adults will like this book because it will teach a lot about life 150 years ago, and the role of these unsung heroes who were major players in the drama of the trek across the plains, deserts, and mountains to a healthier life in the West. These are real young people with a positive message and a willingness to do their part in the struggle for a better life. They are role models for any age, not just teenagers. Perhaps the greatest legacy these parents left was not the taming of the West, but their remarkable children."

*   *   *

KINSEY, Elizabeth
See CLYMER, Eleanor

Autobiography Feature

Sheila Solomon Klass

1927-

A two-dollar permanent wave that covered the head with a capful of tight ringlets was all the rage in the 1930s in Williamsburg, the Brooklyn slum in which I lived. All the girls, longing to be Shirley Temple, went for it. Except me, though I had impossibly straight hair. Like sticks.

I knew I wasn't going to be a movie star. I was going to be a writer! And a writer could have straight hair or kinky hair or even be bald.

That permanent was never a real possibility anyway. My family was too poor for such luxuries. So, long before I ever put pen to paper, I enjoyed the immense pleasure of imagining. That was the first of the many times that fiction offered me escape from hard reality.

I was born on November 6, 1927, to Orthodox Jewish parents, and, immediately, I was a major disappointment. They already had a three-year-old daughter, Marilyn. They'd wanted a son to carry on the name—and for all the other reasons people want sons. In 1932 my brother Arnold was born, beautiful, healthy, and an occasion of joy for all of us.

To know me it is necessary to know my family.

My father, Abraham Louis Solomon, had emigrated from a village in Hungary, a village so small only the mayor owned a jacket; that was why, my father explained, he was elected mayor.

Papa arrived just in time to be an American doughboy in World War One, and he remained intensely patriotic, a Jewish War Veterans member all his life. Originally, his name was Solo-monowitz, but during the naturalization ceremony the judge had said to him, "You leave the witz with me and take away the Solomon." I've always been grateful to that judge, and I've kept the Solomon as my own middle name.

A quiet, religious man, Papa had a terrible temper when roused; these paroxysms of rage during which he shouted and glared at us over his eyeglasses were explained by my mother as "shell shock."

Fluent in Yiddish, Hungarian, and German, Papa had gone to night school to learn English, which he spoke with a slight accent. He was a passionate pinochle player and a very sociable person. He had a trade: clothespresser, very low on the wage scale. A staunch Amalgamated Garment Workers Union man, he worked diligently but was never able to earn a living. Even later, during the booming nineteen forties, when clothing factories had military contracts, he earned little.

With no relatives in New York, he was at the mercy of my mother's family. From them I heard repeatedly that a *man* should be able to support his family. (They didn't seem to notice that all around us was the Great Depression.) I understood that Papa had failed us and was somehow diminished as a man. That saddened me; I loved him.

Sheila Solomon Klass

My mother, Regina Solomon (née Glatter), was American born, the first child of badly matched immigrant parents: my angry, silent, tyrannical grandfather and kind, loving grandmother. (Their marriage had been arranged by a marriage-broker.)

An attractive brunette, my mother had to leave school to help out with her six younger siblings. When she could, she read a lot—mostly romances like *Lorna Doone* by Blackmore and *Ivanhoe* and *The Talisman* by Sir Walter Scott.

She had dreamed of a life filled with gentility and beauty: "A small cottage in the country with roses around it and a white picket fence . . . " Her books had a special place on bookshelves wherever we lived, no matter how run down the apartment. Those beloved books were always there for us to admire and then to read as we were growing up.

Her lovely singing voice led her into years of musical training at Henry Street and other East Side Settlements, so when she went to work it was as a pianist in movie houses, accompanying silent films. No job lasted for more than a week because she was not allowed to work on the Sabbath; this was a continual hardship for her.

She was thirty—and still unmarried—when my father, a "greenie" (foreigner), was introduced to her by a relative. Since early marriage was the norm for young women, she had already endured years of cruel comments about being an "old maid." Saddened and embittered, she married but never forgot or forgave those relatives and acquaintances who had made harsh remarks about her having been single so long.

My parents went through many very hard years. When my father had no work, they had to apply for Home Relief (what is called Welfare today). Investigators came to look in Mama's pots to see if she was cooking luxuries like meat, and they questioned her intensively. How she wept afterward each time!

Then there were years on the WPA—Works Progress Administration—when President Roosevelt's government provided low-salaried jobs for the unemployed.

Always, Mama had to scrimp and deny us all but the basics. She became an expert at finding bruised fruit and vegetables, cracked eggs, and day-old bread and cake in Dugan's Bakery. She never paid a fixed price for anything and was a world champion at bargaining over pennies.

Somehow, every day she managed to improvise ample cooked meals: huge basins of homemade soup, plenty of potatoes and other starches, vegetables, and stews, or meatloaves made largely of bread with a little chopped meat. Improvise is the exact word; I was almost adult before I knew that Italian spaghetti sauce was not simply hot catsup.

And we were all clothed though no garment ever fit or matched anything else. It seems to me that I wore the same dreadful, bright red winter coat all through my childhood. My high school yearbook picture still makes me cringe; as editor on the frontispiece, I am wearing someone's discarded housedress.

Some incredible inner strength kept my mother going: washing, ironing, cleaning, cooking endlessly, though the life she'd dreamed of had completely eluded her. *Nobody Knows Me in Miami,* my first juvenile novel, is a fictional rendering of that difficult Depression world of Williams-burg, along with the imagined never-never land of rich relatives.

My mother and her siblings were an unhappy blend of Victorian morality and Orthodox Judaism along with a passion to be middle-class American, to be assimilated. To be "refined." (I detest the word.)

Since I loved my aunts and uncles, my behavior was molded by desire for their approval. Therefore I learned never to mention body functions or the toilet. I dared not speak of or ask about sex. (Indeed, the word was never uttered in our home. I understood it was *dirty*).

Ain't and slang were forbidden. I had to speak grammatically and be meticulous about my pronunciation. Only ignoramuses mispronounced words. I remember one bitter argument between two of my aunts that went on for hours over the correct way to say tomato.

Constantly, I was reminded to stand straight, bathe frequently, and cover my mouth when I yawned. I had to use silverware properly, so people would know I was a lady. Belching or worse was never even discussed much less done; such vulgarities did not occur among "refined" people.

When I played with the kids on the block—jacks and potsy, hide-and-seek and jump rope, and, later on, punch ball and kick-the-can and ring-a-liev-i-o—I envied them their carefree lives: hanging out on stoops or around the lamp post after dusk and sometimes till late at night, singing loudly, cracking their bubble gum, shouting dirty words, reading comics and trading them, eating Chinese food and hot dogs and knishes.

But such low-class entertainments were not for us. Instead we had art, classical music, and, most of all, we had books. *Great Literature.* Reading was refined.

Willingly, eagerly, I became a reader.

The Public Library on Marcy Avenue was a refuge, a two-story red-brick building, warm and silent, run by librarians who, enviably, seemed to know every single book. I spent many hours there particularly during the winters when our house was unbearably cold.

We had a kerosene heater in our living room, but my mother argued that cold was good for us—healthful—and kerosene a luxury. Besides, kerosene had a foul smell. She owned an icebox, as well, but never bought ice even during the summers. This meant she had to shop for food daily as she needed it.

My early favorite books were fairy tales, *Heidi, Pinocchio,* and *Black Beauty,* all of Louisa May Alcott's novels, and *The Secret Garden, Little Lord Fauntleroy,* and *The Little Princess* by Frances Hodgson Burnett. I moved on to Dickens and Twain and Stowe.

I liked school and was a good student, while my older sister didn't like school particularly and didn't shine there. So we became "the pretty one" and "the smart one," and thus we remained.

Each school day, we came home for lunch, and, after a kind uncle donated a radio when I was about nine, we listened to soap operas as we ate. *Helen Trent* and *Our Gal Sunday,* ongoing hard-luck romances, were broadcast during the noon hour and gave us great joy. The *Lux Radio Theatre* on Monday nights was my introduction to drama. My mother's favorite program was John J. Anthony's *Good*

Father, Abraham Louis Solomon

Will Hour, during which people told their sad stories and Mr. Anthony advised them unctuously. It was an hour of pure heartbreak.

My first published work was a limerick, a simple poetic form I am still very fond of today, perhaps because it marked my beginning in print. My limerick appeared in the *Pen and Ink,* PS 16's magazine:

Mrs. Astorbilt once had a poodle,
She fed him on apple strudel.
He became temperamental;
Wouldn't eat beans or lentils,
So they shot him right through the noodle.

The excitement and happiness of seeing my work in print encouraged me so that I began to try to write poems and essays and stories. As soon as I was allowed to, I joined the magazine staff. Dressed in hand-me-downs, pudgy, nearsighted, I had little self-esteem; I got a great boost in eighth grade when I was chosen editor of my graduation issue.

So I felt very early the bliss that comes from making up an original story which others read and enjoy, no matter where it is printed or how few readers there are; being published works a kind of alchemy: printed words on the page, artfully crafted, are transformed into gold.

One other literary coup: the Stuhmer's Pumpernickel Company ran a contest. Entrants had to finish the sentence "I like Stuhmer's pumpernickel because ... " The first prize was money. I entered and won a consolation prize, a two-pound pumpernickel, which I claimed at the neighborhood grocer and carried home bare in my arms for all the neighbors to see. We ate great thick slices of it smeared with butter in celebration, and my mother was inordinately proud of me. I was ecstatic.

The Louis Sobel Post, Jewish War Veterans, to which Papa belonged, started a drum and bugle corps. My sister and I were eager to join, and that pleased Papa.

My mother and her family were appalled. It was not *refined* to go marching in the streets. However, for once my father insisted, much to their chagrin. We joined and paid dues of ten cents each a week. We participated in the marching band for many years.

When I was first given my bugle, everyone's ears suffered as I practiced endlessly, determined to become an expert bugler. I did master the instrument just as Marilyn took on the bass drum and then the glockenspiel. Later, she moved up to being our drum major leading parades by strutting along with a huge silver baton. Definitely not refined.

We didn't care. Uniformed, marching briskly in massive patriotic parades on holidays, we felt important, glamorous, and adventurous. I began to earn pocket money playing "Taps" in cemeteries each Armistice Day and was proud of my expertise. I was entirely enthralled with this new musical career.

I took it all very seriously. The bandmaster one day, inspecting our instruments, said to me sternly, "You need to use more elbow grease when you polish this bugle." I had not used anything—indeed, we didn't have any kind of metal polish in the house—so I immediately went to several local stores earnestly trying to buy "elbow grease." Finally, a kind hardware store owner took pity on me and explained that it wasn't polish my bugle needed—simply harder rubbing with a cloth.

I attended Eastern District High School, a dilapidated institution in our neighborhood (Mel Brooks is our most distinguished alumnus), taking an academic program though my parents were opposed. They argued that a commercial course would be better for a girl. Their reasoning was that I needed a skill so I'd be employable—until someone married me.

I wouldn't agree. Terrible times at home; endless battles as my sister, desperate for pocket money and clothes—and a life—quit school to work in a factory. (Not very "refined"). The *Gold and White,* the high school newspaper, was my haven and my delight. There I found regular publication and friends; Rosa Felsenburg, who loved puns as much as I more than fifty years ago, remains my friend today.

I wrote a weekly humor column: sample titles, "Knish Be True?"; "Why I Hate Frank Sinatra"; followed the next week by "Why I Love Frank Sinatra"; and "I Cried for You," a discussion on the merits of eating onions. I went out on celebrity interviews: Lena Horne was the most memorable.

The faculty adviser to the newspaper, Seymour Risikoff, was helpful, always accessible, and kind. Happiness was in that newspaper office.

Baby-sitting became my major source of spending money. I liked children and was good with them. The pay varied anywhere from fifty cents an evening on up. For washing the dishes and doing light cleaning, I earned a few cents more. One very good client was a young widow; the problem was that she had no one to walk me home late at night. Since I could whistle very loudly—a result of bugling—I walked myself home, whistling for courage. I'm still a first-class whistler.

During the last two years of high school I picked up odd jobs during the summers and school breaks. I cleared tables in a Bickford's cafeteria; I sold cream-cheese-and-nut sandwiches at Chock Full o' Nuts; I was a waitress in a Catskills resort; I became a camp counselor/bugler.

All through these years I kept reading steadily, mostly fiction: O'Henry, Tarkington, Washington Irving, more Twain, the Brontës, my mother's Blackmore and Scott. I kept writing but it was primarily journalistic. My English classes were a constant joy and my math classes a constant sorrow. I was introduced to Shakespeare, the Brownings, Edith Wharton, and George Eliot and a whole crowd of marvelous writers.

World War Two raged during my adolescence, and I, along with my family, was intensely patriotic. My father's army experience, fear of Hitler and Nazism, sorrow for European Jews and all the other war victims churned within me. So much so that when the Red Cross asked for blood donors, my sister and I volunteered.

She was nineteen then and I just under sixteen (underage). I decided to lie. Alas, whenever I lie, the adrenaline flows and I become overexcited. Always poor in arithmetic, in this situation I proved an absolute fool.

The Red Cross Nurse who enrolled us asked Marilyn's birthdate first.

"September 28, 1924," Marilyn said truthfully, and she qualified as a donor.

I came next. To the same query, I immediately answered, "November 6, 1924."

"Twins?" The startled nurse didn't know what to make of us.

Behind her back, my sister was signaling frantically with her hands.

"Nope," I said, helpfully. "Just sisters."

That nurse gave me one long look then shook her head. "Excuse me, I'll be right back," she said, and hurried out of the room, I guess to hide her laughter.

Interestingly, there were no follow-up questions. When she returned, she waved me on. Qualified to be a donor.

I suppose they needed the blood so badly that even my underage blood was acceptable. After that we donated blood regularly, and I collected silver foil from discarded cigarette packages and rolled it into tight heavy balls to contribute to the war effort. This was because of the metal shortage; I have no idea if the foil was, indeed, useful.

Mr. Risikoff, our *Gold and White* faculty adviser, was drafted and went off to war, leaving his wife and young son. Another English teacher took over the newspaper. He was nice, but it was not the same.

Throughout these years, I had girlfriends but no boyfriends. My sister and I would occasionally—when we could muster up the money—go to the Roseland Ballroom and jitterbug for hours with the soldiers and sailors the city was filled with. We became perilous lindy hoppers. (My mother thought the dance was a kind of insanity. She admired the Viennese waltz.)

For us, dancing was a pleasure and a release from the dreariness of Williamsburg. Often, before these outings, Marilyn would lend me a blouse and skirt from her small wardrobe and stockings and high heels, all paid for with her factory wages; she was always very generous. I was not her size, but that was irrelevant. I somehow managed to fit into anything that was pretty.

In June of 1944, with one more term of high school to go, I caused a major crisis at home. Five of us were living in a three-room apartment with a tiny kitchenette and a bathroom in the hall, where I did my homework often, amid frequent interruptions. It was the only quiet, private room in the apartment.

(In 1996 when the houselights dimmed and the curtain rose for the play *Napoli Milionario,* I gasped in recognition. According to the program we were in a grimy, bombed-out Neapolitan slum apartment in wartime. Not me; I was back in my parents' apartment in Williamsburg, Brooklyn. The lumpy couch with an ill-fitting cover, the rickety table and chairs, the light bulb swinging from center ceiling at the end of a twisted wire, all of the shabbiness was achingly familiar. Lest my memory was playing tricks, I looked at my husband and saw that he too recognized it.

Mother, Regina Glatter

Long after I'd escaped, my parents had continued to live there.)

So, in 1944, because our whole family had a single clothes closet, I took some of my precious baby-sitting savings and bought a cardboard closet for my sister and myself.

I set up this new wardrobe in the bedroom, and when my mother saw it she grew hysterical. A freestanding cardboard closet in her bedroom! How dared I? It was ugly and lower class. It spoiled the "decor." It would have to go at once.

The insanity of the word "decor" for the crowded, cold-water flat—shabby, cracking walls; bumpy linoleum floors; ugly rooms—was too much for me. The closet went and I went with it. I packed a suitcase, took my small savings, and set off absolutely terrified. From a newspaper ad, I found a room in the Hotel Latham, a quiet not-very-expensive hotel in lower Manhattan.

I got myself two jobs; in the daytime I worked in a paint factory pasting labels on cans, and evenings I sold roast beef sandwiches at McGinnis, a restaurant on Forty-ninth Street in Manhattan. I planned to save enough to keep me through my final term in high school. I spent that summer scared but determined.

I was not ready for the loneliness that came with independence. I loved and missed my family—difficult though they were—and I let them know where I was.

As the hectic summer came to an end and the High Holy Days drew near, Papa came up to McGinnis and begged me to come back home. He was terribly sad. "A nice Jewish girl does not live alone," he reasoned. "Tell me one girl you know who lives that way." I couldn't. In those days it was uncommon for *any* single young woman to live alone; one either married or lived with one's family. So I returned.

Then word came that Mr. Risikoff was killed in action; the newspaper staff was desolate. It was unbelievable, terrible news.

That senior term I was editor of the *Eastern,* our high school yearbook. I looked toward graduation with mixed feelings of fear and joy. The day that I heard that Brooklyn College was giving its entrance exam and that the people who passed could go to college *free,* ever the optimist, I raced home overjoyed. College! No one in our family had been to college. One of my aunts had gone to Normal School and was a gym teacher, but this was a real liberal arts college! And it was FREE.

Of course, my parents were opposed to my taking the test and to the whole idea of college. We were poor, they argued quite sensibly. It was necessary for me to contribute to the household expenses. My obligation was to go to work.

Furthermore, they reasoned, a girl didn't need a college education, especially a girl like me. I was too smart already. I had a big mouth. No man would ever marry me. Men did not like smart women. My folks absolutely believed this and repeated it day and night.

I took the test, and I passed.

I started college, but I could no longer be a burden at home. My friend Rosa, already a college student, had left her Orthodox Jewish family to live as a mother's helper with Mrs. Risikoff, our teacher's widow, and her young son.

"With my older sister, Marilyn," 1930

When, in the Job Placement office at the college, I saw a notice that a family living near the campus wanted a live-in babysitter, with terror in my heart, I applied.

The Blum family lived in a handsome private house on East Nineteenth Street in Flatbush, within walking distance of the college. They interviewed me in a huge, booklined living room: rugs on the floor, a working fireplace, paintings and sculpture decorating the place.

They currently had a live-in maid, Ethel Williams, who served us coffee and cake as we talked. She no longer wanted to live in but wanted to continue working for them. Because they went out a lot in the evenings, they needed a baby-sitter for their two young sons.

They liked me; I liked them; I moved into their attic and there I lived for the next four years. Lee Blum was a lawyer turned businessman; Ann Blum, a stunning blonde, had studied drama but was now busy being wife and mother. They were kind beyond belief; they took me in; they made me feel part of their family; they advised me and they cared for me. I reciprocated, and I felt incredibly lucky to have found them.

Flatbush was an alien land, but, fortunately, Rosa's live-in job with Mrs. Risikoff was only a few blocks away. We could support one another.

Since the Blums gave me room and board but no salary, I found a weekend day-job. Planter's Peanuts had a huge store on Broadway looking out on Duffy Square;

sometimes I worked behind the counter selling nuts; more often, clad in a huge white apron, I stood in their vast Broadway window each Saturday and Sunday and roasted huge mesh baskets of nuts in a vat of sizzling oil.

My college friends would come by and wave or stand outside the window making faces at me. Working in the Planter's store was lively, and I had marvelous nuts to eat—brazils, cashews, walnuts, pistachios, pecans. I gained impressive weight on that job.

The first months at college I was dazed. I could not really believe I was on this beautiful campus with a lily pond and a huge library, among people who cared about books and ideas. My scholarship was spotty and not very thorough, but I read and wrote voraciously. I was interested in everything.

My free college education was a privilege, a great gift the city was giving me, and I never took it for granted. That is why I was so sad, many years later, when New York began to charge tuition at its colleges. If I'd had to pay, I could not have gone. How different my life would have been!

I believe that the new tuition fees keep many deserving but poor students away today.

I remained in close touch with my family; my kid brother was suddenly very tall and husky-voiced. Happily, my sister married a nice young man from the neighborhood. They set up their own modest apartment in Williamsburg, warm in the winter and with a refrigerator. I rejoiced for her.

My new brother-in-law, Milton Koster, a truck driver, didn't understand why I wanted to be a writer, but he knew I'd need a typewriter to accomplish my goal, and he got me one as a gift. It was an incredible act of generosity.

Lonely on campus, I sought out the office of *Vanguard,* the college newspaper, and, once again, I wrote my way in. Doing straight news stories, at first, about club meetings and guest speakers on campus, I soon moved on to features and then humor columns.

When Dannon Strawberry Yogurt (the only flavor besides Plain, at first) appeared in the school cafeteria, I tracked this exotic Balkan food down to its manufacturer.

As camp counselor and bugler, 1946

During my interview with the Dannon people, they confided that their advertisements were not as successful as they'd hoped, and they couldn't understand why. Studying their ads—all of which featured the special culture of *bacteria* in their yogurt—I suggested that *bacteria* were not appealing to Americans. (Even *good* bacteria). To Europeans, maybe, but to us, no.

I wrote a column full of bad puns about "an udder food coming from behind the strawberry curtain," a "cultured" food just right for a liberal arts college cafeteria. Several months later I received a truly lovely gift from the Dannon people—a compact—along with a note thanking me for my tip about the bacteria. This was the single advertising coup of my life.

Writing for *Vanguard* brought me good friends, among them Nancy Terrizzi, Norma Lieberman, Shelly Mehlman, and Mike Levitas, all of whom remained interested in writing after graduation: Nancy as poet and editor, Norma as publicist and advertising writer, Shelly as baseball chronicler and travel writer, and Mike as an editor of the *New York Times.*

My happiest college memories are of the noisy, frenzied hours in the newspaper office. And, the *Vanguard* connection, indirectly, led me to my husband.

Summers I continued to work: waiting tables in resorts in the Catskills and the Pocono Mountains, ticketing cloth in a garment factory, bugling in girls' camps.

Lee and Ann Blum believed in my writing, but they cautioned me that I needed a way to earn a living immediately after graduation. Writers, even very good writers, often starve, they warned. Reluctantly, I took education courses, sacrificing precious literature and writing credits for educational psychology and methods courses.

In February, 1949, finished with college, I was uncertain. What next? Teaching jobs were not instantly available. In New York City, for a teaching license one needed to go through a lengthy examination process. There was first a written exam, then a speech exam, and a demonstration lesson.

I took a six-week speedwriting and typing course and got myself a job as a secretary receptionist in a New York school that taught ex-GIs to make false teeth.

I hated the job and was so bad at it, I used to carry home stacks of spoiled letterhead so the boss wouldn't know how poor a typist I was. He knew, but he liked me, and he kept me on, though he marveled at my ineptitude. Try though I did, I couldn't work the intercom. When a call came for him, I would *yell* his name loudly and rap on the office wall instead.

I told myself this could not be my life; I needed to be back on a campus. Boldly, I—along with my *Vanguard* friend Nancy Terrizzi—applied to Paul Engle's Writers' Workshop at the State University of Iowa in Iowa City. We sent samples of our writing; we waited what seemed a cruel amount of time, and then we were accepted into the MFA program: two years of study, comprehensive exams, and a creative thesis.

So Nancy and I, festooned with huge corsages, met in Pennsylvania Station with our entire families in our wake to see us off on this singular daring adventure.

We took the train to Iowa and another world, a flat, spread-out Midwest city, populated large by students. In our courses were many writers or would-be writers, a few with rare talent and a lot who were poseurs.

We, immediately on arriving, found jobs at the psychiatric hospital on campus. From eleven at night to seven in the morning, five nights week, we sat on the wards monitoring desperately ill women and unlocking bathrooms on request.

On quiet nights, we wrote, or read: Sterne, Defoe, Henry James, Forster, Flaubert, Dostoevsky, Kafka, Tolstoy, and Goncharov, among others. On bad nights we did little else but comfort, talk to, restrain, and try to help patients.

One of the perks of the job was the privilege of eating meals, if we chose to, in the hospital cafeteria, which was subsidized so the prices were very low. My first breakfast the was memorable: an orange (five cents), two slices of French toast (four cents), and coffee (two cents). Nancy and I took to eating suppers and breakfasts there. The food was abundant but awful.

Paul Engle, a bluff Iowa poet, headed the workshop, which was staffed by Robey Macauley, Hansford Martin, Ray West, and Verlin Cassill. Cassill, a novelist, was my workshop adviser, and he was helpful, kind, but detached. I was on my own.

I read and wrote—when I could stay awake—and I submitted stories to the workshop, which periodically were mimeographed (without the author's name) and distributed to the fifty or so members. Each Friday, we'd meet and discuss the week's stories; the talk was stimulating, the criticism often outrageous and rarely helpful, but great fun.

I was happier than I'd ever been. Literary lions came along regularly to lecture on the college circuit. By juggling our nights off with other aides, Nancy and I got to hear, among others, Robert Penn Warren, the novelist, who talked about the "bumps" in his prose, and the poets: Dylan Thomas, who read magnificently though he was fearfully drunk, and Robert Lowell, who smoked continuously, fearfully nervous.

We listened to many great scholars including Harry Levin, the James Joyce authority from Harvard; Cleanth Brooks from Yale, whose book *The Well-Wrought Urn* was revered by our teachers; and Malcolm Cowley, the Hemingway expert, who scolded us for being in school. If we wanted to be writers, he said, we ought to follow Hemingway's advice and be out in the world living.

We heard some terrible speakers, too, academicians who did not prepare and bumbled incoherently. I resented them; they knew better; they had stolen my precious sleep time.

Meanwhile things back in Williamsburg took a bad turn. My brother, Arnold, miserable in high school and depressed by poverty and difficult family living conditions, ran away from home and enlisted in the army. He was sixteen years old but very tall and well built, and he looked much older.

My parents, frantic, wanted to tell the army his true age so he'd be discharged, but he urged them not to. He feared he would be dishonorably discharged if they did—and he threatened that he would simply run away again. He wrote to me that he *had* to be away. Home was intolerable. He would finish his high school courses in the army. He

would get his diploma. He would make a life and we'd be proud of him.

They let him stay.

At the end of the first year in Iowa, I took the comprehensive exams and earned the highest grade in my cohort. My friends really teased me, but—once I believed it—I was immensely proud. I submitted my collection of prose, *Sick and Other Stories,* and earned my master's in English with a concentration on American literature.

Life was good. I had a job, a boyfriend, and I was writing. One more year, another set of exams and another thesis, and I would have the coveted M.F.A. in creative writing. There was also a doctorate possible. I could write a novel for my thesis. A novel! I stayed.

My brother, stationed in the peacetime army in Japan, was indeed completing his high school requirements and having a fascinating time. We kept in close touch through letters in which he sounded happy and purposeful and very mature.

Then, in June 1950, the Korean War broke out! The peacetime army men who had been stationed in Japan—without any retraining or warning—were immediately plunged into battle.

So, in the third week of the Korean War—which was not really a war but a "police action"—my brother, Arnold, not yet seventeen years old, was reported missing in action. And so he remained, MIA, for many months.

Numb, I stayed on at Iowa. There was nothing to do but wait and hope. I finished my work, took my M.F.A. comprehensive exams and passed, but could not stay on to finish my thesis. My sister summoned me back to New York. She could no longer cope with the situation at home—my mother was behaving bizarrely—so I went back in the summer of 1951.

Shelly Mehlman and her husband kindly let me sleep on their couch while I looked for a job; I became a contest judge for the Reuben H. Donnelley Company and spent my days judging limericks for a contest sponsored by Colgate, Palmolive, and Peet.

My father and sister were terribly sad, mourning, but my mother—oddly—was secretive and optimistic. She kept smiling inappropriately and saying that she had taken care of everything. But she would not explain.

She, who her whole life had looked down on and been snobbish about people who hung out at the beach or went to amusement parks, had taken to spending every Sunday in Coney Island. *Every Sunday!* Doing what? Nobody knew. Months passed.

Then my brother's "remains" were returned for burial, and at the terrible funeral—a sealed coffin covered by a great flag and guarded by four soldiers with rifles—my mother would not allow the rabbi to cut her garment, a traditional rite. Nor would she "sit shivah" afterward (sit mourning on a wooden box instead of a chair, and remain shoeless). Watching her violate these religious rituals that were so much a part of her life, I realized that she was in desperate trouble.

There was nothing for me to do but to bully her into telling. So I did. I warned her that I would go to the police and bring them to the house (and all the neighbors would see) if she didn't tell me what was going on.

Trapped, and with the greatest resentment, she compromised; she would not tell *me* anything, but she would go

The author's younger brother, Arnold, killed in action in Korea when not yet seventeen

with me to police headquarters. There, with me locked out of the room during the detective's gentle but skillful questioning, she finally showed her bankbook and revealed her secret to them.

My brother was not dead! She knew that because a Gypsy fortune-teller was helping her bring him home alive and well—by burning up her "dirty money," her life's savings: the pitiful few thousand dollars she had scrimped and struggled to save so she would never again have to be on Relief.

This scam had been going on for almost a year. It began on Mother's Day in 1951, when my weeping mother had wandered into the Gypsy princess's fortune-telling store and asked, "Can you tell me why I'm here?"

The seer, after studying this desolate, shabby, middle-aged woman, had not missed a beat. "Someone is missing," she declared. And she had my mother.

The complicated year-long relationship between the two women, and the Gypsy's demands, as well as her rituals and magic, are the materials from which I fashioned my adult novel *In a Cold Open Field.*

The novel, first written thirty years ago and rewritten many times since, was published in 1997 after forty-five rejections. It is fiction; I am nowhere in the book. Of all my books, it is the one I cherish most.

While all this family trouble was going on, I took and passed the New York teaching exam. I began to teach English at Julia Ward Howe Junior High School 81 in Harlem. I enjoyed teaching but was angered by the injustices in the city school system. I started to write a novel set in a school like my own.

I'd found an inexpensive room—share the bath—on Bedford Street in Greenwich Village (upstairs from my friend Rosa), and I was busy teaching and writing.

In 1952, my friend Nancy, who'd married a member of the Writers' Workshop and was living in the South, came to New York on a visit. She dropped in, bringing along with her a young editor she knew, Morton Klass, who, that night, gallantly memorized my phone number.

We began to go out together. Mort was editing pulp magazines days and going to college nights, studying anthropology. He had read, it seemed to me, everything ever written, and we had some heroic literary arguments, the most memorable over why, in the story "Metamorphosis," Franz Kafka turned the protagonist into a roach. Why a roach?

Well, I had—and still have—many deep symbolic reasons. I had just spent two years studying literature and thinking about writing and why writers do what they do. But Mort insisted—and to this day insists—that Kafka was sitting up late one night with one of his headaches, writing, in his miserable Prague apartment, and he just happened to look up on the wall and there. . . .

No way would I allow that theory then nor do I allow it now. We're still arguing.

In Iowa I had learned to live very cheaply, and I continued to live that way in New York, so that in the summer of 1952 I was able to go—with my friend Norma Lieberman from the Brooklyn College *Vanguard*—to Europe inexpensively. Together we wandered through England, France, Italy, Switzerland, Holland, and Belgium.

It was a summer of laughter. We were truly innocents abroad, and we loved every dumb thing we did. She stepped into the canal getting out of a gondola in Venice. On Bastille Day in Paris, we were wandering around the Place de la Bastille and I asked a woman selling pralines where the Bastille was. She looked at me in utter surprise and said, "That is what we are celebrating, Mademoiselle. It is not here. They tore it down!"

During 1953, two wonderful events occurred: I completed my second thesis, a new collection of short fiction called *The Village Harlot and Other Stories,* and I was awarded my master's of fine arts (creative writing) by the State University of Iowa. More important, on May 2, Mort and I were married in Garfein's, an old-fashioned East Side Jewish restaurant.

We had decided that Mort would go to school full-time so he could finish his B.A., then go on to graduate school; I would support us on my teacher's salary.

We set up housekeeping in a two-room apartment on East Fourth Street near Second Avenue; then, it was just the East Side, but it has since become the fashionable "East Village." In one large room we cooked, ate, slept, and entertained; the smaller room became our study, and we bought two huge, old-fashioned desks at which we could each work.

Mort, himself a fine writer of short fiction and much anthropological literature, has from the first been my

"Our wedding day, May 2, 1953"

staunchest fan and critic. Never once has he failed me. He reads whatever I write, he suggests changes, he edits, and he defends himself when I attack. Because, after seeking his advice, I usually get defensive and go after him. Like most writers I know, I don't really want criticism. What I really want is approval.

While initially I often don't agree with my husband's judgment, I respect it and I consider what he says. Often, later, it makes sense. I am very lucky to have his literary expertise.

In 1957 after Mort completed his graduate studies, we went off to live for a year and for him to conduct research in Felicity, a village of East Indian sugarcane cutters in Trinidad. While he interviewed the villagers, I—pregnant then—finished my Harlem school novel and then gave birth to Perri, our Trinidad baby.

Her birth is celebrated In *Everyone in This House Makes Babies,* a humorous memoir. The book tells of our wonderful year spent in a house built on stilts with a sheet of corrugated iron for its roof, without plumbing. Our Hindu neighbors were kind, shrewd, tactful folk who helped us constantly, laughed at our foolish urban ways, and welcomed Perri into their village. They gave her a Hindi name: *Tulsi Devi,* which means sacred flower.

After Trinidad, we returned to New York, where my husband finished his doctoral dissertation; then we moved on to Bennington College in Vermont, his first teaching job. In Bennington in 1960 our son, David, was born.

The Harlem school novel, *Come Back on Monday,* appeared to good reviews in 1960; I had dreamed the book would help correct the injustices in the New York school system, but nothing much happened.

Vermont was pleasant, but I missed New York City terribly, so I felt great joy when we returned, my husband to teach at Barnard College and Columbia University, and I to stay home with my children and write. A happy time.

In 1964, after learning to speak Bengali, we took our children to live for a year in a poor, coal-mining region in West Bengal, India, about a hundred miles from Calcutta. My husband wanted to study the effects on village life of a bicycle factory, built on rice land by the British ten years previously. How, he wondered, had the factory changed the rice farmers' village life?

Because there was no sanitation, potable water, or electricity in the village, we had to live in a small town nearby. In India there is an enormous labor force; each small job is done by a different individual. I had to learn to manage a household staff: cook, dishwasher, and "sweeper" (who cleaned the outhouse). Our cooking was all done on a clay stove; the fuel was dried cowdung. We ate delicious curries three times a day; I am a devotee of curries, but once I asked an Indian neighbor if he didn't tire of having them all the time. He thought the question was mad: who could mind having the same delicious food repeatedly?

That year in the boondocks of India was rich in adventure and sparked two novels: *Bahadur Means Hero* and *A Perpetual Surprise,* comic tales about poor but clever Indians surviving by their wits.

Back home again, and as my children grew older and started school, I began to long for the classroom again—as a teacher. I'd come to love it. In 1965 I took a part-time job teaching English at Borough of Manhattan Community

College of the City University of New York. This new two-year college had no campus. Classes met in office buildings on Fiftieth Street and Broadway overlooking the Winter Garden. My students reminded me of myself when younger; for the most part they were poor, scared, first-generation-to-go-to-college kids. I taught evenings, when my husband was at home with our children.

Our third child, Judy, was born in 1967. Just then there was a full-time job opening at the college, and I applied, not knowing how we would manage. I got the job. This was before the days when casual "day care" was available. We managed, but with a balancing act so precarious I had little time to write.

We were living then in Columbia University housing; the streets around us suddenly erupted with demonstrations—some of them violent—against the university, the government, the Vietnam War. Worried about the safety of our children, we escaped to New Jersey, to a small bedroom suburb, Leonia, just over the George Washington Bridge.

There we lived for more than twenty years. We had a big old house with lots of room, safe streets, and a mediocre school system. I often used my bugle to call my family to meals; I couldn't do *that* in an apartment. We even had a dog, Bingo. The dog was a disappointment, sweet but dumb—and so, to my urban taste, was suburban living.

Since I'd tried to learn to drive but failed because I was too cowardly, I had to depend on my husband and the commuter bus for transportation. I felt locked in, claustrophobic.

I was so busy: commuting by bus to my job, running a house, cooking, doing laundry and cleaning (well, not much) for a family of five, I didn't get to do a lot of writing, and I missed it.

I had a tiny attic room which offered quiet and seclusion; that was really all I needed. (Along with free time.) Those years taught me that the longest distance on earth for the writer is the distance between the kitchen and the attic.

I tried writing in the early mornings or late nights. I could manage only short time periods. So I began to write brief humorous essays about life in the suburbs, journalism once again, which I sold to newspapers: the *New York Times, Bergen Record, Jerusalem Post* among them. I began to review books regularly for the *New York Times Book Review.*

I did complete *A Perpetual Surprise,* my second novel set in India, in 1977—just in time to enter it in the Harvard University Press Short Novel Program. Harvard Press advertised that it was looking for three short novels, each to be published in hardcover and the author to receive $1,000. The judges were John Gardner, Eudora Welty, and Irving Howe.

After a long interval, word came: they loved it!

For the next two years, Harvard Press kept my novel, periodically informing me that it *had been* selected by the judges. All they needed were two more winning manuscripts!

Then—one day I came home to find my mailbox jammed with the returned manuscript, along with a note from Pearl K. Bell, who was newly in charge of *terminating* the Harvard Program.

Sheila and Morton Klass with their three children: (from left) David, Judy, Perri, on a camping trip in 1971

She was so sorry but since mine was the only short novel of the thousands submitted that was worthy of publication, and Harvard had been unable to find at least three short novels worth bringing out simultaneously, the entire short-novel program was being abandoned. "I know this will bring cold comfort to you," Ms. Bell wrote, returning the manuscript with praise for my skill, patience, etc.

Cold comfort, indeed. I was frozen by her words.

I was pretty tough; I had thought I'd learned to handle rejection. Any writer must develop strong defenses to survive the continual "Sorry not for us" slips, but this blow was devastating. Included in the returned work were the comments of the three distinguished judges, wonderful laudatory words that only added to my pain.

Shortly afterward, in his *New York Times* book column, Herbert Mitgang wrote about Harvard Press's treatment of me. Phil Zuckerman, the editor of a small press, Apple-Wood Books, Cambridge, Massachusetts, read Mitgang's article and asked to see the manuscript, and he immediately agreed to publish it.

I was comforted, but for the first time since I'd started writing, I did not have the heart to begin a new novel. Harvard Press's actions had traumatized me. Yet, I desperately needed to write.

I cast about and found a different direction. Deciding to use my teaching experience with young people, I tried my hand at books for them; I wrote *Nobody Knows Me in Miami,* a juvenile novel, and I liked doing it so much I immediately wrote a second one, *To See My Mother Dance.* Both young people's books were published in 1981. At the same time, Apple-Wood's lovely edition of *A Perpetual Surprise* appeared. Critics were kind; the best review—in the *New Yorker!*—called it "a delightful comic novel."

I continue to this day writing books for young people, as well as adult fiction, because both are a great pleasure. Not only do I like to write the juvenile and young adult novels, but I enjoy going into the schools to read from them and talk to students about writing. For many years I have been part of the School Volunteer Program, which sends authors into the New York City schools. I adopt two classes every year and visit each class four times, talking, reading, to them, and working with them.

Unexpectedly, all three of my children have grown up to be professional writers. While it's a great joy, I take no credit for it. I never urged it on them as a profession. I think it means that they saw how much pleasure I get from my writing, they tried it, and it worked for them, too.

Perri, the Trinidad baby, is now a pediatrician who writes novels and short stories and also does much medical and other journalism. Her most recent novel is *Other Women's Children;* her newest nonfiction work is *Baby Doctor: A Pediatrician's Training.*

David writes novels for adults and for young people and is a screenwriter as well. He did the screenplay for the movie *Kiss the Girls,* and his young adult novel, *California Blue,* has won many prizes.

Judy, my youngest child, is a science fiction writer, a playwright, and a poet. She authored *Wild Kingdom,* a collection of poetry, and her "Star Trek" novel, *The Cry of the Onlies,* was a *New York Times* best-seller.

My husband is a prolific writer of scholarly anthropological papers and books. His most recent work is *Ordered Universes: Approaches to the Anthropology of Religion.*

This much family detail is cited here only because *all five* of us are writers. I've given much thought to how it affects us, how we function as a family, how we feel about competition, and one another's success or failure.

My two older children are better-known writers than I—with Judy coming along fast—and they earn far more than I ever shall from writing. Do I mind?

Not in the least. I'm amazed (that those little kids they once were can beat me) and delighted. One's children's triumphs are vicarious delights.

I believe that we are very lucky. Each of us has singular interests and tastes and a very individual writing style, so we each choose to tread a different literary path. We read one another's manuscripts—candidly—and if we can, we offer suggestions. Lively discussions abound and *sometimes* our insights are useful. When one of us has a success, we all rejoice. How we loved it when David's movie was Number One in the whole country!

How I choose what I write about is a continuing mystery to me. Some attractive idea occurs to me then recurs; I find myself thinking of it and I begin to noodle around on paper. Often when I start, I don't know where I'm headed. I rewrite a lot; I move things around and change them. Once I wrote a whole book and then realized I'd not used the best point of view, so I rewrote it from a different character's perspective and then it was right.

I have written books for young people about the terrible longing to know an absent parent: *To See My Mother Dance,* and the uncertainties of friendships for teenagers: *Alive and Starting Over.*

My book *The Bennington Stitch* deals with teenagers and their parents' unrealistic expectations for them. In it a mother wants her daughter to go to Bennington College, a very special "arts" school, and have the chance she (the mother) missed. The daughter has other talents and other ideas but doesn't want to hurt her mother. The book tells of their struggle.

After writing two adult novels from a male point of view, I became interested in doing a young adult novel that way. *Page Four* is told by a young man, a high school senior, with a shoddy academic record who decides he wants a shot at college. He writes his college entrance essay (applications often tell students, on page four, to continue the essay as long as they want to). The book is his honest explanation of what happened in his personal life to destroy his high school career.

I believe that any really good writer can tell a story from any point of view effectively, and we should not limit our possibilities. Men can write romances and women can do adventure novels; what's necessary is commitment, originality, and much reading as well as skill.

All those years I lived in suburbia led me to write *Credit-Card Carole* about a suburban teenager whose comfortable "credit-card life" is suddenly interrupted when

her father gives up his lucrative dental practice to do what he always wanted to do—to be an actor.

These books deal with the rather ordinary situations of life in which adolescents have to make hard choices, and they make them knowing they must live with the results.

And always, from the corny high school newspaper columns to the books I do now, I have remembered the pleasure and importance of humor. I love hearing jokes and, even better, groaning at the bad ones—those are the best. I try to lighten my books. I'm addicted to puns, and I agree with Charles Lamb that a pun "is a pistol let off at the ear, not a feather to tickle the intellect." Sometimes, though, I have to work on my editors a bit till they agree.

And speaking of editors, I have been singularly lucky to work with really fine editors who loved good books: Hal Cantor at Abelard Schuman, Margaret Cousins at Doubleday, Helen Everitt at Gambit, Phil Zuckerman at Apple-Wood, and when I turned to young people's books, Clare Costello at Scribner's and my current wonderful editor, Regina Griffin, whom I first met at Scholastic but who is now editor-in-chief at Holiday House.

Whenever I hear or read complaints about bad editing, I think about my own fine experiences, and I know I have been very fortunate.

I like to write about young people who show their inner strength, perhaps because adolescents get such a bad press generally. *Kool Ada* is a book I am very proud of; it is the story of a girl from Appalachia, who, uprooted from home and living in Chicago, is a truant, mute with misery. The book is the story of how Ada, with the help of a smart, kind teacher, gets herself back on track.

After Ada, I went on to do two other novels about determined young girls: *Rhino,* which tells the story of Annie Trevor who hates her nose and wants plastic surgery, and *Next Stop, Nowhere,* which follows Beth Converse, a New Yorker with angry, divorced parents, who is suddenly shipped from the city to a small Vermont town to live with her father, an oddball ceramist.

"Our fortieth wedding anniversary, with our children: (from left) Judy, Perri, and David," 1993

Sheila and Mort Klass at Borobudur Temple, Java, Indonesia, 1996

There is only one work of mine that I can trace back to the very first moment of inception; it had an exhilarating beginning and the two years it took to write the book were a continuous adventure.

It began early one Saturday morning in October of 1994, when my husband and I set out to drive northward through New York State to see the fall foliage.

Once on our way, I turned on the car radio and came upon a movie voice I recognized—Mel Gibson. He was narrating *Rabbit-Ears Radio,* a program of dramatized stories for children. I had tuned in just at the moment he was saying, "Here now is the story of Little Miss Sure Shot herself—Annie Oakley."

The story was a true one. Annie was born to a Quaker farm family on the Ohio prairie in 1860 and left fatherless when she was very young. Poor and hungry, one day at the age of eight she lifted her father's old rifle down from the wall, loaded it the way she remembered he had done, and shot a rabbit. Her mother cooked a rabbit stew but scolded her severely; women did not shoot.

But Annie Oakley could not stop shooting. She knew that she had a strange and incredible talent, and she perfected it with practice and rigorous discipline.

For years she supported her struggling family by becoming a market-hunter. She paid off the mortgage on the family farm, and she beat a crack-shot named Frank Butler in a shooting contest; then she married him when she was sixteen, and, soon afterward, became the best sharp-shooter in the world.

Before the Mel Gibson broadcast, I known a little about Annie Oakley. The famous Irving Berlin musical *Annie Get Your Gun,* which starred Ethel Merman, was supposedly based on her life. But that hokey story was at odds with much of what I heard that morning on the radio.

What was the truth? I began to read all I could about Annie Oakley (actually her name was Phoebe Ann Moses but she detested it). I decided to try a historical novel based on her life.

Happily, I set to work, and my novel *A Shooting Star: A Novel about Annie Oakley,* appeared in 1996.

Since I hate guns and anything to do with shooting, I'm not sure why Annie Oakley's life fascinated me so. Was it because I, too, grew up in a poor home? Two earlier books, *Nobody Knows Me in Miami* and *Kool Ada,* are also about young girls so trapped—who prevail.

More likely the paradoxical nature of her life intrigued me: the daughter of peaceful Quakers, she remained ladylike, feminine, sedate, and modest throughout her career as an international sharpshooter.

I am, at this writing, celebrating the publication of my eleventh juvenile novel, *The Uncivil War,* about Asa Andersen, a sixth grader with a first crush—on a boy who teases her unmercifully about her name. He's got an uncle Asa, who's a prizefighter. It's a light book heavy with puns.

Doing the historical novel about Annie Oakley was so gratifying, I decided to do another book in that genre. This time I chose Louisa May Alcott, a long-time heroine of mine.

When Louisa was ten, her family went to live with some other like-minded folks on a communal farm they called "Fruitlands." The adults dreamed of making Fruitlands a vegetarian paradise where everyone was equal, money wasn't necessary, and spiritual values and goodness would reign.

So a bunch of strangers, most of whom were city folk and philosophers, tried to live together in one large house and share everything: work, meals, clothes. All kinds of unexpected things happened, many funny and some quite sad. My book looks at this experiment in living from a child's point of view.

Life remains rich and gratifying. We have three grandchildren, Orlando, Josephine, and Anatol—the offspring of Perri and her mate Larry Wolff—who delight us. I continue to teach because I enjoy teaching, and I believe I do it well. I am long past retirement age.

And when I am not teaching, I'm writing or traveling. For though we are inveterate New Yorkers, both Mort and I love to travel, and together we have traipsed through India, China, and Japan; Java, Sulawesi, and Bali in Indonesia; Israel and Egypt; Poland and Czechoslovakia; and much of western Europe.

We do not travel elegantly; we enjoy exploring new (and usually very old) places, eating the local foods, and learning a bit about the way people live. In our youth we went everywhere on our own, but in recent years we've joined organized tours, simply because tours are easier and safer, though there is a loss of flexibility and freedom.

Still, travel is always adventure. Often, on tours we meet remarkable people; in Poland, recently, for example, we traveled with a woman who, though not in good health, was wandering around the world so she could scatter her mother's ashes in various rivers. Her mother, she explained, had emigrated from Scotland to the United States and then never gotten to go anywhere. The daughter was determined that her mother's ashes would travel all over the world.

Also, in Poland we journeyed to the Auschwitz concentration camp with a lovely, delicate lady, a survivor who had come back to mark the fiftieth anniversary of her release from the Nazi death camp.

"Mengele, the evil doctor, stood right there," she said, pointing to a spot on the field before us, "and said I was to die. But I was very small and I slipped away."

"Hitler," her husband said softly, looking out at the bleak open field, "you are dead and *we* are here."

Traveling shakes up our lives and our prejudices; it renews us. A trip abroad always makes me yearn to be back home and writing again. Which is what I like to do most.

Writings

FOR MIDDLE-GRADE READERS

Nobody Knows Me in Miami, Scribner (New York, NY), 1981.
Kool Ada, Scholastic (New York, NY), 1991.
A Shooting Star: A Novel about Annie Oakley, Holiday House (New York, NY), 1996.
The Uncivil War, Holiday House (New York, NY), 1997.

FOR YOUNG ADULTS

To See My Mother Dance, Scribner (New York, NY), 1981.
Alive and Starting Over, Scribner (New York, NY), 1983.
The Bennington Stitch, Scribner (New York, NY), 1985.
Page Four, Scribner (New York, NY), 1986.
Credit-Card Carole, Scribner (New York, NY), 1987.
Rhino, Scholastic (New York, NY), 1993.
Next Stop, Nowhere, Scholastic (New York, NY), 1995.
Little Women Next Door, Holiday House (New York, NY), 2000.

FOR ADULTS

Come Back on Monday, Abelard-Schuman (New York, NY), 1960.
Everyone in This House Makes Babies, Doubleday (New York, NY), 1964.
Bahadur Means Hero, Gambit (Boston, MA), 1969.
A Perpetual Surprise, Apple-Wood (Cambridge, MA), 1981.
In a Cold Open Field, Black Heron Press (Seattle, WA), 1997.

Also author of one-act play *Otherwise It Only Makes One Hundred Ninety-Nine.* Contributor of short stories and humorous articles to *Hadassah, Manhattan Mind, New York Times,* and other publications.

KOLÍBALOVÁ, Markéta 1953-
(Markéta Prachatická)

Personal

Born December 4, 1953, in Prague, Czechoslovakia (now Czech Republic); daughter of Stanislav (a sculptor) and Vlasta (a sculptress; maiden name, Prachatická) Kolíbal. *Education:* Attended Camberwell College of Arts, London, England, 1990. *Politics:* Conservative. *Religion:* Roman Catholic.

Addresses

Home and office—Na Mícance 26, Prague, Czech Republic 160 00.

Career

Freelance illustrator, 1973—. Academy of Fine Arts, Prague, worked as assistant in graphic department, 1990-92. *Member:* IAA-AIAP.

Awards, Honors

Premio Grafico, Bologna Children's Book Fair, 1983, for *Alice in Wonderland; and, Through the Looking Glass;* British Council scholar in England, 1990.

Writings

SELF-ILLUSTRATED

(Under pseudonym Markéta Prachatická) *O kocîĉce, mysîĉce a ĉervené slepiĉce* (title means "The Cat, the Mouse, and the Red Hen"), Albatros (Prague, Czechoslovakia), 1986.

ILLUSTRATOR

(Under pseudonym Markéta Prachatická) Lewis Carroll, *Alice in Wonderland; and, Through the Looking Glass,* Albatros (Prague, Czechoslovakia), 1983.
Roger McGough, *Nailing the Shadow,* Kestrel Books (London, England), 1987.
French Fairytales, Odeon (Prague, Czechoslovakia), 1988.
Roger McGough, *Counting by Numbers,* Penguin Books for Young Readers, 1990.
Roald Dahl, *James and the Giant Peach,* Albatros (Prague, Czech Republic), 1993.
P. Muldoon, *The Noctuary of Narcissus Batt,* Faber & Faber (London, England), 1996.
Sheep Don't Go to School (poetry anthology for children), Bloodaxe Books (England), 1996.
C. A. Duffy, *Rumpelstiltskin,* Faber & Faber (London, England), 1999.
A sbohem, Ikar (Prague, Czech Republic), 1999.
C. A. Duffy, *The Oldest Girl in the World,* Faber & Faber (London, England), 2000.
Lewis Carroll, *Jabberwocky, and The Walrus and the Carpenter,* Aulos (Prague, Czech Republic), in press.

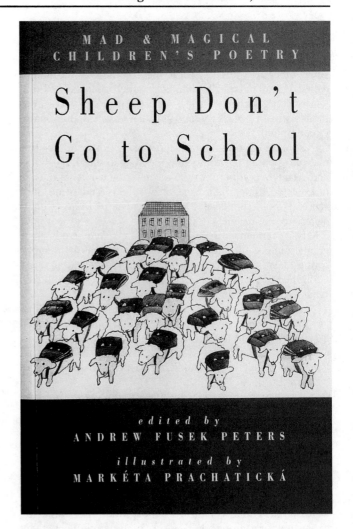

Markéta Kolíbalová (under the name Markéta Prachatická) illustrated this collection of poems by Eastern European writers.

Illustrator of other works published by Albatros (Prague, Czechoslovakia), under pseudonym Markéta Prachatická.

Sidelights

Markéta Kolíbalová told *SATA:* "As both my parents are artists, they took my childhood drawing naturally for granted. In fact I intended to study history at the university. When finishing secondary school, I devoted one summer to drawing, and my father decided that it was worth trying an exam to an art school. I tried then, five times, and was never accepted because my father was a 'persona non grata' for the regime. It normally happened that children of such parents could not study what they wished or what they were gifted for.

"During those five years I worked, using my mother's maiden name as a 'disguise,' for the publishing house Albatros, in Prague, and I won a competition for new post cards. My parents were my tutors at home. I also attended evening classes of drawing for the public and other public courses in art history and languages. I got used to working on books or texts as an exercise for myself. In this way in 1979 I did large drawings for Lewis Carroll's *Alice in Wonderland; and, Through the Looking Glass,* which, in a very complicated way, got published in 1983 and won the Bologna Prize in 1984. This helped me slowly to establish my career, and gradually I have had more and more chances to work for publishers in Prague and abroad.

"I like working for myself. If commissioned I choose to illustrated well-written texts with open imagination, nonsense, absurdity, and wit."

Biographical and Critical Sources

PERIODICALS

Booklist, July, 1988, review of *O kočíčce, myšíčce a červené slepíčce,* p. 21.

* * *

KONIGSBURG, E(laine) L(obl) 1930-

Personal

Born February 10, 1930, in New York, NY; daughter of Adolph (a businessman) and Beulah (Klein) Lobl; married David Konigsburg (a psychologist), July 6, 1952; children: Paul, Laurie, Ross. *Education:* Carnegie Mellon University, B.S., 1952; graduate study, University of Pittsburgh, 1952-54. *Religion:* Jewish.

E. L. Konigsburg

Addresses

Office—c/o Atheneum Books for Young Readers, 1230 Avenue of the Americas, New York, NY 10020.

Career

Writer. Shenango Valley Provision Co., Sharon, PA, bookkeeper, 1947-48; Bartram School, Jacksonville, FL, science teacher, 1954-55, 1960-62. Worked as manager of a dormitory laundry, playground instructor, waitress, and library page while in college; research assistant in tissue culture lab while in graduate school at the University of Pittsburgh.

Awards, Honors

Honor book, *Book Week,* Children's Spring Book Fair, 1967, and Newbery Honor Book, American Library Association (ALA), 1968, both for *Jennifer, Hecate, Macbeth, William McKinley, and Me, Elizabeth;* Newbery Medal, ALA, 1968, Lewis Carroll Shelf Award, 1968, and William Allen White Award, 1970, all for *From the Mixed-up Files of Mrs. Basil E. Frankweiler;* Carnegie Mellon Merit Award, 1971; Notable Children's Book, ALA, and National Book Award finalist, both 1974, both for *A Proud Taste for Scarlet and Miniver;* Notable Children's Book, ALA, and American Book Award nomination, both 1980, both for *Throwing Shadows; Jennifer, Hecate, Macbeth, William McKinley, and Me, Elizabeth, About the B'nai Bagels, A Proud Taste for Scarlet and Miniver,* and *Journey to an 800 Number* were all chosen Children's Books of the Year by the Child Study Association of America; Notable Children's Book, ALA, Parents' Choice Award for Literature, and Notable Children's Trade Book for the Language Arts, National Council of Teachers of English, all 1987, all for *Up from Jericho Tel;* Special Recognition Award, Cultural Council of Greater Jacksonville, FL, 1997; Newbery Medal, ALA, 1997, for *The View from Saturday;* Best Books for Young Adults selections, ALA, for *The Second Mrs. Giaconda* and *Father's Arcane Daughter.*

Writings

FOR CHILDREN; SELF-ILLUSTRATED

Jennifer, Hecate, Macbeth, William McKinley, and Me, Elizabeth, Atheneum (New York, NY), 1967, published in England as *Jennifer, Hecate, MacBeth, and Me,* Macmillan, 1968.
From the Mixed-up Files of Mrs. Basil E. Frankweiler, Atheneum (New York, NY), 1967.
About the B'nai Bagels, Atheneum (New York, NY), 1969.
(George), Atheneum (New York, NY), 1970, published in England as *Benjamin Dickenson Carr and His (George),* Penguin, 1974.
A Proud Taste for Scarlet and Miniver, Atheneum (New York, NY), 1973.
The Dragon in the Ghetto Caper, Atheneum (New York, NY), 1974.
Samuel Todd's Book of Great Colors, Macmillan, 1990.

Samuel Todd's Book of Great Inventions, Atheneum (New York, NY), 1991.

Amy Elizabeth Explores Bloomingdale's, Atheneum (New York, NY), 1992.

FOR CHILDREN

Altogether, One at a Time (short stories), illustrated by Gail E. Haley, Mercer Meyer, Gary Parker, and Laurel Schindelman, Atheneum (New York, NY), 1971, second edition, Macmillan, 1989.

The Second Mrs. Giaconda, illustrated with museum plates, Atheneum (New York, NY), 1975.

Father's Arcane Daughter, Atheneum (New York, NY), 1976.

Throwing Shadows (short stories), Atheneum (New York, NY), 1979.

Journey to an 800 Number, Atheneum (New York, NY), 1982, published in England as *Journey by First Class Camel,* Hamish Hamilton, 1983.

Up from Jericho Tel, Atheneum (New York, NY), 1986.

T-Backs, T-Shirts, COAT, and Suit, Atheneum (New York, NY), 1993.

The View from Saturday, Atheneum (New York, NY), 1996.

Silent to the Bone, Atheneum (New York, NY), 2000.

FOR ADULTS; NONFICTION

The Mask beneath the Face: Reading about and with, Writing about and for Children, Library of Congress, 1990.

TalkTalk: A Children's Book Author Speaks to Grown-Ups, Atheneum (New York, NY), 1995.

OTHER

Also author of promotional pamphlets for Atheneum and contributor to the Braille anthology, *Expectations 1980,* Braille Institute, 1980; subject of a videocassette interview by Tim Podell Productions, *Good Conversation!: A Talk with E. L. Konigsburg,* 1995.

Collections of E. L. Konigsburg's manuscripts and original art are held at the University of Pittsburgh, Pennsylvania.

Adaptations

From the Mixed-up Files of Mrs. Basil E. Frankweiler was adapted for a record and cassette, Miller-Brody/Random House, 1969; a motion picture, starring Ingrid Bergman, Cinema 5, 1973, released as *The Hideaways,* Bing Crosby Productions, 1974; and a television movie, starring Lauren Bacall, 1995. *Jennifer, Hecate, Macbeth, William McKinley, and Me, Elizabeth* was adapted for a television movie titled *Jennifer and Me,* NBC-TV, 1973, and for a cassette, Listening Library, 1986. *The Second Mrs. Giaconda* was adapted for a play, first produced in Jacksonville, FL, 1976. *Father's Arcane Daughter* was adapted for television as *Caroline?,* for the Hallmark Hall of Fame, 1990.

About the B'nai Bagels and *From the Mixed-up Files of Mrs. Basil E. Frankweiler* are available as Talking

Konigsburg offers a glimpse of Renaissance culture in her solution to the mystery of the Mona Lisa. (Cover illustration by Leonardo da Vinci.)

Books. *From the Mixed-up Files of Mrs. Basil E. Frankweiler* is also available in Braille.

Sidelights

An impressive figure in children's literature, E. L. Konigsburg is the only author to have had two books on the Newbery list at the same time. *From the Mixed-up Files of Mrs. Basil E. Frankweiler* won the 1968 Newbery Medal and *Jennifer, Hecate, Macbeth, William McKinley, and Me, Elizabeth* was a runner-up for the award in the same year. Konigsburg has also won not one but two of the coveted Newbery Medals, capturing the 1997 award for *The View from Saturday.* Known for her witty and often self-illustrated works for young people, Konigsburg has carved out a unique niche with her score of published books, generally writing out of personal experience, but sometimes also verging far afield to the medieval world and the Renaissance. As Perry Nodelman noted in *Dictionary of Literary Biography,* Konigsburg is an innovator and tireless experimenter, "a creator of interesting messes." The term "messes" is for Nodelman hardly pejorative; rather, it is an indication of a truly artistic temperament at work.

Konigsburg did not set her sights on writing as a career until later in life. Born in New York, NY, in 1930, she was the middle of three daughters. She grew up in small towns in Pennsylvania, not only absorbing books such as *The Secret Garden* and *Mary Poppins,* but also much unabashed "trash along the lines of *True Confessions,*" as she once reported in *Saturday Review.* "I have no objection to trash. I've read a lot of it and firmly believe it helped me hone my taste." Konigsburg also mentioned that as a child she did much of her reading in the bathroom because "it was the only room in our house that had a lock on the door." She also drew often as a child and was a good student in school, graduating valedictorian of her class. Yet for a young person growing up in the small mill towns of Pennsylvania as Konigsburg did, college was not necessarily the next step. There were advantages to such an upbringing, however. As Konigsburg has commented, "Growing up in a small town gives you two things: a sense of place and a feeling of self-consciousness—self-consciousness about one's education and exposure, both of which tend to be limited. On the other hand, limited possibilities also means creating your own options. A small town allows you to grow in your own direction, without a bombardment of outside stimulation."

And that is precisely what Konigsburg did—she grew in her own way and decided to head for college. Completely ignorant of such things as scholarships, she devised a plan whereby she would alternate working for a year with a year of school. The first year out of high school she took a bookkeeping job at a local meat plant where she met the brother of one of the owners—the man who would become her husband, David Konigsburg. The following year, Konigsburg enrolled in Carnegie Mellon University in Pittsburgh, choosing to major in chemistry. She survived not a few laboratory accidents to eventually take her degree in chemistry. Early in her college career, however, a helpful instructor directed her to scholarships and work-study assistance, so that she was able to continue her studies without break. Konigsburg noted that college was "a crucial 'opening up'" period. "I worked hard and did well. However, the artistic side of me was essentially dormant." She graduated with honors, married David Konigsburg, and went on for graduate study at the University of Pittsburgh. Meanwhile, her husband was also studying, preparing himself for a career in industrial psychology. When her husband won a post in Jacksonville, Florida, Konigsburg picked up and moved with him, working for several years as a science teacher in an all-girls school. The teaching experience opened up a new world for her, giving her insight into the lives of these young girls whom she expected to be terribly spoiled. But she quickly learned that economic ease did nothing to ease inner problems.

Konigsburg left teaching in 1955 after the birth of her first child, Paul. A year later a daughter, Laurie, was born, and in 1959 a third child, Ross. Konigsburg became a full-time mom, taking some time out, however, to pursue painting. She returned to teaching from 1960-1962 until her husband's work required a move to New York. With all the children in school, Konigsburg

then started her writing career. She employed themes and events close to her family life for her books. She also used her children as her first audience, reading them her morning's work when they came home for lunch. Laughter would encourage her to continue in the same vein; glum faces prompted revision and rewrites. Konigsburg once commented that she had noticed that her kids were growing up very differently from the way she did, but that their growing up "was related to this middle-class kind of child I had seen when I had taught at the private girls' school. I recognized that I wanted to write something that reflected their kind of growing up, something that addressed the problems that come about even though you don't have to worry if you wear out your shoes whether your parents can buy you a new pair, something that tackles the basic problems of who am I? What makes me the same as everyone else? What makes me different?"

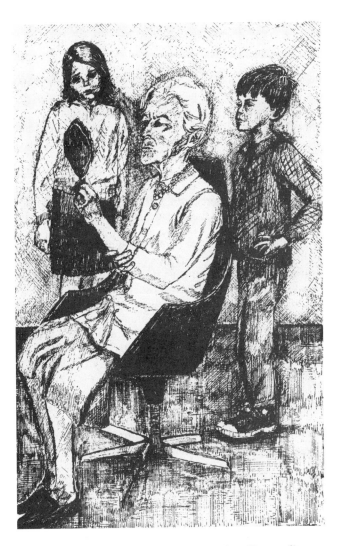

Claudia and Jamie run away to the Metropolitan Museum of Art where a beautiful angel statue inspires them to discover its secret—hidden in the files of the former owner of the statue, Mrs. Basil E. Frankweiler. (From From the Mixed-up Files of Mrs. Basil E. Frankweiler, *written and illustrated by Konigsburg.*)

Such questions led Konigsburg to her first two books, *Jennifer, Hecate, Macbeth, William McKinley, and Me, Elizabeth,* inspired by her daughter's experience making friends in their new home in Port Chester, New York, and *From the Mixed-up Files of Mrs. Basil E. Frankweiler,* which was inspired by the finicky manner in which her kids behaved on a picnic. Konigsburg also illustrated both these books, as she has many of her titles, using her children as models. The first novel tells the story of Elizabeth, who is new in town, and her attempts at finding friendship. It does not help that she is small for her age, and Cynthia, the cool kid in school, is quick to dismiss her. But then Elizabeth meets Jennifer, another classic outsider who styles herself as a witch. Elizabeth soon becomes her apprentice, and suddenly life is full of adventures. Jennifer is a source of mystery for Elizabeth: she never lets the new girl know where or how she lives, and this is just fine for Elizabeth, smitten by Jennifer to the point of declaring that even if she "discovered that Jennifer lived in an ordinary house and did ordinary things, I would know it was a disguise."

Nodelman noted that, baldly told, the story sounds like a "typical wish-fulfillment novel.... [But] as its title suggests this is no ordinary novel. It is too witty." As Nodelman pointed out, Elizabeth comes face to face with the important issue of what it means to be "normal," and decides not to worry about that. "The idea that it is better to be yourself than to be 'normal' and accepted by others transcends the cheap egocentricity of most wish-fulfillment fantasies," according to Nodelman. It is this extra dimension of story-telling that has set Konigsburg apart from other children's writers from the outset of her career. She eschews the easy solution and turns cliches on their head. Critical reception for this first book was quite positive. *Booklist* contributor Ruth P. Bull called it "a fresh, lively story, skillfully expressed," and a contributor for *Publishers Weekly* warned against allowing a too-cute title scare readers away from "one of the freshest, funniest books of the season." This same reviewer went on presciently to say that the reader will have "the smug pleasure" of saying in later years—when the author would surely make a name for herself—that he or she had read Konigsburg when she was just beginning. Writing in *Horn Book,* Ruth Hill Viguers also praised the book, noting that the story "is full of humor and of situations completely in tune with the imaginations of ten-year-old girls."

Konigsburg's second novel, *From the Mixed-up Files of Mrs. Basil E. Frankweiler,* was published shortly after her first. Following a family picnic in Yellowstone Park in which Konigsburg's children complained of the insects and the warm milk and the general lack of civilization, Konigsburg came to the realization that if they should ever run away from home, they would surely carry with them all the stuffy suburban ways that were so inbred in them. This started her thinking of a pair of children who run away from home to the Metropolitan Museum of Art, a safe sort of imitation of far-away places. Claudia, tired of being taken for granted at home, plans to run away and takes her younger brother Jamie—the one with a sense for

finances—with her on this safe adventure. Together they elude guards at the Met, sleep on royal beds, bathe in the cafeteria pool, and hang about lecture tours during the day. Their arrival at the museum coincides with the showing of a recent museum acquisition, a marble angel believed to have been sculpted by Michelangelo. Soon they are under the spell of the angel and want to know the identity of the carver, and this brings them to the statue's former owner, Mrs. Frankweiler. The story is narrated in the form of a letter from Mrs. Frankweiler to her lawyer, and it is she who confronts Claudia with the truth about herself. "Returning with a secret is what she really wants," says Mrs. Frankweiler. "Claudia doesn't want adventure. She likes baths and feeling comfortable too much for that kind of thing. Secrets are the kind of adventure she needs. Secrets are safe, and they do much to make you different. On the inside, where it counts."

Booklist reviewer Bull concluded that this second novel was "fresh and crisply written" with "uncommonly real and likable characters," and Bull praised the humor and dialogue as well. Viguers, writing in *Horn Book,* noted that the novel violated every rule of writing for children, yet was still "one of the most original stories of many

Kidnapped and presumed dead, Caroline returns to her family seventeen years later in this mystery novel. (Cover illustration by Konigsburg.)

years." A *Kirkus Reviews* critic commented that whereas Konigsburg's first title is a "dilly," this one is a "dandy—just as fast and fresh and funny, but less spoofing, more penetrating." Plaudits continued from Alice Fleming, who noted in the *New York Times Book Review* that Konigsburg "is a lively, amusing and painlessly educational storyteller," and from *Washington Post Book World* reviewer Polly Goodwin, who commented that the book is "an exceptional story, notable for superlative writing, fresh humor, an original theme, clear-eyed understanding of children, and two young protagonists whom readers will find funny, real and unforgettable." Award committees agreed with the reviewers, and for the first time in its history, the Newbery list contained two titles by the same author.

In Konigsburg's acceptance speech for her first Newbery, she talked about her overriding feeling of owing kids a good story. "[I try to] let the telling be like fudge-ripple ice cream. You keep licking the vanilla, but every now and then you come to something richer and deeper and with a stronger flavor." Her books all explore this richer and deeper territory, while employing humor in large doses. However, instant success is a hard act to follow, and her third book, *About the B'nai Bagels,* a Little League baseball story with a Jewish Mother twist, was not as well received as the first two. A further suburban tale is *(George),* Konigsburg's "most unusual, messiest, and most interesting book," according to Nodelman. Ben is a twelve-year-old with an inner voice he calls George who acts as a sort of higher intelligence and conscience for the boy. When Ben, who is a bright student, is placed in a high school chemistry class, George starts acting out, causing a crisis of identity.

A fascination for medieval times led Konigsburg to a major departure from suburban themes with her *A Proud Taste for Scarlet and Miniver,* a historical fantasy—told from the participants' points of view in heaven—about the life of Eleanor of Aquitaine. Though some critics found the book to be too modern for the subject, in the *Bulletin of the Center for Children's Books* Zena Sutherland called it "one of the most fresh, imaginative, and deft biographies to come along in a long, long time." Paul Heins, writing in *Horn Book,* also noted that Konigsburg's drawings "are skillfully as well as appropriately modeled upon medieval manuscript illuminations and add their share of joy to the book." Following in this historical vein is *The Second Mrs. Giaconda,* the story of Leonardo da Vinci's middle years. Konigsburg posits a solution to the riddle of the Mona Lisa and serves up a "unique bit of creative historical interpretation" with a glimpse of Renaissance culture she has "artfully and authentically illumined," according to Shirley M. Wilton in *School Library Journal.* Another more experimental novel—though in theme rather than period—is *Father's Arcane Daughter,* a mystery. The novel tells of the return of Caroline after having been kidnapped and presumed dead seventeen years earlier. The story focuses on the effects of Caroline's reappearance on her father, his new wife, and their children in a "haunting, marvelously developed plot," according to a reviewer in *Publishers Weekly.*

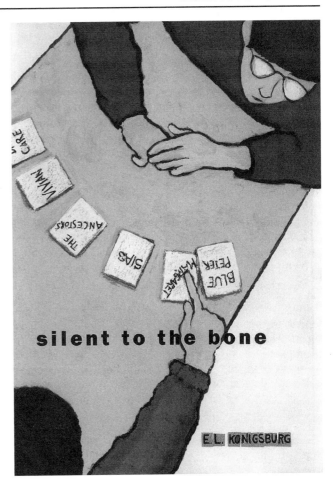

Thirteen-year-old Branwell loses his power of speech after being wrongly accused of injuring his baby sister, and he communicates the truth to his friend Connor using flash cards. (Cover illustration by Konigsburg.)

Konigsburg returned to more familiar ground with *The Dragon in the Ghetto Caper* and *Throwing Shadows,* the latter a group of short stories nominated for an American Book Award. Both *Journey to an 800 Number* and *Amy Elizabeth Explores Bloomingdale's* are vintage Konigsburg, the second of which tells the story of a girl and her grandmother trying to find the time to see Bloomingdale's. A reviewer for *Publishers Weekly* called the book a "vivid portrait of a distraction-filled city—and of a most affectionate relationship." *Up from Jericho Tel* relates the encounter between the ghost of a dead actress and two children, who are turned invisible and sent out with a group of street performers to search for a missing necklace. "A witty, fast-paced story," is how a reviewer in *Publishers Weekly* characterized the novel. A contributor to the *Bulletin of the Center for Children's Books,* reviewing *Up from Jericho Tel,* provided a summation of Konigsburg's distinctive gift to children's literature: "Whether she is writing a realistic or a fanciful story, Konigsburg always provides fresh ideas, tart wit and humor, and memorable characters."

With *T-Backs, T-Shirts, COAT, and Suit,* Konigsburg proved that she not only still had the knack for a weird title but also for telling a story. Young Chloe spends the summer in Florida with her stepfather's sister, who runs a meals-on-wheels van and becomes involved in a controversy over T-back swimming suits. Rachel Axelrod, reviewing the book in *Voice of Youth Advocates,* concluded that Konigsburg "has produced another winner!"

The View from Saturday tells the story of four members of a championship quiz bowl team and the paraplegic teacher who coaches them. A series of first-person narratives from the students display links between their lives in a story that is "glowing with humor and dusted with magic," according to a critic in *Publishers Weekly.* Julie Cummins concluded in *School Library Journal* that "brilliant writing melds with crystalline characterizations in this sparkling story that is a jewel in the author's crown of outstanding work." Konigsburg won the 1997 Newbery Medal for this novel, her second in three decades of writing. Commenting on the connection between *The View from Saturday* and Konigsburg's previous medal winner, *From the Mixed-up Files of Mrs. Basil E. Frankweiler,* the author's daughter, Laurie Konigsburg Todd, noted in *Horn Book:* "Although the inspiration for these Newbery books was as disparate as the three decades which separate their publication, their theme is the same. In fact, every one of E. L. Konigsburg's ... novels are about children who seek, find, and ultimately enjoy who they are. Despite this common denominator, [her] writing is the antithesis of the formula book. Her characters are one-of-a-kind."

More one-of-a-kind characters are served up in *Silent to the Bone,* the story of a thirteen-year-old wrongly accused of injuring his baby sister. Branwell, shocked by such an accusation, loses the power of speech, and it is left to his friend Connor to reach out to him and discover the truth about what really happened. Accused by the English au pair of dropping and shaking his infant half-sister, Branwell cannot defend himself and is confined at a juvenile center. Employing handwritten flash cards, Connor is able to piece together the events leading up to the 911 call that opens the book. By the end of this journey of discovery, not only is the real villain revealed, but both Bran and Connor have come to grips with larger truths in their own lives, including the dynamics of stepfamilies. "No one is better than Konigsburg at plumbing the hearts and minds of smart, savvy kinds," commented *Horn Book* critic Peter D. Sieruta, who called *Silent to the Bone* an "edgy, thought-provoking novel ... written with Konigsburg's characteristic wit and perspicuity." *Booklist*'s Hazel Rochman pleaded for a second reading of the book, not simply for clues to the identity of the real perpetrator, but for "the wit, and insight, the farce, and the gentleness of the telling." Reviewing the novel in the *New York Times Book Review,* Roger Sutton commented that Konigsburg "is one of our brainiest writers for young people, not only in the considerable cerebral powers she brings to her books but in the intellectual demands she makes on her characters."

Some of Konigsburg's characters, such as Jennifer, Elizabeth, and Claudia, have become not only best friends to readers, but also telegraphic symbols of complex emotions and adolescent conditions. "The strong demands Konigsburg makes of her characters and the fine moral intelligence she gives them imply much respect for children, a respect she has continued to express in all of her books," asserted Nodelman. A writer who takes her craft seriously yet who manages to avoid heavy-handed thematic writing, Konigsburg views children's books as "the primary vehicle for keeping alive the means of linear learning," as she wrote in *TalkTalk: A Children's Book Author Speaks to Grown-Ups.* "[Children's books] are the key to the accumulated wisdom, wit, gossip, truth, myth, history, philosophy, and recipes for salting potatoes during the past 6,000 years of civilization. Children's books are the Rosetta Stone to the hearts and minds of writers from Moses to Mao. And that is the last measure in the growth of children's literature as I've witnessed it—a growing necessity."

Biographical and Critical Sources

BOOKS

Children's Literature Review, Volume 1, Gale (Detroit, MI), 1976.

Dictionary of Literary Biography, Volume 52: *American Writers for Children from 1960, Fiction,* Gale (Detroit, MI), 1986.

Hanks, Dorrel Thomas, *E. L. Konigsburg,* Twayne, 1992.

Konigsburg, E. L., *From the Mixed-up Files of Mrs. Basil E. Frankweiler,* Atheneum, 1967.

Konigsburg, E. L., *Jennifer, Hecate, Macbeth, William McKinley, and Me, Elizabeth,* Atheneum, 1967.

Konigsburg, E. L., *TalkTalk: A Children's Book Author Speaks to Grown-Ups,* Atheneum, 1995.

Schwartz, Narda, *Articles on Women Writers,* Volume 2, ABC-Clio, 1986.

Twentieth-Century Children's Writers, fourth edition, St. James Press (Detroit, MI), 1995.

PERIODICALS

Booklist, June 1, 1967, Ruth P. Bull, review of *Jennifer, Hecate, Macbeth, William McKinley, and Me, Elizabeth,* p. 1048; October 1, 1967, Ruth P. Bull, review of *From the Mixed-up Files of Mrs. Basil E. Frankweiler,* p. 199; May 1, 1986, p. 1313; December 15, 1998, p. 751; March 15, 1999, pp. 1349-1350; August, 2000, Hazel Rochman, review of *Silent to the Bone,* p. 2135.

Bulletin of the Center for Children's Books, June, 1967, p. 155; February, 1971, p. 94; September, 1971, pp. 10-11; September, 1973, Zena Sutherland, review of *A Proud Taste for Scarlet and Miniver,* pp. 10-11; January, 1976, p. 80; September, 1976, p. 12; September, 1979, p. 10; March, 1982, p. 133; March, 1986, review of *Up from Jericho Tel,* p. 131; May, 1990, p. 216; September, 1992, p. 16; November, 1993, p. 88.

Growing Point, November, 1983, pp. 4161-4164.

Horn Book, March-April, 1967, Ruth Hill Viguers, review of *Jennifer, Hecate, Macbeth, William McKinley, and Me, Elizabeth,* pp. 206-207; September-October, 1967, Ruth Hill Viguers, review of *From the Mixed-up Files of Mrs. Basil E. Frankweiler,* p. 595; July-August,

1968, E. L. Konigsburg, "Newbery Award Acceptance," pp. 391-395; June, 1969, p. 307; September-October, 1973, Paul Heins, review of *A Proud Taste for Scarlet and Miniver*, pp. 466-467; September-October, 1975, pp. 470-471; May-June, 1982, pp. 289-290; May-June, 1986, p. 327; March-April, 1996, p. 229; January-February, 1997, p. 60; July-August, 1997, pp. 404-414; July-August, 1997, Laurie Konigsburg Todd, "E. L. Konigsburg," pp. 415-417; May-June, 1999, p. 3; November-December, 2000, Peter D. Sieruta, review of *Silent to the Bone*, p. 756.

Kirkus Reviews, July 1, 1967, review of *From the Mixed-up Files of Mrs. Basil E. Frankweiler*, p. 740; July 1, 1973, p. 685; February 1, 1986, p. 209.

New York Times Book Review, November 5, 1967, Alice Fleming, review of *From the Mixed-up Files of Mrs. Basil E. Frankweiler*, p. 44; March 30, 1969, p. 29; June 8, 1969, p. 44; October 20, 1974, p. 10; November 7, 1976, p. 44; July 5, 1980, p. 19; May 25, 1986, p. 25; April 10, 1994, p. 35; November 10, 1996, p. 49; November 19, 2000, Roger Sutton, "In the Blink of an Eye," p. 54.

Publishers Weekly, April 10, 1967, review of *Jennifer, Hecate, Macbeth, William McKinley, and Me, Elizabeth*, p. 80; September 28, 1970, pp. 78-79; July 19, 1976, review of *Father's Arcane Daughter*, p. 13; April 25, 1986, review of *Up from Jericho Tell*, p. 80; July 22, 1996, review of *The View from Saturday*, p. 242; November 11, 1997, review of *The View from Saturday*, p. 30; September 6, 1999, p. 106; September 13, 1999, review of *Amy Elizabeth Explores Bloomingdale's*, p. 86; February 14, 2000, p. 98.

Saturday Review, November 9, 1968, E. L. Konigsburg, "A Book Is a Private Thing," pp. 45-46.

School Library Journal, September, 1975, Shirley M. Wilton, review of *The Second Mrs. Giaconda*, p. 121; September, 1979, p. 141; May, 1982, p. 72; April, 1983, p. 122; May, 1986, p. 93; March, 1990, p. 208; October, 1991, p. 98; September, 1992, p. 206; October, 1993, p. 124; December, 1993, p. 26; February, 1996, p. 42; May, 1996, p. 69; September, 1996, Julie Cummins, review of *The View from Saturday*, p. 204; December, 2000, p. 54.

Teaching and Learning Literature, May-June, 1997, p. 75.

Voice of Youth Advocates, December, 1986, p. 219; December, 1993, Rachel Axelrod, review of *T-Backs, T-Shirts, COAT, and Suit*, p. 254; December, 1995, p. 335.

Washington Post Book World, November 5, 1967, Polly Goodwin, review of *From the Mixed-up Files of Mrs. Basil E. Frankweiler*, p. 22.

ON-LINE

Authors Online Library, http://teacher.scholastic.com/ (June 23, 2001).

E. L. Konigsburg, http://slis-two.fsu.edu/ (June 23, 2001).*

—Sketch by J. Sydney Jones

KURTZ, Katherine (Irene) 1944-

Personal

Born October 18, 1944, in Coral Gables, FL; daughter of Fredrick Harry Kurtz (an electronics technician) and Margaret Frances Carter (a paralegal); married Scott Roderick MacMillan (an author and producer), March 9, 1983; children: Cameron Alexander Stewart. *Education:* University of Miami, B.S., 1966; University of California—Los Angeles, M.A., 1971. *Religion:* "Nominally Church of Ireland (Anglican)."

Addresses

Home and office—Holybrooke Hall, Bray, County Wicklow, Ireland. *Agent*—Russell Galen, Scovil, Chichak, Galen Literary Agency, 381 Park Ave. S., New York, NY 10016.

Career

Writer. Los Angeles Police Department, Los Angeles, CA, instructional technologist, 1969-81. *Member:* Authors Guild, Authors' League, SFFWA.

Awards, Honors

Edmund Hamilton Memorial Award, 1977, for *Camber of Culdi;* Balrog Award, 1982, for *Camber the Heretic; The Legacy of Lehr* was cited as a Best Science-Fiction Title, *Voice of Youth Advocates*, 1986; named Dame of the Military and Hospitaller Order of St. Lazarus of Jerusalem, Dame Grand Officer of the Supreme Military

Katherine Kurtz

Order of the Temple of Jerusalem, Dame of Honour of the Hospitaller Order of St. John of Jerusalem, Dame of the Noble Company of the Rose, and Companion of the Royal House of O'Conor; fellow of Augustan Society and Octavian Society.

Writings

"DERYNI" SERIES

Deryni Rising, Ballantine (New York, NY), 1970.
Deryni Checkmate, Ballantine (New York, NY), 1972.
High Deryni, Ballantine (New York, NY), 1973.
Camber of Culdi ("Legends of Camber of Culdi," vol. 1), Ballantine (New York, NY), 1976.
Saint Camber ("Legends of Camber of Culdi," vol. 2), Ballantine (New York, NY), 1978.
Camber the Heretic ("Legends of Camber of Culdi," vol. 3), Ballantine (New York, NY), 1981.
The Bishop's Heir ("Histories of King Kelson," vol. 1), Ballantine (New York, NY), 1984.
The King's Justice ("Histories of King Kelson," vol. 2), Ballantine (New York, NY), 1985.
The Chronicles of the Deryni (includes *Deryni Rising, Deryni Checkmate,* and *High Deryni*), Science Fiction Book Club, 1985.
The Deryni Archives (stories), Ballantine (New York, NY), 1986, hardcover edition, Science Fiction Book Club, 1987.
The Quest for Saint Camber ("Histories of King Kelson," vol. 3), Ballantine (New York, NY), 1986.
The Harrowing of Gwynedd ("Heirs of St. Camber," vol. 1), Ballantine (New York, NY), 1989.
Deryni Magic: A Grimoire, Del Rey (New York, NY), 1991.
King Javan's Year ("Heirs of St. Camber," vol. 2), Ballantine (New York, NY), 1992.
The Bastard Prince ("Heirs of St. Camber," vol. 3), Ballantine (New York, NY), 1994.
(Compiler and editor, with Robert Reginald) *Codex Derynianus: Being a Comprehensive Guide to the Peoples, Places, and Things of the Derynye and the Human Worlds of the XI Kingdoms,* Borgo Press (San Bernardino, CA), 1998.
King Kelson's Bride, Ace (New York, NY), 2000.

"ADEPT" SERIES; WITH DEBORAH TURNER HARRIS

The Adept, Ace (New York, NY), 1991.
The Lodge of the Lynx, Ace (New York, NY), 1992.
The Templar Treasure, Ace (New York, NY), 1993.
Dagger Magic, Ace (New York, NY), 1995.
Death of an Adept, Ace (New York, NY), 1996.

OTHER

Lammas Night (novel), Ballantine (New York, NY), 1983, hardcover edition, Severn, 1986.
The Legacy of Lehr (science-fiction novel), Walker (New York, NY), 1986.
(Editor) *Tales of the Knights Templar,* Warner (New York, NY), 1995.
Two Crowns for America, Bantam (New York, NY), 1996.
(With Deborah Turner Harris) *The Temple and the Stone,* Warner (New York, NY), 1998.
(Editor) *On Crusade: More Tales of the Knights Templar,* Warner (New York, NY), 1998.
St. Patrick's Gargoyle, Ace (New York, NY), 2001.
(With Deborah Turner Harris) *The Temple and the Crown,* Warner (New York, NY), 2001.

Contributor of stories to anthologies, including *Flashing Swords #4,* edited by Lin Carter, Dell (New York, NY), 1977; *Hecate's Cauldron,* edited by Susan Shwartz, DAW (New York, NY), 1982; *Nine Visions,* edited by Andrea LaSonde Melrose, Seabury Press (New York, NY), 1983; *Moonsinger's Friends,* edited by Shwartz, Bluejay, 1985; *Once upon a Time,* edited by Lester del Rey and Risa Kessler, Ballantine (New York, NY), 1991; *Crafter I,* edited by Bill Fawcett and Christopher Stasheff, Ace (New York, NY), 1991; *Gods of War,* edited by Fawcett, Baen (New York, NY), 1992; and *Battlestation II,* edited by Fawcett and Stasheff, Ace, 1992. Contributor of stories to periodicals, including *Fantasy Book.*

Kurtz's works have been translated into Dutch, German, Italian, Polish, Swedish, Japanese, Spanish, and Romanian.

Sidelights

Katherine Kurtz's love of history has helped to shape the medieval worlds of her fantasy novels, as well as her books set in twentieth-century England and Scotland. Her "Deryni" series, composed of four base trilogies plus additional novels, focuses on the land of Gwynedd in the Eleven Kingdoms, a world based on medieval Wales. There the Deryni, a race of beings with unusual psychic powers, struggle against persecution by humans and attempt to preserve their powers and their culture. In a review of *The Quest for Saint Camber,* a *Publishers Weekly* critic dubbed Kurtz "queen of the proliferating fantasy subgenre that adds a magical element to dynastic historical romances." Kurtz's ability to weave historical detail with themes of magic and sorcery has made her books popular with both adults and young adults; A *Publishers Weekly* contributor declared Kurtz "a master of epic fantasy." Kurtz has also produced the thriller *Lammas Night,* authored a science-fiction novel, and, with Deborah Turner Harris, has written the popular "Adept" series of contemporary mysteries. Comparing Kurtz to British fantasy writer J. R. R. Tolkien in her approach to her imaginary world, an essayist in *St. James Guide to Fantasy Writers* commented that Kurtz's "magic is well realized, the characters [in her novels] much better drawn than in most modern fantasies, and, for anyone with a romantic interest in the Middle Ages, [her 'Deryni'] saga will inevitably have a great deal of fascination."

Born in 1944, in Coral Gables, Florida, during a hurricane, Kurtz once described her first moments on earth to *SATA* as "a whirlwind entry into the world which I like to think was a portent of exciting things to come." Kurtz began her love affair with books at an early age, and since elementary school proved dull, she smuggled library books to school, secreting them "in my lift-top desk or under the book I was supposed to be reading. I also read under the covers at night by flashlight," Kurtz confessed.

During her fourth-grade year, Kurtz discovered her first science fiction novel, *Lodestar.* "After that, no science fiction book in any library was safe from eye-tracking by 'The Kurtz,'" she recalled. Even though, after graduating from high school, Kurtz earned her B.S. in chemistry at the University of Miami, "my tastes always leaned toward humanities rather than hard science. It was during my undergraduate years at the University of Miami that I consciously fell in love with history, and it was to history that I returned when I decided, after one year of medical school, that I would rather write about medicine than practice it." In 1971 she graduated from the University of California—Los Angeles, with an M.A. in English history. "More important than the piece of paper," Kurtz explained, "was the formal knowledge

Kurtz and coauthor Deborah Turner Harris blend real history with fantasy in this novel about a Knights Templar mission to save Scotland's sacred Stone of Destiny so that its spirit may be reborn in warrior William Wallace, the Uncrowned King. (Cover illustration by Greg Call.)

of the medieval and renaissance world that I gained and the sharpening of research skills which would stand me in good stead as I continued writing medievally-set fantasy."

After working for over a decade for the Los Angeles Police Department as a technical writer and curriculum designer—and writing what would become the first six "Deryni" novels in her spare time—Kurtz embarked on her full-time career as a fiction writer in 1980. "I can't imagine a more satisfying life than to be making a living doing what I love," she admitted to *SATA.* "Far too few people get the opportunity to do that, and especially at a relatively young age."

Her first "Deryni" novel, *Deryni Rising,* was published in 1970. The first installment in the three-volume "Chronicles of the Deryni" trilogy, it introduces the reader to the kingdom of Gwynedd and its culture, which is laced with magic. The other trilogies that comprise the "Deryni" series include "Legends of St. Camber," which follows the life of a nobleman as he is first sainted then deemed a heretic; "Histories of King Kelson," which continues the events from the "Chronicles of the Deryni"; and "Heirs of St. Camber," where the magical kingdom suffers a dark age between the time of St. Camber and the rise to power of King Kelson. While *Voice of Youth Advocates* contributor Diane G. Yates expressed personal dismay that in the second part of the "Heirs of St. Camber" trilogy, *King Javan's Year,* "so many of the characters that [readers of the series] have grown to love, lose their lives in an unceasing struggle with the forces of evil," she nonetheless added: "the book is up to Kurtz's usual high standards, is beautifully written, and should appeal to teens as well as adults." In *The Bastard Prince,* the concluding volume in "Heirs of St. Camber," the efforts of the heir to the throne "reflects the atmospheric gloom of a dark and secret land, full of treachery and cruelty but shot through with light and a promise of hope," in the opinion of a *Publishers Weekly* contributor who went on to praise Kurtz for her ability to sustain tension and create vivid characters.

In addition to the "Deryni" novels, Kurtz has made what she terms "several literary forays outside the medieval world of the Eleven Kingdoms." Her historical thriller *Lammas Night,* published in 1983, takes place in England during World War II. As Kurtz explained to *SATA:* "British folk tradition has it that England has been saved from invasion more than once by the magical intervention of those appointed to guard her, Napoleonic and Armada times being cited as two specific examples. Less well-known tradition has it that similar measures were employed to keep Hitler from invading Britain during that fateful summer of 1940, with its sagas of Dunkirk and the Battle of Britain. Whether or not what was done actually had any effect we will never know for certain, but the fact remains that Hitler never did invade, even though he was poised to do so for many months. *Lammas Night* is the story of how and why that might have been."

Together with fellow author Deborah Turner Harris, Kurtz has written several volumes in the "Adept" series. Set in the twentieth century, the novels features members of a secret, three-member brotherhood known as the Adept: former members of the ancient Knights Templar who, now based in Scotland, have sworn to uphold cosmic laws in their reincarnated form. In *The Templar Treasure,* the trio search for the treasured Seal of Solomon, only to discover a host of horrors. And in *Dagger Magic,* the Adept must foil efforts by a reincarnated Tibetan magician to gain absolute power by way of a collection of ancient texts confiscated by the Nazis decades ago and now discovered to exist in a German U-boat hidden in a cave along the northern coast of Ireland. "The plot, though somewhat convoluted, has a Wangerian intensity and a profound moral message chillingly told," maintained *Voice of Youth Advocates* contributor Mary Anne Hoebeke in her review of *Dagger Magic.*

Other works by Kurtz include the science-fiction novels *The Legacy of Lehr,* several collections of short stories focusing on the Knights Templar, and an historical novel set during the American Revolutionary War, titled *Two Crowns for America.* Positing an alternate history, in *Two Crowns for America* Kurtz shows what would have happened had America adopted a monarchy, with factional Jacobites and Freemasons attempting to crown their preferred king while an occult Master has a plan of his own for the new country's future. Calling *Two Crowns for America* an "engrossing and elegant tale," *Booklist* reviewer Roland Green praised the author for her "vivid portrayals" of such characters as Prince Charles Stuart, otherwise known as Bonnie Prince Charlie, George Washington, and Benjamin Franklin. *St. Patrick's Gargoyle,* which *Booklist* contributor Ray Olson predicted would become a "Christmas perennial," finds a guardian gargoyle and a member of the Knights of Malta determined to find those responsible for vandalizing St. Patrick's Cathedral in the days before Christmas.

Kurtz has several interests outside history and writing, although, as she noted, "most of them do tend to relate to my writing or medieval background in some way." A voracious reader, she tackles history, religion, and other books related to her research, while saving time to dip into "the occasional Brother Cadfael mystery for fun." Other hobbies take her away from the printed page; as Kurtz explained: "I delight in counted cross-stitch embroidery and needlepoint, will occasionally crochet, but am totally indifferent to knitting. I can sew just about anything, including medieval costumes and horse bardings." Together with her husband, who she met at a Scottish country dance in Santa Monica, California, she is restoring a historic country house which she bought in County Wicklow, Ireland, in 1986.

Biographical and Critical Sources

BOOKS

Clarke, Boden, and Mary A. Burgess, *The Work of Katherine Kurtz: An Annotated Bibliography and Guide,* Borgo Press (San Bernardino, CA), 1993.

St. James Guide to Fantasy Writers, St. James Press (Detroit, MI), 1996.

St. James Guide to Science Fiction Writers, 4th edition, St. James Press (Detroit, MI), 1996.

PERIODICALS

Booklist, May 1, 1994, Roland Green, review of *The Bastard Prince,* p. 1583; February 1, 1996, Roland Green, review of *Two Crowns for America,* p. 920; December 1, 1996, Roland Green, review of *Death of an Adept,* p. 643; February 1, 2001, Ray Olson, review of *St. Patrick's Gargoyle,* p. 1042.

Kirkus Reviews, April 1, 1998, review of *On Crusade,* p. 452.

Kliatt, September, 1995, Judith H. Silverman, review of *Tales of the Knights Templar,* p. 23.

Library Journal, June 15, 2000, Jackie Cassada, review of *King Kelson's Bride,* p. 121; February 15, 2001, review of *St. Patrick's Gargoyle,* p. 205.

Publisher Weekly, April 10, 1972, p. 60; July 9, 1973, p. 48; May 31, 1976, p. 197; September 11, 1978, review of *Saint Camber,* p. 77; September 25, 1981, p. 87; September 21, 1984, p. 92; July 5, 1985, p. 66; review of *The Quest for Saint Camber,* August 8, 1986; September 26, 1986, p. 69; December 2, 1988, p. 48; December 21, 1990, p. 50; February 8, 1991, p. 54; June 21, 1993, review of *The Templar Treasure,* p. 102; May 23, 1994, review of *The Bastard Prince,* p. 82; November 27, 1995, review of *Two Crowns for America,* pp. 52-53; April 13, 1998, review of *On Crusade,* p. 57; July 27, 1998, review of *The Temple and the Stone,* pp. 58-59; May 29, 2000, review of *King Kelson's Bride,* p. 57.

School Library Journal, January, 1985, p. 92; February, 1986, p. 103; November, 1986, p. 116; December, 1986, p. 126; September, 1991, p. 298; September, 1992, p. 29.

Voice of Youth Advocates, December, 1986, p. 238; April, 1987, p. 38; August, 1989, p. 166; April, 1993, Diane G. Yates, review of *King Javan's Year,* p. 42; October, 1993, Faye H. Gottschall, review of *The Templar Treasure,* p. 230; October, 1995, Mary Anne Hoebeke, review of *Dagger Magic,* p. 234.

ON-LINE

Katherine Kurtz Web site, http://www.deryni.net/ (September 26, 2001).*

L

LACE, William W. 1942-

Personal

Born September 10, 1942, in Fort Worth, TX. *Education:* Texas Christian University, B.A., 1966; East Texas State University, M.A., 1977; University of North Texas, Ed.D., 1987.

Addresses

Home—Arlington, TX. *Office*—Tarrant County College, 1500 Houston St., Fort Worth, TX 76102. *E-mail*—bill.lace@tccd.net.

Career

Tarrant County College, Fort Worth, TX, executive assistant to the chancellor, 1981—. City of Arlington, member of library board, 1993-2000, and of Arlington Public Library Board Foundation. *Member:* Council for the Advancement and Support of Education.

Writings

Sports Great Nolan Ryan, Enslow Publishers (Hillside, NJ), 1993.
Michelangelo, Lucent Books (San Diego, CA), 1993.
The Top Ten Football Rushers, Enslow Publishers (Hillside, NJ), 1994.
The Top Ten Football Quarterbacks, Enslow Publishers (Hillside, NJ), 1994.
The Hundred Years' War, Lucent Books (San Diego, CA), 1994.
Winston Churchill, Lucent Books (San Diego, CA), 1995.
Elizabethan England, Lucent Books (San Diego, CA), 1995.
The Wars of the Roses, Lucent Books (San Diego, CA), 1996.
The Battle of Hastings, Lucent Books (San Diego, CA), 1996.
Defeat of the Spanish Armada, Lucent Books (San Diego, CA), 1997.

William W. Lace

The Houston Rockets Basketball Team, Enslow Publishers (Hillside, NJ), 1997.
The Dallas Cowboys Football Team, Enslow Publishers (Hillside, NJ), 1997.
England, Lucent Books (San Diego, CA), 1997.
The Little Princes in the Tower, Lucent Books (San Diego, CA), 1997.
The Los Angeles Lakers Basketball Team, Enslow Publishers (Hillside, NJ), 1998.
The Nazis, Lucent Books (San Diego, CA), 1998.
The Death Campus, Lucent Books (San Diego, CA), 1998.
The Alamo, Lucent Books (San Diego, CA), 1998.

Tiger Woods: Star Golfer, Enslow Publishers (Hillside, NJ), 1999.

The Pittsburgh Steelers Football Team, Enslow Publishers (Hillside, NJ), 1999.

Ireland, Lucent Books (San Diego, CA), 1999.

World War II Generals and Leaders, Lucent Books (San Diego, CA), 2000.

Hitler and the Nazis, Lucent Books (San Diego, CA), 2000.

The British Empire: The End of Colonialism, Lucent Books (San Diego, CA), 2000.

Scotland, Lucent Books (San Diego, CA), 2001.

Medieval Cathedrals, Lucent Books (San Diego, CA), 2001.

The Atomic Bomb, Lucent Books (San Diego, CA), 2002.

Work in Progress

Oliver Cromwell and the English Revolution and *Joan of Arc and the Hundred Years' War,* both for Enslow Publishers.

*   *   *

LAMSTEIN, Sarah Marwil 1943-

Personal

Born July 28, 1943, in Boston, MA; daughter of Milton S. (a bookseller) and Lenore (a bookseller; maiden name, Zavelle) Marwil; married Joel Lamstein (a management consultant), June, 1966; children: Josh, Emily Rynd, Abby. *Education:* University of Michigan, B.A. (English literature), 1965, M.A. (English literature), 1966; Simmons College, M.L.S., 1984. *Religion:*

Sarah Marwil Lamstein

Jewish. *Hobbies and other interests:* Reading, walking, gardening, painting furniture.

Addresses

Home—45 Pine Crest Rd., Newton, MA 02459-2143. *E-mail*—sarahm45@aol.com.

Career

Lynbrook North Junior High School, Lynbrook, NY, English teacher, 1966-67; Arlington High School, Arlington, MA, English teacher, 1967-69; Sarah Lamstein Puppets, Newton, MA, puppeteer, 1975—; Milton Academy Lower School, librarian, 1982-85; Roxbury Latin School, Boston, MA, librarian, 1985-89; Mather School, Boston, MA, librarian, 1989-94; writer. Newton Peace Vigil, founder, 1990; Temple Emanuel, Newton, MA, Social Action Committee. *Member:* Society of Children's Book Writers and Illustrators, Boston Area Guild of Puppetry, Puppeteers of America, Beta Phi Mu Honor Society.

Awards, Honors

Annie's Shabbat was named to the Top Ten Religion Books for Youth, *Booklist,* 1998.

Writings

(With Kavita Ram Shrestha) *From the Mango Tree and Other Folktales from Nepal,* Libraries Unlimited (Englewood, CO), 1997.

Annie's Shabbat, illustrated by Cecily Lang, Albert Whitman (Morton Grove, IL), 1997.

I Like Your Buttons!, illustrated by Nancy Cote, Albert Whitman (Morton Grove, IL), 1999.

Poems published in *Paintbrush, Genesis 2,* and *Noctiluca,* and performed off-off-Broadway by Clyde, Inc.

Sidelights

Sarah Marwil Lamstein told *SATA:* "From earliest times I was a reader, nestled close to my grandmother, fragrant and ample, on the living room couch, listening as she read *Chicken Little* in her thick Russian accent: '... then dawky, lawky....' I tingled with foreboding at the fox.

"My elementary school library was a house of awe, the librarian, the beautiful Miss Robinson, an angel. She was the caretaker of *Curious George* and the endless volumes of orange biographies with silhouette illustrations, *Sam Adams* and *Clara Barton* among them. In my home library, I pored over picture books of a Native American child, a feather in his headdress, and a boy from Belgium who lived in a stone house on a winding street.

"When I was able to venture off on my own, I made weekly trips to the public library on Saturday afternoons, coming home with books stacked as high as my chin. Wrapped in our home's Sabbath quiet, I became lost in those books, precious companions. I often acted out parts of *Winnie the Pooh* or *Stuart Little* for my brothers and sister, taking delight in their giggles. When my own children came along, I once again savored the chuckles and belly laughs that came with the antics of Winnie and Baby Roo.

"Writing followed reading. All through elementary school, my best friend Judy and I wrote stories together. We combed our parents' picture albums for interesting photos, then wrote about them, trying as much as we could to astonish the other. In school, we wrote and acted in spelling plays, incorporating all twenty words from the weekly list. Our Pilgrim drama was the grisliest. To this day, Judy is a writer. Though she writes stories for adults, we still get together to share our work.

"All through high school I wrote, contributing to the literary magazine, and in college I took a course in creative writing. With the birth of my first child, I stopped teaching high school English and enrolled in a Writing for Children workshop, eager to indulge my old writing habit. A friend led me to a poetry reading course, and from there I began to write poetry. A family trip to Nepal through my husband's work prompted me to explore the folk literature of the country. In collaboration with a Nepali writer, I brought a collection of Nepali tales to publication in the United States, hoping to give Western readers a glimpse of that most beautiful, exotic land.

"With the publication of the folktales, I put poetry aside (not the reading of it!) and turned wholeheartedly to writing for children, remembering the pleasures I felt as a child, nestled close to my grandmother, enjoying the giggles of my brothers and sister, getting lost in a book on a Saturday afternoon. The pleasures included the joy of the story, the words, and the greatest pleasure of all—the understanding. A sense of Belgium. A hint of the Native American way.

"Even the physical book gave me pleasure, the sturdy cover, the pages, the illustrations, the type, the page numbers. Books were glorious to my eye and touch. What better thing than to make something so marvelous? In writing books for children, I could try to recreate those pleasures and understandings for others.

"As a writer, I am most interested in exploring the little known—the courage of ordinary people, the hidden aspects of nature. Being a writer is like being an explorer, for it allows me to discover new things. I try to discover ways of improving my writing, as well, for there is pleasure in the writing itself, and struggle, in the working and reworking and reworking in the hopes of doing it better, getting it right."

Lamstein's first original children's book, *Annie's Shabbat*, celebrates the time-honored rituals associated with the Jewish Sabbath within a warmly affectionate contemporary family. Lamstein's narrative details every aspect of shabbat observances, from the preparatory bath and special clothes, to lighting the candles, special

prayers, traditional meal, and visiting the synagogue on Saturday morning. Thus, "Annie's young and enthusiastic voice" tells a story that is "brimming with facts and sprinkled with Hebrew terms," according to a reviewer for *Publishers Weekly.* Ilene Cooper, who reviewed *Annie's Shabbat* for *Booklist,* similarly focused on Lamstein's narrator, calling Annie's voice full of "both wonder and down-to-earth fun."

In her next effort, *I Like Your Buttons!,* a little girl compliments her teacher's bright buttons and starts a chain reaction of appreciation and goodwill that spreads throughout her school. The good feelings extend out into the community, where they reach the girl's father who brings home an adorable kitten as a present for her. Critics found this a pleasant way to help children learn the lesson that "what goes around comes around." A contributor to *Kirkus Reviews* described the book as "a parade of cheerfulness to make readers grin as they pick up on what's happening and the speed with which it spreads."

Cassandra compliments her teacher and begins a chain reaction of good feeling throughout the school, playground, and neighborhood. (Cover illustration by Nancy Cote.)

Biographical and Critical Sources

PERIODICALS

Booklist, October 1, 1998, Ilene Cooper, review of *Annie's Shabbat,* p. 343; August, 1999, Ilene Cooper, review of *I Like Your Buttons!,* pp. 2064-2065.

Kirkus Reviews, March 1, 1999, review of *I Like Your Buttons!.*

Publishers Weekly, August 25, 1997, review of *Annie's Shabbat,* p. 66.

School Library Journal, December, 1999, Kimberlie Monteforte, review of *I Like Your Buttons!,* p. 102.

* * *

LAROCHE, Giles 1956-

Personal

Born July 1, 1956, in Berlin, NH; son of Romeo and Claire (Huot) Laroche. *Education:* Attended Montserrat College of Art, 1977-81.

Addresses

Home and office—41 Dearborn St., Salem, MA 01970.

Career

Artist and illustrator of children's books, with studios in Salem, MA, and Washington, NH. *Exhibitions:* Paintings, drawings, and illustrations have been exhibited nationally, including at the Society of Illustrator's Show, New York, NY.

Alexander the monkey travels through illustrator Giles Laroche's cut-paper color landscapes in **The Color Box** *by Dayle Ann Dodds.*

Illustrator

Lois Lenski, *Sing a Song of People,* Little, Brown (Boston, MA), 1987.

Rachel Field, *General Store,* Little, Brown (Boston, MA), 1988.

Rachel Field, *A Road Might Lead to Anywhere,* Little, Brown (Boston, MA), 1990.

Dayle Ann Dodds, *The Color Box,* Little, Brown (Boston, MA), 1992.

Lee Bennett Hopkins, editor, *Ragged Shadows: Poems of Halloween Night,* Little, Brown (Boston, MA), 1993.

Philemon Sturges, *Bridges Are to Cross,* Putnam (New York, NY), 1998.

Philemon Sturges, *Sacred Places,* Putnam (New York, NY), 2000.

Sidelights

Giles Laroche's illustrations in cut-paper collage are an ongoing experiment in the possibilities of this technique. Laroche was inspired by his work as an assistant at an architectural firm in Cambridge, Massachusetts, and by his own explorations with paper in his art studio in Salem, Massachusetts, in the 1980s. "I had always enjoyed the collage process," Laroche once told *SATA,* "and I began creating collages depicting scenes of medieval towns and colonial villages. In time my collages became more dimensional, and I found myself hand-coloring my own cut-out collage elements. Then I remembered children's books, and I thought that perhaps my collages (paper reliefs) would lend themselves well as book illustrations if they could be lit and photographed in an interesting and dramatic way." Reviewers of Laroche's published illustrations have suggested that the artist's cut-paper collages do indeed work well as illustrations for children's books, especially when a three-dimensional effect is most desired.

In Dayle Ann Dodd's *The Color Box,* an adventurous monkey crawls into an empty box, only to discover that it is divided into little rooms, each with a hole leading in to the next room, and each room being entirely of one color. As a concept book intended to teach little ones about color, Dodd's text may be almost unnecessary, according to *Booklist* reviewer Kay Weisman, but "Laroche's appealing cut-paper illustrations will entrance them." The three-dimensionality of Laroche's collages is ideal for creating detail in the monochromatic mini-worlds of each two-page spread, reviewers noted. "The layers and shadows effectively distinguish and set off the various shades of the objects," wrote Steven Engelfried in *School Library Journal.* The result is "a clever and splashy introduction to colors," concluded Liz Rosenberg in the *New York Times Book Review.*

Laroche turned his familiarity with the architecture of Salem to advantage in creating the illustrations for Lee Bennett Hopkins's *Ragged Shadows: Poems of Halloween Night.* In this book, fourteen poems by various authors are illustrated by Laroche with images of four young children in costume trailing through Salem trick-or-treating. The architectural possibilities of Laroche's cut-paper collages are again exploited in two works by Philemon Sturges, *Bridges Are to Cross* and *Sacred Places*. In the first of these collaborations, Sturges selected fifteen bridges, from the high-tech splendor of the Golden Gate Bridge in San Francisco to a 2000-year-old Spanish aqueduct, displaying a range of styles across time and materials. A *Publishers Weekly* critic dubbed *Bridges Are to Cross* one of the best books of the year, and highlighted Laroche's "astonishing 3-D collage illustration" in its review. *School Library Journal* reviewer Ronald Jobe was more specific in his praise of the contribution made by Laroche's illustrations: "Each bridge . . . has a luminescent quality to it, as if the light is radiating from within. What an effect!" Jobe observed. In their next book, *Sacred Places,* Sturges offers a brief tour of nearly thirty places across five continents considered sacred by some religion. In her review in *School Library Journal,* Patricia Lothrop-Green remarked that Laroche's illustrations offer more information than a photograph of the actual sites could: "Laroche's rich and detailed art balances architectural impact with situation, use, and cultural context as a photograph could never do," Lothrop-Green stated.

Biographical and Critical Sources

PERIODICALS

Booklist, May 1, 1992, Kay Weisman, review of *The Color Box,* pp. 1606-1607; August, 1993, Kathryn Broderick, review of *Ragged Shadows: Poems of Halloween Night,* p. 2067.

New York Times Book Review, May 17, 1992, Liz Rosenberg, review of *The Color Box,* p. 34.

Publishers Weekly, September 20, 1993, review of *Ragged Shadows,* p. 30; October 30, 2000, review of *Bridges Are to Cross,* p. 78.

School Library Journal, June, 1992, Steven Engelfried, review of *The Color Box,* p. 92; December, 1998, Ronald Jobe, review of *Bridges Are to Cross,* p. 116; December, 2000, Patricia Lothrop-Green, review of *Sacred Places,* pp. 136-137.

*   *   *

LAWSON, Julie 1947-

Personal

Born November 9, 1947, in Victoria, British Columbia, Canada; daughter of Charles A. and Jean V. (Anderson) Goodwin; married Patrick Lawson, August 24, 1972. *Education:* University of Victoria, B.A. (first class honors), 1970. *Hobbies and other interests:* Traveling, hiking, reading.

Addresses

Home—Sooke, British Columbia, Canada. *Office*—c/o Author Mail, Stoddart Publicity, 895 Don Mills Rd., 400-2 Park Ctr., Toronto, Ontario, Canada M3C 1W3.

Julie Lawson

Career

Educator and author. Taught in France, c. 1970-71; school teacher in Saanich, British Columbia, 1972-74, and Sooke, British Columbia, 1975-91; full-time writer, 1991—. Speaker at festivals, workshops, and conferences. *Member:* Canadian Society of Children's Authors, Illustrators, and Performers, Canadian Children's Book Centre, British Columbia Children's Writers and Illustrators, British Columbia Federation of Writers.

Awards, Honors

Ruth Schwartz Book Award shortlist, Canadian Library Association Book of the Year Award shortlist, and National Parenting Publication Award, all 1993, all for *The Dragon's Pearl;* Shelia A. Egoff Children's Prize, and Canadian Library Association Book of the Year Award shortlist, both for *White Jade Tiger.*

Writings

The Sand Sifter, Beach Holme, 1990.
My Grandfather Loved the Stars, illustrated by Judy McLaren, Beach Holme, 1992.
A Morning to Polish and Keep, illustrated by Sheena Lott, Red Deer College Press (Red Deer, Canada), 1992.
Kate's Castle, illustrated by Frances Tyrrell, Oxford University Press (Toronto, Canada), 1992.

Julie Lawson

Paul Mombourquette

Emma wades into a river to claim a piece of silk which is swept away after a train derailment in Lawson's story, based on an actual event in 1927. (Cover illustration by Paul Mombourquette.)

The Dragon's Pearl, illustrated by Paul Morin, Oxford University Press (Toronto, Canada), 1992, Clarion (New York, NY), 1993.

White Jade Tiger, Beach Holme, 1993.

Fires Burning, Stoddart (Toronto, Canada), 1995, published as *The Danger Game,* Little, Brown (Boston, MA), 1996.

Blown Away, illustrated by Kathryn Naylor, Red Deer College Press (Red Deer, Canada), 1995, Orca (Custer, WA), 1996.

Too Many Suns, illustrated by Martin Springette, Oxford University Press (Toronto, Canada), 1996.

Cougar Cove, Orca (Custer, WA), 1996.

Whatever You Do, Don't Go near That Canoe!, illustrated by Werner Zimmermann, North Winds Press (Richmond Hill, Canada), 1996.

Kate's Castle, illustrated by Frances Tyrrell, Stoddart (Buffalo, NY), 1997.

Emma and the Silk Train, illustrated by Paul Mommbourquette, Kids Can Press, 1998.

Goldstone, Stoddart (Buffalo, NY), 1998.

Midnight in the Mountains, illustrated by Sheena Lott, Orca (Custer, WA), 1998.

In Like a Lion, illustrated by Yolaine Lefebvre, North Winds Press (Richmond Hill, Canada), 1999.

Bear on the Train, illustrated by Brian Deines, Kids Can Press, 1999.

Turns on a Dime (sequel to *Goldstone*), Stoddart (Toronto, Canada), 1999.

The Ghost of Avalanche Mountain (sequel to *Turns on a Dime*), Stoddart (Toronto, Canada), 2000.

Destination Gold!, Orca (Custer, WA), 2001.

Sidelights

Julie Lawson is a prolific Canadian writer whose works include picture books as well as young adult novels. "Like a character actor changing her role completely from one performance to the next, Julie Lawson shows a new face in every book," noted Annette Goldsmith in a *Books in Canada* review of Lawson's humorous 1996 picture book, *Whatever You Do, Don't Go near that Canoe!* "Only her love of language and the outdoors remain constant." Among Lawson's picture-book efforts are *Too Many Suns, The Dragon's Pearl,* and *Emma and the Silk Train.*

Born in British Columbia, Canada, in 1944, Lawson was raised in Victoria, but spent her summers at her family's cabin on the Sooke Basin. She loved writing ever since she first learned how to do it. "I decided that when I grew up I'd be an author," she once explained to *SATA.* "I became a teacher instead, but figured I'd be an author during the summer holidays and in my spare time. But I didn't have that much spare time, and in the summer holidays there was always something else to do. But I still kept saying, I'll be an author when I get older. Well, I got older and older, and finally I said to myself, stop thinking about it and do it!" Lawson took a six-month leave of absence and got down to the business of writing.

Her first published book, *The Sand Sifter,* was published in 1990, and would be followed within five years by six more picture books and two novels. Lawson's inspiration springs from a variety of things, as she told *SATA.* "I get ideas from myths and legends and folklore, stories I've always loved to read. I get ideas from my environment.... I get ideas from actual places and experiences: traveling in China, exploring Victoria's Chinatown, seeing the lava flow into the sea on the Big Island of Hawaii, these experiences have all worked their way into my stories. I also get ideas from my childhood memories—memories of people who were close to me, and memories of actual events."

Lawson's picture book *The Dragon's Pearl* was inspired by a trip she took to China. "I became very interested in dragons," she explained. "I'd always thought they were ferocious, fire-breathing monsters. But in China I discovered Oriental dragons are benevolent, good-natured creatures that don't breathe fire; they breathe clouds and make the rain. For thousands of years, dragons have been worshiped as water gods. And from ancient times they have been a symbol of royalty." Loosely based on a folktale from the province of Sichuan, *The Dragon's Pearl* tells the story of Xiou Sheng, a poor boy who lives with his mother. During a terrible drought he finds a pearl which brings his family good luck. When robbers hear of this wonderful pearl and attempt to steal it, Xiou swallows it and is transformed into a dragon that makes rain fall from the sky on the parched earth. Praised by *Booklist* reviewer Hazel Rochman as a story "of shifting reality and glorious change," *The Dragon's Pearl* was also described by *School Library Journal* reviewer Susan

Scheps as a "well-crafted" tale that "successfully presents Chinese tradition and culture in a manner that is both enlightening and entertaining."

In *Too Many Suns,* which Lawson published in 1996, the youngest of ten brothers desires to capture the sun in a painting, while the youngest of ten suns wishes he could shine without having to rotate his position in the sky with his nine older brothers. When the youngest sun convinces his brothers to rise all together, they threaten the future of the earth, until the patient youngest brother finds a way to return the sky to the way it was. Based on a Chinese Yi myth, *Too Many Suns* was praised by *Quill & Quire* contributor Bridget Donald as a read-aloud treat due to its "richly descriptive vocabulary and smoothly flowing syntax." In another picture-book offering, *Midnight in the Mountains,* Lawson describes a young girl's first evening in a cabin in the mountains in language that *Quill & Quire* reviewer Joanne Findon described as "simple yet lyrical, perfectly conveying the meditative mood of the story." And as Hadley Dyer noted in her *Quill & Quire* appraisal of the author's *In Like a Lion,*

In the conclusion of Lawson's "Goldstone" trilogy, Ashley receives the magical goldstone necklace and awakens from within the glacial mountains the presence of Jonathan, who has foreseen the moment he can reclaim the stone. (Cover illustration by Ken Campbell.)

based on a true story about a curious cougar that strolled through a fancy Victoria hotel, "Lawson keeps the text simple, her phrasing short and breathless" in keeping with the suspense of her story.

In addition to her numerous picture books, Lawson has also written a number of novels for older readers, among them *White Jade Tiger, Fires Burning,* and the trilogy that includes *Goldstone, Turns on a Dime,* and *The Ghost of Avalanche Mountain. Fires Burning,* published in the United States as *The Danger Game,* finds Beth, already pushed to her limit by younger brother Field, totally perplexed after her older cousin Chelsea is sent to spend the summer with them. Emotionally distant for reasons Beth cannot understand, Chelsea begins to come out of her shell by playing a game of risks the children call the Danger Game. A *Publishers Weekly* contributor praised the novel for "offer[ing] and intriguing mixture of ordinary and sublime elements," and added that Lawton's portrayal of the "inner torment of a teen who has been sexually abused" should engage teen readers.

Like *The Dragon's Pearl, White Jade Tiger* was inspired by Lawson's research into Chinese Dragon lore. "I was looking through a book on Oriental art and came upon a picture of a white jade amulet carved in the shape of a tiger," the author recalled for *SATA.* "It came from the Han Dynasty, some two thousand years ago. In China, jade has always been associated with magical powers, and the tiger is the mythological animal that rules the West." In the book, which is a combination time-travel story and historical novel, twelve-year-old Jasmine loses track of her class during a visit to a museum in Victoria, British Columbia. Going back in time to 1880, she suddenly finds herself in Fraser Canyon, among the Chinese workers building the Canadian Pacific Railway. Meeting a boy named Keung who is in search of a missing jade amulet, Jasmine disguises herself as a boy and aids Keung on his search, learning much about her own family history as well. "Racism has been an underlying theme in British Columbian history," explained Janice Dawson in *Bookbird,* "and Lawson's novel provides young readers with an opportunity to explore the issue in depth.

Lawson's novel trilogy that begins with *Goldstone* takes place in the early twentieth century, as twelve-year-old Karin rebels against her mother's traditional Swedish clothing and customs. When her mother is killed in a landslide, Karin is wracked by guilt over their relationship, but after wearing her mother's goldstone necklace, the girl begins to dream of another, more deadly landslide and wonders if she is being given the chance to save lives. In *Turns on a Dime* Karin's necklace serves as a link, as it is passed down to Karin's descendant Jo. Described by *School Library Journal* contributor Gerry Larson as "markedly naive and impetuous in keeping with the conservative but changing tenor" of the 1950s, Jo is out of sorts: her friends are caught up in the latest Elvis Presley recording, leaving her to the company of a new boy in her neighborhood. Then her babysitter winds up pregnant, pressure from her friends threatens her friendship with her neighbor, and the worst news of all

hits when she learns she was adopted. The goldstone pendant again changes hands in *The Ghost of Avalanche Mountain,* as Jo, now a mystery author, sends it to niece Ashley for her birthday. When Ashley discovers that dreams she has while wearing the heirloom foretell the future, she becomes nervous: one of her dreams is far from pleasant, and an avalanche near the novel's end brings the trilogy full circle.

Lawson lives on Vancouver Island, in a house she and her husband built in the woods near the sea. "Escaping into books has always been a form of magic to me," Lawson concluded. "As a writer, I hope to create a little bit of that magic for others." In addition to writing, Lawson gives talks and lectures to school children and library groups, and enjoys the question she is often asked. Which book does she like the best? "Well, that's like asking parents which child they like the best. Each of my books is special in its own way." How can someone become an author like Lawson did? "My advice is: read, read, read! And above all, write!"

Biographical and Critical Sources

PERIODICALS

Bookbird, winter, 1996, Janis Dawson, "Telling It like It Was in Western Canada: Postcolonial Historical Fiction for Children," pp. 24-28.

Booklist, April 15, 1993, Hazel Rochman, review of *The Dragon's Pearl,* p. 1513; July, 1998, Shelle Rosenfeld, review of *Goldstone,* p. 1882; November 1, 1998, GraceAnne A. De Candido, review of *Emma and the Silk Train,* p. 504; October 15, 1999, Hazel Rochman, review of *Bear on the Train,* p. 455; February 15, 2001, Roger Leslie, review of *Destination Gold!,* p. 1128.

Books in Canada, summer, 1995, Pat Barclay, review of *Fires Burning,* p. 50; October, 1996, Annette Goldsmith, review of *Whatever You Do, Don't Go near That Canoe!,* p. 28.

Canadian Children's Literature, Vol. 69, 1993, Shawn Steffler, review of *A Morning to Polish and Keep,* p. 80; Vol. 69, 1993, Shawn Steffler, review of *Kate's Castle,* p. 91; winter, 1997, Adrienne Kertzer, review of *Cougar Cave,* pp. 74-76; spring, 1998, Gillian Harding-Russell, review of *Blown Away,* pp. 57-60; winter, 1999, Leonore Loft, review of *In Like a Lion,* p. 105.

Canadian Literature, summer, 1996, W. H. New, review of *White Jade Tiger,* pp. 200-201.

Kirkus Reviews, August 1, 1999, review of *Bear on the Train,* p. 1228.

Publishers Weekly, April 15, 1996, review of *Danger Game,* p. 69.

Quill & Quire, August, 1992; August, 1993; March, 1995, Marie Campbell, review of *Fires Burning,* p. 76; March, 1996, Bridget Donald, review of *Too Many Suns,* pp. 73-74; May, 1996, Maureen Garvie, review of *Cougar Cave,* p. 34; January, 1998, Maureen Garvie, review of *Goldstone,* p. 38; November, 1998, Maureen Garvie, review of *Turns on a Dime,* p. 47; December, 1998, Joanne Findon, review of *Midnight in the Mountains,* p. 35; January, 1999, Hadley Dyer, review of *In Like a Lion,* p. 43.

School Library Journal, July, 1993, Susan Scheps, review of *The Dragon's Pearl,* p. 62; September, 1996, Elisabeth Palmer Abarbanel, review of *Cougar Cove,* p. 204; October, 1998, Ronald Jobe, review of *Emma and the Silk Train,* p. 105; January, 1999, Linda Ludke, review of *Midnight in the Mountains,* p. 97; June, 1999, Gerry Lawson, review of *Turns on a Dime,* p. 134; January, 2001, Heather Dieffenbach, review of *The Ghost of Avalanche Mountain,* p. 132; July, 2001, Ashley Larsen, review of *Destination Gold!,* p. 110.

Tribune Books (Chicago, IL), June 8, 1997, Mary Harris Veeder, review of *Too Many Suns,* p. 7.

Voice of Youth Advocates, October, 1996, Jennifer Fakott, review of *Danger Game,* p. 211.

ON-LINE

Writers' Union of Canada, http://www.writersunion.ca/ (September 26, 2001), biography of Julie Lawson.*

M–N

MARRIN, Albert 1936-

Personal

Born July 24, 1936, in New York, NY; son of Louis and Frieda (Funt) Marrin; married Yvette Rappaport, November 22, 1959. *Education:* City College (now City College of the City University of New York), B.A., 1958; Yeshiva University, M.Ed., 1959; Columbia University, M.A., 1961, Ph.D., 1968. *Hobbies and other interests:* Travel in Europe.

Addresses

Home—750 Kappock St., Bronx, NY 10463. *Office*—Department of History, Yeshiva University, 500 West 185th St., New York, NY 10033. *Agent*—Toni Mendez, Inc., 141 East 56th St., New York, NY 10022.

Career

William Howard Taft High School, New York, NY, social studies teacher, 1959-68; Yeshiva University, New York, NY, assistant professor of history, 1968-78, professor and chairman of history department, 1978—; writer, 1968—. Visiting professor, Yeshiva University, 1967-68, and Touro College, 1972-74. *Member:* Western Writers of America.

Awards, Honors

Notable Children's Trade Book selection, National Council for Social Studies and Children's Book Council, and *Boston Globe/Horn Book* Honor Book, both 1985, both for *1812: The War Nobody Won;* Western Heritage Award for best juvenile nonfiction book, National Cowboy Hall of Fame, and Spur Award, Western Writers of America, both 1993, both for *Cowboys, Indians, and Gunfighters: The Story of the Cattle Kingdom; Boston Globe/Horn Book* Honor Book, 1994, Dorothy Canfield Fisher Children's Book Award, 1995, and Association of Christian Public School Teachers and Administrators Honor Award, 1995, all for *"Uncondi-*

Albert Marrin

tional Surrender": U. S. Grant and the Civil War; Children's Book Guild and *Washington Post* Nonfiction Award for contribution to children's literature, 1995; *Boston Globe/Horn Book* Honor Book, 2000, for *Sitting Bull and His World.*

Writings

FOR CHILDREN; NONFICTION

Overlord: D-Day and the Invasion of Europe, Atheneum (New York, NY), 1982.

The Airman's War: World War II in the Sky, Atheneum (New York, NY), 1982.

Victory in the Pacific, Atheneum (New York, NY), 1983.

War Clouds in the West: Indians and Cavalrymen, 1860-1890, Atheneum (New York, NY), 1984.

The Sea Rovers: Pirates, Privateers, and Buccaneers, Atheneum (New York, NY), 1984.

The Secret Armies: Spies, Counterspies, and Saboteurs in World War II, Atheneum (New York, NY), 1985.

1812: The War Nobody Won, Atheneum (New York, NY), 1985.

The Yanks Are Coming: The United States in the First World War, Atheneum (New York, NY), 1986.

Aztecs and Spaniards: Cortes and the Conquest of Mexico, Atheneum (New York, NY), 1986.

Struggle for a Continent: The French and Indian Wars, 1690-1760, Atheneum (New York, NY), 1987.

Hitler, Viking (New York, NY), 1987.

The War for Independence: The Story of the American Revolution, Atheneum (New York, NY), 1988.

Stalin: Russia's Man of Steel, Viking (New York, NY), 1988.

Inca and Spaniard: Pizarro and the Conquest of Peru, Atheneum (New York, NY), 1989.

Mao Tse-tung and His China, Viking (New York, NY), 1989.

Napoleon and the Napoleonic Wars, Viking (New York, NY), 1990.

The Spanish-American War, Atheneum (New York, NY), 1991.

America and Vietnam: The Elephant and the Tiger, Viking (New York, NY), 1992.

Cowboys, Indians, and Gunfighters: The Story of the Cattle Kingdom, Atheneum (New York, NY), 1993.

"Unconditional Surrender": U. S. Grant and the Civil War, Atheneum (New York, NY), 1993.

Virginia's General: Robert E. Lee and the Civil War, Atheneum (New York, NY), 1994.

The Sea King: Sir Francis Drake and His Times, Atheneum (New York, NY), 1995.

Plains Warrior: Chief Quanah Parker and the Comanches, Atheneum (New York, NY), 1996.

Empires Lost and Won: The Spanish Heritage in the Southwest, Atheneum (New York, NY), 1997.

Commander in Chief: Abraham Lincoln and the Civil War, Dutton (New York, NY), 1997.

Terror of the Spanish Main: Sir Henry Morgan and His Buccaneers, Dutton (New York, NY), 1999.

Sitting Bull and His World, Dutton (New York, NY), 2000.

George Washington and the Founding of a Nation, Dutton (New York, NY), 2001.

Secrets from the Rocks: Dinosaur Hunting with Roy Chapman Andrews, Dutton (New York, NY), 2002.

Dr. Jenner and the Speckled Monster: The Story of the Conquest of Smallpox, Dutton (New York, NY), 2002.

Oh Rats!, The Story of Rats and People, Dutton (New York, NY), in press.

FOR ADULTS; NONFICTION

War and the Christian Conscience: Augustine to Martin Luther King Jr., Gateway (Chicago, IL), 1971.

The Last Crusade: The Church of England in the First World War, Duke University Press (Durham, NC), 1974.

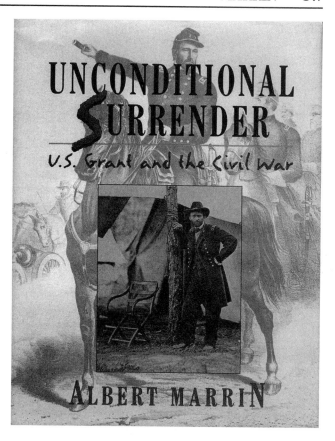

Marrin chronicles Ulysses S. Grant's involvement in the Civil War. *(Cover photo by Matthew Brady.)*

Nicholas Murray Butler: An Intellectual Portrait, Twayne (Boston, MA), 1976.

Sir Norman Angell, Twayne (Boston, MA), 1976.

Work in Progress

Old Hickory, a book about Andrew Jackson.

Sidelights

Albert Marrin is a professor of history who has attempted to make the past accessible to young readers via the many books he has authored. In award-winning books such as *1812: The War Nobody Won, Cowboys, Indians, and Gunfighters: The Story of the Cattle Kingdom,* and *"Unconditional Surrender": U. S. Grant and the Civil War,* Marrin has created an intriguing tapestry of U.S. history by focusing on dramatic moments and famous personalities. With biographies of leaders and tyrants from Napoleon Bonaparte to Adolph Hitler, Marrin has also interpreted the events of a larger world stage for juvenile readers. Additionally, his several books on World Wars I and II provide introductions to many aspects of those struggles. Marrin's books for young readers complement his academic duties as chair of the history department at New York's Yeshiva University.

One of Marrin's first books intended for a young audience, 1983's *Victory in the Pacific,* is indicative of

Marrin's approach to history. Writing in *Voice of Youth Advocates,* Michael Wessells commented on his "straightforward account," highlighted by "lucid capsule descriptions of selected topics" interspersed in the otherwise chronologically organized narrative which follows the war through major battles, from Pearl Harbor to Midway and Guadalcanal and the bombing of Japan. Marrin's treatment, anecdotal rather than detailed, would appeal, the reviewer noted, to "hi/lo readers." And Kate M. Flanagan, writing in *Horn Book,* pointed out Marrin's "fast-paced" accounts of various battles and his balanced narration, looking at history from both sides of the conflict to "provide an understanding of the warrior heritage that made the Japanese such a formidable enemy."

Marrin has dealt with various other aspects of World War II, from the invasion of Europe by the Allies to a history of spies and a study of the air war. With his *The Yanks Are Coming,* he also examines U.S. involvement in World War I. His concentration on military subjects enhanced an even more domestic topic in his *War Clouds in the West: Indians and Cavalrymen, 1860-1890,* which chronicles, battle by battle, the thirty-year war of destruction of the Plains Indians and Apache by the U.S. Cavalry. "The breadth of coverage," along with detailed diagrams and photos "all recommend this book for general readers," noted George Gleason in a *School Library Journal* review. *Horn Book* critic Nancy C. Hammond found Marrin's book to be a "dramatic readable account," with enlightening cultural and histori-

Marrin's informative text discusses the famous Civil War general.

cal perspectives on the struggle, such as the pressures ensuing from demands for buffalo brought on by a new hide-tanning process.

The history of the Native Americans of the Great Plains also figures in several titles by Marrin: *Cowboys, Indians, and Gunfighters: The Story of the Cattle Kingdom, Sitting Bull and His World,* and *Plains Warrior: Chief Quanah Parker and the Comanches.* The award-winning *Cowboys, Indians, and Gunfighters* is a history of the Old West, from the earliest Spanish settlers who introduced horses and cattle to the region to the struggle between buffalo and cattle for the open range. Divided into six chronological chapters, the book includes "minority viewpoints," according to Julie Halverstadt in *School Library Journal,* in its listing of contributions of African-American and Mexican cowboys. "A dynamic look at one of the most exciting and dangerous periods in U.S. history," Halverstadt concluded. With his *Plains Warrior,* Marrin focuses on the Comanche and their losing battle in the nineteenth century for their traditional life on the Great Plains. Providing at once an overview of Comanche history as well as a dramatic representation of the last tragic years of fighting under Chief Quanah Parker, son of a kidnaped settler, *Plains Warrior* "brings the period to life," according to a reviewer in *Bulletin of the Center for Children's Books.* The reviewer also praised Marrin for his even-handed treatment of both parties in the battle. While noting that Marrin's "vivid writing occasionally strays into sensationalism," *Horn Book* contributor Mary M. Burns praised *Plains Warrior* for building on both the "major differences between the Comanche and the white points of view and the tragedy inherent in those differences." In *Booklist,* Chris Sherman commented favorably on Merrin's use of "vivid description" and "compelling anecdotes" in telling his "engrossing" story. In *Sitting Bull and His World,* Marrin frames his biography of the Lakota warrior within "both the nature and substance of one man's resistance to and witness of his nation's enthnocide," according to a contributor to *Horn Book.*

Marrin also investigated an earlier conflict between Europeans and Native Americans in the New World—the wars between the British and French and their Indian allies. *Struggle for a Continent: The French and Indian Wars, 1690-1760,* once again demonstrates Marrin's use of accurate research as well as the use of anecdotes to create a "retelling of history that young people find accessible and appealing," according to Elizabeth S. Watson in *Horn Book.* Paula Nespeca Deal, writing in *Voice of Youth Advocates,* called *Struggle for a Continent* a "fascinating, easy to read overview," and noted that Marrin brings this little-understood battle for power alive with "vivid details of the cultural and social background." Deal also pointed out that Marrin includes the accomplishments of women in the struggle.

A logical chronological companion piece to *Struggle for a Continent* is *The War for Independence: The Story of the American Revolution,* which provides a "detailed account" of the American war for independence, according to Anne Frost in *Voice of Youth Advocates*. "This engrossing narrative gives the reader rare insight," Frost wrote. "Highly recommended." Marrin divides his narrative into eight chapters dealing with various topics such as causes, spies, naval battles, and the front-line skirmishes along the frontier. A contributor in *Kirkus Reviews* remarked particularly on Marrin's use of details that "engage the reader's senses," and a *Bulletin of the Center for Children's Books* reviewer called the work a "spirited and thoughtful account."

Marrin turned to the U.S. Civil War with titles profiling generals on opposing sides. *"Unconditional Surrender": U. S. Grant and the Civil War* uses Union General Ulysses S. Grant to focus on the war years, though it also includes information about the general before and after that conflict. Marrin confines his chronicle to battles and strategies that Grant was personally involved in. Thus Gettysburg and Bull Run are not included, but detailed accounts of Shiloh and Petersburg are, along with a plethora of facts and anecdotes. Neither Grant's racism nor his drinking are glossed over in this account, and the extensive bibliography appended "will be much appreciated by both history students and Civil War buffs," noted Elizabeth M. Reardon in *School Library Journal*.

A view from the other side of the battle lines is provided in *Virginia's General: Robert E. Lee and the Civil War*. Beginning with a brief account of the subject's life before and after the Civil War, it focuses on the war years through the Confederate general's eyes as well as through the eyes of a score of other witnesses. The extensive use of quotations from Lee and his generals, as well as plentiful detail, provides a "vivid picture of the war, its participants, and its effects," according to Deborah Stevenson in *Bulletin of the Center for Children's Books*. Carolyn Phelan, writing in *Booklist*, concluded that *Virginia's General* was "well researched and readable," and Connie Allerton in *Voice of Youth Advocates* noted that Marrin tells "an exciting story." Marrin extended his series on the Civil War with a volume focusing on Abraham Lincoln, *Commander in Chief: Abraham Lincoln and the Civil War*.

With *The Spanish-American War* and *America and Vietnam: The Elephant and the Tiger*, Marrin tackles two bloody chapters in U.S. history. In *The Spanish-American War* he creates "a fine sense of intimacy in his text," according to Margaret A. Bush in *Horn Book*, as he details the events that led up to the war that President McKinley did not want. Raymond E. Houser, writing in *Voice of Youth Advocates*, called *The Spanish-American War* "a good YA history," and a contributor in *Kirkus Reviews* labeled the same work "fresh (and timely)."

Marrin's history of America's longest war, *America and Vietnam*, was both praised for even-handedness and criticized for bias, demonstrating the deep rifts still apparent in U.S. society as a result of that conflict. Initially, Marrin provides an overview of Vietnamese history as one of struggle, beginning with Chinese control of the nation and continuing through the French

colonial system, occupation by the Japanese, renewed conflict with the French, and U.S. involvement in the region. The author also provides a lengthy account of the early life of the leader, Ho Chi Minh, who established Communism in the northern regions of the country following World War II. But the centerpiece of the book is the U.S. presence in Vietnam and the ensuing war. "Marrin covers the Vietnam Conflict in a sweeping fashion," according to Raymond E. Houser in *Voice of Youth Advocates*. "This is an excellent history book. . . . If a YA reader had but one book to read on this subject, this should be the one." Margaret A. Bush in *Horn Book* also found Marrin's account "remarkably even-handed."

Marrin has also written a quartet of biographies on world leaders, including portraits of Hitler, Stalin, Mao Tse-tung, Sir Henry Morgan, and Napoleon, as well as books on the influence of the Spanish in the Americas. A *Kirkus Reviews* critic deemed Marrin's *Hitler* "a dramatic account," and drew attention to the author's inclusion of various topics of recent interest, such as the White Rose resistance group and the fate of Josef Mengele. Margaret A. Bush, writing in *Horn Book*, termed the work a "riveting account that is informative, illuminating, and inescapably painful." Marrin continues his series on world leaders with *Stalin*, dubbed "another fine biography" by Elizabeth S. Watson in *Horn Book*, and with *Mao Tse-tung and His China*. In the latter, Marrin interweaves Mao's life with the history of China from 1911 to his death. From Mao's troubled childhood through the Long March and the days of the Cultural Revolution, Marrin traces the major turning points in the life of one of China's most controversial leaders. "A vivid but inconsistent account," noted Marsha L. Wagner in the *New York Times Book Review*. "This book is actually less a biography than a highly readable historical overview of modern China. . . . Sadly, Mao himself never emerges as a clear historical personalty," Wagner concluded.

With *Napoleon and the Napoleonic Wars*, Marrin took on a project that has been attempted by many other biographers. Marrin's book puts Napoleon's life into the context of his times, and also has the "particular talent for selecting an incident or anecdote" that sums up an individual, according to Margaret Miles in *Voice of Youth Advocates*. "The text is readable, dramatic, and well documented," noted Elizabeth S. Watson in *Horn Book*. And in *Terror of the Spanish Main: Sir Henry Morgan and His Buccaneers* Marrin "has created a narrative of epic proportions," in the opinion of *Horn Book* reviewer Mary M. Burns. Beginning with a history of Spain on the high seas, Marrin focuses on the Welsh-born Morgan as he builds his career from that of lowly pirate to almost-respectable businessman, creating a book that Burns dubbed "addictive reading." In *Booklist* Randy Meyer praised Marrin for doing "a top-notch job of bringing [the seventeenth-century Jamaican] setting to life, describing colonial life in all its grit and glory."

In *George Washington and the Founding of a Nation*, Marrin presents what *School Library Journal* contributor Steven Engelfried called an "engaging" portrait of both

Washington and the times in which he lived. Covering General Washington's military campaigns in detailed fashion, Marrin captures Washington's courage and character by including the words of his contemporaries. Although, as Engelfried pointed out, the author "clearly admires his subject," he "carefully discusses [Washington's] ... flaws and errors ... [and] raises questions and presents different views," among them questions about Washington's ownership of slaves. Washington becomes, through Marrin's lens, "a man of his time," according to *Booklist* reviewer Randy September 19, 2001Meyer, "one who could never reconcile his public philosophy of freedom with his private actions."

With *Inca and Spaniard: Pizarro and the Conquest of Peru, Aztecs and Spaniards: Cortes and the Conquest of Mexico,* and *Empires Lost and Won: The Spanish Heritage in the Southwest,* Marrin examines Spanish incursions in the New World and the clash of cultures such incursions brought about. Kathryn Pierson in *Bulletin of the Center for Children's Books* commented particularly on Marrin's novelistic treatment of *Inca and Spaniard,* which might limit the research value of his book, "but has probably enhanced its appeal," while Zena Sutherland in *Bulletin of the Center for Children's Books* described his *Aztecs and Spaniards* "as dramatic as fiction but well-grounded in fact."

Biographical and Critical Sources

BOOKS

Children's Literature Review, Volume 53, Gale (Detroit, MI), 1999.

PERIODICALS

Booklist, December 15, 1982, p. 565; February 1, 1983, Ilene Cooper, review of *Overlord: D-Day and the Invasion of Europe,* p. 725; June 15, 1983, review of *Victory in the Pacific,* p. 1340; September 1, 1984, p. 68; August, 1985, p. 1668; May 1, 1986, p. 1322; July, 1987, p. 1681; December 15, 1988, p. 700; October 15, 1989, p. 460; December 15, 1989, p. 823; July, 1991, p. 2039; March 1, 1992, p. 1269; August, 1993, p. 2046; April 1, 1994, p. 1440; December 15, 1994, Carolyn Phelan, review of *Virginia's General: Robert E. Lee and the Civil War,* p. 746; March 15, 1996, review of *Virginia's General,* p. 1274; June 1, 1996, Chris Sherman, review of *Plains Warrior,* p. 1723; January 1, 1998, review of *Commander in Chief Abraham Lincoln and the Civil War,* p. 744; January 1-15, 1999, Randy Meyer, review of *Terror of the Spanish Main,* p. 849; January 1, 2001, Randy Meyer, review of *George Washington and the Founding of a Nation,* p. 951.

Bulletin of the Center for Children's Books, April, 1986, Zena Sutherland, review of *Aztecs and Spaniards: Cortes and the Conquest of Mexico,* p. 153; April, 1988, review of *The War for Independence: The Story of the American Revolution,* p. 161; February, 1990, Kathryn Pierson, review of *Inca and Spaniard: Pizarro and the Conquest of Peru,* p. 142; March, 1994, Deborah Stevenson, review of *"Unconditional Surrender": U. S. Grant and the Civil War,* p. 227; January,

1995, Deborah Stevenson, review of *Virginia's General: Robert E. Lee and the Civil War,* p. 173; May, 1996, review of *Plains Warrior: Chief Quanah Parker and the Comanches,* p. 308.

Horn Book, April, 1983, Kate M. Flanagan, review of *Victory in the Pacific,* p. 184; June, 1984, p. 349; March-April, 1985, Nancy C. Hammond, review of *War Clouds in the West: Indians and Cavalrymen, 1860-1890,* pp. 195-196; September, 1986, p. 610; April, 1986, Zena Sutherland, review of *Aztecs and Spaniards: Cortes and the Conquest of Mexico,* pp. 153-154; September-October, 1987, Margaret A. Bush, review of *Hitler,* p. 630; January-February, 1988, Elizabeth S. Watson, review of *Struggle for a Continent: The French and Indian Wars, 1690-1760,* p. 87; March-April, 1989, Elizabeth S. Watson, review of *Stalin,* p. 234; January, 1990, p. 89; July-August, 1991, Margaret A. Bush, review of *The Spanish-American War,* p. 481; September-October, 1991, Elizabeth S. Watson, review of *Napoleon and the Napoleonic Wars,* p. 617; September-October, 1992, Margaret A. Bush, review of *America and Vietnam: The Elephant and the Tiger,* pp. 600-601; September, 1993, p. 625; July, 1994, p. 473; September, 1996, Mary M. Burns, review of *Plains Warrior,* p. 621; March, 1999, Mary M. Burns, review of *Terror of the Spanish Main,* p. 227; July, 2000, review of *Sitting Bull and His World,* p. 474.

Kirkus Reviews, May 15, 1987, review of *Hitler,* pp. 796-797; April 15, 1988, review of *The War for Independence: The Story of the American Revolution,* p. 621; February 15, 1991, review of *The Spanish-American War,* p. 250; April 1, 1992, review of *America and Vietnam: The Elephant and the Tiger,* p. 463.

New York Times Book Review, February 25, 1990, Marsha L. Wagner, review of *Mao Tse-tung and His China,* p. 33; August 17, 1997, review of *Empires Lost and Won,* p. 19; August 13, 2000, review of *Sitting Bull and His World,* p. 16.

School Library Journal, November, 1982, p. 88; April, 1983, p. 126; August, 1984, p. 76; March, 1985, George Gleason, review of *War Clouds in the West: Indians and Cavalrymen, 1860-1890,* p. 180; August, 1986, p. 104; June, 1987, p. 110; December, 1987, p. 108; June, 1988, p. 124; November, 1989, p. 132; February, 1990, p. 116; May, 1991, p. 192; August, 1993, Julie Halverstadt, review of *Cowboys, Indians, and Gunfighters: The Story of the Cattle Kingdom,* p. 199; July, 1994, Elizabeth M. Reardon, review of *"Unconditional Surrender": U. S. Grant and the Civil War,* p. 1122; December, 1994, p. 25; July, 2000, review of *Sitting Bull and His World,* p. 15; January, 2001, Steven Engelfried, review of *George Washington and the Founding of a Nation,* p. 150.

Voice of Youth Advocates, October, 1983, Michael Wessells, review of *Victory in the Pacific,* p. 226; October, 1987, Paula Nespeca Deal, review of *Struggle for a Continent: The French and Indian Wars, 1690-1760,* p. 189; June, 1988, Anne Frost, review of *The War for Independence: The Story of the American Revolution,* p. 103; June, 1991, Raymond E. Houser, review of *The Spanish-American War,* p. 127; October, 1991, Margaret Miles, review of *Napoleon and the Napo-*

leonic Wars, p. 265; June, 1992, Raymond E. Houser, review of *America and Vietnam: The Elephant and the Tiger,* p. 130; April, 1995, Connie Allerton, review of *Virginia's General: Robert E. Lee and the Civil War,* p. 50; August, 1996, review of *The Sea King,* p. 181; February, 1998, review of *Empires Lost and Won,* p. 365.

—Sketch by J. Sydney Jones

*   *   *

MARTIN, Ann M. 1955-

Personal

Born August 12, 1955, in Princeton, NJ; daughter of Henry Read (a cartoonist) and Edith Aiken (a teacher; maiden name, Matthews) Martin. *Education:* Smith College, A.B. (cum laude), 1977. *Politics:* Democrat. *Hobbies and other interests:* "Reading and needlework, especially smocking and knitting."

Addresses

Agent—Amy Berkower, Writers House, Inc., 21 West 26th St., New York, NY 10010.

Career

Elementary school teacher in Noroton, CT, 1977-78; Pocket Books, Inc., New York, NY, editorial assistant for Archway Paperbacks, 1978-80; Scholastic Book Services, New York, NY, copywriter for Teen Age Book Club, 1980-81, associate editor, 1981-83, editor, 1983; Bantam Books, Inc., New York, NY, senior editor of Books for Young Readers, 1983-85; writer and freelance editor, 1985—. Co-founder of Lisa Novak Community Libraries; founder of Ann M. Martin Foundation. *Member:* PEN, Authors Guild, Society of Children's Book Writers.

Awards, Honors

New Jersey Author awards, New Jersey Institute of Technology, 1983, for *Bummer Summer,* 1987, for *Missing since Monday;* Children's Choice, 1985, for *Bummer Summer;* Child Study Association of America's Children's Books of the Year selection, 1986, for *Inside Out,* 1987, for *Stage Fright, With You and without You,* and *Missing since Monday;* Keystone State Reading Award, 1998, for *Leo the Magnificat;* California Young Reader Medal nomination, 2000, and Washington Sasquatch Reading Award nomination, 2001, both for *P.S. Longer Letter Later.*

Writings

Bummer Summer, Holiday House (New York, NY), 1983.
Just You and Me, Scholastic, Inc. (New York, NY), 1983.
(With Betsy Ryan) *My Puppy Scrapbook,* illustrated by father, Henry Martin, Scholastic, Inc. (New York, NY), 1983.

Inside Out, Holiday House (New York, NY), 1984.
Stage Fright, illustrated by Blanche Sims, Holiday House (New York, NY), 1984.
Me and Katie (the Pest), illustrated by Blanche Sims, Holiday House (New York, NY), 1985.
With You and without You, Holiday House (New York, NY), 1986.
Missing since Monday, Holiday House (New York, NY), 1986.
Just a Summer Romance, Holiday House (New York, NY), 1987.
Slam Book, Holiday House (New York, NY), 1987.
Yours Turly, Shirley, Holiday House (New York, NY), 1988.
Ten Kids, No Pets, Holiday House (New York, NY), 1988.
Fancy Dance in Feather Town, illustrated by Henry Martin, Western Publishing, 1988.
Ma and Pa Dracula, illustrated by Dirk Zimmer, Holiday House (New York, NY), 1989.
Moving Day in Feather Town, illustrated by Henry Martin, Western Publishing, 1989.
Eleven Kids, One Summer, Holiday House (New York, NY), 1991.
Enchanted Attic, Bantam (New York, NY), 1992.
Rachel Parker, Kindergarten Show-off, illustrated by Nancy Poydar, Holiday House (New York, NY), 1992.
Chain Letter, Scholastic, Inc. (New York, NY), 1993.
(With Margot Becker) *Ann M. Martin: The Story of the Author of the Baby-Sitters Club,* Scholastic, Inc. (New York, NY) 1993.
Leo the Magnificat, illustrated by Emily A. McCully, Scholastic, Inc. (New York, NY), 1996.
(With Paula Danziger) *P.S. Longer Letter Later,* Scholastic, Inc. (New York, NY), 1998.
(With Laura Godwin) *The Doll People,* Hyperion (New York, NY), 1999.
(With Paula Danziger) *Snail Mail No More,* Scholastic, Inc. (New York, NY), 2000.
Belle Teal, Scholastic, Inc. (New York, NY), 2001.

"BABY-SITTERS CLUB" SERIES

Kristy's Great Idea, Scholastic, Inc. (New York, NY), 1986.
Claudia and the Phantom Phone Calls, Scholastic, Inc. (New York, NY), 1986.
The Truth about Stacey, Scholastic, Inc. (New York, NY), 1986.
Mary Anne Saves the Day, Scholastic, Inc. (New York, NY), 1987.
Dawn and the Impossible Three, Scholastic, Inc. (New York, NY), 1987.
Kristy's Big Day, Scholastic, Inc. (New York, NY), 1987.
Claudia and Mean Janine, Scholastic, Inc. (New York, NY), 1987.
Boy-Crazy Stacey, Scholastic, Inc. (New York, NY), 1987.
The Ghost at Dawn's House, Scholastic, Inc. (New York, NY), 1988.
Logan Likes Mary Anne!, Scholastic, Inc. (New York, NY), 1988.
Kristy and the Snobs, Scholastic, Inc. (New York, NY), 1988.
Claudia and the New Girl, Scholastic, Inc. (New York, NY), 1988.

P.S. Longer Letter Later

A Novel in Letters

PAULA DANZIGER & ANN M. MARTIN

In this work, cowritten by Ann M. Martin and Paula Danziger, Elizabeth and Tara*Starr are inseparable friends until Tara*Starr moves away and the girls must correspond by letter. (Cover illustration by Paul Colin.)

Good-bye Stacey, Good-bye, Scholastic, Inc. (New York, NY), 1988.

Hello, Mallory, Scholastic, Inc. (New York, NY), 1988.

Little Miss Stoneybrook ... and Dawn, Scholastic, Inc. (New York, NY), 1988.

Jessi's Secret Language, Scholastic, Inc. (New York, NY), 1988.

Mary Anne's Bad-Luck Mystery, Scholastic, Inc. (New York, NY), 1988.

Stacey's Mistake, Scholastic, Inc. (New York, NY), 1988.

Claudia and the Bad Joke, Scholastic, Inc. (New York, NY), 1988.

Kristy and the Walking Disaster, Scholastic, Inc. (New York, NY), 1989.

Mallory and the Trouble with the Twins, Scholastic, Inc. (New York, NY), 1989.

Jessi Ramsey, Pet-Sitter, Scholastic, Inc. (New York, NY), 1989.

Dawn on the Coast, Scholastic, Inc. (New York, NY), 1989.

Kristy and the Mother's Day Surprise, Scholastic, Inc. (New York, NY), 1989.

Mary Anne and the Search for Tigger, Scholastic, Inc. (New York, NY), 1989.

Claudia and the Sad Good-bye, Scholastic, Inc. (New York, NY), 1989.

Jessi and the Superbrat, Scholastic, Inc. (New York, NY), 1989.

Welcome Back, Stacey!, Scholastic, Inc. (New York, NY), 1989.

Mallory and the Mystery Diary, Scholastic, Inc. (New York, NY), 1989.

Mary Anne and the Great Romance, Scholastic, Inc. (New York, NY), 1990.

Dawn's Wicked Stepsister, Scholastic, Inc. (New York, NY), 1990.

Kristy and the Secret of Susan, Scholastic, Inc. (New York, NY), 1990.

Claudia and the Great Search, Scholastic, Inc. (New York, NY), 1990.

Mary Anne and Too Many Boys, Scholastic, Inc. (New York, NY), 1990.

Stacey and the Mystery of Stoneybrook, Scholastic, Inc. (New York, NY), 1990.

Jessi's Baby-Sitter, Scholastic, Inc. (New York, NY), 1990.

Dawn and the Older Boy, Scholastic, Inc. (New York, NY), 1990.

Kristy's Mystery Admirer, Scholastic, Inc. (New York, NY), 1990.

Poor Mallory, Scholastic, Inc. (New York, NY), 1990.

Claudia and the Middle School Mystery, Scholastic, Inc. (New York, NY), 1991.

Mary Anne vs. Logan, Scholastic, Inc. (New York, NY), 1991.

Jessi and the Dance School Phantom, Scholastic, Inc. (New York, NY), 1991.

Stacey's Emergency, Scholastic, Inc. (New York, NY), 1991.

Dawn and the Big Sleepover, Scholastic, Inc. (New York, NY), 1991.

Kristy and the Baby Parade, Scholastic, Inc. (New York, NY), 1991.

Mary Anne Misses Logan, Scholastic, Inc. (New York, NY), 1991.

Mallory on Strike, Scholastic, Inc. (New York, NY), 1991.

Jessi's Wish, Scholastic, Inc. (New York, NY), 1991.

Claudia and the Genius of Elm Street, Scholastic, Inc. (New York, NY), 1991.

Dawn's Big Date, Scholastic, Inc. (New York, NY), 1992.

Stacey's Ex-Best Friend, Scholastic, Inc. (New York, NY), 1992.

Mary Anne and Too Many Babies, Scholastic, Inc. (New York, NY), 1992.

Kristy for President, Scholastic, Inc. (New York, NY), 1992.

Mallory and the Dream Horse, Scholastic, Inc. (New York, NY), 1992.

Jessi's Gold Medal, Scholastic, Inc. (New York, NY), 1992.

Keep out, Claudia!, Scholastic, Inc. (New York, NY), 1992.

Dawn Saves the Planet, Scholastic, Inc. (New York, NY), 1992.

Stacey's Choice, Scholastic, Inc. (New York, NY), 1992.

Mallory Hates Boys (and Gym), Scholastic, Inc. (New York, NY), 1992.

Mary Anne's Makeover, Scholastic, Inc. (New York, NY), 1993.

Jessi and the Awful Secret, Scholastic, Inc. (New York, NY), 1993.

Kristy and the Worst Kid Ever, Scholastic, Inc. (New York, NY), 1993.

Claudia's Friend, Scholastic, Inc. (New York, NY), 1993.

Dawn's Family Feud, Scholastic, Inc. (New York, NY), 1993.

Stacey's Big Crush, Scholastic, Inc. (New York, NY), 1993.

Maid Mary Anne, Scholastic, Inc. (New York, NY), 1993.

Dawn's Big Move, Scholastic, Inc. (New York, NY), 1993.

Jessi and the Bad Baby-Sitter, Scholastic, Inc. (New York, NY), 1993.

Get Well Soon, Mallory, Scholastic, Inc. (New York, NY), 1993.

Stacey and the Cheerleaders, Scholastic, Inc. (New York, NY), 1993.

Claudia and the Perfect Boy, Scholastic, Inc. (New York, NY), 1994.

Dawn and the We Love Kids Club, Scholastic, Inc. (New York, NY), 1994.

Mary Anne and Miss Priss, Scholastic, Inc. (New York, NY), 1994.

Kristy and the Copycat, Scholastic, Inc. (New York, NY), 1994.

Jessi's Horrible Prank, Scholastic, Inc. (New York, NY), 1994.

Stacey's Lie, Scholastic, Inc. (New York, NY), 1994.

Dawn and Whitney, Friends Forever, Scholastic, Inc. (New York, NY), 1994.

Claudia and Crazy Peaches, Scholastic, Inc. (New York, NY), 1994.

Mary Anne Breaks the Rules, Scholastic, Inc. (New York, NY), 1994.

Mallory Pike, #1 Fan, Scholastic, Inc. (New York, NY), 1994.

Kristy and Mr. Mom, Scholastic, Inc. (New York, NY), 1995.

Jessi and the Troublemaker, Scholastic, Inc. (New York, NY), 1995.

Stacey vs. the BSC, Scholastic, Inc. (New York, NY), 1995.

Dawn and the School Spirit War, Scholastic, Inc. (New York, NY), 1995.

Claudia Kishi, Live from WSTO, Scholastic, Inc. (New York, NY), 1995.

Mary Anne and Camp BSC, Scholastic, Inc. (New York, NY), 1995.

Stacey and the Bad Girls, Scholastic, Inc. (New York, NY), 1995.

Farewell, Dawn, Scholastic, Inc. (New York, NY), 1995.

Kristy and the Dirty Diapers, Scholastic, Inc. (New York, NY), 1995.

Welcome to the BSC, Abby, Scholastic, Inc. (New York, NY), 1995.

Claudia and the First Thanksgiving, Scholastic, Inc. (New York, NY), 1995.

Mallory's Christmas Wish, Scholastic, Inc. (New York, NY), 1995.

Mary Anne and the Memory Garden, Scholastic, Inc. (New York, NY), 1996.

Stacey McGill, Super Sitter, Scholastic, Inc. (New York, NY), 1996.

Kristy + Bart = ?, Scholastic, Inc. (New York, NY), 1996.

Abby's Lucky Thirteen, Scholastic, Inc. (New York, NY), 1996.

Claudia and the World's Cutest Baby, Scholastic, Inc. (New York, NY), 1996.

Dawn and Too Many Sitters, Scholastic, Inc. (New York, NY), 1996.

Stacey's Broken Heart, Scholastic, Inc. (New York, NY), 1996.

Kristy's Worst Idea, Scholastic, Inc. (New York, NY), 1996.

Claudia Kishi, Middle School Drop Out, Scholastic, Inc. (New York, NY), 1996.

Mary Anne and the Little Princess, Scholastic, Inc. (New York, NY), 1996.

Happy Holidays, Jessi, Scholastic, Inc. (New York, NY), 1996.

Abby's Twin, Scholastic, Inc. (New York, NY), 1997.

Stacey the Match Whiz, Scholastic, Inc. (New York, NY), 1997.

Claudia, Queen of the Seventh Grade, Scholastic, Inc. (New York, NY), 1997.

Mind Your Own Business, Kristy!, Scholastic, Inc. (New York, NY), 1997.

Don't Give up, Mallory, Scholastic, Inc. (New York, NY), 1997.

Mary Anne to the Rescue, Scholastic, Inc. (New York, NY), 1997.

Abby the Bad Sport, Scholastic, Inc. (New York, NY), 1997.

Stacey's Secret Friend, Scholastic, Inc. (New York, NY), 1997.

Kristy and the Sister War, Scholastic, Inc. (New York, NY), 1997.

Claudia Makes up Her Mind, Scholastic, Inc. (New York, NY), 1997.

The Secret Life of Mary Anne Spier, Scholastic, Inc. (New York, NY), 1997.

Jessi's Big Break, Scholastic, Inc. (New York, NY), 1997.

Abby and the Best Kid Ever, Scholastic, Inc. (New York, NY), 1997.

Claudia and the Terrible Truth, Scholastic, Inc. (New York, NY), 1997.

Kristy Thomas, Dog Trainer, Scholastic, Inc. (New York, NY), 1997.

Stacey's Ex-Boyfriend, Scholastic, Inc. (New York, NY), 1997.

Mary Anne and the Playground Fight, Scholastic, Inc. (New York, NY), 1997.

Abby in Wonderland, Scholastic, Inc. (New York, NY), 1997.

Kristy in Charge, Scholastic, Inc. (New York, NY), 1997.

Claudia's Big Party, Scholastic, Inc. (New York, NY), 1998.

Stacey McGill ... Matchmaker?, Scholastic, Inc. (New York, NY), 1998.

Mary Anne in the Middle, Scholastic, Inc. (New York, NY), 1998.

The All-New Mallory Pike, Scholastic, Inc. (New York, NY), 1998.

Abby's Un-Valentine, Scholastic, Inc. (New York, NY), 1998.

Claudia and the Little Liar, Scholastic, Inc. (New York, NY), 1999.

Kristy at Bat, Scholastic, Inc. (New York, NY), 1999.

Stacey's Movie, Scholastic, Inc. (New York, NY), 1999.

The Fire at Mary Anne's House, Scholastic, Inc. (New York, NY), 1999.

Graduation Day, Scholastic, Inc. (New York, NY), 2000.

"FRIENDS FOREVER" SERIES

Kristy's Big News, Scholastic, Inc. (New York, NY), 1999.

Stacey vs. Claudia, Scholastic, Inc. (New York, NY), 1999.

Mary Anne's Big Break Up, Scholastic, Inc. (New York, NY), 1999.

Claudia and the Friendship Feud, Scholastic, Inc. (New York, NY), 1999.

Kristy Power, Scholastic, Inc. (New York, NY), 1999.

Stacey and the Boyfriend Trap, Scholastic, Inc. (New York, NY), 1999.

Claudia Gets Her Guy, Scholastic, Inc. (New York, NY), 2000.

Mary Anne's Revenge, Scholastic, Inc. (New York, NY), 2000.

Kristy and the Kidnapper, Scholastic, Inc. (New York, NY), 2000.

Stacey's Problem, Scholastic, Inc. (New York, NY), 2000.

Welcome Home, Mary Anne, Scholastic, Inc. (New York, NY), 2000.

Claudia and the Disaster Date, Scholastic, Inc. (New York, NY), 2000.

"FRIENDS FOREVER SPECIAL" SERIES

Everything Changes, Scholastic, Inc. (New York, NY), 1999.

Graduation Day, Scholastic, Inc. (New York, NY), 2000.

"BABY-SITTERS CLUB MYSTERY" SERIES

Stacey and the Missing Ring, Scholastic, Inc. (New York, NY), 1991.

Beware, Dawn!, Scholastic, Inc. (New York, NY), 1991.

Mallory and the Ghost Cat, Scholastic, Inc. (New York, NY), 1992.

Kristy and the Missing Child, Scholastic, Inc. (New York, NY), 1992.

Mary Anne and the Secret in the Attic, Scholastic, Inc. (New York, NY), 1992.

The Mystery at Claudia's House, Scholastic, Inc. (New York, NY), 1992.

Dawn and the Disappearing Dogs, Scholastic, Inc. (New York, NY), 1993.

Jessi and the Jewel Thieves, Scholastic, Inc. (New York, NY), 1993.

Kristy and the Haunted Mansion, Scholastic, Inc. (New York, NY), 1993.

Stacey and the Mystery Money, Scholastic, Inc. (New York, NY), 1993.

Claudia and the Mystery at the Museum, Scholastic, Inc. (New York, NY), 1993.

Dawn and the Surfer Ghost, Scholastic, Inc. (New York, NY), 1993.

Mary Anne and the Library Mystery, Scholastic, Inc. (New York, NY), 1994.

Stacey and the Mystery at the Mall, Scholastic, Inc. (New York, NY), 1994.

Kristy and the Vampires, Scholastic, Inc. (New York, NY), 1994.

Claudia and the Clue in the Photograph, Scholastic, Inc. (New York, NY), 1994.

Dawn and the Halloween Mystery, Scholastic, Inc. (New York, NY), 1994.

Stacey and the Mystery at the Empty House, Scholastic, Inc. (New York, NY), 1994.

Kristy and the Missing Fortune, Scholastic, Inc. (New York, NY), 1995.

Mary Anne and the Zoo Mystery, Scholastic, Inc. (New York, NY), 1995.

Claudia and the Recipe for Danger, Scholastic, Inc. (New York, NY), 1995.

Stacey and the Haunted Masquerade, Scholastic, Inc. (New York, NY), 1995.

Abby and the Secret Society, Scholastic, Inc. (New York, NY), 1996.

Mary Anne and the Silent Witness, Scholastic, Inc. (New York, NY), 1996.

Kristy and the Middle School Vandal, Scholastic, Inc. (New York, NY), 1996.

Dawn Schafer, Undercover Baby-Sitter, Scholastic, Inc. (New York, NY), 1996.

Claudia and the Lighthouse Ghost, Scholastic, Inc. (New York, NY), 1996.

Abby and the Mystery Baby, Scholastic, Inc. (New York, NY), 1997.

Stacey and the Fashion Victim, Scholastic, Inc. (New York, NY), 1997.

Kristy and the Mystery Train, Scholastic, Inc. (New York, NY), 1997.

Mary Anne and the Music Box Secret, Scholastic, Inc. (New York, NY), 1997.

Claudia and the Mystery in the Painting, Scholastic, Inc. (New York, NY), 1997.

Stacey and the Stolen Hearts, Scholastic, Inc. (New York, NY), 1997.

Mary Anne and the Haunted Bookstore, Scholastic, Inc. (New York, NY), 1997.

Abby and the Notorious Neighbor, Scholastic, Inc. (New York, NY), 1997.

Kristy and the Cat Burglar, Scholastic, Inc. (New York, NY), 1997.

"BABY-SITTERS CLUB SUPER SPECIALS" SERIES

Baby-Sitters on Board!, Scholastic, Inc. (New York, NY), 1988.

Baby-Sitters Summer Vacation, Scholastic, Inc. (New York, NY), 1989.

Baby-Sitters Winter Vacation, Scholastic, Inc. (New York, NY), 1989.

Baby-Sitters Island Adventure, Scholastic, Inc. (New York, NY), 1990.

California Girls!, Scholastic, Inc. (New York, NY), 1990.

New York, New York!, Scholastic, Inc. (New York, NY), 1991.

Snowbound, Scholastic, Inc. (New York, NY), 1991.

Baby-Sitters at Shadow Lake, Scholastic, Inc. (New York, NY), 1992.

Starring the Baby-Sitters Club, Scholastic, Inc. (New York, NY), 1992.

Sea City, Here We Come!, Scholastic, Inc. (New York, NY), 1993.

The Baby-Sitters Remember, Scholastic, Inc. (New York, NY), 1994.

Here Come the Bridesmaids!, Scholastic, Inc. (New York, NY), 1994.

Aloha, Baby-Sitters!, Scholastic, Inc. (New York, NY), 1996.

"BABY-SITTERS LITTLE SISTERS" SERIES

Karen's Witch, Scholastic, Inc. (New York, NY), 1988.

Karen's Roller Skates, Scholastic, Inc. (New York, NY), 1988.

Karen's Worst Day, Scholastic, Inc. (New York, NY), 1989.

Karen's Kittycat Club, Scholastic, Inc. (New York, NY), 1989.

Karen's School Picture, Scholastic, Inc. (New York, NY), 1989.

Karen's Little Sister, Scholastic, Inc. (New York, NY), 1989.

Karen's Birthday, Scholastic, Inc. (New York, NY), 1990.

Karen's Haircut, Scholastic, Inc. (New York, NY), 1990.

Karen's Sleepover, Scholastic, Inc. (New York, NY), 1990.

Karen's Grandmothers, Scholastic, Inc. (New York, NY), 1990.

Karen's Prize, Scholastic, Inc. (New York, NY), 1990.

Karen's Ghost, Scholastic, Inc. (New York, NY), 1990.

Karen's Surprise, Scholastic, Inc. (New York, NY), 1990.

Karen's New Year, Scholastic, Inc. (New York, NY), 1991.

Karen's in Love, Scholastic, Inc. (New York, NY), 1991.

Karen's Goldfish, Scholastic, Inc. (New York, NY), 1991.

Karen's Brothers, Scholastic, Inc. (New York, NY), 1991.

Karen's Home Run, Scholastic, Inc. (New York, NY), 1991.

Karen's Good-Bye, Scholastic, Inc. (New York, NY), 1991.

Karen's Carnival, Scholastic, Inc. (New York, NY), 1991.

Karen's New Teacher, Scholastic, Inc. (New York, NY), 1991.

Karen's Little Witch, Scholastic, Inc. (New York, NY), 1992.

Karen's Doll, Scholastic, Inc. (New York, NY), 1992.

Karen's School Trip, Scholastic, Inc. (New York, NY), 1992.

Karen's Pen Pal, Scholastic, Inc. (New York, NY), 1992.

Karen's Ducklings, Scholastic, Inc. (New York, NY), 1992.

Karen's Big Joke, Scholastic, Inc. (New York, NY), 1992.

Karen's Tea Party, Scholastic, Inc. (New York, NY), 1992.

Karen's Cartwheel, Scholastic, Inc. (New York, NY), 1992.

Karen's Kittens, Scholastic, Inc. (New York, NY), 1992.

Karen's Bully, Scholastic, Inc. (New York, NY), 1992.

Karen's Pumpkin Patch, Scholastic, Inc. (New York, NY), 1992.

Karen's Secret, Scholastic, Inc. (New York, NY), 1992.

Karen's Snow Day, Scholastic, Inc. (New York, NY), 1993.

Karen's Doll Hospital, Scholastic, Inc. (New York, NY), 1993.

Karen's New Friend, Scholastic, Inc. (New York, NY), 1993.

Karen's Tuba, Scholastic, Inc. (New York, NY), 1993.

Karen's Big Lie, Scholastic, Inc. (New York, NY), 1993.

Karen's Wedding, Scholastic, Inc. (New York, NY), 1993.

Karen's Newspaper, Scholastic, Inc. (New York, NY), 1993.

Karen's School, Scholastic, Inc. (New York, NY), 1993.

Karen's Pizza Party, Scholastic, Inc. (New York, NY), 1993.

Karen's Toothache, Scholastic, Inc. (New York, NY), 1993.

Karen's Big Weekend, Scholastic, Inc. (New York, NY), 1993.

Karen's Twin, Scholastic, Inc. (New York, NY), 1994.

Karen's Baby-Sitter, Scholastic, Inc. (New York, NY), 1994.

Karen's Kite, Scholastic, Inc. (New York, NY), 1994.

Karen's Two Families, Scholastic, Inc. (New York, NY), 1994.

Karen's Stepmother, Scholastic, Inc. (New York, NY), 1994.

Karen's Lucky Penny, Scholastic, Inc. (New York, NY), 1994.

Eighth-graders Elizabeth and Tara*Starr continue their friendship via e-mail as they face big family changes. *(Cover photo by Marc Tauss.)*

A new family of plastic dolls arrives at the house inhabited by a family of one-hundred-year-old porcelain dolls. (Cover illustration by Brian Selznick.)

Karen's Big Top, Scholastic, Inc. (New York, NY), 1994.
Karen's Mermaid, Scholastic, Inc. (New York, NY), 1994.
Karen's School Bus, Scholastic, Inc. (New York, NY), 1994.
Karen's Candy, Scholastic, Inc. (New York, NY), 1994.
Karen's Magician, Scholastic, Inc. (New York, NY), 1994.
Karen's Ice Skates, Scholastic, Inc. (New York, NY), 1994.
Karen's School Mystery, Scholastic, Inc. (New York, NY), 1995.
Karen's Ski Trip, Scholastic, Inc. (New York, NY), 1995.
Karen's Leprechaun, Scholastic, Inc. (New York, NY), 1995.
Karen's Pony, Scholastic, Inc. (New York, NY), 1995.
Karen's Tattletale, Scholastic, Inc. (New York, NY), 1995.
Karen's New Bike, Scholastic, Inc. (New York, NY), 1995.
Karen's Movie, Scholastic, Inc. (New York, NY), 1995.
Karen's Lemonade Stand, Scholastic, Inc. (New York, NY), 1995.
Karen's Toys, Scholastic, Inc. (New York, NY), 1995.
Karen's Monsters, Scholastic, Inc. (New York, NY), 1995.
Karen's Turkey Day, Scholastic, Inc. (New York, NY), 1995.
Karen's Angel, Scholastic, Inc. (New York, NY), 1995.
Karen's Big Sister, Scholastic, Inc. (New York, NY), 1996.
Karen's Grandad, Scholastic, Inc. (New York, NY), 1996.
Karen's Island Adventure, Scholastic, Inc. (New York, NY), 1996.

Karen's New Puppy, Scholastic, Inc. (New York, NY), 1996.
Karen's Dinosaur, Scholastic, Inc. (New York, NY), 1996.
Karen's Softball Mystery, Scholastic, Inc. (New York, NY), 1996.
Karen's County Fair, Scholastic, Inc. (New York, NY), 1996.
Karen's Magic Garden, Scholastic, Inc. (New York, NY), 1996.
Karen's School Surprise, Scholastic, Inc. (New York, NY), 1996.
Karen's Half Birthday, Scholastic, Inc. (New York, NY), 1996.
Karen's Big Fight, Scholastic, Inc. (New York, NY), 1996.
Karen's Christmas Tree, Scholastic, Inc. (New York, NY), 1996.
Karen's Accident, Scholastic, Inc. (New York, NY), 1997.
Karen's Secret Valentine, Scholastic, Inc. (New York, NY), 1997.
Karen's Bunny, Scholastic, Inc. (New York, NY), 1997.
Karen's Big Job, Scholastic, Inc. (New York, NY), 1997.
Karen's Treasure, Scholastic, Inc. (New York, NY), 1997.
Karen's Telephone Trouble, Scholastic, Inc. (New York, NY), 1997.
Karen's Pony Camp, Scholastic, Inc. (New York, NY), 1997.
Karen's Puppet Show, Scholastic, Inc. (New York, NY), 1997.
Karen's Unicorn, Scholastic, Inc. (New York, NY), 1997.
Karen's Haunted House, Scholastic, Inc. (New York, NY), 1997.
Karen's Pilgrim, Scholastic, Inc. (New York, NY), 1997.
Karen's Sleigh Ride, Scholastic, Inc. (New York, NY), 1997.
Karen's Cooking Contest, Scholastic, Inc. (New York, NY), 1997.
Karen's Snow Princess, Scholastic, Inc. (New York, NY), 1997.
Karen's Promise, Scholastic, Inc. (New York, NY), 1997.
Karen's Big Move, Scholastic, Inc. (New York, NY), 1997.
Karen's Paper Route, Scholastic, Inc. (New York, NY), 1997.
Karen's Fishing Trip, Scholastic, Inc. (New York, NY), 1997.
Karen's Big City Mystery, Scholastic, Inc. (New York, NY), 1997.
Karen's Book, Scholastic, Inc. (New York, NY), 1997.
Karen's Chain Letter, Scholastic, Inc. (New York, NY), 1997.
Karen's Black Cat, Scholastic, Inc. (New York, NY), 1998.
Karen's Movie Star, Scholastic, Inc. (New York, NY), 1998.
Karen's Christmas Carol, Scholastic, Inc. (New York, NY), 1998.
Karen's Nanny, Scholastic, Inc. (New York, NY), 1998.
Karen's President, Scholastic, Inc. (New York, NY), 1998.
Karen's Copycat, Scholastic, Inc. (New York, NY), 1998.
Karen's Field Day, Scholastic, Inc. (New York, NY), 1998.
Karen's Show and Share, Scholastic, Inc. (New York, NY), 1998.
Karen's Swim Meet, Scholastic, Inc. (New York, NY), 1998.

Karen's Spy Mystery, Scholastic, Inc. (New York, NY), 1998.
Karen's New Holiday, Scholastic, Inc. (New York, NY), 1998.
Karen's Hurricane, Scholastic, Inc. (New York, NY), 1998.
Karen's Chicken Pox, Scholastic, Inc. (New York, NY), 1999.
Karen's Runaway Turkey, Scholastic, Inc. (New York, NY), 1999.
Karen's Reindeer, Scholastic, Inc. (New York, NY), 1999.
Karen's Mistake, Scholastic, Inc. (New York, NY), 2000.
Karen's Figure Eight, Scholastic, Inc. (New York, NY), 2000.
Karen's Yo-Yo, Scholastic, Inc. (New York, NY), 2000.
Karen's Easter Parade, Scholastic, Inc. (New York, NY), 2000.
Karen's Gift, Scholastic, Inc. (New York, NY), 2000.
Karen's Cowboy, Scholastic, Inc. (New York, NY), 2000.

"BABY-SITTERS LITTLE SISTERS SUPER SPECIAL" SERIES

Karen's Wish, Scholastic, Inc. (New York, NY), 1990.
Karen's Plane Trip, Scholastic, Inc. (New York, NY), 1991.
Karen's Mystery, Scholastic, Inc. (New York, NY), c. 1991.
Karen, Hannie, and Nancy: The Three Musketeers, Scholastic, Inc. (New York, NY), 1992.
Karen's Baby, Scholastic, Inc. (New York, NY), 1992.
Karen's Campout, Scholastic, Inc. (New York, NY), 1993.

"BABY-SITTERS CLUB PORTRAIT COLLECTION" SERIES

Dawn's Book, Scholastic, Inc. (New York, NY), 1993.
Stacey's Book, Scholastic, Inc. (New York, NY), 1994.
Claudia's Book, Scholastic, Inc. (New York, NY), 1995.
Mary Anne's Book, Scholastic, Inc. (New York, NY), 1996.
Kristy's Book, Scholastic, Inc. (New York, NY), 1996.
Abby's Book, Scholastic, Inc. (New York, NY), 1997.

"BABY-SITTERS CLUB SUPER MYSTERIES" SERIES

Baby-Sitters' Haunted House, Scholastic, Inc. (New York, NY), 1995.
Baby-Sitters Beware, Scholastic, Inc. (New York, NY), 1995.
Baby-Sitters' Fright Night, Scholastic, Inc. (New York, NY), 1996.

OTHER "BABY-SITTERS CLUB" SPECIAL EDITIONS

Logan Bruno, Boy Baby-Sitter, Scholastic, Inc. (New York, NY), 1993.
Baby-Sitters Little Sister School Scrapbook, Scholastic, Inc. (New York, NY), 1993.
Baby-Sitters Club Guide to Baby-sitting, Scholastic, Inc. (New York, NY), 1993.
Shannon's Story, Scholastic, Inc. (New York, NY), 1994.
Secret Santa, Scholastic, Inc. (New York, NY), 1994.
Baby-Sitters Little Sister Summer Fill-in Book, Scholastic, Inc. (New York, NY), 1995.
Baby-Sitters Little Sister Jump Rope Rhymes, Scholastic, Inc. (New York, NY), 1995.
Baby-Sitters Little Sister Playground Games, Scholastic, Inc. (New York, NY), 1996.

Complete Guide to the Baby-Sitters Club, Scholastic, Inc. (New York, NY), 1996.
The BSC Notebook, Scholastic, Inc. (New York, NY), 1996.
BSC Chain Letter, Scholastic, Inc. (New York, NY), 1996.
The Baby-Sitters Club Trivia and Puzzle Fun Book, Scholastic, Inc. (New York, NY), 1996.
The Baby-Sitters Club Postcard Book, Scholastic, Inc. (New York, NY), 1996.
Little Sister Photo Scrapbook, Scholastic, Inc. (New York, NY), 1997.
Baby-Sitters Little Sister Secret Diary, Scholastic, Inc. (New York, NY), 1997.
Baby-Sitters Little Sister Laugh Pack, Scholastic, Inc. (New York, NY), 1997.

"THE KIDS IN MS. COLMAN'S CLASS" SERIES; ILLUSTRATED BY CHARLES TANG

Teacher's Pet, Scholastic, Inc. (New York, NY), 1996.
Author Day, Scholastic, Inc. (New York, NY), 1996.
Class Play, Scholastic, Inc. (New York, NY), 1996.
The Second Grade Baby, Scholastic, Inc. (New York, NY), 1996.
Snow War, Scholastic, Inc. (New York, NY), 1997.
Twin Trouble, Scholastic, Inc. (New York, NY), 1997.
Science Fair, Scholastic, Inc. (New York, NY), 1997.
Summer Kids, Scholastic, Inc. (New York, NY), 1997.
Halloween Parade, Scholastic, Inc. (New York, NY), 1998.
Holiday Time, Scholastic, Inc. (New York, NY), 1998.
Spelling Bee, Scholastic, Inc. (New York, NY), 1998.
Baby Animal Zoo, Scholastic, Inc. (New York, NY), 1998.

"CALIFORNIA DIARIES" SERIES

Dawn, Scholastic, Inc. (New York, NY), 1997.
Sunny, Scholastic, Inc. (New York, NY), 1997.
Maggie, Scholastic, Inc. (New York, NY), 1997.
Amalia, Scholastic, Inc. (New York, NY), 1997.
Ducky, Scholastic, Inc. (New York, NY), 1997.
Dawn Diary Two, Scholastic, Inc. (New York, NY), 1998.
Sunny Diary Two, Scholastic, Inc. (New York, NY), 1998.
Maggie Diary Two, Scholastic, Inc. (New York, NY), 1998.
Amalia Diary Two, Scholastic, Inc. (New York, NY), 1998.
Ducky Diary Two, Scholastic, Inc. (New York, NY), 1998.
Dawn Diary Three, Scholastic, Inc. (New York, NY), 1999.
Sunny Diary Three, Scholastic, Inc. (New York, NY), 1999.
Maggie Diary Three, Scholastic, Inc. (New York, NY), 2000.
Amalia Diary Three, Scholastic, Inc. (New York, NY), 2000.
Ducky Diary Three, Scholastic, Inc. (New York, NY), 2001.

OTHER

Martin's books have been translated into several foreign languages. The "Baby-Sitters Club" books have been translated into 19 foreign languages.

Adaptations

The *Baby-Sitters Club* television series was produced by Scholastic Productions and broadcast on Home Box

Office (HBO) and the Disney Channel; *The Baby-Sitters Club Movie,* co-produced by Scholastic Productions and Beacon Communications, was distributed by Columbia, 1995; a "Baby-Sitters Club" board game has been released by Milton-Bradley; several "Baby-Sitters Club" stories have appeared on video and audio cassette.

Sidelights

When the curtain came down on the final act of the "Baby-Sitters Club" series in the year 2000, Ann M. Martin, series author and co-originator, had become one of the best-known names in juvenile publishing. What started in 1986 as an idea for a four-book series to be published over the course of one year had ballooned fourteen years later into a mini-publishing industry with several spin-off titles, a television series, a movie, games, and various "Baby-Sitters Club" (BSC) merchandise to satisfy the needs of legions of faithful BSC readers. With over 180 million books in print in nineteen languages, the "Baby-Sitters Club" had obviously, as Sally Lodge noted in *Publishers Weekly,* "struck a resounding chord with preteen girls all over the world." Martin bid adieu to her readers with the final BSC volume, *Graduation Day,* but not good-bye to publishing. She addressed her fans directly over the Internet on her Web site, *Ann Online,* telling them that "it still amazes me to see the incredible body of work that was a result of that original idea." Those spin-off titles include over 130 of the original "Baby-Sitters Club" editions as well as 120 more titles in the "Little Sisters" series, twenty-five books in the "Mystery" series, a baker's dozen in the "BSC Friends Forever" series, another fifteen in the "California Diaries" series, and dozens of titles in super editions, not to mention twelve books in the "Kids in Ms. Colman's Class" series—a spin-off of a spin-off. Millions of teens and pre-teens have grown up with the antics and adventures of Kristy, Mary Anne, Stacey, and Claudia, and then found new friends with whom to identify with the addition of Dawn, Jessi, Mallory, and Abby to the club. These perennial middle schoolers have found their way into the hearts of young girls worldwide.

Contrary to the way that most multi-volume children's book series are produced, Martin did much of the writing for both of the main series, rising at 5:30 each morning to start her writing day and completing nearly two books each month. As the number of series grew, however, it was impossible for Martin to keep up with the flow of books, and other writers were brought on to help write some of the titles. But after fourteen years both Martin and her publisher, Scholastic, were ready to move on to new projects. Martin already began such a move in 1998 with non-series titles aimed at older juvenile readers and written in collaboration with both Paula Danziger and Laura Godwin. Definitely Martin has not said farewell to writing. "While I am sad on one level to close this chapter of my writing life," Martin wrote, "I am also excited about the new projects that I will now have the time to explore. As you probably know, what I love to do most is write books for children."

Born in 1955, Martin grew up in Princeton, New Jersey, in a tight-knit family of parents and one younger sister, Jane. "I grew up in a very imaginative family," Martin once noted. "My mother was a preschool teacher and my father, an artist. Both liked fantasy and children's literature, so my world was one of circuses, animals, Beatrix Potter, *Winnie-the-Pooh, The Wizard of Oz,* elves and gnomes and fairies. It was a lot of fun, and it stayed with me. I'm often off in some other world, and all my daydreaming goes into my books." In an interview with Kristin McMurran of *People Weekly,* Martin further elaborated on her childhood: "I was moody and temperamental, but those were very happy years ... because I had parents who would ... teach us magic tricks and roast marshmallows in the woods with us. They never cared if we made a mess. My mother called our playroom 'toy soup.'" Martin was an enterprising child, running a library at one point and charging her friends overdue fines. She also was a babysitter; her oddest "client" was a snake which she had to tend one weekend. The reptile did not make it through the two days. The author subsequently modeled many of the events and characters of her popular series from those of her youth, including best friend Beth Perkins who informs much of the character of Kristy, leader of the Baby-Sitters Club.

Reading and writing were among her favorite childhood activities. Martin once commented, "I had always enjoyed writing, even as a child. Before I could write, I dictated stories to my mother. I took creative writing classes and that sort of thing as a kid, but I wanted desperately to be a teacher, so that was what I prepared for." At Smith College, Martin double-majored in psychology and early childhood education. Out of college, Martin taught elementary school for a year, working with students challenged by learning disabilities such as dyslexia. "Working with kids who had special problems or needs, plus seeing the natural way they got along with each other in school—the groups and rivalries that form among children—has all influenced me," Martin once noted.

Soon, however, Martin realized that she wanted to work in children's books rather than in education. Martin cut her literary teeth first on the "other" side of the desk, working as an editorial assistant, then assistant editor, and finally editor and senior editor at publishers including Pocket Books, Scholastic, and Bantam, from 1978 to 1985.

Martin published her first book, *Bummer Summer,* in 1983. A popular story for young readers, this debut is about a first overnight camp experience and paved the way for further teen and pre-teen books such as *Inside Out, Stage Fright,* and *Me and Katie (the Pest).* "Some of my books are based on actual experiences," Martin once said, "others are based more on imagination, and memories of feelings. *Me and Katie (the Pest)* is loosely based on riding lessons I took in the third grade.... *With You and without You* is about the death of a parent. *Inside Out* was based on my work as a therapist for autistic children; it wasn't really something that happened in my childhood. *Stage Fright* is probably the most autobiographical of my books. I had terrible stage fright when I was a kid, ... and that was the inspiration for that book."

Increasingly Martin was coming to see herself as a writer rather than an editor. In 1985, Jean Feiwel, editor-in-chief of the book group at Scholastic, came up with the idea of a mini-series about a babysitting cooperative, and she asked Martin to write four stories. When the inaugural title, *Kristy's Great Idea* quickly sold out its 30,000-copy first printing, Feiwel and Martin thought they might just be on to something. The subsequent books were popular enough that Feiwel suggested Martin write two more stories for the series. "Scholastic decided the books were doing exceptionally well when the sixth book of the series hit number one on the B. Dalton Juvenile Bestseller list, sometime in 1987," Martin once noted. "That was when we decided that we really had something. We stepped up the schedule to one book every other month and eventually one every month."

From the outset the series was a collaborative effort, and Martin and Feiwel, as well other editors determined early on that the series—while sometimes dealing with serious issues such as death, racism, divorce, and peer pressure—would not deal with other hot button issues such as child abuse, alcohol or drug abuse, or the death of a parent. Geared at readers eight through about twelve, the series is intended as entertainment: light, breezy, and conversational. It has often been touted as the perfect introduction to books for reluctant readers. In all of the books, the characters remain the same age. "Two of them are permanently in the sixth grade, and the rest are permanently in the eighth grade," Martin once explained. "I can't let them grow up because the books come out too fast. I try not to allude to birthdays or summer vacations.... Otherwise the characters would soon be thirty-five." Martin was also careful to avoid slang and the use of time-fixers such as the names of current rock groups; the "Baby-Sitters Club" books take place in a time capsule, a sort of all-time and any-time. Neither does Martin talk down to readers in any of her books. "I suppose that somewhere in the back of my mind, I'm always thinking of the audience for whom I'm writing, but I don't talk down to kids, and I don't work with a controlled vocabulary. I just seem to fall into a young voice for Karen, the narrator of the 'Baby-Sitters Little Sister' series, and into older voices for the girls who narrate the 'Baby-Sitters Club' books."

Books in the series deal with the adventures of a group of girls who band together to operate a child-care business, and individual titles have explored a range of topics. *Kristy and the Secret of Susan* deals with an autistic savant, *Claudia and the Sad Good-bye* is about the death of a grandparent, *Kristy and the Snobs* relates the death of Kristy's pet, and *Jessi's Secret Language* finds Jessi baby-sitting for a deaf boy who communicates only in American Sign Language. Such books demonstrate Martin's own interests and proclivities. Her personal favorite among the books is *Kristy's Big Day.*

Martin herself admitted in *Time* magazine that her books were "not great literature," but she has also noted that they "attract kids who are reluctant readers, if not children with definite learning problems such as dyslexia, and turn them into readers. And for kids who are already readers, I don't think there's anything wrong with picking up a series and reading it. I write the books as pure entertainment for myself as well as for the kids, but I am hoping that avid readers who are reading series are reading other things as well, and I also hope that reluctant readers who get hooked on reading through series reading, whether it's the 'Baby-Sitters Club' or another series, will then 'graduate' to other kinds of books."

Over the years, Martin and her editors added new series that would explore different age levels and that might update and enliven the series with a more modern approach. The last such addition was the "Baby-Sitters Club Friends Forever" series, ending with a title in a letters-and-journal-entries format in which the original four members of the club are left to carry on the traditions of their enterprise. The "California Diaries" series, inaugurated in 1997, features Dawn, one of the original baby-sitters, who moves to the West Coast to be with one of her divorced parents full-time. That series is, as the name implies, told in diary format. The eighth grade girls in this series are involved in somewhat edgier and more sophisticated activities than those found in the original "Baby-Sitters Club" books.

All good things, however, come to an end, and so too did the BSC finally call it a day with *Graduation Day.* Martin was prescient about such a demise. She once noted that "as demographics and tastes change, kids do, too, and maybe in a few years they will find that they want pure fantasy and escape, like the C. S. Lewis books. That might signal the end of the 'Baby-Sitters Club'; I can't really think of the BSC characters traveling to an imaginary kingdom or another planet."

Martin continued publishing hardcover novels during the years she was churning out the BSC. One of her personal favorites of these is *Ten Kids, No Pets,* about the boisterous Rosso family. In a sequel to that book, *Eleven Kids, One Summer,* the Rossos spend the summer on New York's Fire Island. Each chapter puts the lens on the activities of one of the "amiable Rosso offspring," according to a *Publishers Weekly* reviewer, who range in age from six months to fifteen years. There is a movie being filmed on the island with a handsome star for eldest Rosso, Abbie, to form a friendship with; there is a house that the sensitive Candy thinks is haunted; and there are plenty of seashells for enterprising Woody to paint and then sell. "Martin ... knows well what pleases young readers," the same reviewer concluded, "and this novel is filled with characters, escapades and dialogue that will do just that."

"One of the most important tools I use in my writing is my memory," Martin has said. "It is very clear. I can remember what that first day of kindergarten was like— the way the room looked, the children, how I felt when my mother left. And I remember my senior prom and my tenth birthday and vacations at the shore and junior high graduation just as clearly. Little things, too—making a bulletin board display in sixth grade and making doll clothes and playing statue after dinner on hot summer nights. It's just as important to be able to transport oneself back to childhood as it is to have a vivid imagination, in order to write believable children's books. When I speak through my young characters, I am remembering and reliving: redoing all those things one is never supposed to be able to redo, having a chance to play out the 'if onlys.'" Clarifying her use of the past in her writings, Martin once commented, "Some of my books have been based on past experiences, although very few of them have been based on actual events in my childhood. But I would say that while I write any book, I'm remembering how I felt when I was a kid. Those feelings definitely go into the books."

The author attributes the success of her books to a combination of humor and relevance. "Kids respond to humor and appreciate it. Secondly, I think the kids find characteristics they can relate to in all the main characters or the topic we've chosen. Whether I'm writing about a handicapped child or divorce, I believe in keeping it down-to-earth. I've received letters from children who have said that the characters in the books are their friends. So something in there makes these books seem real. Some kids have written me, asking for phone numbers because they want to call the characters in the books. Then I sort of sadly explain that they are not real, so they can't get in touch with them. I turned to writing as an outlet for both my emotions and humor. I feel I'm more articulate and funnier on paper, but the more I write, the more comfortable I become speaking. It's a delightfully vicious cycle. The marriage of my love for children's literature with this cycle makes for a continually gratifying creative process."

Humor takes center stage in Martin's picture book, *Leo the Magnificat,* a story based on an actual cat who adopted an entire church congregation. The cat in question sauntered into the yard of a Louisville, Kentucky, church one Sunday and remained there for the next twelve years. Martin, in her book, shows how this cat worms its way into the hearts of the entire congregation and surrounding neighborhood, insinuating itself into events from potlucks to church services. When Leo the cat passes on, he is buried in the church garden. A reviewer for *Publishers Weekly* dubbed this picture book effort a "charmer like its feline hero," and further noted that Martin is a "pro at age-appropriate writing." The same reviewer also praised the "polished, softly focused art" of Caldecott Medallist Emily Arnold McCully who illustrated the book. "An alluring choice for cat lovers of any age," this writer concluded. *Booklist*'s Stephanie Zvirin commented that "Martin's picture book reads just like what it is—a story drawn from life," and concluded that this "gently humorous, poignant (never sentimental)" tale "won't disappoint." Martin told Lodge of *Publishers Weekly* that she "had a wonderful time writing" *Leo the Magnificat,* and was hopeful that she would try the genre again.

In 1998 Martin teamed up with long-time friend and fellow children's book author, Paula Danziger, to write *P.S. Longer Letter Later.* In this book the two authors, who specialize in writing for young girls, blended their disparate writing styles to create an epistolary novel told from two points of view. When two seventh-grade girls, Elizabeth and Tara*Starr, are separated by a family move, they promise to maintain their friendship through letters. The two girls are a study in contrasts: Tara*Starr is the type to put purple streaks in her hair, to joke incessantly, to write scathingly funny columns for the school paper, while staid Elizabeth is into cross-stitching and poetry, and would never think of piercing her ears, let alone her nose. Suddenly Tara*Starr's free-spirited parents become responsible, begin holding regular jobs, think about having another baby, and move to Ohio. Outrageous, flamboyant, creative Tara*Starr—whose letters are written by Danziger—cannot believe the overnight change and subsequently has a hard time of adjusting to a new school and finding new friends. Meanwhile the more reserved, introspective, and affluent Elizabeth—written by Martin—undergoes her own transformations. Her father loses his job, turns to alcohol, and then abandons the family as they are getting ready to move into a small apartment. In letters that are at once humorous and painful, the two girls maintain their long-distance friendship. They survive tiffs and personal crises and even silence when one or the other fails to write for a time.

"If Danziger and Martin had been childhood pen pals," commented a reviewer for *Publishers Weekly,* "their correspondence might have read much like this strikingly insightful epistolary novel." The same writer further observed that the "venerable authors here do a splendid job of creating a story based on … letters." *Booklist* contributor Hazel Rochman felt "the immediacy of the letters format will draw kids in, especially as the tension mounts in Elizabeth's home and her friend replies with humor and heartfelt sympathy." Lynda Drill Comerford, writing in *Publishers Weekly,* commented that the book, "a celebration of friendship, ends on a happy note, with characters overcoming personal conflicts and forgiving each other's shortcomings." Comerford concluded, "For characters and authors alike, it represents the unique meshing of two creative, witty and very different personalities." Renee Steinberg, reviewing the novel in *School Library Journal,* observed that the "authenticity of the well-drawn characters gives life and vitality to the story," and concluded that readers "will thoroughly enjoy this fast-paced story." Reviewing the audiocassette adaptation of the novel, a *Publishers Weekly* contributor noted that Martin and Danziger "breathe life into two of their most richly drawn characters," and that in "a satisfying ending" the two young girls are able to see each other face-to-face once again.

In concluding the review of the book version of *P.S. Longer Letter Later,* the writer for *Publishers Weekly* wished for more: "Given Danziger and Martin's penchant for continuing story lines, readers can only hope that this will be an ongoing correspondence." In 2000 such a hope became a reality with the publication of

Snail Mail No More, a continuation of Elizabeth's and Tara*Starr's correspondence, this time by e-mail. *Booklist*'s Michael Cart dubbed the pair an "epistolary odd couple," and noted that in *Snail Mail No More* "it's business as usual." Martin continues to write the shy, conservative Elizabeth's letters, while Danziger creates Tara's letters. With her mother pregnant, Tara*Starr is not so sure she wants to be a sister. At the other end, Elizabeth's wayward father has shown up again with less than positive results. The girls now turn thirteen, and make new friends, including boys. The green-eyed monster pops up between the two girls for a time, but even jealousy is vanquished by their friendship. "Seasoned pros Danziger and Martin couldn't write a dull book if they tried," noted Cart, "and this one ... is a funny, thought-provoking page-turner that will delight readers and leave them ready for more messages." While *School Library Journal* reviewer Linda Bindner found that *Snail Mail No More* "lacks the energy and freshness" of *P.S. Longer Letter Later,* she also commented that "fans will find it to be an enjoyable sequel." A contributor for *Publishers Weekly* felt *Snail Mail No More* was a "funny and poignant sequel," and concluded that the "two characters approach life differently enough that there will likely be a response or suggestion that resonates with every reader, and both heroines share one important trait: they are all heart."

Teaming up with Laura Godwin, Martin has also written *The Doll People,* the story of culture clash between members of a Victorian doll household who meet their new, plastic neighbors, the Funcrafts. The staid Victorian world of the doll people is turned upside down by the meeting. The Funcrafts are the birthday present of the younger sister of Kate, current owner of the Victorian dollhouse and its occupants. It's barbecues versus parlors now, but Tiffany, the Funcraft doll, is the same age as Annabelle, of the Victorian dollhouse, and the two opposites oddly enough hit it off. Together Annabelle and Tiffany hunt for the missing Auntie Sarah doll from the Victorian dollhouse. Kathie Meizner, writing in *School Library Journal,* commented that a "lighthearted touch and a dash of drama make this a satisfying read," while a writer for *Publishers Weekly* concluded that doll lovers "may well approach their imaginative play with renewed enthusiasm and a sense of wonder after reading this fun-filled adventure."

In addition to writing, Martin is also very active in supporting various community activities. She is co-founder of the Lisa Novak Community Libraries, and founder of the Ann M. Martin Foundation, which benefits children, education and literacy programs, and homeless people and animals. Even without the 'Baby-Sitters Club' on the back burner, it is clear that Martin will not be changing her early rising habits. "I love to feel that every week is full of a lot of different kinds of things," she told Lodge. "I've always worked better when I'm working on many things at one time."

Biographical and Critical Sources

PERIODICALS

Booklist, September 1, 1996, Stephanie Zvirin, review of *Leo the Magnificat,* p. 143; June 1, 1998, Hazel Rochman, review of *P.S. Longer Letter Later,* p. 1765; November 1, 1999, p. 550; March 15, 2000, Michael Cart, review of *Snail Mail No More,* p. 1376, August, 2000, p. 2140.
Book Report, September-October, 1998, p. 51.
Curriculum Review, February, 1995, p. 13.
Emergency Librarian, March-April, 1991, p. 39.
Family Life, August, 1998, p. 89.
New York Times Book Review, April 27, 1986, p. 25; August 14, 1988, p. 28; April 30, 1989, p. 42; May 17, 1998, p. 27.
People Weekly, August 21, 1989, Kristin McMurran, "Ann Martin Stirs up a Tiny Tempest in Preteen Land with Her Bestselling 'Baby-Sitters Club,'" pp. 55-56.
Publishers Weekly, June 17, 1988, p. 37; August 23, 1991, review of *Eleven Kids, One Summer,* p. 62; September 13, 1993, p. 137; May 17, 1993, p. 34; November 21, 1994, p. 42; September 4, 1995, pp. 28-29; September 2, 1996, review of *Leo the Magnificat,* p. 131; September 1, 997, Sally Lodge, "Another Busy Season for Ann M. Martin," pp. 31-32; February 16, 1998, review of *P.S. Longer Letter Later,* p. 212; March 9, 1998, Lynda Drill Comerford, "A True Test of Friendship," p. 26; June 7, 1999, review of *P.S. Longer Letter Later,* p. 53; July 19, 1999, p. 197; January 10, 2000, review of *Snail Mail No More,* p. 68; March 6, 2000, p. 112; July 3, 2000, review of *The Doll People,* p. 71; October 30, 2000, p. 37.
School Library Journal, May, 1998, Renee Steinberg, review of *P.S. Longer Letter Later,* p. 141; March, 2000, Linda Bindner, review of *Snail Mail No More,* p. 234; November, 2000, Kathie Meizner, review of *The Doll People,* p. 128; December, 2000, p. 54.
Time, June 11, 1990, "Wake-up Call," p. 75.
U.S. News & World Report, November 13, 2000, p. 18.
Washington Post, August 17, 1995, p. C1.

ON-LINE

Ann Online, http://www.scholastic.com/annmartin/ (February 26, 2001).

—Sketch by J. Sydney Jones

*   *   *

MARTIN, Marvin 1926-

Personal

Born June 19, 1926, in South Bend, IN; son of Herbert (a furrier) and Esther (Zhiss) Martin; married Gloria Loden (an associate televison producer and office manager), September 9, 1967 (deceased, 1989); children: Michael K., Andrea D., Joshua N., Jessica S. *Education:* Roosevelt University, B.A., 1951. *Politics:* "Independent."

Marvin Martin

Addresses

Home and office—2113 North Dayton St., Chicago, IL 60614. *E-mail*—mmartin102@aol.com

Career

Author and editor. W. D. Allen Co., Chicago, IL, assistant advertising manager, 1951; *Chicago Daily News,* Chicago, IL, advertising account salesman, 1951-56; Bastian-Blessing Co., Chicago, IL, advertising copywriter, 1956-60; *World Book Encyclopedia,* Chicago, IL, editor, 1960-62; *Encyclopaedia Britannica,* Chicago, IL, assistant editor, 1962-68; *Britannica Junior Encyclopedia,* Chicago, IL, executive editor, 1968-83, associate editor, 1984-92. Rochelle Lee Fund, board of directors, publications editor. *Military service*—U.S. Army, 1944-46; became ordnance sergeant, earned Expert Infantryman citation.

Awards, Honors

Children's Reading Round Table citation for books published, 1996; Books for the Teen Age Award, New York Public Library, 1997, for *The Beatles: The Music Was Never the Same,* and 1999, for *Arthur Ashe: Of Tennis and the Human Spirit.*

Writings

The Beatles: The Music Was Never the Same, Franklin Watts, 1996.
Arthur Ashe: Of Tennis and the Human Spirit, Franklin Watts, 1999.
Extraordinary People in Jazz, Children's Press, in press.

Contributor of articles to the *Tribune* (Chicago, IL), Education Today section, 1994-2000.

Sidelights

Marvin Martin told *SATA:* "I have a continuing interest in public affairs and national and international politics. I am an avid reader of the *New York Times, New Yorker,* and *National Geographic* as well as modern fiction and classics. I am a regular goer to movies, theater, and concerts. Music is a passion, particularly classical and jazz (modern and swing).

"My travels have taken me recently to Italy and the Pacific Northwest. I enjoy hiking, rowing, swimming, golf, and tennis. My sports fan following includes baseball (White Sox), football (Bears), and basketball (Bulls), but I enjoy most sports. I also am fond of cooking, particularly Italian and brunch items."

Martin wrote advertising copy and edited encyclopedias before turning to the writing of biographies for young adults. His first effort, *The Beatles: The Music Was Never the Same,* traces the career of the legendary four young men from Liverpool, England, whose music and lifestyle took the world by storm in the 1960s. "The author is most successful at telling the early part of the Beatles' story," observed Tim Wadham in *School Library Journal,* who, like other reviewers, remarked positively on Martin's ability to place the Beatles in the social and cultural contexts of the era. "This is a well-researched overview of the lives and careers of the Beatles," remarked Rhonda Cooper in *Kliatt,* who noted that Martin somewhat neglects the impact the Beatles had on music history in favor of the story of the Beatles as a social phenomenon.

For his next young adult biography, Martin chose tennis champion Arthur Ashe who overcame numerous disadvantages to become a world renowned athlete. "In Martin's informative biography, steadfast and quietly determined Ashe comes across as a noble, if less-than-riveting, subject," proclaimed Roger Leslie in *Booklist.* Leslie went on to call Martin's discussion of Ashe's battle with AIDS "poignant." In *Arthur Ashe: Of Tennis and the Human Spirit,* Martin emphasizes Ashe's early struggles to achieve success in the tennis realm, where he was first thought to be too slight to withstand the physical rigors of the sport. Later, when he began to move up in the ranks, he discovered that no other African Americans had yet competed in the world-class tournaments that were the next step for him as a professional athlete. As a champion, Ashe supported tennis camps for disadvantaged youth, took a public stance against the apartheid government in South Africa, and spoke out against racism at home. He is also remembered for his courage in the face of death, when he discovered he was dying of AIDS. *School Library Journal* reviewer Lynda Short notes that Martin's focus is on Ashe's accomplishments on the tennis court rather than off, and to that end, the biography is "well documented . . . and has an extensive index." Likewise, *Horn Book Guide* reviewer Peter D. Sieruta praised Martin's "clearly written prose," and "thorough" treatment of his subject.

Biographical and Critical Sources

PERIODICALS

Booklist, February 1, 1997, Ilene Cooper, review of *The Beatles: The Music Was Never the Same,* p. 934; July, 1999, Roger Leslie, review of *Arthur Ashe: Of Tennis and the Human Spirit,* p. 1937.
Horn Book Guide, fall, 1999, Peter D. Sieruta, review of *Arthur Ashe: Of Tennis and the Human Spirit,* p. 367.
Kliatt, July, 1997, Rhonda Cooper, review of *The Beatles: The Music Was Never the Same,* p. 34.
School Library Journal, March, 1997, Tim Wadham, review of *The Beatles: The Music Was Never the Same,* p. 204; June, 1999, Lynda Short, review of *Arthur Ashe: Of Tennis and the Human Spirit,* p. 150.

*   *   *

McCOURT, Malachy 1931-

Personal

First name is pronounced "malakee"; born September 20, 1931, in Brooklyn, NY; son of Malachy and Angela (a homemaker; maiden name, Sheehan) McCourt; married Linda Wachsman (divorced, 1962); married Diana Huchthausen (a community organizer), March 1, 1965; children: (first marriage) Siobhan, Malachy; (second marriage) Conor, Cormac, (stepdaughter) Nina. *Politics:* "Left wing." *Religion:* "Collapsed Catholic." *Hobbies and other interests:* Reading, walking, talking.

Addresses

Home—680 West End Ave., New York, NY 10025. *Agent*—IMG, 825 Eighth Ave., New York, NY 10019. *E-mail*—wshare@aol.com.

Career

Worked as a laborer in England and Ireland; also worked as a longshoreman, dishwasher, and truck loader in the New York, NY, area after 1951; actor in plays such as *Mass Appeal, Da,* and *The Hostage,* and on the daytime television dramas *One Life to Life, Ryan's Hope,* and *Search for Tomorrow;* cast in the feature films *Green Card, She's the One,* and *Molly Maguires;* radio talk show host in New York, NY, in the early 1970s; saloon keeper and founder of the first "singles" bar in the United States, Malachy's of Third Avenue in New York, NY; author. *Member:* Manhattan Rugby Club (cofounder).

Writings

A Monk Swimming: A Memoir, Hyperion (New York, NY), 1998.
Singing Him My Song, HarperCollins (New York, NY), 2000.
Danny Boy: The Legend of the Beloved Irish Ballad, Running Press (Philadelphia, PA), 2001.

Coauthor, with Frank McCourt, of the play *A Couple of Blaguards,* 1977; author of foreword to *Through Irish Eyes: A Visual Companion to Angela McCourt's Ireland,* Smithmark, 1998; also writer of a weekly column that appears in local New York publications.

Sidelights

Malachy McCourt's 1998 memoir, *A Monk Swimming,* followed in the wake of his older brother's Pulitzer Prize-winning recollection of their impoverished Irish childhood, *Angela's Ashes.* While Frank McCourt had spent much of his life as a school teacher in New York, the younger McCourt was a well-known New York character whose gift for telling improbable stories made him a favorite of television talk shows for years. He also worked as an actor and saloon keeper, and hosted his own New York-area radio program in the early 1970s.

McCourt was born in the New York borough of Brooklyn, but his parents decided to return to Ireland after his infant sister died, as his brother's memoir recounts. The family settled in Limerick, and their

Malachy McCourt

Storyteller and celebrity McCourt tells his own "darkly funny" story. (Cover photo by Michael O'Neill.)

economic circumstances grew even direr. McCourt left school at the age of thirteen to work as a laborer in England and Ireland; his brother Frank, meanwhile, had returned to America, and by the early 1950s McCourt had decided to join him. As he recalls in *A Monk Swimming,* he was twenty years old, had no money, no formal education, and few salable work skills. Returning to America was something he had fantasized about as a child, he recalled. "When I was growing up in Limerick," McCourt wrote, "my ambition was to come to America and become a convict, because in prison I'd have shoes, a bed to myself."

As *A Monk Swimming* moves forward, McCourt recounts his failed first marriage and burgeoning career as an actor and professional raconteur. He was a favorite guest of television hosts from Jack Paar to Merv Griffin, and was overwhelmed to find that "they're all mad in America—they pay you for talking," as he writes. Unfortunately, McCourt also followed in his father's footsteps and became a heavy drinker. The work concludes around the time of the end of his first marriage in 1962.

A Monk Swimming, which takes its title from the author's title childhood confusion when hearing the "Hail Mary" prayer said aloud—"blessed art thou amongst women"—was a minor publishing success, spending several weeks on the *New York Times* bestseller lists. "This is a book that shows Malachy the blasphemer at his best," observed a *Publishers Weekly* reviewer, and "will have readers smiling and laughing constantly." The review but did point out that the tales of drinking and carousing in the memoir were unsuitable for younger readers—or the older ones "who worshiped *Angela's Ashes.*" A long critique of both Brothers McCourt memoirs from R. F. Foster in the *New Republic* faulted it along several lines, but noted that "From time to time, though, Malachy McCourt's book does convey something of New York in the 1950s and 1960s, as it must have appeared to a healthy and hungry young immigrant: a Manhattan at once intimate and glamorous," Foster remarked. The critic also pointed out that as a memoir, *A Monk Swimming* "confirms the traditional and comforting belief that the Old World is a sow who devours her own farrow, and everything will eventually come right in America, along with creature comforts, blonde women, and hot running water."

Comparisons to *Angela's Ashes* were inevitable. *New Leader* writer Stefan Kanfer found it "not nearly as skilled in composition," he wrote, "but outrageously funny, in the tradition of Brendan Behan and Flann O'Brien." Reviewing it for the *Los Angeles Times,* Susan Salter Reynolds found it "more a tsunami of entertaining, reckless verbiage than a book—the plot a wobbly line of stories drawn through a drunken haze of a life." A *New York Times Book Review* piece from Alex Wichtel declared that McCourt's "writing style is brashly confident, his irreverent brand of storytelling laced with dark humor and sometimes pathos."

McCourt penned a sequel to *A Monk Swimming* in 2000, *Singing Him My Song.* Here he recounts his transformation from an unemployed actor to happily married father and teetotaler. He also reveals his battle with prostate cancer and a somewhat reluctant return to the Catholic faith of his mother. The work also recounts his involvement in a parents' group that called public attention to abuse at a Staten Island institution where his developmentally disabled stepdaughter lived. *Publishers Weekly* termed the follow-up a success. "A surprisingly tender McCourt disarms the reader with his openness and dexterous touch in this winning sequel," and noted that as a memoir, the story "stands on its own." A *New York Times Book Review* assessment from Carolyn T. Hughes lauded this sequel as "more thoughtful," though she added that "McCourt still has the ability to turn a phrase deftly."

McCourt told *SATA:* "Survival has been my main motivation. Accumulating some self-esteem and playing with the English language are nice paths to tread. I love the rough-and-tumble of American politics and despise the chicanery and concomitant religiosity of the right wing."

Biographical and Critical Sources

BOOKS

Contemporary Literary Criticism, Volume 119: *Yearbook 1998,* Gale, 1999.

McCourt, Frank, *Angela's Ashes,* Scribner (New York, NY), 1996.

McCourt, Malachy, *A Monk Swimming: A Memoir,* Hyperion (New York, NY), 1998.

PERIODICALS

Kirkus Reviews, April 15, 1998, review of *A Monk Swimming,* p. 557.

Los Angeles Times, June 8, 1998, Susan Salter Reynolds, "Brother Also Rises from the Ashes," p. E4.

New Leader, June 14, 1999, Stefan Kanfer, review of *American Second Acts,* p. 34.

New Republic, November 1, 1999, R. F. Foster, "Tisn't: The Million-Dollar Blarney of the McCourts," p. 29.

New York Times Book Review, July 5, 1998, Frank Conroy, "Angela's Second Boy," pp. 5N-5L; July 29, 1998, Alex Wichtel, "How a Rogue Turns Himself into a Saint," p. B1; January 14, 2001, Carolyn T. Hughes, review of *Singing Him My Song,* p. 18.

Publishers Weekly, March 23, 1998, review of *A Monk Swimming,* p. 83; September 18, 2000, review of *Singing Him My Song,* p. 94.

*   *   *

McKILLIP, Patricia A(nne) 1948-

Personal

Born February 29, 1948, in Salem, OR; daughter of Wayne T. and Helen (Roth) McKillip. *Education:* San Jose State University, B.A., 1971, M.A., 1973. *Hobbies and other interests:* Music.

Addresses

Home—2661 California, No. 14, San Francisco, CA 94115.

Career

Writer.

Awards, Honors

World Fantasy Award for best novel, 1975, and American Library Association notable book selection, both for *The Forgotten Beasts of Eld;* Hugo Award nomination, World Science Fiction Convention, 1979, for *Harpist in the Wind.*

Writings

FANTASY

The House on Parchment Street, Atheneum (New York, NY), 1973.

The Throme of the Erril of Sherill, Atheneum (New York, NY), 1973.

The Forgotten Beasts of Eld, Atheneum (New York, NY), 1974.

The Night Gift, Atheneum (New York, NY), 1976.

The Riddle-Master of Hed (first book in trilogy), Atheneum (New York, NY), 1976.

Heir of Sea and Fire (second book in trilogy), Atheneum (New York, NY), 1977.

Harpist in the Wind (third book in trilogy), Atheneum (New York, NY), 1979.

Riddle of the Stars (trilogy; contains *The Riddle-Master of Hed, Heir of Sea and Fire,* and *Harpist in the Wind*), Doubleday (Garden City, NY), 1979, published as *Chronicles of Morgan, Prince of Hed,* Future Publications (London, England), 1979, published as *Riddle-Master: The Complete Trilogy,* Ace (New York, NY), 1999.

The Changeling Sea, Atheneum (New York, NY), 1988.

The Sorceress and the Cygnet, Ace (New York, NY), 1991.

The Cygnet and the Firebird, Ace (New York, NY), 1993.

Something Rich and Strange ("Brian Froud's Faerielands" series), illustrated by Brian Froud, Bantam (New York, NY), 1994.

Winter Rose, Ace (New York, NY), 1996.

Song for the Basilisk, Ace (New York, NY), 1998.

The Tower at Stony Wood, Ace (New York, NY), 2000.

SCIENCE FICTION

Moon-Flash, Atheneum (New York, NY), 1984.

The Moon and the Face, Atheneum (New York, NY), 1985.

Fool's Run, Warner (New York, NY), 1987.

The Book of Atrix Wolfe, Ace (New York, NY), 1995.

OTHER

Stepping from the Shadows (young adult novel), Atheneum (New York, NY), 1982.

Patricia A. McKillip

Sixteen-year-old Sybel lives serenely with the magical creatures on Eld Mountain until a baby comes into her care and she is drawn into the human world in McKillip's World Fantasy Award winner.

Contributor of short fiction to anthologies, including *Xanadu 2.*

Sidelights

Patricia A. McKillip is a critically acclaimed author of works in three literary genres: fantasy, science fiction, and the young adult novel. Of her most ambitious project, *Riddle of Stars,* a fantasy adventure in three parts, Roger C. Schlobin wrote in *Science Fiction and Fantasy Book Review:* "The canon of excellent women fantasists must now be expanded to include another superb effort. . . . McKillip's series delves deeply into the rich earth of full human characterization and creates a world elaborate in both magic and mythology." The concentration on basic human traits and themes is a common characteristic of all of McKillip's works, which include such novels as *The Cygnet and the Firebird, The Forgotten Beasts of Eld,* and *Song of the Basilisk.* Noting that McKillip imbues her fantasy worlds with

music and a "sense of history and culture," an essayist in *Children's Books and Their Creators* added that "the main attraction to [her] . . . books . . . remains the irresistible and timeless combination of adventure, magic, and romance."

McKillip was born in Salem, Oregon, in 1948. The second of six children, she soon found she had a talent for storytelling, which helped because, as she recalled, "the baby-sitting duties were pretty constant. I don't know how old I was when I started telling stories to my younger siblings to while away the boredom of sitting in a car waiting while our parents shopped." She began working on her first novel, *The House on Parchment Street,* as a teenager. "I started to write when I was fourteen," she once told *SATA,* "during one of those 'moody' periods teenagers have when they know they want something, but don't quite know what it is. I was living in England at the time (my father was stationed at a local air base) in a big old house facing a graveyard: the 'house on Parchment Street.' The countryside was very peaceful, and evocative of all kinds of tales. I spent that summer, between eighth grade and high school, writing fairy tales, reading them to my younger brothers and sisters, and feeling that I had at least found one of the things I didn't know I wanted."

She wrote constantly after that discovery, "all through high school and college—anything and everything— poems, plays, novels, short stories, fantasies. What I really wanted to be was a musician, a pianist, but I realized finally that I was far better at writing. Since I didn't think I was capable of holding down a full-time job, I thought I'd better get published before I left college, so I could support myself. As she recalled, "no one discouraged me, and I rarely made writing as a career a subject for discussion. I knew the kinds of things I'd hear, so I just kept quiet about it and wrote. My parents never chased me outside when I wanted to write—which was most of the time. They let me grow at my own speed, which strikes me now as an extraordinary way for modern parents to behave."

Although she was determined to be a writer, McKillip did not initially plan to become a children's author. "I never deliberately decided to write for children," she once explained; "I just found them particularly satisfying to write about, and *The House on Parchment Street* happened to be the first thing I sold."

Many reviewers of McKillip's work have noted her ability, regardless of the genre in which she is writing, to touch on basic human traits and themes. *The Forgotten Beasts of Eld,* published in 1974, is filled with the trappings of the fantasy adventure novel: dragons, talking animals, doorless towers, and glass mountains. *New York Times Book Review* contributor Georgess McHargue wrote that "*The Forgotten Beasts of Eld* works on a strictly human level. Trust, loneliness, love's responsibilities and the toxicity of fate are the themes that underlie the fantasy love story." *Riddle of the Stars,* McKillip's famous fantasy trilogy, garnered similar praise. The plot follows the fortunes of Morgan from his beginnings as ruler of Hed, a peaceful, sleepy kingdom, to his ultimate destiny as a trained "riddle-master." Referring to the first volume in the trilogy, *The Riddle-Master of Hed,* Glenn Shea stated in the *New York Times Book Review,* "She understands that we spend much of our time choosing, not between good and evil, but the lesser of two ills."

In 1982 McKillip published the young adult novel *Stepping from the Shadows,* in an apparent departure from her usual fantasy adventure format. Discussing her switch across literary genres, she explained to Charles L. Wentworth in a *Contemporary Authors* interview: "I don't think the changes have been abrupt, but I can't look at it as a reader. I knew while I was writing the trilogy that I wanted to write the modern novel afterward, so to me it was a natural thing to do; it didn't seem like an abrupt switch." *Stepping from the Shadows,* in terms of its concentration on universal human themes, develops naturally from McKillip's earlier work. The book revolves around the private torments of Frances, a young girl who shares, through conversation and writing, her rich fantasy life with an imaginary sister. "McKillip has put an imaginary playmate on paper and the more sophisticated truth that we all have an outside view of ourselves as well as an inside view," noted Charles Champlin in a *Los Angeles Times* review; "McKillip's memory of the coming of age of an author is rich, particular and extremely appealing."

With the publication of *Moon-Flash, The Moon and the Face,* and *Fool's Run,* McKillip achieved distinction in yet another literary genre: science fiction. She explained to Wentworth what she sees as the differences between fantasy adventure and science fiction: "For my own purposes, I try to keep the two separate. If I'm writing fantasy I use elements of epic, fantasy, myth, legend; and if I put magic in it, it's magic out of the imagination and out of the heart. When I write science fiction, ... I try to turn my back on traditional fantasy elements and extrapolate a plot from history, or daily life, or whatever science happens to stick in my head. I am probably more successful at keeping science fiction out of my fantasy than keeping fantasy out of my science fiction. The heritage, the roots and background of science fiction are very different from those of fantasy. The language is different; the images I find in my mind when I contemplate a science fiction plot are different. The stars in *Riddle-Master* are a symbol. The stars in science fiction are real."

In 1991 McKillip returned to fantasy with the debut volume of another series, *The Sorceress and the Cygnet.* The story of Corleu, a young man who is different in appearance and interests from his Wayfolk kin, is "a richly imagined tale of enchantment, intrigue, and romance," according to *Voice of Youth Advocates* contributor Carolyn Shute. The fantasy world of *The Sorceress and the Cygnet* also serves as the backdrop for McKillip's 1993 novel *The Cygnet and the Firebird,* as a mage's plot to steal an ancient, magical key is thwarted after a firebird appears that magically transforms things around it into gold and precious gems but whose

mystery grows deeper still when it is discovered to be a young warrior who returns to his own shape under certain circumstances, but has no knowledge of his name or his past. Sorceresses, dragons, and the power of the dead also figure into this story, which a *Kirkus Reviews* critic dubbed "often charming and inventive." "McKillip weaves a magic spell of words almost as intoxicating as a drug," noted *School Library Journal* contributor Cathy Chauvette, while adding the caveat that while some would like her lush style, others "will be confused and long for a breath of fresh air."

Fantasy has continued to capture most of McKillip's attention. In 1995's *The Book of Atrix Wolfe,* she weaves shape-shifting, the lust for power, and magecraft into the mix as Prince Talis, a student of wizardry, finds a book the spells of which have undisclosed meanings. Returning home, Talis meets a Queen in search of her daughter, Sorrow, and joins with Mage Atrix Wolfe to discover the young woman's whereabouts and dispel a dark power that threatens both the world of humans and that of faerie. Praising McKillip's "masterfully evocative" language, a *Publishers Weekly* contributor maintained that "connoisseurs of fine fantasy will delight in this expertly wrought tale." *Song for the Basilisk* follows a young man named Rook as he survives an uprising that killed the rest of his family and travels to another land to lead a quiet life. However, he is haunted by violent dreams that force him to confront the evils in the land of his childhood, and he discovers his destiny as Caldrius, and his fate: to demand justice from the Prince who killed his family. While calling the novel "a trifle cerebral" for some fantasy fans, *Booklist* contributor Roland Green noted that McKillip works her usual magic, bringing her "archetypal characters and plot ... to life with dozens of subtle touches." And in *Winter Rose,* a young woman who falls in love with a man trapped in a magical otherworld pines away for lack of him, leaving her determined sister Rois to solve the murder that caused him to become a captive in this perpetual dreamworld. Calling her prose a "delightful, delicate filigree," a *Kirkus Reviews* contributor noted that the "frail and undeveloped" plot seemed inadequate by comparison, while in *Booklist,* a reviewer labeled *Winter Rose* "compelling."

In her discussion with Wentworth, McKillip spoke of her strategy as a writer: "I'd like to do more of everything.... There are so many backgrounds and people I'd like to write about—not in any personal way, but just people I know who suggest stories that might be nice to write."

Biographical and Critical Sources

BOOKS

McKillip, Patricia A., interview with Charles L. Wentworth in *Contemporary Authors New Revision Series,* Volume 18, Gale (Detroit, MI), 1986.

Silvey, Anita, editor, *Children's Books and Their Creators,* Houghton (Boston, MA), 1995.

St. James Guide to Fantasy Writers, St. James Press (Detroit, MI), 1996.

St. James Guide to Young Adult Writers, St. James Press (Detroit, MI), 1999.

PERIODICALS

Analog, January, 1980.
Booklist, August, 1995, Sally Estes, review of *The Book of Atrix Wolfe,* p. 1936; January, 1997, review of *Winter Rose,* p. 763; August, 1998, Roland Green, review of *Song for the Basilisk,* pp. 1978-1979.
Bulletin of the Center for Children's Books, January, 1975, p. 82; July, 1979, p. 196; September, 1984, p. 10.
Christian Science Monitor, November 2, 1977, p. B2.
Fantasy Review, November, 1985.
Kirkus Reviews, July 15, 1993, review of *The Cygnet and the Firebird,* p. 898; May 15, 1996, review of *Winter Rose,* p. 718.
Locus, January, 1990, p. 52.
Los Angeles Times, March 26, 1982, Charles Champlin, review of *Stepping from the Shadows.*
New York Times Book Review, October 13, 1974, Georgess McHargue, review of *The Forgotten Beasts of Eld,* p. 8; March 6, 1977, Glenn Shea, review of *The Riddle-Master of Hed,* p. 29.
Publishers Weekly, October 3, 1994, review of *Brian Froud's Faerielands,* p. 54; June 26, 1995, review of *The Book of Atrix Wolfe,* p. 90.
School Library Journal, October, 1991, p. 160; May, 1994, Cathy Chauvette, review of *The Cygnet and the Firebird,* p. 143.
Science Fiction and Fantasy Book Review, May, 1979, Roger C. Schlobin, review of "Riddlemaster" trilogy, pp. 37-38.
Science Fiction Chronicle, July, 1991, p. 30.
Voice of Youth Advocates, October, 1982, p. 32; June, 1991, Carolyn Shute, review of *The Sorceress and the Cygnet,* p. 112; December, 1993, Esther Sinofsky, review of *The Cygnet and the Firebird,* p. 311; April, 1999, review of *Song for the Basilisk,* p. 14.
Washington Post Book World, January 9, 1986; October 23, 1994, Gregory Feeley, review of *Something Rich and Strange,* p. 6.

*   *   *

MODARRESSI, Mitra 1967-

Personal

Born November 22, 1967, in Baltimore, MD; daughter of Taghi (a psychiatrist) and Anne (a writer; maiden name, Tyler) Modarressi; married Gregory Amundson (an editorial/production assistant), September 25, 1998; children: Taghi Jon Amundson. *Education:* Rhode Island School of Design, B.F.A. (illustration), 1989.

Addresses

Home—619 Hayes St., San Francisco, CA 94102. *Agent*—Miriam Altshuler, 53 Old Post Rd. N., Red Hook, NY 12571. *E-mail*—GregMitra@earthlink.net.

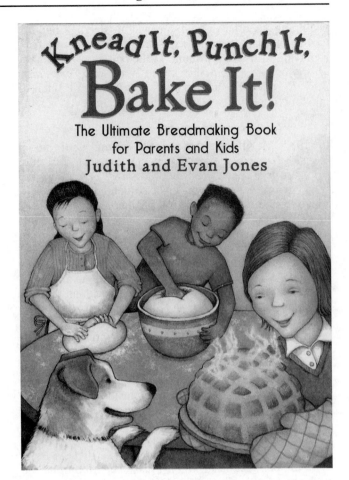

Mitra Modarressi illustrated this cookbook of kid-tested bread recipes. (Cover illustration by Modarressi.)

Career

Illustrator. Previously worked as a children's bookseller.

Awards, Honors

Notable Books for Children selection, *Smithsonian* magazine, 2000, for *Yard Sale!*

Writings

SELF-ILLUSTRATED

The Dream Pillow, Orchard Books (New York, NY), 1994.
The Parent Thief, Orchard Books (New York, NY), 1995.
The Beastly Visits, Orchard Books (New York, NY), 1996.
Monster Stew, DK Publishing (New York, NY), 1998.
Yard Sale!, DK Publishing (New York, NY), 2000.

ILLUSTRATOR

Anne Tyler, *Tumble Tower,* Orchard Books (New York, NY), 1993.
Judith and Evan Jones, *Knead It, Punch It, Bake It!: The Ultimate Breadmaking Book for Parents and Kids,* Houghton (Boston, MA), 1998.

Sidelights

Children's author and illustrator Mitra Modarressi told *SATA*, "I graduated in 1989 from the Rhode Island School of Design with a degree in illustration. After working for several years as a children's bookseller, I found a natural connection between my art and the world of kid's books. I began writing stories that would allow me to paint the kinds of images that I was interested in—magical, slightly eerie, and with a sense of humor."

In 1993 Modarressi began her career as a children's book illustrator by providing the pictures for *Tumble Tower,* the first book for children written by her mother, the award-winning adult author Anne Tyler. Born into a family of clean freaks, Princess Molly the Messy often finds herself at odds with other members of the royal cast. But when a flash flood washes King Clement the Clean, Queen Nellie the Neat, and Prince Thomas the Tidy from their well-kept quarters downstairs, Princess Molly invites her parents and sibling to take refuge in her cluttered upstairs chamber. Despite its disorder, the room turns out to be a blessing in disguise, providing dry clothes, leftover treats, entertaining books, and a comfortable bed for everyone to share. After the waters recede, Princess Molly and her family set upon cleaning up the clutter, this time with a newfound understanding toward Molly's untidy ways. Both Modarressi and Tyler earned rave reviews from critics for this debut picture book. Reviewing *Tumble Tower* in *Publishers Weekly,* a critic wrote, "With . . . the profusion of details, patterns, and objects, [Modarressi's] illustrations hint at the dreaminess of Modigliani and the cosy amiability of Earnest Shepard." Calling the book "good fun," a *Kirkus Reviews* critic noted that the illustrator's "expressive, delicately modeled faces [add] a subtler dimension to Tyler's message."

One year later, Modarressi published *The Dream Pillow,* a work she both wrote and illustrated. Though neighbors, Ivy and Celeste are not necessarily friends in the story. Celeste perceives her schoolmate as snooty and even walks on the opposite side of the street to avoid her. Making matters worse, Ivy gives Celeste a beautiful velvet pillow for her birthday, a pillow that, unknown to Ivy, causes nightmares. Thinking Ivy purposely tried to make her nights sleepless, Celeste transforms the pillow into a stuffed animal and gives it to Ivy at her birthday party a few days later. However, noticing the look of fatigue in Ivy's eyes, Celeste eventually feels guilty about her deception and confesses her trickery to Ivy. The two girls bring their problem to Ivy's mother, who realizes that she doubled the amount of flowers in the recipe for the "Daisy Delightful Dream Pillow." Dividing the pillow in two gives each girl a new pillow, and perhaps more importantly, a new friendship. Writing in *Kirkus Reviews,* a critic remarked that "Modarressi's illustrations, soft and jewel-like, fit her well-paced text." "Mildly dramatic but also calming," wrote a *Publishers Weekly* contributor, "this bedtime book enhances Modarressi's reputation."

Monsters are the featured characters in two other books by Modarressi, *The Beastly Visits* and *Monster Stew.* In *The Beastly Visits,* a young boy named Miles absent-mindedly lets his foot dangle off his bed as he sleeps. In the middle of the night, a gentle monster comes out from underneath the bed and begins poking at Miles' extended foot. Despite the monster and Miles' initial shock, the two strike up an unlikely friendship, with Newton the monster eventually coming to the boy's rescue on the playground. Though finding fault with the book's ending, a *Publishers Weekly* contributor stated that with *The Beastly Visits* "Modarressi has established a unique and haunting style of watercolor illustration." *Monster Stew,* Modarressi's second book about other-worldly creatures, retells three classic tales from the monster's point of view. In the author/illustrator's version of "The Princess and the Pea," the king and queen decide that a delicate princess is no suitable match for their rugged son, while in "Jack and the Beanstalk," the giant of the story befriends the young Jack. The final story of the volume, "Hansel and Gretel," finds two young monsters who, instead of becoming a potential main dish for the witch, eat her "out of house and home." "Modarressi wittily champions monsters" in *Monster Stew,* observed a contributor to *Publishers Weekly,* "and wryly implies that it's some people who need to learn suitable manners."

Commenting upon her 2000 picture book, Modarressi revealed to *SATA:* "With *Yard Sale!,* I wanted to write a story about an entire town rather than focusing on just one or two characters. I wanted it to be big, joyful, and crowded; a story that would be a lot of fun to illustrate. And I've always loved the mystery and promise of a yard sale. You never know what treasure they may hold."

Set in small-town America, *Yard Sale!* focuses on the inhabitants of Spudville, a place where "Nothing strange ever happened." That is until Mr. Flotsam decides to sell off some items he no longer needs. While his neighbors are initially happy with their purchases, the town is turned upside-down when Mr. Flotsam's unwanted things begin to take on a life of their own—a pasta-maker cranks out miles of spaghetti, a typewriter types its own books, and an old telephone receives calls from Amelia Earhart. Residents eventually come to appreciate the magic items, however, and learn to share their newfound gifts with others. Describing the picture book as an "optimistic, creative delight," *Booklist* contributor Gillian Engberg called *Yard Sale!* "a community story that will engage and entertain young ones." "Fun from start to finish" said a *Publishers Weekly* critic, while *School Library Journal* reviewer Karen James added, "This is an amusing bit of magical realism about looking at things in a new way and the joys of the unexpected."

Biographical and Critical Sources

BOOKS

Modarressi, Mitra, *Monster Stew,* DK Publishing (New York, NY), 1998.

Modarressi, Mitra, *Yard Sale!,* DK Publishing (New York, NY), 2000.

PERIODICALS

Booklist, March 1, 2000, Gillian Engberg, review of *Yard Sale!,* p. 1251.

Kirkus Reviews, July 15, 1993, review of *Tumble Tower,* p. 943; September 15, 1994, review of *The Dream Pillow,* p. 1276.

New York Times Book Review, January 17, 1999, Andrew Leonard, review of *Monster Stew,* p, 27.

Publishers Weekly, June 28, 1993, review of *Tumble Tower,* p. 76; July 18, 1994, review of *The Dream Pillow,* p. 244; August 14, 1995, review of *The Parent Thief,* p. 83; July 22, 1996, review of *The Beastly Visits,* p. 241; June 29, 1998, review of *Monster Stew,* p. 59; February 14, 2000, review of *Yard Sale!,* p. 197.

School Library Journal, September, 1996, John Peters, review of *The Beastly Visits,* p. 186; July, 2000, Karen James, review of *Yard Sale!,* p. 84.

Autobiography Feature

Kyoko Mori

1957-

SOMETHING FROM NOTHING: AN AUTOBIOGRAPHY

I

The first house I lived in was at the foot of the mountains in Kobe, Japan. It was a two-story house on a small lot across the street from a river, and my family lived with my mother's brothers and sister. On sunny days when I was four, my uncles and I drew pictures on the low stone wall that was built along the river. We brought a box of chalk—stubby sticks of red, yellow, white, blue, or green—and drew whatever came to our minds. All of my animals looked like fat or skinny turtles, and my cars and ships were variations of the same stacked boxes, but my uncles—Shiro and Kenichi—could draw giraffes, barges, bulldozers, elephants, skyscrapers. In the upper right-hand corner of every picture, I made a huge red spiral with long arrows shooting out in all directions. That was the sun, and it meant that the picture was complete.

Picking up our box of chalk, we would step over to the next blank patch and start a new picture. The wall bordered the river all the way down to the sea. Once or twice a week, my mother and I went to the sea to look at the ships coming in or the seagulls flying overhead, so I knew that the sea was a bus ride away. No matter how much my uncles and I drew, we would never run out of blank space on that wall.

Because it rained a lot in our city, or maybe because a city worker came around now and then to clean the wall, my uncles and I never got very far down the block with our pictures. The wall in front of our house was an unending scroll. The stone had a slightly rough texture, like orange skin, only harder; the soft tip of our chalk went over the little bumps, turning the grey blankness into smooth red

flowers, soft clouds, various animals. Drawing on the wall with my uncles, I came to understand the magic of transformation—a limitless possibility of turning nothing into something.

The house we shared was full of the same magical possibility: my mother's sewing basket stuffed with colorful scraps and threads, my aunt Keiko's red patent-leather purse with silk-lined compartments, old bookcases crowded with our books, cupboards stocked with dried herbs and spices in tiny glass jars. These were earlier versions of what I love now: boxes of beads or yarn, a clean stack of writing paper, a green expanse of meadow where I wait with binoculars for meadowlarks and song sparrows. In the two-story house in Kobe, where I lived with my mother, uncles, and aunt, I learned to look for the small surprises contained in the perfect color red, the delicate shape of a twig, or the *pi-hyororo* call of *tombi*—small black hawks riding the heat currents above our house.

My father, too, lived in the same house, but I saw very little of him. An engineer for Kawasaki Steel, my father worked almost all of his waking hours and took numerous out-of-town trips. Perhaps, at the time, he believed that being hard-working and ambitious were the duties of a Japanese husband and father, though the hours he worked meant he could only be an absentee husband and father. Years later, I would find out that he had affairs throughout his marriage to my mother—going back to the time before my birth—and that he came home late only to gulp down the tea my mother had prepared for him and go to bed in his separate room without scarcely a word to her. As a young child, I took his absence for granted and thought very little of it, or of him.

Too busy to notice his comings and goings, I lived as a pampered child in a large close-knit family. My mother, Takako, was the oldest of six children; she had grown up Kobe, in the same two-story house by the river where we were living with two of her brothers and sister. Before the Second World War, their parents—my grandparents—had lived in the house and my grandfather had worked as schoolteacher. Though my grandfather was the only son of a well-to-do landowning family out in the country, he had wanted to take a job in the city and raise his children where they could attend the better schools. As a young woman, my mother went to one of the best girls' high schools in town and planned become a nurse, a pharmacist, or a teacher. She assumed that she could do whatever she wanted to do in the future since her family had money and she was getting a good education.

During the last years of the war, though, my grandparents had to move back to the country to take over the family business—the management of the land the family owned and rented out to sharecroppers—because my grandfather's father grew sick and then died. Many other families were moving to the countryside anyway, to escape the fire bombs and the food shortage of the cities. Like them, my grandparents meant to return to the city once the war was over, perhaps hiring someone to manage the land for them. My mother and her brother Shiro stayed on in the city because they wanted to finish high school there.

My grandparents never made it back to the city. Right after the war, in a nation-wide land reform, the government required all the land owners to surrender their land for almost nothing, so the government could redistribute it their former sharecroppers. My grandparents were allowed to keep only a few acres to plant with their own crops. The payment they received was not enough to buy the equipment and the supplies they needed to become farmers rather than landowners (who just collected the rent and did not farm). My grandparents knew even less about farming than the average landowners: they were city people who had only visited the countryside for a few weeks every summer to see their relatives. Suddenly reduced to poverty, they could not move back to the city which was flooded with an influx of poor and homeless people after the war. My grandfather obtained a teaching job in the country school in their village, my grandmother tried to farm, and they resigned themselves to being poor country people.

That is why my mother, who was seventeen at the end of the war, had stayed on in Kobe to work as a secretary rather than going to college as planned or moving to the country, where she would only add to her parents' burden. She took in extra sewing, knitting, or mending work and sent home whatever money she could spare. She kept house for her brother Shiro, who had another year of high school. Eventually, two of the other children—Kenichi and Keiko—finished their high school in the country and came to the city to work or to attend school. They, too, lived in their old house and my mother took care of them. Fifteen years older than the youngest—my uncle Kenichi—my mother was like a second mother in the family. She stayed on even after she met and married my father, who made good money but was too young to be able to afford a house of his own.

Kyoko Mori with her cat, Dorian Gray, Wisconsin, 1995

My mother often said that the early years of her marriage, when she still lived with her own family, were the happiest time of her life. Though her parents never got back their fortune, they were still a hardworking and proud family. My uncle Shiro was teaching biology at a high school and taking night classes (he would later earn a Ph.D. in microbiology), Kenichi was about to finish college with a teaching certificate in chemistry, and my aunt Keiko worked at an office downtown. The three of them helped my mother take care of me, and she was happy that she no longer had to work in an office but was able to stay home to plant flowers, to cook and bake, and to take care of all of us.

One of my earliest memories is of my mother sitting by the window of her workroom and sewing a dress for me on a treadle sewing machine. The sun was shining on the metal head of the machine, which looked like a large black cat. As she treadled, the machine made a tat-a-tat-a-tat noise, and the dress draped down more and more, almost reaching the wooden floor. Beyond the sewing machine, on the other side of the large window, was our tiny walled-in garden that had a pond the size of a bathtub and a Russian olive tree my uncles had planted on the day I was born. The shiny red berries of the tree were almost the same color as the *koi* (Japanese carp) swimming in the pond.

I became a writer, I am certain, because of my mother and her family. My grandparents, who had always valued education, did not become bitter and angry people when they lost their fortune. Instead, they cherished reading, writing, drawing, painting, and other forms of education and the arts all the more: these were lifelong pursuits that could never be lost or taken away. When I visited their house in the summer, my grandfather—who had by then

Kyoko with her mother, Takako Mori, Kobe, Japan

retired from his teaching position and was given a modest pension to live on—got up at six or seven every morning to record his thoughts and observations in his journal. Once I was old enough, he helped me with my writing, drawing, or calligraphy. He had a way of making me want to work hard—he showed me that there was real pleasure in a job well done whether it was describing something I saw or making my brush strokes accurate and energetic. My grandmother, too, kept a journal and wrote *haiku* poems, many of which were published in newspapers and magazines. Because of them, I thought of writing as something that was natural and enjoyable, rather than a task to be dreaded.

At the same time, my two uncles who were scientists taught me the habit of observation. When I walked in the woods near our house with Shiro and Kenichi, they pointed out various wildflowers, trees, or insects, so I knew that what looked like a wad of dead leaves was actually a cocoon of a butterfly or that some trees produced burrs that stuck in our clothes so their seeds could be carried to another place. Sometimes, we caught butterflies, dragonflies, or beetles and kept them in wire cages for observation, feeding them slices of fruits and vegetables, before letting them go in a few days. My uncles prevented me from growing up to be the kind of girl who is afraid of caterpillars or frogs; they encouraged me to be curious instead of squeamish.

From my mother, I learned the love of books and stories. Every night at my bedtime, she read to me from the numerous picture books we had: the fairytales of Brothers Grimm and Hans Christian Andersen as well as the traditional Japanese fairy tales about animals who came to repay a debt of kindness or honest men and women who were rewarded for their good deeds. Sometimes, my mother told me stories from memory or invention. One was simply called an unending story and it was about the various adventures of a young boy who had an unending spool of thread.

My mother also filled our house with beauty. She made embroidered and batiked wall hangings, pillow covers, and tablecloths and sewed my dresses and her own blouses and skirts. Every spring, she planted boxes of pansies, forget-me-nots, and jasmine and set them out in our windows and by our front entrance. Even the food she cooked was beautiful. Many of my cousins, to this day, recall the birthday cakes she baked and decorated for us, the intricately shaped and frosted shortbread and sugar cookies she made to serve with tea. A bowl of noodles at my house, one cousin recalls, was a beautiful arrangement of eggs and vegetables sliced thread-thin and sprinkled over the top to please the eye.

For the first five years of my life, I lived in the beauty my mother and her family created around me, whether we were at our two-story house in Kobe or at my grandparents' in the country where most of us spent our summer. During my fourth year, my brother, Jumpei, was born. The first time I ever saw him in the hospital room, I've been told, I was so shocked and outraged to see this small baby in my mother's arms that I ran up to the bedside and tried to hit him. I was carried away from the room, crying, by one of my uncles. I don't doubt that the story is true, but I don't remember anything about my brother's birth except that my mother went to stay at the hospital a few days before the due date. On what must have been the day before my brother was born, I sat with her on her hospital bed, drinking apricot juice from a faceted jelly glass. My mother was holding the empty juice can on which was painted a picture of an apricot—perfectly round, the color of sunset. It looked like the most delectable fruit in the world.

Shortly after my brother was born, my father decided that it was time for us to move. My uncle Shiro and my aunt Keiko were going to be married soon. It was no longer necessary, my father decided, for my mother to take care of her siblings. Because housing was—and still is—scarce and expensive in Kobe, young couples like my parents rented apartments for years before they bought a house of their own. My father went and put his name on the waiting list for one of the apartment houses owned by his company and rented out to its employees. He was told that it would be about a year's wait. In the meantime, he arranged for us to move in with his father, who lived alone in a nearby suburb and was a widower in need of a housekeeper.

The day we moved to the suburb, Ashiya, both my mother and I cried when Shiro, Kenichi, and Keiko were getting ready to leave after helping us unload and unpack our belongings (my brother cried, too, but he was a baby; he cried every day). Both my father and my paternal grandfather were at work. My mother, who had never been close to her father-in-law, had misgivings about living with him. Everyone said that he was a cold and selfish person.

My uncles kept telling her that they would only be twenty minutes away by train. To me, they pointed to the mountains to the north and said, "See those mountains? They are the same mountains we were looking at from the old house, so every day, all of us will still be seeing the same scenery."

Though we only lived in my paternal grandfather's house for a year, I remember the coldness, both of the house and of my grandfather. A self-made man who now owned a small paint company where he had started out as a stock boy, my grandfather had no tolerance for anyone less fortunate than he. He had always held my mother's family in contempt for being poor—never mind that their sudden poverty was not a result of their laziness or mismanagement. My paternal grandfather, Tatsuo, was absolutely unforgiving of any imperfection, from my mother's family's misfortune to my voice breaking the complete silence he required while he was reading the newspaper, or the drop of water my mother had spilled on the counter while preparing tea for him. If he tasted or imagined the slightest tinge of bitterness in the tea, he would call her to come to his room and take it away, to prepare a new pot. Even at five, I could see that Tatsuo was a tyrant, that my mother was terribly unhappy during that year. The house we lived in was orderly, spotless, quiet, and cold.

My father began to take even more out-of-town trips than before, leaving my mother to wait on his own father. Shiro, Kenichi, and Keiko visited now and then but only when Tatsuo was at work; my mother's parents hesitated to even call the house when he was around. My mother must have been so very lonely, spending the whole day alone with my brother and then trying so hard to keep us quiet at night. A month after we moved, I started going to kindergarten. For a week, I cried every morning after my mother walked me there, pushing my brother in a baby carriage, and then turned to go home. Eventually, I got used to being there.

At least, at kindergarten, we were encouraged to sing, run around, and even shout now and then, unlike at my grandfather's house. Most of the games we played, I remember, were some form of tag or hide-and-seek. We had cookies and milk, naptime on the floor, and singing in circles. One morning after our mothers had gone back home, two of my friends—a boy and a girl—decided to jump into the shallow irrigation ditch outside the school gate. The water was only up to their ankles, but they lay down on their backs and began to splash. They were laughing and yelling at me to jump down and join them. The water looked clean enough and it wasn't a cold day, but I didn't want to get my clothes wet. The girl was one of my best friends; her glasses were getting spotted with water. She was having a great time. I hesitated for a long time, annoyed at her for wanting to swim in a ditch. The last thing I remember is jumping down and letting my shoes fill with water—when we went inside together and the other two kids were wet, I reasoned, maybe the teacher would scold me for standing by and watching them do such a stupid thing without trying to stop them. If I was wet, too, the teacher would think that I, too, was just dumb. I can't remember whether I escaped trouble or not.

The summer before I started first grade, my family moved to an apartment house in the same suburb, Ashiya, about a mile south of where we had been living. Our apartment was in a four-story concrete building that had twenty-four units, all the same size and arrangement. Most of the families had children my brother's or my age, so a big group of us played together in the fenced-in yard the size of our schoolyard. Our mothers put up raised flower beds and grew pansies, petunias, chrysanthemums, sweet peas, roses, and even strawberries. My mother was considered to be the best gardener in the building. She and the other mothers visited each other daily, cooking, sewing, and talking in each other's kitchens and living rooms.

For the next five years, we lived in the same apartment building, surrounded by neighbors who seemed more like family. Every afternoon, my brother and I would come home from school and join the group of kids in the yard. We played until it got dark and our mothers came out to call us in for supper. At night, my brother and I did our homework or listened to our mother tell us stories, and in the winter, we helped her bake cookies or pies almost every night; we would make some tea and invite our neighbors for an evening snack. On weekends, our mother planned picnics and hikes, inviting our neighbors and relatives— Shim, Kenichi, and Keiko with their families, my father's sister Akiko and her daughter Kazumi, who was my age. Often, a big group of us would go up to the mountains that bordered our city to the north; we would hike and view the autumn leaves or spring hydrangeas or whatever was

Kyoko with her mother, about 1959, in Japan

beautiful and in season, and then we would have a big picnic lunch.

When I was in third grade, my mother began taking me to museums in Kobe or Kyoto to see the travelling exhibits of Rembrandt, Goya, Van Gogh, Monet, Bonnard, etc. I loved the Old Masters, who painted dark rooms illuminated by a single candle or a table covered with white cloth and a few apples. Their paintings seemed so mysterious, even though the subject matter was so ordinary—a living room, a kitchen table. My mother loved the Impressionists, who seemed to share her passion for gardening and walking in parks or fields to see green trees. I was too young to appreciate their technique of vigorous brush strokes and dots of light. I even thought that they must have been near-sighted to see the world as huge swirls of blurred light. But no matter what we went to see, our outings made me feel important. My mother and I dressed up for the occasion, wearing our good blouses and skirts with hats, jewelry, patent-leather shoes. On the way home, we would have lunch at a pretty coffee shop and also buy a small gift for my brother, who stayed home with our neighbors because he was too young to come along.

In those years, most of my education took place at home, where I read books with my mother and wrote stories, or at the museums and on hiking paths where she taught me to look for pleasing arrangements of colors and

At her maternal grandparents' home in the country, where there was a slide, 1960

shapes. Even though I did not become a visual artist, what I learned from my mother about stories, colors, shapes, and the way they all came together in a composition or arrangement—these were the things that would later inspire me to write short stories, novels, and poems. My mother helped me cultivate an eye for detail, something I now consider essential to my training as a writer.

At the same time I was learning these things from my mother, I was attending a public elementary school, where I did well enough but was mostly bored. Grade school was nothing like kindergarten, where we played games, sang, ate cookies, and generally had fun. Once we were in grade school, we had to sit in orderly rows and never speak unless called upon by the teacher. During recess, too, we had to stay in the designated areas of the yard, we weren't allowed to eat anything unless it was the lunch hour, and then, we couldn't be excused to play outside until we had finished everything on our plate. For all the regimen we were required to follow, we didn't do much at school that I couldn't do just as easily at home, where I was allowed much more freedom.

My life, then, revolved around our home rather than school. It was a home from which my father continued to be absent, but I didn't miss him. On the very few occasions when he went on short family outings with us, my father was irritable and impatient. He would lose his temper and yell at strangers for skipping in front of him at the ticket counter of a train station or accidentally stepping on his shoes in a crowd. When we were on a bus together and the bus had to stop at a railway crossing, I could feel a terrible mood descending on him. He would sit with his jaws and his fists clenched, getting angrier with every train car that went by. If a long freight train was crossing, my brother and I could count on him suddenly lashing out at us, criticizing our poor posture or the clothing we had chosen to wear. So when our family went somewhere and he was not with us, I was relieved rather than disappointed.

My mother seemed well aware of my father's short-comings—never defending or excusing his impatience toward us—and yet resigned to being married to him. Back then in Japan, as it is now, "nice" people in the suburbs who had a comfortable income, like my parents, did not get divorced. Many women—including my mother's close friends—put up with husbands who were indifferent, unfaithful, and ill-tempered. "I have my children and my friends. My own family lives nearby. And my husband, at least he brings home a good income," women said to each other, shrugging their shoulders and making light of the situation. As long as she lived at the apartment and saw other women every day, my mother felt that her life, all things considered, was happy and good. She had no reason to consider herself less fortunate than many of the women she saw day after day.

In the spring of 1967, my family went to look at a two-story house my father's company had offered to sell us. I was thrilled to see that the house was situated up on a hill; my room upstairs would look over the entire city and the bay in the distance. A bush warbler was singing in the evergreens in the yard. The house was still within walking distance of the public school my brother and I attended, so everything seemed perfect.

My mother felt a horrible premonition the moment she entered the house for the first time, though she did not tell me about it. As I would find out later, she called her sister, Keiko, that night after Jumpei and I were asleep. "I don't know," she said to Keiko. "Everything looks just fine with that house, but I can't shake off a bad feeling I have." My aunt, who was known to be somewhat superstitious, advised, "Don't move there if you don't feel right about it. Maybe your feelings are omens or premonitions."

My mother told no one else about her bad feelings, and we moved into the new house a couple of months later. By then, school was out for the summer, and my brother and I helped her plant a huge vegetable garden, perennial and rose beds, and iris patches. My uncles came often to do minor carpentry work, and my grandparents visited, too, bringing bulbs and cuttings from their garden. My mother began to think that her bad feelings had been nothing but nervousness about the move.

Every evening, she and I walked up the hill to a bluff, from which we could overlook the long coastline and the bay at sunset. Somehow, the view—perhaps the sweep and the beauty of it—made us want to talk about the future. By then, I was in fifth grade, as unhappy as ever with the strict discipline of our public school. Junior and senior high schools would give me more of the same, or worse, if I stayed in the public school system: I would have to wear a navy-blue uniform to school every day and take numerous exams, which would prepare me to take more exams. There would be rules about exactly how long my hair can be, what color socks can be worn to school, and how the socks should be folded down over the shoes (and another set of rules about the color, the style, and the make of the shoes).

"I don't want to grow up," I would whisper to my mother when we passed groups of public school girls walking home from school.

My mother told me that I could go to the one private school in the Kobe-Osaka area that did not require any kind of uniform, since this school also had a very good reputation for its English, music, and art education. A school only for girls, it had junior and senior high schools and a college on the same campus, and the students who were admitted to the junior high school were guaranteed an entry into the college—therefore bypassing the complicated system of entrance exams that forced Japanese public school students to spend long hours learning nothing but how to take exams.

"I'll go to that school," I said.

To attend the private school, my mother said, I would have to take an entrance examination at the end of sixth grade, in March of 1969. The school admitted only about a third of its applicants, so I would have to study hard for a while. I didn't mind—since, if I passed, it would be the last time I would have to study for an entrance examination. So when school started in September—the second trimester of my fifth grade—I became a very good student for the first time rather than the "bright but inattentive" smart kid my teachers had complained about. I didn't mind the boring learning-by-rote lessons we had, if they were what I had to learn to get into the school-without-uniforms where I could study to become an artist or a writer.

While I was becoming more absorbed in my studies that winter, my mother began to feel that the move to the new house—and possibly her whole life—had been one big

With her mother, little brother, and maternal grandparents

mistake. She had always hated the cold winter months but had been able to cheer herself up by baking and visiting friends and talking to her parents on the phone. But now, she found herself going back to bed after my brother and I left for school. She would sleep till noon, wake up feeling groggy and muddled, and have a hard time performing her daily tasks of housecleaning or grocery-shopping. Our house was only a few miles from the apartment complex and many of her old neighbors called, but since none of the women had cars, it was hard for them to visit for a short while in the middle of the day, between errands, as they used to. My mother felt lonely and desolate. She began to think that her life had no real purpose.

Still, she got through that first winter and began to feel happy again in the spring. She added new flower beds and grew rows and rows of lettuce and spinach—she loved the fresh greens—so we always had salad from the garden. For a while, with my brother and me home and more of her friends and relatives visiting regularly, she thought that her unhappiness of the past winter had been a bad dream. But when the red and brown leaves began falling from the trees in October, she felt her misery descending upon her.

From the journals she left and from the articles I read when I was older, I know that my mother suffered from depression triggered by the sudden move, the isolation from her friends, and winter weather. Even back then, at ten and then eleven, I knew that my mother was going through a terrible time. I couldn't help noticing her swollen

Kyoko (far left) holding brother Jumpei, with Aunt Keiko, Michiyo, Uncle Shiro, and cousins Eiko, Yumiko, Yukiko, and Takeshi, about 1967

eyes in the morning from crying at night, the vacant way she stared out the window. Sometimes, in what she must have thought was a subtle way, my mother would tell me about children who had grown up without their mothers and turned out just fine, or about famous people who had been orphans. I saw through the supposedly instructional stories about people's fortitude: she was preparing me for a time when she would not be with me, and that time would not be in some far-off future when I myself would be an old woman.

No one else seemed to notice my mother's misery. My brother was only seven and then eight. My aunts and uncles, when they came to visit, brought their children, most of them much younger than I, and there was so much commotion that it was hard to notice anything. Besides, my mother seemed temporarily happy again when we had company. It was the same when her friends visited, bringing their children—my friends.

My father was seldom around, but on the rare Sunday evenings when I saw him reading the paper or watching television alone in the family room, I thought of telling him. But he was irritable when he was home, supposedly trying to "relax." Just like his father, my father did not wish to be disturbed—to him, an ideal home was a place of absolute silence, not of warmth or company or talk. So I gave up the idea of telling him anything. He would only yell at me for disturbing his peace and warn me to mind my own business.

I continued to be the only person aware of my mother's great unhappiness, till one Sunday in March 1969, when my father was forced to spend a day at home because the golf party he planned to attend was rained out. Too restless to sit indoors, he decided to take my brother and me downtown to buy some school supplies, while my mother

insisted that she would stay behind because she did not feel well. We came home in the late afternoon and found her on the floor with the gas pipe in her mouth, her head covered with a black plastic bag. For me, it was like a nightmare come true: I had a horrible feeling that I should have been expecting just this, that I should not have left her alone. My father turned off the gas and called a friend of his, a surgeon, to come and try to resuscitate her. Years later, I would wonder why he did not call an ambulance, whether that would have made a difference, whether she would have wanted us to save her life. But at the time, I sat there holding her hand, which was already turning colder; I swallowed hard to choke down the tears I could taste in the back of my throat. In a few minutes, the doctor would come, take her pulse, and shake his head—and my father would ask me to call our relatives and friends to say that my mother had died. This was the end of my childhood. I was twelve years and seven days old.

II

Ten days before my mother's death, I had been notified of my acceptance for admission to Kobe Jogakuin, the private all-girls' school my mother and I had chosen. In April, when the new Japanese school year started, I began commuting daily to the school, which was in another nearby suburb of Kobe. After getting off the train in that suburb, my new classmates and I would walk to the campus which took up a whole side of a hill. From the school gate at the bottom of the hill, we hiked up a narrow, steep path bordered by flowering trees: azaleas, forsythias, cherries, apples, crepe myrtle. The junior high building was at the very top. On the way, we passed the college buildings. The music building had a brass weathervane in the shape of a trumpeter. Faintly, we could hear a college student practicing the piano inside.

For the next six years, I considered our beautiful campus to be more like a home than the house in which I lived with my father, brother, and stepmother. Only two months after my mother's death, my father asked a woman to move in with us, supposedly to take care of my brother and me. They were married the following spring, a year and a week after my mother's death. Though I did not know the specific details of the so-called "facts of life," it did not take a lot of imagination or knowledge to figure out that my stepmother, Michiko, had been my father's girlfriend before my mother's death.

Shortly after their wedding, my family bought another house in the suburbs and moved there, but it did not matter where we lived—to me, one house was as miserable as another. A few weeks after my mother's death, my father started hitting me every time he thought I was "talking back" to him or looking at him in a way he found objectionable. During my mother's life, my father had spoken sharply at me or even yelled at me, but never actually raised his hand to touch me. Once Michiko was with us, he hit me even more—every time she accused me of being impertinent: talking back, failing to answer right away when she called me, looking at her with the wrong expression, talking too little or too much, almost anything could set her off. At least once a week, Michiko would speak to my father, pretending to be almost in tears, and then he would hit me while she watched, not even averting her eyes. I knew it was wrong to stand around and watch people getting beaten, and though my father never beat me in such a way as to cripple me or cause serious injury, I knew it was wrong to hit people. Even the boys who used to live next door had been cautioned by their mother never to raise a hand against my brother or me because they were older and stronger. For an adult to resort to violence— several hard slaps across the face, a shove into the wall— the way my father did to me, was wrong.

Still, I did not see what I could do to avoid the beatings or to whom I could confide. As soon as my stepmother came to live with us, my father had forbidden my brother and me to see my mother's family and old friends. I no longer had any friends except the new friends I made at school, none of whom had known my mother. For the next several years, I kept my unhappiness to myself and stayed in my room when I was home—reading, writing, doing my homework, hoping not to get into trouble, though eventually, my stepmother would complain about my never coming out of my room and then my father would beat me anyway.

The only thing I could do was to find legitimate excuses to be away from home, and those excuses usually involved some school activity. Though my father and stepmother did not enjoy my company any more than I enjoyed theirs, they were terribly concerned about "appearances" and "what the neighbors would say about us." They did not want me to be away from home all the time to visit

Kyoko with her brother Jumpei, 1961

friends or to do other "frivolous" things because then, the neighbors would say that I was never home because I was a frivolous girl or because my family was not happy together. But if I was away doing things for school, then it was all right: the neighbors would say, "That girl is so studious. She is always at school."

Both in junior and senior high, I played volleyball and ran medium-distance races, which meant that I had after-school practices and did not have to come home till late. I also stayed behind to read in the library, to be coached to participate in speech and debate contests, and to work as an editor of our school magazine and to write scripts for class skits. Even though I was doing these things partly to be able to stay away from home, I enjoyed the activities in themselves. I wanted to grow up to be a writer who was also an athlete.

Even back in grade school, I had often told people that I wanted to be a writer when I grew up. Back then, most of my writing was in Japanese, since I attended a regular public school in Japan. My high school, on the other hand, had been founded in the nineteenth century by two American missionary women who wanted to foster independence and creativity in Japanese girls. A century later, the school still emphasized the arts and bilingual education. We had English classes every day with young American women or Japanese women who had just graduated from American colleges. They taught us to write and speak clearly, correctly, and creatively. Being articulate, our English teachers argued, was an absolute requirement for a woman who wanted to be independent and creative.

In the Japanese language classes that I took in grade school and even at our private school, I had never really been taught how to write. We wrote compositions now and then but we only received grades on them, good or bad, without any comments or suggestions for improvement. Though my grades were usually good, I had no idea what I had done well or what I still needed to improve to be a really good writer. In contrast, my English teachers gave me a lot of specific advice and commentary about what I did well, what I could pay a bit more attention to next time. They encouraged me to write and rewrite my essays and stories both in and outside the classes, and they seemed to be truly interested in what I had to say and how I said it. Because of their help, I was soon more comfortable writing in English than in Japanese, and when I said that I wanted to be a writer, I meant that I wanted to be a writer in English—like the Brontë sisters, Jane Austen, or Emily Dickinson, who were my favorite writers from this time.

From July 1973 to June 1974, I lived with a family in Mesa, Arizona, as an American Field Service exchange student and attended high school there. I remember that year as the only really happy year of my adolescence. The family who hosted me, the Carrs, had a daughter my age and a son my brother's age. I learned, again, what it was like to live in a home where no one hit anyone, where disagreements and hurt feelings were talked about openly and reasonably until everyone felt some satisfaction.

At the high school I attended, my favorite classes were creative writing, American literature, and anthropology. I played on the volleyball team and did volunteer work both at school and at the Methodist church the Carrs attended.

Kyoko Mori, fourth grader, on Sports Day at school in Japan

For the first time in years, I found friends I could really talk to. Back in Japan, I'd had many good friends but felt that none of them truly understood me since I was the only girl at my school who had a stepmother (all the girls at my school came from "nice" families where people didn't get divorced or commit suicide). The girls and boys I met in Mesa were different. Many of them had divorced and remarried parents, so my situation was nothing new. Even the kids whose parents were together sometimes talked about how anxious they were to leave home and be on their own once they turned eighteen.

Obviously, my new friends in Mesa had circumstances and feelings similar to mine. But what I appreciated most about them, as well as about my host family, was that it was all right to *talk*, to voice our feelings and opinions. In Japan, nobody talked about their anxieties or unhappiness. Nobody said, honestly if bluntly, "What you did yesterday hurt my feelings," so that at least some kind of discussion could be started and both sides begin to understand one another's feelings. The "nice" Japanese people I had lived with just pretended that nothing was wrong even when everyone was actually angry and resentful. Instead of confronting each other, they would talk to someone else, so then everyone had to always worry about "what people are really thinking" and "what people might be saying about us in our absence." My father and my stepmother, while beating and criticizing me, still wanted to pretend that nothing was wrong with our family.

After a year of open and free talk with my friends and host family, I wasn't sure how I could go back to the oppressive and false politeness and silence of the "nice" Japanese suburb, where no one was supposed to talk about anything personal or negative. As June 1974 approached, I dreaded having to go back to Japan and vowed to myself that my return there would only be a temporary arrangement.

The next three years in Japan were every bit as difficult as I had imagined. My father continued to hit me, and my stepmother took to packing her suitcase and pretending to leave him, all because she could not stand living with me. She never really meant to leave—she would unpack and make tea for him as soon as he had beaten me and reduced me to tears. Once I finished my Japanese high school and went on to college, I suggested that I could live in an apartment or the dormitory, so none of us had to put up with the misery my presence was supposedly causing the family. My stepmother screamed at me for being insensitive and inconsiderate. "What would the neighbors say if you moved out of the house before you were married? They would say that I, a stepmother, had driven you out of your own father's home." I knew then that the only way I could leave their house—short of getting married right out of college—was to win a scholarship to an American college or graduate school. Then my parents would be able to explain, "Our daughter studied so hard that she won this prestigious scholarship."

I needed to find a scholarship that would allow me not just a year away (junior year abroad) but two years to finish college in the States so I could go on to graduate school without coming back to Japan again. I wasn't a bit afraid of leaving behind everything I'd known in Japan to go to a place I'd never been. I had already done that for a year in Arizona, and besides, there wasn't anyone or anything I thought I would miss all that much.

Since I was not allowed to see my mother's family or even to receive letters from them while I lived with my father and stepmother, I would not miss them any more than I already did—actually, if I went to the States alone, they would at least be able to write to me, as they did during the year I was in Arizona. My brother and I had never been close since our mother's death. By the time I was in college and he in high school, Jumpei claimed that he had no memory of our mother and that he considered Michiko to be his real mother. He seemed more like a stepbrother than a blood brother. Michiko took every advantage of this situation, making sure that only I was beaten, criticized, and blamed for everyone's unhappiness, and repeatedly reminding my brother of every careless, insensitive, or impatient comment I made to him in the last six years. "Remember when your sister wouldn't let you go on that picnic with her and her friends?" she would say to my brother out of the blue, even though the picnic had taken place five years ago. My brother had no chance of thinking well of me.

By the time we were sophomores at college, my friends and I could no longer talk about books or ideas or school in general. In high school, my friends had been serious, athletic, and studious so we could at least talk about school and sports, if not about our personal feelings. But once we were in college, my friends suddenly turned silly—they claimed to have no interest in anything we learned at school; instead, they talked endlessly about attractive boys they saw on the train. Soon, they started skipping our English or philosophy classes to go to movies with boys or to devote more time to the flower arrangement, tea ceremony, and cooking classes they took outside school—classes meant to train them to be nice suburban housewives. Though I knew they still loved me, we often fell into an uncomfortable silence when we were together. My friends, as well as I, thought that the best thing that could happen to me would be a scholarship to go abroad: I would be happier somewhere else, away from them.

I was thrilled, then, to win a scholarship that would allow me to withdraw from my college at the beginning of the third year and transfer to our sister college, Rockford College; the scholarship paid for my tuition and room and board for the next two years so I could earn my B.A. from Rockford and then apply to graduate school somewhere in the United States. Not only would I be able to leave my home under honorable pretense, but I would also no longer be financially dependent on my father, who never let me forget that I was able to attend college only on his

The author with her family: (front row, from left) Aunt Keiko, Kyoko, cousin Yukiko, Mariko's mother; (back row) Aunt Mariko, Uncle Kenichi, and brother Jumpei, Japan, 1993

sufferance and charity—from time to time, he threatened to stop paying for my education, though it was only a ruse to make me cry (doing so would have made him look bad to the neighbors).

The morning I left for Rockford, in July 1977, I already knew that I would never come back to live in Japan. I said good-bye to my friends who had come to see me off at the airport. I cried a little then, but as soon as I boarded the plane and sat down, I felt a tremendous burden lifting off. I would never again have to live with people who screamed at me and beat me, or be with my friends and feel so lonely amidst their company. I knew that the bad part of my life was finally over.

III

During my first semester at Rockford College, I took a creative writing class taught by my academic advisor, Dain Trafton. There were about twenty people in the class. Every week, we read short stories and poems written by contemporary American writers, wrote short stories or poems based on our experiences, and critiqued one another's work in our "workshop" sessions. The first assignment was to write a poem or a short sketch about a childhood experience. Because this was the only creative writing class offered at the college, we could write poems, short stories, or both. Throughout the semester, I wrote short prose sketches about childhood recollections and about the vivid, multi-color dreams I had every night. I wasn't all that interested in a fully realized plot and even less in the "themes" of my pieces. What fascinated me were voice, style, words, images: how my words sounded together, how I could pare down the prose so that a few vivid images stood out in a way that I found stark but pleasing. What motivated me at this early stage was my love of words and images—to this day, this is what is at the core of my writing.

After I finished that class, Dr. Trafton offered to conduct an independent study with me and two other students who had been in the class. We met once or twice a week to workshop our writing in our small group. The same group met for three semesters—so that I had an independent study every semester for the rest of my stay at Rockford. The other two students, one of whom became my best friend, wrote poems. Over time, I worked my way through the prose sketches toward "full-fledged" short stories, complete with a plot and a handful of characters, at least one of whom realizes something toward the end so that the story would have some kind of resolution or epiphany.

By the time I was a senior, ready to apply to graduate schools for masters' programs in creative writing, I had a portfolio of short stories to send along with my application. Though the stories got me into the schools I applied to and earned me a teaching assistantship at the University of Wisconsin—Milwaukee—the school I ended up going to—these stories now seem oddly lacking. They were stark and spare, perhaps well enough written, considering that I was only nineteen and twenty at the time, but they were always about young women who seemed to have no future—isolated figures spending their days in an unspecified town in the American Midwest. Aside from the smooth prose and the well-conveyed mood, there wasn't much to these

Mori with students Marty Block and Callie Schmek, in America, 1996

stories, but I suppose they were at least a good starting point.

In September 1979, I started my master's work at the University of Wisconsin—Milwaukee, and for the next couple of years, I continued to write stories in a similar vein. I did not become close friends with the other fiction writers in the program because they were a little older than I and had children; instead, I socialized with the few poets my age—Nuala Archer, Henri Cole, Ken Pobo. Though I lived alone with my cat, Dorian Gray, in a small efficiency apartment, I was always over at the house Nuala and Ken shared. We ate together, took some of the same classes, went dancing on weekends, and talked a lot about our writing. They introduced me to the works of the poets they loved—Elizabeth Bishop, Adrienne Rich, Denise Levertov, Maxine Kumin, poets I still read with great pleasure. Because Ken and Nuala tried writing short stories now and then, enrolling in the fiction workshop seminars, I decided to take one of the poetry classes. I found that short stories and poems actually had a lot in common: at least for me, they were both about those moments when everything came together into a sudden realization or epiphany, perceived in strong visual images.

After completing my master's, I decided to stay on in Milwaukee for the doctoral program in creative writing, which allowed us to submit a book-length manuscript of fiction or poetry instead of scholarly research. In the summer of 1981, at the beginning of my doctoral work, I took a fiction workshop with Raymond Carver, who came to our school as a visiting writer. The class met every day to read, write, and workshop like any other class, but in addition, each one of us met with Carver once a week to discuss our work. Carver had a way of going over our work with his pen, making minute suggestions about our words and sentences, sometimes rewriting what we had written or adding what we had not. In one of my stories—another one about a young woman who seemed frozen into inaction—he added a sentence to the scene in which the main character goes to say good bye to her boyfriend, who is moving to another town. "We hug," he wrote in.

Maybe that short sentence finally nudged me into realization: my characters had been too elegantly spare, my prose too restrained—I needed more action and emotion in my stories. Or maybe it was simply the encouragement I got from him during our individual meetings. I wrote with added enthusiasm during that summer, and the last of the four stories I handed in to him was a story about an old Japanese woman who was taking care of her grandson on her seventy-fifth birthday. I envisioned the woman to be someone like my grandmother, and the house I described was my grandparents' house as I remembered it. More important, I made the old woman *feel* in the way I had never allowed any of my other characters to. At the beginning of the story, she wishes she weren't alive to see another birthday, with her husband no longer alive and her oldest daughter lost to suicide ten years ago, but at the end, as she watches her grandson running up and down the wooden slide on the sun porch, she experiences a moment of intense joy.

This story, originally called "The First Cicada," eventually became the last chapter of my first book, *Shizuko's Daughter.* After finishing the story, I felt there was more to be said about the granddaughter, Yuki, who appeared only in one sentence as a girl refusing to cry at a Buddhist ceremony for her mother's death. In the next three years, then, I wrote several other stories about the same old woman, her daughter who committed suicide, and the granddaughter who was left alone at twelve. The main events of the stories, obviously, were taken from my own life—my mother's suicide, my grandmother's grief, my own lonely adolescence. But in choosing this material, I was not at all trying to "come to terms with my life" by writing about it; nor was I interested in communicating any big and deep themes about survival, tragedy, or fortitude. Now or then, I do not believe in writing as a form of therapy or a way to give moral instruction. Rather, I wanted to use the characters that were familiar to me—people like my own mother, grandmother, and myself—and the "plot" that I already knew, because these were the things that would allow me to write with understanding or feeling: I needed to turn to my own family stories, in order to take the risk of writing something more than the spare, elegant nothings I had been producing.

In May 1984, I finished my graduate work with a book-length manuscript which was half fiction and half poetry. The fiction part consisted of six stories, some of which were to become chapters of *Shizuko's Daughter;* a few of the poems would later be included in my poetry book, *Fallout.* But I thought of the manuscript as a work in progress—finished enough to earn me a Ph.D. and allow me to move to the next stage of my life, but not entirely finished.

In the last two years of graduate school, I had met and married a man who was studying to be an elementary school teacher. We finished our degrees at the same time and were both ready to move. One of the three places where I was offered a teaching job happened to be in Green Bay, Wisconsin—a town about a hundred miles north of Milwaukee, where my husband Chuck had grown up. In the summer of 1984, old friends of Chuck's came down from Green Bay every week to move our boxes and few pieces of furniture in the back of their pickups or station wagons. Like most people who move, Chuck and I discovered that, although we didn't own much, the little we owned was more than we thought. On the day we left Milwaukee, we loaded his twenty-year-old Plymouth Barracuda with our boxes and house plants. In the car, my cat and I could hardly turn around in our seat without hitting our heads on spider plants and boxes of books. The cat clung to my shoulders and meowed all the way. To switch lanes on the freeway, Chuck had to turn on the blinker and step on the gas, hoping that if someone was behind us, they would slow down and let us pass. With the car crammed to the ceiling, he couldn't see anything outside the window or in the rear-view mirror, so all he could do was to hope for the best. The whole thing made us laugh. It was almost as though we were on some crazy cross-continental adventure instead of moving to a place nearby where we would finally become real adults instead of students.

IV

In Green Bay, we moved into a two-bedroom apartment upstairs from a realty company, before buying a house of our own with a big yard. I taught creative writing and literature courses at St. Norbert College, a small Catholic college, and Chuck found a position with the public school system—teaching first and second grades at an alternative/ open-classroom elementary school in town.

In those early years at my job, I wrote poems during the school year and worked on fiction during the summers. In two years, I finally had enough material to make a complete "collection of related short stories" about the three Japanese women modelled after my mother, grandmother, and myself. I sent the manuscript to short story book contests, with no luck, but was able to find a literary agent interested in representing me.

In the next three years, my agent, Ann Rittenberg, and I had numerous rejections for my manuscript, which was called "The First Cicada and Other Stories." Though the stories were related—in that they were about the same set of characters—the book was a story collection, not a novel. The stories were not arranged chronologically, and there were huge gaps of time that were never filled in. Most of the publishers said that they liked the writing but that they did not publish story collections by unknown writers.

In 1991, Ann gave the manuscript to Marc Aronson, who had just started his work as a senior editor at Henry Holt and was looking for multicultural novels to launch an imprint called "Edge Books"—books that would be on the "cutting edge" of what was so far considered "young adult" literature. Marc liked the manuscript but suggested that I revise it and make it into a novel—a novel that could be read by young adults as well as adults.

To transform "The First Cicada" into a novel, I had to straighten out the chronology of the stories/chapters and fill in the gaps of time. It meant writing some new stories/chapters about the years left unaccounted for in the main character Yuki's life, while embedding a few of the older stories/chapters as flashbacks in other chapters. I also threw out and/or revised some of the stories/chapters I found unsatisfactory. The revision took nearly a year and was immensely rewarding. I was finally being forced to develop the characters and the plot *fully*, in long stretches of meaningful action, rather than in vivid but isolated glimpses that the short story form offered. Revising the book was a milestone in the same journey I had been taking as a writer, ever since Dain Trafton's creative writing class at Rockford, where, at first, I was unwilling to venture beyond the short and almost-perfect prose sketch. As a fiction writer who is also a poet, I tend to gravitate toward an isolated moment in which the images and the words come together into a revelation or epiphany—what I love to capture is a poetic moment, and the kind of writing I find easier to do is an equivalent of a sprint. You go all out and then it's done. What I need to work on, because it does not come to me as naturally, is the long stretch—like a long distance run—of narrative that must be developed slowly and patiently toward the finish in which everything seems clear and inevitable. Revising "The First Cicada" and making it into *Shizuko's Daughter* allowed me to develop my long-distance narrative discipline. Though I had initially written the manuscript for an "adult" market, writing it for an audience that included young adults made sense: the most consistent strand in the various stories or chapters was Yuki's coming of age.

In 1990, the year before I revised *Shizuko's Daughter,* I took an eight-week summer trip to Japan, the first since I left in 1977. I visited my maternal grandmother (my grandfather had passed away), uncles, and aunts, as well as old friends from school. Going back to Japan as an adult and an American citizen—a grown-up outsider—I felt free to exercise much more freedom than I ever thought possible in Japan. I spent a lot of time with my mother's family but saw my father, stepmother, and paternal grandfather just once. I walked all over the country alone in my T-shirt, shorts, and running shoes, even though Japanese women never travelled alone and were not seen in public without their tastefully color-coordinated dresses, nylons, and high heels. While I enjoyed my own freedom—freedom allowed me because I was now an outsider—I was disturbed to see the marriages of my old school friends, who seemed to have no meaningful conversations with their husbands. The men my friends married did absolutely no housework and expected their home to be a quiet place where they could simply "relax," much as my father and his father had done. The few friends who had stayed with their "careers" were unmarried—no man in Japan, it seemed, wanted to marry a woman who was known to be intelligent and ambitious.

I had kept a detailed journal during my eight-week trip and was in the process of turning the entries into a sustained nonfiction narrative, a memoir, when I got the chance to work on *Shizuko's Daughter.* After the revision

was done, then, I returned to the memoir manuscript I had put aside and was happy that I had kept such a detailed journal while in Japan.

The resulting book, *The Dream of Water,* is everything *Shizuko's Daughter* is not, while dealing with some of the same material. While *Shizuko* is a much-fictionalized portrait of a lonely adolescent who must come to terms with a family tragedy, *The Dream of Water* is a nonfiction account of what I as an adult perceived during my visit to the country of my childhood. For the novel, I chose the straightforward chronological sequence of events, except for a few short flashbacks here and there, because that seemed the best way to fully develop the characters and focus on the immediate conflicts they had to resolve. The memoir weaves its way among three layers of time: the present, which is my eight-week trip to Japan as a thirty-three-year-old American woman; the long-ago past, which is my childhood and adolescence in Japan; and the recent past, my adult life as a teacher and a writer in the American Midwest. What is at stake for the narrator of the memoir—some part of me, not a fictional character—is the very balancing act that involves coming to terms with the long-ago past without losing sight of what she values in her life as an adult in another country.

Shizuko's Daughter presents Yuki as an isolated figure, someone who must find her way all by herself, and her journey mostly involves overcoming her past. *The Dream of Water* is about someone who seeks to be reconnected to the past, and this person—myself—is greatly helped along by conversations with old friends and family. The answers come as much from other people as from within. And yet, while *Shizuko's Daughter* has a traditional happy ending—Yuki realizes that her mother would have wanted her to try to overcome her hurt and grow up to love someone—The *Dream of Water* does not. The only resolution that the narrator has about the hurt inflicted by her father and stepmother is that she must make peace within herself—there will be absolutely no reconciliation with them, no real forgiveness. In addition, *The Dream of Water* includes adult reflections about the lives of Japanese women, the meaning of family secrecy, what it means to be Japanese or American, and other reflections I could only pursue in the nonfiction format.

The one thing that both books have in common, though, is that again, I was mostly motivated by the details and observations recorded in my journal or imprinted in my memory. When I start writing anything, I find joy in giving life to these details rather than in teaching a lesson or in coming to terms with things in my own life.

This enjoyment of details is perhaps most apparent when I write poetry, since poems allow the poet to zero in on the most intense and vivid moments. Writing poetry is a discipline I find rewarding between my work on the longer prose projects, so while I was between revisions of *The Dream of Water,* I was also trying to put together a poetry book manuscript to be published by a Chicago press run by the poet Luiz Rodriguez. I revised and "weeded out" the existing poems and came up with a manuscript containing thirty-two poems written between 1986 and 1992. Titled *Fallout,* the book is divided into four sections: "Family Pictures" (poems about people in my family); "In an American Landscape" (poems about living in the Midwest); "Every Woman" (poems about women); "Returning to the Land of Gold" (poems about my trip to Japan). Though I continue to spend more time on prose work, poems give me opportunities to concentrate on isolated but meaningful moments and sudden, intuitive knowledge. At the same time, since each poem is relatively short, the form demands near-perfection: every word must be just so.

I believe that every book I finish prepares me for the next, even though I may not quite realize what is coming up around the bend until I get there. Writing *The Dream of Water* and revising the poems in the first and the last sections of *Fallout* made me realize that, in spite of my long absence, I still knew the landscape around Kobe and Ashiya quite well—that the mountains and the sea of my childhood are imprinted in my memory. In my next book, then, I wanted to revisit this setting and include details about the area my work so far hadn't mentioned: the grade school up on a hill, the old tomb of a fourth-century emperor, the sand beach full of broken seashells, the stores and coffee shops near the commuter train station.

I also wanted to include some details from my adult life. The summer before I started working on what was to become my next novel, *One Bird,* I had worked as a volunteer songbird rehabilitator at a local wildlife sanctuary. I was on call to pick up, take home, and raise or nurse the orphaned and injured robins, house finches, cedar waxwings, cardinals—common birds people found in their backyard and brought to the sanctuary. I fed the baby birds

Mori at Sievers Weaving School, in America, 1996

a concoction of cat food, baby food, and fruit mixed in a blender, and when they were a little older, let them fly around in a large outdoor cage in my yard till they were strong enough to be released back into the wild. I wrote some poems about my work as a rehabilitator, but I wanted to write more about it. That's how I decided that my next character, Megumi, should be a girl who cares for injured and orphaned birds.

Before I could begin my work on the novel, though, I had to learn about the birds of Japan. As an adult rehabilitator and also bird-watcher, I knew a lot about the birds of the eastern United States. In Japan, though, I had been a typical city child—the only birds that came to my yard were house sparrows, swallows, and crows, maybe an occasional bush warbler or white-eye. Many of the common birds of the American Midwest—robins, house finches, cedar waxwings—are not seen in Japan and other Asian countries. If I wanted my character to see or raise birds, I had to first find out which birds migrate through Japan during the various seasons, and which of these birds actually raise their young in southwestern Japan. Even in fiction, I believe, facts are important. I cannot have my characters see a bird in the summer which only winters in Japan, or find nestlings of birds which do not breed there. So to find out the right facts, I read books about Japanese birds and then visited the Chicago Field Museum to consult with a bird specialist and to see the specimens of the birds I was particularly interested in—in order to make sure that I was describing them accurately.

In many ways, *One Bird* brings together details from my past and present. The setting, Ashiya, is the suburb where I grew up, and Megumi attends a private all-girls' high school very much like the one I attended. Megumi's parents are separated and her mother lives out in the country with her own father, so, like me, Megumi is the only girl at her school who does not live with her mother. Like mine, Megumi's father has a girlfriend. But Megumi, who tells her own story as the first-person narrator, is not an isolated character like the adolescent I was or even like Yuki from *Shizuko* 's *Daughter*. Though she complains from time to time, she doesn't feel the kind of despair Yuki feels about life—or I felt, myself, at their age. An optimist with a self-deprecating sense of humor, Megumi is more like the adult I have become than the adolescent I used to be. She is a no-nonsense, take-charge sort of person, something I'd like to think I am in my best moments as an adult.

In the spring of 1993, I spent a week in Japan because my father died of cancer—though I had not known about his illness—and I had to attend to the family division of his property. I spent the week signing everything over to my stepmother so she could live in comfort as a rich man's widow. Since she could at least be trusted to share the money with my brother, whom she considers to be her real son, I didn't mind this arrangement so much in itself. I have never wanted to have anything to do with my father's money, and I certainly was not prepared to take my stepmother to court to get what some people thought was my share—to do such a thing, I would have to stay in Japan for an indefinite amount of time.

What bothered me, though, was the way my family's pretense of "niceness" prevented us from saying anything meaningful to each other most of the time. My brother, my paternal aunt, cousin, and I spoke in polite circumlocution and nice ambiguities even though we didn't intend to be dishonest—or else we fell silent because there was no polite way to say what we wanted to say. My stepmother, on the other hand, told blatant lies, trying to turn us against each other. Because so much in our family went unsaid, it was sometimes difficult for us to know what was the truth and what was the lie. For instance, my stepmother would report conversations that never took place—in which my aunt and cousin had said negative things about me that they didn't say at all—in the hope that I would be too "polite" to confront them with what they supposedly said. Once I began to find out the truth by being slightly more blunt than was polite, I discovered the many lies Michiko had told; I understood how the "nice" surface of my family had given her the perfect cover to lie and manipulate.

Though I was angry and bitter about Michiko's lies and our polite silence, the whole phenomena also fascinated me. What is repulsive is often also fascinating. That's why people slow down on the highway to look at scenes of accidents—hoping and not hoping to get a glimpse. The polite silence of the "nice" Japanese family, the lies, even, fascinated me, as did many of the other things that made me angry about Japan.

These are the thoughts that led to my latest book, *Polite Lies: On Being a Woman Caught between Cultures,* which is a collection of twelve essays about living in Japan and in the American Midwest. Although each essay has a central idea, I saw the essays as long prose-poems that combined narrative, evocative imagery, extended metaphors, and moments of epiphany when ideas come to us in a flash, as experiential and intuitive knowledge. The essay form, at the same time, allowed me to offer more explanation and background information than what is usually possible in a long poem or in fiction. The book gave me opportunities to contemplate the way the language of my childhood, Japanese, silences me; why Japanese bouquets always have yellow, pink, and white flowers; why people everywhere, Japanese or American, feel the urge to build an altar or to offer flowers to the dead. Running through the whole book is my longing to come home, if not to the place of my childhood, then to an imaginary place that has the books and the art work I love, where I can read or hear the stories that make sense to me.

Though I am by no means a shy introvert, I have always been drawn to solitude and to activities that require it: reading, running, weaving, beadwork, bird-watching, writing. In my twenties and early thirties, I was content so long as I could be alone to write a few times a week. In the last five years, I've come to feel a greater need for solitude. To be able to write alone, I first need to be alone to do something else such as bird-watching, running, or weaving. My perfect day would start with a morning run, then a short walk through the woods to see birds, then a few hours of writing, followed by weaving, knitting, or beadwork. Then, at four or five in the afternoon, I might be ready for a few hours of company.

Once I began to feel that way, I found it hard to balance the demands of teaching at a college and being married, with the demands of writing and solitude. At about the same time, I began to take a few trips every semester to promote my books or to speak at conferences, and I finally had a group of friends in Green Bay with whom I socialized regularly. Suddenly, there seemed to be no time to do everything I wanted to do—to be alone and write, to be a good teacher or a partner, and to still be part of the larger community through my books and my friendships.

Though I haven't found a perfect answer, I came to realize that marriage was not something I was suited to. I needed too much time to be alone or to be out and about, giving talks and seeing friends. I needed and was good at solitude and also at community—what I didn't need as much and was not as good at was the one-to-one partnership. Once I knew this, it was unfair to stay married. My husband and I decided to be divorced but to stay friends. I still see him about once a week to play tennis or to have dinner, and I've recently visited his school to talk to kids about poetry. I like to think that I'm doing the exact opposite of what many Japanese women are forced to do. They stay married to people who are not their friends in any way; I decided to be divorced but be friends.

As for my teaching, I try to request a schedule that allows me time to write even during the school year. During the summers and once-in-seven-years sabbatical leaves, I do not teach or give many talks at other schools or at conferences. I use these times to start my books so that I can revise them even while I am teaching. Teaching is work I enjoy for the most part. I particularly enjoy being there when a student makes a discovery or breakthrough, the way I did in Ray Carver's class. In an ideal teaching situation, the teacher is not really so much *teaching* as creating the right environment in which a student can teach him or herself, and giving just a few tips to point the student in the right direction. When a student discovers his or her voice or writes a good poem or story, I am honored to be part of that process. But even the best moment of teaching is not—at least for me—like the moment when my own poem suddenly falls into place or my character makes sense to me, or when I glimpse the yellow and grey breast of a great crested flycatcher in the woods and then the bird flies down, flashing its cinnamon-colored tail.

Many people seem to believe that writers owe something to society *as writers,* that we must teach or give lectures about the important values, themes, and lessons that will improve society. Though I admire the writers whose books have done just that, I do not agree that writers have a special debt—debt other citizens do not owe—to society. As a citizen, like everyone else, of course I do owe something to society. I believe in going to vote, in being informed about issues that affect the welfare of people other than myself, and in offering my time or money to further the common good. These are duties of every citizen, and I, too, am responsible for them. But I do not believe that I *owe* something extra simply because I am a writer. If I want to "contribute to society" by teaching or giving lectures, that is fine, but this should not be a requirement. I write because I enjoy working with words, images, characters, plots, settings—not because I want to improve society.

My future plans include another book of poetry and then a novel, though it will not be a coming-of-age or young adult novel. I take my projects one at a time and don't think much about what my next book will be, until I am ready to work on it. But whatever it may be, any book I write will be inspired by the things I find fascinating in my day-to-day life: the way the colors come together on a piece of fabric or beadwork, the return of the migratory birds, a wildflower on a mountain path that makes us suddenly recall a moment in the past, a whole lifetime away.

Writings

Shizuko's Daughter (young-adult novel), Holt (New York, NY), 1993.
Fallout (poetry), Tia Chucha Press, 1994.
The Dream of Water (memoir), Holt (New York, NY), 1995.
One Bird (young-adult novel), Holt (New York, NY), 1995.
Polite Lies: On Being a Woman Caught between Cultures (autobiography), Holt (New York, NY), 1997.
Stone Field, True Arrow: A Novel, Metropolitan Books, 2000.

MURPHY, Shirley Rousseau 1928-

Personal

Born May 20, 1928, in Oakland, CA; daughter of Otto Francis (a horse trainer) and Helen N. (an artist; maiden name, Hoffman) Rousseau; married Patrick J. Murphy (a U.S. probation officer), August 5, 1951. *Education:* California School of Fine Arts (now San Francisco Art Institute), A.A., 1951.

Addresses

Home—Molena Point, CA. *Office*—c/o Author Mail, HarperCollins, 10 E. 53rd St., New York, NY 10022. *E-mail*—murphy@joegrey.com.

Career

Sam Kweller, Designer, Los Angeles, CA, packaging designer, 1952-53; Bullock's (department store), Los Angeles, interior decorator, 1953-55; San Bernardino Valley College, San Bernardino, CA, teacher of mosaics, 1957-59; Canal Zone Library-Museum, Canal Zone, Panama, documents assistant, 1964-67; writer, painter, and sculptor. *Exhibitions:* Dual show with mother, Helen Rousseau, at Instituto Panameno de Arte, 1964, and eight one-woman shows in California, 1957-63; paintings, drawings, and sculptures also exhibited at group and juried shows in California, Arizona, and Nevada, as well as traveling exhibits. *Member:* Author's Guild, Mystery Writers of America, American Crime Writers League, Society of Children's Book Writers and Illustrators, Sisters in Crime, Cat Writers' Association, Library Cat Society.

Awards, Honors

Received eight awards for sculpture and four for paintings at San Francisco Museum and other exhibitions, 1956-62; Council of Writers and Journalists Awards, 1977, 1978, 1981, 1986, and 1988; Dixie

Council of Authors and Journalists Awards, 1977, for *Silver Woven in My Hair,* 1978, for *The Flight of the Fox,* and 1980, for *Mrs. Tortino's Return to the Sun;* Parents' Choice Award, 1987; Muse Medallion Award, Cat Writers' Association, 1997, for *Cat under Fire,* 1998, for *Cat Raise the Dead,* and 1999, for *Cat in the Dark;* President's Best-of-the-Best Award, Cat Writers' Association, 1998, for *Cat Raise the Dead.*

Shirley Rousseau Murphy

Writings

FOR CHILDREN

White Ghost Summer, illustrated by Barbara McGee, Viking (New York, NY), 1967.

The Sand Ponies, illustrated by Erika Weihs, Viking (New York, NY), 1967.

Elmo Doolan and the Search for the Golden Mouse, illustrated by Fritz Kredel, Viking (New York, NY), 1970.

(With husband, Patrick J. Murphy) *Carlos Charles,* Viking (New York, NY), 1971.

Poor Jenny, Bright as a Penny, Viking (New York, NY), 1974.

The Grass Tower, illustrated by Charles Robinson, Atheneum (New York, NY), 1976.

(Contributor) Sylvia Engdahl, editor, *Anywhere, Anywhen,* Atheneum (New York, NY), 1976.

Silver Woven in My Hair, illustrated by Alan Tiegreen, Atheneum (New York, NY), 1977.

The Flight of the Fox, illustrated by Don Sibley, Atheneum (New York, NY), 1978.

The Pig Who Could Conjure the Wind, illustrated by Mark Lefkowitz, Atheneum (New York, NY), 1978.

Soonie and the Dragon, illustrated by Susan Vaeth, Atheneum (New York, NY), 1979.

(With husband, Patrick J. Murphy) *Mrs. Tortino's Return to the Sun,* illustrated by Susan Russo, Lothrop (New York, NY), 1980.

Tattie's River Journey, illustrated by Tomie de Paola, Dial (New York, NY), 1983.

Valentine for a Dragon, illustrated by Kay Chorao, Atheneum (New York, NY), 1984.

(With Welch Suggs) *Medallion of the Black Hound,* Harper (New York, NY), 1989.

The Song of the Christmas Mouse, illustrated by Donna Diamond, Harper (New York, NY), 1990.

Wind Child, illustrated by Leo Dillon and Diane Dillon, Harper (New York, NY), 1999.

FANTASY NOVELS

The Ring of Fire, Atheneum (New York, NY), 1977.

The Wolf Bell, Atheneum (New York, NY), 1979.

The Castle of Hape, Atheneum (New York, NY), 1980.

Caves of Fire and Ice, Atheneum (New York, NY), 1980.

The Joining of the Stone, Atheneum (New York, NY), 1981.

Nightpool (part one of "The Dragonbards Trilogy"), Harper (New York, NY), 1985.

The Ivory Lyre (part two of "The Dragonbards Trilogy"), Harper (New York, NY), 1987.

The Dragonbards (part three of "The Dragonbards Trilogy"), Harper (New York, NY), 1988.

The Catswold Portal, New American Library (New York, NY), 1993.

"JOE GREY" SERIES; MYSTERIES

Cat on the Edge, HarperPrism (New York, NY), 1996.

Cat under Fire, HarperPrism (New York, NY), 1997.

Cat Raise the Dead, HarperPrism (New York, NY), 1998.

Cat in the Dark, HarperPrism (New York, NY), 1999.

Cat to the Dogs, HarperCollins (New York, NY), 2000.

Cat Spitting Mad, HarperCollins (New York, NY), 2001.

Cat Laughing Last, HarperCollins (New York, NY), 2002.

Author of novella, *Cat on the Money,* serialized in *Cats Magazine,* January-December, 2001. Contributor to *Advocate* and *Writer.*

Work in Progress

Cat Running Wild, Morrow/HarperCollins (New York, NY), expected in 2003; further titles in the "Joe Grey" mystery series.

Sidelights

"The best stories find the author, not the other way around," author Shirley Rousseau Murphy once commented. Murphy, the author of numerous novels for children and adults, has had much experience with such inspiration. Born in Oakland, California, in 1928, she has led as many careers as the cats she often writes about have lives. A decorator, designer, painter, and sculptor before she turned to writing full time, Murphy blended the talents of her parents in her own life. Her father was a horse trainer and her mother a painter, and Rousseau demonstrates the influence of each in her books. Her debut juvenile novels, *White Ghost Summer* and *The Sand Ponies,* both stem from her experiences of training horses with her father as a young girl. Both of these titles also feature young protagonists who find strength as well as friendship through relationships with horses.

Murphy's books for young readers are most often fantasies which take place in other worlds and deal with the elemental battle between good and evil. Five such novels are set in the mythical land of Ere; her young protagonists use their extraordinary power to do battle with dragons, monsters, and sorcerers. The "Ere" novels include *Ring of Fire, The Wolf Bell, The Castle of Hape, Caves of Fire and Ice,* and *The Joining of the Stone.* Another popular set of fantasy novels for young readers is the "Dragonbards Trilogy," in which Tebriel, a so-called dragonbard, and his singing dragon, Seastrider, join voices to free the enslaved world of Tirror, battling the lord of the dark, Quazelzeg. For a younger audience, Murphy has created more fanciful and humorous titles, including *The Pig Who Could Conjure the Wind, Valentine for a Dragon,* and *The Song of the Christmas Mouse.*

Murphy once expounded on the element of inspiration in her writing: "*Wind Child* is a story which came to me unbidden, like a dream.... The theme touches on that within ourselves which searches for answers, for the numinous, for explanations of what and who we are; but it deals as well with our opposite side, with the very practical and everyday disciplines." *Wind Child* is perhaps the most successful of Murphy's children's titles. With drawings, sculpture, and prose, it tells the story of Reeshie, daughter of the east wind, who yearns for companionship with a kindred spirit. "With elements of myth and folklore, this is a satisfying romantic story enhanced by Leo and Diane Dillon's elegant, other worldly illustrations," observed Linda Perkins in *Book-*

list. "This will delight fairy tale fans, inject fine art into climate studies, and invite students to write and/or illustrate their own myths." A *Publishers Weekly* reviewer called *Wind Child* a "haunting, mystical tale" with "carefully honed prose, striking in its spare, direct simplicity." The reviewer concluded, "The stark beauty of both text and artwork are sure to draw sophisticated readers into this stunning meditation on the price of immortality."

"Good fantasy grows from the most elemental within us," Murphy once noted, "from the most basic human strengths and fears, and needs; and the best fantasy is laced with wit, with the warmth of humor and camaraderie that makes us human. All these elements together pull us into a story, whether we are writing a new work or lost in the work of another."

One of Murphy's fantasy titles ultimately led to a new direction for her writing, from children's to adult titles. Murphy once commented: "I'm working on some adult mysteries featuring Joe Gray Cat.... The stories are the exact mix of fantasy and realism which I like best to do; they evolved from *The Catswold Portal,* inspired by my own calico cat who seemed so often to want to speak to me, that I could not help but consider and write about her secrets."

The popular "Joe Grey" mysteries have brought renewed success to Murphy. Set in a small California coastal town, the "Joe Grey" books feature a crime-solving cat duo, Joe Grey and Dulcie, who can think and talk like people. As a reporter noted in the *Monterey County Herald,* "These are not cute, little, furry kitties but rather two shrewd investigators with somewhat caustic personalities." Murphy based her title character on a no-nonsense gray cat she once owned briefly; the crimes and capers he solves are realistically depicted and demonstrate the author's "quick, analytical approach to forensic details," wrote Ann Sharkey in the *Library Cat Newsletter.* Over the course of more than a half dozen titles, Joe Grey and Dulcie have tangled with murderers and conspirators—of both human and cat species—as well as the odd roaming mountain lion. In *Booklist,* Sally Estes declared, "What makes this series so delightful for both cat lovers and readers of offbeat fantasies is ... Murphy's convincing anthropomorphism." Likewise, *Library Journal* correspondent Rex E. Klett commended the series as "a special treat ... for cat mystery fanciers." "Cat lovers will cuddle right up to Joe and his pals," wrote a reviewer for *Publishers Weekly* of Murphy's

sixth installment in the series, *Cat Spitting Mad.* "But the story has plenty of murder and mayhem for those who like to take their detective fiction straight up."

Biographical and Critical Sources

BOOKS

Gallo, Donald R., editor, *Speaking for Ourselves, Too,* National Council of Teachers of English (Urbana, IL), 1993.

Rasmusen, H., and A. Grant, *Sculpture from Junk,* Reinhold, 1967.

St. James Guide to Fantasy Writers, St. James Press (Detroit, MI), 1996.

St. James Guide to Young Adult Writers, 2nd edition, St. James Press (Detroit, MI), 1999.

Something about the Author Autobiography Series, Volume 18, Gale (Detroit, MI), 1994.

Twentieth-Century Children's Writers, 3rd edition, St. James Press (Detroit, MI), 1990.

Twentieth-Century Young Adult Writers, Gale (Detroit, MI), 1994.

PERIODICALS

Booklist, December 15, 1997, p. 695; December 15, 1998, Sally Estes, review of *Cat in the Dark,* p. 728; June 1, 1999, Linda Perkins, review of *Wind Child,* p. 1843; December 1, 2000, p. 697.

Library Cat Newsletter, spring, 2000, Ann Sharkey, review of *Cat to the Dogs.*

Library Journal, December, 1998, Rex E. Klett, review of *Cat in the Dark,* p. 160; January, 2000, Rex E. Klett, review of *Cat to the Dogs,* p. 167; January 1, 2001, p. 162.

Monterey County Herald, February 28, 1999, review of *Cat in the Dark.*

Publishers Weekly, May 17, 1999, review of *Wind Child,* p. 79; December 11, 2000, review of *Cat Spitting Mad,* p. 67.

School Library Journal, August, 1992, p. 189; May, 1999, pp. 158-159.

ON-LINE

Shirley Rousseau Murphy Web site, http://www.joegrey.com/ (January 26, 2001).

*   *   *

NICHOLAS, Louise D.
See WATKINS, Dawn L.

P

PATTISON, Darcy (S.) 1954-

Personal

Born June 28, 1954, in Albuquerque, NM; daughter of Henry Bonneau Foster (a rancher) and Edith (a nurse; maiden name, Legate) Irvin; married Dwight Pattison (a city planner), August 8, 1975; children: Sara, Jinny, Amy, Luke. *Education:* University of Arkansas, B.A., 1974; Kansas State University, M.A., 1976. *Hobbies and other interests:* Quilting, camping.

Addresses

Home—3707 Ridgeroad, North Little Rock, AR 72116.

Career

Author of children's books. *Arkansas Democrat-Gazette,* Little Rock, AR, children's book reviewer, c. 1995—; University of Central Arkansas, Conway, AR, professor of writing. *Member:* Society of Children's Book Writers and Illustrators (Arkansas regional advisor, 1991-96), Arkansas Quilters Guild, Authors' Guild, Science Fiction and Fantasy Writers of America.

Awards, Honors

Pick of the List selection, American Booksellers Association, Best One Hundred Children's Books selection, New York Public Library, and Children's Book of the Year selection, Children's Book Committee at Bank Street College, all 1991, all for *The River Dragon.*

Writings

The River Dragon, illustrated by Jean and Mou-Sien Tseng, Lothrop, Lee & Shepard Books (New York, NY), 1991.
The Wayfinder, Greenwillow Books (New York, NY), 2000.
The Journey of Oliver K. Woodman, illustrated by Joe Cepeda, Harcourt (New York, NY), 2002.

Contributor of articles to several quilting magazines, including *Traditional Quiltworks, Quilting Today,* and *American Quilter.* Contributor of articles about writing to periodicals, including *Writer's Digest, Children's Writer,* and *Children's Book Insider.* Author of nonfiction work for children published in *Kid's Wall Street News. The River Dragon* has been translated into Swedish, Danish, Spanish, and Norwegian.

Work in Progress

How Healthy Is Your Environment?, a children's book coauthored with Elleen Hutcheson, for Millbrook Press.

Sidelights

Darcy Pattison began writing as a way to show her home-schooled children how it is done, but soon the exercise became more than a dutiful task performed as part of her responsibilities as teacher to her four children. "Writing became more and more interesting and I devoured books on how to write," Pattison told *SATA.* "Slowly, I spent more and more time on writing, and then started sending stories to publishing houses."

"*The River Dragon,* my first book, was the result of research about dragons," Pattison continued. "I was studying the differences between European and Oriental dragons when I found some interesting information on Oriental dragons. They love pearls and swallows. They can smell very well, and if they smell swallows in a man's belly, they'll eat him to get to the swallows. They are scared of centipedes and five-colored silk scarves. I knew there was a story in these facts."

Reviewers noted that Pattison does indeed incorporate these authentic details in her fairy tale story of *The River Dragon.* Playing off the traditional plot elements of folktales, in which a young man must overcome impossible obstacles to earn the right to marry his beloved, Pattison created the character of Ying Shao, who desires to marry the daughter of the goldsmith. When the father decides to stop the marriage, however, he does so by inviting Ying Shao to dinner three times, knowing that on the way home the young man must cross the bridge under which the terrible river dragon lives. To ensure the peril of Ying Shao, the goldsmith serves swallows at every meal, which the young man must consume in order to be polite. Luckily, Ying Shao is given a clue to help him outwit the dragon at each banquet in the message written in a fortune cookie.

Pattison traces her love of reading and telling stories to her parents, ranch owners in the mountains of New Mexico. As a writer, she was inspired by Frank Herbert and his science fiction fantasy *Dune.* Pattison told *SATA* that her middle-grade novel, *The Wayfinder,* "was inspired by a hiking trip in the mountains of New Mexico. A hail storm and cloudy weather caused the hiking party to lose their way. Afterward, I started wondering about how people find their way to and from places. I created a fantasy world populated with Wayfinders, a special group of people who are born with the ability to locate anything, 'a lost ring, the way home, a blue dress in the marketplace, a lost child.'"

Biographical and Critical Sources

PERIODICALS

Los Angeles Times Book Review, May 10, 1992, review of *The River Dragon,* p. 14.
School Library Journal, December, 1991, JoAnn Rees, review of *The River Dragon,* p. 99.
Washington Post Book World, December 1, 1991, Ann Thwaite, review of *The River Dragon,* p. 21.

*   *   *

PERSUN, Morgan Reed
See WATKINS, Dawn L.

*   *   *

PRACHATICKÁ, Markéta
See KOLÍBALOVÁ, Markéta

R

REIDER, Katja 1960-

Personal

Born November 22, 1960, in Goslar, Germany; daughter of Horst and Eva Reider; married Frank K. Wittstamm, December 10, 1993; children: Felix, Liva. *Education:* University of Göttingen, M.A. (German literature and journalism), 1987. *Religion:* Protestant.

Addresses

Home—Dorotheenstrasse 141, Hamburg 22299, Germany. *E-mail*—k.reider@designnetzwerk.de.

Career

Trainer in a public relations agency, Bonn, Germany, 1987-89; speaker for the "Young Researchers" competition, Hamburg, Germany, 1989-94. Author. *Member:* German Society of Authors (Verband der Schriftsteller VS).

Writings

Vom Glück ein dickes Schwein zu sein, illustrated by Angela von Roehl, Nord-Süd Verlag, 1997, published as *Snail Started It!,* translated by Rosemary Lanning, North-South Books (New York, NY), 1999.
Der doofe Dieter, illustrated by Heribert Schulmeyer, Patmos (Düsseldorf, Germany), 1997.
Pinguin Pudelmütze macht alles anders, Nord-Süd Verlag, 1997.
Wahre Wolkenwunder, Patmos (Düsseldorf, Germany), 1997.
Der Hase mit der goldenen Nase, Arena, 1997.
Flip und die Fußballfüchse, Arena, 1997.
Die Mäuseprinzessin, Nord-Süd Verlag, 1998.
Nicks kleine Nixe, Nord-Süd Verlag, 1998.
Hanibal, das Schloßgespenst, Arena, 1998.
Liebe sagt das Herz, Angst sagt der Bauch, Dino-Verlag, 1998.
Ein Auto für Pit, Arena, 1999.

Katja Reider

Das Schaf mit dem Zitronenohr, illustrated by Angela von Roehl, Patmos (Düsseldorf, Germany), 1999.
Liebe sagt das herz, Angst sagt der Bauch, Bd. 2, Dino-Verlag, 1999.
Zwei wie Butz und Krümel, Coppenrath, 2000.
Maja ahnt was, Schneider-Verlag, 2000.
Max, der Meisterkicker, Schneider-Verlag, 2000.
Kleine Geschichten aus dem Kindergarten, Loewe, 2000.
Gutenachtgeschichten, Coppenrath, 2000.
Weihnachtsgeschichten, Coppenrath, 2000.
Ein Christkind für Kathi, Arena, 2000.
Geschichten vom kleinen Löwen, Loewe Verlag, 2000.

Die Feder, Patmos (Düsseldorf, Germany), 2000.
Joko und Flo im Zauberzoo, Nord-Süd Verlag, 2001.

Sidelights

Katja Reider told *SATA:* "I am not the kind of author who wrote her first stories as a child and secretly stored her manuscript in a bedside table. Instead, I liked to write letters, none of them less than ten pages in length. And furthermore, if somebody gave me a feed, I could develop a story out of it. For years I thought, that is everybody's skill. . . .

"In 1994, when I was spending a rainy vacation on the North Sea side of Germany, I wrote my first story. My friend, Angela von Roehl, who was with me, developed a story board and after our vacation I contacted various publishers. The reaction was as positive as it could be, and I was motivated to write further stories. At first, I created various stories for picture books, later stories for the beginning readers, for older kids, and later still for the young generation, too. I have still ideas for years.

"Angela von Roehl, who illustrated the pictures for *Snail Started It* and got the reader price of the children book award for that, is still the most important illustrator for me. So far, we have made four books together.

Snail starts a chain of insults but learns to say "I'm sorry" in Reider's spirited story. (Cover illustration by Angela von Roehl.)

"Some of my books, like *Snail Started It!,* have been translated into various languages, e.g., English, French, Italian, Danish, Spanish, Korean, and so on."

Reider is a German writer whose first book, *Vom Glück ein dickes Schwein zu sein,* was translated into English as *Snail Started It!* A child-friendly rendering of the axiom that what goes around comes around, *Snail Started It!* tells the story of Snail, who called Pig fat, and though Pig didn't believe it at first, she began to doubt herself, and then feel bad about herself. So when Pig runs into Rabbit, she calls him timid. Rabbit does not take it to heart at first, but then begins to feel bad and so when he runs into Dog, he calls him lazy. This chain of events continues uninterrupted until someone thinks to insult Snail by calling him slow. Suddenly Snail realizes how hurtful name-calling can be, and apologizes to Pig, who apologizes to Rabbit, who apologizes to Dog, and so forth around the same chain of interactions. A reviewer for *Children's Book Review Service* noted that in telling the story this way, Reider makes it easy for children to predict what will happen in each incident and thus to become involved in the storytelling process. And Marsha McGrath, who reviewed *Snail Started It!* for *School Library Journal* observed that though the story features animal characters, children will easily translate its concerns into their own terms. McGrath concluded: "Also fun for reading alone, this book cries to be read aloud at storytimes."

Biographical and Critical Sources

PERIODICALS

Children's Book Review Service, April, 1997, review of *Snail Started It!,* p. 100.
School Library Journal, June, 1997, Marsha McGrath, review of *Snail Started It!,* p. 100.

* * *

RUELLE, Karen Gray 1957-

Personal

Born June 17, 1957, in Maryland; daughter of Edward (an engineer) and Barbara (an artist; maiden name, Ampolsey) Gray; married Lee Gray Ruelle (an artist), September 18, 1988; children: Nina Sophia. *Education:* University of Michigan, B.G.S. (with distinction), 1979, M.L.S., 1980. *Religion:* Jewish.

Addresses

Agent—Liza Voges, Kirchoff/Wohlberg Inc., 866 United Nations Plaza, New York, NY 10017.

Career

Library Journal, New York, NY, assistant editor, 1980-83; *Publishers Weekly,* New York, NY, associate editor, 1983-85; English-Speaking Union, New York, NY, librarian, 1985-90; freelance editor, writer, and illustrator.

Awards, Honors

First runner-up, Partners and Crimes (bookstore) writing competition, 1994.

Writings

Seventy-five Fun Things to Make and Do by Yourself, illustrated by Sandy Haight, Sterling Publications (New York, NY), 1993.

The Book of Baths, illustrated by Lizi Boyd, Harcourt Brace (San Diego, CA), 1997.

The Book of Breakfasts, illustrated by Lizi Boyd, Harcourt Brace (San Diego, CA), 1997.

The Book of Bedtimes, illustrated by Lizi Boyd, Harcourt Brace (San Diego, CA), 1997.

(And illustrator) *The Monster in Harry's Backyard,* Holiday House (New York, NY), 1999.

(And illustrator) *The Thanksgiving Beast Feast,* Holiday House (New York, NY), 1999.

Snow Valentines, Holiday House (New York, NY), 2000.

Spookier Than a Ghost, Holiday House (New York, NY), 2001.

April Fool!, Holiday House (New York, NY), 2002.

Contributor of book reviews to *Library Journal, Publishers Weekly,* and *Kirkus Reviews,* and of articles to *Stamford Advocate/Greenwich Time.*

Work in Progress

Various picture books, a novel, and poetry.

Karen Gray Ruelle

Sidelights

Karen Gray Ruelle once told *SATA:* "When I was growing up, I wanted to be a writer and I also wanted to be an artist. Since it never occurred to me that I could be both as an adult, I was in a state of constant conflict about what I would be when I grew up. Then a dear friend suggested that I write and illustrate children's books. A great fog lifted, and I've been pursuing that dream ever since!

"I've never had a problem coming up with ideas. My life is filled with little stories, made-up and real. I'm the kind of person who sees the humorous and ironic side of everything, and I'm forever imagining shapes and personalities in everything I see. A fire hydrant is a strange creature breaking through the concrete sidewalk; trees express powerful emotions with their branched arms; birds actually talk; houses listen. And I love the music of language. So it makes sense that I like to put these things down, as pictures and stories.

"My mother, the artist, showed me that the world is filled with magic and beauty; my dad, the humorist and engineer, showed me the funny side of life and that anything was possible. Both raised my brother and me to believe that we could do anything, and they instilled in us a sense of fun and enjoyment. We traveled a lot when I was growing up—moving back and forth across the Atlantic several times—so I often feel as though I belong nowhere, which is to say that I belong everywhere, and home can be anywhere. This is a liberating state of mind, meaning that anything is, indeed, possible. On the other hand, I've also always felt a bit lost, looking for that place called home, and so this motivates me to keep the search going.

"I've always been an avid reader, a flashlight-under-the-covers-at-night kind of person. In fact, for a while I was a librarian, just so that I could be surrounded by books. (I thought of myself as not only a Keeper of the Books, but also as a kind of Private Investigator of Information, answering all sorts of odd and fascinating reference questions.) From a very young age, I started making up my own little books. The first was about penguins and how to dress them up for various special occasions—I think I was six years old at the time! I keep coming back to making up books. It's the only place where I do feel completely at home—with my writing and drawing and painting, making up little stories that develop often from a single image or phrase or sound.

"My first book, *Seventy-five Fun Things to Make and Do by Yourself,* evolved quite naturally. I must have the sensibilities of a ten-year-old because it was easy for me to think from that viewpoint. Brainstorming to come up with projects for the book was an extremely creative time for me, and soon my apartment was filled with a jumble of materials, half-finished projects, junk everywhere. From the midst of this constructive chaos, the book emerged. I like to think that my book is not only a useful resource of activities and projects, but that it also motivates independent and creative thinking in its

Harry and Emily prepare a Thanksgiving feast for the animals in their yard in Ruelle's self-illustrated reader. (Cover illustration by Ruelle.)

readers. In addition, I hope the informal, anecdotal tone reads like a storybook, almost a documentation of the development of the creative process.

"Discipline has always been difficult for me. When I have less time to work on my writing and art, the need to focus becomes imperative. Having a child has helped me concentrate on being more productive—I have no choice but to focus during the brief time allotted to my work in the studio. My mother taught me how important it is to give yourself studio time. My husband, an artist as well, concurs, and has been supportive of my need to have a private and personal workspace.

"It's a joy to see my stories and pictures amuse my daughter. I strive to make my work both entertaining and moving. My goal is to combine sweetness and humor without making my work too sentimental or goofy.

"Tomorrow is my studio day. I'll start off with my usual cup of tea and then immerse myself in the world of a bear-like creature named Harry and his younger sister, Samantha. Perhaps something I see on my way to the studio will appear in one of Harry and Samantha's adventures. Later in the day, I'll work on making stories

and pictures fit together, juggling and trying out different combinations to attain the simplicity and rhythm that I like. Maybe next week I'll work on the mid-grade novel I've begun, or perhaps I'll take out that adult novel I began some years ago. So many ideas, so much work, and not nearly enough time in which to do it all!"

That "bear-like creature named Harry" first appeared in *The Monster in Harry's Backyard,* a first-reader chapter book. By the time the book was published, Harry had become a cat, and his little sister's name had evolved from Samantha to Emily. In Ruelle's first story featuring the feline duo, Harry receives a tent for his birthday and happily plays with it indoors for a week before his mother suggests he try his new tent out of doors. But as soon as Harry beds down for the night in the backyard, the strange noises from what appears to be a masked monster send Harry skittering back indoors to hide under his bed. Early morning investigations reveal the source of the noises to be a raccoon, however, which Harry easily dispenses with. Although *School Library Journal* reviewer Jackie Hechtkopf observed that Ruelle's illustrations make a confusing distinction between animals that act like people and animals that act like animals, she

Harry is anxious to use his new tent to camp in the yard—until it gets dark. (Cover illustration by Ruelle.)

also noted the appropriateness of the author's "easy, repetitive language." This distinction did not appear to bother the contributor to *Kirkus Reviews* who reviewed *The Monster in Harry's Backyard,* and concluded: "The suspense of the story and Ruelle's friendly watercolors make this ... ideal for beginners."

Harry and Emily reappear in *The Thanksgiving Beast Feast,* another short chapter book for early readers. In this story, Harry and Emily learn about Thanksgiving from their mother and decide to make a small feast for the animals that live in their backyard. They distribute peanuts to the squirrels, peanut butter-smeared pine-cones for the birds, and cranberries for the chipmunks. Since Emily can't bear the thought of pumpkin pie, they make pumpkin-shaped cookies and share those, too. "Ruelle's minimalist watercolors give this beginning reader an unusually fresh look," remarked a reviewer for *Horn Book,* who also praised the author's story for its gentle humor and theme of helping others.

Biographical and Critical Sources

PERIODICALS

Booklist, March 15, 1994.

Horn Book, September, 1999, review of *The Thanksgiving Beast Feast,* p. 617.

Kirkus Reviews, February 1, 1999, review of *The Monster in Harry's Backyard,* p. 228.

Publishers Weekly, September 27, 1999, review of *The Thanksgiving Beast Feast,* p. 51.

School Library Journal, April, 1999, Jackie Hechtkopf, review of *The Monster in Harry's Backyard,* p. 108.

S–T

SAVITT, Sam 1917(?)-2000

OBITUARY NOTICE—See index for SATA sketch: Born March 22, c. 1917, in Wilkes-Barres, PA; died December 25, 2000, in North Salem, NY. Artist, illustrator, and author. Savitt specialized in horses and frequently illustrated his own children's books, coffee table books, fiction and how-to books. Among his titles are *Step-A-Bit, Rodeo: Cowboys, Bulls, and Broncos, Sam Savitt's True Horse Stories* and *Wild Horse Running*. In addition, Savitt illustrated one hundred and fifty books by other authors and was the official artist for the United States Equestrian Team. Savitt graduated from the Pratt Institute in 1941 and studied at the Art Students League in Manhattan and the New School. He used watercolors, oils, charcoals, and inks in his work, which could be seen in such magazines as *Sports Illustrated* and on posters at racing events like the Kentucky Derby. Among the honors he received were a Boys' Club of America junior book award for 1958's *Midnight,* and a Lifetime Achievement Award from the North American Horsemen's Association.

OBITUARIES AND OTHER SOURCES:

PERIODICALS

New York Times, December 30, 2000, p. B18.
Washington Post, December 31, 2000, p. C8.

*   *   *

SCHMID, Eleonore 1939-

Personal

Born March 15, 1939, in Lucerne, Switzerland; daughter of Josef and Elise (Wunderli) Schmid; married Aja Iskander Schmidlin (a painter), 1969 (divorced, 1973); children: Caspar Iskander. *Education:* School of Arts and Crafts, Lucerne, Switzerland, degree in graphics, 1961.

Addresses

Office—c/o Nord-Sued Verlag Books, Industriestrasse 837, CH-8625, Gossau, Zurich, Switzerland.

Career

Writer and illustrator of children's books. Worked in graphics in Zurich, Switzerland, 1961-64, in Paris, France, 1965, and in New York, NY, 1965-68.

Awards, Honors

Award of Excellence, Society of Illustrators, first prize for illustration, Bologna Book Fair, and Biennale of Illustrations Bratislava medal, 1969, all for *The Tree;* Honor List for Picture Books, German Children's Book Prize, 1969, for *Fenny: Eine Wüstenfuchsgeschichte;* Award of Excellence, Society of Illustrators, for *The Endless Party* and *Horns Everywhere;* Biennale of Illustrations Bratislava medal, for *Das schwarze Schaf.*

Writings

SELF-ILLUSTRATED

(With Etienne Delessert) *The Tree,* Quist (New York, NY), 1966.
(With Etienne Delessert) *The Endless Party,* Quist (New York, NY), 1967.
Horns Everywhere, Quist (New York, NY), 1968.
Tonia: Die Maus mit dem weissen Stein und was ihr begegnete auf der Reise zu Onkel Tobias, Betz, 1970, translation by Lone Thygesen-Blecher published as *Tonia: The Mouse with the White Stone and What Happened on Her Way to See Uncle Tobias,* Putnam (New York, NY), 1974.
Das schwarze Schaf, Nord-Sued Verlag, 1976, published as *Little Black Lamb,* Blackie, 1977.
Mein Kätzchen Sebastian, Nord-Sued Verlag, 1978, published as *My Cat Smokey* Blackie, 1979.
Maerchenkatzen-Kaetzenmaerchen, Nord-Sued Verlag, 1981, published as *Cats' Tales: Feline Fairy Tales*

from around the World, North-South Books (New York, NY), 1985.

Suess, Sauer, Saftig, Nord-Sued Verlag, 1985, published as *Sweet, Sour, Juicy,* Burke (New York, NY), 1985.

Wo ist der kleinste Kern, Nord-Sued Verlag, 1985, published as *Seeds, Nuts, Kernels,* Burke (New York, NY), 1985.

Geschalt und Geschnitten, Nord-Sued Verlag, 1985, published as *Raw, Cooked, Spicy,* Burke (New York, NY), 1985.

Kennst du uns?, Nord-Sued Verlag, 1985, published as *Farm Animals,* North-South Books (New York, NY), 1985.

Allein in der Höhle, Nord-Sued Verlag, 1986, published as *Alone in the Caves,* North-South Books (New York, NY), 1986.

Wach auf, Siebenschlaefer, Sankt Nikolaus ist da, Nord-Sued Verlag, 1989, translation by Elizabeth D. Crawford published as *Wake Up, Dormouse, Santa Claus Is Here,* North-South Books (New York, NY), 1989.

Eine Wasserreise, Nord-Sued Verlag, 1990, published as *The Water's Journey,* North-South Books (New York, NY), 1990.

The Story of Christmas: From the Gospel According to Luke, Nord-Sued Verlag/North-South Books (New York, NY), 1990.

Winde wehen, vom Lufthauch bis zum Sturm, Nord-Sued Verlag, 1992, translation by J. Alison James published

Eleonore Schmid introduces to young readers the life cycle occurring just beneath the earth's surface. (Cover illustration by Schmid.)

as *The Air around Us,* North-South Books (New York, NY), 1992.

Erde lebt, Nord-Sued Verlag, 1994, published as *The Living Earth,* North-South Books (New York, NY), 1994.

The Squirrel and the Moon, translation by Rosemary Lanning, North-South Books (New York, NY), 1996 (originally published as *Eichhörnchen und der Mond*).

Hare's Christmas Gift, translation by Rosemary Lanning, North-South Books (New York, NY), 2000 (originally published as *Weihnachtshase*).

ILLUSTRATOR

Wendy Ann Kesselman, *Franz Tovey and the Rare Animals,* photographs by Norma Holt, Quist (New York, NY), 1968.

Hans Baumann, *Fenny: Eine Wüstenfuchsgeschichte,* Betz, 1968, adapted from the German by J. J. Curle, published as *Fenny: The Desert Fox,* Pantheon (New York, NY), 1970.

James Krüss, *Die Geschichte vom grossen A,* Thienemann (Stuttgart, Germany), 1972.

Robert Louis Stevenson, *Treasure Island,* McKay (New York, NY), 1977.

Marcel Aymé, *Les contes bleus du chat perché,* Gallimard (Paris, France), 1978.

Marcel Aymé, *Les contes rouges du chat perché,* Gallimard (Paris, France), 1978.

Chantal de Marolles, *Machs gut, Kleiner Wolf,* Nord-Sued Verlag, 1979, published as *The Lonely Wolf,* North-South Books (New York, NY), 1986.

Jerzy Andrzejewski, *Der goldene Fuchs,* Huber Verlag, 1979.

Silja Walter, *Eine kleine Bibel,* Huber Verlag, 1980.

La Vue, Gallimard (Paris, France), 1981.

Le Chene, Gallimard (Paris, France), 1982.

Fritz Seuft, *Unter dem Wiehnachtsfaern,* Huber Verlag, 1982.

Jacob Grimm and Wilhelm Grimm, *Die drei Federn,* Middelhanre, 1984, published as *The Three Feathers,* Creative Education (Mankato, MN), 1984.

Regine Schindler, *... und Sarah Lacht,* Kaufmann Verlag, 1984, translation by Renate A. Lass Porter published as *A Miracle for Sarah,* Abingdon (Nashville, TN), 1984.

Regine Schindler, *Christophorus,* Kaufmann Verlag, 1985.

Regine Schindler, *Jesus teilt das Brot,* Kaufmann Verlag, 1986.

Regine Schindler, *Napoleon the Donkey,* North-South Books (New York, NY), 1988 (originally published as *Der Esel Napoleon*).

Heinrich Wiesner, *Jaromir in einer mittelalterlichen Stadt: Schülerroman,* Zytglogge (Bern, Germany), 1990.

Andrienne Soutter-Perrot, *The Oak,* adapted and edited from the French by Kitty Benedict, Creative Education (Mankato, MN), 1993.

Sidelights

The works of Eleonore Schmid, a prolific illustrator and writer, span a variety of genres, from board books for very young children to elaborately illustrated picture books that present both clever tales and scientific facts.

Many of her books have been published in German, and a number of them have appeared in English translation as well. *Farm Animals,* published in 1986, introduces very young children to various barnyard animals through large, colorful drawings in a board book format. A later work, *Wake Up, Dormouse, Santa Claus Is Here,* presents the tale of Gus the dormouse, who longs to meet Santa Claus.

Some of Schmid's other popular works, including *The Water's Journey, The Air around Us,* and *The Living Earth,* use the picture book format to focus on scientific and serious topics that concern the earth and its various components. The most consistent element of these various works, say reviewers, is Schmid's striking illustrations, which stretch across and fill the pages.

In these books, Schmid depicts the water cycle as it flows from the mountains to eventually reach the oceans, the different forms and qualities of the air as it flows over the earth, and the interactions of plants and animals in relation to the earth's surface. In her *School Library Journal* review of *The Water's Journey,* Kathy Piehl related: "Each two-page spread is a well-crafted painting that invites viewers to delight in the natural world."

In *The Living Earth,* Schmid sets out to inform young readers about the Earth's complex ecosystem and how humans can help keep it in balance. She discusses not only how nature continually renews itself, but also how pollution and misuse by humans potentially threaten the future of the planet. The author's ability to explain "these difficult subjects with ease," noted *Booklist* reviewer Lauren Peterson, "makes this third book about the environment a valuable addition to the 'easy' nonfiction shelf." A critic in *Junior Bookshelf* felt that Schmid's illustrations were the main focus of the book. "These are striking and wonderfully detailed," wrote the critic, "so that the scenes depicted seem to come alive." Writing in *School Library Journal,* Piehl similarly praised *The Living Earth,* writing that Schmid's illustrations "of panoramic views and poetic language emphasize the wonder and beauty of the natural world."

1996 saw the U.S. publication of *The Squirrel and the Moon,* a book about Tiff, a young squirrel, who learns about the rhythms of nature from the Moon. During her first year of life, Tiff is captivated by circles, particularly the beauty of the round moon. As the moon wanes, the young squirrel figures that it must be hungry and buries a store of hazelnuts for her distant friend. Tiff and her brothers do not disturb the nuts, even during the long winter months when food is scarce. For her loyalty, Tiff thinks, the moon repays her with a gift: a ring of trees that eventually grow to shelter her and her family. "A lovely story," observed *School Library Journal* critic Rosanne Cerny, who went on to say that the colored pencil illustrations "reflect the plant and animal life the squirrels encounter naturally."

Another small creature is the focus of Schmid's picture book *Hare's Christmas Gift.* After a brief rest, a young hare sets out to find a meal of herbs in the cool twilight

A hare gives the gift of warmth to the newborn Christ child in Schmid's self-illustrated **Hare's Christmas Gift.**

air. However, he senses that something unusual is happening and sets off to investigate. Following the other animals, he finally arrives at a stable where the baby Jesus has been born. The young hare wishes to offer the newborn child a gift and curls his furry body around the sleeping babe to keep him warm throughout the night. Writing in *Publishers Weekly,* a critic called *Hare's Christmas Gift* "an ideal introduction to the miracle of Christmas." According to a *School Library Journal* reviewer, "Children will delight in recognizing the Nativity story as it unfolds from the hare's perspective."

Biographical and Critical Sources

PERIODICALS

Booklist, December 15, 1992, pp. 741-742; February 15, 1995, Lauren Peterson, review of *The Living Earth,* p. 1088.

Horn Book, June, 1980, pp. 280-281; January-February, 1990, Ethel R. Twichell, review of *Wake Up, Dormouse, Santa Claus Is Here,* pp. 56-57.

Junior Bookshelf, February, 1986, review of *Cats' Tales: Feline Fairy Tales from around the World,* p. 20; February, 1995, review of *The Living Earth,* pp. 26-27.

Library Journal, October, 1968, p. 145.

New York Times Book Review, August 4, 1969, p. 20.

Publishers Weekly, April 8, 1974, review of *Tonia: The Mouse with the White Stone and What Happened on*

Her Way to See Uncle Tobias, p. 83; September 25, 2000, review of *Hare's Christmas Gift,* p. 72.
School Library Journal, March, 1986, p. 158; October, 1989, p. 44; November, 1990, Kathy Piehl, review of *The Water's Journey,* p. 98; December, 1992, p. 107; December, 1994, Kathy Piehl, review of *The Living Earth,* p. 102; September, 1996, Rosanne Cerny, review of *The Squirrel and the Moon,* p. 190; October, 2000, review of *Hare's Christmas Gift,* p. 63.*

*   *   *

SIMONT, Marc 1915-

Personal

Born November 23, 1915, in Paris, France; naturalized citizen of the United States, 1936; son of Josep (an illustrator) and Dolors (Baste) Simont; married Sara Dalton (a teacher of handicapped children), April 7, 1945; children: Marc Dalton (Doc). *Education:* Studied art in Paris at Academie Ranson, Academie Julian, and Andre Lhote School, 1932-35, and in New York, NY, at National Academy of Design, 1935-37. *Hobbies and other interests:* Country life, music, cigars, skiing and other sports.

Addresses

Home—Town St., West Cornwall, CT 06796.

Career

Artist and illustrator; since 1939 has worked in portraits, murals, sculpture, prints, and magazine and book illustration; translator and writer of children's books, 1939—. Advocate of community soccer in West Cornwall, CT. *Military service:* U.S. Army, 1943-46; produced visual aids; became sergeant. *Member:* American Veterans Commission, Authors League of America, Authors Guild.

Awards, Honors

Tiffany fellow, 1937; Caldecott Honor Book citation, 1950, for *The Happy Day; Book World* Spring Book Festival Award, and Child Study Association Book Award, both 1952, both for *Jareb;* Caldecott Medal, 1957, for *A Tree Is Nice;* Steck-Vaughn Award, 1957, for *The Trail-Driving Rooster;* Citation of Merit, Society of Illustrators, 1965; Best Book of the Season citation from the *Today Show,* 1972, for *Nate the Great;* National Book Award finalist, 1976, for *The Star in the Pail;* Children's Younger Book Award, New York Academy of Sciences, 1980, for *A Space Story;* New Jersey Institute of Technology Award, 1981, for *Ten Copycats in a Boat and Other Riddles; New York Times* Outstanding Books citation, 1982, for *The Philharmonic Gets Dressed;* Garden State Children's Book Awards, 1984, for *Nate the Great and the Missing Key,* and 1985, for *Nate the Great and the Snowy Trail;* American Institute of Graphic Arts certificate of excellence; Jefferson Cup, 1985, for *In the Year of the Boar and*

Jackie Robinson; Parents' Choice award, 1986, for *The Dallas Titans Get Ready for Bed; Boston Globe/Horn Book* honor citation, 2001, for *The Stray Dog.*

Writings

SELF-ILLUSTRATED

Opera Soufflé: 60 Pictures in Bravura, Schuman, 1950.
Polly's Oats, Harper (New York, NY), 1951.
(With Red Smith) *How to Get to First Base: A Picture Book of Baseball,* Schuman, 1952.
The Lovely Summer, Harper (New York, NY), 1952.
Mimi, Harper (New York, NY), 1954.
The Plumber Out of the Sea, Harper (New York, NY), 1955.
The Contest at Paca, Harper (New York, NY), 1959.
How Come Elephants?, Harper (New York, NY), 1965.
Afternoon in Spain, Morrow (New York, NY), 1965.
(With members of staff of Boston Children's Medical Center) *A Child's Eye View of the World,* Delacorte (New York, NY), 1972.
The Goose That Almost Got Cooked, Scholastic (New York, NY), 1997.
The Stray Dog: From a True Story by Reiko Sassa, HarperCollins (New York, NY), 2001.

TRANSLATOR

Federico Garcia Lorca, *The Lieutenant Colonel and the Gypsy,* Doubleday, 1971.
Francesc Sales, *Ibrahim,* illustrations by Eulalia Sariola, Lippincott, 1989.

ILLUSTRATOR

Emma G. Sterne, *The Pirate of Chatham Square: A Story of Old New York,* Dodd, 1939.
Ruth Bryan Owens, *The Castle in the Silver Woods,* Dodd, 1939.
Albert Carr, *Men of Power,* Viking (New York, NY), 1940.
Mildred Cross, *Isabella, Young Queen of Spain,* Dodd, 1941.
Charlotte Jackson, *Sarah Deborah's Day,* Dodd, 1941.
Richard Hatch, *All Aboard the Whale,* Dodd, 1942.
Dougal's Wish, Harper (New York, NY), 1942.
Meindert DeJong, *Billy and the Unhappy Bull,* Harper (New York, NY), 1946.
Margaret Wise Brown, *The First Story,* Harper (New York, NY), 1947.
Iris Vinton, *Flying Ebony,* Dodd, 1947.
Robbie Trent, *The First Christmas,* Harper (New York, NY), 1948, new edition, 1990.
Andrew Lang, editor, *The Red Fairy Book,* new edition, Longmans, Green, 1948.
Ruth Krauss, *The Happy Day,* Harper (New York, NY), 1949.
Ruth Krauss, *The Big World and the Little House,* Schuman, 1949.
Red Smith, *Views of Sport,* Knopf (New York, NY), 1949.
Meindert DeJong, *Good Luck Duck,* Harper (New York, NY), 1950.
Ruth Krauss, *The Backward Day,* Harper (New York, NY), 1950.
James Thurber, *The Thirteen Clocks,* Simon & Schuster (New York, NY), 1951.

Marjorie B. Paradis, *Timmy and the Tiger,* Harper (New York, NY), 1952.

Alister Cooke, *Christmas Eve,* Knopf (New York, NY), 1952.

Miriam Powell, *Jareb,* Crowell (New York, NY), 1952.

The American Riddle Book, Schuman, 1954.

Elizabeth H. Lansing, *Deer Mountain Hideaway,* Crowell (New York, NY), 1954.

Jean Fritz, *Fish Head,* Coward (New York, NY), 1954.

Elizabeth H. Lansing, *Deer River Raft,* Crowell (New York, NY), 1955.

Fred Gipson, *The Trail-Driving Rooster,* Harper (New York, NY), 1955.

Julius Schwartz, *Now I Know,* Whittlesey House, 1955.

Janice May Udry, *A Tree Is Nice,* Harper (New York, NY), 1955.

Julius Schwartz, *I Know a Magic House,* Whittlesey House, 1956.

Thomas Liggett, *Pigeon Fly Home,* Holiday House, 1956.

Chad Walsh, *Nellie and Her Flying Crocodile,* Harper (New York, NY), 1956.

James Thurber, *The Wonderful "O",* Simon & Schuster (New York, NY), 1957.

Maria Leach, *The Rainbow Book of American Folk Tales and Legends,* World, 1958.

Alexis Ladas, *The Seal That Couldn't Swim,* Little, Brown (Boston, MA), 1959.

James A. Kjelgaard, *The Duckfooted Hound,* Crowell (New York, NY), 1960.

Ruth Krauss, *A Good Man and His Wife,* Harper (New York, NY), 1962.

Julius Schwartz, *The Earth Is Your Spaceship,* Whitlesey House, 1963.

David McCord, *Every Time I Climb a Tree,* Little Brown (Boston, MA), 1967.

What To Do When There's Nothing To Do, Dell (New York, NY), 1967.

Charlton Ogburn, Jr., *Down, Boy, Down, Blast You!,* Morrow (New York, NY), 1967.

Janet Chenery, *Wolfie,* Harper (New York, NY), 1969.

Janice May Udry, *Glenda,* Harper (New York, NY), 1969.

Edward Fales, Jr., *Belts On, Buttons Down,* Dell, 1971.

David McCord, *The Star in the Pail,* Little, Brown (Boston, MA), 1975.

Richard Kennedy, *The Contests at Cowlick,* Little, Brown (Boston, MA), 1975.

Eulalie Osgood Grover, *Robert Louis Stevenson, Teller of Tales,* Gale (Detroit, MI), 1975.

Beverly Keller, *The Beetle Bush,* Coward (New York, NY), 1976.

Karla Kuskin, *A Space Story,* Harper (New York, NY), 1978.

Joan Lowery Nixon, *Danger in Dinosaur Valley,* Putman (New York, NY), 1978.

Faith McNulty, *Mouse and Tim,* Harper (New York, NY), 1978.

Faith McNulty, *How to Dig a Hole to the Other Side of the World,* Harper (New York, NY), 1979.

Alvin Schwartz, editor, *Ten Copycats in a Boat, and Other Riddles,* Harper (New York, NY), 1979.

Faith McNulty, *The Elephant Who Couldn't Forget,* Harper (New York, NY), 1979.

Marc Simont illustrated Nate the Great's first international case in **Nate the Great Saves the King of Sweden,** *written by Marjorie Weinman Sharmat.*

Mitchell Sharmat, *Reddy Rattler and Easy Eagle,* Doubleday, 1979.

David McCord, *Speak Up: More Rhymes of the Never Was and Always Is,* Little, Brown (Boston, MA), 1980.

Charlotte Zolotow, *If You Listen,* Harper (New York, NY), 1980.

Marjorie Weinman Sharmat, *Chasing After Annie,* Harper (New York, NY), 1981.

Peggy Parish, *No More Monsters For Me!,* Harper (New York, NY), 1981.

Karla Kuskin, *The Philharmonic,* Harper (New York, NY), 1982.

Julie Delton, *My Uncle Nikos,* Crowell (New York, NY), 1983.

Mollie Hunter, *The Knight of the Golden Plain,* Harper (New York, NY), 1983.

Edward Davis, *Bruno the Pretzel Man,* Harper (New York, NY), 1984.

Bette Bao Lord, *The Year of the Boar and Jackie Robinson,* Harper (New York, NY), 1984.

Joan W. Blos, *Martin's Hats,* Morrow (New York, NY), 1984.

John Reynolds Gardiner, *Top Secret,* Little, Brown (Boston, MA), 1984.

Franklyn Mansfield Branley, *Volcanoes,* Crowell (New York, NY), 1985.

Mollie Hunter, *The Three-Day Enchantment,* Harper (New York, NY), 1985.

Karla Kuskin, *The Dallas Titans Get Ready for Bed,* Harper (New York, NY), 1986.

Franklyn Mansfield Branley, *Journey into a Black Hole,* Crowell (New York, NY), 1986.

Wendell V. Tangborn, *Glaciers,* Crowell, 1988, revised edition, Harper (New York, NY), 1988.

Sing a Song of Popcorn, Scholastic, 1988.

Charlotte Zolotow, *The Quiet Mother and the Noisy Little Boy,* Harper (New York, NY), 1989.

Franklyn Mansfield Branley, *What Happened to the Dinosaurs?,* Harper (New York, NY), 1989.

James Thurber, *Many Moons,* Harcourt (New York, NY), 1990.

Willy Welch, *Playing Right Field,* Scholastic (New York, NY), 1995.

Ruth Krauss, *Happy Day,* Harper (New York, NY), 1995.

Betsy Cromer Byers, *My Brother, Ant,* Viking (New York, NY), 1996.

Betsy Cromer Byers, *Ant Plays Bear,* Viking (New York, NY), 1997.

In **Many Moons,** *Simont illustrated James Thurber's tale of a princess who wished for the moon and the court jester who fulfilled the wish.*

Janice May Udry, *Glenda Glinka, Witch-at-Large,* Harper-Trophy (New York, NY), 1997.

Marjorie Weinman Sharmat, *Richie and the Fritzes,* HarperCollins (New York, NY), 1997.

David McCord, *Every Time I Climb a Tree,* Little, Brown (Boston, MA), 1999.

ILLUSTRATOR; "NATE THE GREAT" SERIES BY MARJORIE WEINMAN SHARMAT

Nate the Great, Coward (New York, NY), 1972.

Nate the Great Goes Undercover, Coward (New York, NY), 1974.

Nate the Great and the Lost List, Coward (New York, NY), 1975.

Nate the Great and the Phony Clue, Coward (New York, NY), 1977.

Nate the Great and the Sticky Case, Coward (New York, NY), 1978.

Nate the Great and the Missing Key, Coward (New York, NY), 1981.

Nate the Great and the Snowy Trail, Coward (New York, NY), 1982.

Nate the Great and the Fishy Prize, Coward (New York, NY), 1985.

Nate the Great and the Boring Beach Bag, Coward (New York, NY), 1987.

Nate the Great Stalks Stupidweed, Coward (New York, NY), 1987.

Nate the Great Goes Down in the Dumps, Coward (New York, NY), 1989.

Nate the Great and the Halloween Hunt, Coward (New York, NY), 1989.

(By Marjorie Weinman Sharmat and Craig Sharmat) *Nate the Great and the Musical Note,* Coward (New York, NY), 1990.

Nate the Great and the Stolen Base, Coward (New York, NY), 1992.

Nate the Great and the Pillowcase, Delacorte (New York, NY), 1993.

Nate the Great and the Mushy Valentine, Delacorte (New York, NY), 1994.

Nate the Great and the Tardy Tortoise, Delacorte (New York, NY), 1995.

Nate the Great and the Crunchy Christmas, Delacorte (New York, NY), 1996.

Nate the Great Saves the King of Sweden, Delacorte (New York, NY), 1997.

Nate the Great and Me: The Case of the Fleeing Fang, Delacorte (New York, NY), 1998.

Adaptations

Nate the Great Goes Undercover and *Nate the Great and the Sticky Case* were made into films. An excerpt from *Nate the Great* was adapted and is on permanent display at the Museum of Science and Industry, Chicago, Illinois.

Sidelights

Marc Simont was born in 1915 in Paris, France, to parents from the Catalonian region of northern Spain. He attended schools in Paris, Barcelona, Spain, and New

York City, because his parents kept traveling. Simont's father came to the United States after World War I and decided to become an American citizen. Because that process took five years, Simont, with his mother and two sisters, lived with his grandfather in Barcelona. During this time he sketched bullfighters and soccer players.

This repeated relocation affected his performance as a student. "I was always more concerned with what a teacher looked like than what he said, which didn't do my algebra any good," the illustrator explained in *More Junior Authors.* Simont did not graduate from high school, although he became fluent in French, English, Spanish, and Catalonian. On the other hand, the traveling sharpened his skills as an observer—skills important for an artist. He studied art at the Academie Julian, the Academie Ranson and with André Lhote in Paris, and in New York City at National Academy of Design. But he said his most important art teacher was his father, an illustrator for *L'Illustration* magazine. With a sister and two uncles also making a living as artists, he considers art the family trade.

When he returned to the United States, Simont worked odd jobs, painted portraits, and drew illustrations for pulp magazines. Eventually he became an illustrator of picture books for children. Books by many notable children's writers, including James Thurber, Ruth Krauss, Charlotte Zolotow, and Marjorie Weinman Sharmat, have been published with his illustrations. Simont illustrated Sharmat's book *Nate the Great,* featuring the boy detective who solves neighborhood mysteries, and has won several awards for books in the *Nate the Great* series; two were made into films. His illustrations for Janice May Udry's *A Tree Is Nice* won the Caldecott Medal in 1957, and his pictures for Ruth Krauss's *The Happy Day* earned him a Caldecott Honor Book citation.

Critics have pointed out that Simont's illustrations are perfectly suited to the text in books by a variety of children's authors. George A. Woods comments in the *New York Times Book Review* about Karla Kuskin's *The Philharmonic Gets Dressed:* "Simont has not missed a beat. His musicians are a varied band in terms of age, race and physique. He conveys the awkward stance as well as the graceful pose, the little scenes and moments that are all around us—the hole in the sock, the graffiti inside the subway car as well as the advertising posters." Kenneth Marantz, writing about the same book in *School Library Journal,* notes that Simont's "ability to invest such convincing feelings of life using an almost cartoon-like simplicity is remarkable." *New York Times Book Review* contributor Nora Magid observes that Simont's illustrations in *How to Dig a Hole to the Other Side of the World* have terrific emotional power: "Simont's pictures break the heart. The child voyager is at once intrepid and vulnerable" as he takes an imaginary journey through the earth's crust to China. Other features of Simont's artistic style are a method of composition that gives continuity to the pictures in sequence, and humor that is inviting to readers of all ages.

In addition to illustrating books by other authors, Simont has also written and illustrated his own books for children. *The Goose That Almost Got Cooked* "is a rare treat" by this "veteran author/illustrator" noted Barbara Elleman in the *School Library Journal.* In this work, Simont blends his illustrations with a humorous and suspenseful tale of an adventurous goose who avoids the roasting pan with a narrow escape. A reviewer for *Publishers Weekly* noted that, "the superbly modulated art has no trouble getting this tale off the ground."

Another self-illustrated work, *The Stray Dog: From a True Story by Reiko Sassa,* appeared in 2001. Here, a family on a Saturday picnic finds a stray dog, names him Willy, and plays with him for the day. As the family prepares to leave, the parents will not let their new friend accompany them home, thinking that he probably belongs to someone else. But during the week, the family finds itself thinking about the dog and eventually return to the same picnic spot the next weekend. Here they save Willy from the dogcatcher and decide to keep him in the family permanently. "This picture Books has all the earmarks of a classic," wrote a *Horn Book* contributor, who noted that the text is spare—appropriately so, as the pictures are surprisingly eloquent." *School Library Journal* reviewer Mary Ann Carcich predicted that *The Stray Dog* would be "a great tale for any kid who's dreamed of adopting a pet."

"I believe that if I'm satisfied with something I've done, children will like it also," Simont told *SATA.*

Biographical and Critical Sources

BOOKS

Caldecott Medal Books: 1938-1957, Horn Book, 1957.
Hopkins, Lee Bennett, *Books Are by People: Interviews with 104 Authors and Illustrators of Books for Young Children,* Citation Press, 1969.
Kingman, Lee, editor, *Newbery and Caldecott Medal Books: 1956-1965,* Horn Book, 1965.
Klemin, Diana, *The Art of Art for Children's Books,* Clarkson Potter, 1966.
More Junior Authors, H. W. Wilson, 1963.

PERIODICALS

Booklist, January 1, 2001, Hazel Rochman, review of *The Stray Dog: From a True Story by Reiko Sassa,* p. 974.
Book World, November 5, 1972, p. 4.
Christian Science Monitor, November 11, 1971.
Horn Book, February, 1980, p. 140; April, 1983, p. 158; February, 1984, p. 54; June, 1984, p. 318; May-June, 1985, p. 326; November-December, 1986, p. 737; November-December, 1989, p. 788; January, 2001, review of *The Stray Dog: From a True Story by Reiko Sassa,* p. 86.
New York Times Book Review, October 31, 1965, p. 56; November 18, 1979, Nora Magid, review of *How to Dig a Hole to the Other Side of the World;* October 17, 1982, George A. Woods, review of *The Philharmonic Gets Dressed,* p. 37; November 6, 1983, p. 43; May 20, 1984, p. 28; November 9, 1986, p. 40.

Publishers Weekly, April 20, 1992, review of *The Lovely Summer,* p. 55; June 23, 1997, review of *The Goose That Almost Got Cooked,* p. 91.

School Library Journal, August, 1982, Kenneth Marantz, review of *The Philharmonic Gets Dressed,* p. 99; August, 1984, p. 56; October, 1989, p. 100; June, 1992, Eve Larkin, review of *The Lovely Summer,* p. 103; August, 1997, Barbara Elleman, review of *The Goose That Almost Got Cooked,* p. 142; February, 2001, Mary Ann Carcich, review of *The Stray Dog: From a True Story by Reiko Sassa,* p. 106.

Science Books and Films, November-December, 1988, p. 95.

Time, December 4, 1978, p. 100; December 20, 1982, p. 79.*

* * *

SMALL, David 1945-

Personal

Born February 12, 1945, in Detroit, MI; son of Edward Pierce (a doctor) and Elizabeth (maiden name, Murphy) Small; married Sarah Stewart (a writer), September, 1980; children: five (from previous marriages). *Education:* Wayne State University, B.F.A., 1968; Yale University, M.F.A., 1972. *Hobbies and other interests:* Swimming, traveling, sketching out-of-doors.

Addresses

Home—25626 Simpson Road, Mendon, MI 49072.

Career

Author and illustrator of children's books; freelance artist. State University of New York—Fredonia College, assistant professor of art, 1972-78; Kalamazoo College, Kalamazoo, MI, assistant professor of art, 1978-83, artist-in-residence, 1983-86.

Awards, Honors

Children's Books of the Year list, Library of Congress, Best Books for Spring list, *School Library Journal,* and Parents' Choice Remarkable Book, Parents' Choice Foundation (PCF), all 1982, all for *Eulalie and the Hopping Head;* Notable Book for Children in the Field of Social Studies, National Council of Social Studies and Children's Book Council, 1983, for *Mean Chickens and Wild Cucumbers;* Best Books list, *School Library Journal* and *Booklist,* both 1984, both for *Anna and the Seven Swans;* Children's Books of the Year list, Child Study Association of America, 1985, for *The Christmas Box;* Parents' Choice Award for literature, PCF, 1985, and *Reading Rainbow* selection, both for *Imogene's Antlers; Redbook* Award, and Notable Book, American Library Association (ALA), both 1988, both for *Company's Coming;* Parents' Choice Award for picture books, PCF, 1989, for *As: A Surfeit of Similes,* and 1990, for *Box and Cox;* Caldecott Honor Book selection, ALA, 1998, for *The Gardener;* Caldecott Medal, ALA, 2001,

for *So You Want to Be President?;* Heartland Award, 2001, for *The Journey.*

Writings

SELF-ILLUSTRATED PICTURE BOOKS

Eulalie and the Hopping Head, Macmillan (New York, NY), 1982.

Imogene's Antlers, Crown (New York, NY), 1985.

Paper John, Farrar, Straus (New York, NY), 1987.

Ruby Mae Has Something to Say, Crown (New York, NY), 1992.

George Washington's Cows, Farrar, Straus, Giroux (New York, NY), 1994.

Hoover's Bride, Crown (New York, NY), 1995.

Fenwick's Suit, Farrar, Straus, Giroux (New York, NY), 1996.

ILLUSTRATOR

Nathan Zimelman, *Mean Chickens and Wild Cucumbers,* Macmillan (New York, NY), 1983.

Jonathan Swift, *Gulliver's Travels,* Morrow (New York, NY), 1983.

Burr Tillstrom, *The Kuklapolitan Players Present: The Dragon Who Lived Downstairs,* Morrow (New York, NY), 1984.

Maida Silverman, *Anna and the Seven Swans,* translated from the Russian by Natasha Frumin, Morrow (New York, NY), 1984.

Eve Merriam, *The Christmas Box,* Morrow (New York, NY), 1985.

David Small

Arthur Yorinks, *Company's Coming,* Crown (New York, NY), 1988.

Peggy Thomson, *The King Has Horse's Ears,* Simon & Schuster (New York, NY), 1988.

Milton Meltzer, *American Politics: How It Really Works,* Morrow (New York, NY), 1989.

Norton Juster, *As: A Surfeit of Similes,* Morrow (New York, NY), 1989, revised edition published as *As Silly as Knees, as Busy as Bees: An Astounding Assortment of Similes,* Beech Tree (New York, NY), 1998.

Grace Chetwin, *Box and Cox,* Bradbury (New York, NY), 1990.

Sarah Stewart, *The Money Tree,* Farrar, Straus, Giroux (New York, NY), 1991.

Eve Merriam, *Fighting Words,* Morrow (New York, NY), 1992.

Beverly Cleary, *Petey's Bedtime Story,* Morrow (New York, NY), 1993.

Sarah Stewart, *The Library,* Farrar, Straus, Giroux (New York, NY), 1995.

Sarah Stewart, *The Gardener,* Farrar, Straus, Giroux (New York, NY), 1997.

Bonny Becker, *The Christmas Crocodile,* Simon & Schuster (New York, NY), 1998.

Carl Sandburg, *The Huckabuck Family and How They Raised Popcorn in Nebraska and Quit and Came Back,* Farrar, Straus, Giroux (New York, NY), 1999.

Judith St. George, *So You Want to Be President?,* Philomel (New York, NY), 2000.

Sarah Stewart, *The Journey,* Farrar, Straus, Giroux (New York, NY), 2001.

Russell Hoban, *The Mouse and His Child,* Arthur A. Levine Books (New York, NY), 2001.

Judith St. George, *So You Want to Be An Inventor?,* Philomel (New York, NY), 2002.

Sidelights

Caldecott medalist David Small is known as an author and illustrator of children's books that feature clever text and pictures that entertain readers both young and old. Born in Detroit, Michigan, Small did not intend to become an artist. Although he enjoyed creating his own cartoons as a child, as a teenager he found himself attracted to literature and intended to make a living as a playwright. Setting out on his chosen career path, Small began attending Montieth College at Wayne State University. However, during his sophomore year, Small, with the help of a fellow classmate, realized that his artistic talents were greater at the time than his literary ones and transferred to the university's art school. "I found a real home in the Art Department at Wayne State University," Small once wrote in *Sixth Book of Junior Authors and Illustrators.* "I felt that I had been suddenly washed ashore in a country where people spoke my own language. I felt alive. I grew stronger. I knew that in this world of art I could find a place." In 1968, Small graduated with a bachelor's of fine arts degree, and next attended Yale University, earning his master's degree in fine arts as well.

After finishing his university education, Small remained connected to the academic world, first teaching at the

A young country girl determines to get her city uncle to smile just once in **The Gardener,** *written by Sarah Stewart and illustrated by Small.*

State University of New York—Fredonia College, and then at Kalamazoo College. The same year he stopped teaching, 1982, his first self-illustrated children's book appeared. *Eulalie and the Hopping Head* tells the story of the irrepressible toad daughter and was named to several recommended book lists. Other early works authored and illustrated by Small were also well received by critics, including *Imogene's Antlers,* a silly tale about a young girl who sprouts a rack of antlers on her head one day, *Paper John,* the story of a simple man who uses his paper-folding skills to outwit the devil, and *Ruby Mae Has Something to Say,* a book that features a tongue-tied woman who wishes to share the word of peace at the United Nations. In a review of *Paper John, Booklist* reviewer Ilene Cooper called Small "one of the most inventive illustrators around today."

Small is equally well known for the illustrations he has provided for other children's authors, such as Beverly Cleary, Eve Merriam, Russell Hoban, and his own wife, Sarah Stewart. In 1992, Small provided the artwork for *Fighting Words,* written by the late poet Eve Merriam. Country-boy Dale and city-girl Leda just do not get along. Each envious of the other's life, one day the two decide to settle the score, but with words not their fists. Through the city, across the river, and into the country, the duo try to out insult each other with epithets like "NINCOMPOOP," "BUFFOON," and "POPPYCOCK."

At the end of the tussle, both Dale and Leda, having screamed themselves hoarse, agree to resume their verbal wars on another day. *School Library Journal* contributor Luann Toth remarked that the characters "take center stage in the quirky pen-and-ink and watercolor drawings with perfect facial expressions to match each verbal assault." Calling the book "an original," *Booklist* reviewer Carolyn Phelan wrote that "Small's captivating ink-and-watercolor artwork sets the war in a variety of entertaining settings."

In 1991, Small began illustrating works written by his wife, children's author Sarah Stewart. The first of these collaborations, *The Money Tree,* follows the tale of a tree in Miss McGillicuddy's yard that grows leaves in the shape of dollar bills. All summer long townsfolk and strangers alike greedily pick currency from the tree and even ask for branches of the tree to plant on their own land. A woman who keeps herself busy making quilts, tending her garden, and flying kites, Miss McGillicuddy seems unaffected by all of the attention her new tree receives. But when autumn arrives and all of the tree's leaves are gone, the independent and patient woman decides to take action, cutting down the strange specimen and using its wood in her fireplace. As the weather turns bitterly cold and Miss McGillicuddy warms herself over the fire, readers see that the tree has other valuable

Small hilariously illustrated Judith St. George's **So You Want to Be President?,** *showcasing the variety of characteristics of forty-one U.S. presidents from George Washington to Bill Clinton.*

properties as well. Reviewers praised Small's illustrations for the story. "Often reminiscent of the art of Carl Larsson," observed a *Publishers Weekly* critic, "these evocative, pastel-filled watercolors echo the hushed, mysterious tone of the tale." Noting that *The Money Tree* could be used in discussions with children about "contemporary values," *Horn Book* reviewer Hanna B. Zeigler felt that "Small's charming and detailed illustrations portray a strong, independent woman whose life is graceful and meaningful."

In *The Library,* Small illustrated Stewart's rhyming text about a woman who loves to read. Ever since she was a child, Elizabeth Brown has been collecting books and reading them, intending to read every book ever published. While other girls played with dolls and skates, she occupied herself with piles and piles of books. As a grown woman, Elizabeth continues to buy and consume books until she notices that she has no room for even one more volume in her over-stuffed house. Realizing she has a problem, the bookworm comes up with an idea that helps everyone by donating her life's collection to the town and creating a library for all to enjoy. *New York Times Book Review* critic Rebecca Pepper Sinkler commented on how well Small's illustrations fit Stewart's text. "He never dominates Ms. Stewart's text," Sinkler wrote, "instead, [Small] grounds the action of the story in time and place.... It's a joy to look at, from its delicately framed full-page illustrations to the witty doodads that fill the white spaces around the smaller ones." Other reviewers found kind words about *The Library* as well. A *Publishers Weekly* contributor noted that "Small's ... airy illustrations charm with historical touches and soothing pastel hues," while *Booklist*'s Ilene Cooper said that the illustrator's "framed pastel artwork uses wonderfully unique perspectives.... Reading has never looked quite so delicious."

Taken from Carl Sandburg's *Rootabaga Stories, The Huckabuck Family and How They Raised Popcorn in Nebraska and Quit and Came Back* features a story about a farmer, Jonas Jonas Huckabuck, his wife, Mama Mama, and his daughter, Pony Pony. While in Nebraska, the threesome live on a farm, raising corn, until one day, Pony Pony discovers a silver buckle amongst the squash. Her parents warn that the buckle is a sign of luck, but they are unsure if the shiny object signifies good luck or bad. A fire the next day that turns all of their harvest into popcorn reveals to the Huckabucks that their fortunes have turned for the worse, so the family decides to leave until the blizzard of popcorn clears itself. Many cities later, the family finds a second buckle to match the first and set off for home, realizing that their farm is ready to welcome them back. Several reviewers applauded Small for introducing the *Rootabaga Stories* to a new audience as well as for his accompanying illustrations. Writing in *Horn Book,* a critic predicted that "with a new treatment by David Small in picture book format, this particular selection ... should reach a contemporary audience." Small "depicts the family's peripatetic lifestyle with wry wit and droll details," claimed a *Publishers Weekly* reviewer, "leading readers of this engaging book to feel they've met with the good kind of luck."

Two other books written by Stewart and illustrated by Small, *The Gardener* and *The Journey,* each tell the story of a young girl though a series of letters and diary entries, respectively. In *The Gardener,* Lydia Grace must help her unemployed parents during the Great Depression by working in her uncle's bakery. Lydia does not mind working in the city, though she misses her favorite past time, tending her beloved plants and flowers. Through letters to her family in the country, readers learn how she adapts to city life by turning her uncle's apartment and rooftop into a beautiful garden. "Small controls the action with dramatic angles," suggested *Horn Book* contributor Susan P. Bloom. "Objects placed close up ... afford deep perspective to a page bustling with detail." Noting that the illustrator's paintings "are a bit more softly focused than usual," Stephanie Zvirin of *Booklist* nonetheless said that "they are still recognizably [Small's], with wonderfully expressive characters, ink-line details, and patches of pastel."

The Journey relates the story of a young Amish girl, Hannah, as she visits Chicago for the first time. Through a series of diary entries, Hannah explains all the wonders she sees in the city and compares them to life in the country. She is amazed by the tall skyscrapers, the elevated train system, and the choices of clothing available in the city. However, by the end of her trip, she realizes how much she misses her family and the activities on the farm. Accompanying Hannah's recollections of her daily events are Small's double-page illustrations, with one spread showing the young girl amid the hustle and bustle of Chicago, and the next one offering a contrasting scene from Hanna's Amish life at home. *School Library Journal* contributor Wendy Lukehart found the book's "design perfectly melded to its subtle message." Writing in *Publishers Weekly,* a critic explained that "Small effectively depicts the spare, serene Amish lifestyle and ... underscores the sharp contrast between the two settings."

Continuing to illustrate for other authors, Small provided the artwork for Judith St. George's *So You Want to Be President?,* published in 2000. According to *U.S. News and World Report* writer Marc Silver, Small found the illustrations for this book a challenge. Having only five months to capture the essence of forty-two U.S. Presidents, Small told Silver that, "the handsomer they are, the harder they are to draw." However, "sketching freely, wildly at times," wrote *Horn Book* contributor Patricia Lee Gauch, Small finished the pictures for the book, going on to earn the highest award in children's book illustration, a Caldecott Medal, for his efforts.

So You Want to Be President? offers young readers a great deal of lighthearted information about the men who have held the highest office in the United States. Ranging from trivia about how many Presidents have been named James (six) to how many Presidents have been born in a log cabin (eight), the fact-filled book

gives readers a humorous look at the former occupants of the White House. Small's award-winning illustrations include depictions of Richard Nixon flashing a "V" for victory sign in the White House bowling lanes, a rotund William H. Taft being hoisted by a crane into a bathtub, and the somber Woodrow Wilson doing a little dance, all events based in part on real-life incidents. *Booklist* reviewer Carolyn Phelan claimed that "Small's delightful illustrations, usually droll and sometimes hilarious, will draw children to the book and entertain them from page to page," while a *Publishers Weekly* critic felt that "the comical caricatured artwork emphasizes some of the presidents' best known qualities and amplifies the playful tone of the text."

Whether illustrating his own writings or works by other children's authors, Small has earned a reputation as an artist whose work captures the spirit of the story. With his distinctive style, Small continues to earn praise from reviewers and readers alike. Small concluded in *Sixth Book of Junior Authors and Illustrators* that children's picture books are "the most pleasurable" things he does in art. "Since I take this work very seriously, the real problem is in finding suitable projects.... I want to make a real contribution to children's literature, not simply add to the growing heap."

Biographical and Critical Sources

BOOKS

Children's Literature Review, Vol. 53, Gale (Detroit, MI), 1999.
Merriam, Eve, *Fighting Words,* Morrow (New York, NY), 1992.
Sixth Book of Junior Authors and Illustrators, edited by Sally Holmes Holtze, H. W. Wilson Co. (New York, NY), 1989.

PERIODICALS

Booklist, June 15, 1987, Ilene Cooper, review of *Paper John,* p. 1608; May 15, 1992, Carolyn Phelan, review of *Fighting Words,* p. 1688; March 15, 1995, Ilene Cooper, review of *The Library,* p. 1338; June 1, 1997, Stephanie Zvirin, review of *The Gardener,* p. 1722; September 15, 1999, Linda Perkins, review of *The Huckabuck Family and How They Raised Popcorn in Nebraska and Quit and Came Back,* p. 270; July, 2000, Carolyn Phelan, review of *So You Want to Be President?,* p. 2034; March 15, 2001, Ellen Mandel, review of *The Journey,* p. 1399.
Horn Book, January-February, 1992, Hanna Zeigler, review of *The Money Tree,* p. 62; July-August, 1995, Ann A. Flowers, review of *The Library,* p. 454; November-December, 1997, Susan P. Bloom, review of *The Gardener,* p. 673; September, 1999, review of *The Huckabuck Family and How They Raised Popcorn in Nebraska and Quit and Came Back,* p. 600; March, 2001, review of *The Journey,* p. 202; July, 2001, Patricia Lee Gauch, "David Small," p. 421.
New York Times Book Review, June 4, 1995, Rebecca Pepper Sinkler, review of *The Library,* p. 25; May 20, 2001, review of *The Journey.*

Publishers Weekly, August 30, 1991, review of *The Money Tree,* p. 83; April 18, 1995, review of *The Library,* p. 61; June 2, 1997, review of *The Gardener,* p. 70; July 26, 1999, review of *The Huckabuck Family and How They Raised Popcorn in Nebraska and Quit and Came Back,* p. 89; July 17, 2000, review of *So You Want to Be President?,* p. 193; January 8, 2001, review of *The Journey,* p. 66.

School Library Journal, June, 1992, Luann Toth, review of *Fighting Words,* p. 99; March, 2001, Wendy Lukehart, review of *The Journey,* p. 220.

U.S. News and World Report, January 29, 2001, Marc Silver, "The Cartoonist in Chief," p. 8.

*   *   *

SNICKET, Lemony 1970-
(Daniel Handler)

Personal

Born Daniel Handler, 1970, in San Francisco, CA; married Lisa Brown. *Education:* Wesleyan University.

Addresses

Home—San Francisco, CA. *Office*—c/o Author Mail, HarperCollins, 10 East 53rd St., New York, NY 10022. *E-mail*—lsnicket@harpercollins.com.

Career

Author, poet, and self-styled "studied expert in rhetorical analysis." Comedy writer, *The House of Blues Radio Hour,* San Francisco, CA; freelance book and movie reviewer.

Awards, Honors

Academy of American Poets Prize, 1990; Olin Fellowship, 1992.

Writings

FICTION FOR CHILDREN; AS LEMONY SNICKET; "A SERIES OF UNFORTUNATE EVENTS" SERIES

The Bad Beginning, illustrated by Bret Helquist, HarperTrophy (New York, NY), 1999.
The Reptile Room, illustrated by Bret Helquist, HarperTrophy (New York, NY), 1999.
The Wide Window, illustrated by Bret Helquist, HarperTrophy (New York, NY), 2000.
The Miserable Mill, illustrated by Bret Helquist, HarperTrophy (New York, NY), 2000.
The Austere Academy, illustrated by Bret Helquist, HarperTrophy (New York, NY), 2000.
The Ersatz Elevator, illustrated by Bret Helquist, HarperTrophy (New York, NY), 2001.
The Vile Village, illustrated by Bret Helquist, HarperTrophy (New York, NY), 2001.
The Hostile Hospital, illustrated by Bret Helquist, HarperTrophy (New York, NY), 2001.

A Series of Unfortunate Events (omnibus; contains *The Bad Beginning, The Reptile Room,* and *The Wide Window*), HarperTrophy (New York, NY), 2001.
Lemony Snicket: The Unauthorized Autobiography, HarperTrophy (New York, NY), 2002.

Books comprising "A Series of Unfortunate Events" have been published in England, Canada, Germany, Italy, Norway, Israel, Japan, and Denmark.

ADULT FICTION; AS DANIEL HANDLER

The Basic Eight, St. Martin's Press (New York, NY), 1999.
Watch Your Mouth, St. Martin's Press (New York, NY), 2000.

Handler has also written for the *Voice Literary Supplement, Newsday, Salon,* and the *New York Times.*

Adaptations

The Basic Eight was optioned for a film by New Regency, a division of Warner Brothers; "A Series of Unfortunate Events" was optioned for film and television by Nickelodeon.

Work in Progress

Writing as Daniel Handler, a third novel, about pirates. Writing as Lemony Snicket, more volumes in the projected thirteen-part "A Series of Unfortunate Events." Adaptation of a movie for the Independent Film Channel from Joel Rose's novel, *Kill the Poor,* and a movie script with songwriter Stephin Merritt of the band The Magnetic Fields.

Sidelights

Daniel Handler has a fine sense of timing. As a writer for adults, he has produced two popular novels which have had an eerie prescience to them: his 1999 *The Basic Eight* deals, partly in a tongue-in-cheek manner, with a teenage murder, and hit the shelves just a month before the tragic events at Colorado's Columbine High School focused the nation's attention on teen violence; his second novel, a "mock-operatic incest comedy" as Amy Benfer of *Salon.com* described *Watch Your Mouth,* came out in time to benefit from a similar theme broached at the Oscar awards ceremony of 2000.

However, it is his juvenile writings, penned under the pseudonym of Lemony Snicket, that have most benefitted from chronological serendipity: "A Series of Unfortunate Events" has ridden the tsunami created by J. K. Rowling's "Harry Potter" books, tapping into a youthful readership eager to deal with irony, intelligent silliness, and Goth-like depressing situations in their fiction. When the *New York Times Book Review,* influenced by the huge sales of the "Harry Potter" books, initiated a children's bestseller list, Mr. Snicket weighed in at number fifteen; within a year, all five of the books written by the illusive and mysterious Mr. Snicket had made the top twenty-five, and the series had been optioned by Nickelodeon for a film treatment.

Handler was born and raised in San Francisco, the son of an accountant and a college dean. Growing up, Handler was "a bright and obvious person," as he characterized himself for Sally Lodge in *Publishers Weekly.* However, the incipient novelist "always wanted to be a dark, mysterious person." In books, he preferred stories "in which mysterious and creepy things happen," he told Lodge, hating books "where everyone joined the softball team and had a grand time or found true love on a picnic." The youthful Handler sought out stories à la Roald Dahl or Edward Gorey, and indeed his fiction for juveniles has often been compared to that duo. Snicket enjoyed reading the sort of things "set in an eerie castle that was invaded by a snake that strangled the residents." The first book Handler bought with his own money was Gorey's *The Blue Aspic.*

A student of San Francisco's prestigious and demanding Lowell High School, Handler graduated in 1988, tying for Best Personality of his graduating class. Eleven years later, Handler set his first novel at a barely concealed stand-in for this school, Roewer High with students "pushed to the limit academically, socially and athletically," as Handler wrote. After high school graduation, Handler attended Wesleyan University, winning a Poets Prize from the Academy of American Poets in 1990. His love for poetry soon developed into a passion for novels. "My poems were getting longer and longer, and more proselike," Handler commented to Greg Toppo in an Associated Press story carried on *CNNfyi.com.* Upon graduation, he received an Olin Fellowship which provided him with the financial support to work on his first novel. Publication of that book, however, would come several years later. Meanwhile, there was a living to be earned. Handler spent a couple of years in the mid-1990s writing comedy sketches for a nationally syndicated radio show based in San Francisco, *The House of Blues Radio Hour.*

Things began looking up for Handler when he moved to New York City and began his literary career as a freelance movie and book critic. By 1999, his first novel, *The Basic Eight,* was finally published and earned respectful if not praiseworthy reviews in major media. *The Basic Eight,* though written for adults, caused some reviewers and booksellers to label it YA as it focused on a cast of high school students in a clique called The Basic Eight. The school in question, Roewer High, was plainly a thinly disguised Lowell High in San Francisco. As Handler told Philana Woo in his alma mater's paper, *The Lowell,* "When I was at Lowell, it was called Roewer.... Lowell then was predominantly Asian, ... and Roewer was the name people of all races referred to it. It was sort of the kids' joke about the fact that most of the school was Asian. I guess Roewer could be an offensive way of making a pun on an Asian accent."

Essentially beginning at the end of the action, *The Basic Eight* is narrated by Flannery Culp, who depicts the events of her senior year at Roewer High from her journal written in prison where she is serving time for the murder of a teacher and fellow student. Flan is, as a reviewer for *Publishers Weekly* observed, "precocious"

and "pretentious," and now means to set the record straight. Reviled in the press as a leader of a Satanic cult, Flan has kept her journal to tell the real truth of the tragicomic events that have landed her in prison instead of in some Ivy League school.

At school, Flan, editor of the student paper but having trouble in calculus, relies on her seven friends—the "Queen Bee" Kate, lovely Natasha whom Flan admires, Gabriel, a black student and chef in the making who has a crush on Flan, Douglas, who has access to absinthe, V, whose name has been changed to provide anonymity to her wealthy family, Lily, and Jennifer Rose Milton. These eight form the elitist clique in question. Childhood games turn serious when the group begins experimenting with absinthe; Natasha comes to Flan's rescue by poisoning a biology teacher who has been plaguing her. There is also Adam State, love interest of Flan's, and it is her jealousy that ultimately leads to his murder—by croquet mallet—as well. The talk show circuit quickly picks up on the story, calling these privileged kids a Satanic cult.

Handler's characters are all coming of age and aping the adult world of their parents by throwing dinner parties and toting around hip flasks. "The links between teen social life, tabloid culture and serious violence have been explored below and exploited before," noted the reviewer for *Publishers Weekly,* "but Handler, and Flannery, know that. If they're not the first to use such material, they may well be the coolest." This same reviewer concluded, "Handler's confident satire is not only cheeky but packed with downright lovable characters whose youthful misadventures keep the novel neatly balanced between absurdity and poignancy." *Booklist's* Stephanie Zvirin called the book "Part horror story, part black comedy," noting that *The Basic Eight* shows what can happen to "smart, privileged, cynical teens with too few rules, too much to drink, too little supervision, and boundless imagination." Zvirin felt that *The Basic Eight* "will leave readers on the brink of both laughter and despair." *Library Journal's* Rebecca Kelm found Handler's writing to be "witty and perceptive, especially as schools and society are parodied," and the reviewer also noted his "clever use of vocabulary and study questions" that poke fun at the conventions of literary criticism in high schools. Kelm's admiration for the book, however, was tempered with the brutal murder at its center.

Other reviewers also had mixed praise. A writer for *The New Yorker* commented, "Handler is a charming writer with a lovely mastery of voice, but the book is weakened by his attempt to turn a clever idea into a social satire." Brian Howard, writing in *Citypaper.net,* felt that Handler "beautifully captures the ennui and distorted perspectives of a suburban upbringing, where dinner parties are the biggest concern." Howard also pointed to "a lot of excellent suspense writing" in the book, but concluded that "the oh-my-gosh plot twist, which ultimately ruins Culp's credibility, also does much to undo Handler's otherwise fine debut."

Handler told Woo in *The Lowell* that his theme with his first novel "is that young people are oftentimes full of great ideas and creativity and that those things are often stifled." For his second novel, *Watch Your Mouth*, Handler chose another coming of age crucible, the college years. Joseph is just finishing his junior year at prestigious Mather College. There he has met luscious and lascivious Cynthia Glass, whom he delights in calling Cyn with its intended double meaning. A surfeit of sex has caused Joseph to fall behind in his studies and earn an incomplete in one class. When Cyn recommends that Joseph spend the summer with her and her family in Pittsburgh, he leaps at the chance to stay close to his lover. There the two will work days as Jewish day-camp counselors, Joseph will finish his incomplete, and their nights will be their own.

Once settled in the Glass's home, however, Joseph is filled with a sort of foreboding. "Perhaps it's the summer heat in his attic room," noted Ted Leventhal in a *Booklist* review of *Watch Your Mouth*, "or the overly erotic environment, but Joseph begins to imagine that there is something unhealthy about the family's intimacy." It seems father Ben pines for his daughter, Cyn; that mother Mimi yearns for her son, Stephen, and that Stephen may return the favor. Is this a product of Joseph's warped imagination, or is there any truth in it?

Joseph soon discovers or uncovers a triad of fascinations for the family: science, Kabbalah, and, well, incest. And in the basement, is that a golem Mrs. Glass is constructing? Written in the form of an opera, the novel employs realism and surrealism side by side, references to Judaism and modern literature share the same page. Billed as an "incest comedy," the novel steps perilously close to the bounds of good taste. "Did I hear you right, Mr. Reviewer, did you say 'incest comedy'?" wrote Jonathan Shipley in a *BookBrowser* review. "That's 'comedy'? It can be if you write it right. And who writes it right. Daniel Handler. Handler, the author of the critically-acclaimed *The Basic Eight*, comes back with a very odd, quirky, unusual story." A *Publishers Weekly* reviewer felt that Handler's second novel is so "twisted that even its protagonist can't keep up with the perverse turns of plot," and further observed that "this melodramatic satire of family life trembles between virtuosity and utter collapse." *Library Journal*'s Kelm called the book "quirky" and "offbeat," while *Salon*'s Edward Neuert noted that Handler "is more than ready to pick up the torch [of Kurt Vonnegut] and write the kind of deftly funny absurdist story that both horrifies with its subject matter and hooks you with its humor." Leventhal concluded his review noting that there are "plays within plays and puns within puns.... *Mouth* is clever, witty, and unpredictable."

If Handler has a way of getting away with the quirky novel or two, his alter ego, Lemony Snicket has perfected the gambit. "Try pitching this as a series of children's novels," wrote Toppo. "Three young siblings—handsome, clever and rich—lose their loving parents in a fire that destroys their mansion. Too gloomy? It gets worse." And indeed it does, in the ongoing adventures of "A Series of Unfortunate Events," siblings Violet, Klaus, and Sunny Baudelaire not only lose their parents, but are then set upon by the vile Count Olaf, whose one goal in life, it seems, is to bilk the children out of their fortune. After a close encounter with this dastardly villain in the opening novel of the series, *The Bad Beginning,* the children make their painful way from one relative to the next, each more hideous than the last. The Count, of course, makes reprise appearances in each successive volume, much to the delight of the legion of young readers these books have attracted. The trio of kids is led by inventive fourteen-year-old Violet, her rather bookish brother, twelve-year-old Klaus, and baby Sunny who has incredibly sharp teeth for an infant and employs a baby argot that speaks volumes. Eschewing the magic of Harry Potter, Snicket/Handler has imbued these children with survival skills of a more practical nature, enabling them to defend themselves from a cornucopia of hurled knives, falling lamps, storms, snakes, leeches, and just plain rotten folks. And all of this is related in a deadpan, sophisticated text that has its tongue firmly planted in cheek.

The birth of Lemony Snicket was actually influenced by Handler's debut novel, *The Basic Eight*. Susan Rich, editor at HarperTrophy and a fan of Handler's first novel, decided to try and woo him over to children's books. "I knew we shared a similar sensibility about children's books," Rich told Lodge in *Publishers Weekly,* "which I'd define as a resistance to fall into overly trodden paths of traditional stories, and a resistance to anything that is too sweet or patronizing or moralistic." Handler was at first resistant, but offered the chance to pen books he might have enjoyed reading himself when he was ten, he set to reworking the hundred or so pages of a mock-Gothic novel for adults that he had long ago abandoned. Handler, writing as Snicket—a name he had once devised to avoid getting on unwanted mail lists—was delighted to revamp the entire notion of what constitutes an appropriate novel for juveniles, repealing the old sports or fantasy categories that were available to him as a youth. The result was *The Bad Beginning,* the first of what Handler/Snicket see as a thirteen-volume set chronicling the adventures of the Baudelaire orphans. "If you are interested in stories with happy endings," the author wrote on the first page of that novel, "you would be better off reading some other book. In this book, not only is there no happy ending, there is no happy beginning and very few happy things in the middle.... I'm sorry to tell you this, but that's how the story goes."

When the three Baudelaire children lose their parents in a fire, they become—through the oversight of the ineffectual banker, Mr. Poe—wards of Count Olaf, a distant cousin. He sets them to labor in his house, meanwhile devising schemes with his theatrical troupe to deprive the orphans of their inheritance. The three survive the Count's attacks with spunk, initiative, and, in the case of Sunny, a set of sharp teeth. "The author uses formal, Latinate language and intrusive commentary to hilarious effect," noted a review for *Publishers Weekly* of this first title in the series. The same reviewer felt that the author "paints the satire with such broad strokes that most readers will view it from a safe distance." In the second book of the series, *The Reptile Room,* it seems the orphans will have a chance for happiness when they go to live with Dr. Montgomery Montgomery, a "very fun, but fatally naïve herpetologist," according to Ron Charles in the *Christian Science Monitor.* Unfortunately, their safe haven is short-lived, spoiled once again by the arrival of the oafish Count Olaf. Susan Dove Lempke, reviewing the first two titles in *Booklist,* thought that the "droll humor, reminiscent of Edward Gorey's, will be lost on some children; others may not enjoy the old-fashioned storytelling style that frequently addresses the reader directly and includes definitions of terms." Lempke went on, however, to conclude: "But plenty of children will laugh at the over-the-top satire; hiss at the creepy nefarious villains; and root for the intelligent, courageous, unfortunate Baudelaire orphans." Linda Bindner, writing in *School Library Journal,* noted that "While the misfortunes hover on the edge of being ridiculous, Snicket's energetic blend of humor, dramatic irony, and literary flair makes it all perfectly believable." Bindner also found that the use of sophisticated vocabulary and inclusion of author definitions make "these books challenging to older readers and excellent for reading aloud."

The third book in the series, *The Wide Window,* finds the orphans with elderly Aunt Josephine who lives on a house on stilts which overlooks Lake Lachrymose. Josephine is a widow as well as a frightful grammarian, and when Olaf finally tracks down the Baudelaires, he fools the aunt for a while into believing he is a sailboat captain. When she finally stumbles onto his true identity, he gets rid of her by pushing the good woman into leech-infested waters and the peripatetic children must find a new protector. *Booklist*'s Lempke noted that Snicket writes in "an old-fashioned tone," offering "plenty advice to readers in asides." "The effect is often hilarious as well as edifying," Lempke observed. Most importantly, as Lempke concluded, "readers never truly worry that [the Baudelaire orphans] will be defeated in this or their next adventure."

The fourth in the series, *The Miserable Mill,* begins with the three children on their way to Paltryville and yet another guardian, this time the owner of the Lucky Smells Lumbermill. Here they must work in the mill, survive on gum for lunch and casserole for dinner. Count Olaf, is of course, just off-stage ready to pounce. "The story is deliciously mock-Victorian and self-mockingly melodramatic," noted *Booklist*'s Carolyn Phelan, who also commented on the artwork and "the author's many asides to the reader" which both "underscore the droll humor. . . ." Phelan concluded, "Another plum for the orphans' fans." "This is for readers who appreciate this particular type of humor," observed Sharon R. Pearce in *School Library Journal.* Pearce noted that such humor "exaggerates the sour and makes anyone's real life seem sweet in comparison." The adventures continue in *The Austere Academy* and *The Ersatz Elevator.* In the former title, the Baudelaire children are consigned to a shack at the Prufrock Preparatory School where they

will face snapping crabs, strict punishments, dripping fungus and the evils of the metric system. In the latter book, they must contend with new guardians Jerome and Esme Squalor, while trying to save two friends from the clutches of Count Olaf.

"The Snicket novels are morality tales, albeit twisted ones," observed Benfer in *Salon.* "Among other things, Snicket tells children that one should never stay up late on a school night, except to finish a very good book; he insists that there is nothing worse than someone who can't play the violin but insists upon doing so anyway." He employs continual authorial intrusions, providing definitions, giving stage directions. "I was mostly just knocking the heavy-handedness that I remembered from kid's books that I didn't like as a child," Handler reported to Benfer. "That sort of mockery seems to really appeal to kids." Another Handler trademark is the use of names in the Snicket books which come from literature: the Baudelaire orphans themselves are but the most obvious example of a long list including Mr. Poe and Prufrock Prep. "There's plenty of literary names and the like," Handler told Benfer, "but there's not so many outright jokes. And the literary names are there mostly because I look forward to kids growing up and finding Baudelaire in the poetry anthology and having that be something else to be excited about."

The formula has worked quite well, sending the Handler/Snicket books onto the best-seller charts and establishing a devoted fan base. More than 125,000 of the books in "A Series of Unfortunate Events" are in print, the Snicket Web site is a popular venue in cyberspace, and the elusive Mr. Snicket himself has become a popular speaker at schools. Correction. Mr. Snicket's representative, Mr. Handler, performs stand-ins for his friend, who has variously been injured or delayed or unaccountably held hostage somewhere while Mr. Handler entertains the youthful audience with his accordion and tales of the Snicket family tree. According to the official Snicket web site, "Lemony Snicket was born before you were and is likely to die before you as well."

Lodge wrote in *Publishers Weekly* that obviously "the author's knack for combining the dark with the droll has hit a nerve just about everywhere," and word-of-mouth has greatly contributed to the success of the series. With Nickelodeon working on the film and Handler/Snicket collaborating on an expected thirteen volumes, the future looks surprisingly bright for the Baudelaire orphans.

Biographical and Critical Sources

PERIODICALS

ALAN Review, winter, 2001, Linda Broughton, review of *The Miserable Mill,* p. 35.

Book, July, 2001, *Kathleen Odean,* review of *The Ersatz Elevator,* p. 81.

Booklist, March 15, 1999, Stephanie Zvirin, review of *The Basic Eight,* p. 1289; December 1, 1999, Susan Dove Lempke, review of *The Bad Beginning,* p. 707; February 1, 2000, Susan Dove Lempke, review of *The Wide Window,* p. 1024; May 1, 2000, Carolyn Phelan, review of *The Miserable Mill,* p. 1670; June 1, 2000, Ted Leventhal, review of *Watch Your Mouth,* p. 1857; October 15, 2000, Susan Dove Lempke, review of *The Austere Academy,* p. 439.

Boys' Life, December, 2000, Stephen G. Michaud, review of "A Series of Unfortunate Events" titles, p. 61.

Christian Science Monitor, August 12, 1999, Ron Charles, review of *The Bad Beginning* and *The Reptile Room,* p. 21.

Horn Book, March, 2001, Christine Heppermann, "Angel Wings and Hard Knocks," p. 239.

Library Journal, March 15, 1999, Rebecca Kelm, review of *The Basic Eight,* p. 108; June 1, 2000, Rebecca Kelm, review of *Watch Your Mouth,* p. 196.

New Yorker, June 21, 1999, review of *The Basic Eight.*

New York Times Magazine, April 29, 2001, Daphne Merkin, "Lemony Snicket Says, 'Don't Read My Books!'"

Publishers Weekly, March 1, 1999, review of *The Basic Eight,* p. 59; September 6, 1999, review of *The Bad Beginning,* p. 104; January 17, 2000, p. 58; May 29, 2000, Sally Lodge, "Oh, Sweet Misery," p. 42; June 19, 2000, review of *Watch Your Mouth,* p. 60.

School Library Journal, November, 1999, Linda Bindner, review of *The Bad Beginning,* p. 165; January, 2000, p. 136; July, 2000, Sharon R. Pearce, review of *The Miserable Mill,* p. 110; October, 2000, Ann Cook, review of *The Austere Academy,* p. 171; August, 2001, Farida S. Dowler, reviews of *The Ersatz Elevator* and *The Vile Village,* pp. 188-189.

Time for Kids, April 27, 2001, "He Tells Terrible Tales," p. 7.

ON-LINE

A Series of Unfortunate Events Web site, http://www.lemonysnicket.com/ (March 26, 2001).

BookBrowser Review, http://www.bookbroswer.com/ (July 15, 2000), Jonathan Shipley, review of *Watch Your Mouth.*

Citypaper.net, http://www.cpcn.com/ (June 17-24, 1999), Brian Howard, review of *The Basic Eight.*

CNNfyi.com, http://www.cnn.cm/200/fyi/news/ (May 12, 2000), Greg Toppo, "Wry 'Series of Unfortunate Events' Books Earn Fans, Praise."

Lowell, http://www.thelowell.org/ (February 15, 1999), Philana Woo, "Author Reflects on High School Life."

Nancy Matson's Web site, http://www.nancymatson.com/ (March, 2000).

Salon.com, http://www.salonmag.com/ (July 24, 2000), Edward Neuert, "What to Read: July Fiction"; (August 17, 2000) Amy Benfer, "The Mysterious Mr. Snicket."*

—*Sketch by J. Sydney Jones*

* * *

SOMMER, Carl 1930-

Personal

Born October 17, 1930, in Brooklyn, NY; son of Karl (a butcher) and Elise (a homemaker; maiden name, Hen-

inger) Sommer; married, wife's name Hildegard (a finance manager), May 7, 1955; children: Paul, Esther, Steven, John, Philip. *Hobbies and other interests:* Swimming and fishing.

Addresses

Office—Advance Publishing, Inc., 6950 Fulton St., Houston, TX 77022. *E-mail*—carl@advancepublishing.com.

Career

President and founder of Advance Publishing, Inc.; president and founder of Reliable EDM, Inc.; president and founder of Media One Productions. Former school teacher. *Military service:* United States Marine Corps, Korean War, 1951-53.

Awards, Honors

Several books have been finalists for the Teachers' Choice Awards, *Learning* magazine; Benjamin Franklin Award for Best Children's Picture Book, for *The Ugly Caterpillar; Today's Librarian* award, for *Mayor for a Day.*

Carl Sommer

Writings

FOR CHILDREN

Can You Help Me Find My Smile?, illustrated by Greg Budwine, Advance Publishing (Houston, TX), 1997.

If Only I Were . . . , illustrated by Kennon James, Advance Publishing (Houston, TX), 1997.

No One Will Ever Know, illustrated by Dick Westbrook, Advance Publishing (Houston, TX), 1997.

Tied Up in Knots, illustrated by Greg Budwine, Advance Publishing (Houston, TX), 1997.

The Great Royal Race, illustrated by Dick Westbrook, Advance Publishing (Houston, TX), 1997.

No Longer a Dilly Dally, illustrated by Kennon James, Advance Publishing (Houston, TX), 1998.

Future Trek, illustrated by Greg Budwine, Advance Publishing (Houston, TX), 1999.

George Washington Carver: Making Much from Little, Advance Publishing (Houston, TX), 1999.

I Am a Lion!, illustrated by Greg Budwine, Advance Publishing (Houston, TX), 2000.

Mayor for a Day, illustrated by Dick Westbrook, Advance Publishing (Houston, TX), 2000.

King of the Pond, illustrated by Greg Budwine, Advance Publishing (Houston, TX), 2000.

The Time Remote, illustrated by Greg Budwine, Advance Publishing (Houston, TX), 2000.

The Ugly Caterpillar, illustrated by Greg Budwine, Advance Publishing (Houston, TX), 2000.

Proud Rooster and Little Hen, illustrated by Greg Budwine, Advance Publishing (Houston, TX), 2000.

You Move, You Lose, illustrated by Kennon James, Advance Publishing (Houston, TX), 2000.

The Little Red Train, illustrated by Kennon James, Advance Publishing (Houston, TX), 2000.

The Sly Fox and the Chicks, illustrated by Kennon James, Advance Publishing (Houston, TX), 2000.

Your Job Is Easy, illustrated by Kennon James, Advance Publishing (Houston, TX), 2000.

Three Little Pigs, illustrated by Greg Budwine, Advance Publishing (Houston, TX), 2000.

Light Your Candle, illustrated by Kennon James, Advance Publishing (Houston, TX), 2000.

FOR ADULTS

Schools in Crisis: Training for Success or Failure?, Cahill Publishing (Houston, TX), 1984.

Handwriting Success for Adults: Learning Manuscript and Cursive Writing, Advance Publishing (Houston, TX), 1999.

(With son, Steve Sommer) *Wire EDM Handbook,* Technical Advance Publishing (Houston, TX), 1992, 4th edition, 2000.

Non-Traditional Machining Handbook, Advance Publishing (Houston, TX), 2000.

Work in Progress

"Reading Success for Adults," a phonics-literature based reading program consisting of nineteen books; "Reading Success for Children," a phonics-literature based reading program consisting of twenty-five books; "Number Success," an adult practical math program consisting of

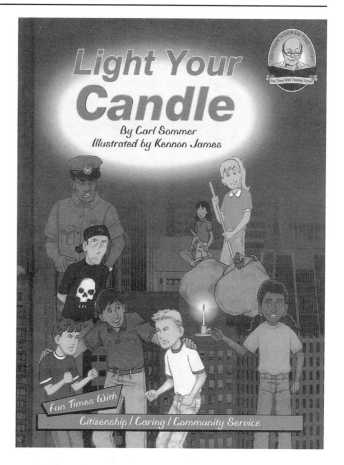

In this work, Stephanie transforms her school and neighborhood by ridding her street of crime. (Cover illustration by Kennon James.)

twelve books on addition, subtraction, multiplication, division, fractions, decimals, percentage, calculator, life skills, algebra, geometry, and trigonometry.

Sidelights

"I wrote about the school crisis and the solutions in my first book, now I want to provide practical solutions for children and adults," Carl Sommer told *SATA*. "My purpose in writing children's books is to teach children by means of exciting stories the virtues that lead to successful living. I am glad to report that the books have received many enthusiastic endorsements. All books have been selected as finalists for the Teachers' Choice Awards given by *Learning* magazine. For best children's picture book, *The Ugly Caterpillar* received the Benjamin Franklin Award, and *Mayor for a Day* received a Today's Librarian award. My purpose in writing the "Reading Success" and "Number Success" series is to provide material for student enrichment and to help adults lacking skills in reading, writing, or math to become literate. Both of these literacy programs are self-directed. "Reading Success" uses audio, and "Number Success" uses video to teach the lessons. I am the practical math teacher who demonstrates math at various sites, such as department and hardware stores, construction sites, NASA, industrial sites, and numerous other places. Four teachers who have won the prestigious

National Science Foundation for Excellence in mathematics for their states teach the lessons. Now anyone who lacks literacy skills can use these self-directed materials and become literate."

* * *

SOREL, Edward 1929-

Personal

Surname originally Schwartz, legally changed to Sorel; born March 26, 1929, in Bronx, NY; son of Morris (a salesperson) and Rebecca (a factory worker; maiden name, Kleinberg) Schwartz; married Elaine Rothenberg, July 1, 1956 (divorced, 1965); married Nancy Caldwell (a writer), May 29, 1965; children: (first marriage) Madeline, Leo; (second marriage) Jenny, Katherine. *Education:* Cooper Union College, diploma, 1951.

Addresses

Home—156 Franklin St., New York, NY 10013. *Office*—c/o Margaret K. McElderry Books, Simon & Schuster Children's Publishing, 1230 Avenue of the Americas, New York, NY 10020.

Edward Sorel

Career

Esquire, New York, NY, assistant art director, 1951-53; Push Pin Studios (commercial and graphic arts studio), New York, NY, cofounder, 1953, staff artist, 1953-56; Columbia Broadcasting System (CBS-TV), New York, NY, art director in promotion department, 1956-57; freelance artist, political satirist, cartoonist, and illustrator of children's books, 1958—. *Exhibitions:* The Push Pin Retrospective at the Louvre, Paris, France, 1970, and other European galleries, 1970-71; one-man shows at Graham Galleries, New York, NY, 1973 and 1978; New School for Social Research, New York, NY, 1974; Galerie Bartsch & Chariau, Munich, Germany, 1986; Davis and Langdale Galleries, New York, NY, 1998 and 2000; and National Portrait Gallery, Washington, DC, 1999-2000.

Awards, Honors

Fifty books of the year selection, American Institute of Graphic Arts, 1958, for *King Carlo of Capri;* ten best illustrated books of the year selection, *New York Times,* 1959, for *Pablo Paints a Picture;* Spring Book Festival Award, 1961, and first prize for illustration of children's books, *New York Herald Tribune,* both for *Gwendolyn, the Miracle Hen;* ten best illustrated books of the year selection, *New York Times,* 1963, for *Gwendolyn and the Weather Cock;* fifty books of the year exhibition selection, American Institute of Graphic Arts, 1972, and U.S. representative, Children's Book International Biennial of Illustrations in Bratislava, 1973, both for *Magical Storybook;* Augustus St. Gaudens Medal, Cooper Union, 1973, for professional achievement; George Polk Award, 1981, for satirical drawing; Page One Award, Newspaper Guild of New York, 1988, for best editorial cartoon (magazines); Notable Books of 1998 selection, *New York Times Magazine,* for *Unauthorized Portraits;* additional awards for illustration from Society of Illustrators, American Institute of Graphic Arts, and Art Directors Club of New York; elected into the Art Directors Hall of Fame, Art Directors Club of New York, 2001.

Writings

SELF-ILLUSTRATED

How to Be President: Some Hard and Fast Rules, Grove (New York, NY), 1960.

Moon Missing: An Illustrated Guide to the Future, Simon & Schuster (New York, NY), 1962.

Sorel's World Fair, New York, 1964, McGraw (New York, NY), 1964.

Making the World Safe for Hypocrisy: A Collection of Satirical Drawings and Commentaries, Swallow Press (Chicago, IL), 1972.

Superpen: The Cartoons and Caricatures of Edward Sorel, edited by Lidia Ferrara, Random House (New York, NY), 1978.

(With Nancy Caldwell Sorel) *First Encounters: A Book of Memorial Meetings,* Knopf (New York, NY), 1994.

Unauthorized Portraits, Knopf (New York, NY), 1997.

SELF-ILLUSTRATED; FOR CHILDREN

The Zillionaire's Daughter, Warner Books, 1989.

Johnny-on-the-Spot, Margaret K. McElderry Books (New York, NY), 1998.

(With Cheryl Carlesimo) *The Saturday Kid,* Margaret K. McElderry Books (New York, NY), 1999.

ILLUSTRATOR

Warren Miller, *King Carlo of Capri* (adapted from Charles Perrault's *Riquet with the Tuft of Hair*), Harcourt (New York, NY), 1958.

Warren Miller, *The Goings-On at Little Wishful,* Little, Brown (Boston, MA), 1959,

Warren Miller, *Pablo Paints a Picture,* Little, Brown (Boston, MA), 1959.

Nancy Sherman, *Gwendolyn, the Miracle Hen,* Golden Press, 1961.

Nancy Sherman, *Gwendolyn and the Weathercock,* Golden Press, 1963.

Joy Cowley, *The Duck in the Gun,* Doubleday (New York, NY), 1969.

William Cole, *What's Good for a Five-Year-Old?,* Holt (New York, NY), 1969.

Nancy Caldwell Sorel, *Word People,* American Heritage Press (New York, NY), 1970.

Jay Williams, *Magical Storybook,* American Heritage Press (New York, NY), 1972.

Ward Botsford, *The Pirates of Penzance* (adapted from the Gilbert and Sullivan operetta), Random House (New York, NY), 1981.

Eric Metaxas, *Jack and the Beanstalk* (with cassette), Rabbit Ears Books (Westport, CT), 1991.

OTHER

Author of introduction to Charles Le Brun's *Resemblances, Amazing Faces,* Harlin Quist (New York, NY), 1980. Contributing editor of *New York, Gentleman's Quarterly,* and *Village Voice.* Creator of syndicated feature "Sorel's News Service," for King Features, 1969-70, and of other cartoon features, including "The Spokesman," for *Esquire,* and "Unfamiliar Quotations," for *Atlantic.* Contributor of artwork and articles to additional periodicals, including *Village Voice, Rolling Stone, Realist, Ramparts, GQ, New York Times Book Review, Forbes, American Heritage, Atlantic Monthly, Nation, New Yorker,* and *Time.*

Sidelights

An award-winning political cartoonist and children's book illustrator, Edward Sorel is known for his pen and ink drawings that have a free flowing, almost scratchy style. In his art, Sorel generally works "direct," explains National Portrait Gallery curator Wendy Rick Reaves to Bruce Hathaway in *Smithsonian.* "That means no tracing or erasing, and little preliminary sketching. With this sudden death approach, Sorel's figures often emerge from a dense, wiry tangle of overlapping pen strokes that crackle with energy." Using this technique, Sorel has developed a unique style, creating satirical portraits and cartoons of world leaders that have graced the nation's top magazines, including *Time, Rolling Stone,* and *New Yorker.*

In his work for children, Sorel also captures this same energy, according to critics. Talking about his entry into the world of children's literature, Sorel said in *American Artist,* "I had for some time wanted to illustrate a children's book and realized that I could not tell a story, could not show those details of costume, expression, or movement which children love, unless I forgot all about style or manner and concentrated on telling a story in pictures.... This need to describe rather than decorate was one turning point in my development." Sorel illustrated his first children's book, the award-winning *King Carlo of Capri,* in 1958, and followed it the next year with *Pablo Paints a Picture,* another award winner.

Throughout the 1960s and 1970s, Sorel continued both paths of his career, illustrating children's books as well as creating humorous, sometimes controversial, political cartoons for an adult audience. In the 1980s, the artist and illustrator began to devote more time to his literary efforts, publishing articles in the *New York Times Book Review, Forbes,* and *GQ.* In 1989, he wrote his first children's book, *The Zillionaire's Daughter,* a self-illustrated work about a young French girl who sails across the Atlantic with her wealthy father. Claire, the daughter of zillionaire Max Maximillion, learns from a fortune teller that one day she will grow up to marry a saxophone player. Her distinguished father is aghast at the thought and spends his time on the ship worrying about the revelation. Claire, however, decides to enjoy herself and makes friends with an Englishman named Charlie. On the night of the Grand Masqued Ball, Charlie reveals himself not only as a superb sax man, but also as the third Duke of Harley, much to the pleasure of Max. Writing in *Booklist,* Barbara Elleman described *The Zillionaire's Daughter* as "a good-hearted spoof on the opulence of the rich that has at its heart a likable young heroine." A *Publishers Weekly* critic commented favorably on the artist's work, saying "brimming with gorgeous Art Deco touches, Sorel's resplendent pen and ink, color-enhanced drawings are perfectly matched by his effortless verse."

A young boy with a fondness for radio captures the attention of readers in Sorel's 1998 work *Johnny on the Spot.* When his family's radio is broken, Johnny takes it to be repaired by the eccentric inventor living in his apartment building's basement flat. Hoping to be able to listen to his favorite adventure programs again, Johnny is amazed when he discovers that the newly-repaired radio now broadcasts news twenty-four hours in advance. Using his new-found knowledge of the next-day's events, Johnny begins to make a name for himself as "Johnny on the Spot," thwarting bank robberies and putting out fires. However, as Johnny becomes tempted to use his forward-seeing radio for shadowy rewards, the young boy's parents decide to junk the "broken" radio and purchase a new one. "Sorel ... constructs an enticing cinematic world of brownstones and sepia-tinted interiors," observed a *Publishers Weekly* contributor. While noting that the book's ending is "perhaps a bit too predictable," *Booklist* critic Michael Cart nonetheless thought that "Sorel's lively pen-and-ink watercolor pictures add panache to a story that is engaging."

Violinist Leo dreams of getting even with the neighborhood bully in **The Saturday Kid,** *written (in collaboration with Cheryl Carlesimo) and illustrated by Sorel.*

Set in New York City during the 1930s, *The Saturday Kid* recalls a time when the last day of the week was spent at the movie cinema, inspiring daydreams about adventures fighting gangsters, flying airplanes, and becoming a pirate. Or at least that is what young Leo likes to do on his Saturdays. However, this pleasure is interrupted one afternoon after Morty, the neighborhood bully, gets Leo ejected from the theater. Longing to repay Morty, Leo brags that he can play the violin and has even shook hands with the mayor. Leo's boasts go unbelieved until a newsreel shows him, larger than life, meeting the mayor after entertaining him with a violin performance. Receiving congratulations from Morty's parents gives the young Leo a feeling that his days of being bullied are soon over. *School Library Journal* reviewer Julie Cummins predicted that "a lot of nostalgia, an appealing underdog, and good old-fashioned moxie will charm any child who dares to dream." Several reviewers applauded the way Sorel's illustrations created a feel for a New York City of yesteryear. A *Publishers Weekly* critic claimed that "Sorel captures old New York in galloping ribbons of ink and sepia-tinted watercolors," while *Booklist* reviewer Denise Wilms, noted "The dynamic pen-and-wash drawings are never static ... their rush of detail captures the city with fond affection."

Biographical and Critical Sources

PERIODICALS

American Artist, May, 1960, Frederic Whitaker, "Edward Sorel," pp. 40-58.
Booklist, May 15, 1990, Barbara Elleman, review of *The Zillionaire's Daughter,* p. 1806; August, 1998, Mi-

chael Cart, review of *Johnny on the Spot,* p. 2017; December 15, 2000, Denise Wilms, review of *The Saturday Kid,* p. 829.
Kirkus Reviews, August 15, 1997, review of *Unauthorized Portraits,* p. 1298.
New York Times Book Review, December 6, 1998, "Notable Books of 1998," p. 90.
Publishers Weekly, February 9, 1990, review of *The Zillionaire's Daughter,* p. 60; September 7, 1998, review of *Johnny on the Spot,* pp. 94-95; August 28, 2000, review of *The Saturday Kid,* p. 83.
School Library Journal, September, 2000, Julie Cummins, review of *The Saturday Kid,* p. 209.
Smithsonian, October, 1999, Bruce Hathaway, "The Gang's All Here," p. 124.

*   *   *

SOWDEN, Celeste
See WALTERS, Celeste

*   *   *

STILLE, Darlene R(uth) 1942-

Personal

Born April 17, 1942, in Chicago, IL; daughter of Theodore E. (a house painter) and Edna Pue (a telephone operator; maiden name, Cook) Stille. *Education:* University of Illinois—Urbana, B.A., 1965. *Politics:* Democrat. *Religion:* Protestant. *Hobbies and other interests:* Travel, scuba diving.

Addresses

Office—World Book, Inc., 233 North Michigan Ave., Chicago, IL 60601. *E-mail*—dstille@worldbook.com.

Career

Encyclopedia Britannica, Chicago, IL, production editor, 1968-69; *Compton's Encyclopedia,* Chicago, IL, staff writer, 1969-71; *World Book,* Chicago, IL, senior editor, *The Year Book, Science Year,* 1971-78, managing editor, *Science Year,* 1978-91, executive editor, *Annuals,* 1991-2000, editor-in-chief, Annual and Online Supplements, 2000—. Worked as a travel writer and Web design consultant for Envoy Travel Inc. *Member:* Women Employed (chair, 1973-76), American Association for the Advancement of Science.

Writings

Extraordinary Women Scientists ("Extraordinary People" series), Children's Press (Chicago, IL), 1995.
Extraordinary Women of Medicine ("Extraordinary People" series), Children's Press (Chicago, IL), 1997.
Jaguars ("First Report" series), Compass Point Books (Minneapolis, MN), 2001.
Snakes ("First Report" series), Compass Point Books (Minneapolis, MN), 2001.

(With Susan Heinrichs Gray) *The White House* ("Let's See—Our Nation" series), Compass Point Books (Minneapolis, MN), 2001.

(With Dana Meachen Rau) *The Statue of Liberty* ("Let's See—Our Nation" series), Compass Point Books (Minneapolis, MN), 2001.

"TRUE BOOK" SERIES

Air Pollution, Children's Press (Chicago, IL), 1990.
Water Pollution, Children's Press (Chicago, IL), 1990.
Soil Erosion and Pollution, Children's Press (Chicago, IL), 1990.
The Greenhouse Effect, Children's Press (Chicago, IL), 1990.
The Ice Age, Children's Press (Chicago, IL), 1990.
Oil Spills, Children's Press (Chicago, IL), 1991.
Ozone Hole, Children's Press (Chicago, IL), 1991.
Space Craft, Children's Press (Chicago, IL), 1991.
The Circulatory System, Children's Press (Chicago, IL), 1997.
The Nervous System, Children's Press (Chicago, IL), 1997.
The Respiratory System, Children's Press (Chicago, IL), 1997.
Trains, Compass Point Books (Minneapolis, MN), 1997.
Trucks, Compass Point Books (Minneapolis, MN), 1997.
The Digestive System, Children's Press (Chicago, IL), 1997.
Deserts, Children's Press (Chicago, IL), 1999.
Tropical Rain Forest, Children's Press (Chicago, IL), 1999.
Wetlands, Children's Press (Chicago, IL), 1999.
Grasslands, Children's Press (Chicago, IL), 1999.
Oceans, Children's Press (Chicago, IL), 1999.

"TRANSPORTATION" SERIES

Airplanes, Compass Point Books (Minneapolis, MN), 1997.
Helicopters, Children's Press (Chicago, IL), 1997.
Blimps, Children's Press (Chicago, IL), 1997.
Big Rigs, Compass Point Books (Minneapolis, MN), 2001.
Freight Trains, Compass Point Books (Minneapolis, MN), 2001.
Race Cars, Compass Point Books (Minneapolis, MN), 2002.

"LET'S SEE—COMMUNICATION" SERIES

Radio, Compass Point Books (Minneapolis, MN), 2001.
Satellite, Compass Point Books (Minneapolis, MN), 2001.
Telephones, Compass Point Books (Minneapolis, MN), 2001.
Television, Compass Point Books (Minneapolis, MN), 2001.

"SIMPLY SCIENCE" SERIES

Electricity, Compass Point Books (Minneapolis, MN), 2001.
Fall, Compass Point Books (Minneapolis, MN), 2001.
Winter, Compass Point Books (Minneapolis, MN), 2001.
Hot and Cold, Compass Point Books (Minneapolis, MN), 2001.
Magnets, Compass Point Books (Minneapolis, MN), 2001.
Sound, Compass Point Books (Minneapolis, MN), 2001.
Spring, Compass Point Books (Minneapolis, MN), 2001.
Summer, Compass Point Books (Minneapolis, MN), 2001.

Sidelights

Darlene R. Stille told *SATA:* "I became a science writer and editor largely because I could not become a doctor. I started out in pre-med in 1960. Medicine, at that time, was not very open to women—to say the least. One needed strong family support to go forth in that direction. My family was dead-set against the idea."

"Fortunately, I had another love in addition to science—writing. I pursued a degree in English, went into the reference publishing field, and was soon able to put together my love of science and of words in science editing and writing."

Stille's interest in science is reflected in most, if not all, of her writing. In *Extraordinary Women Scientists* she presents a history of women's role in science as well as biographies of fifty important scientist from various scientific disciplines, including information on women scientists from numerous countries. Margaret M. Hagel, writing in the *School Library Journal,* noted that while this work can be "used as a reference book, ... it [also] introduces readers to the diversity of science." Her next book for the "Extraordinary People" series is titled *Extraordinary Women of Medicine.* This time, Stille narrowed her focus to present an overview of a history of medicine as well as highlighting women's achievements in the field of medicine. Like its companion volume, *Extraordinary Women of Medicine* also in-

Darlene R. Stille

cludes biographies and covers various ethnic groups, including Americans, African Americans, and Europeans. Reviewing this work for *Booklist,* Lauren Peterson said that it contained a "wealth of information" in an "accessible format."

In addition to books on science, Stille has also written numerous books for her "Transportation" series, including *Airplanes* and *Trains.* In both of these works, she includes information that will be relevant to school-age children who are just beginning to write reports on various subjects. In addition to descriptions of planes and trains, both books also include photographs and a list of sources for further study. Other books by Stille in this series include *Helicopters, Blimps,* and *Trucks.*

Stille's scientific background is once again evident in the books she wrote for the "True Book" series published by the Children's Press. Included among these is *The Circulatory System,* a book that presents basic information about the heart, flow of blood, and the function of lungs. As with her other books, Stille includes a glossary as well as a list of resources for more information. Another book is titled *The Nervous System.* Once again, using simple language and diagrams, Stille explains the interaction between brain, nerves, and muscles. Reviewing this work for *Booklist,* Lauren Peterson noted that Stille does an "admirable" job of explaining a complex subject. Other titles by Stille for the "True Book" series include such titles as *The Wetlands* and *Tropical Rain Forests.* Both follow the

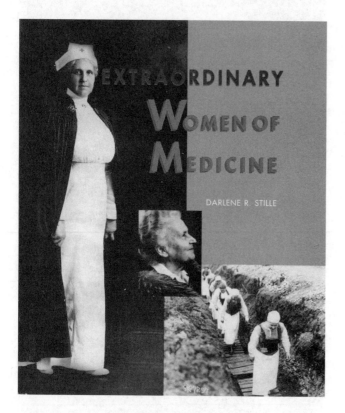

This volume from the "Extraordinary People" series presents biographical sketches of nineteenth- and twentieth-century women of medicine.

familiar, simple format of her earlier books, focusing on presenting basic facts about the topics under discussion, accompanied by photographs and a list of resources for further study.

Biographical and Critical Sources

PERIODICALS

Booklist, October 1, 1997, Lauren Peterson, review of *Extraordinary Women of Medicine,* p. 316; September 15, 1997, Ilene Cooper, review of *Airplanes* and *Trains,* p. 233; December 1, 1997, Hazel Rochman, review of *The Circulatory System,* p. 632; February 15, 1998, Lauren Peterson, review of *The Nervous System,* p. 1006; October 15, 1999, Hazel Rochman, review of *Tropical Rain Forests,* p. 440.
Horn Book Guide, fall, 1997, Peter D. Sierra, review of "True Book" series, p. 360.
School Library Journal, December, 1995, Margaret M. Hagel, review of *Extraordinary Women Scientists,* pp. 125-26; February, 1998, Martha Gordon, review of *The Circulatory System, The Respiratory System,* and *The Digestive System,* p. 105.

*   *   *

STRIKER, Lee
See CLARK, Margaret (D.)

*   *   *

SURFACE, Mary Hall 1958-

Personal

Born June 15, 1958, in Bowling Green, KY; married Kevin Reese (an actor and designer); children: Malinda. *Education:* Centre College of Kentucky, B.A., 1980.

Addresses

Home—2023 Rosemont Ave. NW, Washington, DC 20010. *E-mail*—mhsurface@aol.com.

Career

Freelance playwright and theater director. John F. Kennedy Center for the Performing Arts, Washington, DC, project curator for New Visions 2000: One Theater World (national festival of theater for families); National Endowment for the Arts, member of theater panel, 1998, and on-site evaluator. Speaker at international theater festivals. *Member:* International Association of Theater for Children and Youth (vice president of U.S. Center, 1983-91), Dramatists Guild.

Awards, Honors

Watson fellow, 1980; Helen Hays Award for Outstanding Direction nomination, 1993 and 2000; fellow, District of Columbia Commission on the Arts, 1995; Aurand Harris playwriting fellow, 2000.

Mary Hall Surface

Writings

Prodigy, Anchorage Press (New Orleans, LA), 1988.
What Part Will I Play?, Encore Performance Publishing, 1992.
A Perfect Balance, produced in Lyon, France, 1993.
The Sorcerer's Apprentice (play), Anchorage Press (New Orleans, LA), 1994.
Dancing Solo, Dramatic Publishing, 1996.
The Reluctant Dragon, Anchorage Press (New Orleans, LA), 1997.
Most Valuable Player, and Four Other All-Star Plays for Middle and High School Audiences, Smith & Kraus (Lyme, NH), 1999.
Short Scenes and Monologues for Middle School Actors, Smith & Kraus (Lyme, NH), 2000.
Sing Down the Moon (musical), music by David Maddox, produced in Fairfax, VA, 2000.

Also author of *Broken Rainbows* and *Round Pegs, Square Pegs.* Has collaborated with David Maddox on the musicals *The Nightingale, Ghandara,* and *Perseus Bayou.*

Sidelights

Mary Hall Surface told *SATA:* "I am a theater artist who writes, directs, designs, and collaborates to make theatrical worlds that strive to speak with equal power to young audiences and adults. My early works are rooted in the contemporary world of children. My more recent work is drawn from myths, fairy tales, and metaphor. I

want to engage young people's hearts and minds to feel and think in ways they never have before."

Biographical and Critical Sources

PERIODICALS

Booklist, February 15, 2000, Gillian Engberg, review of *Short Scenes and Monologues for Middle School Actors,* p. 1100.
School Library Journal, December, 1999, Todd Morning, review of *Most Valuable Player, and Four Other All-Star Plays for Middle and High School Audiences,* p. 160; July, 2000, Nancy Menaldi-Scanlan, review of *Short Scenes and Monologues for Middle School Actors,* p. 122.

ON-LINE

Encore Performance Publishing, http://www.encoreplay.com/ (September 23, 2001), biography of Mary Hall Surface.
Nashville Children's Theatre, http://www.nct-dragon-site.org/ (September 23, 2001).
Willie Bell Music, http://www.williebellmusic.com/ (September 23, 2001), biography of Mary Hall Surface.*

*　　*　　*

THALER, Shmuel 1958-

Personal

Born September 20, 1958, in New York, NY; son of Alvin (a television director) and Pat (a university dean; maiden name, Koch) Thaler; married Kathy Cytron (in social work), May 17, 1987; children: Kayla Ariel Cytron-Thaler. *Education:* New York University, B.F.A., 1982. *Religion:* Jewish.

Addresses

Home—1523 Laurel St., Santa Cruz, CA 95060-3522. *Office*—*Santa Cruz Sentinel,* 207 Church St., Santa Cruz, CA 95060.

Career

Freelance photojournalist, 1974—; *Santa Cruz Sentinel,* Santa Cruz, CA, staff photographer, 1988—. *Member:* National Press Photographers Association.

Awards, Honors

First place, Kodak/Parade American Woman Photo contest, 1990; first place, Associated Press News Executive Council, 1991; numerous awards from state newspaper associations for photos.

Writings

Photography: Take Your Best Shot, Lerner Publications (Minneapolis, MN), 1991.
(With Terri Morgan) *Chris Mullen: Sure Shot,* Lerner Publications (Minneapolis, MN), 1994.

Shmuel Thaler photographed a bug's-eye and bird's-eye view of the life cycle of a pumpkin. (*From* Pumpkin Circle: The Story of a Garden, *written by George Levenson.*)

(With Terri Morgan) *Capturing Childhood Memories: Creating an Album to Cherish: How to Photograph Your Child's Most Special Moments,* Berkley Books (New York, NY), 1996.

(With Terri Morgan) *Steve Young: Complete Quarterback* ("Achievers" series), Lerner Publications (Minneapolis, MN), 1996.

(Photographer) George Levenson, *Pumpkin Circle: The Story of a Garden,* Tricycle Press (Berkeley, CA), 1999.

Photographic work published in books, including *Small Inventions That Made a Big Difference,* edited by Donald J. Crump, National Geographic Society, 1984, and in periodicals, including *Time, People, Forbes, USA Today, Los Angeles Times, New York Times, Washington Post, Parade,* and *Landscape Architecture.*

Biographical and Critical Sources

PERIODICALS

Booklist, January 1, 1995, Merri Monks, review of *Chris Mullin: Sure Shot,* p. 817; December 15, 1996, Kathryn Carpenter, review of *Capturing Childhood Memories: Creating an Album to Cherish: How to Photograph Your Child's Most Special Moments,* p. 703.

School Library Journal, November, 1991, p. 142; January, 1995, Janice C. Hayes, review of *Chris Mullin: Sure Shot,* p. 112; October, 1999, Carolyn Jenks, review of *Pumpkin Circle: The Story of a Garden,* p. 118.*

V

VIOLA, Herman J(oseph) 1938-

Personal

Born February 24, 1938, in Chicago, IL; son of Joseph (a carpenter) and Mary (Incollingo) Viola; married Susan Patricia Bennett (a librarian), June 13, 1964; children: Joseph, Paul, Peter. *Education:* Marquette University, B.A., 1960, M.A., 1964; Indiana University, Ph.D., 1970.

Addresses

Home—7307 Pinewood St., Falls Church, VA 22046-2725. *Office*—Museum of Natural History, Smithsonian Institution, Washington, DC 20560.

Career

National Archives, Washington, DC, archivist, 1966-68; *Prologue: Journal of the National Archives,* Washington, DC, founding editor, 1968-72; Smithsonian Institution, Washington, DC, director of National Anthropological Archives, 1972-86, director of quincentenary programs at Museum of Natural History, 1986-c. 1998, curator emeritus, c.1998—. *Military service:* U.S. Navy, 1962-64. *Member:* Society of American Archivists (program chair, 1972), Organization of American Historians, American History Association, Western History Association.

Writings

FOR CHILDREN

(With wife, Susan P. Viola) *Giuseppe Garibaldi,* Chelsea House (New York, NY), 1988.
Sitting Bull, illustrated by Charles Shaw, Raintree Publishers (Milwaukee, WI), 1990.
After Columbus: The Horse's Return to America, illustrated by Deborah Howland, Soundprints (Norwalk, CT), 1992.
Osceola, illustrated by Yoshi Miyake, Raintree Steck-Vaughn (Austin, TX), 1993.

It Is a Good Day to Die: Indian Eyewitnesses Tell the Story of the Battle of Little Bighorn, Random House (New York, NY), 1998.
Why We Remember: United States History, Addison-Wesley (Reading, MA), 1998.

FOR ADULTS

Thomas L. McKenney: Architect of America's Early Indian Policy, 1816-1830, Swallow Press (Athens, OH), 1974.

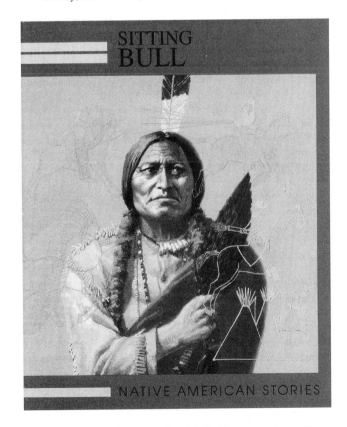

The subject of Herman J. Viola's biography from the "Native American Stories" series, Sitting Bull brought about the defeat of Custer and toured with Buffalo Bill's Wild West Show. (Cover illustration by Charles Shaw.)

The Indian Legacy of Charles Bird King, Smithsonian Institution Press (Washington, DC), 1976.

Diplomats in Buckskins: A History of Indian Delegations in Washington City, Smithsonian Institution Press (Washington, DC), 1981.

The National Archives of the United States, Abrams (New York, NY), 1984.

Exploring the West: A Smithsonian Book, Smithsonian Institution Press (Washington, DC), 1987.

After Columbus: The Smithsonian Chronicle of the North American Indians, Smithsonian Books (Washington, DC), 1990.

Ben Nighthorse Campbell: An American Warrior, Orion Books (New York, NY), 1993.

Why We Remember: United States History through Reconstruction (teacher's edition), Addison-Wesley (Menlo Park, CA), 1997.

Warrior Artists: Historica Cheyenne and Kiowa Indian Ledger Art: Drawn by Making Medicine and Zotum, National Geographic Society (Washington, DC), 1998.

Little Bighorn Remembered: The Untold Indian Story of Custer's Last Stand, Random House (New York, NY), 1999.

EDITOR

(With Robert Kvasnicka) *The Commissioners of Indian Affairs,* University of Nebraska Press (Lincoln, NE), 1979.

(With Carolyn Margolis) *Magnificent Voyagers: The U.S. Exploring Expedition, 1938-1942,* Smithsonian Institution Press (Washington, DC), 1985.

(With Carolyn Margolis) *Seeds of Change: A Quincentennial Commemoration,* Smithsonian Institution Press (Washington, DC), 1991.

(And author of introduction) *The Memoirs of Charles Henry Veil: A Soldier's Recollections of the Civil War and the Arizona Territory,* Orion Books (New York, NY), 1993.

Also general editor (with David Jeffery) of the "Indian Nations" series, Raintree Steck-Vaughn (Austin, TX), 2000-01.

Sidelights

Herman J. Viola has parlayed a childhood fascination with Native Americans into a lifetime career as a curator of Indian documents and an author of histories of the American West for both adults and children. Viola credits this childhood fascination for Native American topics to his parents, who—desperate for a remedy for their baby's colic—would take him to the movies. Italian immigrants, his parents used the movies as an English lesson; a secondary benefit was the fact that young Viola would stop crying while viewing the cowboys and Indians on the screen. Viola told Shirley Leckie in *American History* that he was so absorbed in Native American culture as a kid, that his mother referred to him as "a reincarnated Native American." Going on to college at Marquette University, Viola studied with the noted scholar of Native American and white relations, Francis Paul Prucha, and under his supervision wrote his doctoral thesis on a superintendent of Indian Trade in the early nineteenth century. For much of his professional life Viola was associated with the National Archives—and later the Smithsonian Institution—where he worked with the visual, oral, and written artifacts of American Indians. His writings spun out of the documents he cared for, and many of his books abound with Indian eyewitness accounts of major episodes in their tribal histories.

Little Bighorn Remembered: The Untold Story of Custer's Last Stand is one of those books, twenty years in the planning and writing. Viola persuaded the descendants of the Cheyenne, Sioux, Crow, and Arikara warriors who took part in the battle to talk about their ancestors' recollections. The book contains these oral histories as well as archaeological evidence, drawings, maps, and photographs of the battle in which Custer and his troops were soundly defeated. *Wild West* reviewer Louis Hart noted that the Indian accounts in *Little Bighorn Remembered* are "fascinating" and that the work is "certainly another welcome addition to the field ... a book that makes the battle come alive." In the *Library Journal,* Charles V. Cowling stated that Viola "creates an interesting overview by collecting accounts of the battle by descendants of Indians who fought on both sides." *American History*'s Leckie concluded, "Viola's work provides insights important to historians, but it has enduring value to anyone fascinated by the events of June 25, 1876, and its reverberations in our own time."

Viola also published a children's version of the same book, titled *It Is a Good Day to Die: Indian Eyewitnesses Tell the Story of the Battle of Little Bighorn. Horn Book* correspondent Barbara Bader praised Viola's efforts for younger readers, concluding: "No other juvenile treatment of the battle is nearly as full, authentic, and immediate."

In an interview with Stephen Goode of *Insight on the News,* Viola said: "All of the Indian communities have a history that we should have worked hard to help preserve. That's what I was involved with here at the Smithsonian. I would like to see history programs conducted on all the reservations before the memory is lost. I don't think it's too late, even at this moment, to collect things that are still out there."

Biographical and Critical Sources

PERIODICALS

American History, April, 2000, Shirley Leckie, review of *Little Bighorn Remembered: The Untold Indian Story of Custer's Last Stand,* p. 66; April, 2000, Shirley Leckie, "Talking with: Herman J. Viola," p. 66.

American Spectator, April-May, 1994, p. 74.

Booklist, September 1, 1998, p. 118.

Horn Book, September-October, 1998, Barbara Bader, review of *It Is a Good Day to Die,* p. 625.

Insight on the News, January 3, 2000, Stephen Goode, "Viola Records the View of the American Indian," p. 37.

Library Journal, August, 1998, p. 86; September 1, 1999, Charles V. Cowling, review of *Little Bighorn Remembered,* p. 213.

Los Angeles Times Book Review, September 30, 1984.

Publishers Weekly, August 16, 1999, p. 74.

School Library Journal, March, 1997, p. 210; July, 1998, pp. 111-112.

Washington Post Book World, August 23, 1981; December 5-11, 1999,p. 4.

Wild West, February, 2000, Louis Hart, review of *Little Bighorn Remembered,* p. 62.*

W

WALTERS, Celeste 1938-
(Celeste Sowden)

Personal

Born March 10, 1938, in Melbourne, Australia; daughter of Harold E. (a manager) and Mona E. (a dressmaker; maiden name, Toole) Walters; married Graham Sowden (an engineer), June 24, 1962; children: Ben, Timothy, Annie Strutt. *Education:* Attended Methodist Ladies College (Melbourne, Australia), 1945-54, and Melbourne Teachers College, 1955-57; Trinity College of Music (London, England), L.T.C.L. (with honors); University of Melbourne, L.S.D.A. *Hobbies and other interests:* Jazz, football, beach-walking.

Addresses

Home—461 St. Kilda St., Elwood, Victoria 3184, Australia.

Career

Canberra Grammar, Canberra, Australia, secondary English teacher, 1969-75; Deakin University, Melbourne, Australia, lecturer, 1976-89; La Trobe University, Melbourne, lecturer, 1990-93; Monash University, Melbourne, lecturer, 1994-98. Consultant, Teachers Resource Centre, Melbourne, 1989—; writer-in-residence, Edith Cowan University W.A., Perth, Australia, 1992; honorary consultant, Mental Health Institute of Victoria, 1994—. *Member:* Australian Society of Authors, Fellowship of Australian Writers, Victorian Writers Guild, Australian College of Education.

Awards, Honors

Premier's Literary Award, 1997, and Talking Book Award, 1997, both for *The Killing of Mud-Eye.*

Writings

What Shall I Say?: How to Write Eulogies, Morehouse, 1995.

Who's Who at the Zoo, illustrated by Patricia Mullins, Penguin, 1996.
The Killing of Mud-Eye (young adult novel), University of Queensland Press (Queensland, Australia), 1997.
The Last Race (young adult novel), University of Queensland Press (Queensland, Australia), 2000.
Ossie and Essie (young adult novel), University of Queensland Press (Queensland, Australia), 2002.
The Frog That Went to Safeway (picture book), Hudson Publishing, 2002.
The Rabbiter's Hut, Pascal Press, 2002.

Celeste Walters

UNDER NAME CELESTE SOWDEN

Literacy through Drama, Port Phillip Press, 1977.
End House, Rigby, 1978.
Developing Language through Drama, Nelson, 1985.
Gnome Sweet Gnome, illustrated by John Forrest, Hill of
    Content, 1989.
Pets Day, Pascal Press, 1989.
That's Us, Hudson Publishing, 1991.

Sidelights

"Writing for the young adult market has taught me that
the pen is indeed mightier than the sword—mightier
even than the ubiquitous PC," Celeste Walters told
SATA: "For it is through reading, through identifying
with character, situation, place and time, that attitudes
and behaviors can be changed and a sense of connect-
edness replace that which is born of isolation and of self-
doubt.

"I know. I've seen it happen.

"The two major works that I wrote for this age group,
The Killing of Mud-Eye and *The Last Race,* addressed, in
the first instance, the subject of bullying leading to
mental illness and in the second, the nature of competition and the pressures put upon young people to 'win
gold.'

"I felt that my years of experience at the secondary and
tertiary levels of learning qualified me eminently to
expound upon such issues. In other words, I aimed to
address the dilemmas that young people encounter daily
in the media and, without providing any 'hard and fast'
rules, show ways in which these dilemmas might be
resolved without injury to self or others. This led once
again to 'doing the lecture circuit'; devising role plays as
well as problem solving techniques and strategies for the
free interchange of thoughts and ideas. Observing them.
Hearing the sounds of honesty and openness. Music to a
writer's ears. The hand itches to pick up the pen. Words,
written in love, generate love. And when a writer
receives letters in which the young person of that
wobbly thirteen- to eighteen-years age group states 'I
will never use such terms again for you have shown me
the power of language . . .' then one is both enriched and
humbled. For the writer, in walking 'this way but once,'
somewhere, in some small corner of the world, has used
words that have made a difference.

"I congratulate the publishers of this book who through
their imagination and hard work have exposed these
journeys into words. And the many who live by them."

Walters has written books for a wide range of audiences,
from whimsical rhymes for the picture book crowd to
how-to advice for those composing eulogies. In *Who's
Who at the Zoo,* Walters collects a series of poems that
not only celebrate the uniqueness of the animals to be
found at the zoo, but the joy of playing with language.
Walters' rhymes are often of the nonsensical variety
associated with Ogden Nash. The result is "a witty,
joyous collection guaranteed to lift up the spirits on the
greyest winter day," proclaimed Moira Robinson in

Magpies. In a more serious vein, Walters' young adult
novel, *The Killing of Mud-Eye,* details in realistic prose
the process by which the new boy at a private school in
Melbourne becomes the target for abuse by his peers.
"Walters has captured brilliantly the cruelty and sadness
of adolescence," remarked Cecile Grumelart in *Magpies.*
The narrative is written in a manner intended to provoke
identification between the characters and audience, and
invites readers to question themselves and the power of
peer groups to influence values and behavior, Grumelart
suggested, calling the book a "gripping read."

Biographical and Critical Sources

PERIODICALS

Magpies, July, 1996, Moira Robinson, review of *Who's
    Who at the Zoo,* p. 37; March, 1997, Cecile Grumelart,
    review of *The Killing of Mud-Eye,* p. 38.

*   *   *

WATKINS, Dawn L. (Louise D. Nicholas; Morgan Reed Persun)

Personal

Female. *Hobbies and other interests:* Making costumes,
collecting art and antiques, gardening, photography.

Addresses

Office—c/o Bob Jones University Press, 1700 Wade
Hampton Blvd., Greenville, SC 29615.

Career

Writer. Bob Jones University, Greenville, SC, teacher of
writing and English; Bob Jones University Press, Greenville, SC, editor and supervisor of Elementary Authors'
Division, became director of Marketing Communications.

Writings

Medallion: A Fantasy for Young Readers, illustrated by
    Dana Thompson, Bob Jones University Press (Green-
    ville, SC), 1985.
Jenny Wren (novel), Bob Jones University Press (Green-
    ville, SC), 1986.
A King for Brass Cobweb, illustrated by Holly Hannon,
    Bob Jones University Press (Greenville, SC), 1990.
The Cranky Blue Crab: A Tale in Verse, illustrated by Tim
    Davis, Bob Jones University Press (Greenville, SC),
    1990.
Very like a Star, illustrated by Dana Thompson, Bob Jones
    University Press (Greenville, SC), 1990.
Wait and See, photographs by Suzanne R. Altizer, Bob
    Jones University Press (Greenville, SC), 1991.
Zoli's Legacy (novel), Part 1: *Inheritance,* Part 2: *Bequest,*
    Bob Jones University Press (Greenville, SC), 1991.

Dawn L. Watkins

Pocket Change: Five Small Fables, illustrated by Tim Davis, Bob Jones University Press (Greenville, SC), 1992.

Pulling Together (chapter book), illustrated by Kathy Pflug, Bob Jones University Press (Greenville, SC), 1993.

The Spelling Window, illustrated by John Roberts, Bob Jones University Press (Greenville, SC), 1993.

Once in Blueberry Dell, illustrated by Tim Davis, Bob Jones University Press (Greenville, SC), 1995.

Nantucket Cats, illustrated by Lynn Elam Bonge, Journey Books/Bob Jones University Press (Greenville, SC), 1998.

No Pets Allowed, Bob Jones University Press (Greenville, SC), 1998.

Chickadee Winter, illustrated by Gabriela Dellosso, Journey Books/Bob Jones University Press (Greenville, SC), 1999.

A Winter Secret, Bob Jones University Press (Greenville, SC), 2001.

Other writings include film scripts, narration, and lyrics for a cantata, plays, and poetry. Contributor to education journals. Some books appear under the pseudonym Morgan Reed Persun; some short stories appear under the pseudonym Louise D. Nicholas.

Sidelights

Dawn L. Watkins told *SATA:* "In 1822, as a man named David Cogan came into the region now known by his name, he was so taken with the solitude and the lay of the land that he built a cabin and stayed. As he added 'improvements' over the years, his place—Cogan's House—became a popular rest stop for travelers. By the 1840s many traveling families had decided to stay. David Cogan then packed up and left for less densely populated territory.

"One of the 'crowd' that finally cramped the style of David Cogan was Charles Persun, my great-great-grandfather. Charles descended from the Huguenots who had settled in New England. Charles (and later two of his brothers) came, as God would have it, to Cogan's House, Pennsylvania, to build sawmills.

"By 1880 Cogan House (as the name of the town became shortened by popular use) was a thriving and cultivated community with a band, schools, lecture circles, and a hotel. By the time of my grandfather's birth in 1895, Cogan House was well into the logging boom, the influence of which continues to this day. Today, Charles Persun's original house is occupied by his direct descendants, my great-grandfather's house is the parsonage for the Cogan House Christian Church, and my parents live in what was from 1870 to 1935 the general store and post office.

"I grew up on my grandparents' farm where it was always quiet, despite the buzz of a chain saw or the thrum of a tractor engine. It seems to me now that the drone of insects in the air or the whistle of the wind in the pines was as ceaseless as the sunrises that even in memory take my breath away. I spent most of my preschool days in the woods with my grandfather. While he felled trees and cut wood for our wood stove, I played with Penny (the best collie who ever lived), watched for deer and turkeys, and memorized every rock, fern, and bird on that mountain. Amid such beauty I learned that hard work is good whether it pays well or not; success is being a noble person and is more important than fame or riches; and that while all virtue is not necessarily rewarded, all vice is eventually regretted. I also learned early from caring for animals, from changing seasons, and from Sunday sermons that we are mortal and temporary.

"Growing up in the care of grandparents and living and socializing primarily with older people reinforced this acute sense of brevity. While age gave everything a history, it also gave it something of a shadow. I saw that 'life is fleeting' and things did not last. Except books. They went on for centuries, handed down from generation to generation, a tangible and valuable link to the past and an extension toward the future. Books became companions in a somewhat limited social circle. They answered questions I could not ask, taught me some of the ins and outs of human interaction, and showed me ways of thinking I might otherwise not have explored.

"Grandfather stood staunchly by his beliefs. He paid attention to everything—stars, weather, barn swallows, me. Grandmother paid attention, too. She turned the peach halves over each other just so, to make them 'look nice in the jars.' She made me memorize the family tree. She read me stories and quoted poetry. Stories, I noticed, carried me effortlessly along like a stream. Eventually I entertained myself by making up my own (mostly with me as the heroine).

"Somewhere it began to dawn on me that words were more than just playthings. To satisfy me fully, they had to have an effect on someone else. I realized that all writers—even the ones who say they do not—write to persuade the reader to a way of thinking about the world. I believe that while good may not always appear to prevail in the realm of the temporary, it will always triumph. I do not believe such a view is naïve or foolish. Though human depravity casts shadows, it is only because light is always present. I write from a full heart, not to preach by to delight with words, and along the way my world view reveals itself.

"Whatever I write touches back to Cogan House; it gives me my respect for history and a deep sense of place. Its beauties still inform me, make me try to impress on any who will listen that, despite all evidence to the contrary, I still live there."

*   *   *

Nancy White

WHITE, Nancy 1942-

Personal

Born April 11, 1942, in New York, NY; daughter of George (a textile manufacturer) and Alice (a medical office manager; maiden name, Corner) Selinka; married Mitchell S. White, 1965 (divorced, 1980); married Robert Hirschfeld (an actor and writer), June 9, 1991; children: (first marriage) Daniel E. *Education:* Mount Holyoke College, B.A., 1963. *Politics:* "Liberal Democrat." *Religion:* "Secular humanist/Jewish." *Hobbies and other interests:* Running and swimming, reading, listening to music, playing piano and guitar, kayaking, movies, theater, food.

Addresses

Home and office—300 Broadway, No. C-20, Dobbs Ferry, NY 10522. *Agent*—Susan Cohen, Writers House, 21 West 26th St., New York, NY 10010. *E-mail*—reginawh@aol.com.

Career

Teacher of English, reading, and English as a second language at public schools in New York, NY, 1964-67; Scholastic, Inc., New York, NY, editor for student book clubs, 1967-69; freelance writer and editor, 1969-75; Prentice Hall, Inc., Englewood Cliffs, NJ, editor for

language arts, 1975-77; Macmillan Publishing Co., Inc., New York, NY, supervising editor for language arts and English as a second language, 1981-85; Harcourt, Brace, School Division, executive editor for language arts, 1985-87; W. H. Freeman and Co., New York, NY, development editor for psychology and chemistry, 1987-89; Nancy White Communications, Inc., Dobbs Ferry, NY, founder, 1989, developer, packager, writer, and editor of educational materials and books, 1989—. *Member:* Authors Guild, American Book Producers Association, National Council of Teachers of English.

Awards, Honors

Parents Choice Award, 1995, for *Bears! Bears! Bears!;* Benjamin Franklin Best Education/Teaching Book Award, Oppenheim Toy Portfolio Best Book Award, and Pick of the Lists selection, American Bookseller Association, all 1995, all for *The Kids' Science Book.*

Writings

(With husband Robert Hirschfeld) *The Kids' Science Book: Creative Experiences for Hands-on Fun,* illustrated by Loretta Trezzo Braren, Williamson Publishing (Charlotte, VT), 1995.

(With Louise Colligan) *Rods! Rods! Rods!,* Addison-Wesley (Reading, MA), 1995.

Why Do Dogs Do That?, illustrated by Gioia Fiammenghi, Scholastic (New York, NY), 1995.

(With Louise Colligan) *Bears! Bears! Bears!,* Addison-Wesley (Reading, MA), 1996.

Writing Power, Kaplan Interactive/Simon & Schuster (New York, NY), 1997.

Why Do Cats Do That? Facts about Real Cats and Why They Act the Way They Do, illustrated by Gioia Fiammenghi, Scholastic (New York, NY), 1997.

(Author of adaptation) Joanna Cole, *Scholastic's The Magic School Bus Takes a Dive: A Book about Coral Reefs* (based on an episodes of the animated television series *The Magic School Bus*), illustrated by Bruce Degen, Scholastic (New York, NY), 1998.

The Magic School Bus Explores the World of Animals, Scholastic (New York, NY), 2000.

The Magic School Bus Explores Bugs, Scholastic (New York, NY), 2001.

Sidelights

Nancy White told *SATA:* "Until I wrote *Why Do Dogs Do That?,* I considered myself a writer and editor of textbooks. Then I got my lovely black dog, Fred—a sort of Lab whom I acquired as a puppy from the local supermarket parking lot. Every time I took Fred out, the kids in my neighborhood asked questions about him: Why does he sniff so much? Why is he licking my face? When will he learn how to talk? I told a friend, and she said, 'Write a book,' so I sent off a proposal. Scholastic published the book as well as its sequel, *Why Do Cats Do That? Facts about Real Cats and Why They Act the Way They Do.*

"I still make my living, mostly, working on educational publishing projects, but writing books is really my favorite work. I like the work itself—starting with an idea, revising and developing that idea, and bringing it along to a finished manuscript. Seeing the finished product, complete with witty and charming illustrations by a talented artist, is always a thrill. In addition, each book I've written means something personal and special to me and brings back happy memories. Just a few examples: writing *The Kids' Science Book* with my husband, we filled our kitchen with experiments, ranging from fascinating and amazing (we made plastic out of milk!) to disgusting, foul-smelling, or just a plain mess (our 'volcano' erupted on the kitchen counter ... and floor and walls). *Why Do Cats Do That?* took me to Akron, Ohio, to visit a class of spirited, receptive children and their feline 'pet partner' Woody. It was the first time in my life I experienced having 'fans,' and I loved it! Practically very book I've written has brought me letters from kids who have questions or just want to tell me they liked my book. So I suppose that what I love most about writing are the experiences I've had writing my books and the connections I've made with my audience.

"During my tiny bit of time out from working on books or other projects, I mainly look for time to play—running and swimming (more for fun than fitness), reading, and playing a little piano and guitar are my favorite solitary activities. My best times are spent with my excellent husband Robert Hirschfeld—listening to music, going to movies and plays, taking vacations, eating, kayaking on the Hudson River, walking in the woods with Fred the black dog, and in general having as much fun as we can get out of life. My favorite travel experience, which I repeat as often as I can, is visiting two very wonderful people—my son and his girlfriend, both professors of English literature at the University of Toronto."

Biographical and Critical Sources

PERIODICALS

Booklist, February 15, 1996, Lauren Peterson, review of *Why Do Dogs Do That?,* p. 1024.

* * *

WILCOX, Roger
See COLLINS, Paul

* * *

WINTER, Janet 1926-

Personal

Born June 20, 1926, in Schenectady, NY; daughter of William S. H. and Wilhelmina S. (Clark) Hamilton; married Robert A. Winter. *Education:* Smith College, B.A., 1948; Ohio State University, M.A., 1949; also attended Rhode Island School of Design.

Addresses

Home and office—Box 161, South Orleans, MA 02662.

Career

Writer and illustrator.

Writings

SELF-ILLUSTRATED

Christmas Gingerbread, Medici Society (London, England), 1990.

Christmas Teddy Bear, Medici Society (London, England), 1992.

The Christmas Toy Machine, Medici Society (London, England), 1996.

ILLUSTRATOR

Dianne Pratt, *Hey Kids! You're Cookin' Now! A Global Awareness Cooking Adventure,* Harvest Hill Press (Salsbury Cove, ME), 1998.

Dianne Pratt, *Let's Stir It Up,* Harvest Hill Press (Salsbury Cove, ME), 1998.

Josh Epstein, *Charlie and the Teddy Bear Fire Brigade,* Straight Edge Press, 2001.

Janet Winter

Sidelights

Janet Winter told *SATA:* "I enjoy writing and illustrating for children, especially books about animals and teddy bears. I have also done many greeting cards. I try to avoid a cartoon style—trying to give my drawings a more witty look."

*   *   *

WOJCIECHOWSKI, Susan (Susan Albertson)

Personal

Born in Rochester, NY; daughter of Michael and Regina (Stenclik) Osinski; married Paul Wojciechowski, November 26, 1966; children: Joel, Christian, Mary. *Education:* Nazareth College, B.A.

Addresses

Home—York, PA. *Office*—c/o Author Mail, Candlewick Press, 2067 Massachusetts Ave., Cambridge, MA 02140.

Career

Elementary school teacher; freelance writer, 1981—; school librarian, 1986—. *Member:* Society of Children's Book Writers and Illustrators, Rochester Area Children's Authors and Illustrators.

Awards, Honors

Best Books of the Year selection, Child Study Association, and Book for the Teen Age selection, New York Public Library, both 1988, both for *And the Other, Gold;*

Best Books of the Year selection, Child Study Association, and Book for the Teen Age selection, New York Public Library, both for *Patty Dillman of Hot Dog Fame;* Best Books of the Year selection, Child Study Association, and Book for the Teen Age selection, New York Public Library, both for *Promises to Keep;* Notable Children's Books selection, American Library Association, 1996, Teachers' Choice Award, International Reading Association, Parent's Choice Honor Book, Christopher Medal, and Carolyn W. Field Medal, all for *The Christmas Miracle of Jonathan Toomey;* Parent's Choice Gold Award, and Best Books of the Year List, Child Study Book Committee at Bank Street College, both for *Beany (Not Beanhead) and the Magic Crystal.* Wojciechowski's books have been named to numerous state recommended reading lists.

Writings

And the Other, Gold, Orchard Books (New York, NY), 1987.

Patty Dillman of Hot Dog Fame, Orchard Books (New York, NY), 1989.

Promises to Keep, Crown (New York, NY), 1991.

The Best Halloween of All (picture book), illustrated by Susan Meddaugh, Crown (New York, NY), 1992.

Don't Call Me Beanhead!, illustrated by Susanna Natti, Candlewick Press (Cambridge, MA), 1994.

The Christmas Miracle of Jonathan Toomey, illustrated by P. J. Lynch, Candlewick Press (Cambridge, MA), 1995.

Beany (Not Beanhead) and the Magic Crystal, illustrated by Susanna Natti, Candlewick Press (Cambridge, MA), 1997.

Beany and the Dreaded Wedding, illustrated by Susanna Natti, Candlewick Press (Cambridge, MA), 2000.

Beany Goes to Camp, illustrated by Susanna Natti, Candlewick Press (Cambridge, MA), 2002.

Contributor to periodicals and professional journals, including *Baby Talk, Times Union, National Catholic Education Association,* and *Upstate Magazine.* Has published writings in England under the name Susan Albertson.

Sidelights

With her humorous, true-to-life portrayals of young adults, Susan Wojciechowski has been compared to such authors as Judy Blume and Paula Danziger. One of Wojciechowski's most familiar characters is thirteen-year-old Patty Dillman, a student at St. Ignatius Junior High. Wojciechowski's first three books, *And the Other, Gold, Patty Dillman of Hot Dog Fame,* and *Promises to Keep,* follow Patty's adventures as she discovers boys, learns to value her friends, and becomes involved with social problems.

Wojciechowski introduced another popular character in her 1994 work *Don't Call Me Beanhead!* Bernice Lorraine Sherwin-Hendricks, nicknamed Beany. She is a worrywart and in five chapter-length stories for beginning readers, the author chronicles Beany's troubles, from getting her parents to sign a quiz with a poor mark,

A widow and her young son ask the best wood-carver in the valley to carve a creche in time for Christmas in Susan Wojciechowski's tale. (Cover illustration by P. J. Lynch.)

to standing up to her bossy best friend, to pleading with her mother to keep her favorite out-grown sweater. With the help of her understanding parents, the young character eventually learns to relax a bit and enjoy life. Writing in *Booklist,* Mary Harris Veeder observed that the author "catches Beany's own style and credibly tracks her eventual mellowing." "Wojciechowski captures the feelings, thoughts, and concerns of early elementary-age children in Beany's witty, honest first-person narrative," remarked *School Library Journal* contributor Jacqueline Rose.

Beany's adventures continue in *Beany (Not Beanhead) and the Magic Crystal.* In this episode, a saleswoman gives Beany a crystal from an antique chandelier. Thinking the crystal has magical properties to grant one wish, Beany decides to choose very carefully the one thing she wants to come true. Rejecting wishes for straight hair or finding a lost hamster, the young protagonist finally decides to share her wish with an elderly neighbor. A critic from *Kirkus Reviews* felt that Wojciechowski has created a character that "everyone wants for a friend.... She's likeable and well-intentioned without being a goody-goody." "The characters are nicely drawn," noted *School Library Journal* reviewer Christina Dorr, "and the plot moves along nicely."

Further tales of Beany are recorded in *Beany and the Dreaded Wedding* and *Beany Goes to Camp.* In the first, Beany worries about standing up as a flower girl in her cousin's wedding. She fears the dress will be wrong, or she will run out of flower petals before she reaches the end of the aisle, or that she will not be able to afford the wedding present she has picked out. As in previous books, Beany's concerns turn out to be unfounded, and as always, everything turns out fine. "Simple and satisfying," wrote *Booklist* reviewer Ilene Cooper, "this is a good choice to readers past the beginning-chapter

book stage." *School Library Journal* contributor Julie G. Shatterly favorably compared Beany to Beverly Cleary's popular Ramona Quimby character, going on to comment that "Wojciechowski does have a solid grasp of modern-day children."

Other picture books by Wojciechowski include *The Christmas Miracle of Jonathan Toomey,* illustrated by P. J. Lynch. Called "Mr. Gloomy" by the town children, Jonathan Toomey is considered the best wood-worker in the valley despite his grumpy demeanor. What no one knows is that years before he arrived in the colonial American town, Toomey's wife and child died, leaving him heartbroken and bitter. Then before one Christmas, a boy and his widowed mother ask the town woodcarver to make them a new Nativity to replace one lost during their travels. Though thinking that "Christmas is pish-posh," the carver nevertheless agrees to the job. As Toomey grows closer to the widow and her son, he discovers some joy in his life and finally begins to recover from the loss of his earlier family. "The story verges on the sentimental," noted *Booklist* reviewer Hazel Rochman, "but it's told with feeling and lyricism." In a *New York Times Book Review* article, James

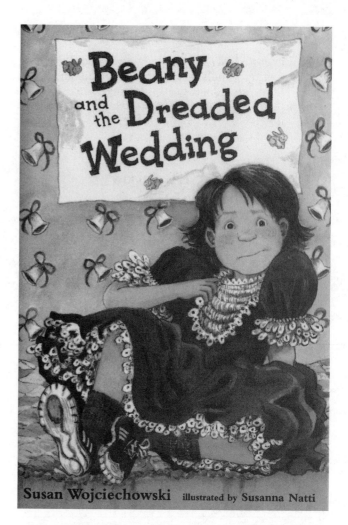

Worrywart Beany is afraid something will go wrong if she agrees to be the flower girl in her cousin's wedding. (Cover illustration by Susanna Natti.)

Howe suggested that "the miracle here . . . is that the tale is unfolded with such mastery, humor, and emotional force that we are entirely in its power."

Wojciechowski once told *SATA:* "As a mother, librarian, and former teacher as well as a children's author, I have always felt the need to touch the minds of children. Through my writing, I try to reach children in a special way, by portraying them as real people—warts and all—and showing them that they are more or less alike, despite their differences."

Biographical and Critical Sources

BOOKS

The Christmas Miracle of Jonathan Toomey, illustrated by P. J. Lynch, Candlewick Press (Cambridge, MA), 1995.

PERIODICALS

Booklist, October 15, 1994, Mary Harris Veeder, review of *Don't Call Me Beanhead!,* p. 429; September 15, 1995, Hazel Rochman, review of *The Christmas Miracle of Jonathan Toomey,* p. 173; March 15, 1996, "Notable Children's Books, 1996," p. 1288; July, 1997, April Judge, review of *Beany (Not Beanhead) and the Magic Crystal,* p. 1820; November 15, 2000, Ilene Cooper, review of *Beany and the Dreaded Wedding,* p. 643.

Kirkus Reviews, July 15, 1992, review of *The Best Halloween of All,* p. 928; June 1, 1997, review of *Beany (Not Beanhead) and the Magic Crystal,* p. 882.

New York Times Book Review, December 3, 1995, James Howe, review of *The Christmas Miracle of Jonathan Toomey,* p. 68.

Publishers Weekly, November 13, 1987, review of *And the Other, Gold;* review of *Patty Dillman of Hot Dog Fame,* May 19, 1989, p. 85.

School Library Journal, November, 1987, Marcia Hupp, review of *And the Other, Gold,* pp. 107-108; October, 1994, Jacqueline Rose, review of *Don't Call Me Beanhead!,* p. 106; July, 1997, Christina Dorr, review of *Beany (Not Beanhead) and the Magic Crystal,* p. 79; Julie G. Shatterly, October, 2000, review of *Beany and the Dreaded Wedding,* p. 142.*

Y

YOUNG, Dan 1952-

Personal

Born October 29, 1952, in Madison, WI; son of Paul and Trudy Young; married, wife's name, Nancy (a consultant), December 28, 1979; children: Dustin. *Education:* Attended Prescott College (Prescott, AZ), 1970-72; University of Wisconsin—Madison, B.A. (economics), 1974; attended Kent State University, 1974-76.

Addresses

Home—7057 East Ln., Pittsville, WI 54466. *E-mail*—youngdn@wi.tds.net.

Career

Marshfield News-Herald, Marshfield, WI, chief photographer, 1979-81, 1990—; freelance photographer. *Member:* National Press Photographers' Association, Wisconsin News Photographers' Association.

Illustrator

Alden R. Carter and Siri M. Carter, *I'm Tougher Than Asthma!,* Albert Whitman, 1996.
(With Carol S. Carter) Alden R. Carter, *Big Brother Dustin,* Albert Whitman, 1997.
(With Carol S. Carter) Alden R. Carter, *Dustin's Big School Day,* Albert Whitman, 1999.

Also creator of the short documentary film, *Invisibly Close,* Filmakers Library, 1995.

Sidelights

In Alden R. Carter and Siri M. Carter's book, *I'm Tougher Than Asthma!,* Dan Young's photographs show young Siri as she goes through her daily activities, including coping with bouts of asthma. In the first-person narration, the young girl describes her first experiences with asthma and what she does to control it.

Martha Gordon, who reviewed the book for *School Library Journal,* described Young's photographs as "large" and "well-composed." Young teamed up with Carol S. Carter and Alden R. Carter for his next book, *Big Brother Dustin,* both a celebration of the joys of a life spent with a child with Down's Syndrome and a heartwarming version of the well-loved subgenre of children's books about the birth of a sibling.

The text of *Big Brother Dustin* is silent on the fact of Down's Syndrome, instead focusing on the normal excitement experienced by a young boy who learns that he is soon to have a baby sister. Young and Carol Carter's photographs depict Dustin as he helps in getting

Dan Young photographs Dustin as he helps his family prepare for the birth of his baby sister. (Cover photo by Young.)

ready for the birth, including decorating the nursery, attending caregiving classes, and choosing the perfect name for the new baby. "Handsome color photographs supplement and extend the narrative in a documentary style," remarked Mary M. Burns in *Horn Book.* The book closes with a collection of photos, arranged as though in an album, of the early days at home with baby and big brother Dustin. "The accent is on Dustin as a boy who experiences many of the same emotions as other big-brothers-to-be," remarked Ilene Cooper in *Booklist. School Library Journal* contributor Maura Bresnahan added that "All librarians will want to put this title on their 'new baby' bibliographies."

In *Dustin's Big School Day,* Alden R. Carter describes a day in the life of Dustin, whose Down's Syndrome does not prevent him from participating in most of the activities at his school. On the day in focus in this book, Dustin is particularly excited because there will be a puppet show for the whole school in the afternoon and he is the performer's host. In the meantime, Young's photos capture the more ordinary details of Dustin's day, attending classes in music, spending time at the library, at recess and at lunch, and then special classes in which he is tutored in math and reading, and spends time with speech and occupational therapists. "Vibrant, full-color photos follow Dustin through his day," remarked *Booklist* reviewer Ellen Mandel, who praised the author and photographer for showing a typical school day for a special-needs child who is fully integrated into the school environment. *School Library Journal* contributor Lucinda Snyder Whitehurst likewise concluded, "the story is valuable for its depiction of a great kid who has special needs but is integrated completely into the life of his school."

Young has also created a documentary, *Invisibly Close,* about his parents and how they coped with the decline of Young's father after he suffered a stroke. Writing in *Booklist,* Sue-Ellen Beauregard described the short film as "a sympathetic profile of an elderly couple facing the challenges of aging."

Biographical and Critical Sources

PERIODICALS

Booklist, May 1, 1996, Sue-Ellen Beauregard, review of *Invisibly Close,* p. 1515; August, 1997, Ilene Cooper, review of *Big Brother Dustin,* p. 1905; April 15, 1999, Ellen Mandel, review of *Dustin's Big School Day,* p. 1534.

Horn Book, May-June, 1997, Mary M. Burns, review of *Big Brother Dustin,* p. 303.

School Library Journal, August, 1996, Martha Gordon, review of *I'm Tougher Than Asthma!,* p. 133; June, 1997, Maura Bresnahan, review of *Big Brother Dustin,* p. 85; June, 1999, Lucinda Snyder Whitehurst, review of *Dustin's Big School Day,* p. 92.*